Interpersonal Communication

Pragmatics of Human Relationships

INTERPERSONAL COMMUNICATION

Pragmatics of Human Relationships

SECOND EDITION

B. Aubrey Fisher
Late Professor of Communication
University of Utah

Katherine L. Adams
California State University, Fresno

McGRAW-HILL, INC.

New York St. Louis San Francisco Auckland
Bogotá Caracas Lisbon London Madrid
Mexico City Milan Montreal New Delhi
San Juan Singapore Sydney Tokyo Toronto

This book was set in Palatino by ComCom, Inc.
The editors were Hilary Jackson and Scott Amerman;
the production supervisor was Denise L. Puryear.
The cover was designed by Charles Peck and Carol A. Couch.
The photo editor was Barbara Salz.
R. R. Donnelley & Sons Company was printer and binder.

Cover photo: Paul Barton/The Stock Market
Text photos:
Page 6, Chester Higgins, Jr./Photo Researchers;   19, Jeffrey
Rothstein/Image Works;   31, Martha Stewart/Picture Cube;
32, Joseph P. Schuyler/Stock, Boston;   36, Hugh Rogers/
Monkmeyer;   46, Miro Vintoniv/Picture Cube;   47, Frederica
Georgia/Photo Researchers;   52, Leo Touchett/Woodfin Camp
& Associates;   64, Spencer Grant/Photo Researchers;
94, Akos Szilvasi/Stock, Boston;   97, Bob Kalman/Image Works;
99, (top) Meri Houtchens-Kitchens/ Picture Cube;   (bottom)
David Strickler/Image Works;   103, Charles Harbutt/ Actuality;
116, Joel Gordon;   120, Susie Fitzhugh/Stock, Boston;
132, Courtesy United Artists;   155, Joel Gordon;   251, Robert
A. Isaaca/Photo Researchers;   292, Peter Vandermark/Stock,
Boston;   297, Michael Kagan/Monkmeyer;   298, A. Collins/
Monkmeyer;   320, Spencer Grant/Picture Cube;
357, Jeffrey Myers/Stock, Boston;   373, Michael Siluk/Image
Works;   379, David Witbeck/Picture Cube;   391, Joel Gordon.

INTERPERSONAL COMMUNICATION
Pragmatics of Human Relationships

This book is printed on acid-free paper.

1 2 3 4 5 6 7 8 9 0 DOC DOC 9 0 9 8 7 6 5 4 3

ISBN 0-07-021103-5

Library of Congress Cataloging-in-Publication Data

Fisher, B. Aubrey, (date).
    Interpersonal communication / B. Aubrey Fisher, Katherine L.
Adams.—2nd ed.
        p.   cm.
    Includes bibliographical references and index.
    ISBN 0-07-021103-5
    1. Interpersonal communication.   2. Interpersonal relations.
I. Adams, Katherine L.   II. Title.
BF637.C45F56   1994
158 '.2—dc20
                                                93-37345

About the Authors

B. AUBREY FISHER completed his Ph.D. at the University of Minnesota in 1968. From 1971 until his death in 1986 he was Professor of Communication at the University of Utah. Aubrey Fisher was a very respected and accomplished communication scholar and teacher. He wrote many articles and chapters on communication theory and group processes and was the author of *Small Group Decision Making, Perspectives on Human Communication,* and *Interpersonal Communication: Pragmatics of Human Relationships.* He was the editor of *Western Journal of Speech Communication* from 1982 to 1984 and was the President of the Western Speech Communication Association in 1985, in addition to holding offices in national organizations.

KATHERINE L. ADAMS is Professor of Speech Communication at California State University, Fresno, where she received a Meritorious Promise and Performance award in 1989. She has served as their Graduate Coordinator since 1989. She received her Ph.D. in Communication from the University of Utah under the direction of B. Aubrey Fisher. She has authored four instructor's manuals in interpersonal and small group communication. She has published articles in the areas of conversational analysis and interpersonal communication. Currently she is an associate editor for *Communication Reports* and *The Western Journal of Communication.* She participates, at all levels, in the Western States Communication Association and Speech Communication Association and teaches in the areas of interpersonal communication, communication theory, small group communication, and research methods.

To Aub Fisher and Irving Feldman

—Wherever you may be, somehow,
we all know you are both getting
the last laugh.

Contents

Preface

This is the second edition of *Interpersonal Communication: Pragmatics of Human Relationships*. I faced the task of revising this text with mixed emotions. One of my dreams had been to write an interpersonal text with Aubrey Fisher, my mentor and friend. What graduate student doesn't dream of someday working with her or his mentor? Little did I know that dreams can come true, but not always in the manner they are dreamed. Aub died suddenly and unexpectedly in 1986, just prior to publication of the first edition of this text. And so, I did get to write my interpersonal text—but without Aub. Nonetheless, his presence was felt during the entire process of this revision. I often imagined him in my den with me, discussing changes in the text and arguing about them. I found it both exciting and frightening to challenge some of his ideas. Somehow, deep down, I know that although he might not have agreed with all I did, he would have been pleased.

The toughest aspect of this rewrite was not the reorganizing, updating, adding, or omitting of material. The toughest job was blending our two voices. I chose to use the pronoun "we" to refer only to the "authors" for continuity. I also chose to keep most of Aub's personal examples. The first edition of this text was Aub's most personal textbook, and I felt that to omit those examples in this revision would be too radical a change. Therefore, all the personal examples in the text are introduced as either "Aub's" or "Kathy's." Blending our two styles of thinking and writing hasn't been easy, but I think that you will understand why it was done and that you will benefit from the different voices present in this text.

The Primary Theme of the Book

All around are signs that contemporary American society is a relationally "sick" society. Interpersonal relationships are floundering. Divorce rates are high. Palimony suits are not uncommon. The lyrics of a country song ask "Doesn't anybody ever stay together anymore?" People can buy a sophisticated computer for less than $20 and hold it in the palm of the hand. People can put a receiving dish in their backyard and watch programs on their own television set from a satellite orbiting thousands of miles above the earth. People live in a glorious high-tech society. But the "state-of-the-art" human relationship is one that breaks up after only a short time and too often is marked by violence.

This book is about literacy—"relational literacy." In other words, it is about the basic skills of interpersonal communication. It is about what people actually do when they communicate with one another in face-to-face interaction—the *pragmatics* of human relationships. It focuses on the evolutionary process of *creating* human relationships through acting toward and with each other. It is about how people *negotiate* the definitions of their relationships through the process of interpersonal communication. It is about the process of understanding how human relationships evolve and it is about developing the skills of interpersonal communication on the basis of that understanding.

A fundamental premise underlying this book is viewing interpersonal communication as a *pattern* of interaction that defines the relationship and binds the individuals together. In this sense, then, communication is not something you *do* as much as it is something you *participate in.* No individual communicator can create *inter*action or define the *inter*personal relationship. An individual communicator *contributes* to the interaction. Together, two (or more) individuals can create the pattern of interaction and thus define their relationship. Hence, it is important that each participant in communication be able to *adapt* to the other person, to the context, and to the particular type of relationship.

When contributing to the pattern of interaction, each communicator enacts a behavior. That behavior will have consequences in terms of how it potentially affects the pattern of interaction and, hence, the relationship itself. Therefore, we will treat each behavior contributed to the interaction/relationship as a "strategy." Every strategy in interpersonal communication attempts to resolve some "issue" or topic question that, when answered, helps define the interpersonal relationship. Developing your skills in interpersonal communication means using relational strategies that are appropriate to the issues in the conversation. When used appropriately and effectively, strategies resolve relational problems, manage relational conflict, answer relational issues, and negotiate relational definitions. Every participant in the process of interpersonal communication uses strategies. The competent communicator uses strategies appropriately.

Communication is a process. Relationship is a process. As people continue communicating, they continually define and redefine their relationship with each other. Hence, we say that a human relationship is constantly in a state of "becoming"—becoming something different from what it was. As a matter of fact, just living is a process. As people grow older and more relationally experienced, they change. And so do their relationships.

An Overview of the Book

Interpersonal communication is conceptualized as a dance between relational partners. This dance metaphor frames the discussion of Parts One and Two. Part One is an introduction to our pragmatic view of interpersonal communication. Chapters 1 and 2 lay out the framework for the study of interpersonal communication. The principles of system theory are explained and then applied to interpersonal communication. The resulting pragmatic model presented and compared to psychological approaches to interpersonal communication. The three components of the model, the individual, context, and relationship are introduced and discussed.

Parts Two and Three are composed of Chapters 3 through 11. Each of the chapters is a detailed discussion of all the major elements of interpersonal communication and human relationships. Some scholars have referred to three of these levels as levels of understanding: the "individual-psychological" level, the "cultural-normative" level, and the "interpersonal-behavioral" level. All of them are necessary for understanding human relationships, or the relational dance. They are best understood as three concentric circles or three boxes of descending size nested within one another.

The "individual-psychological" level (Chapter 3) is the smallest box and deals with the perceptions, self-concepts, schematas, and personalities of the participants that can affect interpersonal relationships. This level is composed of the dancers. The "cultural-normative" level of the physical and social context (Chapter 4) is the largest box. It "deals with the norms, roles, social rules, expectations and ideals that affect personal relationships" (LaGaipa, 1981, p. 72). This level is likened to the dance floor. The individual's behaviors are the primary focus of pragmatics because they are the lifeblood of relationships. Human relationships emerge from these verbal and nonverbal behaviors (Chapter 5). These behaviors are likened to the dance steps from which the dance is created. The "interpersonal-behavioral" level, or the dance, is the middle-sized box nested within the context and contains the individuals nested within it. This relationship level "includes various kinds of interpersonal events, particularly in face-to-face groups" (LaGaipa, 1981, p. 72) and is the central level of interpersonal communication (Chapters 6–11).

New to This Edition

You will find several changes in this edition. This edition is divided into three parts—"Introduction to the Pragmatic View of Interpersonal Communication," "The Individual, The Context, and Language Behaviors," and "The Relationship"—instead of four. The original fifteen chapters have been reduced to eleven in an attempt to omit redundancy and highlight the most important level of interpersonal communication—the relationship.

Parts One and Two contain the most extensive revisions. Part One includes Chapters 1 and 2. The original Chapter 1 was divided into two new chapters. Chapter 1 contains a new discussion of system theory and a definition of interpersonal communication. Chapter 2 is an exclusive, introductory discussion of the pragmatic model used in this text. It contains most of the material from Chapters 2, 6, and 9 of the first edition. This arrangement will allow you to develop a more thorough understanding of pragmatics before you move into the rest of the book.

Part Two is composed of Chapters 3, 4, and 5. The "self" and "other" chapters from the first edition have been condensed into a new Chapter 3 on the individual and interpersonal communication. This chapter includes new material on social cognition and self-schemata with updated information on attribution and perception. The context chapters from the first edition have also been condensed into a new Chapter 4 on the context and interpersonal communication. This chapter includes new material on context and communication and revised discussions of enactment, space, and relational contexts. The chapter on language has been revised and updated into a new Chapter 5 on language use in interpersonal communication. This chapter includes new material on language and context, Don Ellis's code perspective, and revised discussions of indexicality, reflexivity, and nonverbal behavior.

Part Three retains most of the structure of the original relationship chapters from the first edition with one exception. Part Four from the first edition was omitted and a revised chapter on communicative competence was moved to Part Three as Chapter 7. Material in Part Three has been variously shifted, omitted, added, or updated. For instance, discussions of self-disclosure and relational development all occur in Chapter 9 on the ups and downs of relationships. Material that has been added to this part include new discussions on the "dark side" of interpersonal communication, similarity and attraction, the life-span approach, self-disclosure and boundary management theory, turning points, relational accounts, forms of intimate play, and relational maintenance issues. The study of personal relationships has exploded since the mid-1980s, and I have attempted to incorporate some of the new research into this edition. To that end you will find about 300 additional citations which add to and update the material in the book.

All chapters end with a summary and a list of key terms. One of the most requested items by students, a glossary, has been added to the book. In addition, an instructor's manual is available for the first time with test questions, activities, assignments, and discussion questions. These are but a few of the changes made in this edition.

Acknowledgments

The complete revision of this text rested on my shoulders alone. However, several reviewers took time out of their busy schedules and provided numerous helpful comments and detailed feedback about how this book could be improved. Many have fought to keep this book in circulation, which is testimony to the continued impact of Aubrey Fisher's work and thinking in interpersonal communication. The feedback and support from these people were invaluable to me, and I can't thank them enough. In particular I would like to thank Jerry L. Buley, Arizona State University; Judith Dallinger, Western Illinois University; Don Ellis, University of Hartford; Ken Frandsen, University of New Mexico; Edna Rogers, University of Utah; Teresa Thompson, University of Dayton; Laura Stafford, The Ohio State University; Edwina Stoll, DeAnza Community College; and Raymond Young, Valdosta State College. In addition, I couldn't have asked for a better editor than the one I had in Hilary Jackson of McGraw-Hill—"thank you" doesn't quite cover it. Also, thanks to Scott Amerman, editing supervisor and Denise Puryear, production supervisor, who did an admirable job in seeing the manuscript through to completion of the bound book.

Kevin Cabral, a graduate student, was gracious enough to do some of the more tedious work on the book. He was responsible for the Glossary, References, and Indexes, and he assisted in the writing of the *Instructor's Manual.* He deserves special recognition for making my life so much easier.

I am also very fortunate to have an inner circle of friends I consider family. These people listened to me during the rough times and celebrated with me during the good times—very simply, they were there for me. Ironically, this book on "relationships" took me away from some of the most important relationships in my life. However, these special people taught me that some relationships endure—no matter what. Cindy, Gay, and Kerry all deserve a very special thank-you. They kept me going, helped me stay on track, fed me, entertained me, read chapters for me, discussed issues with me, provided numerous examples for the book, and most of all hung in there with me.

I couldn't end these acknowledgments without mentioning Aub. He will forever be a part of my life because he was more than my mentor—he was my friend. The writing of this book has helped me finally say goodbye to him and move on. I have emerged from this experience with a more realistic appreciation and love for this man who meant more to me than I can ever express. Aubrey—you are deeply missed.

                                                        Katherine L. Adams

Part 1   INTRODUCTION TO THE PRAGMATIC VIEW OF INTERPERSONAL COMMUNICATION

"We do not relate and then talk, but relate in talk" (Duncan, 1967, p. 249). Duncan's insight into the nature of human communication and relationships is a succinct summarization of the pragmatic view of interpersonal communication. The underlying premise of this view is an emphasis on patterns of interaction from which emerge human relationships. Interpersonal communication is the ongoing process of individuals jointly creating a single social reality: their relationship. Interpersonal relationships emerge out of the patterns of interaction that pass between the interactants.

This view of interpersonal communication is probably new to many of you and may be difficult to grasp at first, as learning something for the first time often is. Edna Rogers, a leading scholar of the pragmatic view of communication, uses the metaphor of the dance to describe this view of interpersonal communication and relationships. Metaphors can be powerful tools in helping us grasp the character of something new by associating the new with patterns in something familiar (such as the dance). She presented the details of this metaphor in her keynote address for the Sixteenth Annual Student Conference in Communication, at California State University, Fresno, in 1989. Her description is presented in its entirety because it captures so well the essence of a pragmatic view of communication and relationships.

> I ask you to think of how you interrelate with others and to visualize the dances that are enacted in

1

these relationships. How does the dance that you and your mother perform differ from the dance of you and your best friend, you and your "intimate other," or you and a stranger? What are the dances that typify your different relationships?

When we think of the metaphor of dance, we think of movement, rhythm, coming close, moving away; we think of the patterns that relational partners create out of their combined movements. Some couples move freely and fluidly, some cling to one another, step on each other's feet, stumble or seem out of sync. Some move with rigid propriety, while others sensually flow in and out of closeness. These movements are always embedded in context, if you will, the different "dance floors" of life. The dance is influenced by each partner's movement or behavior, but the dance as a relational pattern resides in their mutually produced creation.

As you imagine different dances, the tango, the waltz, the fox trot, bunny hop, jitterbug, recognize that it is the different dance steps of the partners in combination out of which these dances are created and by which they are distinguished from one another. In similar fashion, different social relations emerge and take form from the interactions we have with one another.

The pragmatic approach to the study of communication is guided by the imagery of the dance metaphor. How we move in relation to one another via our communication behavior forms the patterns that underlie and identify our interpersonal relationships. Analogous to dance steps, message behaviors combine into sequences of pattern, recurring interactions, that characterize our different relationships.

Part One is composed of Chapters 1 and 2. These chapters introduce the reader to the pragmatic view of interpersonal communication and detail a model of the pragmatic process of interpersonal communication. Keep the dance metaphor in mind as you explore the pragmatic character of interpersonal communication.

CHAPTER 1

An Introduction to Interpersonal Communication as Relationship

There are two kinds of love: in the first, the heart beats faster, you can't eat, you tremble at the sight of each other. That's puppy love, new love, romantic love. The second kind is the love you have to work at: it's the deeper, stronger love between grown-ups who know that no matter how close they are, they will always be two separate beings. When the romantic love goes, people shouldn't panic because it comes back. In waves or cycles. Like a fever.

—Alan Alda

Few people think of Alan Alda as an expert in communication theory. Most see him (and still do in syndicated reruns of *M*A*S*H*) as Hawkeye Pierce, the wisecracking, woman-chasing, gin-swilling master of one-liners who brought humor and pathos out of the tragedy of war. But anyone who has seen the writer-director-actor's movie *Four Seasons* was treated to a crash course in interpersonal communication. The central concern of *Four Seasons* was interpersonal communication and relationships—how they grew and changed and developed, how they changed the individuals in the relationships, and how they persisted despite and because of the individuals involved in them.

Alda's movie focused on the ebb and flow character of our relationships. Human relationships are not tangible objects forever fixed in time and unchanging. Picture your relationships as living organisms which grow and decay, and are reborn. Ann Morrow Lindbergh in her book, *Gift from the Sea* (1975), captures the dynamic, dancelike rhythm of human relationships:

The "veritable life" of our emotions and our relationships is also intermittent. When you love someone you do not love them all the time, in exactly the same way, from moment to moment. It is an impossibility. It is even a lie to pretend to. And yet this is exactly what most of us demand. We have so little faith in the ebb and flow of life, of love, of relationships. We leap at the flow of the tide and resist in terror its ebb. We are afraid it will never

3

return. We insist on permanency, on duration, on continuity; when the only continuity possible, in life as in love, is in growth, in fluidity—in freedom, in the sense that the dancers are free, often barely touching as they pass, but partners in the same pattern, (p. 108)

Human relationships are characterized by stability and change and by rhythms of patterned movement. And it is in and through interpersonal communication that individuals are able to weave tapestries of message patterns, jointly creating relationships and thus connecting themselves in sometimes profound ways.

The central concern of our book is interpersonal communication and human relationships. We believe that interpersonal communication is composed of actions or behaviors in a series of interconnected and coordinated events, thus reflecting a particular view of human communication—the *pragmatic view*.

THE PRAGMATIC VIEW OF HUMAN COMMUNICATION

A fundamental premise of the pragmatic view of human communication is the identification of *observable behaviors* as the locus of interest. Communication is a social system composed not of individuals, but of the ongoing flow of their behaviors. Human behavior is often treated only as an indicator of internal psychological processes. In the pragmatic view, behavior is appreciated as important in its own right. "Behavior goes *to* other people (it does not just drop off into space). It connects people and thereby creates a new phenomenon" (Bavelas, 1988, p. 1).

The term *pragmatics* is probably most associated with semiotics, or the theory of symbols. Charles Morris (1946) divided semiotics into three areas—syntactics, semantics, and pragmatics. In reference to human communication, the term was probably first used in 1967 with the publication of a book entitled *Pragmatics of Human Communication: A Study of Interactional Patterns, Pathologies, and Paradoxes,* written by Paul Watzlawick, Janet Beavin, and Don Jackson. Sometimes known as the "interactional view" of human communication (see Fisher, 1981; Watzlawick & Weakland, 1977), pragmatics is grounded in the metatheoretical framework of open system theory. Interestingly enough, Ludwig von Bertalanffy, considered the father of system theory, first presented it in 1937 during one of Charles Morris's philosophy seminars (see von Bertalanffy, 1968).

System theory consists of a "loosely organized and highly abstract set of principles, which serve to direct our thinking" (Fisher, 1978, p. 196) about communicative processes. The pragmatic view of interpersonal communication developed in this book is an application of system theory to the study of human communication. The pragmatic perspective, although not the same as system theory, is closely aligned with its central tenets. In order to understand the pragmatic approach better, we will take a brief look at those tenets.

Central Tenets of System Theory

A logical place to begin the discussion of system theory is with the definition of a "system." A *system* functions "as a whole by virtue of the interdependence of its parts" (Rapoport, 1968, p. xvii). There are different kinds of systems. For instance, a galaxy is a type of physical system, the human body is a type of biological system, and a family is a type of social system. Physical systems are not characterized by their elements nor are social systems characterized by their individual, isolated behaviors. A system "is no more adequately characterized by an inventory of its material constituents, such as molecules, than the life of a city is described by the list of names and numbers in a telephone book" (Weiss, 1969, p. 8). The interdependent relationships between the behaviors of a social system, for example, provide it with its unique character separate from the individual behaviors.

Paul Weiss (1969) argues that human beings do have a habit of dissecting their internal and external worlds into discrete, independent elements or parts. People may do this because it may be to their benefit to focus on specific "things" such as an "enemy," and certain phenomena often capture attention because of their "reiterative appearance in relatively constant and durable form" (p. 5), for example, the melody of a bird song or the cadence of a conversation. He goes on to point out that even though people may perceive an individual part as separate from its system, no part is totally independent of the other elements of its system.

Take, for example, five individuals from the same high school who *appear* to constitute a collection of people behaving with no interdependence. If the behavior of these same five individuals were to be sequenced into day-to-day interactions, like that of high school buddies, it would constitute an identifiable single unit or system: The behavior of one friend impacts the behavior of the other four and of the group as a whole. The social system, or "buddy" group, will have emerged from the various communicative patterns of each individual with an identity of its own, separate from each of the five friends. Understanding the interactive dynamics of this group is accomplished by focusing on the patterned interactions of the members, not on their isolated individual behaviors or acts.

Five central properties characterize systems: wholeness, nonsummativity, openness, hierarchy, and equifinality (Fisher, 1978; Trenholm, 1991). These five properties are common to a variety of systems (e.g., biological and social), and taken together they further define the concept of a system (Littlejohn, 1992).

These four individuals have jointly created their "buddy" group by their communication and thus the behavior of one friend impacts the behavior of the other three and their group.

Wholeness   *Wholeness,* the first property, has already been alluded to in the previous discussion. Simply put, the components of a system affect all other components (Hall & Fagen, 1968). Any change, such as a new baby, will affect the interactive nature of a family and thus the unique interactive character of the family system. Have you ever been a member of a discussion group and noticed a change in your group's interactive dynamics when a member was absent or when a new member joined the group? The absence or new presence of behaviors can change the patterns of interactions in a social system such as a small group. This change can be understood by applying the property of wholeness to your group system.

Nonsummativity   Wholeness and nonsummativity, the second property, go hand in hand. *Nonsummativity* refers to the ability of the system to take on an identity separate from its individual components. The whole by virtue of the interdependence of its parts emerges separate from those parts. Any system is more than the sum of the contributions of its components (von Bertalanffy, 1975). Relational partners, for example, sometimes refer to each other and to "the relationship." Relational partners often have a sense of this third entity which is something other than either one of them. How many times have you heard one or both individuals of a pair say something like "Your lies hurt me, you, and most of all *us*"? Nonsummativity refers to the "us." Or take the example of a cake (Infante, Rancer, & Womack, 1990). The cake is a nonsummative product of several ingredients. The ingredients are mixed, and when baked, a "cake" emerges from a chemical reaction that has changed those ingredients into a cake. Once cooked, because the cake is more than the sum of its ingredients, the flour or any of the other ingredients cannot be retrieved from the cake.

Nonsummativity does not imply that the system is "more" than the parts in some measurable quantity (e.g., an increase in number of people or an increase in amount of eggs). When asked how he would rephrase the property of nonsummativity, Weiss (1969) remarked, "The information about the whole, about the collective, is larger than the sum of information about the parts" (p. 43). The system takes on a *quality* that is separate from the individual components and cannot be described solely by information about its parts.

Openness   Any system can be grouped according to its degree of *openness*. Systems do not exist alone but in an environment (Hall & Fagen, 1968), and systems vary in the degree to which they exchange information or energy with their environments. An open system is characterized by a high degree of continuous exchange of information or energy with its environment because its boundaries are permeable, allowing for considerable exchange with the environment. von Bertalanffy (1975) expressed it simply when he explained that our biological system (i.e., our body) takes food and oxygen from the environment and expels waste into the environment. Similarly, a social system such as a work dyad takes information from the environment whenever a memo is read, a report is received, or a telephone is answered, and gives back to the environment when it produces a commodity.

Closed systems have no exchange with their environment and are usually associated with physical systems such as stars (Littlejohn, 1992). Closed systems move toward *entropy*, or an "irreversible force or tendency within a system to decrease its order over time" (Fisher, 1978, p. 201) and eventually end. Stars, for example, do not have the qualities to sustain their lives (Littlejohn, 1992). In comparison, more open systems are capable of self-regulation or operate based "on the principle of correcting their performance on the basis of taking stock of what is happening" (Rapoport, 1968, p. xix). Open systems are characterized by an ongoing renewal or by "dying and becoming" (von Bertalanffy, 1975).

Equifinality   Wholeness, nonsummativity, and openness imply the fourth general property of systems: *equifinality*. Open systems are inherently equifinal. That is, the outputs of an open system are different from the system's initial inputs, whereas the end state of a closed state is determined by its initial state (von Bertalanffy, 1968). Emmert and Donaghy (1981) provide an excellent illustration of equifinality:

> Two small groups may wish to solve the problem of pollution. They may start from different points in their analysis. One may start with an analysis of the problem of emissions from automobiles. The other may start by considering the smog problem in a large city. Both may reach the goal of solving the pollution problem, even though each has started from different points. (p. 39)

The initial inputs of this open social system are not assumed to determine the character of its outputs.

Hierarchy   The fifth general property of systems implied in the previous discussion is *hierarchy*. Systems are not only embedded within environments but also within other systems. There are two different kinds of hierarchies: a vertical hierarchy and a "nested" hierarchy. The first hierarchy can be visualized as a vertical ladder. The hierarchy of a university, for instance, might be visualized in terms of administrative levels on the ladder—the university president at the top and (in descending order) the vice president of academic affairs, the dean of the college, the faculty member, and the student. Although this example places the student at the "bottom" of the ladder, rest assured that your instructor isn't much higher up! But when we discuss social systems such as a dyad, a group, or an organization, we refer to a "nested" hierarchy and not the ladderlike vertical hierarchy. In comparison, picture a collapsible cup that you might use while camping. The cup is composed of connected circles of aluminum which extend into a cup and collapse for easy storage. Those connected aluminum circles, each one smaller than the next, are "nested" within one another.

Complex systems are composed of any number of hierarchical levels or subsystems. Koestler (1978) uses the human body to illustrate this property. The body as a whole includes the digestive system referred to as subwholes, or "holons." The digestive system, in turn, is composed of the organs, and those, in turn, are composed of cells, and so on. Holons are characterized by dual tendencies. Koestler describes this dual tendency by comparing it to the two-faced Roman god, Janus. "The face turned upward toward higher levels, is that of a dependent part; the face turned downward, towards its own constituents, is that of the whole of remarkable self-sufficiency" (1978, p. 27). Human beings are thus unique *and* an integral part of social structures (e.g., dyads, groups) and those social structures are part of larger social structures (e.g., societies). It is not surprising that Koestler considered the tension between an individual's proclivity toward self-assertiveness and synthesis the universal characteristic of living.

Wholeness, nonsummativity, openness, equifinality, and hierarchy are not an exhaustive list of the properties of systems. They are, however, usually discussed in general explanations of system theory. Likewise, in this text, a basic understanding of these properties and how they interrelate will provide a foundation for understanding the pragmatic view of interpersonal communication. Five general principles of pragmatics (Fisher, 1985) and a definition of interpersonal communication will be discussed in the following section that will serve to guide our understanding of the pragmatic process of interpersonal communication throughout the book. The general principles and definition are grounded heavily in the work of Watzlawick, Beavin, and Jackson (1967).

Application of System Theory to the Study of Interpersonal Communication

At the heart of this pragmatic view of interpersonal communication is the conceptualization of interpersonal communication as a social system. Social systems occur any time individuals' actions become interconnected (see e.g., Parsons, 1951). A social system is as small as a social grouping of two people, that is, a *dyad* (see Simmel, 1902), or as large as an entire society. It may include a small group, such as twelve people on a jury assigned the task of deciding the guilt or innocence of an accused person on trial. A social system may include an entire organization, such as your college or university with its many members engaged in instructional, service, maintenance, and research activities. Interpersonal communication as a system is embedded within a hierarchy of systems.

Hierarchy of Nested Systems   The interpersonal communication system is nested within a hierarchy of systems (see Figure 1-1). Each circle represents a system. The smallest system is the individual human being, or *intrapersonal system*. The intrapersonal system is not a social system because it is not composed of individuals engaged in communication. The next circle is a *social system* because it involves at least two people engaged in the process of communication. The pragmatic perspective focuses "on communication properties that exist only at the dyadic system level; relational variables do not lie within interactors, but rather exist between them" (Rogers & Farace, 1975, p. 222).

The number of people and the extent to which these people know one another vary widely from one system to another. Be careful, though, not to confuse the intrapersonal system with the social system of interpersonal communication. As a part of the system, the individual person may affect and be affected by interpersonal communication. But the individual is not and should never be considered the *same* thing as the social system of interpersonal communication. Knowing everything there is to know about

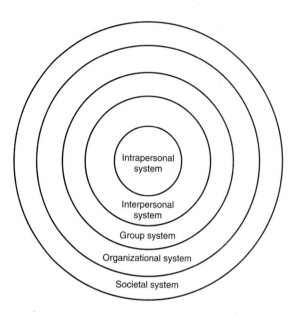

FIGURE 1-1 Nested hierarchy of communication systems.

the individual participants will not enable you to define the social system of interpersonal communication (nonsummativity). An understanding of the interpersonal system "cannot be reduced to, nor predicted from, the lower level" (Koestler, 1978, p. 32). Conversely, the larger systems can affect and can be affected by interpersonal communication, but they cannot and do not define the social system of interpersonal communication. Interpersonal communication is a relationship between and among individual human beings and is, to a larger or lesser extent, different from the individuals who are its members and from the larger systems within which it is embedded.

Principle 1: Behaviors (human actions) are the phenomena necessary for understanding human communication   Underlying this principle is the hypothesis that "in an interactional situation . . . one cannot not communicate" (Watzlawick, Beavin, & Jackson, 1967, pp. 48–49). Even if you've never had a communication course before this one, you may have heard this hypothesis expressed. This hypothesis does not mean that all behavior is communication (see Bavelas, 1990; Motley, 1990), as some have assumed. Rather, this hypothesis focuses on behaviors (rather than on the intrapersonal selves of the communicators) as being most central to interpersonal communication. Within a pragmatic perspective of interpersonal communication, observable behaviors become the phenomena of interest. Thus, communication is now conceptualized as behavior, and behavior has no opposite (Watzlawick, Beavin, & Jackson, 1967). You simply cannot not behave; even holding still and not moving a muscle is a form of behavior. Behavior (unlike emotions, feelings, beliefs, and other elements of the intrapersonal system) is accessible to other persons. You can never know what is going on inside another person, but you can always see and hear (and in some instances feel, taste, and smell) the behaviors of other persons.

Within the pragmatic perspective, all communication is considered behavior; however, whether all behavior is communication remains problematic. Bavelas (1990) has argued that "all behavior is *not* communicative, but that one probably cannot avoid communicating in a social setting" (p. 593). The issue is whether there exists "noninteractive episodes" in interactional situations, and the evidence is inconclusive.

When you engage in communication with another person, you will probably think it is important to discover the feelings and emotions of the other person's intrapersonal system; but actually it is absolutely necessary for you to know the behaviors of the other person in order to gain even a minimal understanding of human communication or the interpersonal system. Remember that the systems are hierarchically nested within one another. The other person's feelings, motivations, emotions, and so on—because they vary in the extent to which they affect the relationship—may or may not be important to your understanding of and participation in human communication. But behaviors or actions, both yours and those of your partner, are absolutely essential to your understanding of the dynamics of the interpersonal system.

A behavior is an event. Because it is an event, it occurs in time and cannot be "taken back." If you hit somebody in the face and break a nose, the event (and its consequences) have "occurred"; you can't roll back the clock and pretend it didn't happen. The most you can do is attempt an additional behavior by saying, for example, "I'm sorry. It was an accident." The new behavioral event (apologizing) does not change the previous behavioral event (face punching). Instead, it provides an additional event in the ongoing sequence of events. It thus becomes part of the sequence of events which may redefine the former event so that it may take on a different meaning. That is, you can change the semantic "reality" (your own intrapersonal meaning) of a behavior with subsequent behaviors, but you cannot change the pragmatic reality (its effects or consequences within the interpersonal system) of any behavioral event. You can apologize all you want, but the nose is still broken.

Another example further illustrates this point about the connection between intentions (intrapersonal system) and behaviors (interpersonal system). Joe, in an effort to reassure his wife, says, "In twenty years, I've never seen another woman I'd rather be married to than you." His wife negatively interprets his comment and replies, "You mean you've been looking for someone for twenty years!?" Joe's meaning of his comment is one meaning; it "belongs to" him. His wife's meaning of his comment is another meaning; it "belongs to" her. If these were the only two meanings, interpersonal communication becomes a simple process of continuing to exchange messages so that "my" meaning gets closer to "your" meaning. Of course, the two meanings will not be the same. The best to hope for is some degree of "overlapping meaning."

Now consider that same meaning within a pragmatic view. The utterance (behavior) occurred. Despite Joe's intention (part of his intrapersonal system) which preceded the utterance and his wife's understanding (also intrapersonal) of his utterance, neither of them can deny the fact that Joe's utterance did occur. And because it did occur, it will have consequences for their future interaction, as will her utterance. A pragmatic view accepts perceptual differences as a very normal part of the process of interpersonal communication. But misunderstanding, confusion, or just different intrapersonal meanings is not really the point of the interpersonal relationship. Given the undeniable truth that intrapersonal perceptions will always be somewhat different, let's move on to the second principle of interpersonal communication pragmatics.

Principle 2: The interpretation or definition of communicative behaviors is to be found in the patterns of how those behaviors interconnect with one another   Interactions are sequences of behaviors connecting the individuals in the interpersonal system (see Fisher, 1978, p. 225; Littlejohn, 1992, p. 55). Bateson (1979, p. 13) referred to a pattern as "a dance of interacting parts." There are two implications of this principle. First, the pragmatic view "accords primary importance to the study of interaction" rather than separate acts (Rogers, 1989, p. 2) because interpersonal communication is conceptualized as a systematic whole or indivisible entity (wholeness and nonsummativity). This holistic conception of communication compared to more individualistic conceptions, suggests that no single entity of the system possesses meaning or significance in and of itself. A former colleague of this book's co-author used to delight in intentionally misinterpreting questions on standardized survey forms. For example, in answer to the routine question asking about "marital status," he would write "Shaky!" On a job placement information form, he once responded to the question "Minimum salary acceptable?" with a decisive "No!" The point is simply this: No single behavior isolated from the stream of interactional events is interpretable or definable unless one jumps to gross and probably inaccurate conclusions. But place that behavior within the interactional stream, and its meaning becomes clearer. "It is the *relations* of the elements or events, the configuration, the pattern we are after" (Scheflen, 1968, p. 10). (One wonders who read those capricious comments on the survey forms and what conclusion was drawn about the person who filled them out.)

Second, patterns themselves may be interpreted differently because they are capable of being ordered differently. *Punctuation* refers to the order imposed on a sequence of behaviors (Watzlawick, 1976; Watzlawick, Beavin, & Jackson, 1967). Different punctuations, or orderings of a sequence of behavior, can create different "realities" for interactants. "Reality" is not an objective reality "somewhere out there" for humans to discover but is a human creation (Fisher, 1978, 1985). Punctuation is the way humans place an order or divide up the stream of behaviors into meaningful patterns (Leeds-Hurwitz, 1992).

An excellent example of the second principle of pragmatics is a favorite comedy routine "Who's on First?" by Bud Abbott and Lou Costello. If you are one of those rare persons who have not had the good fortune to have heard this routine, here is some necessary background. The premise of the dialogue centers on the unusual names of the players on a baseball team: the nickname of the first-base player is "Who," the second-base player is "What," and the third-base player is "I don't know." Abbott understands this, but Costello does not. Thus, Abbott's "Who's on first" is a declarative statement identifying the first-base player by his nickname, but to Costello that same statement is a question asking for the identity of the first-base player. The humor of this dialogue, of course, requires a third interpretation, which comes from punctuating the interaction as a comedy routine. The audience is aware of Abbott's interpretation, Costello's "misinterpretation," and the third interpretation (a comedy routine), which necessarily incorporates both the individual interpretations but is more than their sum.

Toward the end of the dialogue, Costello makes a final desperate effort to discover the first-base player's name. He creates a hypothetical situation in which he is the catcher in a game:

COSTELLO: Valentine gets up, and he bunts the ball. Now when he bunts the ball, to me, being a good catcher, I'm gonna throw Valentine out at first base. So I pick up the ball and throw it to who?
ABBOTT: Now that's the first thing you've said right.
COSTELLO: I don't even know what I'm talking about!
ABBOTT: That's all you have to do.
COSTELLO: Just throw it to first base. Now who's got it?
ABBOTT: Naturally.
COSTELLO: If I throw it to first base, somebody's got to get it. Now who's got it?
ABBOTT: Naturally.
COSTELLO: Who has it?
ABBOTT: Naturally.
COSTELLO: Naturally? So I pick up the ball, and I throw it to Naturally.
ABBOTT: No! No! You throw the ball to first base, then Who gets it.
COSTELLO: Naturally.
ABBOTT: That's right.
COSTELLO: So I pick up the ball and throw it to Naturally.

ABBOTT: No! You don't!

COSTELLO: I throw it to who?

ABBOTT: Naturally.

COSTELLO: That's what I'm saying.

ABBOTT: You're not saying that.

COSTELLO: I said I throw the ball to Naturally.

ABBOTT: You throw the ball to Who.

COSTELLO: Naturally.

ABBOTT: Well, say that.

COSTELLO: That's what I'm saying. I throw the ball to Naturally.

ABBOTT: You don't!

COSTELLO: I throw it to who?

ABBOTT: Naturally.

COSTELLO: I'm saying the same as you! I throw it to who?

ABBOTT: Naturally.

COSTELLO: Okay, I throw it to Naturally.

ABBOTT: You don't.

COSTELLO: Who did I throw it to?

ABBOTT: Who.

COSTELLO: Naturally.

ABBOTT: That's right.

Costello's anguished "I'm saying it the same as you are!" is accurate from his "reality." He interprets "Naturally" as an answer to his interrogative "Who?" given his punctuation of the sequence. He does not see the alternative order of the pattern rendering "Naturally" as a declarative which is an appropriate response to the statement that "Who" is playing first base. Abbot's interpretation is no more accurate than Costello's. After all, the third interpretation of the dialogue is a comedy routine, not a discussion of a particular baseball team. Of course, a "realistic" conversation would undoubtedly clarify this confusion of individual meanings within the intrapersonal systems, but then the dialogue wouldn't be funny. Significantly, the third meaning of the dialogue is quite independent from the perceived meaning of either individual. And that brings us to the third related principle of the pragmatic view of human communication.

Principle 3: The meaning or significance of the communicative patterns is discovered by recognizing that they are context-bound   Gregory Bateson once remarked that "Nothing has meaning except it be contextualized" (cited in Leeds-Hurwitz, 1992, p. 71). Context is not simply a place where interaction occurs. Broadly speaking, context is "anything and everything which needs to be taken into account in order to understand" (Leeds-Hurwitz, 1992, p. 77) the significance of behaviors and patterns of behaviors. Patterns of behavior, like single behaviors, do not occur in a vacuum, they are embedded in multiple contexts.

The third principle seems obvious on the face of it. You are probably aware of the problem of quoting out of context. Often, however, people tend to confuse contexts. Some soap opera fans are notorious for their rabid identification with the fictional characters and have been known to attack physically the "villains" when they see them in real life. Similarly, after the tragic death of Natalie Wood, CBS reportedly received hundreds of letters from fans who wondered why Robert Wagner and Stephanie Powers did not marry. After all, they obviously loved each other, as the characterizations of Jonathan and Jennifer Hart on the CBS series (now in syndication) *Hart to Hart* testified. Naturally, these examples seem extreme because they involve confusing reality with obvious fiction. No normal person with normal intelligence, one might think, would ever do such a thing. But confusing contexts and thereby creating different meanings is not always so obviously "abnormal"!

Aubrey Fisher, the late co-author of this book, had a reputation as a person who frequently (even habitually) engaged in insulting and arguing behavior. His interaction with his closest friends frequently involved mutual, reciprocated insults and fervent arguments. Such interaction was recreational conversation within the context of friendship.

Occasionally, however, Aub would insult someone he didn't know very well. He would realize he was in trouble when he wasn't insulted in return and the conversation either ended abruptly or became exceedingly polite. He was often left with the residual memory of embarrassment. Aub was guilty of confusing the relational context of "friend" with that of "acquaintance," so that his insult was defined within the interactional pattern as a rude behavior (toward an acquaintance) rather than as participation in ritual repartee (with a friend). In other words, the meaning of any interactional pattern varies according to the relational context in which it occurs. A pattern (e.g., "How are you?" "Fine.") that is insignificant in one context (two acquaintances meeting on the street) takes on a highly significant meaning in another context (after a person has fallen off a 10-foot cliff).

Principle 4: To understand communication is to "make sense" of the communicative patterns retrospectively (that is, after they have occurred).   Our western culture has conditioned us to think in "prospective" (past to present to future) ways. People like to think in terms, for example, of causes and effects. Typically, people are not satisfied until they find causes for their own behavior or the behavior of others. What caused me to act that way? Why did I say that? Why did he say those things about me? What can I do to make more money? People like to think and are even rewarded for believing that thought precedes action, but it does not (Weick, 1979). Despite the tendency to seek causes for "why" events happen, people tend to punctuate most (if not all) of their behaviors after the fact, after they occur, in the form of *retrospective sensemaking*.

This fourth principle does not imply that your meanings or definitions of communication are necessarily more correct when they occur after the fact but that retrospective sensemaking is what you typically do to define your behaviors and, hence, your relationships. The "only way a person can sense the separateness of experience is to get outside the stream of experience and direct attention to it" (Weick, 1979, p. 194). The statement "How do I know what I think until I hear what I have to say?" captures the phenomenon of retrospective sensemaking (Fisher, 1985).

Some will scoff at this notion of retrospective sensemaking and point to actions that are directed toward some future goal. Such behavior, they will argue, is driven by some predetermined purpose—to attain the goal. The athlete trains to compete in the Olympics. The student works her way through school to be a lawyer. The sales representative practices his pitch to make the sale. Now don't misunderstand us: We're not denying the fact that much human behavior may be directed toward some goal. But the meaning people ultimately have for their goal-directed behavior will eventually come from *re*defining their behaviors retrospectively, making sense of the patterns of events *after* they have occurred. If the person achieves her goal, she will retrospectively make sense of it, perhaps by saying, "See? It was all worth it. I made it." She thus confirms her original definition. On the other hand, if she does not achieve her goal, she will still engage in retrospective sensemaking, perhaps by saying "What a waste of time" or by redefining her goals—"I didn't really want to do that in the first place."

Several years ago Aub was the faculty advisor of a student who had decided at an early age to become an engineer. He took all the math courses he could take in high school and directed all his activities toward his goal. After earning a D in his first college-level math course, he suddenly discovered that he really didn't want to become an engineer after all. He redefined his goal, became a communication major, and appeared very satisfied when, upon graduation, he entered a management training program with a public utility firm. The goal, like any other part of one's definition of a pattern of events, is also subject to being redefined through retrospective sensemaking. As events change, so do goals.

Specifically, in terms of interpersonal communication, the pragmatic view suggests that individuals retrospectively look back on their interaction with others and define the relationship. Your definitions of the relationships you have with others are derived retrospectively and continuously. Because interactants continue to make sense of the interaction after it has occurred, the meaning, or definition, of their relationships is constantly subject to change, often frequent change. And as the interaction continues, the events of the relationship accumulate and continue to change. But change is the essence of process. Communication is definitely a process and, in the sense that change is constantly occurring, can be said to be constantly in *process*. The "processual" nature of interpersonal communication will be discussed further when the definition of interpersonal communication is presented.

Principle 5: A pragmatic view of human communication involves asking different questions in order to acquire knowledge or understanding What is the question to be asked pragmatically about the meaning of behavior? Is the question *"What* does this behavior mean?" appropriate? At this point in the discussion it should be apparent that this question is the wrong question to ask from the pragmatic view of human communication. Pragmatically, there is no way of interpreting the meaning of a given behavior until it is considered within a pattern or stream of interaction (wholeness and nonsummativity). Behavior, to be meaningful interpersonally, involves finding how that behavior links or connects with other behaviors in the stream of interaction. And even the definition of the interaction pattern is unclear until the entire interaction is contextualized.

The question most likely to be asked if the intrapersonal system was the focus would be "What do people mean by their behaviors?" This question, of course is important and could be quite significant. Unfortunately, it is important primarily for the *intra*personal system. In the context of the *inter*personal system of human communication, it is not always appropriate. To discover what meanings people have for their own behaviors is to ask a question exclusive of the individual, intrapersonal level of analysis. People's meanings are inside their heads. Another person can interpret those meanings, but only on the basis of some inference (filling in the blanks). Remember the examples of Joe and his wife and of Abbott and Costello. The answer to the question of what people mean by their behavior is vitally significant intrapersonally but not very informative if understanding the system of interpersonal communication and human relationships is the focus.

The pragmatic question that informs us about the system of interpersonal communication is *"How* does behavior mean?" Albert Scheflen, in a 1974 book provocatively titled *How Behavior Means,* suggests that people should cease "asking what people mean by their behavior. This is an issue of focus; does one focus on people or behavior forms?" (p. 204). Behaviors "fit together" with other behaviors in the familiar pattern of interaction: that interaction placed within a relational context serves to define that relationship. If you observe one person hitting another person hard on the shoulder, the second person hitting back, followed by both persons laughing and then throwing their arms about each other, you could answer the question of *how* the hitting behavior takes on meaning in that relationship. You might come to the conclusion (retrospectively) that "hitting behavior" serves as a greeting ritual for these two rather close friends. Asking the "how" question focuses the search for the answer on how one behavior meshes within the overall pattern of behaviors and thereby takes on meaning.

You might even go so far as to ask one of the persons who hit the other why the hitting took place, and a likely response might be "I don't know. We just do that whenever we haven't seen each other in a while." If you asked "How did such a greeting get started?" a likely response might be "I'm not sure; it just did. And we've been doing it ever since." Remember how Weiss (1969) rephrased nonsummativity: "The information about the whole, about the collective, is larger than the sum of information about the parts" (p. 43). A description of a behavior does not provide information about the interpersonal system (the whole); information about how the behaviors are integrated with other behaviors to create the whole provides that information. He suggested that the two processes—of focusing on the parts or of focusing on the whole—could be compared somewhat to "two individuals looking at the same object through a telescope from opposite ends" (p. 11). As later chapters will demonstrate, knowing how the intrapersonal level operates, as well as how the interpersonal communication system operates, will provide an even deeper understanding of human relationships—appreciating both views of the telescope or the nested hierarchical nature of the systems.

Definition of Interpersonal Communication   These five general principles capture the essential nature of the pragmatic view of human communication. Central to the pragmatic view is the assumption that in and through the process of interpersonal communication, social relationships emerge. Interpersonal communication has been mentioned frequently, but how can it be summarized into one definition? *Interpersonal communication* is the process of creating social relationships between at least two people by acting in concert with one another. What are the ideas represented in this definition? Answering this question will help you review the core features of the pragmatic view discussed in this chapter.

Interaction and process are two important ideas represented in this definition. First, human relationships emerge through and occur in the actions of *both* members of the relationship, the *inter*personal communication, or *inter*actions. In other definitions, the human relationship has been the context (Gamble & Gamble, 1984, p. 4), the outcome or result (Phillips & Wood, 1983, p. 83), a function (Ruben, 1984, p. 249), and an economic exchange of interpersonal communication (Roloff, 1981)—and more. Our definition of interpersonal communication assumes that it is not greater or lesser than relationship. Interpersonal communication *is* relationship; the events of acting toward and with one another. Remember: "We do not relate and then talk, but we relate in talk" (Duncan, 1967, p. 249).

Your actions are your definition of the interpersonal relationship (Watzlawick, Beavin, & Jackson, 1967, p. 121). In this way, interpersonal communication *occurs* more than it can be said to exist as a "thing." In other words, interpersonal communication is an event (or a series of events) that occurs in time. Like any event that occurs in time, it ceases to exist when the event is over. The only thing left of the pragmatic event is a memory trace in your mind and in the mind of the other person.

But interpersonal communication does not consist solely of your actions, that is, of what you do to create relationship. Nor is it just what the other person does during the communication event. Interpersonal communication is not limited to your actions toward another person; it is interaction created by both your actions and the other's actions in concert with one another. Ray Birdwhistell (1959), a renowned expert in kinesics, summarized this notion very well:

> An individual does not communicate; he engages in or becomes part of communication. He may move, or make noises . . . but he does not communicate. In a parallel fashion, he may see, he may hear, smell, tastes, or feel—but he does not communicate. In other words, he does not originate communication; he participates in it. (p. 104)

The relationship you have with another person is so intertwined with the interpersonal communication you have with each other that the two terms are virtually synonymous.

Human relationships are like a "dance" of interactions situated in time and characterized by constant change, fluidity, and movement.

Second, interpersonal communication occurs in time; it is a process. Interpersonal communication as a social system is open and holistic with interdependent components engaged in a continuous exchange with its environment, accounting for its "dying and becoming" nature. It is "dynamic, on-going, ever-changing, continuous" (Berlo, 1960, p. 24). Referring to the dance metaphor, some dances that begin with the same steps may gradually become quite different and some that start off very differently may evolve into very similar dances (equifinality). The "dance of interactions" is situated in time and denotes constant change, fluidity, movement, emergence, and no beginning and end. The beauty of the tango is found in the *process* of the dance; the ongoing interrelatedness of the steps between the dance partners. Interpersonal communication is constantly in the process of "dying and becoming," and so are our dances (our relationships).

Interpersonal communication itself comprises actions, behaviors, or events which, taken together, form interaction. Interpersonal communication as relationship is so closely linked with human interaction that the distinctions between them become rather arbitrary (Hinde, 1979) and they can be used interchangeably.

SUMMARY

A pragmatic view is used by us as the central perspective for understanding interpersonal communication. Although the term "pragmatics" has its beginnings in semiotics, the principles of the pragmatic view owe no special loyalty to semiotic theory. Instead, its metatheoretical foundation is found in system theory and its central tenets: wholeness, nonsummativity, openness, equifinality, and hierarchy. Pragmatics, applied to interpersonal communication, was first used in 1967 by Paul Watzlawick, Janet Beavin, and Don Jackson in their now-classic book, *Pragmatics of Communication.*

Interpersonal communication is defined pragmatically as the *process of creating social relationships between at least two people by acting in concert with one another.* Interpersonal communication is a social system of interrelated behaviors connecting individuals. As a social system it cannot be reduced to its component parts and has an identity separate from the sum of those parts. It is nested within a hierarchy of other systems, and understanding its dynamics must occur at the dyadic (*inter*personal) level not the *intra*personal level. As a process, it is likened to the fluid ebb and flow of a dance.

Five general principles serve to guide our pragmatic understanding of interpersonal communication. First, behaviors (human action) are the phenomena necessary for understanding human communication. Second, the interpretation or definition of communicative behaviors is to be found in the patterns of how those behaviors interconnect with one another. Third, the meaning or significance of the communicative patterns is discovered by recognizing that they are context-bound. Fourth, to understand communication is to "make sense" of the communicative patterns retrospectively (that is, after they have occurred). Fifth, a pragmatic view of human communication involves asking different questions in order to acquire knowledge or understanding. Interpersonal communication includes not only your actions or the actions of the other person during a communicative event. It is the interaction created by *both* you and the other acting in concert together, just as the essence of a dance is created by the patterning of both dance partners. The pragmatic view shifts the study of human communication from the intrapersonal processes of the individual to the sequences of behavior between people (the interpersonal system). Interpersonal communication, interaction, and relationship are so intertwined with one another that they are considered interchangeable.

KEY TERMS*

pragmatic view

system theory

system

wholeness

nonsummativity

openness

entropy

equifinality

dyad

intrapersonal system

social system

punctuation

retrospective sensemaking

hierarchy

holon

interpersonal communication

process

*Key terms are listed in the order in which they appear in the chapter. Check text for explanation.

CHAPTER 2 A Pragmatic Model of Interpersonal Communication

> A model affords the communication scientist with one of the simplest and oftentimes most useful ways of cutting through some of the enormous complexity of human interaction. A model is, in essence, an analogy, a replication of relationships that supposedly determine the nature of a given event. The logic behind the use of such models is that they are capable of reducing a complex event to a more manageable, abstract, and symbolic form.
>
> —Ken Sereno and David Mortensen

Virtually every textbook ever written about the subject of interpersonal communication has included a model, traditionally in the form of a diagram depicting how communication happens. This book is no exception. Lest it be said that we are making fun of communication models per se, let's digress for a moment and explain our attitude toward them. Imagine for the moment that you have been assigned to devise an "original" model of communication. "No big deal" you say? Let's suppose you have also been told that you are not allowed to use any arrows! Frustrated, you and your fellow students devise models using all sorts of substitutes for arrows. For example, some might use a system of pulleys and ropes, others caterpillar treads, conveyor belts, mathematical equations—in short, anything that would substitute for the arrowlike notion of transmitting and receiving messages.

The lesson of this assignment would have been that to represent a model of communication, diagrammatically, on a two-dimensional sheet of paper is to submit to the limitations of those geometric boundaries of length and width. Asking you to draw a model on two-dimensional paper without using arrows would have been an attempt to get you to think about communication beyond those two dimensions. How would you illustrate other dimensions such as "depth" or "time" in a drawing? How would you capture the dancelike nature of interpersonal communication on a two-dimensional sheet of paper? Try it if you like.

We prefer a verbal *model* of communication that does not involve diagrammatical representation. Where is it written that communication models need to be visual drawings? After all, a model is only an analogy or a metaphor that stands for something "real." And metaphors can be expressed in words as well as in diagrams. In this sense, and contrary to popular cliché, a few words are worth far more than a thousand pictures.

Although we prefer a verbal model, we will include a diagram with our verbal model for those who enjoy seeing what they are learning about and for those who are curious about how we would diagram the "dance" of relationships. Remember, however, that the following diagram is overly simplified because it is restricted to two dimensions and that it actually represents a much more complex process—particularly in its omission of the fact that communication always comprises events that occur in time. The verbal model of communication (which is actually the remainder of this chapter and book) will accompany the diagram and will illustrate that complexity.

A PRAGMATIC MODEL

Most models of interpersonal communication employ a dyad because it is easier to represent the communication process if only two people are involved. Three people (or four or five or more) are also perfectly capable of engaging in interpersonal communication, or having a relationship. However, when more people are involved, the complexity of the process increases substantially and is harder to represent in a diagram. Our model uses a dyad and, for the purposes of discussion, personalizes the human components with human names—Symon and Megan. The complete model possesses three elements: individuals (Symon and Megan), relationship, and context (see Figure 2-1).

Our diagram of interpersonal communication, attempts to illustrate the nested hierarchy of systems discussed in Chapter 1. We do this by using a helix (or spiral) to represent the relationship which connects Symon and Megan. We elected to use a helix shape for the same reasons given by Frank Dance (1970) when he used it to represent the communication process. He explains that

> At any and all times, the helix gives geometrical testimony to the concept that communication while moving forward is at the same moment coming back upon itself and being affected by its past behavior, for the coming curve of the helix is fundamentally affected by the curve from which it emerges. Yet, even though slowly, the helix can gradually free itself from its lower-level distortions. . . . The communication process, like the helix, is constantly moving forward and yet is always to some degree dependent upon the past, which informs the present and the future. (p. 105)

Interpersonal communication, you will remember, is a dynamic fluid process with no beginning and no end. In addition, individuals engage in or

FIGURE 2-1 A pragmatic "model" of interpersonal communication.

become a part of communication with another rather than communication being something individuals do *to* each other.

Symon and Megan represent two *intra*personal systems, components of the relationship, or *inter*personal system. They are immersed within the helix. The helix represented in the diagram is the relationship between Symon and Megan which emerges from the interdependency of their behaviors. The enveloping context represents the broader levels of groups, organizations, and societal social systems within which interpersonal communication occurs. The intrapersonal systems (the individuals), the interpersonal system (the interrelated behaviors, or relationship), and the broader context comprise our *pragmatic model of interpersonal communication.* The primary thrust of our model is a focus on the sequences of interaction occurring at the interpersonal, or dyadic level—a focus that has not guided most of the research in interpersonal communication.

The Pragmatic Model versus the Psychological Models

Our model represents a shift in focus from more traditional models of interpersonal communication. More specifically, our model stands in direct contrast to models grounded in a psychological view of communication. Until recently, these *psychological models of communication* have served as the basis for most of the research in interpersonal communication (Trenholm, 1991), whereas social "interaction has been one of the most talked about and least studied phenomena in the social sciences" (Millar & Rogers, 1987, p. 117).

When you read about the differences between these models, we want you to imagine the shift as a change in a "figure-ground" relationship (Rogers, 1989). The psychological locus of interpersonal communication involves "seeing" the relationship from the point of view of each of the communicators: The relationship serves as the "background" for the individual, which is the "figure." Each person's view of the relationship (the background) is a view from the person's self (the figure). The focus for understanding communication and relationships is found in exploring and explaining personal, cognitive processes: what is going on inside the individual during communication (Fisher, 1978). Fisher referred to these psychological processes as *conceptual filters.* They are the internal states of individuals that can be described as beliefs, attitudes, images, self-concepts, motives, needs, cognitions, personalities, and so on.

Interpersonal communication, from a psychological orientation, is a blend of individual similarities and differences. The word "communicate" is derived from the Latin infinitive *communicare,* which literally means "to make common." From a psychological locus, interpersonal communication involves two or more people whose internal conceptual filters have something in common. For Symon to communicate with Megan, his conceptual filters must have something in common (that is, similar to) Megan's conceptual filters. Figure 2-2 illustrates this overlap or commonality of Symon and Megan's conceptual filters. When Symon and Megan communicate, they extend themselves into the act of communicating through their thinking, perceiving, and believing—in short, through their conceptual filters.

The shaded area in Figure 2-2 indicates that portion of Symon's conceptual filters which are similar to (or in common with) Megan's simultaneously occurring conceptual filters. You might speculate that the communication between Symon and Megan is more "effective" as the amount of this overlap increases. At least the greater amount of overlap does suggest a greater degree of psychological similarity between Symon and Megan.

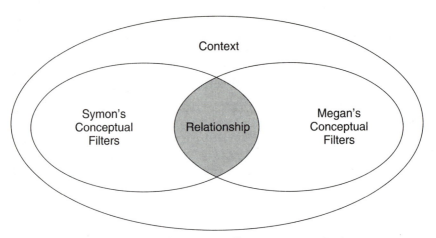

FIGURE 2-2   The psychological processes of human communication.

The greater the overlap, the more things they have in common with each other.

People often use the word "share" to refer to this commonality of communicators. Two people share their experiences with each other; they share our meanings with each other (Fisher, 1978; Trenholm, 1991, p. 37). "Share" is a highly respected word in the language people use every day to talk about interpersonal communication. However, although the word is highly popular, it may be somewhat misleading. Symon and Megan cannot share any psychological process in the sense that they have the *same* psychological process—a single psychological process. There will always be two different psychological processes in action during their communication, even though one person's thoughts, beliefs, and so on may be similar to the other person's thoughts, beliefs, and so on.

To share an understanding is not to have the same understanding but to have two different individual understandings that have some characteristic in common. That common characteristic is a coincidence of two otherwise different understandings. The coincidence is the extent to which the two understandings overlap, but it is not and can never be a single understanding. Psychological communication is thus a coincidence of different conceptual filters and must not be considered to be a single one.

Interpersonal communication, from a psychological orientation, is a blend of similarities and differences; social relationships, from a psychological model, are understood from the individual's viewpoint. If you want to understand the character of a relationship, you would go to one or more participants in the relationship and solicit information about the relationship. Based on this information, inferences would be drawn about the relationship. This reflects the question "What do people mean by their behavior?" introduced in our discussion of principle 5. Individual responses to this question become the basis for insight into relationships.

In comparison, our pragmatic model shifts analysis from the individual (the intrapersonal) to patterns of behavior between people (the interpersonal) as the basis for understanding social relationships. The pragmatic view assumes that "interpersonal relationships are emergent patterns; that they are redundant, interlocked cycles of messages, continually negotiated and co-defined rather than unilaterally caused by personal qualities and/or social role prescriptions" (Millar & Rogers, 1987, p. 118). Now reverse the figure and ground we introduced earlier. In our model the relationship is the "figure" standing out against the individual, now the "background." The question guiding interpersonal communication inquiry becomes "How do behaviors mean?" (principle 5). Interpersonal communication is not the coincidental overlap of two different conceptual filters but the process of creating social relationships between at least two people acting in concert with one another. The locus of communication is not inside a person's head but outside, between people in patterns of behavior.

Lest we be misunderstood, we are not proposing that our pragmatic model is the "right" model for studying interpersonal communication and relationships. We remarked in Chapter 1 that a deeper understanding of interpersonal communication can occur by examining phenomena from both ends of the telescope. In fact, Barbara Montgomery (1984) conducted research with the explicit purpose of integrating "the two models to describe social interaction as it reflects *both* individual consistencies and relational interdependencies" (p. 33). In her conclusions, she does question the inadequacy of either as exclusive models of interpersonal communication and found that they could be used to complement each other. Our issue is not whether the pragmatic model is the "right" model, nor are we promoting the exclusive use of this model in the study of interpersonal communication. However, our understanding of *social* interaction is not likely to be enriched if we study interpersonal communication only from a psychological focus. Instead we believe the pragmatic model to be just as important as other models, and perhaps if our understanding of the "patterns that connect" improves, then both views can be somehow combined (Hinde, 1979).

The pragmatic model of interpersonal communication is made up of three nested systems. In the following sections, we will briefly touch on each of these systems before we explore them at length in Parts Two and Three. You may be wondering why we would discuss separately each of the components of the interpersonal system when we just spent time discussing the nonsummative and holistic nature of systems in Chapter 1. A system *is* nonsummative and cannot be reduced to its component elements. Further, analysis of the system does focus on the connections between component elements. Nevertheless, a holistic analysis does not deny the fact that a system does possess discrete components. Identifying and isolating those components for the purpose of discussion does not destroy the system or its nonsummative nature. What does destroy it is the process of forgetting the interrelatedness of those components.

The Intrapersonal Systems—The Individuals

Interpersonal communication includes individuals who bring to communication their own idiosyncratic differences and similarities. For example, people bring to communication commonsense knowledge about human relationships. This knowledge is gained from retrospectively making sense (principle 4) out of the many experiences they have had. Commonsense knowledge is typical to a wide variety of people who believe it. For instance, everybody knows that relationships vary greatly and have different functions and purposes, that you have to like yourself if others are going to like you, that good friends *really* communicate, that absence makes the heart grow fonder, that out of sight is out of mind—and that this list of commonsense "truths" could go on and on.

It would be a mistake to take the above "truths" or any other set too literally. This is the case for much of what you know based on common sense: Much is blatantly false and often contradictory. Our purpose is not to prove or disprove the commonsense knowledge of individuals but to focus on what people believe to be true about human relationships and to understand how those beliefs affect the way that people interact with one another. To understand fully the phenomenon of interpersonal communication is to know how the individual components of the *intrapersonal system* function to affect the interpersonal communication system (the subject of further discussion in Part Two of this book).

The effect that commonsense knowledge has on any given situation (including interpersonal communication situations) is hardly consistent. For instance, people tend to explain away any instance that doesn't conform to common sense. People typically say "It isn't true" or "That's just an exception to the rule" or "We don't know all the facts." Hence, your commonsense knowledge about communication may or may not have a significant impact on how you participate in interpersonal communication. Perhaps you should treat the commonsense knowledge that you already have about communication as something to be aware of as you pursue your study of interpersonal communication.

We understand that the natural appeal of the importance of psychological processes is so strong that people must constantly remind themselves that the interpersonal processes of the individual communicator is not interpersonal communication; it is psychology. However, the psychological process of each individual communicator can certainly affect interpersonal communication and thus the relationship.

Because Symon and Megan hold particular views of themselves and of each other, their views may lead them to act toward one another in a certain manner. Thus, the *intra*personal process may affect the way each person behaves in the *inter*personal process. The psychology of communication may affect what the individual does (that is how the communicator behaves) during communication. In this way, the psychological process can affect communication, that is, the relationship. And that effect can be either positive or negative: It can help the relationship develop or keep the relationship from developing.

But is the person's communicative behavior always consistent with the internalized self? And what if the external behavior is different from the communicator's internal self? Some commonsense beliefs about personal psychology lead people to think of self or personality in terms of the same old dichotomy: the division between what is "genuine" or "real" and what is "false." You often hear about people in terms of their "public image" and then discover that the public image is in sharp contrast with the "private self." And, of course, you may immediately think that the private self is more real than the public self. (For example, "What is Madonna really like?")

To be perfectly frank, no one knows for sure whether there actually is such a thing as a "real" self—and even if it did exist, it wouldn't have any effect on human communication. To the extent that people's psychological processes can affect how they act and thus affect their interpersonal relationships, the individual is using some internalized self to guide his or her behavior. But if and when the individual's internalized self directs actions, the communicator is acting on the basis of what he or she knows or believes to be true about the internal self. If the individual's inferred image of self is different from his or her "real" self, the individual would have no way of knowing it. The communicator has no choice but to use the inferred self-image, real or false, to affect behaviors. The individual acts *as though* the inferred self were the real self, whether it is or not. In other words, whether there is such a thing as a real self is simply not relevant to communicative behaviors.

Because psychological processes can potentially affect human communication, you cannot ignore them if you want to understand as fully as possible the nature of human relationships. By the same token, you must not think that the psychological processes define the process of human communication. We will consistently treat psychological processes as factors that can affect human communication and social relationships, but they are technically not part of the relationship from the pragmatic view.

One final word before we move on. When two or more people communicate with one another and thereby establish a social relationship, they unite within one single relationship. There is only one social relationship in the interpersonal system, and there are different individual views of that relationship. In fact, there are potentially as many different views of a relationship as there are individuals who are available to view the relationship. Symon and Megan have only one relationship, but individual persons will differ on how they view Symon and Megan's relationship. Symon has one view, Megan has another view, you have a third view, and so on.

Individuals do carry the residues (that is, the outcomes) of the relationship after the relationship ceases to exist. Each individual, even when not interacting with the other, possesses a residue of that relationship internalized in the form of an emotional response, a memory, a perceptual definition of that relationship. Further, that internalized residue of the relationship is reactivated and subject to change when communication (the relationship) occurs later.

To view a relationship is to engage in a psychological process that will often seem more "real" than the relationship itself. But always keep in mind that an individual's psychological process can never be anything more than *intra*personal, and an *inter*personal relationship is always and inherently interpersonal. People will sometimes act *as though* their intrapersonal processes actually defined the "real" relationship, and that is why these discussions are important to an understanding of interpersonal communication.

The Interpersonal System—The Relationship

Remember from our discussion of nested hierarchical systems that interpersonal communication (the social relationship) lies outside and is separate from the intrapersonal systems of Symon and Megan and, conversely, inside and separate from the social systems in which the relationship between Symon and Megan is nested. An individual participant doesn't define a relationship any more than an individual raindrop defines a whole thundershower. Each individual is merely part of the *interpersonal communication system.*

The *relationship* exists between you and another person as a series of connected events in time. A relationship is not a "thing." When you are not interacting, the interconnected events (the relationship) are not occurring. Thus the relationship no longer actively exists except as a residual memory within the intrapersonal systems. The memory is not the same as the relationship event; it is a residue, a footprint, a memory trace of the relationship. Like any residue, it can erode over time and no longer reflect contemporary reality.

Think back, if you can, of some childhood friend whom you have not seen for years. When Kathy Adams, a co-author of this book, was in elementary school, she played constantly with Jimmy, a boy who lived across the street. They would meet after school and hang out together, getting into all kinds of trouble. Kathy moved away, however, and never saw or heard

Human relationships emerge from the patterns of behavior between people.

from Jimmy again. Kathy's only image of him is that of a skinny boy with a blond crew cut. Their relationship ceased to exist when they ceased communicating. The only thing left of that childhood friendship is a residue which grows even fainter with the passage of time. Kathy is quite sure Jimmy no longer resembles her memory of him. Furthermore, he may not even remember her. The relationship, which consisted of sequenced events in time, is gone. Only the individual memories of those "events" remain.

The relationship between Symon and Megan emerges from their inter-action. Symon's actions isolated from Megan's actions are meaningless and can be interpreted only with great difficulty. Have you ever overheard someone talking on the telephone with an unknown caller? You hear only one side of the conversation, the actions of only one person in the interpersonal communication. Sometimes you can "fill in the blanks" and interpret what is going on in the conversation, but more often you really don't know what the conversation is about. Without hearing the actions of the person

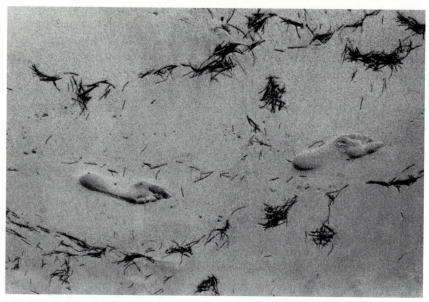

Memories of our relationships are not the event of the relationship but residues that erode over time like footprints in the sand.

on the other end of the telephone conversation, you have difficulty interpreting its meaning. You need the actions of both in the conversation to be able to understand the meaning of the entire conversation.

In the same sense that "in an interactional situation . . . one cannot not communicate" (principle 1), in an interactional situation one cannot not relate. In an interactional situation, together, Symon and Megan cannot avoid having a relationship. Whenever Megan (and Symon) act or behave toward one another, they are relating to and with each other. In fact, they are defining what their relationship is with the other person by the way they act toward and with each other (Watzlawick, Beavin, & Jackson, 1967).

All behavioral messages have two aspects: *content* and *relationship* (Watzlawick, Beavin, & Jackson, 1967). Any behavioral message conveys ideas or information and simultaneously comments on how the ideas are to be taken. The "how" aspect of the message signals how an individual defines the relationship, and that definition serves as a guide for how to take the content, or the "what," of the message. This commenting on messages is what is commonly referred to as *metacommunication*—communication about ("meta") communication. To illustrate, you would describe your relationship with a lover on the basis that your actions toward each other are loving actions and the content of your messages are interpreted in the context of those loving actions.

Several implications summarize the pragmatic view of relationships.

The first implication is that "the relationship" has a single identity different and apart from the identity of either Symon and Megan (remember our discussion of nonsummativity and wholeness in Chapter 1). The bonds that tie Symon and Megan together in a relationship are not feelings or even common experiences, but the events or the actions of each combined with the actions of the other. Moreover, the relationship is not "controlled" or defined by either Symon or Megan as the coincidental overlap of independent partners summed together. The relationship is not something that either Symon or Megan "do" but rather an additional entity that they are a part of and participate in. Furthermore, Symon and Megan cannot "choose" to remain aloof or separate from the relationship; they have no choice but to participate, at least to some extent. Humans are both individuals and social beings at the same time, and are subject to being affected by the relationship and vice versa.

The Relationship between the Intrapersonal and the Interpersonal Systems   Human beings living in a society are constantly torn between what social psychologists like to call the dual interests of "individuation" and "sociation." In plainer terms, every human being is, at the same time, both an individual being with personal desires and a social being with interpersonal motives and desires. These dual interests are not surprising given the "nested" nature of systems. The individual system, as a holon, you will recall, is characterized by dual tendencies resembling the two-faced Roman god Janus: A person is integrative *and* uniquely self-sufficient. In communication, scholars such as Leslie Baxter (1988) and William Rawlins (1989) refer to these dual opposing tendencies as *dialectical contradictions* and place them at the heart of relational dynamics. The opposing tendencies mutually negate each other, and yet they are interdependent.

The dialectic of self-sufficiency and integrativeness is also referred to as autonomy and connection (Baxter, 1988) and is the primary dialectic of relationships (Baxter, 1988; Rawlins, 1983b). If a relationship is to form, participants must give some of themselves to the relationship; yet to give too much would destroy the relationship because the individual self would be lost. Simultaneously, autonomy, or individuation, makes sense only in terms of connection or sociation, but too much autonomy can injure individuals because interpersonal bonds are necessary for self-identity and growth. Dual tendencies such as autonomy and connection are not considered bad forces in a relationship but necessary for growth and change. Other dual tendencies are openness and closedness, stability and change, predictability and novelty, acceptance and judgment, and so on.

Dual individualistic and social interests reflect the reflexive influence between the participant's self and the relationship. Everyone wants to maintain a self-identity and, at the same time, to participate in a relationship that necessitates the risk of redefining that self-identity. An individual might respond to Figure 2-1 and think "if the relationship is that powerful, why risk being in the relationship in the first place?" Or the response might be, "Figure 2-1 is nonsense! I don't change my self-concept so easily—just by having a relationship with someone else. My self-identity is stronger than that." Such responses result from what is a normal human tendency—to see things in either-or, all-or-nothing terms. But the reflexivity of self and relationship is not a choice between "all" (the relationship is omnipotent) or "nothing" (the relationship is impotent). Too much of either tendency (self-assertiveness or integration) is destructive. The tension is found in the continuous managing of some balance between the two.

Relationships neither demand nor could possibly demand all the participant's self. Only part of the self of any participant, and typically a rather small part, is included in even the most intimate of interpersonal relationships. Symon might include more of his self in his relationship with Megan, but he may include much less of his self in his relationship with, say, Bryan.

Remember that, in pragmatic terms, what Symon and Megan give to their relationship are their behaviors, or communicative actions. Committing more of one's self to any relationship involves contributing more behaviors (specifically, more kinds of behaviors) to the relationship. The amount of your self invested in any relationship is thus measured in the number and variety of communicative behaviors you contribute to the relationship. The more behaviors you contribute, the more of your self you invest in that relationship and the greater the impact that relationship will probably have on you. Generally, you contribute more and different kinds of behaviors to a close personal relationship, and you contribute fewer behaviors to a superficial acquaintanceship. On the other hand, someday your acquaintanceship may develop into a friendship. In that case, you will increase your contributed number and variety of behaviors during subsequent interaction in the developing relationship.

Just because the individual recedes into the background of our pragmatic model does not mean that the individual does not matter and is not important. Participants contribute the "lifeblood" of relationships: their behaviors. True, participants cannot avoid contributing some behaviors (in an interactional situation, one cannot not communicate), but they can control the number and variety of those behaviors. Moreover, they *must* control the number and variety of their behaviors in the course of the relationship. Participants will put closure around the kinds of actions they perform in regard to interpersonal communication, whether the relationship involves a close friend or a superficial acquaintance. In every relationship you have, there are certain communicative behaviors you commonly use and others that you don't use. During the normal course of interpersonal communication, you "decide" what your contribution will be in that relationship. Other behaviors that you and your partner are capable of performing (and, indeed, do perform in other relationships) are not relevant to the immediate relationship; only those which create the *inter*action between you and your partner are relevant.

Each individual controls the extent to which her or his self is included in the relationship by putting closure around the types and varieties of behaviors that define participation in the relationship. Your interpersonal relationships are very different in terms of how much of your self-identity you want to contribute in the form of behavior and to what extent you are therefore affected. Your behaviors in concert with those of another impact the emerging relational identity, and at the same time the relational identity affects you and the other. This reflexivity of the intrapersonal and interpersonal systems is a consequence of the nestedness of the systems and is reflected in the opposing tendencies of integration and autonomy. And to discover the meaning or significance of the different communicative patterns of your different relationships, these patterns must be placed in context (principle 3).

The Context of Human Communication

Communication always and inevitably occurs within *context*—the third component of our pragmatic model. And, like any interpretation, the meaning of communication (and hence the meaning of the relationship between people) is influenced by its context. In Chapter 1 we defined context as "anything and everything which needs to be taken into account" (Leeds-Hurwitz, 1992) when attempting to understand patterns of behavior. This definition may appear to some to be a bit overwhelming. "Anything and everything?" you might ask. The definition is not intended to overwhelm you, but to remind anyone interested in understanding communicative events that they are always context-bound. We have already alluded to context when we discussed metacommunication. The relational aspect of our messages comment on how to take the content of our messages; the relationship aspect is a context for the content aspect. Also, patterns of behavior serve as contexts for future sequences, and so on. Consistencies which you label as context are actually patterns of behavior (Bateson, 1972; Leeds-Hurwitz, 1992). Interpersonal communication occurs within a hierarchy of multiple contexts (Barnlund, 1981), and understanding the meaning of communicative events is indeed no small task. Given the complexity of the context-bound nature of communication, we will begin simply by stating the purpose at hand (that is, *introducing* the model) and save our more detailed discussion of context for Chapter 4.

Generally speaking, we think of context as being of two kinds: physical and social. Simply stated, *physical contexts* include material objects, and *social contexts* include people.

The physical context consists of directly observable objects, and so its identification is rarely a problem in interpersonal communication. The social context, however, consists of people and of the influences of those people who make up a particular social system. And those people may not be physically present when interpersonal communication takes place, even though their influences (cultural values, beliefs, norms, and so forth) are certainly present when the participants relate with one another. The empirical identification of social contexts is more problematic than it is for physical contexts. An example might serve better to illustrate the nature of the physical and social contexts.

Let us say that you are a student in a class dealing with interpersonal communication. This is your context, and it includes the room in which your class meets. If it is a typical classroom, it probably contains chairs with tablet-size arms on which to rest notebooks or textbooks. These chairs are probably not attached to the floor but arranged in rows and columns facing one end of the room. In the direction you are facing is probably a desk and chair and a chalkboard mounted on the wall. The instructor stands or sits at that end of the room and is the focal point of your visually directed attention. This classroom context strongly influences the communication, the relationship which occurs within its boundaries, often in subtle ways generally unnoticed but present nonetheless.

You will note that as a student, you are just another one of a group of people. And every member of the group of students has virtually the same orientation. You are all seated, facing the same direction, sitting on similar

The social context of the relationship between this teacher and his students consists of "rules" for what is considered appropriate in their communication.

if not identical chairs, restricted in your actions, and submerged within a group identity of "audience." The instructor, however, is unique. The instructor has a desk and chair, may stand and roam the room, is the only person facing the other participants, has the power to control use of the chalkboard, may stand or sit behind the "barrier" of the desk, and can, from the standing position, "look down" on the seated audience. The context of the classroom itself clearly differentiates the instructor from the students (but not the students from one another).

Whether they choose to take advantage of it or not, instructors in traditional American classrooms are placed in a position of power. The physical context of the classroom itself identifies the instructor as having more power than the undifferentiated individuals in the group of students. The instructor stands; the students remain seated. The instructor can walk around; the students have only restricted movement. The instructor talks; the students listen. The instructor has a desk; the students have tablet-arm chairs. The instructor has a public chalkboard; the students have private notebooks. The physical context of the traditional classroom provides the instructor with a great deal of power. And as you well know, many instructors tend to exercise their classroom power with their actual behaviors, too.

Now the physical context doesn't "make" you behave in a certain way. The physical context of the classroom doesn't require that the instructor act like Julius Caesar. However, the physical context does provide you with a set of expectations which you often use to guide how you behave in the classroom. When you walk into a classroom on the first day, for example, do you sit at the desk or in one of the tablet-arm chairs? Why don't you stand at the front of the room and face the other people who are seated in chairs? But these are dumb questions. You know what the "rules" are on how to behave in the classroom. Well, some of those rules that guide your behavior come from the expectations you have about appropriate behavior on the basis of the physical context itself.

We once knew of a university instructor who often broke the rules of the classroom context. On the first day of class he would enter the classroom early and sit in one of the tablet-arm chairs. He would wear casual clothes, often cutoffs and a T-shirt, and would sit among the rest of the students until after the class bell had rung. After a few moments of grumbling by students about irresponsible instructors who were late for class, he would walk to the front of the room and begin lecturing as though nothing out of the ordinary had happened. The students were invariably shocked by this sudden reversal of roles, and nearly every one of them reacted negatively toward the instructor.

The physical context of your classroom, described above, is but one aspect of your classroom environment. It comprises those cues that are available to your five senses (that is, what you see, hear, touch, smell, and taste). But your class also exists in a social context, which is made up of people. Your class exists, for example, within the context of the university. You are students, and your instructor is a member of the faculty of some college or university. The college itself is a part of the larger context of higher education. Your social role of student is a part of the culture of students within your college and higher education. Your course may be a part of a course of study in your major field or a course designed to liberalize your education beyond that of your major.

Your interpretation of and attitude toward this class is influenced by these elements of the social context. For example, students typically like courses in their major more than courses required to fulfill some liberal education requirement. Students typically like and elect to enroll in courses taught by instructors recommended by other students. We certainly did when we were students, and we assume that your own student culture, with its active grapevine, is not significantly different. Furthermore, the social context of instructor and students and of students and students affects how you interpret the course content. Even though the physical context of the classrooms is similar, you undoubtedly feel closer to some instructors than to others. The degree to which you know and like other students in your class affects your assessment of the value of the course's subject matter. When you like the instructor and/or fellow students, you tend to feel that you learn more from that class. More importantly, you probably do learn more in a favorable social context.

These are the two general types of contexts within which communication takes place. The physical context exists as the tangible surroundings in which the relationship takes place, while the identification of the social context is more problematic than the identification of the physical context. Where does one look for the social context? Its influences are more subtle and reflect cultural or social beliefs, values, norms, attitudes, expectations, stereotypes, roles, and so forth. All these elements are essentially "rules"— ways of behaving or judging behavior as appropriate or inappropriate, good or bad, right or wrong. As we stated in our example, the students whose instructor initially pretended to be a student resented his false role playing. Their expectations, developed over years of experience in the culture of American education, separated students from instructors. These students apparently developed an "us and them" mentality regarding students and faculty in this particular context. Instructors were not meant to be privy to the private conversations of students, especially those addressing the topic of tardy instructors.

Each relational partner carries elements of the social context of the communicative event into the relationship. Moreover, you will typically communicate in only one physical context at a time (such as this particular classroom), but you are subject to the influences of several social contexts (your relationships with fellow students, your college, your social class, your national society, and so forth) at the same time.

The Influence of Context   To say that the physical and social contexts influence communication is to say little of the nature or direction of that influence. Sometimes the context serves to enhance the relationship—to help it along or to allow the communicative relationship to progress. Sometimes the context inhibits the relationship, keeps it from progressing, and actually functions to destroy the relationship. In other words, the context definitely influences communication, and that influence may be either constructive or destructive to the relationship.

To some extent the context always serves to *constrain* the participants in the communicative event. That is, the context serves to narrow down the number of potential interpretations that are available (Bateson, 1972). For example, when you meet someone at a fraternity or sorority "rush party," you already know a number of things about that person (a college student, member of a Greek organization, similar age group) and about what interests you might have in common (value of education, social enjoyment, classes at the college, different majors, etc.). The constraints thus serve as guidelines to tell us how to act and what behavior is considered appropriate within that context. At times the guidelines serve to enhance development of the relationship; at other times they function to retard or even terminate relational development.

Now the term "constraints" may sound somehow "evil" or "bad." After all, as a member of a democratic society, you have come to value freedom and individual choice. The idea of constraints is rather antagonistic to freedom of choice. But think of freedom of choice in the sense that you are at a loss as to what to do or how to act. You look for clues or hints that will provide you with some direction. It's like being lost in a wilderness area. That feeling of freedom of choice is that you are lost. You long for a map of the area that would constrain some of that freedom and allow you to find your way out of your predicament. Constraints that enhance a relationship are like maps that tell you the correct or appropriate thing to do in a given context.

But constraints in the context can function in the interpersonal relationship either constructively or destructively. For example, a typical story line of a romantic novel involves an accidental or unsatisfying encounter as "boy meets girl" for the first time. Boy may collide with girl in a crowded department store, causing her to drop the packages she was carrying. Each is in a hurry to get somewhere and considers the other rude. Later they meet in a different context, perhaps "properly introduced" by a mutual friend at a party, and their love for each other blossoms. The first context was not conducive to continued communication; the other context enhanced it.

Some contextual constraints provide rather clear guidelines for what constitutes appropriate behavior within that context, but others do not. Generally speaking, the number and strength of the guidelines for determining appropriate behavior provided by contextual constraints depend on three factors: the participants' previous experience in a similar context, the amount of information the context provides about the other person, and the amount of similarity or difference between participants that is provided by the context. Let's begin with the first factor.

The number of experiences the participants have previously had in similar contexts provides guidelines for what behavior is appropriate. This constraint of past experiences, typically a positive influence, is a natural outcome of trial and error. As you gain experience in similar contexts, you come to learn which behaviors "work" and which do not. When the situation is new to you, you simply try some tactic, any tactic, because, in the absence of previously learned guidelines, you have no other choice. When the tactic doesn't work (error), you try another and then another. Eventually you discover some tactics that work for you and retain them for future reference. Your previous practice gained from trial and error allows you to select from your repertoire of behaviors those actions which have proved to be successful in the past.

Second, some contexts provide the participants with a considerable amount of information about each other. Two students in the same class, for example, know each other as students because of their context, and the conversational topics relevant to the student culture provide a rich source of information. On the other hand, two strangers meeting on a bus have little information about each other's identity from that context. They are likely to talk about the weather, the bus routes, or other highly general topics; more likely they won't talk at all. Have you ever noticed the fascination people in a crowded elevator have for the lighted floor numbers appearing above the elevator doors? These people certainly have little information about one another and really don't interact at all. In fact, there seems to be an unwritten rule that you just don't talk with other people when you ride an elevator. Staring at the numbers provides an excuse not to communicate.

Clearly, then, some contexts provide more information about fellow communicators than others. The extent to which the context allows the participants to recognize each other's similarities is often the extent to which the context serves to enhance the communicative relationship. The physical context of the classroom, you recall, serves to differentiate the students from the instructor and at the same time emphasizes the similarities among the students. Students are more likely to communicate with one another than with the instructor. Two strangers wearing similar occupational clothing (for example, three-piece suits) are more likely to interact on a bus than persons with dissimilar occupational clothing (for example, three-piece suit versus coveralls). A female is more likely to converse with a stranger who is also female, and a male is more likely to converse with another male. The context can never guarantee what will happen after a conversation begins, but without any communication, no relationship is likely to develop.

Some contexts not only provide little information about the similarities of the communicators but actually involve people who are quite different from one another. The context of intercultural communication is an area of great interest for some students and scholars of human communication. This context, in which a member of one culture interacts with a member of a different culture, is one that maximizes the differences between communicative participants and creates special problems for communication. Some cultures are extremely different from one another. The greater the differences between the communicators' cultures, the fewer the number of guidelines for deciding what behaviors are appropriate. When a member of an Asian culture (for example, Japanese) interacts with a member of a western culture (for example, American), the intercultural context involves extreme differences and few similarities. Communication in such a context would be much more difficult than, say, a context involving an American and an Australian.

SUMMARY

The pragmatic model introduced in this book contains three nested systems: individual human beings, relationship, and context. Two individuals are a part of a relationship, represented in helix form, immersed within context. The helix represents the components of the interpersonal communication process—composed of actions, behaviors, or events—which, taken together, form *inter*action and do so in context. The pragmatic model is in direct contrast to psychological models which focus on the individual as the basis for understanding interpersonal communication.

The pragmatic model reflects the five pragmatic principles discussed in Chapter 1. The intrapersonal systems are the individuals engaging in communication. To understand an intrapersonal system is to understand a psychological view of the interpersonal system. This view is located in the individual self of the communicator and is gained from retrospectively making sense out of many life experiences (principle 4). In other words, to understand the intrapersonal systems, or the individuals, is not to understand the interpersonal system (the relationship).

The relational system exists between the communicators. Pragmatically, the relationship is not the overlap of individual personalities, nor is it located in the heads of individual communicators. Your relationships are created by your behaviors, by events, or by your actions (principle 1) and emerge out of your actions in concert with another's actions—interactions (principle 2). In an interactional situation, participants cannot not relate. Relationships are events in time and as such no longer exist when interactive behavior is not occurring. What is left are residues of the events or memories.

Both systems, the intrapersonal and interpersonal, influence and are influenced by each other because they are nested in a hierarchy of systems. Human beings are faced with the dual tensions of being connected and of maintaining individuality. People do so, in part, by giving only part of themselves—their behaviors—to the relationship. How much you give and what kind of behaviors you give is within your control. In managing the dual tensions, you are both influenced by the relationship and in turn influence it. Communication always occurs within a context, often within multiple contexts.

To discover the meaning or significance of communicative patterns is to place them in some context (principle 3). The physical context consists of the objects in the setting and in other factors external to the participants and available to the senses. On the other hand, the social context is not immediately available to the senses but is internalized, existing within the heads of the communicators in the form of social norms, rules, values, roles, expectations, stereotypes, beliefs, and so on. Both contexts serve to constrain the actions of the communicators by reducing the number of possible interpretations available to each and thus reduce the communicator's uncertainty about which courses of action are appropriate within that context.

Our model of interpersonal communication offers a different view of human relationships in contrast to more conventional, psychological models. Within our model, interpersonal communication is so closely linked with relationship and interaction that we use the terms interchangeably. We no longer look for relationships in the coincidental overlap of individual personalities or in their heads, but in the interaction emerging between communicators. Throughout this book we will be asking *how* behaviors mean within interaction, not what does behavior mean to individuals (principle 5).

KEY TERMS

model

pragmatic model of interpersonal
   communication

psychological models of communication

conceptual filters

intrapersonal system

residues

interpersonal communication system

content

relationship

metacommunication

dialectical contradictions

context

physical context

social context

Part 2 THE INDIVIDUAL, THE CONTEXT, AND LANGUAGE BEHAVIORS

In Part One you were introduced to the study of interpersonal communication as relationship. The fundamental assumptions and principles of the pragmatic view of interpersonal communication were detailed in an introductory discussion (Chapter 1) and in a pragmatic model (Chapter 2). The metaphor of the dance was introduced in Part One as a way of describing the particular dynamics of pragmatics. The dance includes the dancer, the dance steps, the dance floor and the dance. Just as a dance emerges from the interplay of each dancer's steps, so does a relationship (the dance) emerge from the patterns of interaction (dance steps) between individuals (the dancers). And, of course, the dance always happens on some kind of dance floor, just as relationships always occur within some kind of context.

Part Three is composed of three chapters which detail the components of the pragmatic model of interpersonal communication. Chapter 3 is an in-depth discussion of the "dancers," or individuals in interpersonal communication. Chapter 4 discusses the intricacies of "the dance floors," or multiple contexts within which "the dance," or interpersonal communication, takes place. And Chapter 5 discusses "the dance steps," or verbal and nonverbal behaviors which are at the heart of the relationship. The remaining component of our model, the relationship, is the central focus of the pragmatic view and will be the exclusive focus of Part Three.

CHAPTER 3

The Individual and Interpersonal Communication

As a man adjusts himself to a certain environment he becomes a different individual; but in becoming a different individual he has affected the community in which he lives. . . . [I]nsofar as he has adjusted himself, the adjustments have changed the type of environment to which he can respond, and the world is accordingly a different world. *There is always a mutual relationship of the individual and the community in which the individual lives.* [Italics added]

—George Mead

During Aub's lifetime he had the good fortune to run 226 miles of the Colorado River as it winds its way through the Grand Canyon. The trip, made in a five-person inflatable raft, was one of his most vivid memories. He would often recollect the majestic canyon walls—with their technicolor displays of polished white limestone and vivid red wall, shiny black schist, and rugged black lava cones—soaring straight up to the sky and the brownish-red sand-saturated water of the river itself. Long after, he could still hear the sounds of the thunderstorms rumbling down the river and echoing off the canyon walls, the fluttering wings of the bats at night, the splash of the oars in the water, and the deep-throated roar of the rapids.

He remembered the rapids on the Colorado River as truly deserving of the overused adjective "awesome." The sound of all that water was enough to win his respect. The raw power of the sandy water, his eager but reluctant anticipation as he heard the rumble of the rapids ahead of his party (before the rapids could be seen), the flow of adrenaline as his boat slid down the smooth tongue of water straight into the boiling rapids at the bottom, the sight of a brown 15-foot wall of water crashing straight down on top of their heads, and the guide's quite unnecessary shout to "Hang on!"

After his party left the river and climbed to the southern rim of the Grand Canyon, they found themselves having to backtrack nearly 400 miles by automobile in order to return to their starting place. Only a few hours later, after twelve days on the river, they were seeing the canyon from up on the canyon rim. The contrast was remarkable. From their vantage point, they couldn't even see the river. Instead, they viewed the vast expanse of the canyon, a huge hole in the ground that extended forever in front of them and on either side from horizon to horizon; not unlike the last scene in the movie *Grand Canyon*. Aub and his party saw hiking trails switchbacking down nearly vertical cliffs and leading straight down to the canyon floor from dizzying height. Aub was struck with the remarkable difference between his two experiences of Grand Canyon National Park.

Looking down on the canyon from the rim, he could see the enormity of this marvelous work of nature. The feeling he had was one of limitless space and breathtaking size. On the river, he had looked up at the canyon walls flanking both sides of the river and had felt confined, restricted to the water and to the occasional sand beach clinging precariously to the rock walls. From the rim he had the feeling of being a Peeping Tom, looking in on the canyon from his elevated vantage point. All around him were his fellow sightseers, other Peeping Toms with their blow-dried hairdos, wearing clean clothes and eating ice cream cones. Just hours earlier they had been on the river, several thousand feet below, suffering from the oppressive heat and merciless desert sun. Just the day before, any one of them might have done desperate things for an ice cream cone!

They hadn't showered for twelve days. They were wearing the same clothes they had put on earlier. For twelve days they had brushed their teeth in brown sandy water. In fact, they had joked that their biggest problem,

The "outside" view of the Grand Canyon from the rim is but only one view of the canyon.

after the fourth day, was trying to stay upwind of one another. He looked at all the "tourists" peering down at the canyon and felt smugly superior to them. He thought to himself that these tourists were only looking at a long-range view, a slide projected on a giant screen. He, on the other hand, had experienced the "real" Grand Canyon. He had braved the rapids and suffered deprivation on the river. The tourists didn't know what the Grand Canyon was "really" like, but he did.

The "inside" and "outside" views or experiences of the Grand Canyon provide an excellent metaphor for how we understand interpersonal relationships and human relationships. Recall that Aub's initial reaction to seeing the tourists on the canyon rim was one of utter condescension: On the river, he had experienced the "real" Grand Canyon. As TV sportscasters like to say, he had known the Grand Canyon "up close and personal." He didn't realize until later that his river experience had not allowed him to see the enormous expanse of the canyon. From the river he had no grasp of what actually made the canyon "grand." A number of rivers are bound by 300- to 500-foot walls, but they and their canyons would all be insignificant by comparison. From the river he could not see the literally thousands of miles of hiking trails, the variety of geological formations, or the diversity

The "inside" view of the Grand Canyon from the Colorado river is but only one view of the canyon.

of weather patterns that ranged from one end of the canyon to the other. In other words, he couldn't see the canyon for the river.

Understanding human communication, as we pointed out in Chapter 2, is not much different. Your understanding is based on *your* viewpoint. When you are on the inside looking out (as a passenger on a raft on the Colorado River or as a participant in a relationship), you have only one view of what's going on and what it means—your own isolated view. You may think that your understanding is more "real" because you are actually participating in the relationship, but it certainly can't be any *more* real than the view of the other participant. And that view may be very different from yours. So whose view is more real?

Your view of your own relationship is certainly more detailed and more vibrant, at least to you, just as the other person's view is more detailed and vibrant to her or him. But one person's view can hardly be more "real" than another person's. In fact, each of the views (yours and the other person's) is incomplete and distorted precisely because you are both participants in the relationship and are therefore biased. You are both too close to the relationship. The view from the outside looking in (as from the canyon rim or from the vantage point of a nonparticipant in a relationship) is less personal but more complete. The big-picture view enables you to understand just how complex the relationship is, how many different elements it includes, how it resists simple answers that stem from too much knowledge and too little understanding.

What's the difference between knowledge and understanding? One can "know" something very well without "understanding" it at all. One problem of applying what seems like common sense to the phenomenon of human communication is that commonsense knowledge is based on the idea, "I know because I've been there." People can certainly "know" the insider's view, but the insider's view too often lacks the broader understanding that comes from the big-picture view of the outside observer. In a sense, this perspective of the relationship might be expressed by saying "I understand because I haven't been there." For a complete understanding, you need to acquire both the insider's and outsider's views of interpersonal communication, seeing both the self and the relationship.

In this chapter we discuss this "insider's" view of human relationships—interpersonal communication as seen from the participant's vantage point. We have already referred to this part of the relationship as a "psychological" understanding of human communication. The emphasis in this chapter is on elements that lie *within* the individual communicator— the intrapersonal level of communication. That is, we will be discussing concepts that cannot be observed and for which we must rely on assumptions and inferences, the truth of which we can never hope to prove. Also, remember that information about the intrapersonal system reveals little if anything about the interpersonal, or relational, system. Individual behaviors are meaningless with respect to the relationship unless they are understood in the context of patterns of behavior.

Our first task is to explain in more detail than in Part One this psychological understanding of interpersonal communication. We will first critically examine the intrapersonal view. Then we will discuss the perception of self and the other and the ways these perceptual processes can affect the dynamics of communication and the social relationship.

THE INTRAPERSONAL VIEW

As humans, individuals tend to evaluate and use their environment in ways that benefit them. People tend to judge their experiences by the same criterion: "What can it do for me?" It should not be surprising that people tend to judge other people and their relationships with them in a similar manner: "How can this relationship benefit me?" This *intrapersonal view* is reflected in comments such as "Just being with her makes me feel good. She is always there when I need her" and "He just didn't let me grow. I need my own space, and he stifled me."

The psychological part of interpersonal communication locates the meaning of the social relationship "within" the individual, in the communicator's self. When you see your relationship from the viewpoint of your own self, you see it with a sense of ownership or as "belonging" to you. For example, people say *my* wife, *my* boss, *my* friend, *my* classmate, and an acquaintance of *mine.*

In this section we will be dealing with two issues: how to use a psychological view to understand interpersonal communication and how to understand the internal and external self of the individual communicator. When you understand interpersonal communication from the intrapersonal locus of the self, you must keep in mind the fact that this view of the relationship is a *personal* view. It leads to an understanding of an interpersonal relationship that is not really what goes on *between* the communicators but what goes on *within* a participant. The personal view of interpersonal communication is *a* view, but not *the* view. As students of interpersonal communication, you need to understand both views—the insider's (self) view and the outsider's (relationship) view.

Using the Psychological Locus

An individual's personal understanding of interpersonal communication is not wrong. On the contrary, it is always correct (to the participant, that is) and quite normal and natural. Keep in mind, though, that the psychological locus of understanding is not a complete one. Just as Aub could not see the entire Grand Canyon from either the Colorado River or the top, you cannot see an entire relationship as a participant; you see it only in terms of *your* self. There are four potential problems to examining a psychological locus of interpersonal communication which must be avoided when using the pragmatic approach to understand interpersonal communication.

The first problem is to avoid the belief that the insider's view of the relationship is a more accurate definition of interpersonal communication. What you may think, feel, perceive, and know about a relationship or about another person is no more real than what a disinterested observer thinks, feels, perceives, and knows about the same relationship. Your feelings may *seem* more important, and they certainly appear more vivid and stronger. But they are merely more personal or individualized because they are related to your interests, desires, and goals.

The second problem concerns how you understand your experiences. Oscar Levant once said that "happiness isn't something you experience; it's something you remember." Your view of the experience of communication is not the experience itself. It is your sensemaking of the experience (principle 4). The communication, or the relationship (the communicational experience), is not the same as the individual's view of it. Symon and Megan, as individuals, may have quite different views of their relationship with each other, even though they obviously have but one relationship experience. Each view of that experience is their selfish reaction to the relationship *after* the experience, not the experience itself.

This retrospective process through which meaning is derived after the experience also contributes to a third potential problem. Participants' responses are essentially what they remember about the experience, and memories of events can change over time. Once an interaction has occurred, the event itself doesn't change just because the participants have different or even changing understandings of it. But what can change is how each participant defines or understands that interactional experience. In fact, people don't so much reproduce past relational events as much as they "reconstruct" those events, and they do so based on what *they* believe to be true (Miell, 1987). For example, you may remember with fondness your communication with a friend. But if you have a major fight and end the friendship, you are likely to change your memories somewhat and think that you were just fooling yourself during the time you thought the relationship was worthwhile.

A fourth problem concerns confusing an emotional residue with the relationship. People sometimes mistake one for the other and come to think of a relationship in terms of the emotion felt by one or more of the partners. Take, for example, the case of love. As much as people have glorified the notion of "love" in literature and song, and have begun some serious research on the concept (e.g., see Marston, Hecht, & Robers, 1987), people still know very little about the interactive experience of love. Prior to the late 1980s, love was typically conceptualized as a subjective experience or associated with one person's emotional response to another (a psychological locus). Throughout history, *eros* love, for example, has been viewed as a gratification of one's self-interest and desires, whereas *agape* love has been seen as a focus on one's feeling of concern and caring for the other (see Cunningham & Antill, 1981, pp. 30–31). Neither eros nor agape, however, emphasizes the relationship *between* the communicators, the relationship that the two loving partners create by interacting together.

In summary, a psychological understanding of interpersonal communication is only one important part of a thorough understanding, just as the view of the Grand Canyon from either the river or the rim is only one perspective. Several problems, however, may arise from the process through which we derive individual or intrapersonal meaning: This single view is limited to the individual's responses after the communicative experience; one's memory of the experience can change considerably even though the event itself remains unchanged; and people may confuse the relationship with their emotional response. These responses will most likely become problems when people think that the psychological locus of the communicator's self is the most important or "real" understanding of interpersonal communication. This understanding is incomplete by itself. A more thorough understanding includes the external or pragmatic view as well.

The External and the Internal Selves

The psychological locus of human communication considers the individual to have two selves or, more accurately, two parts of the self—internal and external. Central to this locus is the assumption that the individual self is located somewhere within the individual and is not capable of being directly observed. Furthermore, this assumption includes the belief that people can observe their self *in*directly by making inferences about their intrapersonal self on the basis of observable cues offered by the external self.

The psychological task of communication is to decipher cues from the other person in the form of observable behaviors and actions. This task is complicated by the fact that humans don't treat the external and the internal self as equivalent. Individuals must sort through these cues and discover which are fake and which are genuine. The genuine cues, people believe, are those which allow them to discover the "real" self (the internal self) of the other person. Basically, individuals don't trust the external self, probably because they believe it is more difficult for the other person to control external behaviors. Consistent with the personal interest, people tend not to trust other people nearly as much as they trust themselves. The other person, most tend to believe, may be trying to fool them, to manipulate them, to hide his or her true self. The "true" self is thus the internal self—the one that is not so clearly under the potential control of the other person.

Most psychologists tend to discount the belief that a "real" self is somehow hidden in the dark recesses of an individual's psyche. But they will also agree that a person's actual behavior may or may not accurately reflect that individual's true feelings and thoughts. People sometimes behave in ways that are intended to hide more preferred feelings and beliefs. What often comes to mind are the more fraudulent instances of this behavior. For example, a smile on the face of a politician always seems fake, as if it were pasted on. The glad-handing used-car salesperson represents the stereotype of false behaviors masking impure motives. A favorite ploy of political mudslingers is to ask their opponent "Would you buy a used car from this person?" Masking or hiding true feelings and opinions is not necessarily bad. People mask feelings in order to avoid hurting another's feelings. For example, friends work out their own rules for being judgmental and accepting of each other (Rawlins, 1989), which could involve the masking of preferred feelings and beliefs. One of these rules might be, the masking of beliefs about clothing styles. The friends have decided that although one of them does not care for the style of clothes the other wears, those beliefs are masked in an attempt to preserve harmony and not hurt the other's feelings. Complete openness and honesty is not the general rule of even close relationships. Turner, Edgley, and Olmstead (1975) suggest that hiding one's feelings and thoughts may actually help promote intimacy by occasionally allowing partners to protect themselves and avoid conflict. Nonetheless, inferences involve jumping to conclusions on the basis of incomplete information. Some

Masking feelings and opinions is not always bad.

inferences require greater distance in the jumps than others, but all call for a psychological leap to a conclusion.

No one can directly observe another person's internal self. But people all make inferences about other people's internal selves on the basis of what they observe. And the only thing people can observe is the external self—behaviors or actions. As the discussion in this chapter will make clear, this undeniable truth about inferential understanding also applies to the way you come to understand your own self.

THE SELF

For decades western society has reflected a massive effort to glorify the individual and the self. The decade of the 1960s was known as the "me generation." The pop psychology of that era emphasized the individual's right to have "peak experiences" and seek "self-actualization." Ayn Rand, a popular philosopher and author of *Atlas Shrugged*, wrote about the "virtue of selfishness." Hugh Hefner's *"Playboy* philosophy" extolled the means of self-gratification and hedonistic lifestyle. The Staple Singers recorded the highly popular "Respect Yourself," and Mary Travers sang "I Need Me to Be for Me." Even today physical-fitness programs, self-help groups, and self-esteem programs are praised for their effectiveness in self-improvement and helping you "feel good about yourself."

Now just who or what is this inner person (or persons) referred to as *self*? Since the days of Sigmund Freud, psychologists and sociologists have debated the importance of self and created different theories of self. In fact, the late 1940s saw the return of "self" as a legitimate area of research (Lauer & Handel, 1977). For our purposes *self* will be defined as "a person's organization of accumulated experience, which provides the basis for personal action" (Faules & Alexander, 1978, p. 44). Your self is what you know about yourself and what you have experienced. Further, to have a self means that you have the capability of observing, responding, and directing your behavior (Lauer & Handel, 1977). That is, you can act toward yourself just as you do toward other social objects. Behavior toward your self doesn't happen in a vacuum but occurs in interaction with others. There are two important characteristics of self implicated in our definition; self is a process and self is reflexive.

Self is not a physical entity, but a process (Allport, 1962). Gordon Allport explains that self as a process is a present being that is always becoming or moving toward the future. Your self will never arrive at some final destination, and you can change, but not necessarily believe you are being inconsistent. Allport believes that the self is a "wide-open" system responsive to its environment, looking for novel ideas, and capable of the question "Who am I?" (p. 380).

The process of self is found in the tension between two phases of the self: the "I" and the "me" (Mead, 1934). The *I* aspect of your self is self as an active agent, or the subject of action—your active self. Your "I" is novel and unpredictable. When you respond to questions such as "Why are you going to college?" "Why are you picking this major?" and "Why are you writing your paper this way?" you are focusing on your "I." Whereas, your *me* is the aspect of your self as an object—your reflective self. Your "me" reflects the general expectations of your social world (social attitudes, mores, values, and so on) and assists in setting the limits for your "I." You describe your "me" when you respond to the question "Who are you?"

Your self is complete or whole only when these two aspects are *taken together.* The process of self is one of mediation between your I's unpredictability and your me's expectations. What this means is that for your self to be whole, you must behave ("I") and you must think about your behavior ("me") (Faules & Alexander, 1978). For example, suppose a friend did something you didn't like and you decide to tell this friend what you think and how you feel. You find yourself in your interpersonal class where your instructor is going over effective ways to manage conflict. You begin to think about the different ways you could have talked to your friend. Your "I" acted toward your friend in a particular manner, and it is your "me" that is reflecting on the appropriateness of your past behavior. The process of self includes *both* aspects taken together.

Self is also reflexive because you can observe, respond to, and evaluate your own behavior. To have a self means that you can be an object of your own behavior and you are aware of your own qualities (Blumer, 1969). You act differently toward your professors than toward your best friends. If you believe strongly that you are an excellent student, your study behaviors will probably differ from those of someone who believes he or she is a mediocre student. You are capable of defining your self and responding to that definition because self can be observed, evaluated, and responded to on a continuous basis.

One of the supreme ironies of western psychology is that the self, the quality that makes an individual a unique human being, develops through and is probably impossible to attain without social interaction—communication with other human beings. McCall (1987) argues that compelling evidence in social cognition identifies "conversation" as the place one finds self. The idea that an individual's self is socially constructed breaks with American tradition which has typically focused on the idea that self-perception is primarily grounded in the reactions of others to self. Life experiences shape the self of every individual human being. But each person must also be aware of what is happening and what has happened to self. Self-awareness is basically a process of perception that is directed inward. People attempt to perceive and thereby to understand who they are. This section on "the self" explores various intrapersonal processes and their relevance to interpersonal communication by first discussing how humans come to know their "selves" through the psychological processes of perception and awareness and then by focusing on how those perceptions impact their interpersonal interaction.

The Process of Perception

Meaning, humans tend to believe, is equivalent to perception. That is, people generally believe that their meanings are products of an intrapersonal psychological process. This psychological process associated with interpretation and with assigning meanings to persons and objects is known as *perception.* A standard psychological definition of perception might include the following: "Perception is defined as the meaningful interpretation of sensations as representatives of external objects; perception is *apparent* knowledge of what is out there" (Cohen, 1969, p. 6).

This definition contains some key elements of perception that are fundamental to any attempt to understand this intrapersonal process. First, an act of perception requires the presence of some *object* to be perceived. This would include, among other things, another human being as well as one's own self. One's own self is perceived *as though* the self were another person or an external object. The difference is that perception of self includes more information available for interpretation and is subject to more biases and prejudices than is the perception of some other person or object. Second, the only information available for interpretation is *sensory information*—whatever can be gathered by one or more of the five senses. We perceive only what we can see, hear, smell, taste, or feel. Third, sensory information is *representational* in nature. You cannot interpret the meaning of any object directly; you actually interpret the meaning of only the information which you believe "represents" that object. The sights, odors, sounds, tastes, and textures only represent an object, an other, or your self. Thus, any knowledge gained from perception is never of what something *is* but only what it *appears* to be.

Norwood Russell Hanson (1967), a philosopher of science, supported this characteristic of human observation in his philosophical writings. He believed that one can never merely observe and that "pure" observation is not possible; it is virtually impossible to distinguish between sensation and perception. To illustrate, what happens when you smell a rose? Do you first have a physiological sensation (an odor) and then a psychological perception (the pleasant aroma associated with a rose)? Do you first smell then later smell a rose? Not likely. You associate your sensation (the smell) with the familiar aroma of a rose (the perceived object) virtually simultaneously.

If perception is truly subjective, then one never just "sees" anything. The perceiver inevitably and unavoidably *sees* it *as* something or other; the perceiver always interprets what is seen. Furthermore, the interpretation will also affect what you do see. Look at Figure 3-1. It is a familiar optical illusion with two equally valid interpretations: one, a fancy symmetrical vase; two, the profiles of two heads facing each other. Note that you can see the vase, and then you can see the two heads. By changing your interpretation, you can make the drawing "snap back and forth" between vase and heads. Your interpretation allows you to see the drawing as vase, then as heads, then as vase, then as heads, and so on. Note further, however, that you cannot see the drawing as *both* heads and vase at the same time. You continue to "see" the same object, but you see it as one meaning or the other, not both.

Perception then is never more than "apparent" knowledge of reality. And appearances can be deceiving, as you know from mirages, optical illusions, special effects in movies, cases of mistaken identity, and instant replays. Naturally, you should never be overly confident of the knowledge you gain from your perceptions. Quite ironically, the knowledge about which you are most positive is precisely the knowledge you do gain from your perceptions. Perceived reality is the most vivid, personal, important, and credible knowledge to nearly all people nearly all the time. And that is one of the reasons why the process of interpersonal communication and human relationships is so difficult to "understand," yet so simple to "know."

The Nature of Perception   Our discussion of perception has thus far repeatedly emphasized two points: (1) that knowledge gained from percep-

FIGURE 3-1 The two-headed vase—an optical illusion.

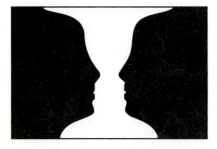

tion is only a reflection of reality and is therefore highly fallible and (2) that knowledge gained from perception is vivid, personal, and thus typically accepted as true, often uncritically. To this point, however, we have not discussed how and why the intrapersonal process of perception works. To understand what is going on when people communicate with one another, you must understand how people come to know about themselves and other people. Perception occurs inside the head of the individual, not in the object, and therefore perception is always "apparent knowledge." Remember: What is absolutely clear to you may be a matter of considerable confusion to someone else. This paradox of perception, the fallibility yet uncritical acceptance of perceived "facts," is vital to understanding the intrapersonal level of interpersonal communication.

Perception Is Experiential   To interpret the meaning of some person, object, or event is to have some basis on which to make an interpretation. That basis will typically be found in your own past experiences with that person, object, or event or with some similar persons, objects, or events. For example, there are movies like *My Mother Was an Alien* or *The God's Must Be Crazy* that have depicted some outer-space creature or person from a long-ago past encountering objects familiar to your everyday experience. These objects are not familiar to the alien or to the anachronistic native, who doesn't know what the objects are or what to do with them. How would people from an earlier century perceive a TV set, for example? If they were from colonial America, say Salem, they might perceive television as witchcraft, a sign of Satan. Perception, even perception of self, is an interpreted meaning based on your experiences.

Perception Is Selective   When people perceive something, they select only certain characteristics of the perceived object and ignore the others. The result is that people perceive only part of the perceived object. Your perceptions are never based on a complete set of sensory data because perception *must* be selective. It is physiologically and psychologically impossible to take into account *all* the information that is accessible to the five senses at any given time. The number of informational items it can take into account at any given time is small (see Miller, 1956). Selectivity in processing information is fundamentally a coping mechanism. Without it you would suffer from massive information overload and almost total chaos of meaning that overload entails. Selectivity, then, is an essential and actually quite beneficial characteristic of perception, while at the same time it also limits the amount of data people have available for perception.

On what basis do you decide which characteristics of the person or object to select and which to ignore? For one thing, you perceive what you "want" to perceive on the basis of your experiences, expectations, attitudes, values, and beliefs. These inputs serve as criteria for selecting which sensory information is important, relevant, or credible—in short, which information to perceive. Expectations, for example, can be a highly potent force in guiding your perceptions. Every Halloween Aub and his church's youth group used to have a party for the junior high kids. The highlight of the party was a spook alley in which the unsuspecting "trick-or-treaters" were led into a dark room and treated to a variety of sensations (not sight) after having been told what to expect. A bowl of cold spaghetti, for example, was described as the intestines of some dead ghoul and cold, peeled grapes were eyeballs, among other tactile sensations and expectations appropriate to Halloween. His role in this party was to don a rubber glove and keep his hand immersed in ice water until it was time to shake someone's hands. At the moment his hand touched that of one of the trick-or-treaters', he laughed his legendary fiendish laugh. For years the group held such a spook party, even though it is hard to accept that adolescents could possibly believe that spaghetti was intestines, that grapes were eyeballs, or that a cold, wet rubber glove was the hand of the living dead!

Relevant to perceptions of self, selectivity also allows the perceiver to select certain aspects of self to be perceived and to ignore others. Of course, selectivity can also function to deny the existence, importance, or relevance of undesired information. When you have information that is detrimental to your self-image, you immediately "circle the wagons" and proceed to ward off the "attack." The selectivity inherent in the process of perception allows you to protect your perceived meaning of your own self. Later discussions will return to the topic of self-protection.

Perception Is Inferential   We have already discussed the fact that perceiving meaning involves jumping to a conclusion that is not fully warranted by the available sensory data. The interpretation that results from perception is, thus, an inference based on incomplete information.

Like selectivity, it is necessary to the interpretive process. It is necessary because acquiring a complete set of details from the five senses is virtually impossible. Take an iceberg, for instance. When above water, you can see only the part of the iceberg that is above water. You are nonetheless apt to infer the existence of the iceberg below the water. When you notice an airplane hundreds of feet above you, you do not see its crew or passengers yet you infer their existence. After all you have seen enough airplanes to feel assured that there is at least a crew flying the plane.

The inferential process of perception allows you to interpret a more complete meaning of an object or a person from any one vantage point. Since complete information is never possible, inferences are necessary if one is to draw conclusions from the incomplete information that comes through the senses. Perceivers must "fill in the blanks" to complete the picture and provide the missing information. Perception, then, is a process of "organizing" available information, of placing the known details within a certain organizational scheme that allows you to perceive a more general meaning that goes beyond the mere details. The organizing character of perception is the process referred to in Chapter 1 as "punctuation."

Droodles, whose popularity has unfortunately waned considerably in recent years, provide an excellent example of the creative inferences available in your power of perceptual organization. A *droodle* is a line drawing that provides minimum information; it is essentially a puzzle. A droodle becomes humorous because the creative solution to the "What is it?" question is a far-fetched inference. Figure 3-2 shows five droodles, each with its own creative organization of a minimum amount of informational details and a huge inferential leap to an interpreted meaning that is straight out of "left field." Droodle A is a trombone player practicing in a telephone booth (on its side, the droodle is a dead trombone player). B is a fried egg for those who like their eggs sunny side down. C is a spider doing a handstand. D has been described as tic-tac-toe for beginners, but we prefer the interpretation that it is a view of two polar bears eating marshmallows in a snowstorm as seen through a frosted window. One of our favorite droodles is the last one; what you see if you've been thrown down a well by two witches. How you organize or punctuate each droodle influences the inference you make about the identity of each droodle (e.g., tic-tac-toe or polar bears).

Droodles represent perceptual inferences fostered by a creative imagi-

FIGURE 3-2 Droodles—case studies in perceptual organization.

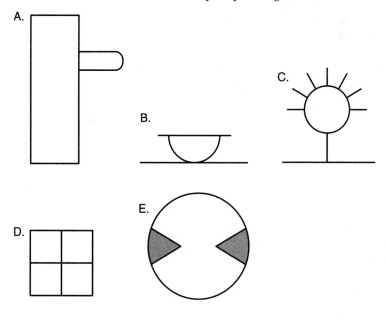

nation or punctuation that affects the interpretation. When one's own self is the object of perception, the organization of details to make the inference logical is often no less creative than the interpretation of droodles. The human being has the ability to organize details into often very extraordinary interpretations of self-image. To illustrate, Aub once talked with a student who was suffering from serious academic problems and in danger of flunking out. The student informed him that he had decided to change his major once again—to communication. While discussing his academic problems, the student organized all the information about his past experiences and inferred a self-image that was, at best, an interpretation at least as "creative" as those for the droodles in Figure 3-2. According to his perceptions, he had not slept well the night before taking the ACT and SAT tests. Besides, he explained, those scores weren't valid because he just didn't perform well on standardized tests. The reason for his poor grades in both high school and college was that he just wasn't interested in those classes and performed far below his ability. But now he had discovered communication and knew that it was the major for him. That, he informed Aub, was why he was doing so well in Aub's class. Aub didn't know how to tell him he was failing the class. He and Aub had the same information, but their respective perceptions of his performance were certainly different. (Incidentally, the student did pass Aub's course with a D, and Aub never saw him again.)

Perception Is Evaluative   To say that anyone perceives something or someone "objectively" or to use the term "objective perception" is to fool yourself. No perception is ever objective. You interpret on the basis of your past experiences and your own personal focus. Perception is an inner, cognitive psychological process. It unavoidably reflects those personal attitudes, values, beliefs, and expectations that you use to assign meaning to the object of perception. Perception is highly personal and thus subjective. The student's self-perception in the above example was not "wrong"; it was different from Aub's highly personal perception.

Steve Duck, an internationally recognized scholar of human relationships, has asserted that "reality cannot be perceived without construal," a process that involves unique and very "personal reasons" for acting in social relationships (1973, p. 136). He goes on to emphasize the "importance of the parallel processes of evaluating what is construed and the inferences from it" (p. 137). Duck makes clear that the inevitable counterpart of subjective interpretation is the process of evaluation. No one perceives just what something "is" without also perceiving how "good or bad" that something is. Rarely, if ever, is a perceived event, person, or object totally neutral.

Perception Is Contextual   Of all the influences discussed that affect your perceptions, context may be the most potent. The context in which you encounter a person, object, or event strongly influences your cognitive structures and expectations and thus your perceptions. Figure 3-3 illustrates just how strong the context is in influencing the interpretation of the sensations. The geometric figure, at the top, is somewhat ambiguous when seen by itself, that is, when it is isolated from any context. But place that identical figure as a sequence of numbers, and its meaning is "13." Place the figure in a sequence of letters, and its meaning is "B."

The geometric figure in Figure 3-3 did not change. What changed was how the figure was "punctuated." The different order imposed on the figure by placing it in a sequence of numbers or letters created the different interpretations. The punctuation of the figure helps guide your perception and makes an alternative interpretation appear difficult. If you chose to place the figure in the wrong sequence of letters or numbers, then "11, B, 15, 17" or "A, 13, C, D" would not make sense. However, if you chose another way to punctuate or frame the figure, then those sequences might make perfect sense to you.

Context and punctuation provide crucial components of the pragmatic view that underlies our entire understanding of interpersonal communication. As you have come to realize, no interpretation of any communicative behavior, verbal or nonverbal, and no meaning of any relationship is possible without placing it within a context and constructing some pattern of interaction. The absence of a pattern is equivalent to having no meaning or, at least, to a confusion of too many meanings. Interpreting meanings within their context is a major factor, perhaps the most important single factor, in understanding interpersonal communication and social relationships (pragmatic principle 4)

Perception is experiential, selective, inferential, evaluative, and contextual. Perception is not like a movie camera or giant videotape recorder that you use to make contact with the world through the senses. When humans perceive, they don't so much *record* the sights, sounds, and smells of their

FIGURE 3-3 Interpretations provided by the context.

world as they actively *create* meanings that are not necessarily present in the external environment. Furthermore, persons, objects, and events have no inherent value or goodness; the act of perception creates an evaluation and attributes it to those worldly phenomena. The movie camera or videotape recorder has yet to be invented that has the creative power of interpretation, evaluation, inference, and subjectivity present in even the most everyday act of human perception.

Awareness of Self

As we mentioned before our discussion of human perception, life experiences shape the self of every human being. Each person must be aware of what is happening and what has happened to self. Self-awareness is a process of perception turned inward and is thus susceptible to the selective, inferential, evaluative, and contextual nature of human perception. People attempt to perceive and thereby understand themselves. Self-awareness can be turned inward because the self is reflexive and can be perceived just as you perceive objects, events, and other people. The general subjective idea or abstraction formed from a "relatively stable set of perceptions you hold of yourself" (Adler & Towne, 1993) is the *self-concept*.

The Self-Concept   Although interest in the idea of "self" and "self-concept" can be traced to the Greeks and experimental work to the early 1900s, not until the 1940s did "self-concept" become a common research topic (Lauer & Handel, 1977). Self being the object of inward awareness is not the same as the self-concept. Your self-concept is that part of your self which you conceive of as a set of relatively stable self-characterizations. To illustrate, how would you answer the question "How do you see yourself?" Generally speaking, people tend to classify themselves in three ways (Kuhn and McPartland, 1954): personal attributes or traits, social attributes or traits, and social roles. Personal traits are characteristics which can be physical (e.g., tall, short, male, female, plain, handsome) or which describe an ability (e.g., dumb, verbal, athletic, smart, skilled, clumsy, educated, musical). Social traits are those qualities you think you demonstrate in your relations with other people or your communicative style (e.g., friendly, introverted, assertive, sincere, manipulative, caring, extroverted). Social roles identify the self in relationship with a particular person in a particular society (e.g., father, mother, sister, aunt, teacher, police officer, Catholic, Hispanic, Democrat). These aspects of your self-concept differ in their importance or significance to your self-concept, their perceived value, and their stability or likelihood of changing.

Even though people may refer to the self as if it were a singular identity, they have a variety of different self-identities in terms of multiple personal traits, interpersonal attributes, and social roles. Your multiple selves relate to different social relationships with different people and should be under-stood as representing your diverse activities, interests, and social relation-ships. Every time you participate in an interpersonal relationship, you deal with who you think you are and who you think the other person thinks you are. In addition, you not only deal with who you think you are, but another part involves who you would like to be—a kind of "ideal" self. An *ideal self* is your imaginative construction of who you want to be or think you ought to be (Argyle, 1969). Attempting to narrow the gap between your "real" self and "ideal" self is probably behind most of the fads relevant to self-im-provement. How many of you have ever gone on a diet to get down to our "ideal" weight? The desire for self-improvement is probably an attempt to get your "real" self closer to your "ideal" self.

During the normal process of living and interacting, people go about developing their self-concept. Self is a process, and because the self-concept is a part of that process it is "processual" in nature as well. It is more stable than self which accounts for its continuity, but the process of "getting in touch with yourself" is continuous, inevitable, and unavoidable. If you are to understand fully the intrapersonal level of your relationships and to be able to take advantage of it, you need to be aware of your own self-concept and how any changes in it come about. Changes in your self-concept come about because the self is reflexive, social, and always evolving.

When you look into a mirror, you see not only your self but your self looking back at you. This illustrates the principle of the reflexive self mentioned earlier. Self-awareness is a cycle of perceiving your actions and being aware that you are engaging in self-perception (Duval & Wicklund, 1972). Because you are a human being, a most sophisticated animal, you are able to act and perceive and to do both at the same time.

It is virtually impossible to be an individual without being involved in interpersonal relationships. Jurgen Ruesch has been quoted as saying, "It is well to remember that all the information a person possesses about himself is derived from others. His impression of the impact he had upon others is what makes up the picture of himself" (cited in Wilmot, 1980, p. 44). The "social self" (Mead, 1913) refers to your use of other people as the criterion for judging your own self-concept. Have you ever told a joke and no one laughed? If that should happen a sufficient number of times, you would begin to wonder about yourself, to lower your evaluation of your self. As you interact with others, the effect is similar to looking in a mirror. Charles Cooley (1922) referred to this effect as the "looking-glass self." You see reflected back to you, in the behaviors of your fellow interactants, an image of your own self. Some people are more sensitive to their own behaviors and to the behavior of others during interaction. The ability to self-monitor (Snyder, 1974) is necessary if you are to be aware of what constitutes appropriate behavior in a social setting. Since it is an ability, it is something which can be improved. Perhaps your instructor may

When you look into a
mirror you see your
self and your self
looking back at you
just as you are able to
act and perceive that
action.

have some ideas concerning ways to improve your own self-monitoring
ability.

Your self-concept never just "is"; it is always in a state of "becoming."
Your self-concept is always subject to change, is constantly developing, is
continually being shaped by the perception and interpretation of new
information. Now that does not mean that your self-concept undergoes
radical changes every time you talk with someone new. In normal day-to-
day activities, your self-concept remains rather constant, without significant changes. You don't enter communicative events with a blank self-concept. Your self-concept is an accumulation of interpretations from past
events intertwined with future expectations. You bring to new events your
self-concept from the past, balance it against the interpretations of yourself
in the present event, and make any appropriate revisions (Wilmot, 1980).

Your self-concept, also, remains relatively stable because perception itself tends to resist massive revisions in your interpretations. Change in your self-concept is typically a very gradual, evolutionary change and not a large-scale modification. Making new friends, getting married, getting a job, graduating from school, moving away from friends, losing a job, getting a divorce, having an argument with someone special—these are all normal fluctuations of life, normal fluctuations in your self-concept, and part of your becoming self.

Self-Esteem   One of the characteristics of perception is that it is evaluative. *Self-esteem* is the term used to denote one's evaluative perception of self and is an inherent part of your self-concept. Self-esteem refers to the positive and negative feelings of worth you give to your self-concept, or "how favourably" (Argyle, 1969, p. 356) you regard yourself. Research suggests that there is a basic human need for self-esteem (Lauer & Handel, 1977). Self-esteem appears to be a central factor in emotional health. Your self-esteem is deeper and longer-lasting than a temporary reaction to a specific event or a temporary low point in your life. For example, if you are temporarily "feeling bad" about something, that doesn't mean that you have negative or low self-esteem. Each of us at one time or another has said, "I hate myself when I do things like that." Your hatred is directed at your action, not your self, and it rarely affects your self-concept and self-esteem. Your self-esteem is part of the interpretation, the inference of self-perception and not merely a simple reaction to an event in your life.

Our view of self is admittedly grounded in the individualistic orientation of western psychology. Although definitions of self may vary within western psychology, self is consistently conceptualized as a "unitary phenomenon" (Johnson, 1985, p. 93) or as peculiar to an individual. As such, the self is treated as an individualistic phenomenon and exists separate from any group the individual may belong to. Members of individualistic cultures such as the United States and Germany tend to experience the self

> As a bounded, unique, more or less integrated motivational and cognitive universe, a dynamic center of awareness, emotion, judgement, and action organized into a distinctive whole and set contrastively both against other wholes and against a social and natural background. (Geertz, 1975, p. 48)

Thus, goals such as self-actualization and self-promotion are indicative of western, individualistic societies. Further, self-esteem is derived from an individual's ability to stand on his or her own; it comes from within.

In comparison, individuals in collectivistic cultures (e.g., China, Japan, Korea) "belong to ingroups or collectivities which are supposed to look after them in exchange for loyalty" (Hofstede & Bond, 1984, p. 419). In China the basis for self, or *jen* (*jin* in Japan), is found in the individual's interactions with others (Hsu, 1985). Whereas self is defined as an intrapsychic phenomenon in the United States, in collectivistic cultures its basis is found in "an intersecting web of social and personal relationships" (Gudykunst, Ting-Toomey, & Chua, 1988, p. 85.). In New Guinea, the Gahuku-Gana, as individuals, are not given any moral value separate from that which is given them by their social status (Read, 1955). Self-promotion is not a goal in these cultural contexts, self-esteem is linked to social networks, and individual success is based on the ability to establish a network of social relationships.

Our treatment of self in interpersonal communication is admittedly individualistic. Although this is our orientation, we do recognize that other cultural views of self do exist and serve to frame different individual experiences of self.

An individual's self, self-concept, and self-esteem are not only related to one another but are also inextricably tied to social interaction. A central feature of our definition of self is that it is the basis for personal action. Your self, self-concept, and self-esteem are developed in social interaction and impact social interaction. In Chapter 2 we touched upon this reciprocal relationship and now will explore it in more detail.

The Self and Interpersonal Behavior

The self cannot itself behave, but it clearly influences behavior. The self is an intrapersonal, psychological part of interpersonal communication. It exists within the individual and comprises beliefs, attitudes, values, cognitions—but not behaviors. But those psychological processes, though they probably can't "cause" people to behave in a certain way (if they did, false roles or unintended behaviors would be virtually impossible), still have implications for understanding how people behave during interpersonal communication. Recall, from our discussion of nested hierarchies of systems, that the intrapersonal system (the self) is nested within the interpersonal system (the relationship) and thus impacts and is impacted by the interpersonal system but is not itself the interpersonal system.

In 1987, George McCall, a sociologist, noted the renewed interest in the role of self in social psychological processes. Of particular interest to scholars of interpersonal communication is the recognition of the field of study called *social cognition*. At the heart of this area of study is the treatment of self as an information processing system (see also Berger, 1987b; Kuiper & Derry, 1981; Markus & Smith, 1981; Rogers, 1981; Sanders, 1992; Snyder, 1981). True, scholars have long recognized a relationship between self and social interaction, but the focus has traditionally been either on the cognitive content of self or on the cognitive processes, but not both—social cognition seeks to examine the dynamic relationship between both (Landman & Manis, 1983). Thus a cognitive scientist would carefully observe behavior and then inductively construct models that would serve as a kind of "map" between the observed social behavior and cognitive structures (Sanders, 1992).

Understanding how people cognitively structure social phenomena is important to our study of interpersonal communication. Trenholm and Jensen (1992) point out that the manner in which you cognitively structure your social world is related to how you perceive and interpret another's behaviors, the behavioral choices you make during interaction, and the amount of control you have over your interaction. In addition, the relationship between your "self" and the social world is reciprocal (Snyder, 1981). That is, there is a mutual interplay between you and the social world you inhabit. Philosophers such as George Mead (1934) have always celebrated the dynamic role individuals play in the shaping of their social worlds and the simultaneous impact which that world has on the individual. "The person continuously influences the "situation" of his life as well as being affected by them in a mutual, organic two-way interaction" (Mischel, 1973, p. 278). Thus, it becomes much more difficult to assume that interpersonal behavior is simply a product of or a reaction to stimuli and psychological processes. People select, alter, and use information as stimuli and in essence create stimuli to the extent that by themselves they do not determine social behavior (Planalp & Hewes, 1982; Watchel, 1973).

Much conjecture surrounds the nature of the cognitive structures which function to help people process social information. Psychologist John La-Gaipa (1981, p. 75) suggests that the intrapersonal process involved in interpersonal relationships comprises several parts: a *memory* of past experiences and *anticipations* of future experiences. The ability to anticipate what will happen to you can be considered an "implicit psychological resource" which the communicator uses to organize past experiences and provide guidelines for behaving appropriately in the present. "Self-schemata," "prototypes," "scripts," and "plans" have been used to refer to those psychological resources people use to produce social behavior. People have conceptualizations of their "selves" just as they do of other individuals, objects, and events. *Schemas* are frameworks into which you place all known information about your "self" in any given situation (Markus & Smith, 1981). *Self-schemata*, then, are "cognitive generalizations about the self, derived from past experience, that organize and guide the processing of self-related information contained in the individual's social experience" (Markus, 1977, p. 64). These self-schemata form the basis for your selectivity when processing social information, your own perception of your social behavior, and they serve as theories about your "self" (Markus & Smith, 1981). Remember that as "resources" these psychological structures do not "make" you behave in a certain way, but they are available to assist you in behaving appropriately.

"Self" as an Information Processing System   Charles Berger's work (1987a & 1987b) exemplifies this kind of thinking in interpersonal communication. He makes note that little is understood about these structures and social action because research tends not to examine social action as a dependent variable but rather focuses on memory, recall, judgments, and related phenomena. He takes the position that a person's self-concept is a mediator between social behavior and information, and thus he is interested in exploring how a person's social behavior is related to social information processing. Particular kinds of cognitive structures central to social information processing function to help individuals judge themselves and others. For example, on one occasion (Berger, 1987a), he has explored the relationship between cognitive plans and a specific kind of social action—asking for a date. Central to his work is a conceptualization of self as an "information processing system" (1987b, p. 289). Such a conceptualization fosters attention on how this system is related to behavior in social interaction.

"Self" as an Anchor Point for Personal Judgments "Self" is a significant anchor point for your judgments of yourself and others. This serves to produce a judgmental bias in your retroactive sensemaking of past events. Since you are the anchor point, this bias is an *egocentric bias*. People remember much more about their behavior in interaction than they do of the behavior of others. A consequence of this bias is that people tend to overestimate their contributions to interaction and thus overestimate their responsibility for the outcome of the interaction. For example, it has been documented that spouses not only report more examples of their contribution to the housework but also overestimate their responsibility for the work around the house (Tversky & Kahneman, 1973). A couple Kathy knows is engaged in a continual battle over who does what around their house and who spends more time and effort on yard maintenance. How much of this relational issue is grounded in distorted notions of contributions and responsibility?

Not only do people tend to reflect an egocentric bias in their judgments, which has implications for their behavior, but they also tend to experience a *false consensus bias,* or *effect* (Berger, 1987b, p. 290). People tend to believe that others would do and say the same as themselves in a given situation. The implication of this bias for interaction is that people often behave as if others would think and behave the same as themselves, when in fact they may not. Many assumptions you have about another's beliefs and behavior, which you use as a basis for your behavioral choices, are not the same.

Self-fulfilling Prophecies Self-fulfilling prophecies (Merton, 1948) characterize a second way in which self, as an information processing system, is related to social behavior. The *self-fulfilling prophecy* begins with your anticipation of some future event. Because you expect something to occur, you behave (often inconspicuously) in a manner that actually contributes to the occurrence of the anticipated event. For example, you "know" that your relationship with that special person just won't work out. As a result of your expectation, you act disinterested, you see that person less and less—and sure enough, the relationship doesn't work out. In essence, a self-fulfilling prophecy is a "behavioral confirmation process" (Snyder, 1981, p. 311). Your actions based on preconceived assumptions and beliefs can set up the behaviors of others to validate those very preconceived notions. Of course, the anticipation of a great relationship can have just the opposite effect. It leads you to work at making the relationship grow: You become more attentive and helpful, and that sequence of behaviors allows the prophecy to come true.

Berger (1987b) points out that people even bias their efforts to gather information about another person. Let's say that you have met someone you really like and you'd like to get to know this person. You have formed an initial impression that this person is really funny. When you are making up your mind about whether this person is really funny, you will tend to ask questions that validate the trait rather than invalidate it. You bias your information seeking in favor of the schematic sense you have of the person, and the person may very well act in line with the bias thus confirming it. As your friend acts consistently with your own schemata (which is already biased toward self), you create an illusion of being similar to your friend.

Self-fulfilling prophecies are present in the larger society as well. In fact, the often-discussed "sex-role stereotypes" may be seen as self-fulfilling prophecies in action. Young girls are often given dolls to play with, told to be clean, and taught to act "feminine." In contrast, young boys are usually given baseball gloves, encouraged to get dirty, and taught to "be a man" and not cry. The traits people come to associate with being masculine and feminine do not "belong" to men and women, but are often the result of trained behaviors throughout the child's growing-up period and thus, instead, reflect a consistent pattern of behaviors (Snyder, 1981).

Aub's daughter was "caught" in a potentially self-fulfilling prophecy regarding sex-role stereotypes. Since she had received exceptionally good grades throughout elementary school, her mother and Aub were somewhat surprised when her sixth-grade teacher recommended her for advanced-placement courses in junior high English but not in mathematics. They asked the teacher why this was so, and he appeared surprised. He responded quite innocently that he wasn't aware of their daughter's interest in math but that he would certainly recommend her if they wished. They asked him whether he had questioned the boys he had recommended for advanced placement about their interest in math. He didn't seem to comprehend why they were asking.

Self-fulfilling prophecies are often difficult to see in operation. Furthermore, people often attribute the results of confirmatory processes to factors other than the behaviors precipitated by the anticipation of future events. Your relationship broke up because that special person was not "right" for

you, not because you were inattentive. Snyder (1981) writes that the consequences of self-fulfilling prophecies to our interpersonal relationships and
social interaction are "both profound and pervasive" (p. 312). He goes on
to say that

> Individuals may construct for themselves social worlds in which the
> behavior of those with whom they interact reflects, verifies, maintains, and
> justifies their preexisting conceptions of other people, including many
> highly stereotyped assumptions about human nature. (pp. 312–313)

Self-Protection A third way the self, as an information processing
system, influences social behavior is demonstrated in people's tendency to
verify and protect their self-conceptions. Those individuals with strong
self-schemata "elicit, attend to, and remember information consistent"
(Berger, 1987b, p. 294) with their self-concepts, especially if they believe
another's perception of them is not consistent with their own. Those individuals with weaker self-schemata are less protective of their self-concepts
and more likely to get caught in another's "prophecies." Generally, then,
individuals go to great lengths to protect their self-concepts from change
and challenge in order to avoid psychological harm. Some individuals,
particularly those with low self-esteem, have rather fragile self-concepts.

Self-protection may take several forms. *Self-handicapping strategies* (Berglas & Jones, 1978) are examples of the lengths to which people will go to
protect their self-conceptions. For example, what strategies will you use to
protect your self-conception of competence? Berglas and Jones discovered
that the male college students in their study who thought they were
intelligent and competent, when faced with the possibility of performing
poorly on a task, chose to take a performance-inhibiting drug before the
task. What they did was handicap themselves so that if they failed the task,
they could blame the drugs, but if they performed well, they could take
credit for overcoming the effects of the drug. Think about the last time you
were faced with the possibility that you might not do as well as you would
like on an exam. What did you do to handicap yourself in order to protect
your belief that you are intelligent? Did you stay up late, party hard the
night before, begin studying the day before, and so on? When you received
your exam grade and discovered you did great, did you pat yourself on the
back because you had done well despite partying hard the night before? Or
upon receiving a terrible grade, did you blame your hangover?

This way of protecting your self in interpersonal communication is
accomplished on a general level by attributing the potential threat to your
self-concept to some cause that doesn't affect your self-concept. When
something undesirable or threatening occurs in communication, your perceptual ability allows you to attribute the "cause" of the undesirable
element to something that does not threaten your self-concept. Psychologist
John Harvey and his colleagues (1982) suggest that

People may sometimes engage in misattribution—probably without much awareness—to dull the experience of self-threatening problems in the relationship. For example, reduction of affectionate contact from a partner can be translated as "He's been under a lot of pressure lately." We can choose to make the attribution situational ("outside pressures") rather than dispositional ("He has a less affectionate nature") or interpersonal ("He is less affectionate *towards me*"). (p. 113)

One of the key elements in *attribution* (designating the cause or reason for some occurrence) is to provide a "locus of control" (similar to a cause). People attribute the occurrence to some controlling factor that is either "internal" or "external" to the self. When the partner wasn't as affectionate as formerly, in the example given above, the person attributed the problem to "outside pressures"—that is, to the situation. The person may also protect the self by attributing the problem to the other person, saying that the partner has a "less affectionate nature." Attributing the undesirable occurrence to the other person or to the situation ("external" locus) allows one to protect one's self-concept. But attributing the occurrence to an "internal" locus ("toward me") is potentially damaging to a person's own self-concept. It seems rather obvious that people would, under "normal" circumstances, tend to attribute the locus of relational problems to some factor other than their own selves. In doing so, they explain the problem and protect their self-concept and self-esteem.

Such protection also occurs on a societal level. Have you ever wondered why our society tends to show little compassion for victims of violent crimes (e.g., rape)? If people attribute the cause of the crime to the victim (she or he should never have gone into that bar), then they can gain a sense of control over violence in their own lives by believing that all they have to do to circumvent a similar situation is not behave like the victim. In contrast, to believe that the victim wasn't at fault (not in control of the circumstances) is to admit that no matter what they may do to circumvent dangerous situations, violence still can occur.

Another form of self-protection is described by sociologist Erving Goffman (1971). He views protecting self as defending one's "territory" from attack. He describes two perceptual "territories of self" that people commonly protect: *"information preserve:* The set of facts about himself to which an individual expects to control access while in the presence of others" and *"conversational preserve:* The right of an individual to exert some control over who can summon him into talk and when he can be summoned" (pp. 39–40).

Goffman's territory of information preserve is very similar to self-disclosure when private knowledge of self is converted into public knowledge, *as the self-discloser chooses to do so.* The second territory of conversational preserve is the self's declaration of the right of privacy, a right to "protect" one's self from relational involvement. Metaphorically, "territory of the self" refers to an individual's right to choose with whom to be involved in a relationship and to what degree in terms of self-disclosure and, when in a relationship, the right to choose the time and place of communicating.

One way to protect your self during interpersonal communication is to exercise your right *not* to self-disclose, or provide in-depth information about yourself, to the other person. Woody Hayes, the late Ohio State University football coach, is alleged to have said about the forward pass that if you throw a pass, three things can happen—and two of them are bad. His football teams were perennial national powerhouses while flying in the face of most coaching philosophy: They rarely passed the ball. A similar statement could be made about self-disclosing communication: If you self-disclose to someone, that person can respond in any of four ways—and three of them are bad. The respondent may reciprocate your self-disclosure, deny it, ignore it, or reject it. To disclose your self to someone else is to risk your self-concept by placing part of it in the hands of another person. When you think the risk is too great, you will try to protect it by not self-disclosing.

There is a mutual interplay between your self, or intrapersonal system, and the social systems you inhabit. Self-schemata are valuable psychological resources which do not make you behave in any particular way, but assist you in making sense of behavior, choosing appropriate behavior, and influencing your ability to control interaction. These resources are reflected in your self, serving as an anchor point for personal judgments, self-fulfilling prophecies, and self-protection strategies. You play an active role in shaping your social world, but do not forget that components of that world simultaneously influence the nature of your self-schemata.

The self provides a wealth of resources that people use to evaluate their behavior and in turn to interpret the meaning of this behavior after it has been performed. At the same time, your behavior is a source of information to the other person and provides him or her with information about your self. Every time you act or behave during communication (and you are continuously behaving during communication), you are "presenting" your self (at least as perceived by the other) for public inspection. Of course, you (as the perceiver of other people's behaviors) also consider every action performed by your partners to be a public display of their selves. As soon as you take the other person into account, all communication is unavoidably and inevitably a presentation of your self and the other's self. "The other" is our focus in the last section of this chapter.

THE OTHER

In any two-person communication there is an engagement of two selves: yours' and the other's. Assuming that you are now relatively well acquainted with the concept of "self," we turn to "the other" and the process of how people get to know the other. We will talk about some specific problems involved in perception when the perceived object is another person. Of course, "knowing" the other is only part of the process of interpersonal communication. The other part is the actual communicating, the behaving toward that other person.

Perceiving the Other

Getting to know the other person is not a simple task. It involves the psychological process of perception, of course, and you already know that perception is a highly subjective basis for securing knowledge. That is, perception is experiential, selective, inferential, evaluative, and contextual. When people perceive another person, they must make inferences on the basis of information available only through their five senses. After all, you can't see, feel, hear, taste, or smell what is going on *within* the other person. The only sensory information you can obtain from other people is contained in their behaviors or actions.

In addition, the process of perceiving people (as opposed to inanimate objects) is a special kind of perception, accurately (but not imaginatively) labeled as *person perception*. What is true of all perceptions (experiential, inferential, evaluative, and so on) is also true of person perception. Person perception is unique in that it includes some elements that are not present with other objects of perception. Unlike a mere object, for instance, a person is a unique, reflective, thinking, talking, behaving human being, and he or she doesn't sit still waiting to be perceived. To put it another way, person perception is "transactional." We live in a world of meaning, not objects.

Wilmot (1980) puts it plain and simple, "there is no objective world of persons" (p. 61). He explains that person perception is transactional because it is a mutual perception process, occurring *between* the perceiver and the other (the perceived). You don't respond to a person but to what the person means to you. When you admire a car, your admiration (a perception) is not affected by what you may think about how the car feels about being admired. This is not the case with another human being. The process of person perception is heavily impacted by what each perceiver thinks about how the other feels about being perceived.

Wilmot writes that person perception occurs in a *mutually shared field*. When you perceive another, the other person is engaged in the same process of person perception you are. The implication of this mutually shared field is that your behaviors in any given situation with another may be the basis for another's behaviors which in turn become the sense data for your perception of the other.

We discussed, in the previous section, how the self is an important resource used to process social information about ourselves (see e.g., Markus & Smith, 1981). The self serves you again as an important resource for your perception of others. Wilmot (1980) explains that "what we see is as much a function of us as it is of the qualities of the other person" (p. 63). To say that your friend behaves consistently, for example, simply means that your own image of your self has remained relatively consistent with your friend, thus consistently impacting your friend's behaviors (Gergen, 1968) which serve as the basis for your perception. Hugh Prather (1970), writing of his own experiences, captures the essence of person perception:

> When I'm critical of another person, when I see his behavior as a "fault," my attitude includes these feelings: I think of him as one thing (instead of having many parts). I "just can't understand" his action. He seems justified. And I think he "knows better." If I feel this way I am in reality seeing my own self-condemnation. "Fault" means failure to meet a standard. Whose? Mine. Another person's behavior is "bad" or "understandable" according to my experience with *myself.* My feeling of censure means that if I had acted that way *I* would think of myself as selfish, opinionated, immature, etc. A part of me wants to act that way or thinks of myself as acting that way and condemns this. If I could see clearly why I also behave like that, or want to, and was no longer attacking myself for it, I wouldn't be critical of this person now. I'm getting upset because there is something in me I don't understand and haven't yet accepted.

When perceiving the other person, you try to draw perceptual inferences from the other person's communicative behaviors. Steve Duck (1977, pp. 102–103) suggests that the behavioral cues of the other person are important for three reasons. One, the cue may be pleasant and rewarding in itself. People like being the recipients of smiles and compliments. Two, the cue provides information that you can then use to form some impressions of that person's inner self—personality, beliefs, attitudes, values, reasons for his or her behavior, and the like. Three, the cue may provide some implications about the future of the relationship, hints of things to come.

When you engage in initial person perception, you may implicitly ask yourself questions concerning your potential relationship, such as whether you will like the person. At best, your inferences in person perception are guesses about what the other person is like. In other words, you use your perceptual guesses as the principal basis, accurately or inaccurately, for liking or disliking the other person.

To convert behavioral cues of your communicational partners into inferences concerning their personality and inner self is to engage in a guessing game, a gamble that your inference is correct. And it can never be more than a guessing game, despite the claims made by a number of popular paperback books. To devise a list of "things to do" in order to increase your ability to interpret behavioral cues correctly is like creating a system to beat the odds in Las Vegas. Even though someone may claim to have a sure-fire system to beat the odds, the chances that there is such a system are slim.

To be an effective communicator is to play the guessing game of person perception with full awareness of what goes into your guesses. Your guesses are based on incomplete information (they are perceptions) and are created using your self as a primary resource. After additional interaction, you will be able to judge the other with more confidence and revise earlier perceptions, remembering of course that you will never come to know the "real" person.

With an understanding of the process of person perception, you are more likely to realize that your perceptions are tentative and that they are likely to be in a state of constant change during continued interaction. The best way to improve your ability in person perception is to realize its inherent fallibility, relative instability, and self-centeredness. There is no "real person" out there waiting to be discovered. Your perceptions of others may appear to you to be stable, but they are based in uncertainty (Wilmot, 1980). In addition, as the perceiver, you control the inferences you make about the other person. To understand the process of person perception is to be aware, like Hugh Prather was, of what is going on within you when your attention is directed to another person. Two significant cognitive processes are involved in perceiving other people: perceptual sets and attribution processes (Wilmot, 1980).

Perceptual Sets   Remember the droodles in our discussion of perception? You assigned a pattern or an imposed structure on those lines and circles to make sense of them. You do the same thing with the behavior of others. Another's behaviors, like the lines and circles, provide you with incomplete information. In order to make sense of incomplete information, you have to go beyond the information. You infer from the incomplete information an overall impression—or *perceptual set*—of the other, thus making sense of the other. In essence, people are amateur psychologists of a sort.

People carry around in their heads an entire set of personality profiles that they use to impose structure on and give meaning to another's behavior. Research suggests that children by four years of age are developing perceptual sets regarding the intentions, feelings, motives, thoughts, and knowledge of others (Gelman & Spelke, 1981). People may not have as many personality types as the well-equipped professional psychologist, but they do have their list of personalities. You use your five senses and the other person's behavioral cues to make your inferences. Your psychological assessment may not be as precise as that of the professional psychologist, but it is no less useful to you when you are deciding how to interact with the other person.

Implicit Personality Theory   This amateur psychologizing is typically known as using *implicit personality theory* (Cronbach, 1955), as part of the psychological "set" used to perceive others. Because of your past interactional experiences, you have encountered a variety of different kinds of people. When you interact with people and observe their behavioral cues, you are able to reduce your uncertainty about them by evaluating them according to these perceptual sets.

Just as you have categories of perceived objects that you use to differentiate chairs, tables, trees, and the like, you also have categories of personality traits that you use to differentiate people. Each personality trait is likely to fall somewhere between two extremes on a given scale. You then look for cues in the other person's behaviors so as to assess such characteristics as warm or cold, friendly or unfriendly, stuck-up or humble, sincere or insincere, trustworthy or unreliable, fun or dull, quiet or talkative, shy or assertive, awkward or coordinated, and many more. The categories that you use are likely to be the same set of categories you use in perceiving yourself. How well you understand another is related to the degree to which you can tie your understanding to your personal experiences (Walster, 1970). And the "traits" you infer in another are not really owned by them but are grounded in your perceptions of what you believe to be consistent behavior. You prefer consistency in another; you behave accordingly, producing consistency in the other; and then you perceive a consistent impression of the other person in the form of a "personality trait" (Ichheiser, 1970).

As you attribute personality traits to the other person, you place yourself in the position of knowing how to interact. Your first perceptual judgment is likely to be whether you wish to continue interacting with someone having these "personality traits." If you like people with these traits, then you will want to foster additional interaction. Your second judgment is to determine what behaviors are appropriate when you are interacting with another person who has such traits. You behave differently with shy people, for example, than you do with talkative ones. For one thing, you have to spend more time "carrying" the conversation. You are also, with sufficient confidence in your personality assessment, capable of distinguishing behavioral cues that don't fit with the personality ("facades," or false roles). With confidence in your assessment, you are able to say, for example, "I know he seemed unfriendly, but he isn't really like that at all."

Response Sets   Another part of the perceptual set, relevant to person perception, includes *response sets*—certain predispositions to respond to the other in a certain way. Response sets involve making inferential leaps from the other person's behavior to our own behavioral response. Knowing that you will never have sufficient information to know all that you want to know about the other person, you use response sets as inferential shortcuts. We refer to them as "shortcuts" because they require inordinately huge leaps of inference, in fact, much larger leaps than typical perceptual inferences. Because of this fact, response sets typically involve errors in person perception. The following paragraphs discuss some of the most common response sets used in interpersonal communication.

One common response set that affects the accuracy of person perception is known as the *halo effect*. People perceive a halo effect when they generalize the other's behavior in one situation to other situations about which they know nothing. For example, you notice a colleague who behaves quite irresponsibly at work—this person is often late, doesn't get work done on time, and appears to take no pride in personal accomplishments. You then infer that this irresponsibility extends to other areas of his or her life as well. You assume that the person is irresponsible at home—stays away a lot, contributes little time to the family, and may even cheat on the spouse. The halo effect can work the same way with positive perceptions.

The problem with perceiving other persons with a halo effect is not simply that it is an inference. All perceptions are inferences. The halo effect is a problem because it is an inference that extends beyond the bounds of reason. It unfortunately enables people to ignore differences in situations that are likely to affect a person's actions. As a result, people fail to take into account the fact that others behave differently and perform different roles in different situations and with different people. The halo effect is an overgeneralized inference based on the false premise that people behave similarly in different situations. People baselessly assume a consistency of behavior. Although, halo effects are judgmental errors, their occurrence is not surprising, given the tendency to expect consistency in behavior.

The *leniency effect* is another response set in which people allow their relationships with persons to affect their perceptions of them. People tend to idealize their friends and are lenient in judging them. That is, you tend to give your friends a high (probably too high) score on all favorable traits and a low (probably too low) score on traits that are socially undesirable. In this way, you may perceive few faults in your friends and overestimate their positive attributes. You just can't understand why everyone doesn't like them and that they might be less than perfect. Hall and Taylor (1976), for example, found a strong tendency among marital couples (1) to rate spouses more favorably than themselves, (2) to judge spouses more favorably than acquaintances, and (3) to give their spouses personal credit for their good behavior and blame the situation for their bad behavior. Kathy has a friend who, charmingly, is rather delighted with the idealization the leniency effect produces and would expect nothing less from her close friends and spouse.

Naturally, the reverse is true of persons with whom you are unfavorably impressed. You tend to judge them too harshly—scoring them too low on positive attributes and too high on their negative attributes. Do any ex-boyfriends or -girlfriends come to mind? Of course, you shouldn't refer to this response set as "leniency." Perhaps, it could be termed a "cruelty effect," although we have never seen that term used by any psychologists.

Person perception, like all perception, is experiential, inferential, selective, evaluative, and contextual. Sometimes person perceptions benefit the relationship; sometimes they are detrimental. The thing to remember is to be open to additional information, use it to revise your own person perceptions, and remain sensitive to the personal grounding of those perceptions. Communicative skill does not really develop from making the "accurate" or "right" person perception, which, as we have said, is not possible. Rather, you develop your communicative skills by developing a keen and accurate awareness of your own perceptual processes and, of course, their limitations.

Attribution Processes   Let's review for a moment. In our discussion of self we alluded to the intrapersonal process of attributing the cause or control of events to someone or something. Typically, we have said, these perceptual processes place the "locus of control" within a person (dispositional) or within the context (situational). As a form of self-protection, people typically see themselves in situational terms. That is, you attribute your undesirable behaviors to the situation rather than to yourselves, as in "It wasn't my fault; I had no choice under the circumstances." Conversely, you tend to perceive the other person in dispositional terms (see Jones & Nisbett, 1971). That is, when you observe another person's behaviors, you tend to attribute them to some intrapersonal process—something occurring within the person. In this way, you perceive that "she is really stuck up. She passed me in the hall twice today, and she didn't even say hi."

Although the bulk of attribution theory and research has focused on understanding how people interpret and explain the causes of behaviors and events, little attention has been given to exploring the relationship between these attributions and patterns of behavior (Eiser, 1983; King, 1983). Despite this neglect, it is recognized that attribution processes are important to communication for several reasons. Hewstone (1983) identifies three attributional functions. One is the protection of your self-esteem. We discussed some behavioral implications of this function when we talked about individuals handicapping themselves when faced with a difficult task. Second, attributions may function to help you achieve some control over your world. For one thing, as a human being you need to construct explanations for how and why things occur. This apparent need for explanations stems in part from a need to reduce uncertainty, and the simplest explanation of all is causal. For example, the use of attributions appears to be one reason that parents sometimes blame themselves for a child's disease.

In the early stages of interaction, and consistent with implicit personality theory, the behaviors of the other person always seem to be cues that reveal innermost dispositions, intrapersonal feelings, emotions, personality traits, beliefs, attitudes, and values. Apparently you know yourself well enough so that you don't inevitably believe that your own behaviors always reflect your intrapersonal dispositions. But you don't know the other person that well. Therefore, you perceive every behavioral cue as an insight into the other's self. Hewstone, suggests that self-presentation and enhancement is the third attributional function. Others will communicate designed, positive attributions of themselves for public approval and the avoidance of embarrassment.

Emotions are part of those intrapersonal processes people look for in another's behaviors. You want to know how he or she feels about you, for example. Therefore, the other person's cordial behavior toward you often seems to be perceived as a behavioral cue for liking. On the other hand, you tend to attribute your own emotional displays toward the other person as being caused by the other person—as in "You make me angry" or "You bother me" or "You bring out the best in me."

Such an attribution is somewhat unusual because, after all, emotions are intrapersonal. People create their emotions internally, and dissolve them internally. They are part of the relationship only when you attribute them to the other person or yourself. Curiously, though, you often think of a relationship in terms of your emotions, at least as you perceive that relationship internally. You might say "We have a loving relationship" or "We love each other." But you need to remain aware that the intrapersonal emotion is not the same as the interpersonal relationship. An emotion is your perceptual attribution of an emotion to the other person (or to yourself). A popular song of many decades ago certainly conveyed that notion of attribution. The lyrics went something like "You made me love you. I didn't want to do it."

Attribution processes are important to communication in that they accurately depict the reflexive association between psychological states and behaviors. Popular belief has it that your actions always reflect your psychological states. People often think that, because they think or feel something, they act on the basis of that feeling or belief. However (as earlier discussions have revealed), the connection between psychological states and behaviors is more reflexive. You no more act because you believe than you believe because you act. The two, psychological state and action, function together in a cyclical and reflexive loop of influencing and being influenced.

How do attribution processes depict the reflexivity between psychological states and behaviors? Remember how you attribute cause to your own actions and to the actions of others? You often see others' behaviors in dispositional terms and your own behaviors in situational terms. Thus, you perceive others on the basis of causal connections between psychological states and behaviors, but you tend not to perceive the same causal connection with respect to yourself. In this way, you are likely to respond to others and perceive them on the basis of their behaviors, which you perceptually translate into their personality traits. You may not think that psychological states control your own behaviors, but you tend to think they do for other people, and you behave toward them accordingly.

Even though we recognize a reciprocal relationship between attributions and interaction, not much research has explored the relationship between the two. When attributional processes are examined in close relationships, the focus tends to be psychological: attribution of another's traits or attribution of blame in interpersonal conflict (Sillars, 1985). Underlying the work in attribution and interaction is the assumption that your actions tend to be based on your inferences about the other and that these inferences are self-confirming. Sillars concludes his examination of the research with this observation:

> When intimate couples and members of other dyads attribute relationship problems to the negative traits of each other, they are then likely to communicate in a negative, verbally competitive or ambiguous manner that often provides the other person with additional confirmation for his or her attributions about the source of these communications. (1987, p. 290)

He goes on to conclude that these patterns are self-perpetuating and that if the patterns become deeply entrenched, they may be very difficult to change.

Attribution processes are also important to communication because of their additional reflexive association with the interpersonal relationship. Your attributions will influence the outcomes of a relationship (as in wanting to continue interacting), and the developing relationship will also influence your attributional processes. When a relationship is in its early stages or when a relationship is not extremely close (such as that with an acquaintance, "just friends," and the like), you tend to perceive events in either situational (when pertaining to self) or dispositional (when pertaining to other) terms. But in more fully developed relationships or in relationships characterized by genuine liking, you tend to attribute a third cause to the success of your relationship—the relationship itself. In this way, the intrapersonal (attribution) and interpersonal (relationship) levels of communication thus influence each other reflexively.

Fincham (1983), a noted attributional theorist, argues that when applying causal attributions to the processes of close relationships, we do not find them to be logical products of an individual's cognitive activity: "On the contrary, they are part of the fabric of the relationship, altering and being altered by its course" (p. 201). Causal attributions may be a central part of the dialogue between couples and may remain unarticulated. Unarticulated attributions can pose problems in relationships especially if they go untested. Untested attributions are most problematic when you attribute your partner's behavior as significant in relation to you when in actuality the behavior reflects your partner's own problems or unique character.

Moreover, relational partners tend to perceive events in terms of how they affect their relationship—not just how they affect their individual selves. If they perceive events as threats to their relationship, they judge the events to be bad and avoid them. If they perceive the events as beneficial to the relationship, they judge them to be good and seek them out. In more intimate relationships, the partners tend to define their own selves (both self and other) in terms of their relationship, so that the social relationship itself assumes its own identity—in a way, it assumes its own "self." And that "relational self" or the relational identity of the participants is highly significant in maintaining close relationships (see Newman, 1981).

Attributional processes are thus vitally important to interpersonal communication. Furthermore, they are important not only in the way they can affect interpersonal communication, but also in the manner in which they can indicate the quality of that communication. As long as, and insofar as, the participants continue to perceive themselves situationally and others dispositionally, their communication indicates a "holding back" or a tentativeness of relational commitment. Such attributions probably reflect a less intimate relationship or one in the stages of getting started. When participants interpret events and their own self-identities in terms of the relationship as a whole, then the relationship begins to take on its own identity and demonstrates a rather highly developed level of intimate connections between the relational partners.

Interpersonal Perception   We have spent considerable time discussing the nature of person perception and its two components: perceptual sets and attribution processes. We would be remiss if we did not discuss the process of *interpersonal perception*. Too often, person perception is not studied in the context of social interaction. Often those who are studied do not even know one another, and the interactional consequences of their perceptions are not examined. Thus, when we talk about interpersonal perception, we are talking about perception and the social coordination of partners toward each other and a common issue: congruency (Sillars, 1987).

Why are close relationships filled with so many contradictions? After all, aren't people supposed to be able to count on these relationships for predictability, compatibility, and congruency? The safety that people so often seek in their intimate relationships is threatened by the fact that the partner they rely on to know them so well, does know them to a point but is also their least objective partner. Whether you like it or not, ambiguity concerning anything from who has garbage duty to what each partner feels about a conflict is common in close relationships.

Sillars (1987) identifies characteristics of close relationships which produce the ambiguity or incongruence of interpersonal perception so often experienced in personal relationships. First, *familiarity* may serve as a basis for understanding, but it also can be very misleading. Generally, over time, people in a close relationship do become more familiar with each other. For example, the pair's communication may become more efficient, as unique ways of interacting are developed (Knapp, 1984). Have you ever been around a couple whose communication makes sense to them but it doesn't to you because you don't have the details to fill in what is to you missing information? However, familiarity doesn't always facilitate congruence. If partners begin to take for granted their understanding based on the presumed familiarity, then change in close relationships can be hampered when partners do not see changes in each other's thoughts and actions— each partner sees the other in the "same 'ol way." Recently a friend of Kathy's was having some personal problems. Kathy suggested that the friend talk to her spouse about her problems and get some feedback. Her friend commented that she does not disclose much about personal issues to her spouse anymore because she doesn't think it would do any good. She believes that her spouse will think it is her "same old stuff," even though to her the situation seemed very different.

Second, although people typically strive for some degree of *interdependence* in their relationships, it can produce problems when they forget that the reasons for their partner's behavior can no longer be simply explained. As we discussed in Chapter 2, interdependence, or connection to another, is something all people strive for in some degree. This is reflected in joint identities, the frequent use of "we," inside jokes, similar dress, unique ways of doing things together, and so on. However, as the interdependency increases, it becomes more difficult to assign simple causes to each other's behavior because the interdependency complicates the reasons for behaving. For example, it becomes easier to blame the other when responsibility has become ambiguous because of increased interdependence. Remember the couple Kathy knows who have trouble determining who should be responsible for what when it comes to keeping their house and yard in order? Inevitably, whenever the issue is raised about the messy house, they blame each other, and rarely do they ever take responsibility for their own contributions to the mess. It is far easier to overlook your behavior when interdependence is a key characteristic in your relationships.

Third, close relationships are often characterized by their *uniqueness.* However, a pair's shared reality will be threatened to the degree that the couple depends on its own codes for validation. That is, consensus about the important characteristics of each partner (e.g., friendly, open, supportive, caring, and so on) and of the relationship (e.g., it will last, they belong together, and so on) is more likely to be threatened if the manner in which those characteristics are validated is not supported by others. For example, Kathy knows a couple who don't do many things with others; in fact, they spend most of their time in separate careers, operating on individual schedules, and when together, they are usually alone. For the most part, their shared belief in their relationship and positive impressions of each other are a function of their own, unique set of standards and generally don't involve others. Now the problem is, one of the spouses is not liked by the other's friends. As a consequence, a great deal of stress is experienced by the couple due to the perceived threat to their private consensus. Her response to the threat is that the friends just don't know her spouse the *way* she does nor do they see how well she and her spouse interact in the privacy of home.

Fourth, close relationships are characterized by a high degree of *emotionality*. Close relationships can be very involving, and the constraints on emotional expression are lowered. All of you are probably familiar with the saying "You always hurt the one you love." In fact, "strong negative emotions are seen as leading to a less accurate, more one-sided, and more negative perception of the partner" (Sillars, 1987, p. 283).

To summarize, interpersonal communication, pragmatically, occurs at the dyadic level and at the very least involves two interacting selves. Getting to know the other is a complicated task involving inferences based on incomplete information. Person perception, although similar to all perception (i.e., it is selective, inferential, experiential, evaluative, and contextual) is also unique as compared to the perception of inanimate objects. It is a transactional process involving a mutual process that occurs between people. Two significant cognitive processes involved in this transactional process are perceptual sets and attribution processes. Perceptual sets are overall impressions you form of people such as the implicit personalities or categories of people that you attribute to reduce your uncertainty about others you encounter. Attributions refer to the inferences you make about another's reasons for behaving. Whether you infer a personal or situational cause for another's behavior has implications for the behavioral choices you make and thus the way you define the relationship. Interpersonal perception is important because of its focus on person perception in the context of social interaction. Too often, person perception is not studied in an interactional setting. Thus the interactional or pragmatic consequences are not examined. The study of interpersonal perception reminds us once again of the reciprocal influence between perception and behavior.

Behaving toward the Other

To be an effective communicator, you want to be able to influence the other person's perceptions of you. You would like the other person to think highly of you, perhaps, or at least to have an impression of you that is consistent with your own purpose in communicating. You may want the other person to see you as a friend, a boss, a sexual partner, an acquaintance, or in any number of different social roles. Even though you can't force the other to perceive you in a certain light, you can behave in a manner that fosters the impression you want the other person to have of you. Thus, your communicational task is to provide the other, through your behaviors, with information that the other person can use in perceiving your self—information that is consistent with the perception you want the other to have of you.

You may react negatively to the suggestion that people try to influence other people's perceptions during communication. You might think that you should not try to be so manipulative but should, instead, strive to "be natural," to "be your own self." Such a reaction assumes that your self and the way you present your self are somehow different and even unrelated. However, you already know that you have many different selves and many social roles in many different interpersonal relationships. Furthermore, every one of your selves *is* your "natural" and "real" self. When you are being natural and your own self with members of your family, you wouldn't deny that the way you interact (quite differently) with your friends is also very natural and consistent with your own self.

We're sure you have heard the cliché "You are what you eat." (If it were true, we all know of people who would be Big Macs and others who would be pepperoni pizzas. And just think of how many Cokes there would be in this world.) If we reword the saying, though, it is much more sensible: "You are what you *do.*" You behave as a friend, and you are a friend. You behave as a lover, and you are a lover. But that doesn't mean that you are a friend or a lover with everyone you meet or that being a lover is not "natural" because you don't behave that way with everyone. Remember that part of your self-concept—a large part of it—is defined in terms of the social attributes you display when behaving with others and in the role relationships you have with others. Therefore, your behaviors with others constitute a very natural part of being your own self.

Of course, some of your behavior might be a facade, a false face, or false role presented to others. When you interact with some people, you sometimes pretend to be someone you are not. But we would hesitate to condemn any role as being "false." Let us illustrate. In a group decision-making class several years ago, a student confided that she simply could not be a leader of her group because she just wasn't a "leader type." She felt that being a leader was not natural for her. However, she did behave as a leader in her group and later recognized that she performed that role. She also said that she did so only because she wanted her group to do well and receive a good grade. Throughout the entire term, she insisted that her leadership role was false and that she wasn't her true self. She attributed a situational locus of control for her behavior and believed that she was the group leader only because the situation demanded it. After having experienced success and rewards from her fellow group members, though, she indicated that she was likely to assume other leadership roles in the future. Apparently, her "false role" had become a natural part of her self, but only after she had experienced it.

The reflexivity among behaviors, the self-concept, and person perception is quite strong. True, these processes have tended to be studied separately from the dynamics of social interaction. Wilkinson (1987) reminds us, however, that impressions of others and of ourselves evolve and are interconnected in the context of a social relationship. There is a reciprocal influence between the relationship and the perspectives of both partners (see also Sillars, 1987). Further, your impressions of others are intimately tied to your own self-impressions. Impression formation is an "instrumental activity," or a way in which people each construct a self in relation to their impression of the other and to their impression of the other's impression of them. After all, you create your self-concept in large part from your social experiences. With new and different social experiences, you tend to create a new and different self-concept. As you proceed to influence other people's perceptions of you through your behaviors, you influence your perceptions of your own self at the same time. Person perceptions influence interpersonal communication, and interpersonal communication reflexively influences person perceptions (both of the other, the self, and the relationship).

Impression Management   Erving Goffman (1959, 1963), a sociologist, wrote extensively on how people in everyday life engage in "presenting" their selves to others. He did not regard such presenting of self as manipulative but rather as a natural part of social interaction he called *impression management.* Goffman suggested that every time people behave socially with another person, they manage the impressions of that person. Most importantly, people really have no choice but to manage others' impressions of them. By behaving toward another person, you are unavoidably attempting to affect that person's impressions of you. You don't have any choice in the matter: You simply cannot not behave! The only issue in impression management is whether you are aware of *how* you go about managing the impressions of others, not *whether* you do so.

Impression management involves thinking of interpersonal communication as a drama or play. As a participant in communication, you are not only an actor in the drama, you are also the playwright—the author who is writing the script of the real-life drama while engaging in interpersonal communication. When you manage the impressions of the other person in communication, you present your self in two regions of behavior: front and back. *Front* refers to that part of your self that is observable or publicly visible to the other person. Your front region of impression management reveals the part of your self that is "onstage." The *back* region refers to your "behind-the-scenes" behavior, the part of your self that you display when not in the presence (or when you don't know that you are in the presence) of another person.

An example of "front" and "back" may serve to illustrate this difference between onstage and behind-the-scenes regions of impression management. Sometime ago Aub walked into the office of a faculty colleague who was engrossed in evaluating some term papers and was clearly distressed by the one he was reading. He scowled through his reading glasses, muttered some epithet under his breath, scribbled on the paper, and even scratched himself absentmindedly. Although Aub was standing across the desk from him, no more than 5 feet away, he was apparently not aware of Aub's presence and was behaving in a behind-the-scenes manner. When he looked up and saw Aub standing there, he immediately behaved with his "front." He removed his reading glasses (the funny ones with only half lenses), smiled broadly, pushed himself away from the desk, and greeted Aub heartily.

Don't be misled into thinking that this teacher's onstage (front) behavior was a false role and his behind-the-scenes (back) behavior was more real. He was behaving quite naturally in both instances, but he was in two different situations—one private (at least he thought so) and the other social. In the social setting, the act of communication, he was engaging in impression management, and this behavior was quite natural. In the private setting, or back region, he was not engaging in impression management. After all, he wasn't aware that anyone was there requiring that he manage his impressions.

Managing impressions, then, is equivalent to interaction behavior. In fact, we could say that all interaction behavior (that is, all communication) is impression management, whether the communicator is aware of that fact or not. The difference between front and back behaviors, then, is the difference between the two situations of social interaction or private behavior. This means that impression management is behavior directed not so much by your internalized self but by the presence of another person.

Aub's colleague behaved as he did because Aub was there—not just anybody, but Aub. If a stranger had walked into his office, he would have behaved quite differently. He may have looked expectantly toward the stranger or inquired as to whether he could be of assistance. He may have stood up and moved to shake the hand of the stranger as a form of introduction. In the case of Aub, a friend and frequent "intruder" into his office, he simply shoved his chair back and welcomed Aub. This "front" was quite familiar to him; Aub often walked into his office uninvited. He had memories of many previous experiences similar to that one, and he fell easily into that role.

To say that impression management is other-directed rather than self-directed is to say that your interactive behavior focuses on what impression you want the other person to have of you. Often you have some specific goals in mind for a communicative encounter, and you have ample time to prepare your "front" behaviors beforehand. There is nothing unethical in preparing your impression management. In fact, in many situations, you prepare and expect the other person to have prepared for your communicative behavior. When engaging in an employment interview, for example, you attempt to present yourself in the role you think will impress the interviewer most favorably, and the interviewer expects that you have prepared yourself.

The most potent influences on impression management will always be the interactive behaviors. Aub's instructor in an undergraduate acting class repeatedly stressed the point that more acting is accomplished through *re*acting to others. Impression management could well use that dramatic point as an axiom. When you become aware of your own behaviors and allow another person to direct them, you begin to judge the appropriateness of your behaviors *as responses to* the other person's behaviors. In impression management, you are less concerned with manipulating the other person and more involved with behaving responsively. That ultimately means that you focus on responding to the other's behavior. By being consciously aware that your every action is a response to the other's behavior, you are interacting quite normally and are certainly engaged in managing the other's impressions.

Attributional Responses   We have pointed out that traditionally attributional processes are treated almost exclusively as perceptual processes that locate the cause or control of events within a person (dispositional), in the context (situational), or in the relationship. However, you know that attributions may also be evident in the behavior you use to respond to the other's actions. That is, the communicator may respond in a way that clearly attributes some implied meaning to the other's preceding behavior. For example, consider the following conversational sequence:

"What are we having for dinner tonight?"

"Stop nagging me!"

"I was only kidding."

The response to the initial question about dinner clearly attributes a dispositional meaning to that comment. The person is saying "You are only asking about dinner because you are nagging me to get ready." The original questioner responds by denying the attribution and is saying "I wasn't nagging. My question was perfectly innocent, a matter of curiosity."

Often, close friends believe they know each other so well (familiarity) that, they respond to the other's comments with implied attributions. You may have been involved in a conversation similar to the following:

"You look tired. Did you have a hard day?"

"You don't really want to go out tonight, do you?"

"No, it's not that. But we don't need to go out tonight if you're tired."

The respondent attributes a meaning to the first question by suggesting that it seemed to be an excuse for not carrying through on their original plan to "go out." The response to that comment actually denies that attribution but does not leave the door open to not going out, that is, by making the same dispositional attribution ("tired") of the other person.

Both these examples of conversation provide dispositional attributions for the other's behaviors. The attribution, though, could also be situational or relational. Whatever the attributed locus of control, the attribution (by being expressed or implied in the interactional behaviors) is no longer just part of the psychological or perceptual process; it is now a part of the pragmatic behavioral level of communication.

When the perceptual process of attribution becomes expressed or implied in communicative behaviors, it affects the interactional behaviors of both communicators. For instance, attributing a dispositional locus to the other person places responsibility for the action on that person: The other person now feels compelled to respond. The response may attempt to shift the attributed locus, thereby avoiding the responsibility, or it may attempt to deny it. For example, the above conversation might continue:

"Do you still want to go out tonight?"

"You'd rather not go, wouldn't you?"

"Actually I do, but it's been a really bad day. I'm beat."

The second comment attributes an implied dispositional locus to the first speaker who responds by denying it, saying "Actually I do." Your dispositional attribution is erroneous, goes this response, but a situational attribution is accurate—the "really bad day." The final comment says, in essence, "I personally want to go, but I am a victim of circumstances" or "My spirit is willing, but my flesh is weak."

Any communicative act during a conversation may include an expressed or implied attribution by inferring an underlying meaning to the other's prior behavior. The communicator, in responding to the other person's implied or expressed attribution, has several choices available. The communicator may deny the attribution contained in the other's prior comment by saying, for example, "No, that's not it." The communicator may accept the other person's attribution by saying, for example, "Yeah, I'm really tired." Or the communicator may shift the attributional locus by saying, for example, "I'm just a victim of the situation." Attributions, then, may be employed as a conversational strategy as well as a perceptual process. And when used as a strategy, attributions affect the entire conversation.

SUMMARY

Looking at interpersonal communication and social relationships from the viewpoint of the individual participants is to locate the understanding of the communication within the psychological process (the intrapersonal system). Each individual member of a relationship possesses a personal understanding and meaning of every social relationship in which that person is a member. Because that understanding is so personal and so meaningful to the individual, the psychological or intrapsychic understanding is often seen as the "real" meaning of the relationship. In fact, it is not more real so much as it is more vivid. This view is essentially an internal residue or memory of the interpersonal relationship, a personal reaction or response to the experience of the relationship that the individual carries around after the fact. That residual memory often takes the form of an emotion, an individual response to a relationship, which is often mistaken for the experience of the relationship itself.

The intrapersonal, or psychological, process relevant to interpersonal communication focuses on the self of the individual communicator. Each person has two selves, or a self in two parts: the internal self and the external self. The internal self is not capable of being observed, but the external self (the behaviors or actions) are observable during communication. The psychological task of interpersonal communication, then, is to observe the behaviors of the external self and to use those actions as cues to make inferences about the internal self. On the basis of another's behaviors, we make inferences about what that person is like or what that person is thinking or feeling.

The intrapersonal level of communication concerns the self and the nature of acquiring meaning of self. The psychological process in self-meaning is perception, an internalized process of assigning meaning to sensations of objects, persons, or events. Perception, the process by which people acquire all personal knowledge, is experiential, selective, inferential, evaluative, and contextual. Perception, often considered to be valid without qualification, is a subjective portrayal of reality gained from interpreting sensations and is, thus, only apparent knowledge.

When one's own self is the object of perception, the task is to become aware of self through the same process of perception used to acquire knowledge of physical and external objects. The identity of one's self is known as the self-concept, a product of self-reflexivity in social interaction. The way one values, positively or negatively, one's self-concept is known as self-esteem. The process of developing an awareness or perception of your own self involves reflexivity, social interaction, and continuous evolutionary change.

The self is a psychological component of interpersonal communication. The self cannot behave, but it can influence behavior. The self and behavior reciprocally influence each other, which means that the individual shapes his or her social world and the social world simultaneously impacts the individual. Self-schemata serve as important resources which help people process social information. People use these resources as anchor points for personal judgments, in self-fulfilling prophecies, and in the protection of their self-concept. As grounds for social behavior, these social cognitive processes may benefit or harm the development of social relationships.

The psychological process of perceiving the other person during interpersonal communication is called social cognition or person perception. When the object of perception is another person, the perceptual process is somewhat different than when the perceived object is inanimate. Person perception is a transactional process involving a mutually shared field. A person's perception of another is grounded in his or her own self and, thus, the perception says as much about self as it does about the qualities of the other. Two important cognitive processes in the perception of others are perceptual sets (implicit personality theory) and attribution processes.

Perceptual sets are personality profiles that people use to impose structure on and give meaning to another's behavior. They can affect the quality of person perception. Two kinds of perceptual sets are implicit personality theory and responses sets. Implicit personality theory is the assumption that certain characteristics of individuals are related to others. Response sets involve assumptions that individuals have about how certain behaviors are related to other behaviors. Those response sets include the halo effect, or generalizing the other's behavior to situations about which we have no information, and the leniency effect, or overestimating positive traits of friends and underestimating their negative traits. All perceptual sets may affect how you behave toward the other.

Person perception also involves attributing factors of cause and responsibility for behaviors. People often attribute dispositional (intrapersonal) causes to the behaviors of others but situational (controlled by the context) causes to their own behaviors. When relationships attain a more fully developed state, relational partners tend to view events and other persons in terms of how they affect the relationship itself, thereby creating a third locus of attributional control—the relationship.

The behaviors people perform when communicating with another person are designed to give that person the impression of their selves that they want that person to have. Each person attempts to manage the impressions the other perceives through the behaviors performed during interaction. In impression management, each selects which self to portray, what information to present, and the manner in which to present that information. No communicator can avoid making these types of choices. Communicative behavior thus involves selecting responses to the other person. Specific kinds of responses involve making and responding to attributions implied or expressed in the other's behavior, confirming the other person's value as a self.

KEY TERMS

intrapersonal view

internal self

external self

self

I

me

perception

self-concept

"ideal self"

self-esteem

schema

self-schemata

egocentric bias

false consensus bias

self-fulfilling prophecies

self-handicapping strategies

attribution

information preserve

conversational preserve

mutually shared field

perceptual sets

implicit personality theory

response sets

halo effect

leniency effect

interpersonal perception

impression management

front region

back region

CHAPTER 4   # The Context and Interpersonal Communication

We rely on context to understand the behavior and
speech of others and to ensure that our own behavior is
understood, implicitly grounding our interpretations of
motives and intentions in context.

—Elliot G. Mishler

Our third principle of communication pragmatics states that to discover
the meaning or significance of communicative patterns is to place them in
some context. This principle should not be surprising to any student of
human behavior. How many times have you appealed to the context when
you have found yourself in the midst of a misunderstanding or difficult
encounter? How many times have you countered with "My comment was
taken out of context" when you found your intentions misinterpreted?
And how many times has a teacher advised you to consider context when
you were trying to figure out just what to say or do in any given circumstance?

Let's take these questions even further. Imagine, for the moment, what
it would be like to not be able to rely on context to help you understand
what has been said and done. Imagine not being able to *ground* your
interpretations—you have no road map, no cues to help you interpret
behavior. If you have no grounding for your interpretations, you would
have no basis for your choices concerning how to behave. Imagine being
incapable of any retrospective sensemaking during an ongoing interaction
with another. Can you imagine not being able to make sense of the previous
actions and thus not able to behave in a relevant and appropriate manner?
Going crazy? By now you should be feeling a little crazy and out of control.
Isn't that what happens when you don't know what to expect? The importance of context may not be surprising to any of you, but its unique place
in a pragmatic perspective of human communication needs to be explored.
This chapter will discuss more precisely the nature of physical and social
contexts and their influence on the process of interpersonal communication.
But first it is necessary to address the adaptive capabilities of the human
being.

ADAPTING TO THE ENVIRONMENT

You are capable of making sophisticated adaptive responses to your environment. Although the total number of human cognitive skills is much larger than this, we will discuss only two of them at this point: sensemaking and self-reflexivity. Both are important to you when it comes to making adaptive responses to your environment.

We introduced the notion of *sensemaking* with the fourth pragmatic principle. It is an extremely vital part of human communication and, for that matter, everyday living. Human sensemaking is our ability to make sense out of everything, even nonsense. Central to our sensemaking, you will remember, is the ability to "organize events into some patterns that endows the events with meaning" (Fisher, 1985, p. 517). Human beings absolutely detest being confused or being unsure of what something means. The late Isaac Asimov, one of the world's premier science-fiction writers, once said, "I'm on fire to explain, and happy when it's something reasonably intricate which I can make clear step by step. It's the easiest way I can clarify things in my own mind." Making the complicated simple, reducing the confusion, is sensemaking, and he made sense of our past and future in 477 books!

Human beings possess a remarkable ability (perhaps even need) to reduce their uncertainty and confusion by making sense of any context they encounter (Berger & Calabrese, 1975). Contrary to common sense, you don't "seek out" information in order to grasp the meaning of something (that is, to achieve certainty) as much as you seek information in order to eliminate the number of potential meanings you might have for it (that is, to reduce certainty) (Shannon & Weaver, 1949). You already possess a repertoire of potential meanings that are applicable to virtually every context of communication. Your problem is not that you have no idea of what something means but that you have too many such ideas. Hence, you take in information available to you in the context, interpret that information in terms of what it means for your own actions in regard the context, and adapt your behaviors accordingly.

True, it has been demonstrated that people are capable of *mindlessness*, or acting as if information were true regardless of its context (Langer, 1989). Have you ever driven somewhere and once you reached your destination wondered how you got there? This kind of automatic behavior is a form of mindlessness. On the other hand, remaining open to the variety of possible interpretations in any given context and being willing to create new interpretations is *mindfulness*. You can do this because you are a sense maker; you are capable of punctuating events in order to furnish those events with meaning.

You learned in Chapter 3 that every individual possesses a self and that

Human beings tend not to like being confused and are capable of
sensemaking or organizing events into patterns that give the events
meaning.

self is a process and reflexive. Self-reflexivity implies that people make
sense of their environment not so much as it *is* but in terms of what it means
for them. If the environment is not conducive to your own needs and
desires, you can change it. A relationship that was once the "best thing to
happen to you" can become "your worst mistake" in the painful experience
of termination.

The human attributes of sensemaking and self-reflexivity constitute a
normal and taken-for-granted characteristic of day-to-day existence. Think
of your first day at college. You wondered not so much about other people
or the school but more about how you yourself would fit in. As you heard
your instructor expound upon the values and requirements of this course,
your first reaction was probably "What is this course going to do for me?"
It shouldn't be particularly embarrassing to admit that you have often taken
a required course and thought it was a waste of time. You felt that you
weren't able to "do anything" with it. You may have chosen your major on
the basis of what you could do with it in order to earn a living upon
graduation. These thoughts do not make you a bad person; you are merely
behaving normally and exercising that remarkable ability possessed by all
humans—sensemaking, combined with a unique personal focus.

These two human attributes are at work whenever the context enters
into the process of human communication as a *potential* influence. One of
the most important issues of this chapter is that the individuals (the in-

trapersonal systems) as well as the relationship (the interpersonal system) are not influenced by the context so much as humans respond adaptively to their contextual environments. During the past few decades the conservation and environmental movement has focused attention on the term "ecology." The word is often confused with the mere environment: with forests, national parks, air quality, whales, sea otters, eagles, and so forth. But ecology is a more precise field of study in biology and sociology and deals not with the environment (that is, the context) alone but with the *relations* between living organisms (most notably, humans) and their environment. Fundamental to this ecological perspective (Capra, 1982) is the belief that the world you live in is interconnected and that its psychological, biological, social, and environmental aspects are interdependent. The human adaptive response is quite different from other organisms.

Proactive and Reactive Responses

One way to describe this difference between humans and nonhumans is to note the difference between *proactive responses* and *reactive responses* to the environment. Humans are capable of being proactive and thus "acting toward" their environment. Other organisms may be more reactive and thus "react to" their environment. For example, "Cheese is cheese, and that's why mousetraps work." In other words, a mouse smells cheese, recognizes it as food, and proceeds to eat it in a reactive response. A human would also recognize the cheese as food but would see the danger involved in attempting to eat it. The mere presence of some sensory stimuli does not "cause" the human to respond. Humans can act proactively, and therefore they can act on the basis of their sensemaking and what it means to them.

As you read about the physical and social context, keep in mind that contexts do not cause you to behave in a certain way but instead are an integral part of behavior (Werner, Altman, & Brown, 1992). As a human communicator, you are a sensemaking organism engaged in seeking out ways to act appropriately. You act toward the context and adapt your behaviors to it on the basis of your having made sense of it. The context is not simply an environment but a situation in which you must find your own way.

There are fundamentally two ways in which humans can adapt to their environment: determinism and interactionism. These two views of environmental influence correspond roughly to reactive and proactive responses. According to a *deterministic* view, the environment contains numerous stimuli that channel the perceptual responses of humans within that environment in a specific direction. Stated another way, aspects of the context influence the behaviors and perceptions of humans, perhaps without their conscious awareness, who are exposed to them. Determinists believe that the meaning of the context resides in the factors that are available in the context itself.

People often find it difficult to resist the simplicity of the deterministic view. They can easily find examples of how the context "determined" their "reactions" (your behaviors). Many people, for example believe that TV and magazine advertising works on their subconscious and "leads" them to buy the product "because" of those hidden appeals.

On the other hand, an *interactional* view suggests another explanation: humans create or control their environment as much as they are influenced by it. Remember from our discussions in Part One that the systems which concern us are living, open systems. These systems are self-organizing and self-renewing, which means that they are somewhat autonomous *and* somewhat dependent on their environments (Capra, 1982; Jantsch, 1980). They maintain a dynamic, continuous exchange with their environment.

In *environmental interactionism,* the meaning of the context is socially created or defined by humans in their actions toward and within the context. There is a reflexive relationship between context and behavior (Beach, 1983; Heritage, 1984; Leiter, 1980). In terms of their communicative behavior, humans typically define their environment on the basis of their activities within it and at the same time those activities are defined by the context. This idea may be easier to grasp when we discuss social contexts and discourse, but it also holds true for physical contexts. A friend of Aub's, an architect, told him repeatedly that the first thing he wants to find out about a new building project is what people are supposed to be *doing* in it. Then he tries to design a physical context that is conducive to those activities. He doesn't believe that the environment he designs will determine anyone's behaviors, but he fervently believes the environment should serve the activities that serve to define the environment for the participants.

Environmental interactionism is the view of contextual adaptation in our pragmatic view of communication. People's actions are partially defined by their environment, and they simultaneously create the social meaning of their environment when they act toward it and among themselves. If your conversation with "that special someone" is likely to be important and intimate, you search for an environment that is conducive to this interactional purpose. But even if the environment is not the best, you can define it as being special. When Aub was dating the woman he later married, they first kissed in the front seat of his old Dodge. The context was a rather busy intersection in a downtown metropolitan area. However, for them, that place was very special and even intimate.

Interactants are sensemakers and self-reflective. They respond proactively; that is, they act toward their context and in so doing create the social meaning of the context. We are discussing the individual because the context that constrains the individual thus helps shape the interaction of the interpersonal system. We will spend the rest of this chapter exploring

People are capable of acting toward their environment and thus capable of defining the social context to fit the relational event.

in more detail the role of the physical and social contexts in interpersonal communication.

THE PHYSICAL CONTEXT

Generally speaking, three elements make up the *physical context* that humans define interactionally: design, decoration, and presence or absence of other people. *Design features* comprise those elements which are "built into" the setting. Elements of the interior design of a room, for instance, include its size, shape, lighting, soundproofing, placement and shape of the doors and windows, and ceiling light. The *decoration features* typically include those elements which can easily be manipulated or changed; they are not permanent. Such features might include the furniture (size, number, color, texture, placement), wall coverings, pictures, window treatments, floor coverings, room accessories, color, and virtually anything that comes under the heading of room furnishings. The physical context also includes *other people,* in the sense that the mere presence or absence of others, the number of people present, their proximity to one another, the amount of crowding, and so forth are as much a part of the physical context as the inanimate objects.

Various combinations of these three factors make up the physical context which is, in turn, defined by the human interactions. Compare the two photographs in Figure 4-1. Both depict dining places in a public restaurant, but the physical contexts differ considerably. The photo on top depicts a private, cozy rendezvous for intimate dining and conversation. The lighting is subdued and falls just on this table; the table is well separated from the others; the tablecloth and candle contribute to an ambience for private conversation.

The photograph on the bottom suggests a dining environment that differs considerably in the three elements of the physical context. The booth doesn't allow for discretionary movement of furniture, the lighting is overly bright, and people sitting in adjacent booths encroach on one another's privacy. The hard plastic tops of the table and benches contribute to a feeling of harshness. Any conversation in such a setting is likely to be less intimate than the interaction of the people in the top photograph.

We don't mean to imply that the settings illustrated in Figure 4-1 will "determine" or "cause" the people to behave in a certain way. The two people in the "intimate" setting may actually want some excitement, frivolity, and gregarious fun. They would then find this setting inappropriate for those interactional functions and might find the setting of the second picture more appropriate. Settings don't cause behavior, but rather they may encourage and be well suited to certain actions that people wish to perform. And this is the point made by Aub's architect friend. The designer of a building attempts to discover what the "normal" interactional activities of the occupants are likely to be and then tries to provide a physical setting that is compatible with those activities.

People notice the physical context and in their interaction with the context define it as "intimate or nonintimate," "good or bad," "friendly or unfriendly." Whether they behave any differently when engaged in interpersonal communication in these settings, however, is a matter of some dispute. Humans think they behave differently when, in fact they really don't. Apparently the physical context is a highly significant influence on communicator's *perceptions* of what they do in them but much less significant in influencing their actual behavior when communicating.

Context and Behavior

Two social psychologists, Maslow and Mintz, conducted research in 1956 investigating people's reactions to "beautiful" and "ugly" rooms. They manipulated the elements of the physical context by creating rooms that differed in terms of size, color, illumination, furnishings, and accessories.

FIGURE 4-1 Two contrasting restaurant scenes

They assigned subjects either to a beautiful or an ugly room, and they asked the subjects to rate pictures of people's faces. Their findings indicated that people tended to perceive significantly higher levels of "energy" and "well-being" for the faces when assigned to the beautiful room than they did for the same faces when the ratings were performed in the ugly room. Mintz (1956) found in a follow-up study that these ratings persisted over time.

Related research (Kitchens, Heron, & Behnke, 1976) found that people in more aesthetically pleasant rooms tended to like their conversational partners more than did those in an unattractive room. This research tends to support Maslow and Mintz's inference that, other things being equal, some physical contexts tend to encourage more positive interpersonal reactions.

Research indicates that people perceive some settings as friendlier than others, and it is equally clear that they perceive their interactions in such settings to be "friendlier" as well. The question still remains whether humans' perceptions of their communication are consistent with their actual communicative behavior.

Reviewing the literature, Pendell (1976) found that nearly all the studies had observed the influence of the physical context on how humans *perceive* their environment and one another, and a few studies attempted to observe some isolated factors often associated with human communication (e.g., interpersonal attraction and number of messages sent and received). She found no study that sought to observe the impact of the environment on how humans actually communicate with one another in conversation. In her research, Pendell placed groups of three people in three different rooms that varied in terms of interior design and decoration. The rooms were shaped differently (rectangular, square, and oval) and varied in aesthetic appeal (from bare walls and metal chairs to attractive wall coverings and comfortable seating). She then directly observed the interactive behaviors, the communication, of three-person groups as they discussed a problem-solving exercise. After the discussions, she asked them individually whether they had noticed their physical context and whether they thought it influenced their conversations.

Not surprisingly, she found that the participants definitely "made sense of" both the design and the decorative features of the rooms. Furthermore, the people generally perceived that the environment did influence their conversations, although they didn't think that the degree of influence was necessarily great. The surprising result of her study concerned the actual influence of interior design and decoration on interpersonal communication. In every comparison made, Pendell was unable to find even the slightest difference in communication caused by the different rooms!

What sense is to be made of this rather confusing difference between perceptions of the physical context and communicative behaviors? On the one hand, people have very active sensemaking abilities. They are certainly aware of their physical contexts and may even perceive their own behaviors and reactions to (or judgments of) other people differently on the basis of their environments. But when it comes to the question of whether humans actually communicate differently in different settings, the influence of the environment in this study was apparently minimal.

Some of you may be thinking, "But wait a minute don't my perceptions influence my behavior in interpersonal communication?" Common sense would tell you that you typically behave on the basis of what you perceive. Certainly what you perceive and how you perceive it must be important to interpersonal communication. And they are. But you need to keep in mind that commonsense knowledge tends to simplify what is really much more complex. Apparently your perceptions are an influence, but not as strong an influence on how you communicate. Remember also the nested hierarchy of communication systems discussed in Chapter 1. The individual (the intrapersonal system) is only a part of the interpersonal system (the behaviors, communication, relationship) and may affect and be affected by the interpersonal system. But these systems are not the same, and knowing about the perceptions of the individuals does not enable you to define the system of interpersonal communication.

Communicative Functions of the Physical Setting

The fifth pragmatic principle reminds you that studying interpersonal communication from a pragmatic perspective places you in a position to ask a different kind of question. You are no longer interested so much in the issue of *how much* the physical context affects communication but rather *how* and *in what way* communication functions within a given physical context. Your question becomes "How do people communicate with one another, in regard to certain aspects of their physical context?" not "How much does the physical context affect communication?" In adapting a different perspective, we switch our emphasis from a deterministic explanation to an attempt to understand the pragmatic, environmental interaction between physical contexts and human communication. Recall that people are proactive (not reactive) and "act toward" rather than "react to" their environments in order to create meanings, and thus come to understand their environment in terms of the actions they perform within it. Just how do you use your environment—that is, how do you function communicatively in regard to your physical context?

The Function of Space   Scholars involved in the study of nonverbal behavior have coined the term, *proxemics*, to denote the use of space and distance in human interaction. *Territoriality* and *personal space* are two uses of space and distance important to our understanding of physical context and interpersonal communication.

Not too many years ago it was quite fashionable to compare the behavior of other animals with that of humans and, by analogy, to discover alleged insights into human behavior. Biologist Robert Ardrey (1970) wrote several best-selling books on the topic of animal-human comparisons and reflected the popular interest in, among other things, the concept of "territoriality." According to this principle, animals, including household pets, stake out geographical areas to which they claim ownership and will challenge any intruders who don't "belong." A friend of Kathy's owns two cocker spaniels: Nuggett and Shadow. When they are taken for a ride, both will claim their territory in the car. Shadow will take a position between the seats and Nuggett, seeking a position closer to "Mom," will sit in the driver's seat. Moving these two dogs is quite a chore because they will both steadfastly defend their positions.

Territoriality, in human communication, is "the assumption of proprietary rights toward some geographical area, with the realization, at least for humans, that there is no basis for those rights" (Rosenfeld & Civikly, 1976, p. 147). Humans are not exempt from the kind of behavior displayed by Shadow and Nuggett as evidenced by the proliferation of "No Trespassing" signs in many neighborhoods. Although humans do not necessarily claim their territory in the same manner as Shadow and Nuggett, it has been found that people claim ownership of territory in four ways (Knapp, 1978). First, people "mark" territory with objects. When Kathy was young, her brother and sisters use to grab the cereal boxes each morning so each one could eat behind a "fortress" of boxes. Second, people use "labels" to identify ownership. Kathy uses the label "Doc Adams" on her license plate and mailbox to identify her property. Actually friends of hers don't buy that explanation and instead believe the label reflects the grandiose side of her. Third, people use "offensive displays" such as fists, scowls, glaring, and so on in an attempt to prevent invasion of territory—sounds like Shadow and Nuggett!? And fourth, people stake out territory with "tenure." When was the last time you got upset when another classmate sat in "your" seat, the one that you had been sitting in for quite some time?

You must, however, guard against the natural tendency to accept too uncritically the analogy between human and animal behavior. One problem of assigning the "territorial imperative" to humans is that it defines space only in terms of mere ownership and then compounds the problem by interpreting ownership negatively. The person feels "violated," then, if a "nonintimate other" enters more private territory. But humans, you will remember, are remarkably adaptive. People often experience total strangers within private territory and think little of it. When people go to a movie theater, the person sitting in the next seat, millimeters away, is likely to be a stranger, but they don't feel violated (although they may "fight" over who gets the arm rest). When people enter a crowded elevator, they are often actually touching total strangers; but no one feels a need to attack anyone else, (unless of course one of them is Hannibal Lector from *Silence of the*

People mark their
territory with objects.

Lambs). People "make sense" of the situation and adapt their behaviors accordingly, without particularly feeling the negative imperative of territorial protection.

Space does not function solely as an issue of ownership. Rather, *personal space* is more like a "bubble" around each person which they carry around with them as they move. The bubble analogy is not totally accurate either. For one thing, the size of your bubble varies with the situation. It is probably rather large when camping in a wilderness area; people resent the intrusion of any other camper, even one who may be hundreds of yards away. The bubble is very small, virtually nonexistent, in the crowded elevator. Moreover the bubble is not really round, either, but is much larger directly in front of you and quite small behind you.

Edward T. Hall (1966) adapted the principle of territorial distance to humans and postulated four concentric circles, which he characterized as progressively closer degrees of interpersonal relationship: public distance (12 feet and more), social distance (4 to 12 feet), personal distance (1½ to 4 feet), and intimate distance (0 to 1½ feet). These distances may actually vary according to culture, age, status, sex, physical size, and so on.

The term "proxemics" is probably unfortunate because it implies that the key factor in how space functions in human interaction is proximity—how near you are to another person in terms of distance. But studies have consistently demonstrated that mere distance or ownership is not what space is about and, further, that it is not particularly significant to interpersonal communication. The more relevant attribute of how humans use their space is *accessibility*. A classic sociopsychological study of housing for married students on a university campus was conducted by Festinger, Schachter, and Back (1950). These researchers found that friends consistently had more interpersonal contact with one another. Even though other people might have lived physically closer by, they were actually less accessible and did not offer as many opportunities for interaction. This study may have been the first clue that accessibility, rather than distance, was the key to understanding how space functions in human interaction.

Robert Sommer (1969) discovered a similar phenomenon when he observed people's choices of seating arrangements around a rectangular table (see Figure 4-2). He found that people tend to choose different arrange-

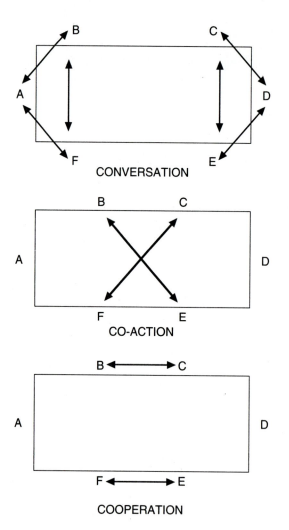

FIGURE 4-2 Seating arrangements and communication purposes

ments on the basis of their purpose for interaction. For example, people choose to sit diagonally with another for conversation (A with B or F, D with C or E) or directly across from each other (B with F, C with E). These arrangements, as expected, provide maximum accessibility. People choose to sit side by side when they are interacting in a cooperative manner. Two students studying for an exam do so "together," yet the cooperating friend does not "intrude" on the other's field of vision and distract the other's attention (B and E or C and F do not intrude on each other). Clearly, the most important factor relevant to space is accessibility, not mere distance.

How humans use space and distance during interpersonal communication is also influenced by a variety of other factors. Some of these factors are primarily relevant to the social context but deserve mention because they also deal with the physical context of space. For example, anthropologists are quick to point out that different cultures use space differently. Italians, for example, are said to stand closer than Americans when they talk with each other (Watson, 1970). But subcultural differences among people within our own country also abound. A friend of Kathy's always gets the feeling that she has to lean over backward when talking with a friend from Louisiana.

There is also some reason to believe that males differ from females in their use of space. Females in American culture tend to have a smaller zone of personal space than do males (Heshka & Nelson, 1974; Rosegrant & McCroskey, 1975). We urge you to be skeptical, though, of allegations of behavioral differences between males and females in American culture. First, sex-role stereotypes in American society are slowly but surely changing. Second, most of the research has relied on perceptions of both observers and observed, and the results of those perceptions are apt to be influenced more by expectations, based on the sex-role stereotypes, than on actual behaviors—another area in which perceptions and behaviors differ. Women, stereotypically, are more socially oriented than men and people tend to perceive their personal space as smaller. However, no research has established any link between the possession of certain anatomical attributes or hormones and interactive behaviors.

The type of relationship also affects how humans use space. Hall's (1966) different distances would lead you to conclude that friends and lovers would tend to stand or sit closer than acquaintances and strangers do. They proactively define the context in terms of their purposes and sit together because they are intimates. They aren't likely to react to the context and become intimates because they sit closer together. Open families complement their informal communication (e.g., rotating of family chores, sharing good news, and doing enjoyable things together) with informal physical environments (e.g., open bedroom doors even at night and some members eating in the kitchen even if guests are present) (Altman, Nelson, & Lett, 1972).

The point to remember when considering space and distance as a function of the physical context is that the actual physical distance separating interactants is a less important factor in human communication than the accessibility of communicators. With greater frequency of interpersonal contact, your opportunity to develop a closer relationship increases.

The Function of Expectations   Physical settings also provide clues as to what type of interaction you should expect to take place. Remember from our discussion of context in Chapter 2, that people possess a repertoire of potential meanings that are applicable to virtually every context of communication. People assess the physical context for clues that will help them narrow down the possible meanings of the situation and thus provide expectations about how to interact socially.

When you encountered a stranger on the first day of class, for instance, you already knew a great deal about that person on the basis of this physical context's influence on your expectations. You knew, for example, that the person was probably an undergraduate student, had some interest in the subject matter of the class (either as relevant to a major or as an elected course to satisfy a requirement), was currently living at or near school, and so forth. In other words, you reduce your uncertainty about the other person by using the clues available in the physical context, thus influencing your expectations about how to interact with this person. You can expect, for instance, that "What's your major?" "Where's your hometown?" and "Did you see the game last week?" are all appropriate topics of conversation associated with this physical context. Often the first place people look for informational clues is the physical setting. It can provide general information about who the other person is and how to behave appropriately.

Actually human expectations and physical contexts probably exert a reciprocal influence on each other. That is, people's prior expectations of appropriate interaction within a particular context are probably as much a factor in how they will function in it as are the clues provided by the physical context. Take, for instance, the notion of personal space as it influences the accessibility of interpersonal communication. When you enter the crowded elevator, you expect to be crowded and don't really resent what would, in other circumstances, be violations of your personal space. In a context with vast quantities of available space, you would probably resent much less formidable intrusions on your private bubbles. The expectations you have as you enter a context are as much a factor of how you function within it as is the way the physical context functions to direct your expectations.

The Social Impact of the Physical Setting

The physical context is not just a physical setting composed of visual, oral, and olfactory stimuli floating around waiting to be turned into sensations and perceptions; it is much more than that. It is also a place where human communication takes place and has taken place.

The physical context often contains subtle clues about the social relationship of people within it, too. We have already suggested that the traditional classroom context implies a status or power distinction between teacher and students, and our prior experience in other classrooms serves to reinforce that status difference. Also, if you walk into a living room with a white carpet and white furniture, you are likely to expect that the adults in the house don't allow their children to play in this room. Kathy has a friend who has often remarked that she grew up in an immaculate *Better Home and Gardens* home. In her home she came to expect long periods of "sterile" silence between family members shattered by moments of intense family interaction. This section discusses other ways in which the physical contexts of communication impact the social expectations of people.

As a setting of interpersonal communication, a physical context contains clues about interpersonal relationships that have taken place or will occur within it. The context, for instance, may be someone's "turf"—that is, someone may "own" the setting and consequently have greater power in the relationship that occurs within it, at least in the introductory stages of the communication. A physical context may function to encourage or discourage a developing relationship between people who meet as strangers and engage in interpersonal communication. Or a physical context may include environmental objects or other "residues" that tell people who enter the environment something about the interpersonal relationship of the people who are in that setting. In all cases, the physical context itself may reflect or influence the relationships of people who use that context for interpersonal communication. And this is what is meant by "the social impact of physical contexts."

"Ownership" of the Setting   If you are invited into someone's home for a party or a social engagement, you know who "owns" that setting. The residential setting "belongs to" the host or hostess. You are an outsider invited into the territory of the other person and consequently tend to defer to the other's direction. The host/hostess is entitled to tell you what to eat or whether to eat, when to eat, what to do, when to do it. That is the "right" of the host/hostess. You, as a guest, would be very rude if you did not defer to the owner's directions. Even though guests may appear to be in a position of honor, they are expected to ask permission to use the phone, tour the home, use the bathroom. Of course, the good host/hostess always accedes to such requests but still has the "power" to do so. The hostess/host–guest relationship creates a clear social distinction in terms of power and status, a social relationship that influences at least the early stages of the interaction.

Defining ownership of the physical context in the above example is easy. But what about the ownership of the setting in a public place, a context that is not the residence of one of the communicators? A scene in an old, tawdry spy novel involves a clandestine meeting between the spy chiefs of the United States and the Soviet Union during the cold war. Naturally, each person distrusts the other and does not wish to allow his counterpart and enemy to have an advantage at this meeting. They have agreed to meet alone (without supporting personnel), in a neutral country (not "owned" by one of their respective countries), and in a public restaurant (clearly no ownership in this public setting). The American quickly discovers that he has been placed in a position of disadvantage as he observes the Russian (through his communicative behavior) usurp "ownership" of the setting.

The Russian, who arrived first (a good tactic), has already ordered a wine that he proceeds to offer to the arriving American (who begins to feel more and more like the Russian's "guest" in the public restaurant). The Russian, apparently a connoisseur of good food, then proceeds to recommend certain items on the menu as being particularly good when prepared by this particular restaurant. He has obviously been there before. The Soviet spy chief has thus gained a social advantage by behaving in a way that lets him claim the ownership role of the public setting.

Keep in mind that the relationship between the physical context and interpersonal communication is interactional, not deterministic. If the setting had determined the behaviors of the participants, the American and the Russian would have been on socially equivalent grounds. But the meaning of the physical context was not just the sensory stimuli present in the restaurant; it was created socially by the people who interacted within its boundaries. The Russian *acted as though* he were the host of the setting. The American, by deferring to the Russian's invitations (he really had little choice without appearing boorish), also *acted as though* he were the guest. The result? The physical context, even though it was a public setting, was defined *through interpersonal communication* to create a difference in status or power between the two men who were peers/equals in all other respects.

To be the "owner" of the setting is to be in a position of greater power. Often sales representatives try to usurp contextual ownership, even though they may be making the sales pitch in the prospect's living room. A sales pitch is certainly interpersonal communication. In the seller-buyer relationship, it is often to the seller's advantage to be in a more powerful social position.

How can a seller attempt to usurp ownership of the potential buyer's living room? One way is to direct where the potential buyers should sit to discuss the product. ("Let's sit at the table here. I can lay out all my materials.") Then the seller takes over the table by covering the available space with visual aids, notebooks, and so on. It's even better if a centerpiece (belonging to the buyer) must be moved in order to make room for the materials (belonging to the seller). One sales technique is to ask the potential buyer for a glass of water, thereby forcing the buyer to "wait on" the seller and play the less powerful role of "servant." A good sales representative will gain "ownership" of a setting in a matter of moments.

Sometimes, however, you may find it to your advantage (depending on the goal or purpose of your communication) not to be in the role of ownership. For instance, hosts and hostesses may own the setting when they invite guests to a party, but they often attempt to shed their ownership role. They allow guests to serve themselves refreshments, give them the run of the house, urge them to act as though they were at home, and generally attempt to share ownership of the setting with the guests. You have been to parties or dinners in which you felt "at home." They are in direct contrast to other parties at which you felt inhibited, stiff, and unsure of how to behave. The one party may appear to be more formal than the other, but perhaps the most appropriate definition of "informal" is the shared ownership of the setting.

Several years ago Aub's daughter went out for the first time with a new young man. When he asked her how she had enjoyed it, she told him it was "weird." Apparently the boy did everything in a very proper manner. He told her where they were going to eat. He opened doors and pulled out chairs for her. He asked her to choose what she'd like from the menu and then proceeded to give the waiter both their orders. He told her what movie they were going to see, and so forth and so forth. Her previous dating experience had apparently been with boys who shared their ownership of the date's physical context. They abdicated their "right" to dictate her behavior, and she apparently preferred that kind of relationship. Thus, she didn't think her date did anything wrong, but she did think he was "weird." To repeat, depending on one's purpose or goal in communication, abdicating ownership may be advantageous.

The Role of the Stranger   What about interpersonal communication situations in which the interactants have had no prior experience in communicating with each other? How might the physical context influence the expectations of strangers when they communicate for the first time? Public settings (restaurants, department stores, shopping malls, transit buses, etc.), you might think, are typically populated with strangers. But if you think that all strangers are alike in all settings, you are surely mistaken.

Strangers are so called because you have had little or no prior acquaintance with them; some strangers, however, remain strangers even after prior acquaintance. You may notice a specific person in a shopping mall and then recognize the same person later in another part of the mall. Even though the prior experience is present in your mind, you continue to consider the stranger as a stranger because the physical context of a shopping mall has directed your expectations regarding your relationship with that person. The stranger remains a stranger, and little opportunity for further communication is available in this setting.

The key to understanding how the physical context influences your expectations of interpersonal communication with strangers is in discerning whether the context encourages or discourages future relationships and further interactions. Some public contexts discourage, or at least don't encourage, continued development of relational interaction. The public elevator remains a good example. Even when it is crowded, people don't have the feeling that they know much about their companions. Even though they may converse with one another (usually about how crowded the elevator is), they have little expectation that they will have interactions with one another after they have gotten off the elevator.

The stranger in the elevator or in the shopping mall is more like a part of the physical context, a virtual "nonperson." The stranger has no discernible identity as a specific person and remains a part of the context in your memory even after the elevator ride is over. You may talk about "the person in the elevator" in the same manner as you might discuss the advertisement on the wall of the elevator. The stranger in this context is not much different from any other object in the physical context. Hence, you might identify this setting as defining the expectation of the communicators to regard the stranger *as object*.

Other physical contexts, though, actively encourage the development of social relationships among strangers. The most blatant example of such settings is the ever-popular "mixer." The purpose of such a public context is to enable strangers to become acquainted, to engage in small talk, to get to know something about one another. The expectation is that participants in a mixer will have future contacts with one another and that future interaction will be easier because of this prior interactional experience.

High schools, colleges, and universities are notorious for having such get-acquainted parties during the first weeks of the fall term. Fraternities, sororities, and other campus social organizations regularly sponsor parties and mixers. The other person in such a setting is certainly a stranger, but the context defines the stranger not as an object but as an acquaintance. And acquaintances are potentially future friends.

Of course, some chance encounters in stranger-as-object contexts may develop into future friendships. A TV commercial for a breath mint popularizes the myth of boy meets girl in public context, but even this commercial acknowledges the role of typical expectations of such settings. The message is to keep on chewing those little mints because you may need them when you least expect it. The point is that the physical context helps define the role of the stranger. Whereas some settings discourage continued interaction and thus define the stranger as object, others encourage further interaction and thereby define the stranger as acquaintance.

Social Residues in the Settings   Articles in popular magazines providing advice on "how to decorate your home" typically tell the reader to give the home that "personal touch." Your home, these authors say, should reflect you and your personal tastes. Most of you would probably believe that you can tell a great deal about people as soon as they walk into their homes, dorm rooms, or apartments. You can tell whether they're neat or messy, whether they're formal or informal—in short, whether you would like to get to know them better or not. People who own physical contexts (typically the home) can modify the physical stimuli of the setting directly by decorating and designing this space to reflect their own individual ideas and tastes—their very identity (see Hayward, 1977).

When you derive expectations and inferences about what people are like from the appearance of their homes, you are not unlike archaeologists who study past civilizations. Because these researchers exist in the present and attempt to understand a society or culture that no longer exists, archaeologists have no choice but to search for physical residues of past cultures, physical objects that have lasted through the ages and function as the "footprints" of the past. The archaeologist digs into the earth and finds tools, pottery, buildings, statues, jewelry, and other physical objects. From these physical residues, the archaeologist makes inferences about actual behaviors of members in a society that is now no more. In the absence of interactive behavior to observe, the archaeologist looks for residues of those behaviors in the form of physical artifacts—not real facts but residues of facts in the form of physical objects.

Artifacts of social relationships also exist in many physical contexts in which interaction has taken place. Clark Olson (1981) studied artifacts of social relationships in the homes of a young married couple, an unmarried couple, and an older married couple. He then generated some intriguing insights into the social residues as well as the nature of some potential differences in these three types of relationships.

Artifacts in the home, Olson discovered, reflect the identities of both individuals and relationships. Prominently displayed photographs, for example, may be the most obvious artifacts, and they may be individual or relational—that is, they may be pictures of one of the individuals or of the couple together as a unit. A displayed trophy is more likely to reflect an individual, but wedding gifts or gifts to "the couple" are often displayed with pride as a reflection of relational identity. Olson suggested that displaying the relational artifacts might reflect the stability or strength of the relationship, the effectiveness of past communication or interaction. Often the artifacts are displayed in a prominent place, such as a fireplace mantle or a wall collection, so that they seem to constitute a "shrine"—a place of honor and reverence.

Olson also discovered that certain sections of homes might contain residues of specific interactional or communicative functions. A kitchen desk with a convenient wall calendar, for instance, was reserved for communication that involved planning activities. In that particular context, the couple compiled grocery lists, talked about their activities for the day, rehashed activities of the past day, and made plans for the weekend. Other areas of the house were reserved for other functions. Each member of one couple had her or his own personal desk which contained the materials "belonging to" that person. That setting was for private functions—reading, studying, meditating—a place of solitude in a physical context whose ownership was otherwise shared.

A marriage counselor in a radio interview once expounded on the necessity of never arguing in bed. Her point was that the bedroom was a place for intimate sharing and should not be "defiled" with the blasphemy of arguing. Not only did she appear to recognize the concept and function of artifacts, residues of past interactions in the physical setting, but she also talked about the bedroom in quasi-religious tones—as though it were a place of worship and the marital relationship the focus of reverence. In any case, she clearly recognized the sometimes-close connection between the "owned" environment or physical context, the social relationship, and the people within it.

What is the relative strength of the physical context's influence on interpersonal communication? As you have undoubtedly inferred from our discussions, elements of the social context and of the physical context sometimes conflict. Sometimes social factors work against the increased opportunity for interaction that is present in the physical context. At times, the social context is so powerful that the physical context's influence is minimized.

THE SOCIAL CONTEXT

To use "social context" as a singular term, though, is somewhat misleading. Whenever communication takes place, numerous *social contexts* are present: the relationship of the participants, cultures in which the participants hold a common membership, and additional cultures to which only one of the participants belongs. And those contexts are too often thought of as exogenous to the interaction or something external to the participants. Priests, ministers, and rabbis are fond of telling their congregations that the church is not the building, nor the scriptural writings, nor the body of knowledge. When the Jews and early Christians were persecuted, their scriptures burned, and their buildings destroyed, their religion continued to flourish. Why? Because their religion was not (and is not) external to the members in the form of a building or dogma; it is endogenous or made real in and through the interaction of the members (Heritage, 1984). The influences of all the relevant social contexts are present in any given event of human communication and exert positive and negative influences.

But if so many social contexts influence interpersonal communication and if those influences are both positive and negative, which influences are the strongest? It is a truism that the strongest influence of all is typically the most immediate social context, the smallest one. The most immediate context, of course, is the relationship created by the participants themselves through their interaction with one another. Recall that Romeo and Juliet's interpersonal relationship ultimately proved to be stronger than the highly potent social contexts of their families. The closer the social context is to the immediate relationship, the greater its influence.

Our discussion of social context of interpersonal communication is divided into three sections. The first section identifies the various types of social contexts potentially present during every act of human communication. The second section recalls that humans are proactive and details how people use the social context for purposes relevant to interpersonal communication. Finally, the third section deals with how social contexts specifically influence your communicative choices. You will note in this section the absence of any detailed discussion of language and discourse—which function "*in* context and *as* context" (Beach, 1983; Ochs, 1979). This is because the powerful influence of language and discourse is so significant that it deserves its own discussion in Chapter 5.

Types of Social Context

We distinguish between two general types of social contexts: socializing and relational. One socializing context differs from another on the basis of the kinds of things members learn from belonging to it. A relational context focuses on the nature of the interpersonal bonds that tie members to one another within the social context. These social contexts overlap one another in the sense that a particular relational context (such as family) will also socialize its members by teaching them certain customs, traditions, norms, rules, and so on.

Socializing Contexts A society does not come into existence by coincidence. Societal members do not just wake up one morning and magically possess the norms, values, beliefs, and traditions of a society. They learn or are socialized about these values and customs from experienced social members. In our large society, *socialization* functions through our social institutions: schools, churches, mass media, and—most important, perhaps—the family.

Bernstein (1972, p. 1970), a sociolinguist, has classified four social contexts in which the socializing process occurs: regulative, instructional, imaginative or innovative, and interpersonal. Bernstein suggests that these socializing contexts occur primarily in the family, as parents or guardians teach children about society; but they are just as relevant to schools, mass media, street gangs, and peer groups.

Regulative Context   *Regulative context* involves the learning of authority relationships and the rules of conduct that regulate the larger society as well as a small group of friends. For instance, children learn not to cross the street before looking both ways, adolescents learn the rules for dating, adults learn how to get ahead in their jobs, and students learn how to get good grades.

Instructional Context   *Instructional context* involves learning about the nature of objects and other people. From the adolescent who takes the first drive in a car to the adult who tries to master the intricacies of a personal computer, members of a society continue to learn in instructional contexts throughout their lives. Every new social situation, also, constitutes an instructional context in which the individual discovers more social knowledge about the nature of other human beings. You do so either by other people telling you about others or through your own observations or direct experience with others.

Imaginative, or Innovative, Context   *Imaginative, or innovative,* context encourages creativity and innovation on the part of the person becoming socialized and is thus the farthest removed from regulative socialization. Recall that open systems are self-organizing (regulative) and self-renewing (creative). When you innovate or learn a creative behavior, there are no rules for that particular situation. These contexts are recognized as "exceptions to the rules"; they require spontaneity, innovation, trial-and-error techniques. People learn from imaginative contexts how to interact with each other without conforming solely to the influence of some larger social context. By participating in personalized relationships, the participants learn how to create their own rules that are idiosyncratic to their interactions and recognize that their rules may not be appropriate for other social interaction. Kathy and two of her friends often engage in what they consider "playful" games with their squirt guns—behavior that would be considered "juvenile" and perhaps "weird" in another situation. Innovative socialization, in essence, encourages individual members of a society to develop their own individual identities and unique relationships.

Interpersonal Context   In *interpersonal context* individuals learn to become aware of their own emotions, their inner selves, and their innermost feelings, and they learn how to deal with such personal awareness. The teenager who breaks up with his or her "steady" learns the pangs of adolescent heartbreak. Individuals also learn to be sensitive to and aware of the internal states of other people and how to deal with other people's emotions as well as their own. What do you say to a person who tells a racist or sexist joke? How do you respond to a friend whose parent has just died? Kathy will never forget the moment when a friend of hers, Mary, came to her dorm room, sat down on her bed, and in shock revealed that Kathy's mother had died. Kathy learned a lot on that cold, winter morning about empathy and compassion. In these contexts people learn the nuances of perceiving what is going on inside themselves and understanding what that means to their own behavior. It also allows them to perceive what is going on inside other people on the basis of what they can observe in their behaviors. For these reasons this context as an "interpersonal" context is probably more accurately described as *intra*personal, despite the fact that it nearly always occurs within a social setting.

Socializing contexts offer members of a society the opportunity to learn what it means to belong to a social community. Further, this process of socialization continues throughout life, although the greatest proportion of socialization probably occurs prior to adulthood. Once you learn the rules and customs of a society in a socializing context, you can then apply elsewhere what you have learned in a specific kind of society—a particular kind of social context identified by the nature of the bonds that hold the members of that context together.

Relational Contexts   You will be surprised to learn that relationships are like laundry detergents. There are a large number of detergents on the market, but they are produced by only a small number of companies. Likewise, you will probably have dozens, perhaps hundreds, of different relationships in your lifetime. However, all these relationships fall into relatively few kinds of relational contexts. The following discussion will briefly touch upon five types of *relational contexts*, or "connections," between participants in interpersonal communication: kinship, friendship, work, social contract, and acquaintance. We will discuss these, in more detail, in Part Three of this book.

Kinship   *Kinship* involves a relational context based on the connections of biological (including adoptive) relations. The family is an important context for socialization and is typically the longest-lasting relational context as well. People tend to keep in contact with their families long after they leave home. Furthermore, unlike other relationships, the family can regenerate itself with each succeeding generation of children and, perhaps, has the greatest stability of all possible relationships.

Friendship   *Friendship* is also a common social relationship, although the differences among different friendship contexts is enormous. Since it is a context people each invent, they have different definitions of it and yet

The family is an important context for socialization.

they use the term as if it were understood by everyone (Pogrebin, 1987). There are five common characteristics of this context (Rawlins, 1992). Friendships are voluntary, personal or privately negotiated, mutually involving or collaborative, equally balanced as opposed to exploitative, and conducive to affective ties. The characteristics of choice and privacy as well as others (such as social mobility) threaten the stability of this context more so than kin relations. As strange as it may seem, the relational context of friendship includes some of the closest and most intimate social ties. But at the same time, it is a highly unstable social relationship.

    Work   *Work* relations develop when people work together and their relationship is considered a matter of coincidence. When people "live" together for eight hours a day, forty hours a week, they have frequent opportunities to talk with one another. With this frequency of interpersonal contact, the work context may create rather close interpersonal relationships. These relationships usually are not friendships because *you* choose your friends; the place of work chooses your work relationships *for you*. Of course, work colleagues may also be friends, but only if and when they expand their relationship beyond the boundaries of the work environment and choose to have frequent interpersonal contact outside the work setting.

    Social Contract   *Social contract* involves a special type of relational context quite different from any of the others. The contractual relationship contains an overt obligation on the part of the members that just isn't present in any other relational context. A wife and husband are "legally married" and, therefore, subject to obligations (such as financial support, communal ownership of property, legal responsibility for actions of children) prescribed by law. The lawyer-client and the priest-confessor relational contexts share an obligation of confidentiality. The attorney's obligation is sanctioned by law, the priest's obligation by the doctrines of the church. Other social contracts might include employer and employee, buyer and seller, lender and borrower, therapist and client, landowner and tenant, among others. Many social contracts invoke the proverbial "piece of paper," others do not. The social contract is not the document at all; it is the identifiable sanctioned influence of some larger social context.

Acquaintanceship   Each of the above relational contexts are common and familiar ones involving interpersonal communication. However, *acquaintanceship* is the most common (by far) of all social relationships. The average individual, over a 100-day period, has a pool of acquaintances numbering between 500 and 2500 people, and yet only three to seven of these may be considered "friends" (Pogrebin, 1987). Acquaintances are referred to as "bit players" in our lives, the "familiar strangers" who come and go. Perhaps the most definitive attribute of acquaintanceship is the lack of depth in these interpersonal encounters. Interaction tends to remain on a superficial level.

These, then, are the social contexts, both socializing and relational, embedded in and available to the participants in any given act of interpersonal communication. The interactant brings to the act of interpersonal communication the socializations of a number of larger cultures as well as other relational contexts that implicitly function to influence the communicative behaviors in some way, and that influence is present to some extent in every act of interpersonal communication. The precise nature of these influences is the subject of the following discussion.

Using the Social Context

The social contexts of interpersonal communication provide natural guidelines for your communicative behavior in the "Who are you?" and "Who am I to you?" stage of relational development. When you encounter another for the first time you set out to discover who the other is by identifying the other as a member of certain social contexts. Work: "What do you do for a living?" Kinship: "Are you married?" Acquaintanceship: "Do you know so and so?" And, of course, there are the usual issues of social identity that come from a larger social context: identity by political affiliation, religious belief, socioeconomic status, fraternity affiliation, and so on. But when you engage in interpersonal communication, there are additional uses you can make of the social context in the early stages of interpersonal communication. Proactively, you can use the social context as a means of comparing or evaluating your present relationships, of providing opportunities for further interpersonal contact, and of offering support when intrapersonal problems arise.

Evaluation of Present Relationships   Social psychologists James Thibaut and Harold Kelley (1959; see also Kelley and Thibaut, 1978; Kelley, 1979) have developed a model for understanding how and why people form relationships with others. Their model, called "social exchange," is based upon perceived "costs" and "rewards," positive and negative values, associated with interacting with another person. Individuals are "economically" motivated to evaluate any specific interpersonal relationship along a scale that ranges from "very good" to "very bad." In addition, the individual uses the costs and rewards to compare each individual relationship with other relationships and discover which one is more valuable.

The assumption is that social exchange between individuals is consistent with individual self-interest. "Self-interest is defined as the tendency to seek preferred resources from others" (Roloff, 1981, p. 25). People tend to relate selfishness with exploitation and assume that altruistic behavior is better. However it has been shown that altruism is often disguised selfishness (Homans, 1961), and may even be harmful to relationships (Walster, Walster, & Berscheid, 1978). Altruistic relationships are fundamentally inequitable in that the altruistic partner is giving and receiving another in return. This inequity can produce overdependence in the receiver of the altruism and possible humiliation. As we pointed out in Chapters 2 and 3, people, to some degree, make sense of their environment in terms of what it means for them. People evaluate their friends and acquaintances, partially, on the basis of "Who can do the most for me?"—a profit motivation. Realistically most people are not at either extreme; totally altruistic or profit peddlers. The well-being of a relationship requires relational partners to act in concert with each other; to blend self-interest with other-interest and relationship-interest.

According to Thibaut and Kelley (1959) individuals typically compare their immediate relationships with the social context of other relationships (friends with other friends, acquaintances with other acquaintances, etc.). During and after the process of interpersonal communication, each communicator tends to evaluate the worth of that transaction. Whether people make their comparisons on the basis of personal motives or for other reasons, every relationship is judged retrospectively as to its degree of worthiness, and the judgment process occurs simultaneously in the minds of each participant.

Think about the last time you were at a party with people you did not know very well. You engage in idle chatter with someone, but you are both aware that you will probably never see each other after this party. You run out of things to say and begin looking around to see where you might wander next. You notice the other is also scanning the room for alternatives. After all, if you don't think the other is worthy of more of your time, why should you think the other is evaluating you any different? The process of social exchange, judging the relationship against others in the social context, is going on in the minds of both communicators during the process of interpersonal communication.

Opportunity for Interpersonal Contact   Your interpersonal relationhips change drastically during the course of your life for many reasons including changes in social contexts. For the first few years, your social context is restricted to kinship relational contexts. The very small child has very few social contacts outside the boundaries of the immediate family. The child's social context expands somewhat with the addition of neighborhood playmates of a similar age, but the social context does not extend far beyond the people who live in the home and the immediate neighborhood. When the child enters school, however, the number of people in the social context increases dramatically. High school acquaintances expand the social context even more. The social context continues to increase, but individuals will experience fluctuations in social context over the life span. For example, young adults experience more contact with friends than at any other adult stage except that of the elderly (Rawlins, 1992).

Very simply, you can use only the social context that is available to you. When your social context offers the opportunity for a variety of contacts and repeated contacts with people, you have variety and closeness in your interpersonal relationships. Social contexts vary in size, not according to the number of people, but according the degree of interpersonal accessibility. Beginning in junior high, and increasingly during high school and college, the social context encourages an extremely large number of interpersonal contacts. As you grow older, factors such as career, marriage, retirement, and health can help or hinder the interpersonal accessibility to others offered by your social contexts. Further, the social context itself will change as you enter a different phase of your life and thus your opportunity for increased interpersonal contact.

Support Systems   Individuals use their social contexts for social support. The individual who experiences a problem in some relationship often seeks out someone else in order to "talk out" problems. Teenagers who have problems with boyfriends or girlfriends often tell their troubles to other friends, typically the same sex, and look for help. Support systems need not require a friendship relation. The plethora of support groups in this country, such as Alcoholics Anonymous, Codependent Anonymous, Parents

Individuals use their social contexts such as the family for social support.

without Partners, Weight Watchers, and so on, are formal support systems designed to assist people with particular problems. The individuals that people seek for support are usually the ones who have some familiarity with the problem, have gone through the problem, or somehow know what it is like to experience the problem.

Although there are exceptions to the rule, people tend to use relational contexts that include members of the same sex as their support system; our society is primarily homosocial (Pogrebin, 1987). Members of American society tend to view male-female relationships as "romantic involvements." People encourage boys to play with boys or risk being called "sissies," and girls to play with girls or risk being called "tomboys." The opportunity for interpersonal contact provided by social contexts in American society can be very sexist. As people grow older, is it any wonder that they may find it difficult to seek support from the opposite sex? Yet there are variations in this preference. Young men confide more to their best female friend than to their best male friend and consult them more on major decisions (Olstad, 1975). Young women, however, are happier in close same-sex relationships (Helgeson, Shaver, & Dyer, 1987). Both young men and women tend to seek women in times of stress (Buhrke & Fuqua, 1987).

The tendency to dismiss the other half of the population as potential members of support systems is perhaps an unfortunate commentary on our society.

Influence of Social Context

This final section discusses more specific ways in which the social context of interpersonal communication actually influences your choice of what communicative behaviors to perform. Keep in mind, though, that social contexts do not "cause" people to behave in a certain way. Rather, you can gain information from the social context in order to know which behaviors are appropriate and which are not. Since you are a proactive individual, the behaviors you actually perform during the process of interpersonal communication are *always* the result of your choosing to perform them. But your choice is influenced by information, some of which comes from the social context. And remember that information functions to restrict the number of behavioral options available to you.

Social Expections   To be a member of a social community is to subscribe to its norms and values. Every member of a society has been, to some extent, socialized to accept normal social beliefs, to value normal social values, to act normally in social roles, and so forth. Society provides its members with rules to guide their conduct and beliefs. The socializing contexts provide a rather large proportion of the individual's cognitive framework, the intrapersonal level of communication. Socialization gives the individual member of society the cognitive background to interpret objects, people, and events. Interpreting the meaning of any event, object, or person is often attributable to the expectations that an individual has acquired through the process of socialization. Our discussion of these social expectations will fall generally into two categories: roles and stereotypes.

   Roles   *Roles* provide guidelines for behavior; or they are what the social context designates as appropriate behavior in specific relationships. A teacher-student relationship, for example, is defined by roles that the social context of the school has created and defined. The instructor is the instructor and the student is the student because those are the roles the school context has assigned them. The context of the school provides the interactants with expectations as to the behaviors that are and are not appropriate to the instructor's and student's roles.

   Other relational contexts comprise roles that influence the behaviors of the communicators within them. The contracted relationship of husband and wife defines roles designated by the social context of marriage and family. The same is true of the boss-subordinate relationship in the work context. Because of these role designations, the social context influences interpersonal communication by providing the participants with guidelines for what constitutes acceptable and unacceptable behavior during interpersonal interaction.

Andreyeva and Gozman (1981), both social psychologists, provide one example of the contextual influence of roles on interpersonal communication:

> At a certain period of an individual's life the norms of society prescribe that he should fall in love with another person of the opposite sex. But if this does not occur then the individual is exposed to all the pressures felt by someone subject to group influence who violates group norms. Hence, attraction [of one person to the other] is presumed to be not only determined by external influence but also normative in its essence, and the behaviour that accompanies it is, to a great extent, role behaviour. (p. 56)

What are these people trying to say in this paragraph? You "know" from common sense that people "fall in love" or become friends because of some mysterious ability to discover attractive or admirable personal qualities in the other person. But maybe you "fall in love" because our society expects you to do so. Certainly society tends to treat people who reach the age of thirty without ever having been married as having something "wrong" with them. Moreover, our society tends to punish women more than men who fail to fulfill their "proper" roles in society. Unmarried women are called "spinsters" or "old maids," not highly desirable names; whereas men are merely "bachelors," a more neutral term.

During their teenage years, boys and girls are expected to date, to fulfill the roles expected of them at that stage of their lives. Dating after the age of forty can pose real problems, because what is "expected" and socially very "normal" for teenagers may be quite abnormal for people beyond that age. Somehow the roles expected of participants in a dating relationship are probably much more normal and thus more comfortable for teenagers than for mature adults.

Although you may not want to think so, much of your relational behavior is guided by your reliance on the social context to tell you what roles you are expected to and "should" perform. Social contexts serve as valuable frames of reference by providing you with role guidelines. By conforming to them, you know that you are doing the normal thing. During much of your relational life, you are (at the same time) both a victim and a beneficiary of the influences of your social context.

Stereotypes   When you hear the word "stereotype," you are filled with all sorts of negative reactions. A stereotype, you tend to believe, is a "wrong" belief that you should avoid. Stereotypes provide the reasons for sexism, racism, anti-Semitism, and social prejudices of all kinds. As a matter of fact, though, stereotypes are no more likely to be in error than any other belief that has its basis in "common sense." That is, a *stereotype* is little more than a widespread belief based on common sense. Recall that common sense is only something considered "sensible" because it is consistent with what many people conventionally believe. In other words, many members of a society believe in a stereotype, and that fact of widespread belief is fundamental to the nature of a stereotype.

Like your belief in stereotypes, you believe common sense without exercising any critical judgment toward it; you accept it without evaluating it on the basis of what you believe to be true because of your own trial-and-error experiences. Uncritical acceptance is also a characteristic trait of a stereotype, something you believe to be true because it is conventional—a lot of other people also believe it is true. Like any commonsense belief, a stereotype is a bias or prejudice because you tend to accept it uncritically, without rendering any independent judgment as to its accuracy or truth value.

A stereotype is also a generalization. That is, you attribute some property to an entire class of people or objects. "The English drink tea" is a stereotype of people from Great Britain. The stereotype attributes the "tea-drinking" property to the entire class of "English." When people indiscriminately apply the stereotype to absolutely every member of the class, they often make errors. And it is the indiscriminate application of stereotypes, as well as the fact that some stereotypes (such as racist and sexist stereotypes) are simply false, that gives "stereotype" its well-deserved bad reputation.

Like all commonsense beliefs, a stereotype often has some basis in truth. Otherwise, why would so many people believe it to be true? Adults often have a stereotypical image of teenage behaviors. Not only are teenagers "boy crazy" and "girl crazy," but they stereotypically use the telephone for recreational purposes with greater frequency than any other single group in our society. We know of no statistics compiled by the telephone company to support this belief, but many adults do subscribe to this stereotype of teenagers. What's more, this stereotype may have some basis in fact. A friend of Aub's once confided that when he called Aub's home and actually heard the telephone ringing, he assumed that no one was home and hung up. He assumed (quite correctly, too) that if one of Aub's daughters had been home, he would have heard a busy signal.

You will notice that in this discussion of stereotypes we have not advised you to guard against their evil influence or to realize that stereotypes are harmful to effective interpersonal communication. In fact, such advice is not always good advice. We cannot deny that stereotypes do exist and that people use them as guidelines for their behavior in interpersonal communication. In other words, social stereotypes (whether they are true or false) do influence the process of interpersonal communication, despite the fact that their influence is sometimes detrimental to effective communication. On the other hand, some stereotypes actually serve to assist the process of interpersonal communication by giving the communicators some notion of what to expect from their interaction with a new acquaintance.

Social Rules   Every social context has its own rules. They are an important part of understanding the interplay between social context and interaction. A *rule* is "a followable prescription that indicates what behavior is obligated, preferred, or prohibited in certain contexts" (Shimanoff, 1980). Let's take a closer look at this definition. First, individuals have a choice about whether to follow or not to follow the rule. If there exists no choice, then there exists no rule; that is, rules are *followable*. Second, rules imply some course of action, and criticism can be expected if the course of action is violated. Rules *prescribe* the obligated, the preferred, and the prohibited. Third, rules guide more than a single event, yet they do not guide everything: They are *contextual.* Finally, rules help you decide what behaviors are appropriate. They *specify* appropriate actions rather than require appropriate actions.

Social rules operate like the rules of any game. When you learn a game for the first time, you first learn the rules. But there are two kinds of rules for every game. Some rules are called *constitutive rules* (Searle, 1969) because the game exists because of the establishment of the rules. The constitutive rules of basketball, for instance, specify five members to a team, allow movement of the ball by passing and dribbling, require that the basket be precisely 10 feet above the playing floor, specify 2 points for a field goal and the length of playing time, and so on. In addition to allowing certain behaviors, the rules of basketball also prohibit certain behaviors such as personal fouls, possession of the ball beyond the boundary lines of the playing surface, interference with the flight of the ball in the cone above the basket, and so on. The constitutive rules of basketball tell you what will count as "basketball."

Social contexts of interpersonal communication also have constitutive rules, even though few social contexts provide a written rule book (although we may often wish for one). Individuals can enact promises, for instance, because certain rules are recognized to constitute promises. Suppose a friend has shared something very personal with you and you, in turn, remark "I will never reveal your secret to anyone." Your action is recognized as a promise because of five constitutive rules (Searle, 1969). First, it is an action that indicates a future act—never to reveal the secret (propositional content rule). Second, you have made this promise to your friend only because your friend would prefer you not to tell than to tell (preparatory rule). Third, you have made the promise because it is not obvious to either of you that you would not normally do this (preparatory rule). Fourth, you must be sincere in not revealing the secret (sincerity rule). Finally, your action must involve an obligation on your part not to reveal the secret (essential rule).

The second kind of rules are called *regulative rules* (Searle, 1969) and are created during the playing of the game. Referring back to our basketball analogy, the regulative rules would be the 1-3-1 zone defense, give-and-go plays, location of passing lanes, fast-break plays, and the like. The players of basketball develop their own rules for playing the game within the guidelines of what makes the game basketball (the constitutive rules). In the same way interactants engaged in interpersonal communication develop their own regulative rules during the process of "playing the game" of interpersonal communication. You and your friend develop your own way of promising given the nature of your friendship and your purpose. These regulative rules are the strategies you actually use, the behaviors you perform when you engage in interpersonal communication. In Part Three of this book, on the relationship level of communication, each chapter will include a discussion of those strategies, the regulative rules of interpersonal communication.

Relationship Models   The concept of the "role model" is a well-established tradition in sociology. Small children are said to look up to professional athletes and emulate their behavioral styles. Muhammad Ali serves as a role model for many boxers and black youth even today, years after his retirement as heavyweight boxing champion of the world. Adolescents emulate rock musicians, although imitating Michael Jackson seems more like a masquerade. Movie and television stars are often selected as role models. When people pattern their individual appearance and behaviors on those of someone else in their social context, they are said to be using that person as a role model. But the social context may also provide interpersonal relationships that serve as models for the interpersonal relationships of others.

If you are a typical member of our society, the relationship you are most likely to use as a model is that of your parents. Statistics show that the children of divorced parents are far more likely to end up divorced themselves, as opposed to children of parents with stable marriages. But as strong as parental relationships are as relational models for the next generation, the most influential of all in society may be the relationships depicted by the mass media. Popular music, TV, and the movies often emphasize the power of an intense emotional attachment to another person, typically of the opposite sex. They help to establish a societal model of "love" that is far removed from the reality of actual interpersonal relationships.

For over a hundred years, romantic novels have told a similar story: boy meets girl, boy marries girl, boy and girl live happily ever after. Love is said to conquer all. If you love the other person enough, according to this popular myth, all your troubles will be overcome. The unfortunate fact is that this story *is* mythical. Yet people continue to regard it as a norm and attempt to model their own relationships on its virtually unattainable standard.

Relationship modeling works like this. The individual enters a relationship believing in the live-happily-ever-after myth. The individual behaves in the relationship as though this relationship were the same as the mythical relationship. The individual also seeks out relationships that are expected to manifest the model they have seen on TV or at the movies and that is immortalized in popular music. As a result, the individual comes to feel the emotional attachment that the media have associated with the relationship and indirectly with the myth. In other words, if you believe that your relationship with this other person is consistent with the relational model, you come to believe that you must be feeling the emotion that is consistent with such a relationship. In this way, relational modeling tends to influence not only what people *do* but also what they *feel*—emotions as well as behaviors, intrapersonal as well as interpersonal.

Relational modeling often results in disappointment when the participants discover that the "real" relationship is not the same as the "ideal" depicted by the model. When relational problems arise for whatever reason, the participants become disillusioned and the relationship suffers. They may withdraw their commitment to the relationship; they may seek another relationship in their ongoing search for the ideal; they may resent the other person for not living up to the model; or they may seek assistance from a social support system. Whatever the outcome of the "rude awakening," the actual relationship becomes extremely vulnerable and unstable when the interactants discover that it is not like the model.

There are two problems associated with relational modeling. One is the myth that the ideal relationship need only be "attained." The model tends to define the relationship as a "goal." Once the partners have achieved that goal, they supposedly have nothing more to do. Stories may end at the point of "living happily ever after," but the "real" relationship continues. In other words, the relational model typically ignores a fundamental principle of evolutionary development: the inevitability and constancy of change. Relationships ebb and flow, rise and fall, have peaks and valleys. A relationship cannot sustain a honeymoon period for very long. When the honeymoon is over, the problems of *maintaining* the relationship begin. Maintenance is by far the most crucial stage of relational development (as Chapter 11 will show). The relational myth popularized by the mass media creates a problem by ignoring the maintenance stage completely.

The second problem with relational modeling concerns the glorification of suffering in the typical model depicted by the mass media. Movies and popular songs portray sadness and individual suffering in a way that seems beneficial and even rather enjoyable. Many of you enjoy a good cry during movies that portray a lost love or that show the agony of loving someone who doesn't deserve that love and may not even return it. Popular songs, both rock and country, tell tales of unrequited love. "He is a no-good cad, but I love him just the same" goes the story. "She doesn't love me, but my love is strong enough for both of us" is another common theme. These mythical lovers are made stronger ("become better persons") as a result of their painful experience. What the individual who engages in relational modeling doesn't understand is that suffering doesn't feel good. In fact, it isn't fun at all. But the mass media don't tell us about that.

We hasten to add that we are not suggesting that relational modeling should be avoided by interpersonal communicators. Although it often results in ineffective communication and disconfirmed expectations, no quick-and-easy techniques are available to help you avoid modeling your relationships on mythical ideals. But that isn't really the point. Modeling a relationship on the basis of some mythical ideal is a "normal" contextual influence on the process of interpersonal communication. Increasing your effectiveness as an interpersonal communicator does not mean avoiding doing something that is normal. Rather, you should become aware of and sensitive to these influences of social contexts. You must learn to deal with them because they do, in fact, exist.

One way of dealing with relational modeling is to understand, as fully as possible, the maintenance process of relational development and to work to increase the effectiveness of your communication skills during that stage. You can't deny or ignore the reality of contextual influences on the process of interpersonal communication and pretend that such influences don't or shouldn't exist. You develop your interpersonal skills as you engage in the process of interpersonal communication and behave in a manner appropriate to the recognizable stage of relational development. First comes awareness; then comes practice. Then these two factors (awareness and behaviors) become inseparable so that our interpersonal communication becomes second nature to us. Eventually you won't realize where one (the intrapersonal or the interpersonal) leaves off and the other begins.

SUMMARY

Pragmatic principle 3 reminds you that to discover the meaning or significance of communicative patterns is to place them in some context. Communicative patterns do not emerge in a vacuum. Although you may act mindlessly or as if information were context-free, it is not: Context and interaction are intricately related. Because you tend to reflect a proactive rather than a reactive nature, the role of the context is probably not as often deterministic as it is interactional. Thus context may be said to influence and to be influenced by the human interactions that take place within it.

We discussed two types of context: physical and social. The physical comprises three elements: design, decoration, and the presence or absence of other people. Design features of the context include those elements which are less resistant to change; the decoration features include elements that are easily manipulated such as movable objects or furnishings; and other people are elements of the physical context to the extent that their presence or absence and their location in reference to the communicators provides another context resource. Human beings are also social animals. As a natural consequence of being a member of a social community, they become subject to its influences on their behaviors and beliefs. Socializing contexts such as the instructional, the regulative, the innovative, and the interpersonal (i.e., intrapersonal) teach their members the rules, roles, values, beliefs, and norms of that society. Relational contexts such as kinship, friendship, work, social contract, and acquaintanceship are identified by the nature of the interpersonal bond that unites the members within a definable relationship. The boundaries of these contexts overlap and the closest context to the encounter is the most influential.

The physical setting functions to affect and be affected by human communication to the extent that it provides information about the other person and guidelines as to what constitutes appropriate behavior within that context. Space functions to affect behavior to the extent that it allows greater accessibility and opportunities for interpersonal contacts between communicators. Although the actual influence of the physical context on human communication is probably less than you might think, the context does affect human perceptions relevant to interpersonal attraction and judgments of the other person. Some rooms can be manipulated to encourage a friendly atmosphere. People's expectations upon entering a setting may affect their definition of the setting, and the setting itself may direct one's expectations of the sort of interaction that will take place. People typically search for clues in the physical context in order to reduce their uncertainty or confusion about what to do and how to behave.

The physical context also reflects some elements of the social context or at least provides subtle clues that identify the social relationship among the interactants in the setting. The "owner" of the setting is in a position of greater power or status. When the ownership of the setting is a prior condition of the setting, as when it is the residence of one of the communicators, the host/hostess may abdicate the ownership role in order to minimize social differences. On the other hand, when the context is a public setting, one of the participants may secure a social advantage by acting as though he/she were in the ownership role. Many public settings include the role of social stranger, but strangers differ from one physical context to another. Some settings define the stranger as an "object"; and in others, the stranger is defined as an acquaintance. The difference between physical contexts is based on whether the context encourages or discourages (or does not encourage) furthe-r interaction and relational development. Finally, past interactions and relationships within a physical context may leave residues of the nature or stability of that relationship as physical objects (akin to archaeological artifacts) present in the physical context.

Participants in interpersonal communication use their social contexts to provide guidelines for how they should behave during interpersonal communication, to provide information about the other person, and to influence the opportunities for interpersonal contact. In addition, the social context functions at the intrapersonal level of interpersonal communication by providing a baseline that allows the individual to compare and evaluate the worth of any particular interpersonal relationship. The social context also functions to increase the opportunities for interpersonal encounters. Because the social context varies as a result of the particular period of one's lifetime, some stages of life provide greater opportunities for interpersonal encounters than do others. The norms and standards used to define appropriate interpersonal behavior, therefore, differ during different stages of life.

Individuals also use their social contexts as support systems when they need help in solving relational problems and validating existing relationships. Contexts that serve as support systems typically include members of the same sex. Social contexts serving as support systems to provide help for individuals with relational problems are not necessarily made up of friends but rather of people who share the same problem.

The social context influences behavior during interpersonal communication by providing a set of general expectations, including rules of conduct, role relationships, and stereotypes. Because one's social context tends to change during the course of a lifetime, the social expectations of rules, roles, and stereotypes also change. People look to the social context to provide them with constitutive and regulative rules for interaction. Members of our society are also susceptible to the social influences popularized by the mass media in terms of idealized relationships, which then serve as models that individuals use to guide their own "real" relationships. Relational modeling affects not only the behaviors but also the feelings and emotions of relational partners. Unfortunately, the mediated model of the ideal relationship tends to ignore the problems associated with the maintenance stage of relational development and to overemphasize the power and significance of the intrapersonally felt emotional attachment.

KEY TERMS

sensemaking	proactive responses
mindlessness	reactive responses
mindfulness	determinism

environmental interactionism

physical context

design features

decoration features

proxemics

territoriality

personal space

social context

socialization

regulative context

instructional context

imaginative, or innovative, context

interpersonal (intrapersonal) context

relational contexts

kinship

friendship

work

social contracts

acquaintanceship

roles

stereotypes

rule

constitutive rule

regulative rule

CHAPTER 5

Language Use in Interpersonal Communication

> Language enters life through concrete utterances (which manifest language) and life enters language through concrete utterances as well.
>
> —Mikhail Bakhtin

The story of Helen Keller is a fascinating one. With neither sight nor hearing, two vitally important senses in "normal" communication, Helen nevertheless learned to read, write, and speak (through sign language, of course). *The Miracle Worker*, a movie based on the stage play dramatizing the early life of Helen Keller and that of her teacher Anne Sullivan, should not be missed. The movie illustrates the enormous difficulties that were associated with teaching her to communicate.

The problem was that Helen had no language, nor did she have any idea of what language was. Anne Sullivan, truly a miracle worker, constantly used sign language, to "spell out" names of objects in Helen's hand. Sullivan consistently repeated to the child Helen, "Everything has a name. Every word has a meaning." The climax of the drama was Helen's realization that the finger game was actually a game of words that stood for objects: In an electrifying scene, Helen is overjoyed to learn her first crucial word "water."

A fundamental, if not the most popular, function of language is probably the labeling function depicted in *The Miracle Worker*. Words are labels that you attach to persons, objects, and events. Everyone has a name, a linguistic label used for the purpose of social identification. People also apparently have more things to name than there are names to go around. At least it may be said that people use the same linguistic label to refer to a number of different objects. To call someone a "turkey," for instance, is not to suggest that he or she possesses large tail feathers and gobbles a lot. And "sucker" generally refers to a person who has nothing in common with a piece of candy on a stick. On the other hand, people have numerous words that they use to refer to the same object. "Couch," "sofa," "divan," and "davenport" all label the same piece of living room furniture.

John Stewart and Gary D'Angelo (1988) remind people that words also perform actions (recall our discussion of a promise in Chapter 4), evoke emotions, help to create social realities, reduce uncertainty, express abstract

131

The climax from the movie *The Miracle Worker* when Helen learned her first word, "water."

ideas, and promote human contact. Words are "a flexible and richly varied part of many communication contexts" (p. 153). Everyone possesses an amazing repertoire of communicative abilities that are generally taken for granted. For example, as communicators, people have access to four functional vocabularies: listening, speaking, reading, and writing (Wolvin & Coakley, 1985). Despite the varying size of each of these vocabularies, your personal vocabularies are rather limited. They average about 20,000 words which is small when you consider that the English language is estimated to have anywhere from 600,000 to a million words (Berko, Wolvin, & Wolvin, 1981). People have the capability, as a result of being socialized in their linguistic culture, of knowing and using a large repertoire of the fundamental tools of human communication—words.

LANGUAGE-IN-USE

Our focus in the following pages will be on discussing how people modify and, in a very real way, actually "create" their language when they use it for purposes of communication. We will be less concerned with language *as language* than with language *in use,* that is, with how people use language in the act of interpersonal communication. To illustrate, when Aub was a first-year college student, one of his roommates, from a small German community in the midwest, spoke only German until he entered the first grade. Even though he was a fourth- or fifth-generation American, his English was heavily accented with German pronunciations. He, of course, immediately enrolled in elementary German, thinking he would have at least one snap course while he became oriented to college life. However, he dropped his German course before midterm because he was failing it miserably. Apparently the German he spoke at home, corrupted by generations of living in America, was quite different from the "pure" German taught in the classroom.

Aub's roommate was mislead by thinking that language is language is language. Four terms—langue, parole, competence, and performance—will help you understand our distinction between language *as language* and language *in use* and thus to grasp our focus.

Langue and Parole

Years ago a French linguist by the name of Saussure who later became known as the father of modern linguistics, distinguished between formal language, or *langue,* and language use, or *parole* (1916). *Langue* refers to an abstract system shared by all members of a language-speaking community which enables them to speak (Ellis, 1992a). *Parole* refers to language use in communication. Parole is the way members of the community actually speak. Parole is more varied and fluctuates more often than the formal language it actualizes. Parole is *language-in-use* (hyphenated to indicate its singular meaning). The rules of parole reflect the linguistic choices of the people who use the language. These rules are constantly changing because changes in usage create new rules, and they vary from one subgroup to another.

Early studies of language focused on the understanding of langue. Scholars such as Noam Chomsky (1965) sought to show how new sentences are created and understood. Chomsky spent a lifetime developing a description of a rather complex set of grammatical rules which explain how streams of sentences are generated and understood by individuals. Such work, valuable in its own right, nonetheless ignores the study of language-in-use, or the pragmatic level of language.

Linguistic Competence and Performance

Noam Chomsky (1965) once defined two different kinds of competence in regard to language. He referred to the understanding of the grammatical rules and proper use of standard language as *competence.* He reserved the term *performance* to mean the social use of language, including all the revisions and violations of standard rules typical in any given social context.

According to Chomsky, any individual may adapt to a present social context and use the language in a manner appropriate to that context. He called that use of language "performance." Chomsky was suggesting that although language users may be very competent in knowing what constitutes proper use of the language (their *langue*), their actual *performance* in using the language (their *parole*) does not necessarily reflect that knowledge. The truly competent communicator is aware of the rules of language-in-use within any given context and behaves appropriately. Aub once knew an African-American student, by the name of Ed, from an urban ghetto. They spent quite a bit of time together in different social contexts, and Aub marveled at the competence Ed displayed in adapting his language (and accompanying nonverbal behaviors) appropriately to the specific social context in which he found himself. In the classroom he invariably employed standard English (parole 1), was consistently attentive, and spoke articulately and with serious purpose. In conversations with Aub, he "lost" some of his articulateness, often spoke in run-on and fragmentary sentences, used common slang, and acted rather casually (parole 2). When he encountered an African-American acquaintance, his speech slurred and slowed down, his voice went up a full octave, the words and phrases were grammatically black English (parole 3), and even his posture changed. Ed was truly a competent communicator. He entered the social context, developed an understanding of what the rules were in that context, and behaved appropriately. He obviously understood the rules of standard English (competence), and was able to adapt appropriately (performance) to various social contexts.

Since your major interest is in interpersonal communication, language-in-use (parole/performance) is more important to you than language as language (langue/competence). "If possession of a language is the most essentially human of all attributes, then the *use* of language in its appropriate social context must be the most essentially human of all activities" (Beattie, 1983, p. 1; emphasis ours). Our discussions will focus on understanding how people use language in the act of interpersonal communication.

We shall also discuss in this chapter a concept crucial to human communication—the concept of meaning. As will become increasingly apparent throughout your reading about interpersonal communication, the concept of meaning is highly complex. It is a part of language, a part of the individual communicator's internalized self, a part of the social relationship and the communicative behaviors during communication and a part of the context. All these different "places" of meaning (places to look for meaning) are important in understanding the process of interpersonal communication.

LANGUAGE-IN-USE AND CONTEXT

Language has a very close and special connection with the society and its members who use the language. As it is used in social contexts, language takes on the characteristics of the community of people who use it. Actually there are really two English languages: one that is taught in the schools and defined by dictionaries and one that is used during communication. Language, when used, is defined by the social context or by the people who use it. It also serves to help define the social context. This reflexive relationship between language use and the social context was introduced in Chapter 4 when we noted a reflexive relationship between behavior and context. In this chapter our primary focus will be on the relationship between verbal behavior and context.

In the United States, English is the national language, even though some segments of the country speak another tongue. But the fact that most Americans speak English does not imply that every social context in the nation uses English in the same way. In fact, the problems of translating one language into another (for example, Spanish into English) sometimes pale in comparison to the problems of translating one English-speaking social context into another (for example, gang talk into cop talk). This "translation" is sometimes more difficult because the communicators are unaware that they are experiencing a translation problem. And even when they are aware, their first tendency is to accuse the other person of using the language incorrectly. Translation is no easy task and even a "correct" translation of say gang talk entails some loss. Language conveys information and a worldview (Watzlawick, 1976), and "correct" translations, while accurate, lose the "intangible essence of any language, its beauty, imagery and metaphors for which there is no one-to-one translation" (p. 9).

Kenneth Leiter (1980) addresses this translation issue when he explains how context helps interactants with the literal meaning of the content of their expressions and supplies the sense of of their expressions or how the expressions are to be taken in a particular situation. We turn to Abbott and Costello again, this time, to illustrate the issue of translation and context:

ABBOTT: A nice soft pillow filled up with down.
COSTELLO: Up with down?
ABBOTT: Certainly. See that pillow up there? It's down.
COSTELLO: How can it be down if it's up there?
ABBOTT: That pillow is down, Costello. You get down off a duck's back.
COSTELLO: That's a lie. I never even got on a duck's back.

ABBOTT: I didn't say you got up on a duck's back. I said you get down off a
duck's back.

COSTELLO: How can I get down off a duck if I never got on a duck?

Abbott and Costello do not have to hear their interaction literally as a
discussion of the content of pillows. They in fact play with the concrete
sense of "down" to create a comedy routine that is funny because of the
different ways these two comedians "hear" each other. Context in association with behavior, in this case verbal behavior, is indefinitely elaborated
and thus helps interactants with more than the meaning of the content of
their expressions.

Since the focus is on the pragmatics of language-in-use, the social
context must not be taken as a given and as external to interaction but as
inseparable from the study of language. If you study only langue, in essence
you have removed language from social context and have done little to
recognize language as a "social instrument used for communicative purposes" (Giles & Wiemann, 1987, p. 352). Giles and Wiemann summarize
over twenty years of research focused on the nature of language-in-use into
three approaches of language and social context.

Language Reflects Context

The first approach, *language reflects context,* is probably the most extensive
and arose in response to the nonpragmatic treatment of language. This
approach is the cornerstone of sociolinguistics and is premised on the belief
that communicators utilize speech repertoires to adapt to the constraints of
any given situation. The social context largely prescribes and proscribes
language use (e.g., Gumperz & Hymes, 1972; Labov, 1966). Characteristics
of the individual, relationships, cultural subgroups, and society are reflected in language use. For example, Mark Knapp's (1984) widely cited
ten-stage model of relational beginnings and endings is built upon the
assumption that language use reflects different stages of relational development. Specifically, communicative behavior varies along eight dimensions (i.e., narrow-broad; stylized-unique; difficult-efficient; rigid-flexible;
awkward-smooth; public-personal; hesitant-spontaneous; and judgment-
suspended–judgment-given) with the relational stages. It is not unusual,
for example, for intimates to begin to use personal idioms when "intensifying" their relationship (Bell, Buerkel-Rothfuss, & Gore, 1987; Hopper,
Knapp, & Scott, 1981). "Futtbutt," "Tooty," "Boo," "Pizza King," and
"Wuzzer" are just five examples out of over 545 idioms used by couples as
signs of affection, teases, nicknames, and sexual euphemisms (Hopper et
al., 1981). In Malaysia the speech repertoires of the ethnic Chinese have been
documented to contain at least six varieties of language use serving quite
different functions in various social contexts (Platt, 1977).

Language Builds on Context

The second approach, *language builds on context,* is illustrated in the assumption that "language derives much of its meaning from the context in which it is spoken" (Giles et al., 1987, p. 362). Fundamental to this approach is the recognition of intersubjectivity, or shared knowledge of interactants, without which communication would be impossible (e.g., Garfinkel, 1967; Leiter, 1980). A basic problem people face as communicators is that "not everything that is available or transmitted is taken up, and not everything that is taken up is shared" (Kreckel, 1981, p. 20). Thus you are constantly at work making sense of your interaction with others, relying on background understandings or on what Hopper (1981) refers to as "taken-for-granteds." This knowledge remains implicit and unspoken, which is why context can provide a sense of the interaction beyond the explicit content of our interaction. Tyler (1978, p. 459) summarizes this idea nicely:

> Every act of saying is a momentary intersection of the "said and the unsaid." Because it is surrounded by an aureola of the unsaid, an utterance speaks of more than it says, mediates between past and future, transcends the speaker's conscious thought, passes beyond his manipulative control, and creates in the mind of the hearer worlds unanticipated. From within the infinity of the "unsaid," the speaker and hearer, by a joint act of will, bring into being what was "said."

Your language builds on the background understandings of your social contexts. One of the characteristics of your developing relationships is that you create these taken-for-granteds which, in turn, help you make sense of your interaction. The personal idioms and verbal shortcuts of the intensifying stage of relationships are examples of unspoken, implicit background understandings. During termination of a relationship, an individual may actually legitimize his or her exit by calling into question otherwise-taken-for-granted understandings with comments such as "What do you mean?" (see Baxter, 1985). On the other hand, Giles et al. (1987) point out that the more interactants share background understandings, the more they can take advantage of the unsaid. Inside jokes work as "inside" because much is left unsaid, but those who share the background understandings "get" the joke and those who don't won't. Those in powerful positions in society, such as doctors, may not need to use explicit commands to influence patients, but may instead use a "polite" request because both have a particular understanding about who is the more powerful.

An extension of the idea that language builds upon context is found in the recent work of Nofsinger (1989). He demonstrates how it is that the social context is collaboratively achieved or created by both interactants. The social context is actually only part of an interactant's background understandings and becomes a "reality" in the interaction. Any aspect of context, such as the physical setting, roles, stereotypes, models, rules, and so on, are not "context" until "they are invoked or made momentarily relevant by the participants" (p. 228). He explores how it is that interactants can do this by merely alluding to their background understandings rather than bringing them up explicitly. His position that context is achieved by interactants in and through interaction is important because it is uniquely communicative; interactants communicate to one another which contextual particulars have interpretive value.

Language Mediates Context

The third approach, *language mediates context,* is exemplified in the argument that utterances which precede other utterances function as their context (Nofsinger, 1976; Schegloff & Sacks, 1973). The language people use in interaction to talk about people, places, and things greatly influences their sense of those phenomena. Giles et al. (1987) originally referred to this approach as language determines context, but we actually prefer the term "mediate" to "determine" because of the strong causal implications of "determine." We prefer to view language as mediating reality; your reality is not experienced directly but rather in and through your language use. For example, have you ever wondered why your sense of some of your relationships is full of ambiguity and uncertainty? One answer to this question is that the English language is lacking in the number of words available for the description of relational phases and feelings about our close relationships (Bradac, 1983). Your experience of close relationships may be unclear because you are missing the necessary language to mediate a clearer and more textured reality of close relationships.

Even more far reaching is the concern that powerful groups in American society (e.g., media, church officials, politicians, interest groups) use language as a way of "establishing, maintaining, and legitimizing the status quo" (Giles et al., 1987, p. 365). Remember the events in Los Angeles, California, after four police officers were acquitted of charges in the first trial in the Rodney King case? In retrospect, a group of African-American journalists discussed the implications of the media's tendency to use "riot" rather than "rebellion" to describe those events. Their concern centered on the different experience people would have of those events (or reality) as a result of the different semantic environments "mediated" by using only the term "riot."

Language reflects context, language builds on context, and language mediates context—these approaches, though different, are not mutually exclusive. All three approaches describe in some fashion the intricate relationship between language and context. Your next question may well be "Which of these approaches, then, accurately describes that relationship?" Deciding whether language reflects, builds upon, or mediates context is actually dangerous because it assumes that only one of the approaches is correct. None of the approaches are correct and in fact their overlap has too often been ignored (Giles et al., 1987). Interaction not only "reflects" a relational phenomenon but also "builds upon" that phenomenon and "mediates" it. To repeat, language can be shown to simultaneously reflect, build upon, and mediate social context.

Ellis's Code Perspective

Donald Ellis's work in language behavior is an example of how these three approaches can be integrated. His *code perspective* (Ellis, 1992b; Ellis & Hamilton, 1985) rests on the assumption that individuals do not directly experience "reality" but construct meaning. Individuals do so with *codes*. These codes are an important element of the intrapersonal system *mediating* language and social reality. They are "systems of signs that are interactionally relevant to contexts, appropriateness, genres, and situation" (Ellis, 1992b, p. 1), and thus connect individuals to their social reality and help them construct and interpret situated meaning. His perspective is also an excellent example of the complex interplay between the intrapersonal and interpersonal systems. The code perspective is a pragmatic perspective; its focus is on understanding the interaction by placing it in its relational or patterned environment (Ellis & Hamilton, 1985).

There are three important communicative characteristics of codes outlined by Ellis and Hamilton. First, since codes are cognitive models, they are highly individual and *reflect* among other things your experiences and shared knowledge. Second, codes are flexible and highly adaptable. The nature of codes and your use of them changes with the demands of your needs, various experiences, and the complexities of face-to-face interaction. Third, codes although cognitive, are activated in interaction and provide communicators with various choices; but they do not determine those choices. Meaning is constructed in the unfolding interaction.

Central to the code perspective is the recognition of two kinds of codes: syntactic and pragmatic (Ellis, 1992b; Ellis & Hamilton, 1985). The *syntactic code* is consistent with formal, planned, literate language use. It is more explicit, orderly, and integrated than the pragmatic code. The *pragmatic code* is linked to the oral tradition and resembles spoken language. It is therefore, more fragmented, more personalized, and informal. This code's association with unplanned discourse means more dependency on context and background understandings, looser structure, and more pauses, repetition, and use of paralinguistic clues. Much more is left unsaid or assumed in the pragmatic code. Both codes coexist in language use and can be used interchangeably during interaction, given various conditions and interactant experience with language use.

Ellis's work with codes has concentrated on their use in interpersonal communication. If codes connect people to their social world, then as mediums, they should reflect the categories people use to characterize their relationships and other people. In the 1985 study with Hamilton, Ellis tested the ability of these codes to differentiate between the language use in various kinds of marital relationships. They found correlations between various code indicators (e.g., pronoun usage, pauses, structure) and marital types (Fitzpatrick, 1988). To illustrate, we will look at two marital types: traditionals and independents.

Traditionals were distinguished from independents by their use of different codes. Traditional couples are characterized by their conventional beliefs, resistance to change, psychological and physical sharing, high interdependence, and low individual autonomy. Much is left *unsaid* by traditionals because of their well-developed background understandings (Fitzpatrick, 1988). Note the following excerpt of traditional couple talk taken from the work of Ellis and Hamilton (1985, p. 274):

A: Shouldn't let 'em talk back
B: He sez too much
A: There's still a fear of you comin' down on 'em
B: It's these schools
A: It's not like before

In this excerpt, April and Bryan are addressing their son's talking back. April begins with the new issue and the sequence ends with April's final comment; the excerpt is the complete handling of the issue between Alice and Bryan. Simply put, traditionals do not need to be very explicit or elaborate in their interaction because so much is assumed. An outsider to their interaction probably would have difficulty understanding what they are talking about unless he or she had some knowledge of their shared codes. Their language *builds upon* clearly understood shared assumptions. These code characteristics become even more obvious when compared to an excerpt of talk from an independent couple.

Independents are characterized by their acceptance of change, limited attention to traditional values, and high degree of individual negotiated autonomy (Fitzpatrick, 1988). These couples have to be more tightly organized in their talk and more explicit about what they are referring to because their background understandings are not as clearly negotiated or well-developed. Note the following excerpt taken again from the work of Ellis and Hamilton (1985, p. 275):

L: I have this strong feeling that there are people in nursing homes, and no one comes to see them
M: Well, that's because nursing homes are depressing
L: Look at my situation, speaking of nursing homes, my grandmother is in one and it is burdensome to visit her
M: Isn't it a little different because you never got along with her?

In this excerpt, the topic is much more explicit between Leon and Marsha. For example, the noun phrase "nursing homes" is repeated three times referring to the topic at hand. Compare this to the excerpt between April and Bryan in which there are no explicit references to the topic at hand. An outsider would probably have an easier time understanding the interaction between Leon and Marsha because so much is included in the interaction and less "goes without saying."

If our focus remains only on the impact of language-in-use on the social context and not the impact of the social context on language-in-use, then only half of the story is told. Language and context are *reflexive*. In Chapter 4 we recognized the reflexive character of language behavior by pointing out that language behavior functions *in* and *as* context, that is, "meaning and context are produced simultaneously by the actors in and through their interaction" (Mishler, 1979, p. 15). Thus, language-in-use influences context, and context simultaneously influences language-in-use. For example, consider one of your close friendships. That close friendship (social context) influences your language-in-use, and in turn those language behaviors define the close friendship, and so on. The *reflexivity* of human behavior (in this case verbal behavior) is a product of the *indexical* character of behavior. Your behavior is indexical because it is contextual (Leiter, 1980). More often than not, your expressions are vague and potentially open to many meanings, and so your behavior serves to index the context that is needed to make sense of your behavior. Your understanding of the indexical and reflexive character of human behavior is important to your understanding of how people construct social meaning.

SOCIAL MEANING

The concept of meaning has, itself, a number of different meanings. None of the meanings of "meaning," of course, is any more "correct" than any of the others. Like many words in the dictionary, "meaning" has several different definitions. One of the principal reasons for the variation in the meaning of "meaning" is the issue of location: *Where* is the meaning located?

Depending on where you look, you will find different meanings. Those more conventional meanings are typically referred to as *denotative meanings*. The dictionary is typically the last place to look to discover the meaning that is important or even relevant to interpersonal communication. The dictionary is generally a source of standard English as accepted by the larger society; it does not describe language-in-use in specific social contexts. The model of communication used to guide the discussion in this book specifies three potential "places" where you can find meaning: in the context, in the individual (the intrapersonal system), and in the relationship (the interpersonal system). In each of these you will find a different as opposed to a "correct" meaning of "meaning" in interpersonal communication.

For the moment we will distinguish two kinds of meaning—one inside the heads of the communicating individuals (intrapersonal) and the other in the language-in-use during the act of communicating (interpersonal). Those intrapersonal meanings are commonly referred to as "denotative" and "connotative" meanings. As you will recall, denotative meanings are the formal definitions of words found in dictionaries. These help individuals classify phenomena into a variety of categories (Goss & O'Hair, 1988). *Connotative meanings* are individuals' affective meanings or their emotional experience of words (Osgood, Suci, & Tannenbaum, 1957). "Mother," for example, has a formal definition which helps you classify different kinds of caregivers, and you may have various feelings associated with "mother." For some, "mother" is associated with warmth and safety, and for others, "mother" may be associated with coldness and harm. These kinds of meaning are intrapersonal and say very little about the dynamics of social meaning.

More precisely, intrapersonal and interpersonal meaning can be described this way: (1) people "mean something" by what they say and (2) what people say "has some meaning." Intrapersonal and interpersonal meanings are basically the difference between locating meaning in the intrapersonal system and locating it in the interpersonal system or in the patterns of behavior in context.

People commonly think of meaning as defined by the intentions of the individual. But for those who continue stubbornly to insist that the most important meaning is what people intend their behaviors to mean, we ask you to recall the case of James Watt. For those of you who have forgotten, Watt was secretary of the interior under President Reagan. He uttered a number of things in public that got him in deep trouble: He referred to the people who attended Beach Boys concerts as an "undesirable element," and his description of the minorities represented on a national commission created a public outcry similar to that toward the Reverend Jesse Jackson when he referred to New York as "Hymie town." Despite Watt's insistence that his *intended* meaning was perfectly honorable, the language itself apparently had its own meanings in a number of differing social contexts. The public outcry resulted in Watt's resignation from the cabinet post in 1983. As for Jesse Jackson, some Jewish supporters of Jerry Brown for the 1992 Democratic presidential nomination withdrew their support because Brown considered Jackson as a possible running mate. Indeed, intent is extremely difficult to ascertain by either the sender of a message or its receiver (Andersen, 1991; Bavelas, 1990).

No one should dispute the existence or importance of psychological meanings. Similarly, no one should dispute the existence and importance of social meanings that are embedded in the situated language-in-use. Since our focus in this book is on the interpersonal system, our concern will be on the social meaning created by and embedded in interpersonal interaction. We begin our discussion of social meaning by discussing the central features of social meaning: indexicality and reflexivity.

Indexicality

Retrospectively, people make sense of the voluminous patterns of behavior they find themselves immersed in, and by doing so, render their social "reality" momentarily stable, structured, factual, and orderly. We say "momentarily" because the ordered and factual character of your social reality is not a fixed, independent quality of social reality separate from your interpretations. Your sense of social structure is a continuous, ongoing accomplishment. This is the case because all behavior, including verbal behavior, is indexical (Garfinkel, 1967; Leiter, 1980).

Indexicality, simply, "refers to the contextual nature of objects and events" (Leiter, 1980, p. 107). Objects and events which are not embedded in some context are said to have multiple potential meanings as opposed to being meaningless. People reduce the uncertainty about their potential meaning by providing a context. When you refer to verbal behavior, you recognize that interactants do not normally specify their intended meanings (recall the "said" and the "unsaid"). Your expressions are potentially equivocal and a sense of meaning emerges only within the context. Thus the language's range of social meaning is partially constrained by that social context. In order to reduce the number of possible meanings, and thus remedy the indexical nature of behavior, the communicators must give "hints" to each other or index the language-in-use. The linguistic techniques that perform the indexing function are called "indexical expressions" (Bar-Hillel, 1954, p. 363).

Indexing is something like putting subscript numbers on sociological symbols (words and expressions) whose social meaning is otherwise ambiguous (too much uncertainty, too many possible interpretations). Consider also a book's index. Each subject and author is "marked" with page number(s) which guide you to their location in the book. Speakers employ *indexical expressions,* and in so doing, they essentially inform the hearer, "I am using meaning 1, not meaning 2." The solution to the indexing problem, reducing the uncertainty of meanings, lies with identifying the social context in which "meaning 1" is conventional. A colleague of Aub's, interested in sociolinguistic questions relevant to interpersonal communication, was once intrigued with indexing notions pertaining to time. What was meant, he wondered, by the phrase "next Wednesday"? When someone used the phrase on a Sunday, he discovered that few people would misunderstand that this indexical expression ("next") indexed the time three days in the future. On a Tuesday, he discovered that most people interpreted the indexical expression to mean "eight days." But on a Monday, the expression that indexed time was quite ambiguous, and its meaning differed accordingly to relatively small social contexts.

Wayne Beach and Robert Nofsinger are two communication scholars who have explored the nature of indexicality. Nofsinger (1989) investigated how people invoke aspects of their shared knowledge as part of the context to be used to help them situate their expressions. Obviously, you can directly or explicitly index your shared knowledge. One way you can do this is to directly describe the knowledge by identifying a particular category. For example, the speaker might say, "Overall, I think John is a neat person, but as a date I found him rather boring." "As a date" is the relevant category indexed by the speaker and thus specifies what shared knowledge is to be invoked for contextual use. Also, when you request clarification of what someone has referenced, you are directly invoking shared knowledge. Consider the following example taken from work by Beach (1983, p. 202):

F:　This place reminds me of that restaurant, remember, Our House?
G:　What? That reminds you of our house?
F:　No! The restaurant Our House
G:　Our house?
F:　No, that restaurant where we ate pie, over by Baskin Robbins, with a lot of older people
G:　Oh

The shared knowledge of Frank and Gloria is directly referenced by Frank with "that restaurant" and "remember, Our House." However, Gloria is confused because of the similarity between the restaurant's name "Our House" and the common phrase "our house." Gloria requests clarification in her first two lines, and with additional information the shared knowledge is clarified (Nofsinger, 1989).

The significance of Nofsinger's work was to show that people do not have to refer directly to index-shared knowledge; they can simply allude to it. That is, you need not ever explicitly mention those background understandings that help you situate and make sense of your interaction. This would be easier for communicators who share many aspects of background understandings. Recall the conversations between the traditional and independent couples we discussed earlier.

Beach and Dunning (1982) examined the communicative properties of "pre-indexing methods" (p. 171), or preparatory strategies, used by interactants to set up particular understandings and interactant purposes by setting up relevant sequences of behavior. Disclaimers, for example, are used by communicators as hedges against possible negative impressions or threats to their identity (Hewitt & Stokes, 1975). You may know that anything can and might be used against you in interaction. Disclaimers help you avoid this possibility. See if you can find the disclaimer, or pre-index strategy in an interaction from Beach and Dunning (pp. 177–178):

A:　I know you're going to say this is none of my business, but what you're trying to do with her/
B:　I think she's a great girl, and I'm going to marry her if I can. A team like the two of us/

A: Don't you think that's a little selfish?

B: Why don't you just stay out of this and leave us alone

Did you find the disclaimer? The pre-index occurs in the first line with the phrase "I know you're going to say this is none of my business." Other methods of pre-indexing are prompts, hints, teases, conditional disclosures, small talk, and so on. Beach and Dunning found that disclaimers function to begin sequences; structure sequences in explicit, implicit, playful, devious, effective, and ineffective ways; set up a particular sense of social structure; sustain community among interactants; and avoid or decrease the possibility of negative impressions (p. 185).

Indexical expressions provide interactants with frames of reference or markers to help clarify the social meaning of the language-in-use. "In everyday language use, indexical work is necessary to ensure that utterances and their meanings are situated and understood" (Beach & Dunning, p. 170). When +understanding occurs, the interaction appears to possess "stable" meaning. Remember, however, that "the context itself is made up of indexical expressions, which means that sense has to be made of the context as well" (Leiter, 1980, p. 109). The context is not fixed and independent of the interaction. Its nature is open-ended, and it can be indefinitely elaborated. Indexicality may be bothersome and something people always seek to remedy, but it defies resolution because every attempt you make to remedy it is in itself indexical. Thus social meaning and indexicality exist side by side (Leiter, 1980), and indexicality is normal work for communicators (Garfinkel, 1967). This brings us to the reflexive character of language-in-use.

Reflexivity

The open-ended chain of indexicality actually produces the reflexive nature of language-in-use (Leiter, 1980). "The setting gives meaning to talk and behavior within it, while at the same time, it exists in and through that very talk and behavior" (p. 139). The classroom setting helps gives meaning to the talk within it, while at the same time "classroom" exists in and through that very classroom talk and behavior. Behavior and talk utilize indexical expressions and in part depend on the context for their meaning, while, simultaneously, aspects of the context are produced by the behavior and talk.

Several years ago there was a movie on television that contained a conversation that went something like this:

"Now that's truly awesome!"

"Where?"

"I'd say a ten."

"Hunk city."

"Oh, get off it! He's nerdsville!"

"Just cool out, beach breath."

These indexical expressions and the teenager behavior help to make features of the youth culture and the setting observable. This conversation, or one close to it, occurred at Fort Lauderdale during spring break. A group of females were sunning themselves on the beach and observing the passing parade of males. The teenagers' behavior and talk are creating a context of revelry and ribaldry during spring break. In turn those very same features and the behavior of the teenagers are made meaningful by the spring break setting. Behavior and talk and context are mutually elaborated, thus producing the reflexive character of language-in-use.

Language-in-use influences the people who use it and is in turn influenced by these people. As people use language to create special meanings, that language then changes to reflect the additional meanings created by its use. The special meaning of the language also reflects the social context in which it is used. People, through the use of their special-meaning language, exhibit their membership in that social context as well as their thoughts and feelings toward that membership (Giles, Scherer, & Taylor, 1979). CB-radio talk, cop talk, rapper lingo, youth gang talk, black English, Valley-girl talk, teentalk, and Waynespeak are examples of special social contexts with their own language-in-use. The CB-radio craze gave society an entire new vocabulary with such words as "handles" (nicknames), "smokies" (highway patrol), "double nickel" (55-mph speed limit), "seat covers" (female drivers), "hammer" (accelerator), and others. Teentalk is filled with expressions such as "me an'," (meaning someone else *and I*), "goes" (for "says," as in "She goes 'How ya doin?'"), and the notorious "Ya know?" (a modulated pause, literally translated as "Huh?"). One of the newest "talk" to work its way into the mainstream in the early 1990s was "Waynespeak," spoken by Wayne and Garth of *Saturday Night Live's* "Waynesworld." Test yourself and guess the meaning of the following terms: "baby pop," "do damage," "dead presidents," "knot," "jockin'," and "hooptie." If you are stuck, ask the Wayne and Garth fans in your class to help you out!

Interestingly enough, as the usage of a special language extends beyond the boundaries of the original social context and becomes more common in a larger society, it soon disappears from use in the social context that created it. Language, you recall, is said to be reflexive when it serves to identify members of a particular social context and in turn the members of that particular social context identify with it. However, as more language users outside the boundaries of that social context pick up the expressions and use them as their own, the reflexivity of language within its social context becomes less apparent. Consequently, the special language, no longer reflecting its particular social context, dies away through erosion or benign neglect. Take, for example, "colors" worn by youth gangs. Once those special "colors" become fashionable in the mainstream culture, they no longer are unique to a particular youth gang and no longer serve to delineate the gang from the larger society. As a result, the youth gangs may stop wearing those now-fashionable colors and select others. The same would hold true for their verbal behaviors. Terms which once were used exclusively by the youth gangs, like "taggers" (graffiti artists), are already finding their way into mainstream talk, and the reflexivity between some of those special terms and the youth gangs (the social context) is becoming less apparent.

Members of some social contexts, however, try to deny the essential character and influence of linguistic reflexivity. Some members of social contexts, for instance, want to believe in the existence of some central social standard for "proper" language use. According to this belief, a body of rules exists in schools, dictionaries, and grammar books, and those rules serve as the standard for language usage throughout the entire society. "Standard English" appears to function, for example, as the norm for network radio/TV announcers and newscasters. Network news reporters overwhelmingly speak with little trace of a regional accent (except perhaps Peter Jennings, who is not always successful in hiding his Canadian accent) and use almost no special linguistic labels or slang. But if standard English does exist and the standard is to be followed universally, then the language-in-use within specialized social contexts is "nonstandard"—that is, language usage that is not up to the level of, or as good as, the standard or "proper" usage. And normally the "establishment" determines the proper language usage in public situations (Giles & Wiemann, 1987). Cross-culturally, what is considered standard language usage is that of the upper class (Trudgill, 1975) or the language of the most economically and politically powerful (Drake, 1980). How many cases can you cite where the ethnic majority and minority live side by side and where, as a result, the majority learn the language behavior of the minority?

Within the last few decades the *deficit hypothesis* which refers to "substandard" language-in-use (Raph, 1967) has been generally rejected, at least by linguists and sociolinguists (people involved in the study of the interplay of society and language). Although many educators and psychologists viewed the language-in-use of different varieties of English as "*sub*standard," "verbally destitute," and "lazy speech," it was the sociolinguists who argued that these different languages were neither deficit nor substandard (Baratz, 1970). These varieties of language-in-use are not less than standard English but are recognized as a "well-ordered, highly structured, highly developed language system which in many respects is different from standard English" (Baratz, 1970, p. 13). Black English is now recognized (unfortunately not by everyone) as a type of language-in-use rather than a problem to be overcome (a "deficit" in the literacy education of young urban African Americans). In a similar vein, the language use of the working class is considered different and no less rich than the language use of the middle class (Labov, 1972; Trudgill, 1975).

Some sociolinguists have found that these differences may reflect a social group's (e.g., French Canadians in Montreal) attempt to gain power and a valued social identity (Mercer, Mercer, & Mears, 1979; Taylor, Meynard, & Rheault, 1977). Attention in sociolinguistics now seems to concentrate on recognizing that these different languages-in-use provide "markers" (Giles & Wiemann, 1987) which help distinguish membership in various social groups or contexts (e.g., work, religious, gender, ethnic) as well as express and sustain positive group identity (Edwards & Giles, 1984; Milroy, 1980). Here again you see that language-in-use and social context mutually elaborate each other because of the indexical and reflexive nature of language. Individuals use different indexical expressions in their language to mark or index their membership in various social contexts and use language to achieve valued group identity. In turn, language-in-use creates the very social context that is being marked and valued.

We would like to believe that the number of people who think in terms of "verbal deprivation" gets smaller with each passing year. Not everyone, however, holds to the view of Martin Joos, a distinguished linguist, who begins his book *The Five Clocks* (1967) with this quote (p. xvii):

> Ballyhough railway station has two clocks which disagree by some six minutes. When one helpful Englishman pointed the fact out to a porter, his reply was "Faith, sir, if they was to tell the same time, why would we be having two of them?"

Joos uses the metaphor of the clock for language and demonstrates five different kinds of English (five clocks) that are characteristic of speaking and writing. His often-entertaining analysis is an attempt to ease the "English-usage guilt-feelings" (p. 4), or the insistence that "the clocks of language all be set to Central Standard Time" (p. 4) and that people must feel bad, if their clock is not set to the one in the English department! No single standard for determining "right" and "wrong" usage exists. But be aware of the tremendous influence of society's economically and politically powerful elite who use what is considered "standard" language.

Language users often have the knowledge of other standards of usage but don't necessarily perform according to those standards in all social contexts. Let's take a look at an example of conversation between two professors of communication that on the surface may appear rather "sloppy." The two interactants are car pooling home from work and plan to stop at a tavern on the way and drink beer because their workday has been unusually difficult.

A: Need a ride?
B: Yeah. Gotcher car?
A: Unh-huh. The Chevy. How 'bout My Wife's Place on th' way?
B: I sure could use a draft. Bad day!
A: Yeah. Me, too. S'go.
B: Hot daa-yum! Yer on!

Some characteristics typical of conversation, particularly among friends, are quite apparent in this brief conversation. Note the use of the pragmatic code (Ellis, 1992b). Each person's turn is grammatically "impure" in the sense that neither tends to converse in complete sentences. One of the few complete sentences occurs in the fourth line of dialogue, and it is grammatically incorrect. The "proper" sentence would be "I could *surely* use a draft."

A nonparticipant in this interaction would find it difficult to understand the objective meaning of each turn, but the interactants themselves would have no difficulty at all in interpreting each other's remarks because they can build on their background understandings and thus achieve their own conversational coherence (Beach, 1983). Apparently they are both familiar, for example, with the understanding that "My Wife's Place" is a business establishment that serves beer, rather than the residence of an estranged spouse. Both communicators realize that the ambiguous "How about My Wife's Place on the way?" is an invitation to interrupt their journey homeward in order to stop and drink beer. "Bad day" is certainly ambiguous on the face of it, but the next speaker/hearer clearly has understood that the phrase meant "I have experienced an unusually difficult day here at work." Each one of them worked reflexively with their presupposed background understandings. That is, they are influenced by aspects of the context such as who they were talking to, the physical setting, and what they were doing while talking, and in turn, they influenced the relative importance of each of those aspects on the achievement of their conversation's coherence.

Sloppy speech patterns, ambiguity of objective meanings, grammatical errors, and sentence fragments are just a few of the characteristics that are typical and "normal" in conversation or unplanned discourse, the primary act of interpersonal communication. Remember the outrage and disgust people expressed upon hearing, for the first time, the Nixon Watergate tapes? Americans were appalled by the "defective" speech because they expected to hear the leaders of the nation speaking in the "proper" language of formal, planned discourse. It is not that interactants in conversation aren't competent in the rules of standard language; in fact, to converse in the manner reflected in the conversation above is to reflect one's competence in performing conversation and doing what comes naturally. They were merely following the rules and norms of what conversation looks like and sounds like. Janet Bavelas (1990) quite pointedly remarks that people do not communicate poorly. "What we do mostly is face-to-face communication, and the most ordinary of us do that elegantly, precisely, rapidly, and with great subtlety and complexity" (p. 601). That includes the two professors of communication with superb interpersonal and public speaking skills!

Individuals not only work to place themselves within various social groups but also seek satisfaction from those memberships. Since language use and particular nonverbal behavior have been documented to be important elements of ethnic identity (Edwards, 1985), it is suggested that one way individuals accomplish positive social identities is to use their language to differentiate themselves from those who are considered outside the group (Giles & Johnson, 1986; Gudykunst, 1987). One way we accomplish this differentiation is by "style switching" or code switching (Giles, Bourhis, & Taylor, 1977).

Style Switching

An individual's interpersonal *style* is his or her language-in-use in a particular social context, or the way he or she participates in communication. Occasionally, people think of interpersonal style in terms of some internal quality or individual personality quirk. People treat style as personality when they refer to someone as "extroverted" or "introverted," "sociable," "a show-off," or "shy." What people have come to know as personality traits, though, are more likely to be the ways they have learned their language-in-use, the ways they have learned to communicate in a particular social context. Moreover, they have learned to switch their styles when moving from one social context to another. *Style switching* refers to the ability to change your use of language from the conventions of one social context to another. Joos (1967) reminds you that you need not confine yourselves to any one style, that you can shift styles to meet any occasion, and that you can do so in midsentence if you choose. It is a "notorious fact that more than one kind of English is likely to be used at the same time and place" (Joos, p. 3).

   Speech accommodation theory (Giles, 1973) has been developed to explain the reasons for and the consequences of such speech accommodating phenomena as style switching. During interaction, people accommodate their styles in order not only to differentiate themselves from others and maintain a valued social identity but also to increase communicative efficiency and approval (Giles, Mulac, Bradac, & Johnson, 1987). Speech shifts are said to be "convergent" and "divergent." *Convergence* occurs when interactants use language to adapt to any number of features of another's speech style (e.g., utterance length, pauses, slang, speech rates, pronunciation, etc.). *Divergence* occurs when interactants use language to stress the speech differences between them. Speech accommodation is not simply a matter of speech shifts which converge or diverge; the picture is far more complex than that. When convergence with another is mutual, the result is style matching. Interactants do not always match, however. One person may attempt to adapt to the style of another, while the other may not attempt to adapt at all. Both interactants may maintain their own styles and not attempt to converge or diverge. Divergence, itself, can also be mutual. Further, interactants may only partially converge or diverge (Street, 1982).

For example, you may only partially match another's frequency of pauses. Consider also that interactants converge or diverge on any combination of linguistic features.

Speech accommodation between interactants is a complex speech phenomenon, which permeates human interaction. Giles et al. (1987) further suggest, based on findings in Asian settings (e.g., Beebe, 1981; Platt & Weber, 1984), that speech accommodation tendencies may be a widespread phenomenon. It has important consequences for both the intrapersonal and interpersonal systems. For example, we have discussed how a person's divergence from another's speech style can increase the person's sense of identity. Also, when interactants perceive that another is accommodating to their style, they will attribute positive qualities to that person (Coupland, 1985). In turn there are communicative consequences to the interpersonal system because perceptions initially influence the behaviors of the interactants.

Switching styles, the individual's language-in-use, is one part of being competent in interpersonal communication. Knowing when to switch styles and what style is appropriate to the context constitutes an essential first step in becoming a more effective communicator. Of course, your competence is also a function of your ability to perform the appropriate style in each social context. Not everyone is equally competent in all interpersonal styles (O'Keefe & Delia, 1985; Ward, Bluman, & Dauria, 1982). However, research has shown (LaGaipa, 1981, p. 85) that people who are rich in one relational context are also rich in others. That is, people with close family relationships also, generally speaking, have many close friends and acquaintances. Communicators competent in one style tend to be competent in other styles, as well.

The way you interact with others is undoubtedly not a single style. You actually have many styles that you use in different social contexts. The members of one social context classify you within a style that may be quite different from the way your fellow members in another context have classified you. A former student of Aub's switched styles so successfully that she could easily have been two different people. She was a marginal student in several classes—bright enough, but so painfully withdrawn (she spoke only when spoken to, with her eyes downcast and her voice barely above a low murmur) that her classroom performance was far from excellent. She completed a major in communication with a grade-point average barely above the minimum. Aub and his faculty colleagues stereotyped her, attributing her behavior and classroom performance to her status as a minority (African American) student intimidated by being in a predominantly white culture. They were wrong!

Aub subsequently discovered that this student was very active in African-American organizations on and off campus and politically active in intercampus and community organizations—a capable and highly respected member of those social contexts. He had the opportunity to see her "in action" (after her graduation) during a banquet in a downtown hotel. She was articulate, forceful, energetic, even extroverted. Her style was almost the exact opposite of her classroom behavior. She had switched styles, to be sure, and her style switching was extreme. When Aub discussed her classroom style with her, she agreed that it was probably inappropriate, but she had never developed any other style for the classroom context.

This student is probably not typical, but her experience does illustrate that competence in interpersonal communication involves both knowing when to switch styles and how to perform a style appropriate to the context; but not everyone feels comfortable or confident in every occasion. Competence in interpersonal communication is undoubtedly relevant to all three aspects of our communication model—self, context, and relationship. Feeling uncomfortable or lacking confidence in your own communicative behavior is equivalent to locating communicative competence in your self, the intrapersonal level of interpersonal communication. But if the relationship "works" or is competent, the intrapersonal feeling of incompetence may not be significant.

The fundamental view of meaning as it exists in interpersonal communication is its social nature—the "sharedness" of individual meanings. The idea of "shared meaning" pervades virtually all the perspectives of interpersonal communication. However, everyone does not view "shared meaning" in the same manner. Shared meaning from the pragmatic perspective is found in the pattern of interaction and located in events. Traditional psychological approaches to interpersonal communication locate meaning in the minds of individuals and shared meaning, as you will recall, in the cognitive overlap of individual experiences. But pragmatically, meaning does not exist in isolation from its use; it always "occurs" (Fisher, 1985). Thus shared meaning belongs not to the person who uses it or to the one who responds to it; it belongs to the context of events. Thus any judgment about the worth or value of an interpersonal event isolated from the situated event is meaningless. Individuals, you will recall, are faced with any number of possible interpretations during interaction. The reduction of alternative interpretations to some workable interpretation (evident in the pattern of behavior) is pragmatic meaning (Fisher, 1978). It is cocreated by individuals only through interaction with others. Thus a pragmatic perspective is always focused on exploring *how* behavior means, not asking people *what* they mean by their behavior.

NONVERBAL ELEMENTS OF COMMUNICATION

You may think it unusual to be discussing nonverbal elements of communication in a chapter on language. Recall, though, that we are discussing language-in-use, and no one can *use* language in a social context without using the nonverbal behaviors which are conventional within that context. Referring to the dance metaphor introduced in Part One, your dance is created by both verbal and nonverbal dance steps. But there is a problem with discussing nonverbal behavior: Researchers know very little about it. Unfortunately, people think they know much more than they actually do. Edward Sapir captured this dilemma with this famous quote: "We respond to gestures with an extreme alertness and, one might say, in accordance with an elaborate and secret code that is written nowhere, known to none, and understood by all" (1949, p. 556).

Our society abounds with commonsense "knowledge" of nonverbal communication. Much of that "knowledge" is included in the large number of "how to" paperback volumes available in nearly every neighborhood bookstore. You know the ones. Books titled *How to Pick Up Girls* and *How to Close the Sale* promise you success in achieving your interpersonal goals (from seduction to marketing) primarily on the basis of being able to "read" the other's "body language." These books treat the other person as essentially a "victim" of the reader's newly acquired "power." Unfortunately, they promise much more than they can possibly deliver.

Nonverbal Behavior Compared to Verbal Behavior

"Nonverbal" is a catchall term that refers to a confusingly large number of potential nonlinguistic behaviors. Dick Crable (1981) identifies some areas of nonverbal behavior and illustrates the fantastic breadth of this area: "kinesics, proxemics, haptics, oculesics, objectics, chronemics, vocalics, environmental factors, or physical appearance" (p. 66). And Crable's list of jargonistic terms denoting nonverbal elements of interpersonal communication is highly incomplete! To understand all nonverbal behaviors as they function in communication is to understand bodily movements and postures (kinesics), use of space (proxemics), touching (haptics), pupil dilation (oculesics), and on and on.

Nonverbal behavior, like verbal behavior, does not consist of a series of isolated occurrences, but rather occurs within a system or a code which helps give structure and meaning to the behavior. We discussed two different kinds of verbal codes earlier; nonverbal behavior has a code as well. While both nonverbal and verbal behaviors occur within a code, their codes are different. The nonverbal behaviors you use, for the most part, are nonlinguistic and analogical. *Analogical codes* are made up of "(1) infinite and (2) a continuous range of (3) naturally derived values" (Burgoon, 1985, p. 350). Verbal behaviors, on the other hand, are linguistic, and the *code* is *digital*, made up of a "(1) finite set of (2) discrete and (3) arbitrary defined units" (Burgoon, p. 350) (see also Watzlawick, Beavin, & Jackson, 1967).

To get some idea of the difference between analogical and digital codes, think about the difference between the face of an old-fashioned watch and that of a digital watch or imagine the difference between a picture of a tree and a verbal description of a tree. Better yet, think about the difference between "dancing" your relationship and verbally describing the relationship. The hands of an old-fashioned watch move continuously through time (the analogical code). Often this is best represented by the "sweeping" of the second hand. In contrast, the digital watch presents time by discrete on-and-off "readouts" of the time (digital). When Kathy was in graduate school, one of her colleagues decided to make up a "dance" to portray the process of small-group decision making. Sarah had been frustrated in her attempts to describe the fluid, dynamic process of small-group decision making in words (in a linguistic, digital code). She decided to put her new-found interest in ballet to good use by creating a "dance" of decision making that was better suited to communicating the continuous, dynamic flow of the process. She actually performed the dance as her first ballet recital.

The distinction between the two codes is important because each one is better suited for different kinds of communication (Watzlawick, Beavin, & Jackson, 1967), and humans are capable of using both codes simultaneously. The words you use are digital and function better when communicating content information and thus are better suited for such things as abstract thought (e.g., theorizing and conceptualizing about interpersonal communication). These codes are involved in the content dimensions of messages. On the other hand, the nonverbal behaviors you use are analogical and function better when communicating your feelings; analogical codes invoke relationships. These codes are involved in the relationship dimension of messages. Do you understand better now why we chose to use the dance metaphor to capture the relational dynamics of interpersonal communication? On a more personal level, have you ever tried to tell someone how you felt and in your struggle remarked "I just can't put my feelings into words; I'll have to find another way to show you!"

Make note that not all nonverbal behavior is nonlinguistic and, therefore, truly analogical. Some behavior categorized as nonverbal is linguistic and more digital. Emblems, for example, are a type of kinesic behavior which are preplanned, arbitrary, highly intentional, and used in place of verbal behavior (Knapp, 1980). Examples of emblems are the American Sign Language, or the sign language for the deaf, and the nonverbal signals used by airport or aircraft personnel to direct planes. Nonlinguistic behavior is analogical, linguistic behavior is digital, and most nonverbal behavior is nonlinguistic.

Nonverbal nonlinguistic and verbal linguistic behavior are characterized by two different codes and by other features as well (Burgoon, 1985). Many nonverbal behaviors are iconic, or can visually resemble their referent. We're sure you are thinking of some now—those graphic gestures some

Interaction between people is comprised of verbal and nonverbal behavior.

people use to get attention. Some nonverbal behaviors, like the smile, transcend cultural differences with their universal meaning. People are also capable of conveying, simultaneously, several different meanings through a vast array of nonverbal signals. On the other hand, those interacting with you have all kinds of nonverbal cues to use to make sense of the interaction. Nonverbal behavior can stimulate your senses directly without cognitive mediation. For example, seeing a car accident may produce a stronger sensory response in a person than if that person were merely to read about the car accident. Your senses process many nonverbal signals very rapidly. This may be one of the reasons why people tend to favor the nonverbal signal over the verbal signal in communication. Kurt Hegre, a photographer for a California newspaper, had this to say about whether photographs of death and dying should be used as news (Glaser, 1992, p. B5):

> I believe that some photographs can so anger and affect people that they will move to change some of the ills of society. The two most powerful and memorable images from the Vietnam War are the picture of a naked girl and the photo of a man shooting another, point-blank in the head. These two Pulitzer Prize–winning photos delivered the ugly truth of war *like no written story ever could* [italics added]. Were they offensive? You bet. And so was the war.

Our next question: To what degree are nonverbal behavior and verbal behavior similar? Whether nonverbal behavior is like verbal behavior is an issue that has not been resolved. Burgoon (1985), however, has argued that nonverbal behavior does appear to be characterized by varying degrees of linguistic properties. First, there are many nonverbal behaviors that can be broken down into phonetic and morphemic units. Birdwhistell (1970) uses a linguistic model to classify nonverbal behavior. For example, a basic unit of movement is a kineme, analogous to the phoneme, or basic unit of sound. Second, nonverbal behavior follows syntactic, semantic, and pragmatic rules. Many nonverbal behaviors follow certain sequencing rules (syntax). People do not, for example, display a scowl and a smile at the same time. Nonverbal behavior in isolation and together often have conventionalized meanings (semantics). And the use of nonverbal behavior is a function of cultural norms. Third, the meanings given to nonverbal behaviors are a function of context (pragmatics). Contextual particulars such as the type of interaction, the verbal behavior, and other nonverbal behaviors aid in making sense of the nonverbal behavior.

In these and other ways, nonverbal behavior is similar to—but not the same as—verbal behavior (Burgoon & Saine, 1978). First, although nonverbal behavior can be said to follow rules, its analogical code makes it very difficult to successfully specify its rules: Have you ever taken a class in the grammar of nonverbal behavior? Second, nonverbal behavior can't comment on itself like verbal behaviors can. When someone verbally interrupts, you can verbally comment on that interruption; you can talk about talk. Can you think of any instance in which you have commented on a nonverbal message with a nonverbal message? Third, your nonverbal codes are restricted to the present tense, whereas verbal codes can refer to the past, present, and future. Fourth, you can't address the absence of something in a pure analogical code, whereas you can do so in a digital code.

Regardless of the similarities and the differences between the two, the importance of nonverbal behavior to the construction of social meaning in an interaction has not gone unnoticed. Burgoon (1985) has summarized the informative significance of nonverbal behavior into five propositions (p. 347):

1. As a general pattern, adults place more reliance on nonverbal than verbal cues in determining social meaning.
2. Children rely more heavily on verbal than nonverbal cues. Prior to puberty, however, they shift to greater belief in the nonverbal signals.
3. Adult reliance on nonverbal cues is greatest when the verbal and nonverbal messages conflict; verbal cues become increasingly important as the messages become more congruent.
4. The function of communication mediates channel reliance. Verbal cues are more important for factual, abstract, and persuasive communications, whereas nonverbal cues are more important for relational, attributional, affective, and attitudinal messages.
5. Individuals have consistent biases in channel reliance. Some consistently depend on verbal information; some consistently depend on nonverbal information; and some are situationally adaptable.

Nonverbal behavior provides you with a rich and invaluable set of contextual cues to help you interpret verbal messages. The verbal behavior, in turn, helps you with your interpretation of the nonverbal behavior. Both are reflexive partners in the work of helping you make sense of your interpersonal communication. We will treat nonverbal elements as a part of the social context and its conventions of language-in-use.

Nonverbal Behavior in Social Interaction

Despite the plethora of research into the nature and use of nonverbal behavior, our understanding of nonverbal behavior in interpersonal communication is sadly lacking. Wiener, Devoe, Rubinow, and Geller, in 1972, wrote an important article arguing that most past research equates nonverbal behavior with nonverbal communication. The primary emphasis is on the receiver and the significance he or she gives to some nonverbal behavior. They were concerned because the psychological approaches tended to consider any nonverbal behavior that was given some significance by a receiver to be communicative. Every time people cross their legs or fold their arms they are not necessarily communicating anything. Analogously, they point out that just because a person infers that a group of dark clouds are a sign of rain, doesn't mean that the clouds communicated that it would rain. Nonverbal communication is a subset of nonverbal behavior and occurs only when nonverbal behaviors are interpretable within some social context of language-in-use.

Nonverbal Behavior and Nonverbal Communication

There are fundamentally two ways that nonverbal behavior functions in interpersonal communication. Albert Scheflen (1972), a psychiatrist widely read by people interested in communication, referred to these as the *psychological* and the *communicational* viewpoints of nonverbal behavior:

> If the observer focuses on one member of a group and considers that member's thought or purpose he will see his behavior as an expression [of a psychological state]. But when the observer looks at this behavior in terms of what it "does" in the larger group then a communicational point of view has been adopted. (p. xiii)

Psychologically, nonverbal behaviors are interpreted as expressions of an individual's states, such as the individual's emotions. People feel sad (internal emotion), and so they cry (nonverbal behavior). They feel happy, and so they smile. In interpersonal communication, then, the communicators interpret each other's nonverbal behaviors as "messages" that one "gives off" to inform the other what he or she is feeling.

Communicationally, the interactants use nonverbal behaviors to organize their interpersonal relationships on the basis of how the nonverbal behaviors of one person "fit together" with the nonverbal behaviors of others. To understand how these behaviors are organized interpersonally is to understand how the interactants integrate or regulate themselves as they create their interpersonal relationship. Scheflen (1972) demonstrated how, by observing only the nonverbal behaviors of kinesics, someone could make the interpretation that a close interpersonal relationship was developing or failing to develop. For instance, during their conversation, Symon leans closer to Megan and smiles. Megan leans closer to Symon and returns the smile. Symon puts his arm around Megan. Megan smiles and places her hand in Symon's. The behaviors of both participants "fit together" to organize a developing, more intimate relationship.

Another way to describe the "psychological" and "communicational" views of nonverbal behavior is to describe them as *intrapersonal* and *interpersonal*. When a communicator uses the other's nonverbal behavior to infer an emotional state, the nonverbal behavior is an integral part of the intrapersonal aspect of communication. In this case the nonverbal behavior is said to be informative. When the behaviors of both people fit together in an organized and meaningful fashion, nonverbal behaviors are functioning within the interpersonal or relational part of the communication process. In this case the nonverbal behaviors are said to be communicative. Nonverbal behaviors that are informative are not necessarily communicative (Bavelas, 1990; Wiener et al., 1972). These views, though different, are compatible with each other. Nonverbal behaviors are both expressive and relational, psychological and communicational; they are located in both places in our model of interpersonal communication.

Awareness of the critical distinctions between these two types of behaviors doesn't guarantee that researchers interested in the dynamics of nonverbal communication will in fact study nonverbal communication. In 1985, thirteen years after the Wiener et al. article, Burgoon (1985) lamented:

> Too often, the nonverbal component of interpersonal interchanges has received only passing reference or has been ignored entirely. Such oversight can lead to some erroneous conclusions about the interpersonal communication process. (p. 344)

She goes on to give several examples of some of these erroneous conclusions. One area of interest she mentions is self-disclosure. One of the widely accepted guiding principles of self-disclosure is the norm of reciprocity— that is, that if a person discloses intimate, verbal information to you, you will reciprocate with intimate, verbal information. The assumption is that your verbal behavior influenced the reciprocation of verbal behavior. This assumption doesn't take into consideration how the verbal messages may be changed, modified, strengthened, negated, or tempered by the nonverbal messages. That which may appear to be verbally intimate may not be, and vice versa. If researchers ignore the presence of nonverbal behaviors in the process of self-disclosure, this could lead to erroneous conclusions about which messages influenced the reciprocity: the verbal messages or the nonverbal messages, or any combination of both. Burgoon goes on to say that our interpersonal research is lacking in the investigation of how conversational structure can change the nature and meaning of certain nonverbal expressions; how multiple (not single) nonverbal cues operate in interaction; how various relational contexts may change the meanings of nonverbal behavior; and how the duration, frequency, and meaning of relational nonverbal behavior may be altered as a relationship changes over time.

Bavelas, in 1990, echoes a similar, though distinct, concern from that of Burgoon:

> Even when called nonverbal communication, it is not usually treated (by communication researchers, much less by linguists) as *real* communication. Rather, it is treated as a separate and considerably lesser communicative "channel," studied for what it reveals rather than for what it conveys. (p. 595)

Bavelas addresses this issue by demonstrating that some nonverbal behaviors traditionally considered only informative are in fact communicative. She comments that although numerous nonverbal actions are only informative, many can be shown to be communicative. One example of such research is her own study of the communicative dynamics of motor mimicry (Bavelas, Black, Lemery, MacInnis, & Mullett, 1986a; Bavelas, Black, Lemery, & Mullett, 1986b; Bavelas, Black, Chovil, Lemery, & Mullett, 1988).

Her University of Victoria research group began studying this nonverbal action in the early 1980s. They were interested in collecting empirical evidence to support the pragmatic hypothesis that one cannot not communicate in an ongoing interactional setting (Bavelas, 1990; Clevenger, 1991). You will recall that this hypothesis is the cornerstone of our first pragmatic principle. Bavelas (1990) has argued that cases in which verbal behavior in an interactional setting would not be considered communicative are "infrequent and trivial" (p. 600); however, such is not the case for nonverbal behavior. Research interests should be focused on substantiating which of the many nonverbal behaviors in interaction are in fact communicative. She sees this research as a new and exciting trend in the study of communication simply because so many nonverbal behaviors appear to be only informative. Motor mimicry was a place for her group to begin this line of research.

Motor mimicry (Allport, 1968) has been traditionally conceptualized as only a reflexive nonverbal reaction appropriate to the circumstances of another (Bavelas et al., 1988). This behavior was considered a reflection of the empathic experience of an individual in response to a situation that someone else is experiencing. Examples of motor mimicry include wincing when you see someone stub a toe, leaning forward as you watch a runner cross the finish line, and smiling at another's delight. This behavior functions as an indication of an observer's vicarious experience of another's situation; the behavior functioned to inform.

Bavelas's research group was interested in testing the hypothesis that "such apparently reflexive actions are not merely expressions of private emotional experience but are communicative displays conveying our empathy analogically" (Bavelas, 1984, p. 6). The group did not negate that motor mimicry is informative but wanted to find out first whether nonverbal behavior is communicative, and if it is, whether that function is primary to its intrapsychic function. Bavelas, Black, Lemery, & Mullett (1986b) demonstrated that motor mimicry is processed by interactants as nonverbal communication. They did so by showing that

> (i) motor mimicry is differentially affected by the visual availability of a receiver, (ii) its display is synchronized to this visual display, (iii) it occurs too rapidly to have required prior inner processing, and (iv) it is consistently decoded by receivers. (p. 297)

Very simply, individuals interpret motor mimicry to mean "I am like you." By displaying the behavior appropriate to another's situation, "the observer conveys, precisely and eloquently, both awareness of and involvement with the other's situation" (Bavelas et al., 1988).

The next task facing the group (Bavelas et al., 1988) was to investigate whether the communicative function of these behaviors was indeed their primary function. They found this to be the case. This finding is a very important one for the pragmatic study of human behavior. A widely accepted position among scholars of human behavior is the belief that the major causes of our behavior are psychological. That is, elements of the intrapersonal system (such as emotions, attitudes, motives) determine the behavior. Motor mimicry and other nonverbal actions are treated simply as "leaks" from the internal experience. Bavelas et al. (1988) have shown that motor mimicry has a function of its own and that while someone's situation (e.g., stubbing a toe) may elicit both an internal experience in an observer and communicative behavior, these two functions are independent. Further, and most important, the communicative function is the reason for the nonverbal behavior (e.g., the wincing). Thus, motor mimicry (and possibly other nonverbal behaviors) can "serve to convey, analogically, the nature of the relationship between communicants" (the interpersonal system) (Bavelas et al., 1988, p. 279). Thus these expressions are not *of* an observer's internal state, but subtle relational messages *to* another. Chovil (1990) has recently shown that facial mimicry occurs only when the behavior can be seen.

Bavelas goes on to conjecture that many other nonverbal behaviors may also prove to be communicative. She lists, for example, blushing, facial disgust, gestures, and various kinds of facial displays. Her group cautions that in order to explore the communicative function of nonverbal behaviors, these behaviors need to be studied in ongoing interaction, not in isolation. Bavelas and a colleague are working on a research method for identifying nonverbal communication based on the methods used for motor mimicry (see Bavelas, 1990).

SUMMARY

Verbal behavior, a fundamental part of the social context of interpersonal communication, is embedded in the social context and varies from one context to another. The same language, such as English, involves two different types of meaning and rules that govern its use: (1) the rules that are universal in the language and (2) the rules that are created as the language is used in communication. Language-in-use creates social meanings interpretable by members of the social context as a result of their conventional (highly frequent and typical) use during interaction among members of that social context.

Virtually every social context develops its own social meanings and conventions. Language is said to reflect, build upon, and mediate context. Language and social context are reflexive in that language-in-use aids in the creation of the social context and in turn the social context influences the language-in-use of that context. Language-in-use includes indexical expressions that inform the hearer of the social convention and reduce the uncertainty concerning which meaning is workable in that context. Social meanings are either universal or specialized, depending on their applicability to the social meaning of language-in-use in the social context. Universal meanings, though fewer in number, apply to every social context that includes the use of that language. More particularized social meanings are limited to the members of that social context, and although different from the universal form and meaning, they are not substandard.

Individual communicators develop their own individual adaptations of language-in-use and interact with that style. Each individual has the ability to perform many different styles and switches from one style to another upon entering a different social context for a new stage in a developing interpersonal relationship. Understanding which style is being performed and when to switch to a new style is a part of being competent in interpersonal communication.

Using language in interpersonal communication involves using non-verbal behaviors that coexist with the verbal behaviors. Nonverbal behavior, while similar to linguistic verbal behavior, is also unique. Nonverbal behaviors function in two ways in interpersonal communication. Psychologically, this may be interpreted as external expressions of some internal or emotional state. Communicatively, the nonverbal behaviors of one communicator "fit together" with those of the other to "organize" and define their interpersonal relationship. These two functions exist side by side and are independent of each other. That means that some nonverbal behaviors, such as motor mimicry, thought to be only psychological, are communicative. Their primary function is communicative, and the nonverbal behavior is not caused by a person's internal state but is brought on as a way of displaying a relationship with another. Thus, many nonverbal behaviors in interaction that were in the past only considered behaviors may in fact be communicative in the truest sense of the word.

KEY TERMS

langue

parole

language-in-use

competence

performance

code perspective

code

syntactic code

pragmatic code

reflexivity

denotative meaning

connotative meaning

indexicality

indexical expressions

style

style switching

speech accommodation theory

convergence

divergence

analogical code

digital code

Part 3   THE RELATIONSHIP

In Part Three of this book we examine in detail the central focus of the pragmatic view of interpersonal communication—the relationship. The relationship has been likened to a dance and now that we have examined the dancers, the dance floor, and the dance steps, it is time to explore the dynamic nature of the dance. The preceding five chapters have prepared you for the chapters that follow. From your earlier reading you know, for example, that communication takes place in a context that may influence the relationship either positively or negatively. You know too, that the context includes both physical elements of the environment and, more importantly, social elements of cultures and co-cultures to which the communicators belong. You know that the individual participants possess unique self-identities that they both conceal from and reveal to the other. You know that communication takes place between two or more thinking, breathing, perceiving people who are affected by being a part of the relationship process. But between the beginning and the end of the interaction is the "stuff" of which the relationship is made, created, enacted, and maintained. And that stuff—the content of the relationship, the practical "doing" of communication, the interaction, the interpersonal behaviors—is the focus of the next chapters.

You will recall that your dances or relationships are composed of events (dance steps) and that events "occur"—that is, they exist in time. Once an event is over, it's over. On the other hand, your attributions of the relationship (such as your emotions or feelings toward the other person) seem to be more "real." But you must keep in mind that those internal and individualized feelings are not the relationship itself but the residual effects that remain inside the heads of the participants (dancers) after the interaction with the partner has already created the relationship (the dance).

These two elements—the relationship and the effects of the relationship on individuals—must remain separated. You must continue to see the relationship as interpersonal communication and resist the temptation to see the relationship as *thing*like, or having some material substance. The characteristics that serve to define the relationship are created and reflected in the pattern or sequence of communicators' actions toward one another. These actions are the external behaviors that occur between people. They occur in time and are related to one another in time.

We will introduce Part Three by detailing five axiomatic characteristics that describe all interpersonal relationships from a pragmatic view. Together, these axiomatic characteristics summarize the fundamental characteristics of relationships discussed in Parts One and Two, and they serve to frame our discussions in Part Three.

Relationships Are *Created*

A relationship is not something that just "happens." It is something that results from the communicators' overt acts which create it. Having once been created, a relationship continues to exist with a life of its own, nurtured by the participants and affecting the participants within it. Like any created life, though, a relationship does not stand still. It continues to change, to grow, to develop over the natural course of time. Every relationship is constantly evolving so that it may progress to a new and more intimate stage, or it may regress to a new and less intimate stage. Like flowing rivers, events continue to change normally with the passage of time, and so do relationships.

Relationships Are *Enacted*

The term "enact" is central to the nature of communication and relationships (Weick, 1979). To enact a relationship is to create the relationship through actions. The components of any relationship are ultimately those actions performed by the participants while communicating within the relationship. Combined, the actions create meaningful patterns of interaction. Symon can individually create his meaning of Megan, but he can do so only acting toward Megan. Conversely, Megan's meaning of Symon results from her having acted toward Symon. But neither person's definition of the other, though also enacted, is the same as the definition of the relationship as a whole. Their relationship is the interaction that is created by the particular combination of actions performed by Symon and Megan.

Relationships Are *Becoming*

To say that relationships are created is to emphasize the *process* of relating. Any process, by definition, embodies the notion of time and change over time. A relationship, then, is constantly *in process;* it is continually evolving and becoming something different. Thus a relationship is not so much a goal to be attained or never just *is;* it is constantly changing, constantly moving, constantly becoming something else. To maintain a relationship is to keep changing it.

Many of you may hold steadfast to the fairytale of the beautiful young princess and the handsome young prince who married and "lived happily ever after." As a result of such fairytale tradition—reinforced in novels, movies, and TV shows—many people have been led to believe that "falling in love" or "finding that special someone" is all they need do in order to "live happily ever after." The practical truth of the matter is that maintaining a loving relationship requires a considerable expenditure of energy—energy spent in interpersonal communication. Change is normal and inevitable. When left alone, relationships atrophy, wither, and die. They need to be revitalized to keep them at the same level of development.

Relationships Are *Consequential*

You have probably heard someone say something like the following: "Yes, I'm still seeing him [or her], but it's nothing serious. I don't want to get involved. And he [or she] respects my wishes." Such a comment assumes that the speaker is somehow aloof from and unaffected—that individual persons are somehow separate from the relationships in which they participate. Relationships, as you learned in Chapter 3, are inherently consequential.

To behave toward another person is to get involved with that person. Two people acting toward each other create the phenomenon known as *inter*action—the connections between actions and, thus, between the persons who perform those actions. The only way you can avoid getting involved with another person is not to have any communication, that is, not to have a relationship at all. A relationship can, does, and must affect both Symon and Megan as a consequence of their having been in that relationship. Furthermore, there is nothing that Symon and Megan can do about it short of not communicate at all.

Relationships Are *Qualitative*

All relationships are different. You, the same person, have many relationships with many different people. But each of your relationships is different, in some respects, from any of the others. Your relationship with your mother is probably different from that of your sister, father, or brother. Yet, all can be described as "kinship" relationships. There are many different people you would call "friends," but some of those relationships are "friendlier" than others. In other words, every relationship, as an open system, has a certain quality that makes it different from other relationships.

The quality of a relationship is created by the communicative behaviors, the interactions you and the other person perform toward each other. You, together with your relational partner, "enact" a relationship which is, to some extent, unique. And that relationship, in turn, exerts an influence on your definition of your self.

Some scholars (Graziano & Musser, 1982, p. 101) have suggested that the quality of interaction can be assessed along three dimensions: *performance, closeness,* and *relevance.* For instance, you may find the performance of the relationship itself very satisfying. You enjoy being with that person. Second, you may experience a feeling of being very close with that special person, but you don't have that feeling with people you don't know very well. Finally, you may conclude that some people are simply more relevant to certain areas of your self than are others. Your academic advisor, for instance, may be very relevant to your educational life but not very relevant to your having fun.

The remaining chapters of Part Three generally follow these five characteristics. Chapter 6 discusses the "enacting" of relationships, in which communicative behaviors, because of their "consequential" nature and impact on the participants, become strategies as the individual selves of the partners negotiate their interpersonal relationship. Depending on the nature of the interactional patterns people enact with their partners, that relationship develops a quality that distinguishes it from some relationships and makes it similar to others.

Individual communicative competence and relational competence is the focus of Chapter 7. What does it mean to be a competent communicator? What is relational competence? Can two incompetent communicators enact a successful relationship? Can two competent communicators enact a failed relationship?

Chapter 8 begins at the beginning of communication. How do people initiate the creative process of developing an interpersonal relationship? What happens during the early stages in the process of interpersonal communication?

The developmental process of continual change is the major theme of Chapter 9. Why and how do people develop closer relationships with some people and grow farther apart in their relationships with others?

Some relationships, of course, just don't make it. They simply end, sometimes abruptly and sometimes gradually, as the partners (independently or mutually) decide to terminate the relationship rather than keep a relationship going. The creative phase of terminating a relationship is the topic of Chapter 10.

The "becoming" phase of interpersonal relationships is the focus of Chapter 11. In many ways, it is far easier to begin a relationship than to keep a relationship (particularly a close one) going. The strategies involved in maintaining relationships, too often ignored but highly significant nonetheless, are explored in this chapter.

These next chapters are really the "guts" of this book. In order to gain the fullest understanding of and appreciation for how interpersonal communication works and how you can apply the principles of effective communication in the actual process of relating to others, the preceding discussion of self and context is a vitally important prerequisite. In order to be practical and apply the principles of interpersonal communication in your day-to-day experiences, however, you must know and understand what you *do* when you actually engage in communication—that is, what you do when you participate in interpersonal relationships. The questions you and another will be asking of yourselves in any communicative situation will be "What do I want out of this relationship?" and "What do I do in order to help me get it?" The answers to those questions should become more apparent when you have completed your study of the remaining chapters.

CHAPTER 6

Enacting Relationships: Communicative Strategies and Patterns

> Interpersonal relationships develop upon the basis of reciprocal knowledge, and this knowledge upon the basis of the actual relations. Both are inextricably interwoven.
>
> —Simmel

Among the pithy pieces of folk wisdom uttered by the late humorist Will Rogers is the famous statement "I never met a man I didn't like." The most common interpretation of this implies some enviable property of Will Rogers himself, a property that allowed him to see something likable within every other person or which gave him extraordinary skill as a participant in interpersonal communication. Despite these worthy implications of Rogers's statement, you should probably not ignore the possibility that, in uttering these words, Will Rogers probably did not expect anyone to take him literally.

For most people, communication with others includes the entire range of interpersonal reactions. You rate some people high on your liking scale. You rate others rather low and react to them with supreme indifference. But why? Why do you like some people and not others? Why do you want to get to know some people more than others? Why do you have favorable first impressions of some people, while others "turn you off" immediately? To answer such questions, you must first rephrase the "why" questions and substitute the subtly though significantly different question "How come?"

To ask "why" is to look for the easy cause-effect answer, such as looking for something in the other person (or in you) that causes you to react favorably, unfavorably, or with indifference. A "why" question is probably more appropriate to understanding your reactions to inanimate objects in your environment. You like a movie or a popular song because of something within you that perceives the movie or music as pleasing. You dislike it because of something you perceive as displeasing. In fact, human perceptions probably provide a fairly complete explanation for understanding your reactions to such objects.

When you communicate, though, you do more than merely perceive. You "act toward" the other person and experience the other person's acting toward you. Consequently, it is more accurate to say you *enact* your communication (Weick, 1977), your relationship. That is, you *create* relationships through your acting toward the other person and that person's acting toward you. Moreover, because actions are events, they take place over a period of time. Your first impressions of the other person may (and often do) change from one moment to the next, as your interaction continues. What seemed important at one time may, during interaction, turn out to be trivial, and vice versa.

Because interpersonal communication is constantly changing, constantly in a process of becoming, you need to rephrase your "why" questions to consider fully the time factor. Hence, understanding the process of enacting relationships requires asking "how come" questions. How does your reaction of liking come about through interaction? How does your relationship develop over time to become what it is right now? How do your relationships with some people come to be pleasant while those with others are unpleasant? Unlike "why" questions, asking "how come" questions forces you to address the issue that you, through your own actions and those of others, are responsible for the relationships you have with others.

The best way to understand how relationships come about is to think of interpersonal communication as a process of negotiation. Each individual communicator possesses individualized motives, wants, desires, interests, and so on. Your individual list of these things is different from every other person's list. Yet very different individuals, communicating with each other, develop an interpersonal bond or relationship that becomes more significant than the differences that separate them.

Interpersonal communication involves a blend of individual differences and interpersonal bonds. Interpersonal communication highlights the independence of individual members within a unified relationship. In Chapter 2 we discussed these dual interests of individuation and sociation as dialectical tensions (Baxter, 1988; Rawlins, 1983b) characteristic of any relationship. These opposing, yet valued, tensions of independence and interdependence are central to the social process of negotiation.

As individual communicators act toward each other, they create the process of negotiating their own individual selves toward the natural goal of achieving some "settlement" or "contract" that unites their independent selves within a relationship. Like negotiation, communication involves individuals functioning to further their own interests. Yet, these same individuals continue to seek elements of commonality with the other, elements that make them similar and on which they can agree.

This chapter describes the process of enacting interpersonal relationships through communication within the framework of a negotiating process. To see interpersonal communication as a process of negotiating differences of individual selves is to focus on the quality of the interaction that inevitably contributes to the quality of the ongoing settlement or the relationship, the interpersonal bond. Communicative behaviors are not just idle chatter. They are *strategies* you use when acting toward another person. Every time you communicate, you make an offer to the other person, an offer that may affect the quality of the settlement or the relational contract that is the outcome. As in any process of negotiation, interpersonal communicators achieve a settlement *after* a lengthy process of talk. At different stages during their interaction, they come closer to a settlement, move farther away, or make no progress. A settlement or contract defining their relationship, however, is always the temporary outcome of this evolutionary process of interpersonal communication.

All negotiated relationships, of course, do not arrive at the same settlement. They are characterized by equifinality. Some relationships, like negotiated contracts in general, are more acceptable to the participants than are others. Some contracts enjoy more commitment on the part of the negotiators than do others. The outcome of any particular interpersonal communication, like the outcome of any process of negotiation, is never guaranteed at the beginning. It evolves to some outcome, but the outcome is never final; it is constantly changing. These are the major topics to be discussed in this chapter.

QUALITY OF INTERACTION

What is it about the interaction that makes it satisfying to you or that generates your feelings toward the other person? After all, you interact with strangers in generally the same manner, regardless of who the stranger is. You are guided by those conventional norms of your society that tell you how to engage in let's-get-acquainted talk with new people. With some people you seem to hit it off right away; with others, you spend much more time getting acquainted; and with still others, you come quickly (or eventually) to the conclusion that this relationship won't ever "get off the ground." "How come?" you ask yourself. The answer lies in those characteristics of the *inter*action that identify it as being different from (or similar to) other interaction—in other words, the *quality* of the interaction.

Primary Characteristics

The primary characteristics of the quality of interaction describe interaction in terms of events. Events occur in time and hence are related to each other in time. Events may occur with certain lapses in time between them. Thus, interaction is *discontinuous*. Events may fit together in a logical progression. Thus, interaction is *synchronized*. Events may occur again and again at different times. Thus, interaction is *recurrent*. One event may reflect back on or remind you of an earlier event. Thus, interaction is *reciprocal*. These are the four primary characteristics of interactional quality: discontinuity, synchrony, recurrence, and reciprocity.

Discontinuity   The most obvious characteristic of interactional quality is the fact that it is discontinuous. Even with your closest friends, you do not interact all the time. Hours will go by—days, weeks, months, even years—between the times when you and your relational partner are actually engaged in communicating with one another. During any typical day, even husbands and wives are separated for many hours between periods of interaction. However, the fact that interaction in even the closest and most intimate relationships is discontinuous isn't particularly interesting. What *is* intriguing is that the relationships continue to prosper during the periods of noninteraction, so that when interaction again occurs, the relational partners take up where they left off—often as though nothing had changed or time had not intervened.

Just recently, Kathy experienced a revival of an intermittent and discontinuous relationship. She received a phone call from a high school friend she had not seen or talked with in over ten years. Kathy had kept track of her friend through her friend's sister, who has remained one of Kathy's closest friends. Her friend had been thinking about Kathy and decided to call and catch up on old times. Coincidentally, Kathy was going to be flying through Salt Lake City where her friend lived, and they made arrangements to meet each other at the airport. Although time had changed them emotionally and physically, they both remarked how pleased they were that their friendship picked up where it had left off. They laughed, reminisced about their escapades in high school, gave each other the usual hard time, and were immediately comfortable in their conversation. Their relationship continued as though ten years of only minimal interpersonal contact had not intervened.

Ray Birdwhistell (1970, p. 88) once remarked that communication is composed of "isolable discontinuous units" which appear as one continuous whole when the interactants put those units together. Kathy's friendship may have felt as though it had gone on forever, but the relationship really hasn't. Her friendship appears as one continuous relationship only when the many separate discontinuous units are strung together (Leeds-Hurwitz, 1992). Relationships thus appear to persist during long periods of noninteraction and absence. Of course, Kathy's incident may be somewhat unusual. After all, the typical interpersonal relationship does not involve highly discontinuous communication. Periods of hours, days, or weeks intervene between comparatively brief periods of interaction; then the relationship is reactivated by communicating.

Synchrony   A second characteristic of relational quality is the *synchrony* of interpersonal communication. Two people synchronize their actions so that, together, their actions create a recognizable *inter*action—a dance. Leeds-Hurwitz (1992) discusses "interactional rhythms" created by two people coordinating, or synchronizing, their individual rhythms. When you interact with a close friend, you always seem to know what to say or how to respond. And your friend knows how to respond to what you say and do. Together, your actions and your friend's actions "dovetail," or fit together, to create a synchronized pattern of actions or an interactional rhythm during your communication.

The rhythm, or synchrony, of speech and movement between interactants is called *interactional synchrony* as opposed to self-synchrony (Condon & Ogston, 1966; Davis, 1982). *Asynchrony* is the opposite of synchrony and in its extreme form has been associated with psychiatric problems such as autism (Condon, 1980). In its less extreme form it can characterize interaction between people of different cultures. Many patterns of movement and timing are cultural; thus, the timing of your movements with another from a different culture may not match. For example, Doug Kirkpatrick, a middle school teacher and a local "feminist of the year," has observed that female response time to his questions is slower than male response time and that it is this kind of quickness that is often rewarded in the classroom (Koury, 1993). Synchrony between teacher and student can have a profound impact on the character of the educational experience of males and females.

With even a slight acquaintance, you are likely to know what response is appropriate because you and an acquaintance also create a synchronized pattern of interaction. But this pattern is one of acquaintanceship rather than friendship. The appropriate response to your friend is often not appropriate in your acquaintanceship interaction. In addition, you don't usually notice these rhythms. What you do notice is the impression you gain from the synchronized patterns. Have you ever gone away from an interaction and felt uncomfortable? Perhaps you have even remarked about how pushy and irritating the other person was? What about those interactions when you felt comfortable and perhaps noted how tender or loving the other was? Those remarks are ways interactants have of recognizing asynchronized and synchronized interaction (Byers, 1977).

Recurrence   But how do you know how to synchronize your communicative actions with those of your partner? How do you know when an action is "out of sync" with the pattern? The answer is the third characteristic of interactional quality: *recurrence.* You have compiled years of experience as interpersonal communicators. By the time you entered kindergarten, you had already been communicating for years. You had known kinships, friendships, acquaintanceships, and a variety of other communicative experiences. At the present stage of your life, you are already a rather sophisticated interpersonal communicator, even though you may not be aware of just how sophisticated you really are.

Your years of communicative experience have allowed you to enact relationships with others, to create synchronized interaction patterns, and to recognize when some action (yours or another's) is "out of sync" with the pattern. You have learned interactional synchrony as a result of the most common of learning modes: sheer repetition. You have participated in so much interpersonal communication, so many interpersonal relationships, that you already know a great deal about what is appropriate and what is not.

You also know, based on your communicative experiences, what criteria to use in order to evaluate interactional synchrony in any relationship. In interaction with a new acquaintance, for example, you know that the criteria for assessing synchrony come from the cultural context—the rules for doing "small talk" in acquaintanceships. In interaction with a close friend, you know that the criteria for assessing interactional synchrony come from your history of past interaction with that friend.

In other words, you can recognize a perfectly appropriate synchronized interaction of acquaintanceship as appropriate to that kind of relationship. But if that same interaction occurred between you and your friend, you would both know that something was wrong. That is, you and your friend would know that your interaction was "out of sync" because you were both using the same criteria to evaluate its synchrony. Those criteria are found in the recurrent, familiar patterns that have characterized your interaction (that relationship) in the past.

The interaction of close friends is so synchronized that other persons, outside that particular relationship, would experience great difficulty in understanding or interpreting the behaviors of either partner, let alone the particular synchrony of their patterns or interactional behavior. Persons outside their relationship are not familiar with the distinctive pattern of synchronized actions because they did not participate in enacting or creating those patterns. On the other hand, the relational partners themselves did create those patterns and hence are very familiar with their own recurring patterns. To outsiders, each partner may appear to be highly sensitive to what the other is feeling inside. In reality, they are just familiar with the synchronized "flow" of their interaction and are thus sensitive to any action that deviates from their own familiar synchronized pattern.

Reciprocity   Earlier we discussed reciprocity as a norm of social behavior characteristic of all interaction (Gouldner, 1960). Reciprocity can mean responding to another's action in kind. If Symon self-discloses to Megan, Megan reciprocates by self-disclosing to Symon. If Symon insults Megan, Megan reciprocates by insulting Symon. But reciprocity involves additional ways in which participants enact or define their relationship with each other (Adams, 1985).

Generally speaking, *reciprocity* is the quality of interaction in which each interactant reciprocates the other's definition of their relationship. If Symon asks a question of Megan, for example, then Symon is defining his relationship with Megan as one of questioner and answerer. Megan would be reciprocating Symon's definition of the relationship by providing an answer to Symon's question. Responding in kind (the "do-unto-others" definition) would suggest that Megan would reciprocate a question by asking another question. But reciprocity, as a quality of interaction, maintains the synchrony of interaction. By responding to Symon's question with an answer, Megan reciprocates Symon's definition of the relationship as one of questioner-answerer. In this way, both Symon and Megan have the same definition of their relationship. Symon provided the initial definition of their relationship with his question, and Megan reciprocated that definition with an answer.

You might think that this example of a questioner-answerer relationship is rather outdated, given the contemporary cultural tendency to use questions as indirect answers. Consider, for example, the following conversation of Symon and Megan:

SYMON: Hey, Megan! Want to go get a cuppa coffee?
MEGAN: Is the Pope Catholic?
SYMON: Great! How about the cafeteria?
MEGAN: Aw, come on! Do submarines have screen doors?
SYMON: Yeah, you're right. Why stay on campus? That pizza place across the street shouldn't be busy this time of day. Want to try there?
MEGAN: You wanna lead the way?

This conversation illustrates a high level of synchrony, with Symon consistently in the role of questioner and Megan consistently providing answers. Even though every one of Megan's answers appears grammatically as a question, both relational partners are clearly aware that inquiries as to the Pope's religious preference or a submarine's accessibility function as answers to previous questions and not as serious interrogations requiring answers.

In contrast, the following conversation includes little reciprocity of relational definitions and, consequently, is not highly synchronized:

SYMON: Hey, Megan! Want to go get a cuppa coffee?
MEGAN: Why? Are you hungry?
SYMON: Does that mean you don't want to go?

MEGAN: Did I say that?
SYMON: Shall we go or not?
MEGAN: How long do you want to stay?
SYMON: Did you know that you always answer questions with a question?
MEGAN: Do I?

This conversation is apparently going nowhere. Symon maintains his role as questioner, but Megan resists his relational definition and consistently redefines their relationship with herself in the role of questioner. Symon appears frustrated at the lack of reciprocity in their conversation and, in his final comment, overtly recognizes that lack of reciprocity by introducing it as a topic of their conversation. His overt attempt to enforce reciprocity doesn't work, though. Megan responds with yet another question.

These, then, are the four *primary* characteristics of interactional quality: *discontinuity, synchrony, recurrence,* and *reciprocity.* Of these four, synchrony is probably the most important to improving your communicative skills. To the degree that the patterns of interpersonal communication are synchronized, your interpersonal relationship is well defined. The lower the level of synchrony, the less clear is the definition of the relationship.

Most definitions of interpersonal relationships focus on the central importance of interaction and these major characteristics of the quality of that interaction. Denzin (1970) provides such a typical definition:

> A relationship exists between two or more people when those people engage in recurrent forms of either symbolic or co-present interaction. . . . For a relationship to exist[,] the parties involved must share the same or [a] similar set of reciprocal definitions about the other. Further, these definitions must extend through time so that the influence of the other does not disappear when he is out of physical, face-to-face presence. . . . It is possible to speak, then, of relationships that are reciprocated and those that are nonreciprocated. Further, there are those that are reciprocated, but unevenly so. (pp. 67–68)

One final note. These characteristics of interactional quality are *variable.* That is, each characteristic is present in all interaction, and it is present to some extent or in some amount. Some interactions are more synchronized than others, for example, but every interaction possesses some level of synchrony that varies from "very low" to "very high." All interactions are discontinuous, but some relationships have more frequent and longer periods of noninteraction than do others. All interactions involve reciprocity, but some relationships have more reciprocity than others. Some interaction patterns are more familiar or more recurrent than others, even in the same relationship. Each characteristic will exist in greater or lesser amount in a particular interaction.

Secondary Characteristics

The secondary characteristics of interactional quality include those qualities you typically attribute to the internalized feelings of one or more individuals. These secondary traits characterizing the quality of interaction result directly from the discontinuity, synchrony, recurrence, and reciprocity of interactional quality. A partial list of these secondary characteristics is discussed in the following pages: *intensity, intimacy, trust,* and *commitment.* When used to characterize a relationship, these traits describe the interpersonal bond created by interaction.

Intensity   The strength or potency of a relationship indicates its degree of *intensity.* To the extent that the interpersonal bond of the relationship (whether friendship or enmity) is strong, that relationship might be said to be very intense. A relationship with high intensity is likely to influence the participants even when one is not in the immediate physical presence of the other.

Intimacy   *Intimacy* refers to the depth of individual attachments or close associations. Intimacy in Latin is *intimus,* which means "innermost" or "inner." We are using "intimacy" here to describe the relational process of achieving closeness with another (Hatfield, 1984). People often use this word in their everyday speech and imply a connotation of a purely physical or sexual relationship. "Intimate relations," for instance, is often used as a euphemism for sexual intercourse. Intimacy, however, does not rest on the content of behaviors (Simmel, 1950), although some behaviors such as expressions of love, appreciation, and caring are necessary components of intimacy (Helgeson, Shaver, & Dyer, 1987). A stranger in the grocery store may share very personal information with you, yet you would not say that you have an intimate relationship with this person. Intimacy is the process of attempting closeness, and it is based on the degree to which the other is used to confirm the self and one's sentiment associated with that self-confirmation (Millar & Rogers, 1987). Intimate relationships hold the promise of creating selves from the previously unknown. Viable intimacy, then, is the degree to which partners maintain a balance between the boundaries of individual self and the relationship.

Trust   To the extent that the partners freely engage in high-risk behaviors when interacting with each other, their relationship is characterized by *trust.* Trust exists in the interaction to the extent that the partners mutually risk their selves (that is, their own definitions of self) when they interact with each other. Remember that relationships are dynamic and evolving and, thus, inherently fragile. Although the actions of partners are interdependent, partners cannot be entirely certain of each other's actions. Thus, relational partners attempt to limit each other's choices, and each limitation—whether that involves, agreements, rules, contracts, or promises—implies an "obligation to live up to the 'confidence' implicit in that agreement" (Millar & Rogers, 1987, p. 122). To trust is to risk the possibility that the other will not live up to the confidence in the agreement. Of course, trust (like every other secondary characteristic of interactional quality) is synchronized or reciprocated to some extent in the interaction. The interpersonal trust may exhibit a high level of reciprocated trust (for example, Symon trusts Megan to the same extent that Megan trusts Symon) or a low level of reciprocity (for example, Symon trusts Megan much more than Megan trusts Symon).

More importantly, perhaps, interpersonal trust is typically limited to a specific area of interaction or interpersonal behaviors. Symon may trust Megan to be discreet in maintaining a confidence, and so he might tell her a secret (thereby risking his self) and trust her not to blab it to everyone else. On the other hand, Symon may not trust Megan to catch him if he should fall down, precisely because he knows that Megan does not have the ability (that is, the physical strength) to be worthy of that trust. Within the same relationship, Symon and Megan may exhibit high trust in some of their interaction patterns and a low level of interpersonal trust in some others.

Commitment The quality of the interaction that reveals the extent to which relational partners are dedicated to the relationship indicates their "commitment." In a broad sense, we identify *commitment* as "those situations in which one or both parties either accept their relationship as continuing indefinitely or direct their behaviors towards insuring its continuance" (Hinde, 1979, p. 132). Commitment has been found to be reciprocal; that is, both partners must commit to achieve a relational sense of commitment (Piland, 1986). As such, a relationship with a high level of commitment is one that is more likely to persist (that is, to last longer) than is another with a lower level of commitment. Relationships with high commitment tend to endure through periods of adversity as well as contentment, through good times and bad, in sickness and in health, despite long periods when there is no interaction.

Relationships with high levels of commitment may not be the most intimate relationships, although they often (perhaps typically) are. Couples who have been married for thirty, forty, or fifty years often remark on the fact that being together is like a habit they can't break. They feel comfortable with each other and have never even considered the alternative of being apart. Such relationships reflect a high level of commitment, even though their interaction may not exhibit much intimacy or intensity. The most appropriate definition of commitment, then, is probably persistence over time—endurance, even though relationships with the highest levels of commitment (that is, identification of self with the relationship) are also likely to be those with correspondingly high levels of intimacy, reciprocity, intensity, and synchrony.

These are some secondary characteristics of the quality of interaction that can be used to describe any and every interpersonal relationship. These characteristics are variables that are present, to some extent, in every interaction. Describing their interaction in terms of these variables defines the interpersonal relationship between the interactants. Two relationships may have some characteristics in common (just as two people may have the same color of hair or eyes), but they will always differ to some extent in one characteristic or another.

When relationships are similar to one another in a variety of these characteristics, we tend to classify those relationships as being of a certain type. For example, relationships with relatively high levels of synchrony, intimacy, reciprocity, commitment, and recurrence are likely to be classified together under a general category of *friendship*. A relationship with relatively low levels of these same characteristics is apt to be classified as *acquaintanceship*.

NEGOTIATING INTERPERSONAL RELATIONSHIPS

Nearly all of you are familiar with "negotiation." People have a general idea of what this word means: people sitting down and talking with one another in order to reach some sort of agreement. But negotiation is much more common than people might think. It occurs very frequently in everyday situations. You undoubtedly engage in negotiation yourself. At one time or another, you may have entered into negotiations with your parents to get a higher allowance or to use the family automobile. You may have negotiated with an instructor concerning the grade received on an assignment or in a course. You and your friends negotiate with one another in order to decide what to do on a given night: go to a movie, go to a dance, go to the basketball game, go cruising, and so on. Negotiation is a much more common and routine occurrence than people often think.

A process of negotiation begins with the participants fully aware that they are very different from one another. Negotiation is essentially a process of talking together in order to resolve those differences or reach agreement on some point of commonality. It often involves disagreement, compromise, and argument; but it always involves communication. In fact, all interpersonal communication is, to some extent, a process of negotiation. Two human beings who are different from one another negotiate their individual differences and come to some understanding or settlement that defines their interpersonal relationship.

In formal settings, negotiation is typically viewed as a context of communication in which negotiators representing larger social systems, such as the workers or the company itself, labor or management, meet for the purpose of resolving conflict (Sawyer & Guetzkow, 1965). Diez (1986) and Donohue, Diez, and Hamilton (1984), for example, have investigated the communicative character of negotiation as a particular type of situation. Donohue (1981, p. 107) defines negotiation as a "mixed motive" situation in which people must reach incongruent goals beneficial to both. Those larger groups have different interests, different desires, different motivations, different goals. When two people engage in interpersonal communication, each person represents his or her own self in negotiating interpersonal relationships. Each communicator has interests, desires, motivations, and goals that are quite different from those of the other. The purpose of the communication process is to arrive at some sort of agreement on areas common to both communicators. That agreement is the interpersonal relationship. It is created neither because of nor despite differences in goals, motives, and interests of the individual selves. Rather, the interpersonal relationship is *in addition to* these individualized differences.

Communication as a Negotiated Relationship

In creating their relationship, communicators enact a process of negotiating their individual differences (their selves) in order to achieve some common goal (the definition of their relationship). The process of creating interpersonal relationships through negotiating individual selves involves a unique blending of opposites—a blending of opposing forces that are present during communication. Two different individual selves engage in the same activity and talk in order to reach agreement on things about which they differ at the outset. Each communicator attempts to protect his or her self and at the same time risks self by engaging in the social activity of communication, by relating with the other person. To understand negotiation is to understand how it blends opposites together into the common interpersonal activity of communication. Each of the following characteristics of interpersonal communication is based on viewing the process of enacting relationships as a process of negotiating individual differences.

Interpersonal Communication Is a Blend of Cooperation and Competition, of Unity and Diversity   Every time you communicate with another human being, you are engaging in an act that contains elements of both cooperation and competition. You compete with the other person in the sense that you have a self-concept to protect and maintain. Of course, the other person competes with you at the same time and for the same reason: to protect his or her self-concept. While you are competing, you and your partner are cooperating too. You both speak the same language, you use the same social skills learned in previous encounters, you follow essentially the same cultural rules, you recognize the same social environment, you are both oriented to the same act of communication and topic under discussion, and you follow the rules of turn taking in conversation. You both recognize the indisputable fact that you are individually different at the same time that you seek areas of similarity.

During communication, you and your partner are negotiating the differences that separate you. Without necessarily being aware of it, you and your partner are creating something that did not exist when you began interacting; a social unit which is something different from either of you (McCall, 1988). Inevitably, you and your partner will negotiate a settlement, a relationship, that binds you together in some definable and recognizable way. Your relationship, even an undesirable one, will evolve as you continue to engage in interpersonal communication. The precise nature or definition of your interpersonal relationship evolves as you continue your interaction. Whatever the relational settlement, it will contain elements of both cooperation and competition, unity and diversity. Your relationship binds the two of you together into a social unit but maintains the self-identities that make you both different. Both the assimilating and the differentiating elements of communication continue to exist throughout your interpersonal relationship.

Interpersonal Communication Assumes a Future Agreement on Some Potential Settlement or Contract   The title of an old show tune depicts the potential development of any relationship: "This Could Be the Start of Something Big." Who knows what is going to happen in the future when two people interact for the very first time? An appropriate saying, often attributed to Confucius, suggests that "A journey of a thousand miles begins with but a single step." The point is that the eventual outcome of a relationship between any two persons is simply not apparent or predictable from their interaction in early conversations.

Every act of interpersonal communication does assume the existence of a potential future, some outcome, some relationship. Some interactions develop into close friendships; many more do not develop beyond the initial meeting. At the time of their first encounter, even the participants have no idea what the relational outcome is likely to be; but the potential for further development is always present, even from the first "Hi, how are you?" greeting. When you begin talking with an automobile sales agent, for example, neither of you knows whether the negotiation will conclude with the purchase of an automobile. But the potential for such a contract, settlement, or agreement is present from the very first.

Relationships that persist, that involve commitment (such as close friendships or marriage), never do achieve a "final" stage of development. They are continually negotiated and renegotiated throughout the passing months and years. Just as every individual changes somewhat during the course of a lifetime, so do the relationships in which that individual is a partner. Changes in relationships are a part of the natural process of the evolutionary development of interpersonal communication and require continued negotiation and renegotiation. Remember that relationships are always in a process of becoming, constantly being enacted.

Each Participant Brings to Interpersonal Communication a Self That Is Offered as the Basic "Commodity" to Be Negotiated through Communication   When labor representatives sit down at the bargaining table, they have a "commodity" that they can offer to management representatives—the efforts of their members to produce the services or products of the company. Similarly, management has a "commodity" that it can offer to labor—wages and benefits. Each "side" in the negotiating process has commodities desired by and offered to the other as "bargaining chips." The same principle holds true when individuals negotiate their interpersonal relationships. Each person brings to the situation a "commodity" desired by and offered to the other. In the case of interpersonal communication, that personal commodity is the self of the individual communicator.

In Chapter 2 we discussed that part of each communicator's self is included in the relationship to the extent that the participant contributes actions to the relational patterns. Furthermore, the relationship neither demands nor desires more than a small portion of the actions of any individual participant. You thus negotiate a relationship with another person by offering certain actions (parts of your self) extended toward the other person. Other persons also "offer" actions or parts of their selves to you.

Together, you and your relational partner create a pattern of interaction that defines your interpersonal relationship. The more actions you offer and that are synchronized with the actions of the other person, the more of your self is included in the relationship and the more likely it is that your relationship reflects a high level of intimacy and intensity. In other words, you risk part of your self every time you act toward the other person during interpersonal communication. In essence, you offer that part of your self to the relationship and obligate that part of your self to the relationship.

Interpersonal Communication Involves an Interactional "Settlement" That May or May Not Incorporate All the Offers of Each Participant's Self   Interpersonal communication as negotiation always involves some element of risk. Negotiation renders individuals susceptible to certain obligations. By engaging in interaction, people automatically subject their selves to some obligations and restrict somewhat their own absolute freedom of choice. No longer do you have the right to do *anything* that you please; you give up some part of that right when you respond to the actions of another person. Your offering of your self to the relationship in the form of communicative actions does not necessarily mean that you have synchronized your offer into the interactional patterns. The other person has the choice of accepting your offer, rejecting it, ignoring it, or making a counteroffer. You may feel very attracted to the other person and offer a commitment that he or she may not wish to accept. For example, Symon suggests to Megan that they "go steady" and give up dating other people (an offer incorporating obligation and commitment). Megan likes Symon but she also likes dating Charlie and Dave and Eddie. Hence, she makes a counteroffer that they continue dating and think about going steady at some time in the future. The result, in terms of the definition of the relationship, is that Symon has offered a part of his self (his behaviors), but Megan does not accept his offer. After all, the acceptance of any offer from the other person typically obligates the selves of both partners. When Symon offered an obligation on his future behavior to forsake dating other people, Megan, by accepting his offer, would also be obligating her own future behavior.

Self-offers, by themselves, do not define the relationship. But the synchronization and reciprocity of self-offers in the pattern of interaction (requiring self-offers of both partners) does define the relationship. In this case, Symon has self-offered and Megan has also self-offered. Because Megan's self-offer is not congruent with Symon's, it is more aptly described as a counteroffer. At this point the relationship is not well defined because no reciprocity or synchronization is evident. The definition of their relationship will depend on their further interaction and, of course, the recurrence of the reciprocated and synchronized self-offers.

Further, not all offers involve commodities of significant value. That is, not every offer of your self involves a significant part of your self. Your contributions to any conversation may involve topics or interests that do not vitally concern you. Your interactions with friends at work, for example, may be restricted to conversational topics involving your work. You don't discuss topics, such as religion or politics, that you consider important to your self-concept. You don't invite your work partners to your home. You don't offer any part of your self to the relationship that goes beyond the time spent at work. And the other people at work offer no vital parts of self to you.

The result of restricting your self-offers is to limit your interpersonal communication to the work environment. Thus, your relationship does not extend beyond the boundaries of your work context. But your relationship may not demand any greater variety of self-offers; any greater degree of commitment may not even be desirable. You and your relational partners may have highly synchronized and reciprocated work-related interaction patterns that are satisfying.

When two people get together in an act of interpersonal communication, what do they do? Primarily, they talk. When people communicate, what do they talk about? If you answer this question by merely listing topics of conversation (such as the weather, last night's basketball scores, Johnny's new girlfriend, Joan's new car), you are looking at communication only superficially. When they are negotiating what their relationship is going to be, people use such topics in order to discover the answers to questions they consider essential to their eventual "settlement"—the definition of their relationship. Those questions important to negotiating the relationship are known as *issues*.

ISSUES

Interpersonal communication is principally talk about specific issues that need to be addressed so that some agreement is possible. In formalized negotiations (such as those between labor and management in a collective bargaining situation), the negotiators begin by trying to discover their points of agreement and disagreement. Each of these points is an issue—a question that, until answered, is a topic to be negotiated or resolved (Rieke & Sillars, 1993). Some issues are common to virtually every act of interpersonal communication, while others are common to particular stages of the developing relationship. Still other issues are unique to the specific individuals and the relationship they have negotiated. But all interpersonal communication revolves around one or more relational issues.

In the following pages we will discuss two general types of issues that are typical of most interpersonal communication: *informational issues* and *relational issues* (Adams, 1985). Some of these issues need to be resolved before people can move on to others, and some are typical of particular types of interpersonal relationships. But all involve questions that will guide much of the talk occurring during interpersonal communication.

Informational Issues

Recall that the beginning stages of interpersonal communication involve the need to reduce uncertainty (Berger & Calabrese, 1975). The situation is new to both participants, and each person is new to the other. The opening stages of such conversations include attempts to reduce uncertainty about the situation and the other person. At such times, certain relational issues are of paramount importance: Who am I? Who is this other person? Do we have anything at all in common? Is it worth my time to continue talking with this person? Will I ever see this person again? Do I want to see this person again? Each of these questions (and many more like them) is an issue that the participants attempt to answer during their initial conversations.

The informational issues peculiar to the beginning stages of interpersonal communication are rather simple. They arise from the newness of the situation and the other person; they arise from a simple lack of information. Hence, communicators find such issues rather easily resolved. All they need to do is acquire information about the other person.

Most of you are fairly skilled at resolving informational issues. You engage in small talk. It is difficult to imagine that the issues addressed by small talk are potentially points of disagreement or conflict. They are simply questions that arise from a state of ignorance—that is, a lack of information. But it takes more than just information to resolve other issues. When their conversation begins to involve issues of each person's self in relation to the other, the communicators find that they need more than information to resolve *relational issues.*

Relational Issues

Two relational issues are fundamental to all interpersonal communication: Who am I in relation to you? Who are you in relation to me? Of course, these are the issues as each individual communicator would phrase them interpersonally. At the interpersonal or relational level, these same issues describe the talk between the communicators and involve three different classes of issues: (1) *self-as-object,* (2) *self-as-other,* and (3) *self-as-relational* issues. Although other issues may be important to specific stages of development or specific situations, these three classes of issues are basic to all of interpersonal communication.

Self-as-Object Issues   When interacting about self-as-object issues, neither participant is really taking the other person's experiences, attitudes, or interests into account. Figure 6-1 illustrates a conversation between Symon and Megan when they are addressing self-as-object issues. Symon and Megan are engaged in conversation about some topic (denoted as "X" in Figure 6-1). Symon orients his self toward the topic X, and Megan also orients her self toward the common topic X. Symon contributes to the conversation about X only his own personal experiences, attitudes, and interests. Similarly, Megan contributes only her own personal experiences, attitudes, and interests to the conversation about X.

Interpersonal communication addressing self-as-object issues might look something like this:

SYMON: I really had a tough day at work today. Virtually everything seemed to go wrong.

MEGAN: My day was pretty normal. I don't know why that is. Some days seem to go pretty fast; others seem to just drag.

SYMON: The first thing that happened was I walked in the door, and the boss

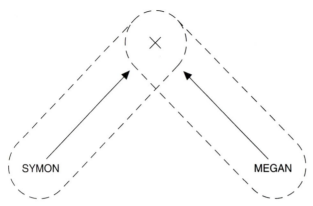

FIGURE 6-1 Orientation of interaction regarding
self-as-object issues.

> was all over me. He wanted to know why I was late. I wasn't late, at
> least not very late.
> MEGAN: Yeah, I know what you mean. I remember last week I was just two
> minutes late, and Jeri wanted to know whether I tied one on the night
> before.
> SYMON: Yeah, really. Then I just couldn't seem to concentrate. I kept looking
> at the clock all day. It just didn't seem to move.
> MEGAN: Yeah, I've had days like that, too. Sometimes 5 o'clock just never
> seems to come.

Self-as-object interaction is essentially conversation in which each communicator defines his or her self in relation to a common topic. Individual selves are offered as experiential beings or as objects embodying a vast repertoire of experiences (Adams, 1985). Each person takes turns addressing the topic, but rarely do they talk about the other person's comment as it relates to their own individual experiences. The above conversation is a series of that-same-thing-happened-to-me comments. Neither person attempts to define his or her self in relation to the other. As a result, two individual selves are related coincidentally to a single topic of conversation. Such conversation means repeatedly taking turns, with each person using the turn to "do his or her own thing."

Have you ever had a joke-telling session with friends? The interaction is very similar. One person tells a joke, the others laugh, and then another person takes a turn telling a joke. You contribute to this conversation as respondent to the other person's joke, but your real contribution is your own joke. So you "wait your turn" to tell it. You have probably often found yourself in such conversations and may get the feeling that each person is trying to top the others. As a result, you probably begin paying less attention to the others' jokes and spending more effort trying (often desperately) to remember the good jokes that you heard at some time in the distant past.

Any individual's experience of a topic is "offered," in a number of different ways (Adams, 1985). First, interactants can specify the degree of their direct involvement with the topic with comments such as, "I have to admit I started looking through the poems today" or "I really had a tough day at work today." Second, interactants can indirectly connect themselves to the topic with comments such as, "My brother lives in Flagstaff" or "I have a sister-in-law who has that condition." Third, interactants can offer personal claims drawn from their experiences with comments such as, "I'd stick with exercise for fitness" or "I think it's a lot more open for discussion now than it was years ago." Fourth, interactants can offer conjectures about possible future decisions made on the basis of their experience with comments such as, "I hope to do marriage and family counseling" or "I would never move to a snowier place."

The self-as-object issue reflects the repertoire of individual's experiences. Each interactant orients self toward a topic defined by some personal experiences. The interactants then can indicate the nature and extent of their experiences, draw claims from their experiences, and project hopes, dreams, and decisions yet to be made. Since each person's experiences are different from those of anyone else, self-as-object issues define the relationship in terms of independent selves.

Self-as-Other Issues Interaction concerning *self-as-other issues* takes the form of one person telling the other about his or her experiences and the other person talking about those same experiences (Adams, 1985). Figure 6-2 illustrates conversation surrounding self-as-other issues. In attempting to resolve self-as-other issues, Symon orients his self toward some topic and Megan orients her self toward Symon. (Of course, either Symon or Megan could be oriented to the other person who is, in turn, oriented to the topic.) The communication addressing self-as-other issues is similar to the interaction of a therapist with a client. The client contributes self experiences and the therapist encourages the client's talk about those experiences. The therapist is a helper, a respondent, a sympathetic listener—but not an active contributor of self experiences.

The following conversation between Symon and Megan is reminiscent of self-as-other interaction:

SYMON: Boy, this finger hurts! I was playing basketball yesterday, and I jammed my little finger on the ball. It's really sore!

MEGAN: Have you tried soaking it in cold water? That's what I always do—to keep it from swelling.

SYMON: Yeah, I did that right away, and I think it helped some. Actually, it didn't hurt too much last night. I mean I didn't have any trouble sleeping. But I woke up this morning, and I could hardly move it.

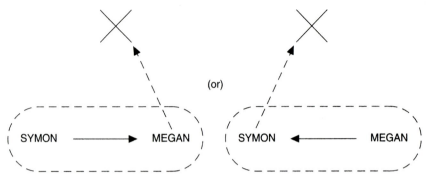

FIGURE 6-2 Orientation of interaction regarding self-as-other issues.

MEGAN: Maybe you bumped it in the night while you were sleeping.
SYMON: I don't think so. But I was sleeping. How do I know if I bumped it?
MEGAN: Maybe you ought to see a doctor. You could have broken a bone
    or something.
SYMON: No, I don't think so. I've jammed fingers lots of times.
MEGAN: Still, it can't hurt to see a doctor. You'd probably feel better.
SYMON: Well, maybe you're right.

Both Symon and Megan are contributing to the same topic—Symon's
jammed finger. But that topic "belongs to" Symon in the sense that it is his
personal or self experience. Megan thus contributes to the topic indirectly.
She does not contribute her own experiences concerning jammed fingers;
rather, she attempts to provide assistance to Symon's experience. She is the
sympathetic listener, the "therapist" attempting to help Symon.

Of course, self-as-other interaction doesn't require Megan's contribution to be positive or helpful. She could also be totally unsympathetic and
confrontative, as in the following interaction:

SYMON: Boy, this finger hurts! I was playing basketball yesterday, and I
    jammed my little finger on the ball. It's really sore!
MEGAN: Why didn't you soak it in cold water? Any fool knows that's what
    you do to keep it from swelling.
SYMON: But I did that right away, and I think it helped some. Actually, it
    didn't hurt too much last night. I mean I didn't have any trouble
    sleeping. But I woke up this morning, and I could hardly move it.
MEGAN: You should have taped it to the next finger. Then you wouldn't
    have hurt it while you were sleeping.
SYMON: I didn't hurt it while I was sleeping. It just felt worse this morning.
MEGAN: How do you know you didn't bump it in the night? You were
    sound asleep.
SYMON: Well, I don't think I did. I've jammed fingers lots of times. I don't
    know why this one hurts so much.

MEGAN: Oh, don't be such a crybaby. It's just a little finger sprain. You'd
    think you broke your leg or something.
SYMON: Well, it hurts just the same.

This interaction continues to revolve around Symon's personal experience and Megan's indirect contributions to the topic as she responds to
Symon's experience. The interaction continues to address a self-as-other
issue, but Megan's "therapeutic" role has changed. She is no longer sympathetic, no longer helpful. She is unsympathetic and confrontative. But the
relational issue being negotiated during this interaction, self-as-other, remains the same.

Self-as-Relational Issues   When communicators attempt to negotiate
their relationship through *self-as-relational issues,* their orientation is not to
the topic or the other person so much as it is toward the relationship that
binds them together (Adams, 1985). Figure 6-3 illustrates the interaction of
Symon and Megan as they attempt to resolve self-as-relational issues. They
continue to be talking about some topic, X, but they are actually addressing
it from the viewpoint of their interpersonal relationship. The following
interaction reflects Symon and Megan engaging in interaction addressing
a self-as-relational issue:

SYMON: I've been thinking. Maybe we ought to go to summer school next
    year. I think we could get out a lot sooner if we could pick up a few
    credits during the summer.
MEGAN: Oh, I don't know. I think we could really have a lot of fun during
    the summer if we didn't have to be hitting the books all the time.
SYMON: Aw, come on! It could be great. We'll still have time to have fun.
    We could play tennis after classes are over; we could swim during the
    noon hour. And we'd still have the weekends.
MEGAN: Maybe so, but can we afford it? Tuition and fees are pretty high for
    just a few credits.

FIGURE 6-3
Orientation of
interaction regarding
self-as-relational issues.

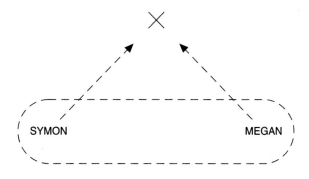

SYMON: It's gotta be paid sometime—either during the summer or next spring.

MEGAN: Well, it's something to think about, anyway.

Most importantly, self-as-relational interaction assumes that the two selves of the communicators are interconnected. That is, the self of one relational partner defines (and is defined by) its relation to the self of the other. Self-as-relational offers function to show recognition of what is "between" interactants. Interactants recognize coincidental selves by explicitly demarcating the boundaries of overlap between the selves with remarks such as "but I know by what you are telling me that we're two of a kind." Interactants also recognize the mutuality of their individual selves by discussing joint activities, for example, "I've been thinking maybe we ought to go to summer school next year," and joint activities with others, "That's another couple we should have over." Their conversation includes more than a few references to "we" and "us."

By contrast, self-as-object interaction may include the same experience (such as having a tough day at work), but each person's experience is separate from the other's. The fact that both communicators have the same experience is coincidental. That is, Symon had a tough day at work and Megan had a tough day at work. Self-as-object interaction includes two experiences, Symon's and Megan's. Their interaction concerns the coincidence that Symon's experience was similar to Megan's. But in self-as-relational interaction, only one experience is at issue: the single experience of Symon and Megan doing something together.

The issue addressed by the communicators in self-as-relational interaction is the common orientation of both participants: the relationship, rather than the individual self of the communicator. Often the relational partners focus their self-as-relational interaction on a joint experience or activity that involves both communicators, but they could be talking about any topic that emphasizes their togetherness.

In other words, self-as-relational issues may also involve interaction in which an individual communicator expresses his or her own individual desires or opinions but bases those intrapersonal desires or opinions on criteria derived from the relationship. The following interaction concerns the topic of Symon's personal desires, but both participants address Symon's desire from the viewpoint of their interpersonal relationship:

SYMON: Did I tell you I've got a line on another job? It means I would be making more money, too.

MEGAN: That's great.

SYMON: I'm not so sure. It also means that I'll be working every other weekend. We wouldn't be able to see each other much.

MEGAN: But still, more money and all. We'll probably survive.

SYMON: I don't wanna just survive. I want to keep seeing you.

MEGAN: Well, how late do you work? We can still get together when you're not working.

SYMON: I don't get off until 10 at night. And you're working all day. We'd never see each other.

MEGAN: We can still work it out. After all, we'll have all Sunday afternoon to be together.

SYMON: I'm not sure that's enough. I don't think I'll take that job.

MEGAN: But it means more money. Just think what we can do with that.

This conversation concerns only Symon's experience—his new job. But Symon and Megan discuss his new job *not* in terms of Symon or Megan individually but in terms of their relationship. They continue to talk in "we" terms: *we* will survive, *we* can use the extra money. All the advantages and disadvantages of the new job become topics associated with its effect on their relationship and their relationship's effect on it. The issue addressed in this interaction continues to be self as relational, even though the topic under discussion concerns only the activity or experience of a single communicator rather than one involving both.

If communicators are talking about self-as-relational issues, they must already have negotiated some relationship in the past. Clearly, two people who have just met and are getting acquainted with each other would hardly be engaging in self-as-relational interaction. Only when a relationship has been established somewhat and both parties recognize that some relational settlement has occurred can they address self-as-relational issues.

In summary, self-as-object issues may occur at any time during the developing relationship. New acquaintances seeking areas of common interest will engage in discussions concerning coincidental experiences. Highly developed relationships will also include a fair amount of self-as-object interaction. A husband and wife will typically discuss their experiences when they get together at the end of the day. They will "catch each other up" on what happened to each of them during the day (Adams, 1985). And those discussions involve taking turns in telling each other what they did since they saw each other last. You already know that interpersonal communication is discontinuous. When friends get together after a period of separation, they will typically engage in "whatcha been doin'?" interaction, which will appear amazingly similar to the interaction of self-as-object issues.

Self-as-other interaction can also occur at virtually any stage of relational development and in virtually any kind of relationship. You often find yourself needing just to talk with someone. When you feel that need, you often seek out a trusted friend who you know will take on the role of a sympathetic listener. But you will also find yourself discussing self-as-other issues even with a new acquaintance. To illustrate, Kathy's interactions with her students are almost entirely devoted to self-as-other issues. Her students, for the most part, are acquaintances, and they often relate to her their experiences and observations about class or school work. Kathy discovers a great deal about her students, and she suspects that they learn little about her in comparison to what she learns. She is, after all, only an indirect contributor to any central topic, which focuses almost exclusively on their experiences.

Self-as-object, self-as-other, and self-as-relational issues are three basic relational issues inherent in any communicative event. The task of the relational partners is to continuously negotiate these individual orientations cooperatively into an ongoing relational definition. Interactants enact negotiation through strategies. Enactment, you will recall, is itself a process involving interactants acting toward each other and their informational environment.

STRATEGIES

The fundamental unit of interpersonal communication is the *strategy*. Every time you offer your self to the other person during the process of interpersonal communication, you are using a strategy. Why call it a strategy? Because you are always trying to manipulate the other person? Absolutely not! Because interpersonal communication is inherently *consequential* (Kellermann, 1992). Every time you offer a comment to a conversation, you potentially affect the negotiated outcome of the interpersonal relationship. Each strategy focuses on one of the issues that must be resolved in order to negotiate the relationship. To the extent that the comment helps resolve that issue and fits into the pattern of interaction, it is a strategy.

Normally the term "strategy" brings to mind some notion of warfare in which the general adopts a strategy (or tactic) in order to "win" the war (or, at least, the battle). And some strategies in interpersonal communication are similar to that. When you feel that the competing part of communication is greater than the cooperative element, you may be very aware of adopting some strategy to "win" the game of interpersonal communication (such as topping the other person's joke with a funnier one of your own). When you are engaged in an interpersonal situation in which you want to persuade the other person or control the other person's response (such as trying to impress your new acquaintance), you will develop strategies with a high degree of awareness. But probably most often, you communicate with other people strategically, even though you are not aware that our comments (and those of the other person) are strategies.

When you use a strategy during interpersonal communication, you are not always aware that you are doing so (Kellermann, 1992). You aren't always aware of what portion of your self you have offered to the conversation at the time you offer it. For instance, you often say some things that you later regret having said. You often say some things without thinking about them and later have them come back to haunt you.

At other times, though, you are very aware of what self you are presenting to the other person. In certain situations, you choose your words carefully (that is, are highly aware of what you are saying) in order to get some desired response from the other person. For example, you might want to impress that new acquaintance (you know, the attractive one you'd like to get to know better) with some clever comment in the hope that he or she will respond favorably. The important point is not whether you are aware of what you are saying or doing during communication but that every comment (that is, every self-offer) made during interpersonal communication fits into some pattern and potentially affects the subsequent relationship that is negotiated.

According to at least one psychologist (Mangam, 1981), people are quite unaware of most of the strategies they use in interpersonal communication:

> Much of what is deemed to be "normal" interaction . . . is nonproblematic. Social actors . . . approach interaction already influenced by past social experience and, to a marked extent, their choices (insofar as they are aware of choice at all) are limited, if not determined, by the patterns of behaviour most frequently used by other social actors past and present in what are taken to be similar circumstances. (p. 198)

In other words, you don't negotiate your interpersonal relationships with other people as though you were totally inexperienced. You don't attempt to negotiate relationships anew on each and every social occasion. To a large extent, you are the product of your own past experiences. You know what strategies to use in virtually every interpersonal situation because you've "been there" before. You approach the new communicative situation from your experiences of having been in similar situations in the past. Consequently, you use the strategies that proved successful in the past, and you probably aren't even aware that you are doing so. Only when the situation is new or when some change in the relationship is occurring are you likely to be aware of the strategic choices you are making as you communicate (see Special Section: Communication and Consciousness, *Western Journal of Speech Communication*, 1986, vol. 50, pp. 1–101).

The number of potential strategies you could use in any given situation is undoubtedly extremely large. And, of course, the same comment may function as one kind of strategy in one pattern of interaction and as a different kind of strategy when it occurs within a different pattern of interaction. It is probably best to think of strategy, then, as an *action* you contribute to the pattern of *interaction*. Therefore, your strategy performs some function because you direct your action toward some relational issue.

In the following pages we shall discuss the various types of strategies in terms of how a particular strategic comment functions within the inter-action pattern—whether you direct your strategy toward your self, toward the other person, toward the relationship, toward the situation or context, toward the communicative goal, or toward a specific issue. The following sections discuss each type of strategy and provide some representative examples of each.

Self-Directed Strategies

One class of strategies focuses the topics of the interaction on your own self and your self-offers. The purpose of such a strategy is to inform the other person of a direct connection between your behavior and your self. When you use a *self-directed strategy,* you are essentially telling the other person how to interpret your self-offer. Most of your strategies do not include an explicit rationale for the behavior. You leave it to the other person to draw some inference about the internal motives or desires that prompt you to behave as you do. On the other hand, you also have the option of telling the other person "how come" you're doing what you're doing. When you choose that option, you are employing a self-directed strategy.

Account Giving   Probably the most common self-directed strategy is giv-ing *accounts.* The communicator strategizes the comment by telling the other person explicitly the reason or reasons for the behavior. In other words, the communicator *accounts for* his or her behavior. Accounts often occur when one of the communicators is reproached for committing some offense or error in a previous comment. (Antaki, 1987; McLaughlin, Cody, & Rosenstein, 1983). As a reply to the reproach, the accounts serve to somehow disconfirm, confirm, placate, mitigate, aggravate, or somehow manage the reproach (McLaughlin et al., 1983).

When accused of committing some offense, the communicator has several options or strategies to account for the alleged erroneous behavior (Semin & Manstead, 1983). One, the offender can provide an account that tells the other person that the alleged offense did not, in fact, occur, such as, "I didn't say that at all." Two, the offender can account for the offensive behavior by attributing the problem to the other person's faulty perception or hearing, as in "I think you misunderstood what I was saying" or "You didn't hear me correctly." Three, the offender can attribute the alleged offense to the situation that forced the improper behavior—"I know that was wrong, but I didn't have any choice." Four, the offender can account for the problem by denying responsibility for the problematic behavior, as in "I didn't mean to say that," "That's not what I intended to say," or "I'm sorry, that was a stupid thing to say." These kinds of accounts attempt to provide excuses or justifications for one's own behavior, particularly when that behavior was erroneous or offensive.

Account giving may also be a strategy to make your intentions or purposes clear to the other person. In other words, you include with your comment the reason (that is, your internal motivation or intention) for making that comment. You will often hear yourself saying something like "I'm just trying to help you" or "I'm saying this only because I really like you." You may also tell the other person how to react to your comment (for example, "You can take it or leave it. That's up to you") or how you will react to his or her response (for example, "You can certainly disagree with me. That won't hurt my feelings").

By using accounts you attempt, in every case, to inform the other person explicitly of the connection between your observable behavior and your unobservable intentions, desires, motivations, attitudes, and so on. Of course, saying what your intentions are does not make your statement any more or less truthful. You have probably heard people tell you that they wouldn't be upset if you didn't follow their advice. But then, when you disagreed with their advice, they did become upset. Adapting normally to the benefits of past experience, you probably agreed with their advice the next time, even when you really disagreed. In that case, both of you used strategies that were not truthful, but you succeeded in maintaining your relationship.

Flagging   A second type of self-directed strategy is called *flagging*. If you want the other person to be clear in interpreting the function of your comment, you can "flag" it by telling the other person what its *function* is in the interaction pattern. Flags are a form of pre-indexing (Beach & Dunning, 1982) discussed in Chapter 5. By telling the other person this, you assure yourself that the other will find it difficult to misperceive your comment. Typically, flagging is used to introduce your contribution, as in the following: "This is just an idea off the top of my head." "I'd like to say something in support of that." "I'm going to disagree and explain why I'm disagreeing." "Let me check to see that I've got this straight." "Let me tell you what I think you are saying."

Flagging is a strategy that attempts to avoid the problems that ensue when the other person misperceives how your comment functions during the interaction. Hewitt and Stokes (1975) refer to these flagging strategies as *disclaimers*. Disclaimers function to manage impressions and protect the identities of individuals by attempting to avoid potential problems such as misunderstandings, misinterpretations, conflict, embarrassment, and so on. By introducing your comment with a flagging strategy, you are informing the other person of what to expect and how to interpret your comment. Because it tries to avoid misperceptions on the other person's part, flagging is often helpful. Of course, a flagging strategy is no guarantee that your statement will not be misperceived. As Peter Honey (1976) points out, "What is fatal is to flag a piece of behaviour incorrectly." You have probably encountered people who continually flag their behavior with introductory comments such as "I'm not really disagreeing with you. I just want to understand." You just know that this "flag" is problematic. These people don't want to understand; they want to disagree and use the flag in a transparent attempt to appear open-minded. Soon you come to expect this strategy from these people, and you react in exactly the opposite way the other person had hoped. You hear the person say, "I'm not really disagreeing with you," and your immediate reaction is "Here comes the disagreement."

Whether it is giving accounts or flagging, the use of a self-directed strategy attempts to make explicit what is otherwise implicit during the process of communication. You give accounts for your behavior and explicitly tell the other person what portion of the hidden self has prompted your behavior. You flag your comments with an explicit description of how your comment functions within the pattern of interaction and try to shape the other person's response to it. By choosing self-directed strategies, you attempt to control, shape, or influence the other person's reactions to your interactive behaviors.

Keep in mind that the self-directed strategy is a type of self-offer that the other person may accept or reject. In attempting to shape the other person's perceptions of your self and your self-offer, you have no assurance that your strategy will do so successfully. Whether your strategy works as you intended it to can only be discovered in the interaction patterns that follow.

Other-Directed Strategies

You may also negotiate your relationship with another person by using an *other-directed strategy* that focuses the interaction on the other person. Other-directed strategies function to "do something to" the other person and may be either competitive or cooperative. Other-directed strategies are often competitive in the sense that you are attempting to control the other person's response, to get the other person to do what you want him or her to do. On the other hand, such strategies may also be cooperative if they function to tell the other person that he or she is important or valued. Other-directed strategies often fall into one of two categories: those designed to gain the other person's compliance and those designed to confirm or disconfirm the other person's self.

Compliance Gaining   The class of strategies known as *compliance gaining* involves an attempt to persuade or manipulate the other person (Miller, Boster, Roloff, & Seibold, 1977, 1987). Using a compliance-gaining strategy implies that you see the interpersonal communication situation as a competitive "game" that you are "playing to win." That is, you want the other person to do something. When you want to persuade the other person toward a particular action or belief, you use a compliance-gaining strategy. When you want to control or manipulate the other person's response, you use a compliance-gaining strategy. Simply put, compliance-gaining strategies are "performed in the service of a personal or interpersonal agenda" (Miller et al., 1987, p. 93).

Compliance-gaining strategies implicitly view the other person as an object of your persuasive attempts. Compliance-gaining strategies are, of course, the life blood of advertising agencies. Their task is to get the consumer (the TV viewer, radio listener, or magazine reader) to purchase a given product. In other words, advertisers want the consumer to comply with their purpose in communicating with them. Advertising strategies are inherently directed at the "other person"—the consumer.

Two decades ago, psychologists Marwell and Schmitt (1967) developed a list of potential compliance-gaining strategies. Their list (or some variation of it) remains a relatively complete list of such strategies and continues to be used today by scholars interested in exploring how communicators attempt to manipulate each other during interpersonal communication. The following list is adapted from Marwell and Schmitt's original typology:

1. *Promise:* "If you comply, I will reward you."
2. *Threat:* "If you do not comply, I will punish you."
3. *Debt:* "You should comply because you owe me past favors . . . because of all we have meant to each other."
4. *Liking:* "I am pleasant and friendly toward you so that you will be in a good frame of mind and will comply."
5. *Moral appeal:* "You should comply because it is the right thing to do."
6. *Self-feeling:* "You will feel better about yourself if you comply." (positive) "You will feel worse about yourself if you don't comply." (negative)
7. *Altercasting:* "If you were a good person, you would comply." (positive) "Only a bad person would not comply." (negative)
8. *Altruism:* "I really need you to comply, so do it for me . . . do it for someone else, not for yourself."
9. *Social esteem:* "People will think highly of you if you comply." (positive) "People will think poorly of you if you do not comply." (negative)

Each item on this list of compliance-gaining strategies contains basically one of two strategies—reward or punishment—to persuade others to do what is wanted. Whatever compliance-gaining strategy is chosen, the aim is essentially to reward or punish the other person. The idea is to gain the compliance of other people by saying something like "If you do what I want, you will be rewarded in some positive manner" or "If you fail to do what I want, you will be punished in some negative manner." Most people would probably consider such strategies rather heavy-handed and too blunt to be effective. But it is amazing how many people are swayed by such appeals, especially when used subtly.

Not infrequently, however, people use compliance-gaining strategies in a less-than-subtle manner, and their strategies have a boomerang effect. Aub was "pitched" by an insurance sales agent years ago. His attempts to gain Aub's compliance were not at all subtle and were almost exclusively based on punishments rather than rewards. He asked Aub the same question countless times. He phrased the question differently each time, but the question always came out sounding like "If you *really* loved your family [moral appeal], you would buy additional life insurance—not for yourself, but for them [altruism]." In Aub's interpretation of his compliance-gaining strategy, the insurance agent was saying, "If you don't buy more life insurance, then you don't really love your family." This strategy boomeranged. Aub reacted very negatively to it and remembered the name of the insurance company represented by that agent. When Aub did buy additional life insurance some years later, he made sure that he did not purchase it from that company.

A too obvious attempt to gain the other person's compliance may create a negative reaction. People typically don't like the feeling of being manipulated. They resent not only the persuasive strategy but also the person who attempts to manipulate them. Some advertising agencies have apparently recognized this fact and seem to have discarded many of their traditional "hard sell" strategies. The most successful TV commercials today are subtle. They appear to persuade consumers by entertaining them. You tend to remember the commercials that are funny, clever, and often better than the program they are interrupting. A strategy for selling the product is effective, of course, only insofar as the consumer remembers the product being advertised in the commercial and actually purchases it. The continuing success of "lite" beer commercials suggests that subtle compliance gaining through entertainment may be a very effective strategy in communicating with a mass audience.

Miller et al. (1987) warn that on the surface, the compliance-gaining strategies appear rather simple. However, these strategies are used in interaction and often in circumstances that are rather complex. Miller et al. point out that most research investigating the selection of strategies has ignored the interactive character of compliance gaining. Too often only an initial compliance attempt or opening strategy is studied separate from the larger sequence of behaviors.

Interpersonal Confirmation/Disconfirmation A second type of other-directed strategy involves the act of *confirmation* and its negative form *disconfirmation*. We discussed in Chapter 3 that part of the work in interpersonal communication is the management of impressions by both participants; both present their selves to each other. There are three responses to offers of self-presentation: confirmation, rejection, or disconfirmation (Watzlawick, Beavin, & Jackson, 1967). Confirmation attempts to tell the other person that her or his self-image is worthwhile or acceptable. For example, you might respond, "You have an excellent point there. Good idea." When you respond with rejection, you recognize the other person but you deny their self-presentation—"You can't possibly mean what you are saying!" A disconfirming strategy, on the other hand, goes beyond rejection and attempts to deny the other person as a source of the message and even her or his existence or significance. For example, when you disconfirm you may ignore the other person's message completely and treat it as though it had never been said.

The other-directed strategies of confirmation and disconfirmation have not been systematized satisfactorily or consistently demonstrated by researchers. However, a general list of how a person might go about confirming or disconfirming the other person in interpersonal communication has been developed. The following one is derived and adapted from the work of communication scholars, Ken Cissna and Evelyn Sieburg (1981):

Confirming Strategies	Disconfirming Strategies

A. Showing respect
  1. Seriously responding to other's comments
  2. Paying attention when other is speaking
	A. Showing indifference
	  1. Silence, refusal to respond
	  2. Attention wanders or engages in unrelated activities

B. Showing involvement
  1. Maintains eye contact
  2. Maintains closeness, leans toward other
  3. Uses personal language, expresses feelings
	B. Denying involvement
	  1. Avoids eye contact
	  2. Avoids touch, uses "distancing" behaviors
	  3. Uses impersonal language, avoids expressing feelings

C. Accepting communication
  1. Dialogue, awaits turn to talk
  2. Makes relevant comments
	C. Rejecting communication
	  1. Monologue, interrupts, "talks over" other
	  2. Makes irrelevant comments

D. Accepting the other
  1. Expresses praise or agreement
  2. Uses clear and complete messages
  3. Verbal and nonverbal modes of expression agree
	D. Disqualifying the other
	  1. Expresses insults or name calling
	  2. Uses clear and incomplete messages
	  3. Verbal and nonverbal modes are incongruent

A confirming response performs four functions in responding to the other person's self-definition:

1. It expresses recognition of the other's existence.
2. It acknowledges a relationship of affiliation with the other.

3. It expresses awareness of the significance or worth of the other.
4. It accepts or "endorses" the other's self-experience (particularly emotional experiences). (Cissna et al., 1981, p. 259)

A disconfirming response, on the other hand, may be a(n):

1. *Indifferent response* (denying existence or relation).
2. *Impervious response* (denying self-experience of the other).
3. *Disqualifying response* (denying the other's significance). (Cissna et al., 1981, p. 261)

The following conversation includes an indifferent response:

MEGAN: Is dinner ready? I've had a rough day and nobody paid any attention to what I said all day long.
SYMON: That's too bad. What do you want for dinner?

An impervious response might include something like "You don't really mean that; what you're really trying to say is . . ." The impervious response denies the validity of what the other is saying. A disqualifying response is really a put-down of the other's intelligence, trustworthiness, significance, competence, worth, or whatever. Adults disqualify children when they say, "When you're older and have lived a few more years, you'll think differently."

What makes a comment disconfirming or confirming in interpersonal communication? No comment is either confirming or disconfirming until and unless the other person perceives the impact it has on his or her self-concept. You may respond with what *you* think is a confirming statement (such as "That's a good idea"), but the other person may perceive your statement as condescending or insincere. Whether a response confirms or disconfirms the other's self is ultimately a matter of the other's perception of the response.

Research by Smilowitz (1985) into confirming and disconfirming responses may serve to explain this point more clearly. His study sought to discover whether effective managers in business organizations "confirmed" their subordinates more often than ineffective managers. It seems reasonable to assume, as Smilowitz did, that effective business managers would tend to be more confirming when they interacted with their subordinates. The results of this research, however, were not totally consistent with this assumption. Subordinates of effective managers perceived that their managers were somewhat (but not much) more confirming than the subordinates of ineffective managers. But the only differences in the way effective managers actually interacted with their subordinates was in their use of disconfirming responses, which were unexpectedly (but only slightly) more frequent than those of ineffective managers.

So what do the results of this study mean for confirming responses in interpersonal communication? One inference is that what *appears* to be a confirming or disconfirming response and what *functions* as a confirming or disconfirming response in conversations are not necessarily identical. Stewart and D'Angelo (1988) concur when they point out that confirming or disconfirming responses are not simply acts that one individual does to another. Disconfirmation and confirmation happens between relational partners; these acts are communicative phenomena. Each partner's actions, intentions, and different ways of interpreting behavior are important.

Although confirming and disconfirming strategies often appear to be the difference between being rude and being polite, a more appropriate interpretation of these other-directed strategies may be the difference between being cooperative and being competitive. When your orientation toward the other is one of cooperation, you tend to participate in the interaction by confirming the other person both verbally and nonverbally. But when you are competitively oriented toward the other person, you will probably tend to use disconfirming strategies.

Be careful of interpreting cooperative and competitive orientations toward the other person to imply that confirming means agreeing and disconfirming means disagreeing. In fact, quite the opposite is often true. When you disagree, you often confirm the worth of the other person's ideas. When disconfirming others, you would be more likely to ignore their comments and, by so doing, tell them "Your ideas aren't important enough for me to disagree with them."

Cooperation and competition, as used in interpersonal communication, are essentially the relationship of one's self to another's self. When you sense that your self is in competition with the other person's, you select strategies that tend to disconfirm the other person's self. In conversation with a persistent and "hard sell" sales agent, you may very well use disconfirming strategies. But if there is no need for your self-concept to compete with the other person's self-concept, you may be likely to be more cooperative. In those situations, you use strategies that keep the interaction flowing smoothly. Those strategies are cooperative and tend to confirm the worth of the other person's self-concept.

Other-directed strategies generally attempt to "do something to" the other person. You can do something good or you can do something bad. Consequently, other-directed strategies tend to have two sides: reward and punishment, cooperation and competition, confirmation and disconfirmation. Although they may originate from a highly personal goal, such as getting others to do what you want them to, other-directed strategies are oriented to the other's self and not your own. This class of relational strategies may be the most familiar of all those discussed in this chapter. And other-directed strategies may be the most commonly used when people communicate. People may be more aware of using other-directed strategies than they are when they use strategies of other types.

Relationship-Directed Strategies

A comment that functions directly to define your relationship with the other person is a *relationship-directed strategy*. Some of these strategies are obvious; others are subtle. Some function to create or initiate change in the relationship; others serve to maintain the existing definition of the relationship. Like all strategies, some relationship-directed strategies are successful; others are complete failures. There are probably hundreds of different kinds of relationship-directed strategies, but our discussions will include only two types: "tie-signs" and "control modes."

Tie-Signs   Sociologist Erving Goffman (1971) coined the term *tie-signs* to refer to objects, acts, events, and expressions that provide evidence of a relational bond that exists between two or more people. Tie-signs may include either verbal or nonverbal behaviors, or both, and function in several different ways. One, they serve to inform the other participant of how you have defined the relationship. Two, they confirm the existing definition of the relationship for the benefit of both participants. Three, they inform people who are within the social context but outside your relationship of the nature of your relationship.

Tie-signs generally fall into one of three different categories: *rituals, markers,* and *change signals.* A ritual is a set of behaviors or events that have been repeated so often that both partners know the meaning of how it confirms the existence of the relationship. To participate in a ritual tie-sign is to have inside information about what to do. And the only way to acquire that inside information is to have participated in the past interactional experiences that created the ritual. A ritual tie-sign "belongs to" the people who created it. An outsider cannot participate in the ritual without appearing out of place. And the ritual of one relationship will not be the ritual of another except by pure coincidence. A ritual is the direct result of repeated interactional experiences by the people in that relationship who then come to identify the ritual with their relationship.

To illustrate, when Kathy was growing up and still living at home, her family had a number of rituals (as does virtually every family) that now often conflict with the individual family rituals of her brother and sisters. For example, on Christmas Eve only one present was opened by each family member. Then on Christmas, before breakfast, Dad would play Santa and hand a present to one family member at a time to open. Everyone else watched as that person opened a present. This would continue until all presents were open. Her brother and sisters all have their own families now, and they have developed their own Christmas rituals. When all the families gather at her folk's house for Christmas, there is quite the discussion on how to "do" Christmas in the attempt to blend the different rituals, which often are very different and appear strange to the other families. Somehow the details always get worked out in the long run. But the point is that these rituals belong to each family and are clearly one of the tie-signs that are identified with family membership.

Tie-sign "markers" are acts or events that lay claim to a territory—in this case, the "territory" of a relationship. When people hold hands in public or walk with their arms around each other, they are telling the world that they have a loving relationship that excludes other people. People often wear similar clothing ("his" and "hers" shirts, for example) that says "We belong together in this relationship, and you aren't part of it." A tie-sign marker may also take the form of idioms, like the ones discussed in Chapter 5 which denote the relationship (as in "I love you") or pet names for each other (most commonly "dear," "sweetheart," or "honey").

Individuals place a great deal of importance on these rituals and public markers of the bonds between people (Duck, 1991). This can be particularly distressing for couples whose relationships are not always approved by society, for example, homosexual couples. Their use of particular markers such as holding hands, dressing alike, and even rings can be particularly problematic and troubling.

Change signals are tie-signs that function quite differently from rituals and markers. Unlike change signals, rituals and markers are not single acts performed by single persons. They are sequences of acts that members of the relationship create and in which they participate together. It is difficult and rather nonsensical, for example, for one person to hold hands. Rituals and markers involve members of the relationship acting out a "script" that is unwritten, but each member of the "drama" knows his or her part. When one of the members fails to perform his or her role adequately, all members of the relationship know that something is wrong. When that happens, the ritual or marker fails to confirm the relationship and, rather, signals to the participants that some change has occurred or is occurring in the relationship.

A change signal, then, is not necessarily an overt "Dear John" announcement, although such an obvious and direct approach would also signal a change in the relational definition. *Change signals* are more typically variations in rituals or markers that become meaningful for the participants because the rituals and markers are so familiar, having been repeated so often in the past. If the rituals and markers define and confirm the relational bonds for the participants (and for observers in the social context), then a variation in those rituals and markers signals that some change is taking place in the relationship.

Control Modes   Relationship-directed strategies that implicitly define the relationship in terms of which participant is "in charge" are known as *control modes* (Millar & Rogers, 1976, 1987; Rogers & Farace, 1975). A comment phrased as a command or an imperative (such as "Shut the door") implicitly defines the relationship with the speaker in charge and the listener deferring to the speaker. A comment that contains an imperative or gives instructions is sometimes called a *one-up comment,* also known as *domineering* or *structuring* the flow of the conversation. One-up comments function to restrict the choices of the recipient, who then has the option to defer to the speaker's control with a *one-down comment.*

Control-mode strategies seem similar to compliance-gaining strategies, but there is a major difference. Whereas an attempt to gain the compliance of the other person assumes that the speaker has some persuasive or manipulative purpose in mind, control-mode strategies are not manipulative. Control modes seek to define the basis of the relationship in one of two ways: equality or difference. For example, the person who was told to shut the door could easily respond with "Shut it yourself." This interaction reveals a relationship based on equality. Neither party gains or relinquishes the position of control or changes who is in charge in the relationship. This relationship, based on equality, is termed a *symmetrical relationship.* If the person had responded to the above command by actually shutting the door, then the respondent would have deferred to the one-up comment with a one-down comment. The resulting relationship is based on difference (one person in charge and the other person agreeing with the definition). It is therefore called a *complementary relationship.*

But not all control-mode strategies are one-up or one-down strategies. Some comments (indeed, most comments in everyday interaction) define the relationship as one of equivalence—neither person defines self as "in charge" and neither defers to the other's control. Naturally, the use of academic jargon demands that such comments also be given a label. Domineering comments are known as one-up comments, deferring comments are known as one-down comments, and equivalence-defining comments are called *one-across comments.*

In most interpersonal relationships, participants move rather easily from symmetrical (neither person in charge) to complementary (one person in charge) interaction and back again. During certain periods of their communication, they may engage in competitive symmetry (one-up comments responding to one-up comments), and at other times they will engage in complementary interaction (one-down comments deferring to one-up comments). Much of the interaction of people in long-term relationships will probably be equivalent symmetry (one-across comments responding to one-across comments) in an "I'm OK and you're OK" pattern of communication. In fact, healthy relationships that maintain themselves over a long period of time will include frequent changes between symmetrical and complementary interaction (see Fisher & Drecksel, 1983). This is a topic for Chapter 11.

Situation-Directed Strategies

Situation-directed strategies are coping strategies that allow the communicator to define the situation so that he or she no longer feels a victim of circumstances. Occasionally you may become involved in a communicative situation and feel helpless, not in control of the situation. The situation may be one that is new to you or not similar to any communicative situation in your past experience. The situation may be one in which you feel threatened. You feel that the other person is attempting to exert control, and you don't want to defer to that control. For whatever reason, you may find yourself in a situation that requires the use of relational strategies aimed at defining the situation itself. You would then use coping strategies to regain some control over the definition of the context, typically a social context.

Coping, or situation-directed, strategies are comments that make explicit what is typically a problem of perception. Recall that individual human beings are amazingly skillful at perceiving what they want to perceive. When the situation is unfavorable, humans cope by perceiving selectively and creatively so as to perceive the situation in a more favorable light. A list of representative coping strategies, then, might include the following:

Reframing: Explicitly redefining the other person's comment so that your comment provides an interpretation that differs from the intended meaning of the other person.

Confronting: Explicitly telling the other person that his or her comment was out of line or inappropriate.

Attributing control: Explicitly telling the other person what prompted his or her comment; may involve disconfirming.

Ignoring: Continuing the interaction as though the other person's comment had never occurred; may involve changing topics.

Being fatalistic: Accepting the situation as beyond your control (as in "It's God's will") and minimizing your own discomfort.

Using humor: Making fun of the other person's comment or explicitly refusing to take the comment seriously.

Countering: Responding to the other person's controlling comment with a controlling comment of equal or greater intensity.

Withdrawing: Terminating the conversation with a comment that explicitly indicates that you are leaving the situation.

Situation-directed strategies are probably less common than other kinds. They occur only at those times when the individual doesn't know what to do. As a result, they rarely occur in relationships that have had some time to develop. They are probably most appropriate in those first encounters with strangers in which you don't feel comfortable. They may also occur with people (for instance, in a work context) who "bug you" but with whom you cannot avoid social encounters.

Goal-Directed Strategies

To understand how *goal-directed strategies* work in the process of interpersonal communication, we need to have a clear sense of what we mean by the word "goal." Robert Hinde (1979, pp. 25ff) has distinguished between what he calls "ballistic behaviour" and "goal-directed behaviour." Ballistic behavior is like hunting pheasants or shooting down enemy bombers. You have a desired outcome (hitting the target), you aim your weapon, and you fire your gun. The result of ballistic behavior is a hit or a miss, success or failure. Goal-directed behavior is quite different. According to Hinde, "The minimum requirement for behaviour to be regarded as goal-directed is a feedback loop capable of assessing the discrepancy between the present situation and the goal situation, and of initiating appropriate corrections to the current behaviour" (p. 25).

A goal-directed strategy is an attempt to adapt to a communicative situation that does not appear to be fulfilling your goals. But if the relationship is to achieve your goal or desired outcome, you need to modify the current pattern of interaction. You won't achieve your goals by merely setting your sights on some desired outcome and "shooting for it." You first need to know what is wrong with the current situation. In other words, you need a feedback loop that first allows you to gain an understanding of the problem in the status quo and then to devise a strategy to correct it.

For example, you have a relationship with a certain person and think that your relationship is not going the way you want. You want to do something about it. What do you do? First, you have to compare the present relationship with the relationship you want. Second, you have to devise some strategy to change the direction of the developing relationship. Goal-directed strategies thus function to *change* the direction of the developing relationship from the status quo. Naturally, if the present relationship is consistent with your goal, you don't need to use a goal-directed strategy.

It is quite impossible to provide a list of goal-directed strategies. Any strategy designed to change the relationship must be adapted to the specific relationship, and no two interpersonal relationships are exactly alike. However, three criteria can help you judge whether a particular goal-directed strategy is likely to be successful: One, is the strategy consistent with your relational goal? Two, is your goal realistic? Three, is your goal challenging?

Basically, the relational goal is a rather clearly defined relationship that you want to develop at some relatively specific time in the future. Furthermore, the goal you set for yourself should be realistic in the sense that the chances of the relationship developing to meet your relational goal are genuinely possible. And, finally, the relational goal you set for yourself should be challenging in the sense that it will require some interactional effort on your part. You are likely to see your relational goal as worthwhile only to the extent that you have to "earn" it. If your relational goal is too easy, you won't find it very satisfying.

When you choose a goal-directed strategy, you generally attempt to raise the level of intensity or intimacy in your relationship. Of course, you could also want to lower the level of intensity or intimacy, but goal-directed strategies that function to deintensify the relationship are typically less challenging. It's easy to lower the intensity or intimacy level of a relationship—just reduce the amount of interaction or stop interacting altogether. It is much more challenging to adopt a goal-directed strategy aimed at intensifying the relationship. But such strategies can be discovered only after a reasonably accurate assessment of the current status of the relationship (the feedback loop) and will vary considerably from one relationship to another.

Issue-Directed Strategies

We shall refer to those comments which relate directly to the information being discussed as *issue-directed strategies.* These strategies attempt to exert some control over the content of the information or the flow of information being discussed. Specifically, issue-directed strategies function to do something to the issue under consideration during discussion. After all, the issues are the "stuff" that communication is about.

You will recall that an issue is a question or point of discussion about which there is some potential controversy. Communication allows the participants to manage the issues or come to some agreement on them. Issue-directed strategies address specifically any potential controversy surrounding the question or point being discussed. They contribute or evaluate information and thereby seek to control the information pertinent to the issue. In this way, issue-directed strategies attempt to provide a rational basis for discussion. They seek and provide information concerning the issue while also evaluating the information concerning the issue. They attempt to control the amount and quality of the information that is relevant to conversational topics.

So what can you do with an issue when you contribute to the conversation? The following is a list of issue-directed strategies that attempt to control the relevant information:

Take issue: Express an opinion that supports one side of the issue under discussion. (Example: "I don't think you're being fair to her. She's really a very nice person.")

Challenge the issue: Express an opinion that questions the relevance or significance of the issue. (Example: "I understand where you're coming from, but I can't see why you're so upset. After all, it seems pretty trivial.")

Seek information: Indicate that the issue cannot be resolved without more information; ask the other person if he/she has any additional information. This functions to delay resolution of the issue. (Example: "I'm not sure. Have you heard anything new? Doesn't anybody know any more than we do?")

Provide information: Express additional information concerning the issue under discussion. (Example: "I was talking to her brother yesterday. He said that she was really sick, and nobody knew what was wrong with her.")

Avoid the issue: Delay resolving the issue by changing the topic under discussion. (Example: "I really don't know anything about that: let's talk about something else.")

Seek resolution or compromise: Invite the other person to provide a definitive answer. This may be accompanied by a promise to support the answer. (Example: "You just tell me what to do, and I'll do it.")

Provide resolution or compromise: Suggest a definitive answer to the issue. (Example: "I think we've talked long enough about where we're going to eat. Let's just go to McDonald's and be done with it.")

Combine two (or more) issues: Indicate the similarity of two different issues. Suggest that the issue is part of a broader one. (Example: "You know, all this terrorism sounds just like the 1960s. Remember all the killings that seemed to come all in a row? John Kennedy, Martin Luther King, Robert Kennedy?")

Issue-directed strategies attempt to manage issues by dealing with information that may or may not affect the intrapersonal self of one of the communicators. Despite your best intentions, it is not always possible to avoid affecting the self of the other person when you use an issue-directed strategy. Such strategies may appear to be objective in their focus on only the information, but they may also affect the self of one or more of the communicators. For example, what happens when you take issue with an idea advocated by the other person? You disagree not only with the information but also with the person who contributed that information. Hence, any issue-directed strategy may also function as an other-directed or relationship-directed strategy at the same time.

The only way to understand how any self-offer or relational strategy works to negotiate interpersonal relationships is to place it within the context of the *inter*action, the sequential pattern of communication involving the exchange of comments from both communicators. Then and *only* then will you be able to understand what is going on in the communication. The remainder of Part Three focuses on how the strategies contributed by both communicators "fit together" to create some recognizable pattern of negotiated relationship. Our discussions will consistently emphasize *how* the behaviors mean, *how* people negotiate their interpersonal relationships, *how* relationships develop. When you understand the "how come" question, you will have taken a giant step toward becoming more effective and competent communicators.

SUMMARY

Participants in interpersonal communication negotiate their relationship with each other as they enact behaviors toward each other. Together, they create interaction patterns that define their relationship. When those patterns are described in terms of their existence as actions or events, the quality of the interaction includes the primary characteristics of discontinuity, synchrony, recurrence, and reciprocity. Secondary characteristics of interaction quality refer to the intrapersonal perceptions of the participants and include intensity, intimacy, trust, and commitment.

When viewed as a process of negotiating relationships, interpersonal communication reflects the following characteristics. It is a blend of cooperation and competition. It assumes a future agreement on some potential settlement or relational contract. Each participant brings to the communicative situation a self, which is the basic commodity to be negotiated. The relationship that is negotiated by interpersonal communication may or may not incorporate all the "offers" of each participant's self.

All interpersonal communication focuses on certain issues or questions indicating potential points of controversy that need to be resolved through negotiation. Some issues are informational only and require only information from the communicators in order to resolve them. Informational issues are typical of the early interactions of strangers who are highly uncertain about one another and need to acquire information in order to reduce their uncertainty. Relational issues concern questions of how each person identifies self with the relationship or the other person; they include self-as-object, self-as-other, and self-as-relational issues.

During the process of interpersonal communication, each person "offers" his or her self to the other person when contributing to the enactment of the interaction patterns. Because every action potentially contributes to the resolution of an issue and the eventual relationship definition, the actions contributed during interpersonal communication are called strategies. Relational strategies include self-directed strategies that attempt to tell the other person the precise connection between the implicit self and the explicit behavior. Giving accounts and flagging are two kinds of self-directed strategies. Other-directed strategies attempt to "do something to" the other person and include compliance gaining and interpersonal confirmation/disconfirmation. A third type of strategy is relationship-directed; it attempts to change or maintain the existing relationship. Relationship-directed strategies include tie-signs and control modes. Situation-directed strategies are coping strategies that allow the individual to define a situation that is threatening or confusing. Goal-directed strategies seek to change the current undesired state of the relationship to an outcome that is more consistent with the individual's goals. These strategies call for a "feedback loop" connecting an assessment of what is wrong with the status quo with the future desired state. Issue-directed strategies attempt to control the quality and evaluation of information contributed to the interaction.

KEY TERMS

enact

discontinuity

synchrony

asynchrony

recurrence

reciprocity

intensity

intimacy

trust

commitment

issue

informational issues

relational issues

self-as-object issue

self-as-other issue

self-as-relational issue

strategy

self-directed strategy

accounts

flagging

disclaimers

other-directed strategy

compliance-gaining strategies

confirmation

disconfirmation

indifferent response

impervious response

disqualifying response

relationship-directed strategy

tie-signs

rituals

markers

change signals

control modes

one-up comment

one-down comment

symmetrical relationship

complementary relationship

one-across comment

situation-directed strategy

goal-directed strategy

issue-directed strategy

CHAPTER 7

Communication
Competence and
Interpersonal
Communication

The interpersonally competent communicator is seen as
responsible for not only being able to perform
appropriately, but also for choosing relationship partners
who will find satisfaction . . . with the performance
options the individual has in his or her repertoire. . . .
Interpersonal competence then becomes more a matter of
avoiding errors or traps that lead to relational distress (or
impasse) than of getting things just right communicatively.
. . . The relationship is the context in which
communication takes place (and in which meaning
emerges).

—Wiemann & Kelly

COMPETENCE

Brian Spitzberg (1993a, 1993b), a leading communication scholar of competence, contends that the success or failure of our significant social relationships rests heavily on individual competence for three reasons. The first
reason is that competence as an ability can directly promote the growth and
management of social relationships. Spitzberg and Cupach (1984) have
shown that skilled individuals can be at an advantage in relational interaction. The second reason is that perceptions of competence by relational
partners can influence how each responds to the other's behaviors. For
example, the nature of the impact of one partner's conflict behaviors
(whether good or bad) is related to the perceived competence of that partner
(Canary & Spitzberg, 1989). The third reason is that self-perceptions of
competence can influence a person's motivation and passage of relational
pursuits. Individuals who do not perceive themselves as competent have
been found to more likely resist relationships and subtly undermine those
they are in (Kolligian, 1990).

We have alluded to the issue of competence in relationships throughout
the first two parts of this book. No doubt as you read about such strategies

211

as confirmation and disconfirmation, you concluded that confirmatory strategies were more effective and appropriate and were probably associated with competence in relationships. You will see in the following discussion of competence, however, that such conclusions are problematic. People generally have a strong sense of competence when they have achieved it, yet their efforts to describe competent phenomena are rather disappointing. If you were to read all the popularized "how to" books on being effective in interpersonal communication, you would discover hundreds of different answers to the question "What does it mean to be a competent communicator?" But this how-to material is also confusing, because much of the advice on improving your communicative effectiveness is in direct conflict with other advice. Communication scholars have not fared much better in explaining what Parks (1985) describes as a "slippery" concept. Spitzberg (1993b) himself admits that work in competence lacks focus and direction, and is problematic. Yet, questions about competence in interpersonal communication are important and deserve attention. Our discussion will attempt to make some sense of competence in interpersonal communication.

Our first step in this sensemaking process is to identify the myths surrounding competence. We use the term "myths" because society has established hundreds of beliefs about the nature of human communication that have proved to be false in actual practice. Much of what you believe to be true about competent communication makes good, sound common sense. But it often doesn't work that way in real life.

The second step in our discussions of increasing competence in interpersonal communication is to define precisely what we mean by the terms. You will discover that a simple definition of communicative competence is not immediately apparent. Interpersonal communication is much too complex to be understood in terms that are overly simple. For instance, does competence in interpersonal communication mean being a competent communicator (the personal view)? Or does it mean participating in a competent relationship (the interpersonal view)? In this chapter, we discuss both views.

Some Myths about Communicative Competence

There is an old saying that "Fifty thousand Frenchmen can't be wrong." The sentiment underlying this adage is the notion that what most people believe must be correct. That sentiment is often not true and misleading. For centuries, entire societies have believed many things about phenomena they did not fully understand. Such beliefs have extended from "the earth is flat" to "moonlight causes people to go insane" (the derivation of the word "lunacy"). Commonly held beliefs concerning communication and specifically communicative competence are numerous and fervently held. The tenacity of the general belief in them, however, is not a measure of their truth.

In order to understand what it means to be a competent participant in interpersonal relationships, you need first to recognize the myths surrounding competence. To be aware of what you "know" and to dispel such false knowledge is the first step on the road to understanding. The following items provide only a partial listing of myths of communicative competence, phrased in the form of "good advice" to would-be interpersonal communicators:

1. Be honest.
2. Be yourself.
3. Express your true feelings.
4. Be open in communicating with others.
5. Believe in yourself.
6. Do not give advice to others, even when asked.
7. Avoid evaluating the other person.
8. Develop good listening habits.
9. Be attentive.
10. Think before you speak.
11. Develop effective communication skills.
12. Study communication.
13. Relax.

For different reasons, most of these statements are myths. Some are patently false. Some are probably good ideas but aren't very practical or are very difficult to put into practice. Some are based on truth but are overstated and need to be qualified. Some are so general and vague as to be totally impractical.

The Myth of Openness

Each of the first five statements listed above reflects the myth of openness. According to it, the best relationships are those with "open" communication in which the partners confide in each other their innermost secrets and intimate details of their lives. A cartoon in a national magazine some years ago derived humor from this myth. The cartoon depicted a marriage counselor with a couple, obviously his clients, sitting on the other side of the desk. The husband (or the wife) is saying to the new counselor, "But if we were to 'really communicate' with each other, our marriage would be in even more trouble!"

The myth of openness is not that those five "good advice" items are somehow wrong. To the contrary, being open with your partner is beneficial to the evolving relationship *at certain times*. But being open at all costs is not beneficial. We will discuss in Chapters 8 and 9 how partners get to know each other through being open and self-disclosing to each other. In fact, this open communication is one of the principal characteristics of a relationship in its integrating stage. Each of the partners needs to reduce uncertainty by gaining information about the other person's self. In Chapter 10, however, we will discuss how couples who have already established a rather high level of interactional quality (intensity, intimacy, trust, and commitment) don't really self-disclose to each other very much. In other words, openness and self-disclosure in communication characterize an *integrating* relationship but do not play a significant part (and, indeed, can be harmful) in *maintaining* a close relationship. In fact, Baxter (1988) contends that openness in developing relationships does not occur to the extent people presume. Indirect strategies occur far more than open ones. Direct openness, although assumed necessary initially, does not usually occur in great amounts because it threatens the fragile nature of early relational bonds. Later in the relationship, partners are not particularly open. They have come to believe that they do not have to be "open" because their partner should already know what they are thinking and feeling. Nevertheless, people tend to accept the myth that all good interpersonal relationships are always open. Only bad relationships are not open. This myth ignores the process of evolutionary development in interpersonal communication.

There is another view concerning openness in interpersonal communication. Two communication scholars, Mac Parks (1982) and Barbara Montgomery (1988) have warned against what they call the "ideology of intimacy." Parks illustrates (with supporting evidence from research studies) that "Most of us tell lies and most of our statements are less than completely honest" (p. 90). He also suggests that

> interpersonal relationships are established as much by privacy, secrecy, and deception as by self-disclosure, empathy, and openness. . . . Privacy and secrecy maintain relationships by allowing individuals to hide their inadequacies, thereby making themselves more attractive to their partners. . . . Moreover, deception can promote intimacy by protecting others, helping maintain a focus in conversations, and by avoiding tension and conflict. (pp. 90–91)

Another communication scholar, Bill Rawlins (1983a), also refers to the unquestioned belief in openness as "problematic." He discusses how communicators are constantly caught in the dilemma of deciding when to be open and to what degree and when and how much to lie to their partners. Moreover, a group of communication scholars discovered that, when communicating, "People lie a lot, and they justify their white lies with ease— especially in certain social contexts" (Camden, Motley, & Wilson, 1984, p. 321). They even went so far to suggest that, since communicators often view "white lies . . . as a practical effective way to cope with certain situational demands," perhaps we should "view lying [as well as openness] as a particular sort of communicative competence" (p. 321).

Contrary to what you might presume, research consistently demonstrates that interpersonal relationships are not only rife with deception (Cochran & Mayes, 1990), but also with suspicion (Levine & McCornack, 1991), intentional miscommunication (Johnson, Palileo, & Gray, 1988), the withholding of information (Berger & Kellermann, 1989), and a reluctance to speak one's mind (Roloff & Cloven, 1990). Would you find it surprising, then, to discover that relational partners typically achieve only 25 to 50 percent accuracy in representing their behaviors (Spitzberg, 1993a)? Perhaps any more accuracy would only serve to expose partners to those issues which separate them and thus endanger the relationship (Spitzberg, 1993a).

In addition, competence researchers are only beginning to grapple with the realization that behaviors normally presumed to be incompetent actually perform valuable adaptive functions over the course of the relationship. Roscoe, Cavanaugh, and Kennedy (1988), for example, reported positive consequences to the exposure of a partner's deception regarding his or her unfaithfulness. Undoubtedly, and more often than you might think, partners do lie to each other and deceive their partners in some way. Openness in the process of interpersonal communication is often helpful to the evolution of a close relationship. But when you think of openness as a noble idea toward which you should constantly strive, you contribute to the myth of openness. Few people, though, are willing to accept the precept "When in trouble lie to your partner" as one of the "ten easy steps" to developing effective skills in communication.

The Myth of Objectivity

Items 6 and 7 in the list of "good advice" statements foster the myth that people should look at other people (and the entire world, for that matter) with an objective eye. It is better, you might think, to avoid making judgments. Therefore you shouldn't evaluate other people or give them advice on what they should do. As in the case of openness, the myth is not that objectivity is wrong per se. However, there are times when being objective is not only problematic but absolutely impossible. And communicating with another person is one of those times. In fact, all interpersonal behavior is inherently evaluative (Laing, 1971). In addition, individuals typically perceive either negative or positive intentions in the behaviors of others toward them (Rawlins & Holl, 1988).

Every time you perceive something, you inevitably evaluate it. When you perceive another person, you automatically evaluate that person. You wonder whether your relationship with this person will evolve into something more than casual acquaintance. You judge other people on the basis of how much you like them, and you apply your implicit personality theory to them. You cannot avoid making evaluative judgments of other persons. And certainly when your relationship has developed beyond casual acquaintance, you have already evaluated the other person as a person whom you like. To tell people to avoid evaluating others is to tell them to avoid doing something that is impossible to avoid.

More importantly, though, you shouldn't avoid evaluating your partner in an interpersonal relationship. Judgment, for example, can be confirming in that you are demonstrating that another person is worth evaluating (Laing, 1971). Also, if the relationship is going to get off the ground, you *must* evaluate the other person. Developing a relationship and continuing interpersonal communication is a matter of judgment. You don't continue interacting with someone unless you have judged that the other person is worth it. The only exception is the environment (such as your place of work) that requires interaction. But even in such an environment, you will still be making judgments about your acquaintance in order to determine whether you want the relationship to develop into something more than work acquaintance.

The Myth of Listening Techniques

Engaging in interpersonal or face-to-face communication requires the use of communicative skills involving both sending and receiving messages. People send messages with verbal and nonverbal behaviors, and they receive messages through their five senses. Hearing, of course, is one of those senses. Items 8 and 9 in the above list encourage the practice of using the sense of hearing. No one will deny that listening is an important and valuable communicative skill (Wolvin & Coakley, 1985). The *myth* of listening techniques assumes that competence in listening is simply a matter of learning and practicing certain techniques (Roach & Wyatt, 1988).

For instance, what does being attentive mean to you? Does it mean to focus your mind in total concentration on what the other person is saying? Does it mean looking into the eyes of the other person and having an interested expression on your face? These are techniques that should not be confused with the skill of listening in interpersonal communication. Listening in a relationship is not merely paying attention or maintaining eye contact. In fact, it is a mistake to separate listening skills from speaking skills in the process of interpersonal communication. Listening and speaking together involve the use of verbal and nonverbal communication skills in being a partner in the interpersonal relationship.

Perhaps an example might best illustrate the point of what we might call "relational listening." The following hypothetical conversation might occur between (who else?) Symon and Megan:

SYMON: I just can't believe that guy.

MEGAN: What guy?

SYMON: My English prof. I spent hours on that paper, and he only gave me a "C."

MEGAN: Really?

SYMON: Yeah. I went to his office and showed him my notes and everything. He didn't even look at them hardly.

MEGAN: Is that right?

SYMON: And after all that work, too. I just gotta get a higher grade than that. I could lose my scholarship if I don't get a 3.3 this semester.

MEGAN: Don't worry, you'll make it up in the other classes. You interested in a cuppa coffee or something?

Megan may be very attentive to what Symon is saying and may even be practicing excellent techniques of good listening. But her comments do not demonstrate very good *relational* listening. See what happens in the following conversation:

SYMON: I just can't believe that guy.

MEGAN: What's wrong? You seem upset about something.

SYMON: Well, I am. My English prof gave me a "C" on my term paper, and I spent hours on it.

MEGAN: Oh, no. That's terrible. How could he give you a "C"? You always get the highest grade in the class. If I were you, I'd go see him. Maybe he made a mistake.

SYMON: I already did. I showed him my notes and everything. I don't even think he looked at them.

MEGAN: Oh boy! That doesn't sound good. How are your other grades in the class? With a good final, you might still pull your grade up.

SYMON: Well, I did pretty good on the midterm. And the final is worth about 30 percent of the grade.

MEGAN: Okay, you can't do anything about the term paper now. The thing to do is ace the final. I can help you study if you want. Throw questions at you or something. I only have one final, and I don't really need to study for it.

SYMON: Yeah, maybe you're right. No use crying over spilled milk. I really need to study for that final, though. I could lose my scholarship.

MEGAN: No way! We're gonna show him on the final. Let's go get a cuppa coffee and talk about when we get together to study.

In the second conversation Megan is demonstrating effective skill in *relational listening*. She is not merely being attentive or using good listening techniques. She *contributes* (speaking) to the interaction on the basis of her listening. Every one of her comments is *responsive* to the needs and feelings expressed by Symon. She listened for what Symon was feeling and thinking and responded as a relational partner, not just as an attentive receiver of messages. She goes beyond the appearance of being sympathetic; she reaches out to offer assistance and advice. She acts (speaks) on the basis of the relationship. In fact, the relational listening she demonstrates serves to define the relationship as a rather close one. On the other hand, the listening skills she demonstrated in the first conversation point more to a relationship of casual acquaintance. In other words, Megan exhibited casual listening. Perhaps that kind of listening was appropriate to that relationship, but it certainly doesn't serve to enhance it.

Listening is too important to be treated so casually, as a mere collection of learned techniques. When you think of listening as a skill different from the entire process of interpersonal communication and practiced independently of it, you are missing the point of how listening functions in interpersonal relationships. Stewart and Thomas's (1990) notion of "dialogic listening," an excellent example of what we mean by relational listening, captures the integral role of listening in social relationships. *Dialogic listening* displays a genuine awareness of "our," with a concentration on what happens between partners and the relational present. Dialogic listeners play with the open-ended improvisation of dialogue recognizing no predetermined end to the dialogue. Dialogic listening celebrates the cocreation of relationship. The more important ability of listening in interpersonal communication is being responsive to the other person in terms of how the relationship has been defined in the past interaction patterns.

The Myth of Formula Answers

The final four statements in the list of communication skills are our favorites. They say everything without saying anything. They are solutions to all problems without providing any direction or guidance for solving the problems. Telling a nervous or apprehensive person to relax is like saying "Don't drown" to a person who doesn't know how to swim. It's good advice, but it isn't very helpful. You need to know more than the formula for solving the problem. You need to know how to use the formula, how to put it into effect. You need to know what the formula means in practice.

Let us illustrate. A few years ago Aub was talking with an advisee just before she was to take an oral examination. She was a very good student who tended to get excited in the situation of an oral exam and to talk herself into a hole that was difficult to crawl out of. Basically, she needed to relax and allow her abilities and intelligence to work for her. He advised her ("commanded," actually) never to answer any question immediately but to pause for a minimum of two seconds before she replied. Two seconds is about the time needed to take a single deep breath, but it seems like an interminable length of time during a normal conversation. The two-second pause was a practical way of telling her to relax and to think before she provided an answer. She passed her exam with flying colors and confided to me afterward that she had never felt so much confidence, so much in control of the situation.

There is certainly nothing wrong with the final four comments on the list. In fact, we endorse every one of them. But formula answers simply aren't very specific and certainly aren't very practical as a way to enhance your competence in interpersonal communication. In fact individuals can take analysis and practice too far. Spitzberg and Cupach (1984) caution that overly conscious individuals can spend more time than necessary analyzing their communication and not nearly enough time simply doing it and having fun with it. Further, too much attention to overlearned responses can actually be detrimental to a person's motivation and performance (Andersen, 1986). Item 12 ("Study communication") may be the single most important guideline in developing your competence and skills in interpersonal communication. In a very real way, this entire book deals with developing communicative competence.

To understand the process of interpersonal communication fully is to know what and when to communicate appropriately and effectively. Acquiring an understanding is the best way to achieve competence. Practice based on understanding may be the most useful and practical definition of competence. Getting rid of myths (which are really misunderstandings) is the best way to begin acquiring that understanding. All that remains is practice.

DEFINING COMPETENCE

Competence or skill in interpersonal communication is easier to recognize than to define. You know of people, we are sure, who are very competent or skilled communicators. But you probably have a difficult time putting your finger on precisely what makes them competent. Some things come to mind that might be included in your definition. For instance, the competent communicator seems poised or at ease, appears natural, is articulate or fluent, uses grammar correctly, has a pleasing voice, coordinates verbal and nonverbal behaviors, and so forth. People typically tend to define competence in terms of the interactive behaviors produced by the communicator, although sometimes they define it quite differently.

Definitions of communicative competence will differ because each uses a different basis for assessment. Consider the following definitions:

Individual ability: Competent communication is "the ability to engage in appropriate and effective interpersonal interaction" (Spitzberg & Cupach, 1984, p. 14).

Individual goals: Competent communicators "accomplish tasks successfully" (p. 53) or are successful in "exerting control over the environment to achieve certain outcomes" (p. 54).

Instrumental behaviors: "Interactive skills are the skills you or I use in face to face encounters to arrange our behavior so that it is in step with our objectives. . . . Our behavior is a means that can, depending on our skill, either help or hinder us in achieving our ends" (Honey, 1976, p. 13).

Adaptation: "Persons who are able to adapt to different relational situations are 'rhetorically sensitive' and seen by others as competent communicators" (Wilmot, 1980, p. 194).

Whatever the basis used to define communicative competence, any definition (including those above), implies that competence is either an *ability* or a *quality* (Spitzberg, 1993a, 1993b). The dominant synonym for competence has been "ability." "Competence as ability" refers to an individual's capacity to produce and reproduce skills necessary for the accomplishment of relational goals. The competent communicator must be able to perform appropriate behaviors. Interactive behaviors that are appropriate in one relationship may be quite inappropriate in another, and no two interpersonal relationships are exactly alike. In addition, behaviors that are appropriate during one stage in the evolutionary development of a relationship may be quite inappropriate during another.

Performing certain behaviors in order to achieve individual and relational goals is also problematic, especially when your goals change during the development of the relationship. A behavior that was instrumental to one objective may turn out to be detrimental in the long run, or one that at the time was detrimental may in the long run be beneficial. Retrospective sensemaking often entails the revising of goals in the relationship.

"Competence as quality" is found in the interpretation of the individual. Competence is an inference or judgment made about effectiveness and appropriateness that is based on any number of standards for determining what is competent. Within this tradition the question is not which behaviors (skills) are competent but which *skills* are interpreted as competent and why. The position is that if competence changes across context, then competence must be found in the different interpretations of competence in others.

The movie *Being There* dramatizes one of the most persistent problems associated with perceptions of competence—the fact that such perceptions are often irrelevant to either ability or performance of competent communication. The character portrayed by Peter Sellers in *Being There* was a gardener by trade and a bumbling idiot in his behavior. Despite his almost total ineptitude in communicating, nearly everyone around him *perceived* him to be a genius. He even became as advisor to the President of the United States.

Perception of competence is likely to be problematic for various reasons. For one thing, people will generally agree with one another on an overall evaluation of how competent or skilled another person is, but they are likely to disagree on the components or definition of just what competence is (see, for example, Wiemann, 1977; Rubin, 1985). Second, the "fit" between what people perceive and what the other person is actually doing can be problematic. Rubin (1985), for example, is not alone in her discovery that peoples' perceptions of competence are often unrelated to the behaviors they have observed. Certainly the people who thought Peter Sellers competent in *Being There* exhibited little correlation between their judgment and his communicative behaviors. Third, the nature of person perception is problematic. Recall our earlier discussions in Chapter 3. You tend to see other people in terms of yourself. When you perceive other people as being competent communicators, you perceive them more in terms of your own feelings than according to what they are actually doing when they are communicating. Perceiving your relational partners to be competent communicators may be a significant factor affecting how satisfied you are with your relationships, but the perceptions you have of their competence may have little to do with their abilities or performance in interpersonal communication.

Obviously, competence as "quality" or "ability" serve to locate communicative competence in the intrapersonal system, that is, in the individual. Little research has attempted to locate the phenomenon of communicative competence in the *social unit*—the interpersonal level (Spitzberg, 1993a). Research in this area would attempt to "identify the mutual, *relational* sources of actor and coactor competence, and the factors that influence these sources" (p. 12).

What then is communicative competence? The obvious truism concerning communicative competence is, perhaps, expressed by two authors who wrote an entire book on defining social competence. Rathjen and Foreyt (1980) introduced this work with the statement, "The choice of which behaviors should be included in the repertoire of a socially competent person is not clear" (p. 1). Few people will deny the obvious truth, however frustrating, of such a statement.

Despite the problem of providing that clear definition, communicative competence is a powerful force in the process of enacting interpersonal relationships. Research into communicative competence (for example, Spitzberg & Cupach, 1989) has consistently demonstrated the fact that competence conceptualized as ability and quality in interpersonal communication will significantly affect how satisfied people are likely to be with their interpersonal relationships. *Communication competence,* for our purposes, will be defined as "appropriate and effective interaction whether enabled by personal abilities and performance or attributed by observer(s)" (Spitzberg, 1993b). In the following section we will take a closer look at this definition.

Dimensions of Communicative Competence

No discussion of communicative competence occurs without directly mentioning or implying three predominant components of competence: *appropriateness, effectiveness,* and *flexibility.* Our definition of communicative competence directly mentions the first two, and we have alluded to the notion of flexibility, or adaptability.

Appropriateness   When you engage in *appropriate* interaction, you don't violate any expected rules or norms of others or the interaction between individuals (Spitzberg, 1993a, 1993b). Your behavior "fits" the context, and yet you don't have to conform to be considered appropriate. Some situations you will encounter are new with no clear rules, other times you may want to renegotiate rules, and in still other situations you may desire to conceal the importance of the rules in your interaction. We mentioned earlier, for example, that in some situations clarity is called for and in others deception may be the most appropriate behavior. We also discussed masking in Chapter 3 and situations in which you may not want to reveal how you feel in order not to hurt another person.

Effectiveness   *Effectiveness* is related to appropriateness in that it is the "accomplishment of desirable or preferred outcomes" (Spitzberg, 1993a, p. 13). Spitzberg (1993a) clarifies that these outcomes need not be positive; that is, accomplishing that which is the least detrimental may be the most competent.

Discussions of communicative competence invariably include discussions of various degrees of effectiveness and appropriateness. Ideally, it would stand to reason that optimal competence occurs when it is both effective and appropriate. Certainly you can recall a situation in which you may have effectively accomplished something, but your actions were considered inappropriate. Recently one of Kathy's colleagues was angry over a decision made by the chair of their department. Her colleague sent a memo to the faculty and expressed his concern over the decision. He was effective in getting his message to the faculty, but some considered the angry accusations in the memo inappropriate. Was this competent interaction? The answer is not simple because, as Spitzberg (1993a) points out, competence is often equated with only the positive—clarity and understanding. And, as we have discussed before, interpersonal communication is rife with suspicion, deception, inaccuracy, tentativeness, and so on. Researchers have been reluctant to consider these tactics within a competency framework because they are not socially and politically acceptable (Spitzberg, 1993a). Only recently have communication scholars begun to examine the "dark side" of communication from within a competence framework (see, for example, Miceli, 1992). And this leads us to the issue of flexibility.

Flexibility   *Flexibility,* or behavioral adaptability, is recognized as the most vital dimension of competence—so much so that it is often used synonymously with competence (Spitzberg & Cupach, 1989; Spitzberg, 1993a). The underlying assumption is that people face a variety of situations, relationships, and social partners, and to the degree that they are capable of adapting their repertoire of behavior to the guidelines of those situations, relationships, and partners, they are competent. However, flexibility poses a dilemma for interactants. People are expected to act in a consistent manner in relationships (Hoelter, 1985). Yet, people are also expected to be flexible across situations and relationships. Adding to this dilemma is the expectation that individuals are to act in a consistent manner with another in order to facilitate their partner's competence (Athay & Darley, 1981). Yet, rigidity of behavior can point to a lack of concern for the partner! "The trick then, is to adapt to the co-actor by altering one's behavior, but simultaneously provide sufficient consistency to behavior to permit the co-actor to adapt to self" (Spitzberg, 1993b, p. 147).

Phillips (1984) notes that conceptualizing competence "is like trying to climb a greased pole" (p. 24). Competence in interpersonal communication is not any one thing or any one list of things to do when communicating. Rather it involves a number of different dimensions, ranging from having a repertoire of behaviors to choosing appropriate relational partners and even to deciding which relationships to continue and which to end. It involves having the ability to perform appropriate behaviors, having a repertoire of behaviors from which to choose, having appropriate partners, having realistic goals to be realized in the relationship, and so forth. Competence is found in the interplay between the intrapersonal and the interpersonal. In the following sections we will examine in more detail the intrapersonal (the competent communicator) and the interpersonal (the competent relationship). We will end our discussion with some guidelines for improving competence.

THE COMPETENT COMMUNICATOR

Relational Strategies

In this chapter, we have emphasized that everyone uses relational strategies when communicating and forming interpersonal relationships with other people. It follows, then, that the competent communicator will use relational strategies in a competent manner. By demonstrating competence in using relational strategies during the process of interpersonal communication, the communicator is demonstrating an ability for competence, is giving the other person information that can then be used to perceive competence, and is adapting the communicative style that is appropriate to the situation. Using relational strategies while communicating is, perhaps, the central element of communicative competence.

To understand how to use relational strategies competently, you need to look at what people actually do when they communicate in the "real world." To be practical, you need to discover what researchers have discovered in their observations of interpersonal communication. John Wiemann and Cliff Kelly (1981), two of the foremost researchers in communicative competence, have summarized the research findings and indicate two primary and four secondary characteristics of communicative competence. When people use relational strategies competently, then, they demonstrate (primary characteristics) *control* and *empathy* as well as (secondary characteristics) *affiliation/support, behavioral flexibility, social relaxation,* and *goal achievement.* Now we need to translate these terms (jargon) into what competent communicators actually do when they communicate with other people.

Primary Characteristics   To use a strategy of *control,* you perform an action that implicitly defines your relationship or your interaction in terms of which relational partner is in control. (Recall the discussion of control modes earlier.) A control strategy is an implicit relational definition. For example, you might say to your partner, "What do you want to do tonight?" In essence, you have used a relational strategy that gives control of your future plans for the evening to your partner. On the other hand, you might use a relational strategy that defines yourself in control: "Let's go bowling tonight." The following conversation defines control in the hands of Megan:

MEGAN: Let's go bowling tonight.
SYMON: Okay. Where do you want to go?
MEGAN: I like those new computer alleys at Cottonwood Lanes.
SYMON: Sounds good to me. I haven't bowled in ages.
MEGAN: Neither have I, but it should be fun. Pick you up at 8?
SYMON: Sounds good. I'll be ready.

This conversation reflects what is known as a *complementary* pattern of relational control. Both persons agree on the definition of their relationship in terms of who is in control. Megan uses control strategies that indicate she is planning their activities, and Symon agrees with Megan's plans and thereby defers to her control. The complementary pattern of relational control is based on a difference between the partners. That is, Megan is the controll*er*, and Symon is the controll*ee.* Megan uses strategies to control their interaction, and Symon uses strategies that agree with and accept her control strategies.

On the other hand, a control pattern may be based on equality as well as difference. When the interaction pattern defines the partners in equal control of the relationship, it is called *symmetry.* The following hypothetical conversation is symmetrical. Symon uses strategies that define the relationship with himself in control of the interaction. Megan's strategies define herself in control. Both define themselves as controllers, a relational equality. However, they disagree on who is in control. The result is an interaction pattern of relational control known as *competitive symmetry:*

MEGAN: Let's go bowling tonight.
SYMON: Naw, bowling is no fun. Let's go to a movie.
MEGAN: I don't like any of the movies playing. Bowling is fun.
SYMON: That new Eastwood movie sounds good. Let's go see it.
MEGAN: I don't like him. Besides, I want to *do* something.
SYMON: I just wanta relax, like in a movie. Bowling is for nerds.

Both Symon and Megan try to gain control over the interactional topic and their evening plans. But neither relinquishes control to the other. The result is an interaction pattern that exhibits not only equality but also competition in terms of who is in the position of control in their interaction.

The type of control pattern that reflects communicative competence is not necessarily either symmetrical or complementary. You will recall that most relationships develop by evolving through patterns that include both symmetrical and complementary interaction. That fluctuation, you will recall, is one of the characteristics of relationship maintenance (further developed in Chapter 11) and helps the partners avoid cultural schismogenesis. Communicative competence, then, is not an issue of who is in control but whether the control patterns "follow the rules" established in the interaction.

Competent communicators know the rules and interact with their partners while observing the rules they have developed during the evolutionary process of the relationship. Some of those rules, of course, come from the larger society and deal with such social customs as how to take turns in interaction. Although rules of control patterns will vary from one relationship to another, a general rule is that relational partners take turns at being in control. Competence, then, is knowing the rules governing when to enact a symmetrical control pattern and when to enact a complementary one.

The second primary characteristic of communicative competence, *empathy,* borrows a psychological term referring to a person's ability to understand and mimic the feelings of another (Hickson, 1985). If you're sad, your friend is sad. When empathy is used to characterize communicative competence, though, it goes beyond the psychological feeling. It includes the strategies that the competent communicator contributes to the pattern of communication.

Empathic communicators are probably sensitive to the emotions and internalized feelings of their relational partners. But knowing when your partner is sad or depressed, for example, does not make you a competent— that is, an empathic—communicator. Competence requires performing your empathy in the interaction patterns. The empathic *person* knows when the partner is sad or depressed; the empathic *communicator* attempts to cheer up the relational partner who is sad or depressed. The empathic communicator probably has good empathic skills and is able to detect or to be sensitive to the partner's feelings. Being sensitive to a partner's thoughts and feelings doesn't imply that the empathic communicator knows what to do or whether to take any action at all (Spitzberg, 1993a).

Secondary Characteristics

The secondary characteristics of communicative competence are called secondary not because they are less important but because they derive from the characteristics of control and empathy. Communicators who exhibit affiliation and support demonstrate empathy. Communicators who exhibit social relaxation are probably in control of their selves during the process of communication. When they achieve goals, they are also probably using control strategies competently, so that their relationships with other people are consistent with their personal goals.

Behaviorial flexibility, as we stated earlier, may be the most important characteristic of communicative competence. The truly competent communicator undoubtedly possesses a large repertoire of relational strategies to use in communicative situations. Furthermore, the truly competent communicator has experienced a variety of different communicative situations with a variety of relational partners and has thus developed the ability to judge what strategies are most appropriate in which situations and with which relational partners. Being able to adapt and communicate appropriately is the flexibility that the communicator has in choosing strategies and adapting them to specific interpersonal relationships. The truly competent communicator is more than merely skilled, but is capable of knowing what "skill" means in a specific situation. In other words, the truly competent communicator has the ability to perform competently and to define competence for each specific situation.

THE COMPETENT RELATIONSHIP

If one of the participants in interpersonal communication is competent but the other is not, is the relationship likely to succeed? If both communicators are not highly competent, is the relationship doomed to failure? If both participants exhibit a high level of communicative competence, is the relationship assured of a long and healthy existence? Or is the relationship itself competent? Is it possible for two incompetent individuals to enact a competent relationship? Can two highly competent individuals enact an incompetent relationship? What on earth is meant by a "competent relationship"? Will the following pages provide the answers to all these questions?

Our discussions throughout this book have consistently emphasized that the relationship is different from either or both of the communicators individually. Neither communicator, as an individual, can determine what the relationship is or will be. Each individual communicator participates in and becomes part of the relationship, but the individual communicators cannot define the relationship by themselves. The whole relationship, because it is a whole, is likely to be quite different from the sum of its parts. A competent relationship may result from the interactive combination of two participants who are individually quite incompetent. Conversely, two individually competent people may not be able to create a relationship that is competent. The relationship may be more or less than the sum of its individual participants, but it almost certainly will be different from them.

Remember that competence is typically conceptualized as a judgment, an assessment, or an evaluation of what somebody is or does. Little is known about the dyadic, nonsummative nature of competence (competence as a social unit). Judgments of competence occur after the communication has taken place—not prior to communicating. When one contributes to communication, the action or behavior becomes an event that fits together with the actions and events of the partner to create the pattern of interaction. According to anthropologists Orvis Collins and June Collins (1973), "In the knife-edged present in which we all live, none of us knows at that moment when he issues an act exactly how that act is to fit into the emergent future of interaction sequencing" (p. 122). Yet "what we do mostly is face-to-face communication, and the most ordinary of us do that elegantly, precisely, rapidly, and with great subtlety and complexity" (Bavelas, 1990, p. 601).

Competence is a judgment made on the basis of retrospective sense-making and characterizes the interpersonal relationship. When you participate in interaction, you don't know what the pattern or "interaction sequencing" will be. At some point in the future, though, you look back on the interaction that you've already enacted and make sense of what the interaction pattern (and, hence, the relationship) means. In this way, the partners evaluate the competence of the interpersonal communication patterns (the entire relationship) as they evaluate each other's competence. The following discussion, then, shifts our focus from judging the competence of the individual communicator to judging the competence of the entire interpersonal relationship in which the individual communicators are members.

Relationship Rules

Whenever you learn a new game, your first reaction is to ask "What are the rules?" In order to play the game, you must first be aware of what you can do and what you can't do. The rules of the game provide the information that is necessary to play the game. There are basically two kinds of rules: those that define the game itself and those that you use to play the game. (Recall the earlier discussion of constitutive and regulative rules in Chapter 5.) Chess, for example, is a game that has certain rules that define the game. The game is played on a square board divided into sixty-four smaller squares. Each player begins with the same sixteen pieces arranged in the same way at either end of the board. Each piece can move in only one way, and so forth. But some people are much better chess players than others. Why? After all, they all follow the same basic rules. The difference is that all chess players use another set of rules that guide what they do during the playing of the game. And this second set of rules—rules that regulate the playing of the game—is a central characteristic of relationship competence.

When you communicate with someone else, you follow rules that define how you communicate. You are rarely aware of following rules, but you follow them anyway. You use the same language. You follow the same norms of your culture. You take turns when speaking. In short, you follow the rules that define the game (or culture) itself. Following those rules doesn't mean you are a highly competent communicator, though. It means only that you have been acculturated within a society and have learned the customs and traditions of that society. That is, you are influenced by the social context. As in the game of chess, you can be aware of all the rules that define the game and still play it poorly. To be a good chess player, you need to learn rules that enable you to play the game well. To be a competent communicator, you need to learn rules that guide what you do when you are engaged in the game of interpersonal communication.

Unlike the rules that define the game, rules that regulate the game don't exist until and unless they are created by the players. Furthermore, one person cannot create rules to play the game, because interpersonal communication is not a game of solitaire. It takes two (or more) people to play the game, and it takes two (or more) people to create the rules. Hence, the rules for playing the "game" of interpersonal communication are enacted by the "players" (the communicators themselves) during the process of developing their relationship. Rules are, in essence, the patterns of interaction that you have developed in cooperation with your partner during the process of communication. The rules of your relationship are the sequential patterns of interaction that you (and your partner) come to identify with your relationship. Identifying rules as patterns of behavior stands in contrast to the typical identification of rules as cognitive structures within individual communicators which serve to explain the reasons for individuals' behavior. For example, Pearce, Cronen, and Conklin (1979) use this conceptualization of rules in their theory, the coordinated management of meaning, to explain how individuals create and manage meaning in everyday interaction. Within the pragmatic approach, rules are the interaction patterns that make your relationship different from other interpersonal relationships.

John Van Maanen (1979) has suggested six "characteristics associated with all rules" of a relationship:

> *First,* rules cannot transcend the situation in which they are applied (though we often try). . . . *Second,* and relatedly, all rules have exceptions. . . . *Third,* rules not only change over time, they are also selectively enforced at any given time. . . . *Fourth,* rules, like all meaningful aspects of the social world, are negotiated. . . . *Fifth,* rules serve as resources to justify behavior after the fact as well as to guide behavior before the fact. . . . *Sixth,* shame more so than any form of direct punishment is the great enforcer of the rules. (pp. 74–76)

The first characteristic indicates that the interaction patterns of a specific interpersonal relationship *belong to* that relationship and even to that particular stage of the relationship. Even though you may try to mimic the interaction patterns that proved to be so successful in one relationship, you soon learn that you can't do so successfully. Each relationship is different and has its own rules. Furthermore, when a relationship starts to go sour, you may want to go back to the way it used to be, but you soon learn that you can't go back. It's just never the same. You need to move forward and create new rules to invigorate your relationship.

The second characteristic indicates that interaction patterns which define your relationship do not constitute the entire interaction you have with that person. Those patterns happen frequently, but they don't occur all the time. If they did, you would soon find them monotonous and dull. The interaction patterns occur *as a rule,* but all rules have exceptions. That's what makes the relationship interesting. The interaction patterns don't violate the rules, they just aren't typical or normal in your relationship. Rules are the defining characteristics of your interpersonal relationship. The rest of your interaction is part of your relationship but is not as important to defining it.

The next three characteristics of relationship rules emphasize the evolutionary development of relationships and, thus, of rules also. Rules change over time (a fundamental characteristic of the evolutionary development and constant state of becoming) which means, of course, that rules do not have the same strength all the time. You may have one set of relationship rules with your very close relational partner that applies when you are all alone and another set that applies when you are in public. The fourth characteristic emphasizes the process of negotiation, also a fundamental characteristic of the pattern of relationship development that has been discussed in earlier chapters. The fifth characteristic suggests that rules help provide guidelines for behaving in any given situation, but they still come about through the process of retrospective sensemaking.

The final characteristic suggests how people in a relationship "enforce" the rules or interaction patterns that guide their interpersonal communication. Certainly relational partners do not conform to the rules of their relationship because they have to but rather because they choose to. It is not fear of punishment that guides their interaction patterns but rather the free choice of partners to use the relationship rules to guide their participation in communication. When a partner breaks or violates one of the relationship rules, the individual is not punished by the partner so much as he or she becomes intrapersonally aware of having broken a rule. The individual, then, provides his or her own punishment. The rulebreaker feels shame or embarrassment at having done something wrong in the relationship.

A competent relationship is interpersonal communication in which the interaction patterns are clearly established and demonstrated in the interpersonal communication of the relational partners. The more competent the relationship, the easier it is to see the relationship rules in the interaction patterns of the participants. Partners in a competent relationship know what the rules are (even though they may not realize it) and interact accordingly. They experience the intrapersonal pangs of shame or embarrassment when they break the rules. They negotiate changes in the rules in order to maintain the continuity of the relationship. The stronger the relationship rules in the interaction patterns, the more competent the interpersonal relationship.

Characteristics

At this point, we can summarize what we mean when we say that a relationship is competent. A relationship is competent to the extent that

1. It endures.
2. It is continuous.
3. It meets the expectations of its partners.
4. It serves various functions.

A Competent Relationship Endures   Simple endurance or longevity may not be a sufficient reason to call a relationship competent. On the other hand, a competent relationship is likely to be a long-term relationship. In addition, communication researchers (for example, Wheeless, Wheeless, & Baus, 1984) have discovered that people tend to be most satisfied with relationships that have evolved to a stage of advanced development. The fact that the relationship has lasted a long time is a sign, though not a necessary sign, that it is a competent one. If it were less competent, it probably wouldn't have lasted as long. We will have more to say about endurance in Chapter 11.

A Competent Relationship Is Continuous   Recall that continuity is a key factor in maintaining a close relationship. Partners who maintain the closeness of their relationship keep the interaction from stagnating, from becoming too monotonous and repetitive. They maintain their relationship by constantly changing it to something new. The continuous relationship remains in a constant state of becoming. It remains fresh, vital, and new—regardless of how old and enduring it has been.

A Competent Relationship Meets the Expectations of Its Partners   No one is really sure which comes first—the expectations individuals have of their relationship or the relationship itself. Perhaps individuals enter a relationship expecting it to be a particular kind. When interaction fulfills those expectations, the individuals are satisfied with it. On the other hand, the process of interpersonal communication may provide the individual participants with some sense of what the future of their relationship will be. In that case, the process of interpersonal communication (the relationship) serves to create or guide the expectations of the relational partners. In either case, to the extent that retrospective sensemaking results in the partners' feeling that their relationship is consistent with their expectations, the relationship is competent.

A Competent Relationship Serves Various Functions   Every interpersonal relationship that endures for any length of time does something to and for the participants or society. A family, for example, serves the social function of raising children for the next generation and of teaching that new generation the cultural norms and traditions of the society. The family also serves the intrapersonal functions of providing affection, support, and companionship for participants in the kinship relation. The competent interpersonal relationship may serve recreational, spiritual, economic, sexual, or any of a variety of other social functions. But it is functional.

SOME GUIDELINES FOR IMPROVING COMMUNICATIVE COMPETENCE

Despite the claims of some people to the contrary, no one has any way of knowing precisely what to do in order to ensure effective and enduring interpersonal relationships. Too much depends on the specific relationship, the specific situation, the specific relationship stage, the specific person to guarantee confidence in any list of "things to do" in order to demonstrate competence in interpersonal communication. Our discussions in this chapter have strongly suggested that competence is just as much a characteristic of the relationship as of the individual communicator. The eight recommendations discussed in the remaining pages of this chapter are certainly no guarantee that you will have happy, healthy, and successful interpersonal relationships from this time forward. They are intended only as principles of good advice that, given what is known about the nature of interpersonal communication, seem to be practical and to make sense.

1. Avoid Generalizing from One Interpersonal Relationship to Another
It is a common human tendency to analyze, to break something down into its parts, in order to understand it. When you have a relationship that goes sour, your first reaction is likely to be to try to find out what went wrong. When you have a relationship that is good, your first reaction is likely to try to find out what made it that way. Then you tell yourself to avoid the wrong things and to do the right things in your other relationships. Unfortunately, no two relationships are exactly the same. Generalizing from one relationship to another often leads to a false understanding based on the *error of assumed essence*.

You commit the error of assumed essence when you observe a difference between two things (in this case, two different relationships) and then assume that the difference you observed is the "reason why" the two relationships are different. But although the difference you observed is probably genuine, it is often not the critical distinguishing factor. You often hear of athletes who wear "lucky socks" or "lucky jackets" or do "lucky behaviors" in order to keep a winning streak going. An athlete might, for example, have begun wearing those socks on the first day of his winning streak. But only a superstitious fool would believe that wearing those socks was the critical factor that brought about the winning streak. In other words, just because two relationships are different, don't assume that the observed difference makes any difference.

2. Develop and Practice a Wide Variety of Relational Strategies   Using one strategy does not guarantee that the relationship will develop in the way you want it to develop. Nor does using a lot of strategies guarantee the outcome you want. After all, the relationship will evolve over a long period of time. You can't guarantee what will happen in the future any more than you can guarantee how your partner will respond to a particular strategy. On the other hand, if the relationship evolves slowly, it stands to reason that you need to be prepared for whatever happens in the future—both the expected and the unexpected. The more strategies you have in your repertoire of communicative behaviors, the more likely you are to have an appropriate strategy for whatever situation develops in the future.

How do you know what strategy is appropriate? The answer to that question is simple. Use the "scientific method" to determine appropriateness—trial and error. In other words, try something. If it doesn't work, try something else until it does work. Of course, the success of the trial-and-error method in interpersonal communication depends on the number of items in your repertoire of strategies. The more strategies you have to try, the more likely you are to find one that is effective in any given situation of interpersonal communication.

3. Avoid Confusing Relational Outcomes with Emotional Residues   This point has been made repeatedly in previous discussions. The emotion you feel toward the other person is not the same thing as the relationship. You may love the other person even though the relationship is a lousy one. Battered wives, for example, do not have "good" relationships with their sadistic husbands. Paradoxically, though, they often express an emotional love toward their partners who use them as punching bags. The emotion felt by relational partners is a residue resulting from the process of retrospectively making sense of the interaction patterns that create the relationship. Two people may have the same emotions about their relationships, even though the relationships are very different. Conversely, two people may have very different emotions, even though they are participants in the same relationship.

Every relationship that progresses to a rather high stage of development proceeds through different emotional stages. There is excitement and anticipation during courtship; emotional bliss during the honeymoon; an emotional roller-coaster ride during the ups and downs of relational development; and comfort and ease of the long-term familiar relationship. The relationship is the same, even though it is constantly in a state of becoming and changing, but the emotions felt by the participants vary widely from one stage to the next.

Two people in the same relationship with the same relational outcome may have differing emotions. Their interpersonal relationship (and don't forget there's only one relationship) has only one outcome; their intrapersonal emotions (at least two people are included) may have a variety of outcomes. The intrapersonal feeling is simply not the same thing as the interpersonal relationship. Despite all the directives of common sense, you should never confuse these two quite different elements of interpersonal communication.

4. Know the Relationship Rules, and Follow Them   The key to all relationship rules is appropriateness. When you participate appropriately in interpersonal communication, you are following the rules that define the relationship. To participate appropriately also implies a sense of timing. To participate in interpersonal communication appropriately is not only to perform the appropriate behavior but to perform it at the appropriate time. As long as you follow the rules, you will keep the relationship at its current stage of development. Of course, when you know that the relationship is beginning to get stale, you know that you need to change the rules. And sometimes, for purposes of maintaining continuity in the evolving relationship, you will find it appropriate to break the rules. Of course, timing is again the crucial factor in knowing and following the rules of the interpersonal relationship.

5. Be a Relational Gambler Some years ago Kenny Rogers taught you—through the medium of popular music—that living is similar to gambling. In interpersonal relationships, as in playing poker, the "secret to surviving is knowing what to throw away and knowing what to keep." All relationships are not good ones, and some relationships are never going to be good ones. If a relationship is incompetent, then why keep it? Being competent, then, is being able to distinguish competent relationships from incompetent ones. When relationships are competent, the gambler decides "to hold 'em." When they are incompetent, the gambler decides "to fold 'em." The secret to being a competent relational gambler is simply knowing when to do which.

You might think that a person who terminates a relationship rather than trying to work out the problem is probably not a competent communicator. In other words people who are competent communicators never have unsuccessful relationships. Such a belief is quite absurd. Anyone and everyone can and does have unsuccessful relationships. Sometimes, as you know, relationships terminate as a result of circumstances that are beyond the control of either participant. More importantly, though, take seriously the notion that the *relationship* itself is competent, rather than the notion that competent individuals participate in a relationship.

When the relationship is competent, neither individual can guarantee what the outcome of the relationship is likely to be. The development of the relationship is the pattern of interaction enacted by both participants together, not by any single person. When you view the relationship as the source of communicative competence, then the individual participant can take neither credit for a successful relationship nor blame for an unsuccessful relationship. The key to being a good relational gambler is working at potentially successful relationships and ending unsuccessful relationships. Under no circumstances does the relational gambler feel guilty when a relationship doesn't work out. After all, you have to play the cards that are dealt to you.

6. Participate in a Variety of Different Relationships An acquaintance once told Aub of the difficulties she had experienced following her divorce. According to her story, she had really had only one boyfriend throughout her high school years. Since they were together constantly, her friendships with other people (such as girlfriends) were very limited. She married her long-time "steady" shortly after high school graduation and was divorced a few years later. She was, according to her self-analysis, relationally naive. She didn't know how to act with other people. She didn't know how to act on dates. She didn't know how to make friends. In fact, she wasn't even sure what friendship meant. She suffered from low self-esteem and had little self-confidence. She proceeded to remarry (twice, in fact) and get divorced (also twice). At the time she talked to Aub, she was just beginning to solve her relational problems.

This woman's problem, perhaps more than anything else, was a lack of relational experience. That is, she had years of relational experience, but she had very little variety in these experiences. The same experience repeated over and over is still a single experience. Variety comes from having had many different kinds of experiences.

The more different kinds of relationships you have, the greater the variety of relational strategies you learn and the more likely you are to have encountered whatever relational experience may be in your future. People often talk about a "well-rounded" person without really knowing what that means. One significant part of being well-rounded is the variety of interpersonal relationships you have experienced and from which you have learned. After all, relationships with other people probably exert the most significant impact on the development of an individual's personality. Want to be a more well-rounded individual person? Then participate in a greater variety of interpersonal relationships.

7. Manage the Tension Created by Opposing Forces in the Relationship
The development and maintenance of a competent relationship involves a series of roller-coaster changes. Participants in every relationship are constantly being faced with dilemmas and choices between what to do and what not to do. Interpersonal communication during the evolutionary development of a relationship involves a constant effort to establish some equilibrium or balance between dialectical tensions (Baxter, 1988; Rawlins, 1989). For example, how open should you be in disclosing private information about yourself to your partner? You want to be open, but you also want to protect your self. How involved should you get in the relationship? The more you identify with your partner in the relationship, the greater the risk you run of changing your unique self or personality. Throughout the process of relational development, each of the partners is torn between such opposing forces: conflict versus cooperation, openness versus self-protection, involvement versus privacy, integration versus differentiation, monotony versus mystery.

If you are successful in establishing a competent relationship, you will have devised ways of managing the tensions created by these opposing forces (Baxter, 1988; Rawlins, 1989). You will have learned to take the good things with the bad. You will have experienced the ups and downs of relational maintenance. You will have balanced your private life with your relational life (by "shmoozing," for example). You will have discovered what you want to disclose and what you want to conceal about your self. In other words, you will have learned to cope with tensions.

Under no circumstances will you have an absence of tensions in a competent (or incompetent) relationship. To experience no tensions in a relationship is to have a lousy relationship, one that you couldn't care less about. Participants in competent relationships manage tensions; they learn to cope with the problems created by tension.

8. Stop and Smell the Roses   Some years ago Irene and Aub (marital partners in a very close relationship) were struck with the fact that so many of their friends were getting divorced. Not only were neighbors getting divorced, but colleagues at work, friends from graduate school, friends from high school years, nearly everybody in the world (or so it seemed at the time) was getting divorced. If it could happen to other people, they thought, then it could happen to them. They began to watch carefully the "seven danger signals" of marital unhappiness. They assumed that this relational unhappiness was like a virus. Without proper immunization, they were vulnerable to the disease and wondered when it would strike. Apparently they came to the conclusion that they weren't getting anywhere trying to "psych out" other people's unhappy relationships or their own happy one. Without thinking about it, they finally just quit worrying about it.

In trying to decide why your relationship is the way it is, you are wasting your time using your critical-thinking skills. You probably won't ever know the reasons for your happy relationships. Moreover, even if you did know why your relationship was happy, you wouldn't be any happier. The only possible approach, then, is to quit worrying about it. Stop and smell the roses while they are in bloom. Whatever makes your relationship a good one just isn't very important if searching for it takes all your energy. Don't analyze your relationships so much. Enjoy them! We hope you keep this in mind as you read the rest of this book. As you explore further the dynamics of relational beginnings (Chapter 8), development (Chapter 9), endings (Chapter 10), and endurance (Chapter 11), we hope you keep in mind the competence issues we have introduced in this chapter.

SUMMARY

Competence in interpersonal communication is recognized as being crucial to the success and failure of our relationships. Competence can directly promote the development of relationships. Perceptions of competence by relational partners can impact their behavioral choices. And self-perceptions of competence can influence an individual's willingness to be a participant in relationships as well as his or her behavior in those relationships.

Although important to relationships, competence is very difficult to define. For one thing, defining competence is problematic because of the commonsense myths that surround it. The myths of communicative competence include those of openness, objectivity, listening techniques, and formula answers. These myths reflect strongly held beliefs about the presumed nature of competent communication. These presumptions are being questioned by some scholars in communication who have begun to look at the "dark side" of communication within a competence framework.

Any definition of competence typically either reflects ability or quality. Ability refers to a person's performance of appropriate behaviors. Quality refers to the recognition that competence is often a personal judgment of another's competence or of one's own competence. These judgments are made about effectiveness and appropriateness based on a number of standards and are highly problematic. Both these approaches to competence reflect a focus on the individual. Little if any significant work has explored the nature of competence in the social unit or the coenacted nature of competence.

Inherent in competence or in appropriate and effective interaction are three predominant dimensions: appropriateness, effectiveness, and flexibility. Competence in interpersonal communication is not a list of things to do but rather a number of different dimensions, ranging from having a repertoire of behaviors to choosing appropriate relational partners and even to deciding which relationships to continue and end.

The competent communicator uses relational strategies with appropriateness and timing. These strategies are primarily characterized by control and empathy and secondarily by affiliation/support, behavioral flexibility, social relaxation, and goal achievement.

The entire relationship, jointly created by the participants through their interaction patterns, may also be considered a source of competence. A competent relationship has clear relationship rules or patterns of interaction. A relationship is said to be competent to the extent that it endures, is continuous, meets (or guides) the expectations of its participants, and serves various functions. Although no list of "things to do" can guarantee effective interpersonal relationships, some good advice for improving communicative competence can offer guidelines for improving their effectiveness.

KEY TERMS

relational listening

dialogic listening

communicative competence

appropriateness

effectiveness

flexibility

error of assumed essence

CHAPTER 8

Creating
Relationships—
Initiation, or
"Getting Started"

Don't knock the weather. Without it, 90 percent of the
people wouldn't be able to start a conversation.

—Anonymous

Despite the fact that friendships are so common, many will say they have
difficulty making friends. Meeting new people and making new acquaintances is, for many people, a stressful experience. Of course, some people
always seem to make friends easily and are constantly meeting new people.
Salespersons, for example, learn the knack of making conversation with
many different kinds of people, but many sales representatives claim to
have difficulty in making new friends. Perhaps they repeat the initial stages
of relationships so often in the day-to-day activities of their jobs that they
treat every person as a "client." Consequently, they have difficulty in
moving beyond the early stages of acquaintanceship.

This chapter deals primarily with the "getting acquainted" stage of
relationship development. Initial stages occur under three conditions
(McCall & Simmons, 1978). One, you are born into relationships. Some of
the most basic of our interpersonal ties (e.g., kinship) begin this way.
Second, reputations or prior knowledge set in motion circumstances which
bring people together. Given what you have heard about someone, you
may seek this person out, for example; or another may seek you out.
Sometimes third parties, such as well meaning friends, bring you together
with another. Third, without any prior knowledge of someone, you meet
her or him by accident. But it is vital for you to understand what goes on in
the process of creating a relationship from scratch. You will discover the
things that influence you during this initial stage and what you can do to
influence the way in which your new relationship will evolve. Our discussions in this chapter will include managing the first impressions you have
of others and they have of you, following the rules of social conduct, making
opening moves when initiating conversations, and doing small talk. As in
each of the remaining chapters of Part Three, we will conclude with a
specific description of the issues and strategies that are normal to and
typical of this stage of relational development. The purpose is to recognize

238

the interaction of each evolutionary stage so that you can adapt your interactive behaviors and become more competent communicators.

MANAGING FIRST IMPRESSIONS

It is difficult to overestimate the importance of first impressions on a developing relationship—yet people make quick estimates of others all the time. One psychiatrist (Zunin, 1972) has claimed that the outcome of any relationship was evident in the first four minutes of interaction. And at least one textbook has asserted that the first *five seconds* of interaction determine the outcome of a relationship.

Such claims are, of course, incredible. The first impressions people have of others are certainly significant in terms of their potential effect on what will transpire in the interaction. Getting started "on the right foot" is important to any relationship if you expect it to evolve into anything more than a casual meeting (Duck, 1991). If the first impression is negative, you will probably remove yourself from the situation and not allow the relationship further opportunities to grow. Whether that time frame is five seconds, five minutes, or five meetings is not important. What *is* important is being able to make appropriate judgments about the other person and doing all you can to make your first impression on the other person a favorable one, if you so choose.

Your task in the opening moments of conversation with a stranger, then, is twofold. One, you want to make sure your first impression on the other person is favorable. Two, you want to make sure your first impression of the other person is appropriate. The first step in managing first impressions, then, is to be aware of what goes into the first impressions you and the other person have of each other. Recognizing that individuals are their own public relation firms may turn some of you off. Remember, however, that interpersonal relationships are communicative accomplishments, and as such they require your skills in attracting, creating, sustaining, and keeping them (Bochner, 1984). Fostering and managing favorable impressions is important throughout your relationship, especially so in the beginning. In this section we discuss the three most significant influences on your first impressions: expectations, physical attractiveness, and similarity.

Expectations

The expectations you have prior to interacting with the new acquaintance will influence what you are likely to experience in those first moments of interaction. Thus, if you are going to manage your first impressions in interpersonal communication, you need to manage your expectations of that initial encounter. Generally speaking, you have three sets of expectations that influence your first impressions: expectations regarding the situation, the other person, and your goals.

Expectations regarding the Situation   The situation itself will provide you with a set of expectations that influence your social encounters. If you don't want to be there in the first place, you will probably find that nearly everyone you meet "there" confirms your expectations. You already know enough about the process of perception to know that you tend to perceive what you expect to perceive. If you go to the social event with the expectation of enjoying yourself, then you are likely to encounter people who are enjoyable. The expectations you have regarding the social situation will go a long way toward influencing your impressions of other people in that situation.

When you recognize which situations and circumstances are best for fostering first impressions, you understand the *ecology of attraction,* and this is the first concern in developing relationships (Duck, 1991). Do you have a sense of which situations are best and which are probably not suitable places or circumstances for "laying out your relational wares" (p. 35)? Duck (1991) points out, for example, that some people who may appear, to you, unfriendly and unapproachable at parties may not have a good understanding of the ecology of attraction. Often individuals who are actually shy appear unfriendly to strangers (Burgoon & Koper, 1984). For some reason their behaviors are mistakenly interpreted. We need not remind you that these mistaken impressions do impact reciprocally subsequent behavior and impressions.

Duck (1991) explains further that understanding the ecology of attraction is not simply a matter of knowing which situations are good for fostering impressions but also which are suitable for the beginnings of different types of relationships, which are suitable for different individuals, and which are suitable for only the beginnings of relationships but don't remain suitable after the relationship is on its way. To illustrate, contrary to what you might expect, Duck and Miell (1986) found that people will meet more often in public not private places (about six weeks) when developing intimate relationships.

Duck (1991) concludes by saying, "If we seek to become friends with someone it is essential to enter situations, and create opportunities, where activities that 'feel friendly' can be done" (p. 37). Remember, of course, that the trick is to figure out what situations and activities count as "friendly." For example, if men tend to focus on joint activities as a central component of their intimacy and women tend to focus on length of talk and subject matter (Hegelson, Shaver, & Dyer, 1987), then these differences can set up potential problems in initiating cross-sex relationships. Men may construct situations which involve joint activities, and women may construct situations conducive of talk. In addition, men do not fare as well initiating a relationship when they are being watched or overheard. For women this does not appear to pose a problem (Duck, 1991).

Expectations regarding the Other Person   You also have a set of expectations concerning other people, an "implicit personality theory," that influences whether you like them or not. You carry around a set of expectations for categorizing people into types that you like and other types that you don't like. In other words, you expect to like some types of people because they are likely to meet your expectations. Specifically, your expectations take the form of criteria or qualities of persons you "like" as well as criteria or qualities that you "dislike." In most cases, your liking criteria stem from the qualities you have perceived in your friends. You tend to like new acquaintances if they are similar to persons you already like. On the other hand, your criteria for disliking someone are not necessarily the opposite of your criteria for liking people. These negative criteria tend to come from a variety of sources and are quite distinct from your criteria for liking.

Psychologist Miriam Rodin (1982) believes that people typically have two sets of criteria *(dislike criteria* and *disregard criteria)* that they use to exclude people from their list of potential friends. Far more people tend to meet your disregard criteria than your dislike criteria. That is, you tend to dislike very few people, but you disregard a whole lot of them. To understand your set of expectations regarding other people, then, your disregard criteria are probably more important than your dislike criteria.

How do you interact with people who meet your criteria of like, dislike, and disregard? If people meet your like criteria, you have a favorable first impression and seek out continued interaction with them. If people meet your dislike criteria, you tend to ignore them and avoid interacting with them. On the other hand, you "don't necessarily ignore people who meet [your] disregard criteria. In ordinary social situations [you] may treat them quite courteously, and even interact with them at some length. . . . [But] the interaction is ritual and carried out with glazed attention" (p. 35).

When your first impressions of other people are consistent with your dislike criteria, you never have the opportunity to become friends. More significantly, far more potential friends never have that chance because you disregard them. It is estimated, for instance, that in a typical 100-day period in a city, a person can meet anywhere from 500 to 2500 people and only somewhere between 3 and 7 will eventually become friends (Pogrebin, 1987). That is, you tend to carry on conversations with these new acquaintances without ever giving them a chance to become friends. You don't take seriously your interaction with them. You aren't rude to them; on the contrary, you are very courteous. But courtesy is a way of coping with new acquaintances who aren't meaningful to you, whom you disregard. It is just your way of failing to engage them in meaningful interaction. Consequently, your interaction with people who meet your disregard criteria never goes beyond the "getting acquainted" stage.

Recall from our discussions in Chapter 3 that you are very much a part of those first impressions and can't divorce your self from your impressions of others. Your own needs may create a situation in which you overaccentuate or underaccentuate the characteristics of another. Knapp and Vangelisti (1992) provide an example. Presume for the moment that you have a particularly high need for affection and in addition you underestimate how much someone likes you. You may then find yourself very happy with any behavior from this person which you interpret as acceptance. You also may not be very disappointed if they reject you. On the contrary, suppose you overestimate how much this person likes you. Based on this perception you act accordingly, and these actions could reciprocally elicit from the other more liking. Does this cycle sound familiar? It should because we have just described an example of the self-fulfilling prophecy or behavioral confirmation.

Taylor (1989) has discovered an optimistic bias in many individuals' perceptions of others. People tend to see the pleasant and the positive much more readily than the ugly and the negative. Knapp and Vangelisti (1992) suggest that people do this because they are attempting to create a pleasant social situation for themselves. They warn, however, that going overboard with optimistic impressions could produce negative impressions of yourself by others. Also, consider that individuals are inclined to weigh more heavily negative characteristics and events than positive ones when forming *first* impressions. Perhaps it may be that negative events are more informative because they are the exception and positive events are the norm (Fiske, 1980). However, Kellermann (1989) has discovered that negativity of events alone in initial interaction aren't the key to their information value. Rather, typicality or the unusualness of an event is the key to its informativeness. An atypical event will remain with you and, thus, you will be more likely to use it than typical events in forming first impressions.

Just as you must be able to recognize which situations and circumstances are suitable for initiating relationships favorably, you must also be able to recognize individuals who are likely to become relational partners. The criteria discussed above help explain how you may do this. The story that emerges from research reveals that, overall, people tend not to be very creative when it comes to selecting relational partners and that those who get inventive may be wasting time (Duck, 1991; Rodin, 1982). You tend to select individuals who are similar to you in job, education, religion, income level, race, recreational activities, sexual orientation, and so on (McCroskey, Richmond, & Daly, 1975). We will discuss the significance of similarity to initial interaction later.

Expectations regarding Goals   A third set of expectations will also affect your potential relationship with new acquaintances: the goals you have for the future of this relationship. What kind of relationship are you looking for? Whatever it is, your expectation will influence your first impressions of the other person. For example, a friend once told Aub that he had joined a country club. He actually didn't like golf very much, but his country club membership, billed as a business expense, was intended to help him make new acquaintances and find new clients for his sales. Aub asked him whether he had made any new friends among the "upper crust" at the country club, and he replied, "Not at all. They're really stuffy. I wouldn't have anything to do with them if they weren't such good clients."

To this person, every person he met was a potential client. He didn't make any new friends at the country club probably because he didn't expect to make friends. He expected salesman-customer (instrumental) relationships, and those were the relationships he developed. Rather surprisingly, he couldn't seem to understand why he didn't develop any friendships (that is, communal relationships). His clients remained clients, and he regretted the fact that they didn't become friends.

Some people continually ask themselves "What can this relationship do for me?" For them, it is likely that relationships will become individualized. They drive freeways, eat in chain restaurants, and stay in chain motels. They get no surprises; they have no unexpected experiences; they play it safe. For persons who expect to gain a set of new experiences and possibly even new definitions of self from new acquaintances, relationships will more likely develop into communal ones. They drive on side roads, look for new and different places to eat and stay, and are open to new and unexpected experiences. They run a greater risk of being disappointed and having unsatisfying social experiences. But they will also, more often, have closer and more satisfying personal relationships. For them, interpersonal communication (and probably life) is pretty risky, but it is not boring.

Physical Attractiveness

Psychological research reveals that people are likely to have a more favorable first impression of persons who are physically attractive than those who are physically ugly (Berscheid & Walster, 1974). You probably do not find this statement surprising. But don't be too quick to reject it as overly obvious. It does not mean that good-looking people generally have satisfying interpersonal relationships. For instance, people have been found to evaluate unattractive couples as happier than attractive ones, and good looking men don't score any higher than unattractive men when they are tested for self-esteem, happiness, and psychological well-being (Berscheid & Walster, 1974). It also does not mean that you should have cosmetic surgery if you want to create a favorable first impression on others. In fact, physical attractiveness is not just what you see on a person's outside. It is a set of expectations you have about people and must be understood in the context of what happens in the early stages of interaction.

Some extremely attractive people have publicly stated that their physical assets were actually detrimental to the formation of personal relationships. Actresses or starlets seem continually to be telling interviewers that they are really lonely because people tend either to be intimidated by their beauty or to treat them as sex objects, and not as friends. Most people don't have that problem. They are condemned to live a life of normalcy—somewhere in the middle between "gorgeous" and "yucky." For the vast majority of people in American society, the influence of physical attractiveness on the beginning stages of interpersonal communication is even more problematic.

In the first place, what is physically attractive to one person may not be to another. For instance, teenage girls will often differ from their fathers on the criteria by which to judge "cute" boys. On more than one occasion, Aub was surprised when he actually set eyes on a fellow who had set his teenage daughter's heart aflutter. He often found him quite unattractive (if not downright ugly). But what is cute to one person may meet the disregard criteria of another. Therefore, physical attractiveness certainly does not influence all people in the same way.

Perhaps the most important fact concerning your expectations regarding physical attractiveness is that they are often not defined in terms of outward appearance or anatomical features. For instance, when Aub asked his daughters what they found attractive in a certain boy, they often responded in terms of behaviors and not physical features. They often thought a boy was cute because he was "fun to be around" or he had a "nice smile." And this is the point that is most important in people's expectations concerning physical attractiveness and managing first impressions.

Physical attractiveness is not just what you see when you look at someone; it is also the impressions you acquire during the opening moments of interaction. A person who smiles, for example, is often perceived as more attractive than one who remains glum-faced. A person who appears "natural" is often perceived as more attractive than one who appears too formal or "stuck up." Behaviors are often as much a part of attractiveness as are physical features. At the very least, the behaviors of the other person will affect your judgment of that person's physical attractiveness, and your behaviors will affect the other person's judgment of you. Hence, the first moments of interaction are significant in terms of how they influence each communicator's expectations regarding the other's physical attractiveness.

Physical appearance more than anything influences only the opportunities for social interaction. For example, attractive males interact more with females than males, and attractive males and females report having more fun in social interaction than unattractive individuals (Reis, Nezlek, & Wheeler, 1980). Duck (1991) argues that the impact of physical attractiveness can recede over time, and although it may increase the opportunities for meeting people, it doesn't help form relationships. "It is just another circumstantial factor that affects opportunity rather than doing the creation of relationships for people" (p. 53).

Similarity

Consistent with the saying that "Birds of a feather flock together," people tend to be attracted to those people whose interests, attitudes, experiences, and beliefs are similar to their own. In other words, people tend to be drawn to people who are most like themselves. There appears to be at least three reasons to explain this apparent attraction (Knapp and Vangelisti, 1992). One, you expect first-time interaction to be less difficult with people who are similar to you. After all, you should have lots to talk about. In initial interaction with dissimilar others, there may be more questions about the meaning of phrases and expressions, how to open the interaction, what to say during the interaction, and how to say what it is you want to say. Gudykunst and Kim (1984), however, point out that dissimilarity, in particular cultural dissimilarity, need not thwart efforts to develop close relationships. In fact, they contend that cultural similarity "is not a necessary prerequisite for friendship formation" (pp. 178–179), although, other kinds of similarity (e.g., motives, socioeconomic class, education, beliefs, and so on) may be important. Second, similar characteristics may be the basis for assuming that another holds a like worldview, and you would assume that this person would reinforce your own beliefs, attitudes, and so forth rather than disagree with you—and being agreed with is often preferable to being disagreed with. Finally, your chances of being liked may often appear to increase with similar others.

But actually how strong is the relationship between attitude similarity and attraction? There is no doubt that "perhaps the most well known and well established finding in the study of interpersonal relations is that attitude similarity creates attraction" (Cappella & Palmer, 1990, p. 161). On the other hand, although the old adage "Birds of a feather flock together" may lead you to believe that attitude similarity is closely linked to attraction, there is also the recognition that "opposites attract." This issue has generated a tremendous amount of research and theorizing, and yet the exact nature of the relationship between attitude similarity and attraction remains elusive. At one extreme, Bochner (1991) believes it makes sense to proclaim the similarity-attraction relationship dead. Sunnafrank (1992) refers to the relationship as a "myth." He explains that research in platonic, romantic, and marital relationships doesn't substantiate the precept that general attitude similarity causes attraction. For example, friends in comparison to spouses and lovers have less attitude similarity. Friends do typically come from the same social class, the same geographical area, and the same social groups precisely because they have more opportunity to get acquainted and become friends. In that case, the fact that friends are similar is a consequence of coincidence or demographic matching. In addition, friends may be similar because they have frequently interacted in the past. With increased interaction, friends create their own similarities and have similar outlooks on the world. In such cases, friendship creates a similarity between people rather than being created by their similarity.

Understanding the role of similarity in relationship development has been problematic because similarity and attraction have been studied as isolated variables independent of interactional processes. Sunnafrank (1992) and others (e.g., Cappella & Palmer, 1990, 1992) have come to recognize that the impact of attitude similarity on attraction is weak and questionable when studied in the context of naturally occurring relationships. For example, does the initial period of interaction allow the communicators to discover similarities and thus lead to a favorable first impression? Or does initial interaction create a favorable first impression and thus lead to perceptions of similarities? Sunnafrank and Miller (1981) actually compared the relative influence of attitudinal similarity and initial conversations on strangers' first impressions of each other.

They found that, before the strangers interact, people tend to have a more favorable first impression of those who are similar to them. But they also found that only a few minutes of conversation between dissimilar persons counteracted many of the negative first impressions such people had of each other. In other words, before you talk with them, you will probably expect to be drawn to strangers to the extent that you think they are similar to you. However, when you actually talk with strangers who you thought were "different," you discover they aren't so different after all. The "getting acquainted" interaction actually intervenes and dilutes the impact of attitude similarity on attraction.

In fact, Sunnafrank (1992) posits that a consistent pattern does emerge from the studies of initial interaction in naturally occurring relationships. That is, communicative contact—even the smallest amount—will weaken and sometimes eliminate the impact of similarity on attraction. Although it has been found that dissimilarity can be repulsive (Rosenbaum, 1986), communicative contact can serve to increase the attraction between dissimilar strangers. Cappella and Palmer (1992), while recognizing the importance of initial communicative contact, caution individuals against assuming that it is the only interactive factor mediating the similarity-attraction relationship.

The relationship between similarity, attraction, and favorable first impressions within naturally occurring interaction is complex to say the least. Duck and Barnes (1992) offer some concluding thoughts about similarity and relationships. They argue provocatively that humans are faced with a dilemma. On the one hand, people recognize that their world (in this case their relationships) are fluid and changing. This realization is coupled with their fundamental need for order. So how do you resolve this dilemma? Your solution to the problem is to *create* a sense of order and rationality. Duck and Barnes (1992) claim "simply that the creation and application of meaning to the world are the driving force behind human life as human beings face the blooming, buzzing confusion that would otherwise exist without some applied construct system of meanings" (p. 203–204). People are thus influenced by similarity since it reflects meaning. Similarity is important not because it *exists* but because relational partners *recognize* it to exist. Similarity does not exist between partners, instead relational partners "come to be" similar through the process of negotiated interaction. Recall our comment earlier about the friendship creating the similarity. Relational partners come to recognize in their similarity a sharing of meaning which provides the framework for creating an orderly and therefore manageable world. For instance, research in marital communication consistently demonstrates that similarity per se is not as important as is the realization of a shared reality. This can explain why couples often presume that they are more similar than they are in actuality. "It is not similarity of attitudes, and all the rest, that is important of itself, but KNOWING that you are deeply similar in the meaning that you attach to things that counts" (p. 206). Similarity is necessary but not sufficient to the negotiation of relationships, and perhaps so, for far different reasons than has been assumed.

MAKING OPENING MOVES

Opening moves are required in three different situations (Bochner, 1984), one of which will be our focus. Openings are required when interactants begin a conversational episode, when an interactant discovers that a presumed acquaintance is really a stranger, and during the initial meeting of two strangers. We will be focusing on the third opening situation. The opening moves occur during the first few exchanges of interaction and serve as the "ignition" for relational "liftoff." They may not determine what the outcome of the relationship will be, but they will certainly affect whether the relationship will ever get off the ground and have a chance to develop into something more because openings build a framework for the rest of the interaction (Schiffrin, 1977). In this sense, the opening moves of "getting acquainted" communication can set the tone for the continued negotiation of the interpersonal relationship.

Initial interaction between strangers involves a number of opening moves which, like the other kinds of openings, serve to recognize the other participant, indicate involvement, and signal accessibility in the interaction (Schiffrin, 1977). These openings are accomplished in numerous manuevers. For the most part, opening moves involve the performance of *rituals*. But do not think of ritual as simply "going through the motions" of insincere and trite behaviors. "Ritual," according to sociologist Erving Goffman (1971), "is a perfunctory, conventionalized act through which an individual portrays his respect and regard for some object of ultimate value to that object of ultimate value or to its stand-in" (p. 62). In the case of interpersonal communication, that "object of ultimate value" includes both the other person, the relationship between them, and the culture in which they both reside. "Ritual," in the sense we use it here, is a celebration of those "objects of value" and is a way of demonstrating respect for them.

When communicators participate in rituals, they are celebrating the value of their culture and the worth of every individual human being who is a member of that culture. In a real sense, to perform a ritual is to confirm the influence of the social context and let both communicators know that this social context is important. Our discussions will consider two varieties of ritual that are important to the early stages of getting-acquainted interaction: *rituals of the situation* and *rituals of greeting.*

Rituals of the Situation

Each situation has its own rituals that are frequently repeated when people enter that situation. When you find yourself in one of these situations, you enact that situation's ritual. According to Goffman (1971), social contact occurs in one of three different situations: *business, accident,* and *ceremony.*

Business A *business* situation "requires" social contact and focuses the conversation on topics that are part of the situation. For example, two people who are colleagues in a work situation need to talk with each other so that they can perform their jobs. When you walk into a store to purchase something, your interaction with the salesperson is a business situation that governs how you behave. You and the salesperson are both aware that the nature of your relationship is "all business." That is, you came into contact in the first place because the situation demanded it. Neither of you has any expectation of further interaction concerning other topics or other areas of interpersonal contact. The result is that you both enact the ritual of seller-buyer interaction.

Accident The second situation involves accidental social contact. You just "happen" to bump into another person because you are both riding on the same bus, standing in the same ticket line, using the same elevator, walking on the same street, or attending the same social occasion. In these situations, social contact may be nothing more than a perfunctory exchange of greetings, or it may lead to further contact at some future time. That is, accidentally meeting someone at a party may be the occasion of your first interpersonal contact, but you may also make plans to continue your relationship before you break off that contact.

Some situations may lead to "accidental" meetings that tend to happen almost regularly. You meet someone at the regular meeting of a club, a social organization, or a church. Because you seem to be "accidentally" meeting the same person again and again, you eventually develop a relationship that extends beyond the limits of the accidental situation. The interaction ritual of the accidental situation may not cause you to maintain interpersonal communication, but its contact allows the relationship to develop into something further.

For example, a student once told Aub that he had noticed a fellow student in a class he was taking from Aub. He apparently found her physically attractive, but his problem was how to make social contact with her. Because of his work schedule, he typically arrived a few minutes late for class and could not select a seat next to her. He frequently waited after class in order to "accidentally" bump into her on the way out the door, but (according to his story) she always seemed to walk out the door while engaged in a conversation with some other student. The day finally arrived, however, when he waited to ask Aub a question after class, and also waiting to talk with Aub was the object of his frustrated affections. They talked with Aub about some common issue related to the class and walked out the door together, continuing to interact between themselves about topics related to the class. The two students began seeing each other regularly after that day, but it wasn't until much later that he told her that their first social contact was no accident. He had planned it all along.

Ceremony   *Ceremony* is the third type of situation and involves a ritual in which one person supports the other. The ritual is a ceremony in the sense that it accomplishes a particular purpose of interpersonal support. Such situations might frequently occur in relationships that have already established some level of trust or intimacy. For example, one person has a problem and frequently comes to a friend for help. A ceremonial ritual may also involve any person giving assistance to another, even if they were both strangers prior to that time. One person stops to help a stranded motorist, and they establish social contact. One person drops a load of books or packages, and another person performs the ceremonial ritual of helping retrieve the objects. In any case, the ceremony provides a reason for the social contact that places each person in a specific role relationship—the helper and the helpee, the supporter and the supportee. And who knows what will happen when a relationship begins on such a positive note?

Greeting Rituals

Greetings are a common ritual in opening moves and at the very least signal accessibility. The following interaction is a variation of the familiar opening moves that begin a conversation between friends or strangers in contemporary American culture:

A: Hi.
B: Hi.
A: Howya' doin'?
B: Pretty good. How's yourself?
A: Just fine.

No more perfunctory or cliché-ridden interaction ritual appears in daily life. Saying "Fine" or making some similar response to "How are you?" is as much a part of your unthinking ritualistic vocabulary as saying "You're welcome" to "Thank you." This is the greeting ritual that frequently constitutes the opening moves in a conversation between two people who bump into each other for the first time or between two friends who have not seen each other for a while. You enact the ritual without thinking about it. It comes easily to almost everyone.

Communication scholars Paul Krivonos and Mark Knapp (1975) have studied the American greeting ritual and suggest that, despite its perfunctory performance and conventional usage, it performs some highly important functions in your relationships. According to these authors (pp. 117, 118), the greeting ritual functions in American society: (1) "to mark a transition between a period of absence and a period of increased access" (for interactants who have already developed at least an acquaintanceship with each other), (2) "to reveal important information about the state of the relationship between the participants" (although the inquiry into personal health rarely seeks or reveals very important information), and (3) " to serve a maintenance function for interpersonal relationships" (especially the greetings between acquaintances who meet in passing).

When you say "How are you?" and the other person responds "Fine," you are telling each other that you have a relational bond that connects— even if that bond is only that you are members of generally the same culture. Of course, some specific cocultures have their own unique greeting rituals (such as the ritual handshake between blacks or fraternity brothers). When you greet each other, both of you expect that more interaction will follow, no matter how brief that interaction. If for no other reason, the greeting ritual is the absolutely first impression either of the interactants has of the other during interaction and is, therefore, important.

Greeting rituals include both verbal and nonverbal components, of course. These elements, when used by both interactants in concert, combine to form the complete ritual. Common greetings typically include such elements as a verbalized recognition of the existence of the other person (such as "Hi" or "How are you?"), a nod of the head typically accompanied by a smile, and some tactile (touching) contact typically of the hands (with all the variety of different handshakes and touching for various cultures). In some cultures, in fact, the tactile contact may include a kiss, smelling the facial cheeks (e.g., Burmese and Mongols), "friendly sniffing" or breathing

Most of us perform greeting rituals without thinking about them.

deeply (e.g., Balinese lovers), an embrace and rubbing of the backs (e.g., Polynesian men) (Gudykunst & Kim, 1984). Members of the French culture typically greet each other with both an embrace and a kiss on both cheeks—men and women alike. Female guests on late-night talk shows frequently greet their male hosts with a kiss, which suggests the existence of some "show business" culture that considers the kiss to be a part of a perfunctory greeting ritual. Many families also use the kiss as part of their greeting ritual. In other cultures or social situations, however, kissing implies a much more intimate relationship. The greetings of Asians involve moves which more clearly delineate status than the typical American handshake (Gudykunst & Kim, 1984). In Japan the bow, central to their greeting, is much more complicated than might be expected. The bow should appropriately reflect the status between the interactants. The interactant of lower status is expected to "shrink" in size compared to the "greatness" of the other. Therefore, the interactant of lower status begins the bow, bows deeper than the other, and the higher status interactant determines when the bow is completed. When interactants are of equal status they mirror each other's bows.

According to Krivonos and Knapp (1975), the greeting ritual is different for strangers than for pairs who have been previously acquainted. Their observations revealed that previous acquaintances typically greet each other with the following verbal and nonverbal behaviors, in this order:

mutual glance, head gesture (such as nodding to the other person), smile, verbal salute (such as "Hi"), a reference to the other person (such as calling the other person by name), a personal inquiry (such as "How are you?"), an external reference (such as "How's the family?"), and a topic initiation ("I've been meaning to speak to you about . . ."). Previously acquainted partners thus use the greeting ritual as a means to move directly into conversation. The ritual is rather complex (that is, contains a variety of different elements), rarely includes any gaps between elements, and is accomplished without much fuss or attention being paid to it.

Strangers generally use a greeting ritual that typically involves the same *types* of behaviors but differs in the *variety* of elements included in the ritual. Strangers tend to enact the following greeting ritual: mutual glance, head gesture, verbal salute, and personal inquiry. As you can see, the greeting ritual for strangers is much less complex and does not always lead smoothly into an extended conversation. Once strangers complete this rather simple exchange of behaviors, they have no rules to guide them in deciding where to go from there.

You rarely rehearse greeting rituals or prepare them in advance. You just naturally "fall into" the ritual because you know it so well. *Sixteen Candles,* one in a series of movies that tells the story of adolescent love, contains an episode in which the sixteen-year-old heroine rehearses the greeting she will use when she meets her dream boyfriend for the first time. She practices a variety of greetings in the hallway during a school dance until she decides on the "perfect" opening line. But when the big moment arrives, she becomes flustered and says absolutely nothing. Some time later, when the two adolescents actually do meet for the first time, she has prepared nothing. But they enact their greeting ritual with no problem whatsoever.

The greeting ritual is a convenient and important way to open the interaction, whether the communicators are strangers or good friends. For previous acquaintances, however, the greeting ritual is a natural and smooth way to introduce the conversation. For strangers, the greeting ritual is neither very natural nor sufficient. Strangers meeting for the first time face a very uncomfortable and risky situation. The opening moves in initial interaction are potentially threatening to each interactant's *face* (Laver, 1981). Your face is the public self-image you claim for yourself (Brown & Levinson, 1978). *Negative face* is your claim to carry out actions without interference by others (desire for autonomy) and *positive face* is your claim to a self-image (desire to be approved and appreciated by other interactants). Opening moves potentially threaten your claim to an appreciated and approved self-image or identity. Any routine behavior, by virtue of its "routineness," allows interactants to easily and safely enact appropriate roles which can indicate an acknowledgment and acceptance of each other's self-image, that is, being polite (Brown & Levinson, 1987). Greetings, as routine behaviors, function (Laver, 1981) to express positive *politeness* (protect positive face) and provide a way for strangers to manage the potential threat to face in initial interaction.

After the exchange of verbal salutes and personal inquiries, the greeting ritual for strangers concludes. At this point, strangers must be prepared to continue their interaction or conclude it. What comes after the opening greeting in the getting-acquainted stage of interpersonal communication? You guessed it—small talk! The small talk ritual is another form of routine, polite behavior. The early getting-acquainted interaction with strangers is often a matter of reducing uncertainty by following the rules of some social context and being polite. You know what the rules are from having been acculturated into that social context. The problem of negotiating your interpersonal relationships is rarely one of not knowing the rules of politeness in the early stages. Rather, it is a matter of knowing how and when to get the interaction moving beyond and into the later stages.

DOING SMALL TALK

Silence in the middle of a conversation can be an uncomfortable experience for strangers. It is awkward for both communicators. They have concluded their greeting ritual and are not sure what to expect next. They don't even know whose turn it is to talk. This period of relational discomfort is frequently a part of dialogue in comedy sketches. After an appropriate period of silence to establish the fact that everyone is uncomfortable, the sketch includes some comment that instantly draws laughter. "So . . . ," says one of the characters in a voice that is louder than normal and that draws out the response longer than necessary to enhance the feeling of relational discomfort. Or the comment may be a complete non sequitur, an obviously inappropriate act that introduces a topic without sufficient preparation: "How about them Dodgers?"

Why does the audience invariably laugh when this comedy sketch appears on some televised "sitcom?" The situation isn't particularly funny, and the line itself isn't very funny. Perhaps everyone in the audience has been in a situation just like that one. They are familiar with the awkward feeling of "What do I do now? Why doesn't he speak? Should I say something? What do I say?" Vanlear and Trujillo (1986) characterize this time period of the acquainting stage as "uncertainty." Tentativeness, uncomfortableness, and awkwardness characterize the interaction. At this point, somebody *must* do something. And for the relationship to move to some further stage of negotiation, both people have to do something *together* in the interaction. Fortunately, people have developed a whole repertoire of things to do in such situations. People have even given this "things to do until we can find something better to do" a name. People call it *small talk.*

Misperceptions of Small Talk

Virtually no one likes small talk. Virtually no one likes to do small talk. Virtually no one thinks small talk is important. If it were why is it called "small" talk? Perhaps people have come to condemn small talk because of some unfortunate but common experiences they've had in the past. Hence, people tend to overgeneralize their experiences as being a problem inherent with small talk. They don't like to do small talk because they think they aren't very good at doing it. So they tell themselves that it is not important. That is unfortunate.

The first step in improving your skill in doing small talk is to become aware of the misperceptions you may currently have of it. The next several pages will discuss three common reactions that people have to doing small talk. We will treat these objections as problems to be overcome in order that you may improve your interpersonal communication skill and get better at doing small talk.

Objection 1: "It's all so boring. Just one cliché after another. It's just so superficial. I never get to know the 'real' person."

Response: "Well, what do you expect? You just met the person, for heaven's sake. You want her or him to give you her or his entire autobiography right away? Don't be so impatient. Let things coast for a while. After you get to know each other, things will work out."

Small talk is a "reconnaisance dance" that allows each person to get to know the other in a low-risk context. This is a time for gathering information. In fact, small talk is much more informative than has been presumed. Kellermann (1989) discovered, in her studies of acquainting, that it is the observers of small talk interaction who tend to judge it as boring and uninformative, not the participants. This acquainting stage is referred to as "exploration" (Vanlear & Trujillo, 1986). Small talk, uncertainty reduction, and increased comfortableness characterize this stage as well as initial affective judgments (e.g., trust and attraction). Judgments about the "real" self of the other person and about your feelings toward them come later. This happens during the "interpersonal growth" acquainting stage (Vanlear & Trujillo, 1986).

Only after uncertainty reduction and increased comfortableness does it appear that interactants increase their judgments, especially their positive ones—trust and attraction. This stage could become the basis for intimacy at later stages or serve as the foundation "for the enduring relationships many acquaintances enjoy" (p. 389). The only way to make such judgments is to gather information from the other person and give information about your self to that person. Then both of you will have some basis on which to make an informed judgment. Without the safe opportunity that small-talk rituals provide for you to gather such information, you will have no basis for establishing any kind of relationship at all.

Objection 2: "All I ever seem to do is small talk. I meet one person, and just as we're getting to know each other, it's all over. Time to move on to the next person. Then we start all over again."

Response: "You're suffering from the 'cocktail party syndrome.' There are certainly some occasions that virtually force you to have too many and too brief encounters with too many persons. You need, then, to be more discriminating. Select the person or persons you want to spend more time interacting with, and then seek them out again. When the fish are biting, you don't keep all of them, do you? Of course not. You put only the big ones in your creel and throw the little ones back. You ought to be as discriminating with people as you are with trout."

Some situations, like the proverbial cocktail party or "rush" party in fraternities and sororities, include just too many interpersonal contacts and too little time for any of them to develop any depth. This situation may make you feel as helpless as the person who made the objection quoted above. This person is frustrated because the situation seems beyond his or her control. To avoid the feeling of being helpless or not in complete control, you need to develop coping strategies.

Small talk is not the problem here. The problem lies in the excessive demands of the situation. The solution to the problem is to discover strategies to cope with it. The simplest coping strategy is the one provided in the response. Seek out the persons who interest you and initiate another conversation. It should also be easier the second time around. You may also cope with the situation by getting away from the crowd. Suggest to the other person that you continue your conversation in a more secluded place, away from the hustle and bustle of the party. If you are standing, find a place to sit down. When both of you are seated, it is more difficult for other people to interrupt you or for your conversation to be terminated prematurely. Each of these coping strategies is aimed at controlling the situation by providing you with the opportunity to keep the small talk going.

Objection 3: "Boy, what an ego! All she wanted to talk about was herself. I couldn't get a word in edgewise, even if I had wanted to." *or* "Boy what a drag! He just wouldn't say anything. I had to do all the talking, and he just stood there like a dummy. I'll bet being married to him is really exciting!"

Response: "I can't believe it! Did you ever consider what the other person was thinking about you? Probably just the opposite! You oughta know that when you're nervous, you tend to either talk a lot or to say nothing. People are different that way. You probably showed how nervous you were by not saying anything (by talking all the time). And she (he) showed how nervous she (he) was by talking too much (by not saying anything). Right now, she's (he's) probably telling a friend about you and saying just the opposite. Now who's the dummy?"

When one person in the interaction carries too big a burden in doing the small talk, the interactants are not demonstrating competence in communicational skills. Both partners should feel that they are contributing equally to the conversation, even though the actual proportion of behaviors will never be exactly equal. The problem in such a situation is undoubtedly that the partners do not feel very comfortable.

You need to employ some communicative strategies that tend to equalize the conversational burden and make both of you feel more comfortable. If you think you are "carrying" the conversation, strategize your behaviors to encourage the other person to talk more. Ask open-ended questions, ones that require more than a simple yes-no response. Find out what interests the other person. Soon you will have a common area to talk about. If you think the other person is carrying the conversation, interject some comments that tell about your self. Give the other person the opportunity to get to know you. After all, the other person has already told you about her or his self. Now it's your turn. Take it.

The point to be made here is that small talk is probably more significant than people typically give it credit for being. Small talk is a major part of your interactional life. You will find yourself doing small talk perhaps more than any other kind of interaction. Therefore you really should be good at it.

The way to improve your skills in doing small talk is to practice them. Determine for yourself what the problem is and solve it for yourself by selecting some strategy appropriate to the occasion. You will probably find it amazing just how easy doing small talk is and how significant it is in helping you to negotiate your own interpersonal relationships. At the very least, you'll be invited to more parties. And that can't be all bad!

The Nature of Small Talk

You are all probably familiar with what small talk is like. You can certainly recognize it when you are doing it, and you can recognize it when you observe other people doing it. Small talk is routine behavior which transpires in conversation, often but not necessarily, between new acquaintances and in the very first phase of developing relationships—the getting-to-know-you stage. Small talk appears superficial, focuses on a topic of only minor importance, reveals very little of the speaker's inner self, and is guided by the rules of the social context. Because small talk engages in only trivial subject matter (e.g., the weather) in an apparently superficial manner, it can be considered to be virtually meaningless and without any special purpose except for killing time during conversation. As we pointed out earlier, however, small talk is an important ritual of politeness used by acquaintances to manage the early threatening moments of meeting and the later stages of acquainting. There are probably four general characteristics of interaction that provide a general description of what people have come to recognize as small talk:

1. "Interviewing interaction"—asking and answering questions.
2. "Safe" topics—removed from self and involving minimal risk.
3. Exchange of demographic information—who you are and where you're from.
4. Variety of different topics—little time spent on each.

Small talk is highly predictable. The exchange of questions and answers, of information about each person's self, is almost a ritual, it is so predictable. But underlying the familiar sequence of interaction is the expectation that something could potentially develop from this conversation. Small talk does more than just kill time until something better comes along. It allows time and opportunity for each partner to size up the other. It keeps the conversation going until the partners discover something that interests them both. Small talk gives communicators an opportunity to "practice" relating with each other. It is the rehearsal for some future performance—a prelude to a more fully developed relationship or the foundation for an enduring acquaintanceship.

Perhaps the principal function of small talk is to allow the participants to reduce their uncertainty about each other. Whenever you meet someone, especially for the first time, you undoubtedly have a number of questions running through your mind. Just who is this person? What does this person want of me? What do I mean to this person? What does this person mean to me? How should I act with this person? Where are we going? The problem is that neither partner knows much about the other and uses small talk to reduce that uncertainty. This stage is filled with uncertainty. On the other hand, due to the highly ritualized structure of initial interaction, characterized by stock actions and topics (Douglas, 1984), getting acquainted is neither totally unpredictable nor uncertain. Individuals are faced with uncertainty about the other (a high degree of novelty) and certainty about the structure of the interaction (predictability). One way interactants manage this tension between novelty and predictability is in small talk (Baxter, 1988). Small talk is ritualistic and affords the interactants safe opportunities for revealing themselves to each other.

Berger and Calabrese (1975), two communication scholars interested in early stages of communication, call this attempt to discover appropriate communicative behaviors a process of *uncertainty reduction*. Your inability to explain or predict the other person's actions, they argue, is the primary reason for your actions during this period (see also Berger 1979; 1987c). The goal of early interaction is to find out about the other person, and this concern for uncertainty reduction can be especially high if you anticipate seeing her or him again (Kellermann & Reynolds, 1990). To know how to act is to know who the other person is and who you are in relation to that other.

Recall from our discussions in Part One that when you encounter someone, even for the first time, the problem is not that you have no idea about what to expect. Rather, your problem is that you have too many such ideas. In your memories of the past are hundreds, perhaps thousands of social experiences; you've known many people fairly well and you've known *about* many more. Your problem is not what to expect, but which of your expectations is more likely to come true. Selecting an appropriate action in the pattern of initial interaction is not, then, a matter of discovery but of uncertainty reduction. Your problem is to select those actions appropriate to the present situation. You don't lack information, you want information (Kellermann & Reynolds, 1990). You want information to reduce the number of alternative behaviors by eliminating those actions that are inappropriate. And small talk affords each interactant the opportunity to ease into the relationship in gradual, incremental steps.

Small talk can resemble an "interview." After all, an employer interviews prospective job applicants in order to determine whether to hire them. A communicator interviews prospective relational partners in order to determine whether to include them as eligible friends. In a sense, each person in the getting-acquainted stage of communication is an actor auditioning for a role in an upcoming production called *Our Relationship*. Of course, each person is also judging the audition of the other to determine whether to continue with the drama. Small talk serves as a trial-and-error series of conversational topics until the participants create a shared reality from which to build a potential relationship.

You might think that directness during this getting-acquainted stage would be the best way to cut to the chase and find out about the other person. Certainly the idea of "interviewing" another would lead you to believe that direct questions would be the answer to the problem of initial interaction. In addition, directness is highly valued in many circles in some contemporary western societies (Tannen, 1990). Although compared to the Japanese, Americans are more interrogative in initial interaction with strangers (Gudykunst & Nishida, 1984), a closer examination of the research, doesn't support directness as the preferred informational strategy of American interactants in this phase of relational development. Indirectness is the dominant pattern, with periods of selected directness (Baxter, 1987a).

Remember that small talk affords interactants the opportunity to manage both the novelty and the predictability of initial interaction. Too many

direct questions to the other and/or increased openness from both participants may very well reduce uncertainty about the interactants, but it would
violate the norms of small talk (Baxter, 1987a; 1988). Small talk is a safe,
polite ritual of acquaintance. Interactants are expected to engage in superficial openness which signals a willingness for openness but protects self
from the threat of increased vulnerability due to the disclosure of private
information.

Appropriate indirectness works well in initial interaction because it
allows for the seeking and providing of information "off the record"
(Baxter, 1987a). Direct indications of involvement or rejection, for example,
don't allow participants to save positive or negative face. Indirect strategies,
however, provide "slippage," allowing a participant to deny the attributed
meaning of the message. For example, you may indirectly signal your
interest in a romantic relationship by talking about friends of yours who
are involved and happy. If the other negatively responds with "Relationships are great to have but right now I'm not ready," you can still maintain
your face because you didn't directly ask for a relationship. Whereas if you
directly said something like, "I really like you and want to go out with you,"
and the other rejects that remark, it would be much more difficult for you
to maintain your positive face. There is no slippage in avoiding the rejection.

Further evidence of indirectness in initial interaction is found in the
occurrence of "taboo topics," or those topics which are left unspoken
between the interactants. Baxter and Wilmot (1985) discovered that opposite-sex interactants, inbetween platonic and romantic stages, considered
direct discussion of the state of the relationship a closed topic. Participants
revealed that discussion of the status of the relationship placed it at risk.
The reasons they gave for avoiding direct relational talk included: (1) the
potential of revealing unequal commitment levels; (2) the potential loss of
face due to rejection by the other; (3) the introduction of a level of relational
work not presumed in acquainting; and (4) the signaling of greater closeness than expected in platonic relationships. Other topics that are not
directly talked about in the getting-acquainted stage include previous
romantic relationships, relationship sexual norms, and activities the other
does with other people. Baxter and Bullis (1986) have also found that direct
expressions of liking are not appropriate in the getting-acquainted stage.

A predominant pattern of indirectness in initial interaction doesn't
mean that the desired information can't be uncovered; you just are wise to
do it indirectly. For instance, how do you find out if someone likes you if
direct expressions of liking are not considered appropriate in these initial
stages? Baxter (1988) suggests that affinity-seeking (Bell & Daly, 1984) is
often indirectly achieved. You can keep the other's confidences, demonstrate adaptability by following conversational rules, signal similarity
through agreement, be supportive, and make an effort to be around the
other.

In a study of affinity testing in initial interaction, Douglas (1987) found that although direct questions (interrogation) occurred, they were found to be socially inappropriate. He discovered the predominant use of indirect strategies to test another's liking which included asking third parties (that is, utilizing the individual's social networks) and becoming less talkative (that is, being quiet and seeing if the other will continue the conversation). Initial interaction participants, as compared to participants in close dyads, must be able to test their liking for each other rather quickly. This may be why they consider actions which maintain the conversation highly appropriate for testing whether another likes them.

During small talk, each interactant attempts to draw some inferences about the "inner self" of the other person. You already know that inferences about a person's self on the basis of that person's behavior are highly prone to error. But that does not prevent people from trying to "psych out" the other person. People are so good (or bad) at perceiving things that you don't need much information in order to make some inferential judgment or perception. Recall that you always use perception to "fill in the blanks" between incomplete information and make judgments even when you don't have sufficient information. This means only that perception can be different not that you can't and don't make perceptions on the basis of insufficient information.

Small talk must begin somewhere, and it typically begins with areas of conversation that afford minimal risk of self. After all, one doesn't immediately plunge into an unfamiliar swimming hole without first testing the waters. And if the water is frigid, one typically wades in knee deep and allows the body to adjust gradually. There are always some people who dive into freezing water and claim that such practice is better than gradually acclimating the body. But this behavior can be considered foolhardy and obviously places the potential of a relationship at high risk.

Small talk should be allowed to run its course. Communicators will find subjects to talk about that include common interests or self-offers of a more significant nature. Until that happens, the best advice is to remain patient. And if it never happens? Well, not every acquaintanceship is meant to develop into a more extended relationship. Be satisfied with what you have. The greater risk is to accelerate a relationship prematurely or to give up on a relationship too soon. Probably the longest-lasting relationships are the ones that develop gradually over a comparatively long time. "Getting to know you" should be an enjoyable experience in and of itself. So give yourself the necessary time.

Scripts

When we used the term "audition" to refer to how acquaintances function in small talk, we are using the metaphor of the theater. We can extend this dramatic metaphor by referring to small talk as a similar process of enacting dramatic dialogue. Unlike a script prepared by a playwright, though, the scripts involved in the getting-acquainted stage of relationship development are improvised by the social actors even as they speak their lines (see Douglas, 1984). As in the improvisation exercises used in acting classes, actors don't prepare their scripts in advance, but are all aware of a common situational premise. Partners then create their own roles as they cooperate in acting out their common premise. The "premise" of initial interaction, of course, is "two strangers meeting for the first time for the purpose of getting acquainted."

A script of initial interaction has several characteristics that guide the acquaintances in making their opening moves. One, a script involves not just the actions of one person but a sequence of actions that are organized meaningfully. Two, a script provides the acquaintances with a set of expectations to guide them in creating their "roles." Three, a script is standardized and generally known to the social actors because they have experienced the same or a similar script in past interactions. Acquaintances do not know precisely what will occur next in the sequence, but they have a general idea of where the interaction is going. Of course, they can use their own comments to influence the future sequence of interaction patterns, but the basic idea of scripting their small talk is to allow each actor to adapt an appropriate response to the behavior of the other person. Scripts deal primarily with generalized experiences, those common to the widest variety of people. Therefore, virtually everyone is qualified, by past experiences, to contribute to the interaction.

Naturally, there are "good" scripts and "bad" ones. A good script allows both social actors to contribute equally from the same set of expectations. A bad script violates expectations and forces one of the participants to adapt to a situation that is out of control. The following hypothetical interaction is typical of a good script and should be familiar to all of you. In fact, good scripts are always familiar. That's what makes them "good":

A: Hi. I don't think I've seen you around here before.
B: No, this is my first time. Do you come here often?
A: Not as often as I'd like. Enjoying yourself?
B: Oh, yeah! That band is really hot!
A: They *are* good, aren't they?

This script takes advantage of the immediate environment to provide a topic for conversation. Both interactants are experiencing the sounds of the music and agree on their judgment. Of course, their script may also be following the rule of politeness, which tells them not to disagree with each other during this early stage of getting acquainted.

The following script is also a good one, but it involves little more than a greeting ritual. Nevertheless, the greetings lead the participants immediately to a point of commonality, which they quickly exploit:

A: Hi. My name is Symon.

B: Hi. I'm Megan. (They shake hands.) Hello, Symon.

A: Call me Sy. Everybody else does.

B: Okay, Sy. Do you live around here?

A: Yup. I went to high school just down the street.

B: You went to Olympus High? I had a lotta friends go there.

A: Really? Who were they? Maybe I know them.

Not all conversations "luck into" a topic of commonality so quickly. Often the script must proceed through the weather and a host of other "safe" topics before the actors find a topic of common interest. The point is not *when* the area of common interest is introduced; it's whether the actors take advantage of it when it does come up. At that point, the actors don't need the script anymore. They can branch out into more creative exploration of their potential relationship.

The following interaction is a "bad" script. It illustrates a creative opening line, but creativity is rarely of value in scripts of getting-acquainted interaction. To be too creative is to violate the set of common expectations. It typically leads to a premature termination of the interaction, and the chance for extended development is lost:

A: Well, how do you like me so far?

B: What?

A: I asked you how you like me so far.

B: But I've never seen you before in my life!

A: Yeah, I know. How'm I doin' so far?

B: How should I know? You're kinda weird.

A: A lotta people feel that way at first, but I grow on you after a while.

B: Yeah, so do warts. Excuse me. There's somebody I need to talk to.

You can just bet that the sudden compulsion to talk to "somebody" is a direct result of the desire to get away from the "weirdo." The actor had the option of attempting to cope with the script by "going along" with what is an obvious violation of the rules for greeting rituals. Actor B might have thought that the "opening move" was clever and could have reciprocated with clever comments such as "I don't think you're doing so hot. But I'm really doing great!" In this way the actor might have coped with the unexpected by using a strategy designed to regain control of the interactive situation. In the script above, however, the actor elected to use a coping strategy designed to withdraw from the situation as quickly as possible. But she couldn't resist taking that "parting shot" and letting "the weirdo" know just how she felt about his deviant behavior. But even after that retort, she continued to adapt to the rules of politeness and terminated the conversation in the ritualized form of asking permission ("Excuse me") to leave.

When interactants are using a script, they are communicating with a common set of expectations. Both communicators know what each is supposed to do. After all, they have played out this script numerous times in the past. But the script is always subject to change, and the wording of each line is not typically prepared beforehand. Each social actor improvises while enacting the script and is prepared to depart from the script at any time during this beginning small talk. When the script is a bad one and violates the expectations of one or more of the social actors (as in the example above), the departure from the script is often an exit line.

Obviously, there are good and bad scripts of initial interaction. Douglas (1991) provides one reason why some go bad. Interactants develop scripts of initial interaction from their numerous participation in this kind of interaction. Interactants' accounts of initial interaction experience reflect an awareness of uncertainty, not so much as a part of getting acquainted, but as an overall uncertainty about acquaintanceship in general that is, *global uncertainty*. Further, interactants vary in their degree of global uncertainty. Those interactants high in global uncertainty are comparatively less competent in enacting initial interaction episodes and don't relax easily during acquainting. Douglas (1991) concluded that these individuals aren't very successful getting acquainted with others because of inefficient initial interaction scripts.

When Opportunity Knocks . . .

The expectations or social norms that govern "getting acquainted" interaction are both advantageous and disadvantageous to interpersonal communication. They have the advantage of making possible interaction between two highly diverse people in a variety of situations. Small-talk interaction is polite and "safe" in the sense that it is unlikely to threaten anyone's self-concept. The social rules of politeness and use of scripts make interaction easy, but they also make continued evolution of the relationship difficult. After all, "Nothing ventured, nothing gained." Baxter (1988) cautions, for example, that the interactional predictability of small talk may forestall getting to know the other. Some appropriate novelty is required in order to learn about the other and reduce the uncertainty on the interactant level. In other words, if the relationship is going to evolve into something other than casual acquaintance, the interaction must move away from rules of politeness and persistent use of low-risk topics.

According to sociologist Suzanne Kurth (1970), "In forming a friendship individuals must 'move' away from what is required to what is clearly voluntary. For this movement to occur, one must make an initial move to indicate that he desires a change in the relationship" (p. 152). Now making that "initial move" from the safety of small-talk interaction is a risky business. Three things can happen, and two of them are bad. One, the other person may not reciprocate your move to a further stage of relational development, and you run the risk of damage to your face. Two, you may develop a relationship that is not satisfying, and you have a more difficult problem of extricating yourself from a developed relationship (the topic of

Chapter 10). Three, you may develop a friendship with the person, and you can't have too many friends.

So how do you make that initial move? How do you know that it is the "right" move? How can you make sure that the two "bad things" don't happen? These questions have no sure-fire answers. You simply don't *know* that the move away from small talk is the "right" move. You simply don't *know* that the two bad things won't happen to you. There is no list of "initial-move strategies" that you can memorize and use when the time is right. You have only the option to keep the small talk going until the opportunity comes along to change the direction of the interaction pattern and take advantage of that opportunity. Taking advantage of opportunities also means either making the initial move away from "safe" interaction or responding to your partner's initial move. You cannot change the direction of the relationship alone; only both partners working together can accomplish such a feat.

A typical opportunity to make an initial move away from the tension-filled interaction can occur when one or both of the partners violates one of the rules governing the situation. An instance of this kind of rule breaking, though, must not appear to be conscious and willful (as in the preceding example of the "bad script"). But accidental rule breaking occurs frequently in polite and stereotyped interaction. The most common violation is probably in the rules of turn taking. Silence is awkward and uncomfortable. Both social actors feel some responsibility to keep the conversation going. Therefore, when a pause occurs in getting-acquainted communication, both will simultaneously be thinking of a comment that fills the gap. And that means that both may simultaneously take the turn, so that both end up speaking at the same time—a potential violation of turn-taking rules.

When a turn-taking violation occurs, the typical response is to laugh—nervous, not fun-filled laughter. The following hypothetical interaction involves the opportunity to move away from the small talk. It occurs immediately after a period of silence when both partners attempted to speak at the same time. Both partners are aware that they have violated turn-taking rules and attempt to use strategies that repair the damage:

A: I'm sorry. You go ahead.

B: No, it was my fault. You go first.

A: Well . . . [pause] I can't remember what I was going to say. [laughs]

B: [also laughing] Really? Do you have these memory lapses often?

A: No, not usually. But it couldn't have been very important. Now what were you saying?

B: [pause] Now I can't remember what *I* was talking about. [both laughing through the next several comments]

A: Can you believe it? Neither one of us has a memory that's worth a darn.

B: You know, you're right. Come to think of it, I seem to remember that I had this same problem when I was taking my final exams last week.

A: You, too? I'm always suffering from loss of memory, then, too. I think it's called "academic amnesia."

B: [getting serious] You know, it's really fun talking with you.

A: Yeah. Me, too.

Now this conversation seems rather ludicrous. Nothing happens to make the conversation fun except that the partners have released a lot of tension by laughing about their "mistake." Neither partner knows much more about the other person's similarity in attitudes or interests, but they have combined to "break the ice" that inhibited their relational development. Releasing tension, for whatever reason, is a pleasant feeling. And whenever it occurs, the interactants will experience a personal feeling of relief and a joint feeling of being closer together. Releasing tension means that they don't have to be "on guard" anymore; they don't have to be so careful of what they say and do; they don't have to play it so safe anymore. In other words, the interaction is more fun.

The opportunity to make an initial move away from small talk may also occur by identifying some mutual interest or acquaintance as the small talk wanders from topic to topic. The form of the initial move is simply not very important. What is important is being ready to take advantage of any opportunity to make the initial move. That move must be unusual in the sense that it is somehow noticeably different from the interaction that preceded it during small talk. The initial move away from getting-acquainted interaction is out of the ordinary; it is not expected.

Turning points are "any event or occurrence that is associated with change in a relationship" (Baxter & Bullis, 1986, p. 470). They are considered central to change in relationships, and understanding them can vastly improve your understanding of the process of relating. Baxter and Bullis (1986) found that the "getting-to-know time" for romantic couples comprised three major turning points which promoted their getting to know each other. The first was when they first met, the second were times they spent doing things with each other, and the third was their first date. Direct relational talk occurred less during this time period than during any other, as stated earlier in our discussion of small talk.

Most importantly, both interactants must participate in the change in relational development. One person can make an initial move, but it means nothing unless and until both partners enact the interaction pattern that departs from small talk. If that change in interaction pattern does not occur, then the relationship continues as one of acquaintanceship. If and when it does occur, a potential change in the definition of the relationship occurs.

PATTERNS OF INTERACTION

Often people think of getting acquainted as only a preliminary stage they have to pass through on their way to a more interesting relationship. Hence, people tend to think of those relationships that remain acquaintanceships as somehow "retarded"—relationships arrested in the "normal" process of development and therefore not as "good" as other relationships such as, say, friendships. Such an attitude toward acquaintanceships is undoubtedly mistaken. Throughout your lifetime, you will have far more acquaintanceships than friendships. Even though every acquaintanceship has the potential of developing into a friendship at any time, far more acquaintanceships remain acquaintanceships.

Whether the relationship is a long-term acquaintanceship or a friendship in some early stage, the patterns of interaction that define the relationship are virtually the same. Partners in long-lasting acquaintanceships tend to enact the same communication patterns as partners in the initial stages of a developing friendship. The only difference is that acquaintanceships continue those interaction patterns for longer periods of time and friendships change the patterns to something else.

Acquaintances in one research study (Adams, 1985) of strategic interaction in interpersonal relationships tended to define their relationships in a similar manner:

> "Sue is easy to talk with, but a lot of 'newness still' in the relationship. A real nice person I am enjoying getting to know."
>
> "I don't know Joe particularly well. We are acquaintances because a context brings us together; otherwise I would not have instigated the relationship on my own."

Partners in acquaintance relationships may feel that the relationship is still "new" and that it could develop into something more. Or they may feel that the acquaintanceship is merely the result of circumstances, such as happening to meet at work as colleagues, and will never develop beyond its present state. Despite the differences in these expectations, though, their definitions of the relationship are quite similar. Most importantly, the interaction patterns of acquaintances are amazingly similar. They generally talk about the same issues in much the same manner, and they generally use the same strategies in accomplishing their interaction.

Relational Issues

Not surprisingly, Adams (1985) discovered that acquaintances enacted their relationships by relying heavily on *self-as-object* issues. Each person takes a turn telling the other about personal experiences and interests. For example, "I'm really into cameras. I'm constantly taking pictures of interesting things and blowing them up and framing them and things like that." Each person takes a turn asking the other about personal experiences and interests but rarely identifies with the other's experiences.

Acquaintances tend to define other people through their own individualized personal experience or relationship. For example, "I have a friend who works for IBM." And each person tends to draw conclusions or generalizations derived from personal experiences. For example, "So as a result, most females don't really establish a career for themselves until they're around thirty." The result is a lot of "I" and "me" (or "you" and "your") talk, but little "we" and "our" talk in reference to the joint relationship of the interactants.

Each acquaintance tends to define his or her self quite independently from the other person or the relationship. Each retains "possession" of his or her self and does not offer much of that self to the relationship. Participants in an acquaintanceship rarely tend to define their selves in terms of the relationship they have with each other. Consequently, each self remains distinct from the other during interaction. Even though the partners may exchange confidences (as in self-disclosure), each person keeps his or her definition of self intact and separated from that of the partner.

The interaction patterns of acquaintances reflect the phenomenon of *parallel selves.* Imagine two parallel lines running side by side into the far distance, much like a pair of railroad tracks. The two rails maintain the same distance from each other, never touching or crossing at any point. The self-offers of acquaintances interacting with each other are similarly parallel. Neither partner typically identifies his or her self with the relationship. Neither partner typically responds to the other person's self-offer as anything but an offer that "belongs to" the other person. Consequently, the interaction continues as a parallel development of each person's self. An interpersonal relationship with which the partners identify themselves is never allowed to develop.

Relational Strategies

Getting-acquainted interaction often includes patterns similar to those of "interviewing." One person serves as the questioner and the other person is the answerer. This pattern of interaction addresses the self-as-object issue by allowing each person to tell the other about personal experiences and opinions. The following hypothetical interaction is typical of this interviewing pattern:

A: Are you a skier, then? It seems like everyone is around here.

B: Yup. I gotta admit I really do enjoy skiing.

A: Cross-country or downhill?

B: I do both actually, but mostly I enjoy downhill. That's really a rush when you're flying downhill in deep powder. There's nothing like it in the whole world.

A: You must be a pretty good skier then.

B: Oh, I don't know about that. I got a lotta friends who are better, but I keep up with them pretty good. Do you ski?

A: Some, but mostly cross-country. It's a lot cheaper, and I like to get outside in the wintertime. Most people I know seem to do nothing but watch TV when there's snow on the ground. I've gotta be doing something, or I get bored stiff.

B: Where do you go? In the touring centers, or do you get off in the back country?

A: I've been to a lot of places, but generally I go on established trails. I'm a little leery of avalanches. How about you? Do you like to break your own trail?

Interviewing allows each partner to tell the other about personal experiences and opinions. Furthermore, each person easily switches roles in this interviewing pattern, from being the interviewer to being the interviewee and back again. The answers tell about personal experiences, and the questions ask for or invite the other person to tell about personal experiences. The result is a pattern in which each person tells the other (whether asked or not) about things that are personal. These exchanges tell each partner a great deal about the other's self while keeping that self separate from the other person and the relationship.

The interaction patterns can also reflect parallel selves when the response to the other's personal experience says, in essence, "Me, too." For example, one person may respond to a personal experience with a comment that says, in essence, "That same thing happened to me:"

A: I just can't stand the dentist chair. I get so tensed up.

B: I know what you mean. I'm always gripping the arms of the chair.

A: The last time I went, the dentist told me, "Ease up. I'm not going to hurt you." Dentists always lie like that.

B: Oh yeah. Whenever he says that, watch out. You know that pain is coming.

A: Isn't that the truth? I remember once the dentist started to drill before the Novocaine started working, and I thought I was gonna go through the ceiling.

B: Oh, that's terrible! I can imagine how that felt. It's bad enough when the stuff wears off and every tooth in your head hurts.

A: He said he was sorry, but that didn't help much. It still hurt.

B: Don't you just hate it when he says he didn't mean to hurt you? I don't think I could ever be a dentist. To be hated by everybody, even little kids.

A: Really. I don't think I would want to look in people's mouths all day, either. Especially when they have halitosis.

This interaction reflects a personal experience that is common to many people. Each person contributes to the interaction by drawing on his or her own individual experience. But the experience is personal to each acquaintance individually rather than one that they shared together. In other words, each of the acquaintances had an individual experience, and the coincidence or similarity of those individualized experiences provides the basis for their interaction. The selves of the acquaintances overlap only because of coincidental experiences. Each partner's personal experience parallels the personal experience of the other, and their interaction continues to reflect a parallel-selves pattern.

Even when acquaintances exchange personal opinions, their interaction continues to reflect the same pattern of parallel selves. To be polite, the respondent feels obligated to agree with the other's opinion, even though agreement may not accurately reflect his or her opinion. The obligation to agree, regardless of what you may really think, is greatest when the other person invites (and implicitly expects) you to agree. The following hypothetical interaction reflects such obligatory agreement of opinions:

A: I just don't understand how we can continue to knuckle under to all these terrorists. Like the airplane hijacking in Lebanon and the bombing of the World Trade Center in New York. I think we should just go over there and bomb 'em all to pieces. Don't you think so?

B: We gotta do something, that's for sure.

A: Those guys are just trying to get some publicity, that's all. I think the government oughta tell all those TV guys and journalists that they can't give them any air time. Every time one of these things happen, they just oughta make a big news blackout, right?

B: I admit a lotta those terrorist guys like to get on camera a lot. You're right, they seem to play to the media parading the hostages around, shooting their guns and everything.

A: Yeah, just go over there and drop an atomic bomb or something. I bet we wouldn't have so many hijackings and stuff any more.

B: Well, I don't know about that, but something's gotta be done.

When you engage in "polite" interaction, you feel compelled to abide by the social rules that govern such interaction. One rule that seems implicitly to govern "good manners" is not to disagree too much with the other person. Disagreeing is tantamount to showing disrespect. Consequently, even when the other person states absolutely outrageous opinions (such as "nuking" entire countries), you don't want to run the risk of appearing disrespectful. Rather than say the obvious "Are you out of your mind?" or "That's the most asinine thing I've ever heard," you bide by the rules and behave as the person in the above interaction does. Although you may not express wholehearted agreement, you don't disagree either.

The rules of politeness obligate you to respond in a manner that avoids rudeness. Acquaintances just don't know each other well enough to disagree very much. And besides, interaction with acquaintances just isn't important enough to spend the effort to disagree. The result is a continuation of the parallel-selves pattern, even though it may not reflect your "real" self.

The obligation to be polite does not mean that you don't ever disagree with your acquaintance-partner. It means that the obligation to avoid disagreeing is so strong that you feel the need to justify or apologize for your disagreeing response. Hence, when you are about to disagree with an acquaintance, you may flag the answer with a precise statement that a disagreement is coming (for example, "You may be right, but . . ." or "I have to disagree with you about that, but . . ."). Your flagging strategy will also tend to minimize the importance of the disagreement. You may also use a strategy that disclaims responsibility for the disagreement by attributing it to some other person or aspect of the situation (for example, "I was reading an editorial in the paper the other day that didn't agree" or "I'm probably wrong, but . . .").

In any case, the acquaintance who wants to disagree still has the freedom to do so. But the obligation of observing the social rules of politeness is so strong that the acquaintance feels the need to phrase the disagreement in such a way as to avoid potentially negative reactions. It is apparently better to ignore the outrageous opinions of others than to let them think you are rude.

Reciprocity has been discussed earlier, particularly in regard to communication and enacting relationships. That is, when someone tells you something about his or her self, you are likely to tell that other person something about your self on the same topic and with about the same depth of disclosure. This kind of reciprocity associated with self-disclosing communication involves the tendency to respond "in kind." In-kind reciprocity is essentially analogous to the golden rule—"Do unto others as they do unto you."

Acquaintances tend to reciprocate each other's self-offers in kind. They seem to be saying "You tell me something about your self, and I'll tell you something about my self." You and your acquaintance-partner then take turns telling each other about personal experiences, opinions, interests, and the like. This kind of interaction, typically in terms of self-disclosing communication is another symptom of a parallel-selves pattern. The self-offers that are embodied in in-kind reciprocity do not include a definition of self based on the relationship but, rather, a definition limited to one's personal self-concept. The comments may disclose a little or a lot about one's self-concept, but they offer a definition of self that is quite separate from the relationship. The pattern reflects the characteristic of two distinctive self-concepts moving through the interaction on parallel tracks—in other words, parallel reciprocity.

In summary, interaction patterns of acquaintances reflect comments that address self-as-object issues. Comments consistently reflect each person's orientation to his or her own self-concept. The result is an interaction of parallel selves, with each person maintaining and, to some extent, protecting his or her individual self-concept. Self-offers consistently refer to personal experiences, interests, and even opinions that belong to the individual. When acquaintances discuss the same experiences, their interaction reflects general but individually distinct experiences that merely happen to coincide with each other. Reciprocity in the interaction, like that of self-disclosing communication, is merely a response in kind, in which acquaintances take turns relating similar experiences or opinions.

The interaction patterns of acquaintances may reflect the interpersonal communication of partners who have just met and will ultimately move into a relationship of greater intensity and intimacy. Or they may reflect a long-term acquaintanceship, in which partners maintain their relational definition for an extended period of time (often for years). At any point in time, though, the interaction patterns of acquaintances or acquaintanceships are subject to change and further development—toward increasing or decreasing communion or toward increasing or decreasing intimacy, intensity, and trust.

As their definition of their relationship evolves to something new and different, the communicators enact different interaction patterns to reflect that new and different definition. In fact, as the participants enact a new and different interaction pattern, they tend to create a new and different definition of the relationship. In other words, "interaction patterns" and "definition of the relationship" are equivalent terms. And those changes of interactional patterns and relational definitions, for better or for worse, are the subject of discussion in the next chapter.

SUMMARY

The initial stage of developing a relationship is commonly known as the getting-acquainted phase of communication. This interaction may include newly acquainted partners who move through this first stage on their way to friendship or partners who are maintaining a long-term relationship of acquaintance. Getting-acquainted interaction involves the mutual attempts of each partner to manage the first impressions of the other person and requires them to be able to recognize which situations and circumstances are best for fostering first impressions. Common influences on first impressions include prior expectations, physical attractiveness, and similarity of the relational partners.

The interaction of this first stage typically reflects the rules and norms from some larger society or social situation to which both relational partners belong. Opening moves serve to recognize the other participant, indicate involvement, and signal accessibility. Greetings are typical rituals in opening moves which are polite and orderly.

The commonly recognized term for getting-acquainted interaction after greetings is "small talk." Small talk is another routine behavior in which participants are focused on reducing uncertainty on a personal level. Small talk includes an exchange of demographic information, conversational topics involving little risk, and generalized discussions about situationally prominent interests. Small talk is highly predictable, functions to reduce each partner's uncertainty about the other, and allows the opportunity for the partners to safely "audition" each other to determine the potential for further development of their relationship. Indirectness is preferred to directness allowing interactants greater opportunity to maintain face.

The polite and stereotyped interaction of small talk often reflects the use of a "script" in which the sequence of actions is meaningfully organized; both partners have a common set of generalized expectations based on being familiar with the pattern because of their previous interactional experiences. Small talk, while making interaction easy, actually inhibits development of the relationship unless the partners depart from their script and precipitate some change. To move away from small talk requires one of the partners to take advantage of some opportunity for change (typically a release of tension) and make an initial move. The departure from small talk also requires an appropriate response that allows both partners to modify the interaction pattern and the definition of the relationship.

Interaction patterns of acquaintances and acquaintanceships reflect discussion of self-as-object issues. Strategies include comments that inform the other person about personal experiences, interests, and opinions as well as prompting or inviting the personal experiences, interests, and opinions of the other person. These interaction patterns place obligations on the communicators to follow the rules of good manners and inhibit disagreement which, when it occurs, is typically flagged with disclaimers or attributions or responsibility away from self.

Patterns of small talk indicate interaction that emphasizes the parallel selves of the interactants. Each partner consistently retains a personal orientation to the conversational topics and avoids a self-offer that incorporates the relationship into his or her definition of self. Reciprocity in small talk reveals a similar parallelism of self-concepts in which each interactant responds in kind to the other's comments, a pattern typical of the reciprocity commonly associated with self-disclosing communication.

KEY TERMS

ecology of attraction	face
dislike criteria	negative face
disregard criteria	positive face
opening moves	politeness
rituals	small talk
business	uncertainty reduction
accident	global uncertainty
ceremony	turning points

CHAPTER 9

Creating Relationships— Integration/ Disintegration, or "Ups and Downs"

> The outcome of the contracts of two individuals is not mechanically predetermined either by the relation of their personality characteristics or the institutional patterns providing the context for the development of their relation—though these are both certainly to be taken into account—but . . . the outcome is an end-product of a sequence of interactions characterized by advances and retreats along the paths of available alternatives, by definitions of the situation which crystalize tentative positions and bar withdrawals from certain positions, by the sometimes tolerance and sometimes resolution of ambiguity, by reassessments of self and other, and by the tension between openendedness and closure that characterize all human relationships that have been reduced to ritual.
>
> —Bolton

This chapter is about changes in developing relationships. It is about the relational bonds which unite two or more people within a relationship and serve to define the selves of the individuals as a result of their being so related. To enter a new stage of a relationship with another person is to travel into the unknown. You have no guarantee that the relationship will develop into one that you find satisfying, just as you have no guarantee that you won't be hurt by or disappointed in the relationship that develops. In some relationships, you are consciously aware that you and your partner are becoming something more than casual acquaintances. In most relationships, though, you may be quite unaware of any significant relational change until after you have enacted a new definition of that relationship.

This chapter deals with multiple directions of change—integration and disintegration. Such growth and decline, however, are not necessarily the same things in reverse. That is, the decline of a relationship is not merely a matter of backtracking the road that once led to intimacy (Baxter, 1983). This chapter will discuss the function that emotions play (and don't play) in integrating and disintegrating relationships. We will also discuss the characteristics of both increasing intimacy and declining intimacy, as well as the factors that precipitate the rise and fall of interpersonal relationships. Most importantly, of course, we will discuss the issues and strategies of changes in relationships, the actual communicative behaviors that people use when enacting their relationships. We can never overemphasize that the term "interpersonal relationship" is just another way of saying "interpersonal communication."

THE RISE AND FALL OF INTERPERSONAL RELATIONSHIPS

An implication of equifinality is the realization that no two relationships develop in exactly the same way. One highly intimate relationship may have seemed like "love at first sight." Another may have been a slow and gradual process in which each person "sorta grew on" the other. Another relationship may have had a stormy beginning in which intimacy came about despite a "bad start." Similarly, two relationships rarely decline in precisely the same way. One relationship may decline traumatically and dramatically from a state of mutual bliss, while another may reflect a slow and gradual process of drifting apart. Still another relationship may decline after the partners realize that their integration never reached the point that they wanted, so they quit trying and allow their budding relationship to wither and die.

Bolton's (1961) study of newly married couples in Chicago did in fact reveal several different patterns in their movement toward marriage. For some couples one partner or both, had an identity crisis and used marriage as a way of managing the crisis. For example, one of Kathy's closest friends once told the story about why her mother married her father. Her mother's route to marriage didn't follow the romantic ideal of love at first sight. When her mother met her father she was a young woman feeling very trapped in a small town in Iowa. When her mother met her father, a young naval officer, she found him very exciting. Marriage was her ticket out of town. They eventually married and have remained together for over sixty years. Other couples, he found followed patterns of relational addiction, analyzing their relationship to the altar. In still other relationships, one partner was particularly ready for marriage and pressured the other into marriage. Sometimes an event occurs (such as sexual intimacy or living together), which, once undertaken, propels the couple toward marriage. Other times, couples who see each other for an extended period of time begin to objectify the relationship. They differentiate themselves as a couple, others see them as a couple, and over time the support for their "coupleness" leads to a formal commitment. One of Kathy's best friends followed this pattern to commitment. During the three years before their marriage, they dated, traveled together, alternated between apartments, supported each other in times of crisis, and interacted with friends and family as a couple. One weekend, while she was knitting and he was reading, he looked up from his magazine and said, "Why don't we get married?" They did so, and after two children and ten years they are still married. Bolton's (1961) research recognizes several process patterns out of which marital commitment emerges: Couples can get to the same place (that is, the altar) in a variety of ways. Although Bolton studied newlyweds, the same can probably be said of the development of any close commitment.

Regardless of the dissimilarities in how relationships develop, one characteristic is overwhelmingly typical of nearly all: They fluctuate back and forth between good times and bad. They have high points and low points. There are many periods of growth and decline. Alan Alda characterized his marital relationship as fluctuating back and forth unpredictably between periods of mutual neglect to "waves" of emotional attachment. Ann Morrow Lindbergh (1975) writes, "We have so little faith in the ebb and flow of life, of love, of relationships. We leap at the flow of the tide and resist in terror its ebb . . . when the only continuity possible, in life as in love, is in growth, in fluidity" (p. 108). Nearly every relationship that develops some noticeable degree of intimacy and involvement (that is, any relationship beyond casual acquaintanceship) will experience its ups and downs. How do you chart these ups and downs? In this section we will take a closer look at change in relationships, some typical developmental models, the issues often faced by those who seek to explain how human relationships develop, and some new ideas about relationship development.

Relationship Development

Part Three is primarily devoted to different stages of developing relationships: the "getting started" stage, the "growing together/apart" stages, the "let's end it all" stage, and finally "keeping it all together." Taken together, the chapters in this part emphasize the evolutionary aspect of relationships. As communication continues, the relationship is constantly changing, constantly in a state of becoming something different from what it was, constantly evolving. Evolutionary change is an inherent and inevitable fact of all relationships, all interpersonal communication. As long as interpersonal communication continues, the relationship is continually undergoing change. Change is constant in interpersonal communication. In other words, change is "normal."

Characteristics of Relational Change

One communication scholar, Dick Conville (1983), has speculated that the development of a relationship inherently involves change, that change in one part of the relationship affects the entire relationship. He proposes that there are four typical characteristics of relational change: Change is "predictable," change is "unique," change is "oblique to its happening," and change involves "exchange . . . of securities." Whether the change is toward increasing integration (growth) or disintegration (decline), the process of change is similar in these four respects.

Change Is Predictable   To say that change in a relationship is *predictable* is not to suggest that the relational partners are aware of what the outcome of the relational change will be. Nor does predictability, as the word is used here, imply that relational change is irreversible. Once change toward integration or disintegration has begun, a relationship can and frequently does reverse its trend and head in the opposite direction. It may be more appropriate to say that change is *inevitable.* Change *will* occur; that's highly predictable. Furthermore, any change in a relationship also leads to a change in how each partner evaluates and assesses that change and behaves.

What happens when two newly married people, for example, experience their "first fight"? That experience will inevitably affect their interaction in future episodes, and it will lead them both to assess their relationship differently. The partners realize that change is occurring or has occurred. After the episode, they know that the honeymoon is over, and their relationship will not be the same as it was before. That single experience may lead to a stronger relationship or a weaker relationship. In either case, both partners will evaluate their relationship differently.

Change Is Unique   The second characteristic indicates that relational change is *unique.* You already know, however, that relationships develop differently for different people and at different times. That certainly is not news. The point here is that because relational change is unique, no one possesses sure-fire techniques for dealing appropriately with change when it occurs. Hence, every time a change occurs in a relationship, both partners have to struggle with it. It is not enough simply to rely on your past experiences to provide guidelines for how you deal with a particular relational change. Each relationship is unique, and so the behaviors that worked in past relationships may be totally inappropriate to the present one. Nearly everyone appears to have a tacit understanding of this fact, too. Although people in the midst of a change in a relationship may seek advice from someone else, they are likely to respond to advice by thinking, "Yeah, but this time is different."

Change Is Oblique to Its Happening   The third characteristic of relational change is that development *is oblique to its happening.* People in the midst of relational development often cannot get beyond the immediate situation to see what is happening. In other words, when in the midst of a change in the relationship, the partners may be aware that some change is occurring, but they are so caught up in the immediate details of their relationship that they are unable to do anything about it. Only upon reflection, *after change has occurred,* are they able to understand the nature of the change and how it has affected them personally and their relationship.

Let's illustrate this notion. Imagine yourself being stuck on a deserted highway with a car that is out of gas. That situation is so significant that nothing else seems important. But you can't do anything about it. Some time later, you may recall being on that road and you may be able to analyze what you were thinking and feeling at the time. You may even look back on the situation with some amusement or tell the story as an interesting experience. But at the actual time of your disaster, you have no thoughts except how to get yourself out of it.

That understanding which comes from retrospection is as true when a relationship is escalating toward intimacy as when it is "on the skids." When two people are in the midst of an integrative change, they are so caught up in the euphoria of the moment that they may not be able to assess what is happening. When the relationship sours, the partners are so caught up in their predicament that all they can think about is how to get out of it. As a matter of fact, about the only way one can understand developmental change of anything (including relationships) is retrospectively. The demands of the immediate situation virtually always take precedence over other factors.

Change Involves Exchange of Securities   The fourth characteristic of relational change concerns the participants' *exchanging one set of securities for another.* What is a "security"? It's just the opposite of a risk that is inherent in interpersonal communication. Securities, then, are the compensation for the risks in interpersonal communication. Each communicator risks his or her definition of self, among other things. To compensate for that risk, each partner assesses the relationship in terms of some securities that compensate for taking that risk. For example, the potential outcome that "this could be the start of something big" may be sufficient security to warrant taking some risk in extending additional self-offers to the other person.

At any stage of relational development, the partners have established a set of such securities for themselves. For an adolescent couple "going steady," securities involve the availability of the other for the next school dance or weekend date. Each is secure in the knowledge that the "steady" is not dating someone else. However, if the relationship goes through some change (toward either further integration or disintegration), the partners must give up the securities they have established for another set of securities.

That adolescent couple cannot continue going steady indefinitely. At some point they will undergo a turning point (Baxter & Bullis, 1986) in their relationship toward greater integration or disintegration. They may escalate toward a relational stage of marriage or living together. During the period of change the partners need to decide whether to give up their present securities (guaranteed dates, low cost of living with parents, freedom to go where and do what they please when not with partner) for another set of securities (more time together, independence from parental guidance, sense of permanence in the relationship). The couple may, however, decide to break up. If they do, their transition period also involves greater risk (such as going through the pains of finding a new partner, wondering what your friends think, experiencing a sense of loss) but also carries with it a new set of securities (such as freedom to date anyone, more time for other friends, increased independence).

In the case of either growth or decline, relational partners must assess their relationship in terms of the degree of interpersonal risk and the compensating securities. Furthermore, each partner typically assesses the relational change retrospectively (that is, after the fact), and it always involves a struggle. Relational change is always a time of increased stress, both on the relationship and on the partners individually.

Every interpersonal relationship will involve some change. Even stable relationships undergo periods of individual stress and mutual bliss. Relational change will always involve a struggle—with the relationship, between each partner, and with each partner's retrospective evaluations of the relationship. The partners must learn to struggle with relational change by making careful assessments of the risks and securities involved, and they will evaluate relational changes after they have occurred—that is, retrospectively. The adage that "hindsight is typically 20-20 vision" is appropriate here, as well as the realization that only by taking a retrospective view can relational partners assess their relationship. At least, it is the only way they can assess their relationship with any degree of understanding or accuracy.

Developing interpersonal communication skills involves an awareness of evolutionary change and a repertoire of optional strategies. With an awareness and a sensitivity to the change that is occurring in the developing relationship comes the knowledge of what to select in order to keep the relationship developing in the direction you want it to go. But even the most skillful communicator, the person with a heightened sensitivity to the interaction and a variety of strategic choices at her or his disposal, cannot guarantee the continual evolution of desirable or even satisfactory relationships. Recall that relationships are nonsummative and thus continually emerge as something other than the relational partners taken together. In addition, one person cannot create a relationship; it takes a minimum of two.

The competent communicator (Chapter 7) is not necessarily a person whose interpersonal relationships are always satisfactory, even though most of them probably are. It is probably more accurate to think of the competent communicator as one who is aware of the evolutionary stages of interpersonal relationships and is skilled at knowing when and how to end relationships as well as how to begin them.

Models of Relationship Development

Even though no two relationships evolve in exactly the same way, phases or stages can be used to characterize the evolutionary process of most interpersonal relationships. First, two people meet and are initially drawn to each other (Chapter 8). They experience a sense of possibility and wonder whether "this could be the start of something different." Next comes what Miriam Rodin (1982) calls the "reconnaissance dance, the set of exploratory moves which allow one to sample the other's company on what might be thought of as trial occasions" (p. 38). These opening moves or "trial occasions" allow each partner to "test the waters" before plunging headlong into the relationship. This testing period may even disconfirm the initial attraction, and one or both partners will decide to get out of the relationship while they can easily do so. After this first stage, the relationship can go either way—get stronger or grow progressively weaker and eventually die out. Models of relationship development chart these changes over time. Two such models are typical of the work in relationship development from 1973 to the late 1980s.

Altman and Taylor's Social Penetration Model   Relationship research before 1973 didn't examine its developmental character (Wilmot & Sillars, 1989). In 1973 Altman and Taylor introduced a model of interaction that they called *social penetration*. Their model provides insight into the way self-disclosure is linked with developing intimacy or liking. By 1977, the social penetration model was referred to as "the most comprehensive, substantive theory seeking to explain the growth of interpersonal relations" (La Gaipa, 1977, p. 142).

According to the concept of "social penetration" the human self can be visualized as similar to an onion, with an inner core surrounded by a layer of self, surrounded by another layer, surrounded by still another layer, and so on, until the outermost layer is visible to the other person. That outer layer may be considered the "public knowledge of self" visible to other people. Self-disclosure, then (in the sense of the other person's discovering the inner layers of self otherwise hidden from view), is tantamount to peeling away the outer layers of self, "penetrating" the layers to reveal a more private layer of self-knowledge.

Social penetration becomes relevant to interpersonal communication in regard to the topics chosen for conversation. Topics may be said to have two dimensions: breadth and depth. Figure 9-1 illustrates the onionlike self (appearing as a circle but more appropriately as a cross-section of a sphere) and the conversational topics. *Breadth* refers to the number of different topics covered during interpersonal communication, and *depth* refers to a deeper or more personal level of conversation within any given topical area. Naturally, the breadth of topics (the number of topics discussed) is related somewhat to feelings of closeness, in the sense that the more you know about another person in different areas, the more likely you are to perceive that you "know" the other. But depth of topics—penetration to more personal attitudes, beliefs, and values of self—is probably more closely related to feelings of liking or intimacy.

As people interact and maintain relationships, they can move toward core areas of their personalities. Altman and Taylor (1973) related this movement to a pin moving through the onion without skipping layers (depth). The metaphor is extended to include the process of adding more pins (breadth) entering broad categories of personality as individuals unfold more of their onions or personalities to each other.

All topics are not alike in terms of their levels of intimacy. That is, some topics are more likely to be more intimate and private than others. Marriage and family matters, for example, are likely to be perceived as more private than demographic and biographical information about self. Furthermore,

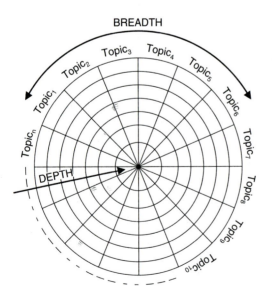

FIGURE 9-1 Breadth and depth of topics in self-disclosing communication.

some people will disagree on which topics are more personal or private. Once Aub was advisor for a graduate student who was interested in the topic of self-disclosure and who was observing the interaction between groups of people and tracking the types of topics they discussed. She found that "sex and dating" was a topic rarely discussed by newly acquainted college students, who considered it a "very intimate" topic. However, she also observed a women's consciousness-raising group that discussed the most private details of their lives with one another. She concluded that a topic considered intimate by one group in one situation might be considered very nonintimate by another group in another situation.

The discussion thus far has considered only differences among topics (breadth). Within a topic (depth), however, partners may disclose a deeper level of their private selves to the other. A statement within the topic "marriage and family" could be at a very low level of intimacy (e.g., "I am married and have two children") or a rather high level of intimacy (e.g., "My husband beat me last night. I don't know what to do. I'm terrified of him, but I can't leave him. Where would I go?"). This latter comment discloses much more depth—a layer deep in the private self and far removed from the outermost "public" layer.

Disclosing to another person a deeply penetrating layer of self typically makes you feel vulnerable. Self-disclosing communication with depth is risky in most relationships, especially in the beginning. Your self, especially that innermost core of your private self, is your final refuge of privacy. To disclose a highly personal piece of information about your self is to stand psychologically naked before the other person. Thus, many people interested in self-disclosure suggest that trust may be as important a factor in the relationship as liking or intimacy. Rawlins's (1989) analysis of communication in young adult friendships, for example, reveals that trust is vital to the management of the tension between openness and closedness. To reveal your private self is to reveal where you are vulnerable. You are, in essence, trusting that other person not to reveal that private information to others, not to hurt you with that information at some later time. To restrain from hurting the other with the disclosure builds trust, and offering private disclosure confirms the trust.

Altman and Taylor (1973) investigated the question of whether development of social relationships proceeds gradually and systematically from superficial to intimate topics. They also researched whether new and different topics are discussed and whether more intimate items within each topic become accessible as the relationship progresses. The depth and breadth of self-disclosure is, obviously, central to the process of peeling away the onion layers of another. Further, they use reward and costs to explain why any changes occur. Rewards and costs determine which self-disclosure behaviors are appropriate to any given point in time.

Altman and Taylor (1973) describe four stages of relationship development: (1) The *orientation* stage is characterized by the reciprocal exchange of superficial "outer layer" information. The participants exercise caution in their penetration of each other's onions. (2) The *exploratory affective exchange* stage is characterized by increased relaxation and exploration of the inner layers as well as increased breadth of the outer layers (that is, more topics at the outer layers). (3) The *affective exchange* stage is characterized by significant increases in depth of disclosure (penetration to the core) and increases in evaluative behavior. A history of rewarding behavior is necessary to reach this stage. (4) The *stable exchange* stage is characterized by substantial private knowledge and understanding of each other as well as efficient and idiosyncratic interaction.

Knapp's Staircase Model of Relationship Development   Mark   Knapp (1984), a communication scholar, has speculated that interpersonal relationships evolve in a parallel fashion. His model is a derivation of Altman and Taylor's social penetration theory. Partners experience a *coming together* evolutionary process parallel to a *coming apart* evolutionary process. Each stage in coming together has its counterpart in coming apart. Figure 9-2 illustrates this parallel development of interpersonal relationships in the form of parallel staircases that show how a relationship evolves through stages of *initiating, experimenting, intensifying, integrating, and bonding.* As the relationship deteriorates or comes apart, the evolutionary process is re- versed in the parallel stages of *differentiating, circumscribing, stagnating, avoiding, and terminating.* Figure 9-2 shows how each "coming together" stage has a parallel stage of development in the "coming apart" process. That is, "initiating" is to the "coming together" process what "terminating" is to the "coming apart" process; "experimenting" is to the "coming to-gether" process what "avoiding" is to the "coming apart" process, and so forth.

    Knapp's staircase model accepts the ideas of depth and breadth of interaction as well as the reward or cost explanation for movement on the staircase. His contribution was his explicit focus on detailing the qualitative

FIGURE 9-2   Knapp's stages of "coming together" and "coming apart."

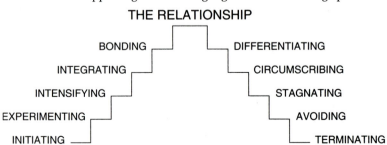

THE RELATIONSHIP

nature of partner talk in each of these stages. He speculated that each stage is characterized by dialogue that represents strategies peculiar to that stage. In fact, the stages may also serve to identify a list of strategies used by participants in the "coming together" and "coming apart" stages. The following table illustrates Knapp's (1984, p. 33) conceptualization of the stages of a developing relationship:

Process	Stage	Representative Dialogue
	Initiating	"Hi, how ya doin'?" "Fine. You?"
	Experimenting	"Oh, so you like to ski . . . so do I." "You do?! Great. Where do you go?"
Coming together	Intensifying	"I . . . I think I love you." "I love you too."
	Integrating	"I feel so much a part of you." "Yeah, we are like one person. What happens to you happens to me."
	Bonding	"I want to be with you always." "Let's get married."
	Differentiating	"I just don't like big social gatherings." "Sometimes I don't understand you. This is one area where I'm certainly not like you at all."
	Circumscribing	"Did you have a good time on your trip?" "What time will dinner be ready?"
Coming apart	Stagnating	"What's there to talk about?" "Right. I know what you're going to say and you know what I'm going to say."
	Avoiding	"I'm so busy, I just don't know when I'll be able to see you." "If I'm not around when you try, you'll understand."
	Terminating	"I'm leaving you . . . and don't bother trying to contact me." "Don't worry."

Knapp's model of interaction stages is obviously speculative and, as Knapp admits, "simplifies a complex process." Relationships in real life are certainly not nearly as orderly, and the stages of relational deterioration are not necessarily the reverse of the stages of coming together (Baxter, 1983). Nevertheless, Knapp's model does show how relationships evolve through the passage of time and the continuing experience of interpersonal communication. Knapp's model also emphasizes that any relational stage (or change from one evolutionary stage to another) is identified by the interactional patterns (the dialogue) that the participants create while negotiating their relationships.

Several conclusions about relationship development are to be gleaned from these models and others (e.g., Berger and Calabrese's uncertainty reduction theory):

1. Relationships develop and change gradually over time in an evolutionary manner. The speed of development varies according to a number of factors (e.g., proximity, need, situation), and development is not linear but sequential (Bochner, 1984).
2. Distinct stages of a relationship are created and reflected in sequences of interaction enacted by relational partners (Bochner, 1984).
3. Relationships evolve toward fluctuations in quality of the characteristics of interaction (that is, rising or lowering of intensity, intimacy, trust, and commitment), and the change may be in either direction.
4. Competence in interpersonal communication requires some awareness of the relational stage and sensitivity to which strategies would be appropriate to that stage (e.g., small talk initially and personal talk later).

Relationship Development Issues

Several communication scholars (Baxter, 1990; Bochner, 1984; Wilmot & Sillars, 1989) have taken a critical look at the relational development research of the 1970s and 1980s and taken issue with a number of assumptions in the research. First, the research, taken together, presents a rather sterile, uniform approach to development (Bochner, 1984). For example, the models tend to place the individual at the center of analysis rather than the relationship (Bochner, 1984; Wilmot & Sillars, 1989). Individual assessments of reward and cost are typical explanations for change even if the theorists try to claim that the relationship emerges from the interaction. Again, characteristics of relational development are reduced to the insider's view only or to the view from the intrapersonal system.

Second, relational growth is often equated with an increase in the good things in relationships and a decrease in the trivial and superficial (Bochner, 1984). The stereotypical assumption is that as partners grow in a relationship, they get more personal, become more certain about each other, and understand each other more. A decline in a relationship is equated with negative things like distrust, uncertainty, pain, and so forth.

Research, however, is beginning to tell a different story. For instance, people often assume that increased development is accompanied by increased understanding between partners. However, when the negotiated views of relational partners as opposed to the individual views are studied, understanding is not constant in developing relationships. In a five-week study of couples, Stephen (1985) found an "emergent couple reality" created by *both* partners which influenced patterns of behavior and, in turn, was shaped by those patterns. In other cases, intimates have been found to be less than understanding on sensitive topics, and direct communication doesn't necessarily guarantee greater understanding between intimates (Sillars, Pike, Jones, & Murphy, 1984).

Wilmot and Sillars (1989) point out that all relationships contain some asymmetry or divergent partner viewpoints. Divergent viewpoints are not particularly an issue during times of relational stability but can become quite an issue during personal and relational tension and crisis. The co-negotiation of these divergent viewpoints between partners is the essence of relating and should be studied from the interpersonal view as well as from the individual standpoint.

Previous discussions in this book have also revealed another relational reality. Close relationships can be the place where people find incongruence instead of the expected congruence (Chapter 3—Sillars' interpersonal perception), deception instead of honesty, and ambiguity instead of certainty (Chapter 7—the dark side of communication competence). In addition, many of you have probably come to realize that often the person who knows you best is your enemy, not your lover or best friend.

The models of relationship development too often depict what *should* happen in relationships rather than explain what is actually *done* in social relationships (Bochner, 1984). What happens when researchers examine what relational partners actually do in relationships?

In 1986 Duck and Miell set out to chart male and female friendships over a period of eighteen weeks. They believed that little had been done to chart the "actual conduct" of friends over time. Contrary to what would be expected, these college-age friends met mostly in public (e.g., coffee houses) not in private, and their talk occurred in short, not long, episodes and with gossip, not personal matters as the essential feature of their talk. Duck and Miell (1986) also found that these friends reported a vagueness and uncertainty about the constancy of their friendships, reflecting a "mild existential terror" about their friendships. They concluded that friendship development is characterized by an uncertainty and fluctuation as friends negotiate the speculative nature of their relationships.

More important to our discussion is their conclusion that the long-term evolution of human relationships contain elements that have been ignored in most of the discussions of relationship development. Researchers too often presume important relational elements, such as openness, intimacy, and certainty, without having discovered the relevant elements relational partners encounter in the everyday job of making their relationships work.

Leslie Baxter (1990) is another communication scholar to take issue with the assumptions that have come out of past work in relationship development. She too believes that an overemphasis has been placed on openness, uncertainty, and predictability. Her research provides evidence that the essence of a relationship is found in the management of dialectical tensions such as openness *and* closedness, novelty *and* predictability, and autonomy *and* connection. She speculates that one reason these dual tensions have been ignored is that when asked for their accounts of relational development, partners will often "smooth out" the fluctuations in the movement of their relationship (Miell, 1987). Baxter (1990) poses the challenge that if these dual tensions are prevalent in relationships (as her work is beginning to suggest), then any model of relationship development that claims growth in the direction of only openness, connection, and predictability should be altered to account for the reverse pulls of closedness, autonomy, and novelty.

Casting relational development within the framework of dialectical tensions has continued to raise several questions about how relational development is understood. Another framework which is changing how relational development is understood is the *life-span developmental communication perspective* (Bettini & Nussbaum, 1991; Nussbaum, 1989).

Adopted from psychology, life-span theory is being used by communication scholars (see e.g., Nussbaum, 1989) to argue that understanding any communicative phenomena is predicated first on understanding the development of that phenomena. This theory posits that human development is a continuous life process and that it is multidirectional; it includes both growth and decay; it is unique in some aspects from person to person; it is influenced by historical, cultural, and social factors; and it is contextual.

Granted that the focus of the life-span theory has been on the developmental changes of the intrapersonal system or the individual. Communication scholars, however, recognize that this theory can be used to understand the development of interpersonal, group, and organizational systems (Bettini & Nussbaum, 1991). Its implications, then, are that no communicative system, including social relationships, are static. Any understanding of relationships must be framed by the point in time within which that relationship exists. Young adult same-sex friendships can't be expected to function the same as elderly same-sex friendships. Second, relationships develop multidirectionally, not unidirectionally. Thus, not all initial interactions may develop in the same neat predictable ways toward the same goals. The initial interaction between two 82-year-old men in a retirement community may not move the same way as the initial interaction between two 8-year-old boys at school. Third, relational development will produce simultaneous growth and decay, and *both* these processes are normal developmental processes within the overall communicative context. Fourth, relationships can be characterized by unique communicative change special only to that relationship. If these idiosyncratic patterns are not considered, then the generalizations about relational patterns become suspect. Fifth, relationships are influenced by social, economic, political, and cultural conditions. Pat O'Connor's (1992) book on female friendship examines the dynamics of female friendship over the life span and as it is embedded within the social, political, economical, and cultural. Sixth, as you learned in Part One, communicative messages can't be understood or given significance outside of the context within which they occur.

So if you are interested in friendship, then you would be interested not only in how friendship develops but also in how it develops within the life span which frames the friendship. In other words, it does make a difference if the communicative accomplishment of friendship is occurring between young adults or between elderly friends. For instance, Bettini, Patterson, Nussbaum, and Norton (1991) have found in their study of the young and of the elderly that the meaning of friendship does differ across the life span. Communication with friends is a central component of friendship at a young age. However, their data suggests that as individuals age, communication with friends is not a defining component of friendship. Instead, the idea that friendship is something unique emerges in the elderly's conceptualization of friendship. Friendship is not easily put into words, but it is clearly separate from other relationships (e.g., family). Constant communication with friends is not possible for some elderly, and with the death of friends some friendships remain only as psychological constructs (in the mind in memories).

Understanding relational change is undoubtedly a difficult task compounded by the realization that social relationships fluctuate through cycles of growth and decay and will do so throughout the life of the relationship. Stages of development, then, function only as artificial and arbitrary distinctions used by theorists to discuss development (Bochner, 1984). We will be using the concept "stages" in the same manner. Relationships can't be broken down into neatly packaged stages with the assumption that every one of your relational actions must pass through a stage. Stages are tools we will use to discuss global, qualitative changes of relationships over time. Always keep in mind that patterns will vary. The challenge is to describe and ultimately understand the variations. Regardless of which perspective of development you select, change in relationships involves continual choice and negotiation of commitment.

Choice and Commitment

The famous American jurist Peter Marshall once said, "In a modern society there is no real freedom from law. There is only freedom in law." On a similar theme is the saying, "If you have a good friend, let him go. If he is a true friend, he will come back to you. If he doesn't, then he was never your friend in the first place." The point of both sayings is the same. Freedom to make choices includes, above all, choosing to place constraints on the choices you make. The most precious choice of all is the choice to commit yourself to something. Without the freedom of choice, of what value is commitment?

Each participant in interpersonal communication continually exercises freedom of choice. Each communicator chooses relational partners, chooses to escalate or deescalate the relationship, chooses to make self-offers to the other person, chooses strategies to enact during communication. The fact that people are usually unaware of making these choices at the time they make them is really unimportant. The process of interpersonal communication is a continual succession of one choice after another. You know you have freedom of choice in a relationship when you choose to commit yourself to that relationship. And there is the paradox. Freedom of choice and commitment (limiting choice) are inextricably interwoven. They are one and the same. To have one is to have the other, and to deny one is to deny both.

The processes of increasing commitment and limiting choice characterize every relationship that is becoming more integrated. Commitment is one of the principal characteristics of intimate, loving, or close relationships. And commitment is inherently a constraint on your freedom of choice—one that is chosen freely. The more committed you are to a relationship, the more constraints you place on yourself, the greater your sense of responsibility, the less actual freedom you enjoy, and the greater the sense of freedom you feel. The truly open relationship is one to which the partners are firmly committed. Commitment necessarily involves reducing your freedom of choice and closing off options that had been available to you.

If increasing commitment characterizes escalating relationships, then what characterizes declining relationships? The obvious answer is "decreasing commitment," but what does that mean? Decreasing commitment may appear to be too much constraint on choice. The relational partners feel "hemmed in" by the relationship, "prisoners" of it. Interestingly enough, the same constraints that lead to *in*creased commitment also lead to *de*creased commitment. How can this be? The answer is that the participants use different attributions for their behaviors.

The difference between increasing and decreasing commitment is the difference between attributing an internal or external locus of control for your constrained actions. When your commitment to a relationship increases, you attribute your behaviors to an internal locus of control—your self. "I know I don't run around as much these days," you say, "but I *want* to stay home more. I'm in love." When your commitment to a relationship decreases, you attribute your behaviors (often the same behaviors) to an external locus of control—the situation or the other person, some cause outside self. "I never get out of the house anymore," you say, "because she (or he) won't let me go. I never have time for myself."

What may have been commitment at one time in your relationship may be understood later, retrospectively of course, as stifling—a loss of personal control or choice. In this sense, then, constraint on your personal freedom of choice characterizes both commitment and lack of commitment, both increasing commitment and decreasing commitment to an interpersonal relationship. The behaviors may be the same, but your attributions of those behaviors differ.

Relational change, toward or away from intimacy, will always involve constraint of choice. Both increasing and decreasing commitment to the relationship are characterized by constraint. In the case of increasing commitment, the communicator attributes commitment to the free choice of self and assesses the relationship as satisfying. In the case of decreasing commitment, the communicator attributes the constraint to the situation or the other person and considers the relationship unsatisfying.

Here again is the blend of the individual and the relational, the self and the relationship, that is necessary to understand the process of interpersonal communication. The relationship affects the individual just as the individual affects the relationship. To understand interpersonal communication is to understand both Parts Two and Three of this book and how they fit together to enable you to develop a more complete understanding of interpersonal communication.

THE FUNCTION OF EMOTIONS

Sometimes people use the term "in love" to identify a relationship characterized by the emotion. Unfortunately, people also tend to think that being "in love" may be a delusion and isn't really the emotion of love at all. But "in love" may be a more accurate term than simply "love." It suggests that "love" is something that partners are "in" together rather than something each feels separately. They are equal members "in" a relationship; they participate "in" a relationship rather than just feel something toward the other person. As a matter of fact, this term more accurately describes membership in a variety of relationships. If you can be "in love," then why can't you be "in like," "in hate," "in acquaintance," "in indifference?" Using the term "in" emphasizes the relationship that includes both the partners and is, to a considerable extent, different from either partner's emotional interpretation of it.

The emotions felt by communicators during and following their interaction are certainly a part of interpersonal communication as much as are the patterns of interactional strategies. Emotions, often thought of primarily as individual phenomena, are also undeniably social and thus are an intricate part of the fabric of relationships (Bowers, Metts, & Duncanson, 1985). The emotions felt by the interactants are created by participant actions, and their displayed presence, in turn, influences participant actions. They may affect the future of the relationship as each interactant assesses it retrospectively and intrapersonally. The following discussion describes the important functions performed by emotions during interpersonal communication but does not consider the emotions to be synonymous with the relationship. Fundamentally, emotions belong to individual communicators as they retrospectively make attributions about the relationship and inferences about the other person.

As Attributions

Humans seem constantly to be in the process of making assessments and evaluations of their experiences. When confronted with some novel experience, people attempt to make sense of it. Perhaps that is the reason underlying the Rorschach inkblot test used by psychologists. People attempt to find some meaning in even a random ink stain. People read the *Peanuts* comic strip and find humor, and not just a little familiarity, in Charlie Brown's attempts to see animal shapes in cloud formations. Human beings are notorious for trying to make sense out of everything they encounter. They just can't stand uncertainty and take every opportunity to reduce it.

A relationship has no emotions. Only individual people have emotions. The behaviors that people perform when engaging in interpersonal communication have no emotions. The people who perform those behaviors have emotions. You can feel some emotion when you communicate, but your feeling can never be part of your behavior. As feelings, your emotions are inevitably internalized and hidden within you. You will naturally experience some feeling, as one of the communicators, about a relationship you have with someone else. And you will naturally project your feeling to the other person and, consequently, to the relationship itself. When you project your feelings outside yourself, you are engaging in attribution; you attribute the cause or locus of control of your internalized feeling to an external source—the other person and the relationship.

When you feel good or at ease interacting with another person, for example, you want to attribute that feeling to the other person and to the relationship. Your attribution thus allows you to see the other person and the relationship in terms of the emotion you are feeling. You are likely to call the other person "friend" and the relationship "friendship." You may even call the other person "lover" and the relationship "love." As sense-making attributions go, your assessment of the relationship typically occurs after the interaction. That is, you tend to make your attributions retrospectively, after the fact. Those attributions then guide your expectations of what will happen in further interaction.

People are so good at attributing their own emotions and feelings to someone and something else that they think everyone else does it, too. Hence, when you feel some emotion and attribute it to someone else, you often believe that the other person feels the same emotion and attributes it to you. "I love you," for example, is tantamount to saying, "We love each other." When we feel some emotion toward another person, we think the other person reciprocates that emotion. When you think someone likes you, you also tend to like him or her in return. If you think someone hates you, you almost automatically hate that person back. Consequently, emotions attributed *to* another person ("I love you") go hand in hand with emotions attributed *from* the other person ("You love me"). Therefore, the emotions people feel become virtually synonymous with emotions felt by both communicators, and they use them to characterize the interpersonal relationship.

As Inferences

Most people subscribe to the conventional wisdom that they can tell what a person is thinking or feeling by observing what that person does. You think you can "read" what people are thinking or feeling, for example, by looking closely at their eyes. "The eyes," it is said "are the mirror of the soul." Of course, you also know that some people try to hide their emotions. To the extent that they do so, you consider them good poker players. Some people fake their emotions so well in their behavior that you may even make errors in your inferences with regard to their internalized emotions.

The point to be gleaned from this discussion is that people do attempt to infer intrapersonal dispositions in the behaviors of other people during interpersonal communication (see Kelley, 1979, pp. 3–6). Whether they can infer emotions from behavior or whether they are correct when they do so is not important. They *think* they can, and therefore they do. To understand the process of interpersonal communication is to understand how, from observing their behaviors, people make inferences about what others are feeling inside.

A study of marital relationships (Sillars, Pike, Jones, & Murphy, 1984) provides some insight into the inferential process that participants use when they are engaged in interpersonal communication. The following discussion summarizes the conclusions of their study.

1. *The most immediate information available is the information with the greatest influence on inferences.* The term "immediate" refers to the information that is most readily accessible. You tend to think the information that is available to you is the most important and therefore accurate information. Obviously, the most immediate information about feelings are the statements that actually express feelings (such as the words "I love you"). You know it's easy to fake this behavior, but you still consider it very important information.
2. *Nonverbal behaviors are the primary source of information used to infer the partner's feelings and emotions.* This result is not surprising. Our previous discussions have indicated that people tend to think that others cannot control (and thereby fake) their nonverbal behaviors as easily as their verbal behaviors. People also tend to think that nonverbal behaviors are more likely to reflect emotions and feelings than are verbal behaviors (also, probably, because people think it is easy to lie about their feelings verbally). Perhaps because nonverbal behaviors allow so much

room for interpretation, you also like to use them to infer what you want to infer about the other person's emotions.

3. *People infer negative feelings much more easily than positive feelings from nonverbal behaviors.* This finding is more surprising than the others. Apparently you think it's easy to tell from the nonverbal behavior of others that they don't like you, but it's usually difficult to tell whether they do like you. Perhaps you are more receptive to negative emotions than to positive ones. Perhaps you want to avoid the risk of offering too much of your self, and so you infer negative feelings in others. Perhaps you just tend to look on the bad side of things rather than the good. For whatever reason, your inferences (based on observing nonverbal behaviors) about other people's emotions and feelings are more likely to be negative than positive. And you are more likely to be more assured of your judgments of other people if the judgment is negative. No wonder people have trouble developing long-time interpersonal relationships!

4. *People strongly overestimate the similarity between their own and their partner's feelings.* The tendency to think that your partner reciprocates your feelings is very strong. You are probably most likely to overestimate your similarity with your partner during periods of relational change, particularly when the change is in the direction of increasing

We infer other's feelings primarily from their nonverbal behaviors.

intimacy. After discovering some similarities in the getting-acquainted stage, you tend to think that the two of you are much more similar than you really are. Continued interaction and more development of the relationship will probably reveal more similarity, but it is also likely to reveal more differences. In other words, during that period of excitement when the relationship is escalating, you will probably judge your partner to be more similar to you than she or he actually is.

Emotions and feelings are part of the intrapersonal level of communication and thus are hidden from view. However, the fact that emotions are not observable does not mean that you don't *think* they can be observed. Therefore, you use your capacity to make attributions and inferences in order to perceive the emotions of your relational partners. Since you have only the behaviors of your partners to observe, you use those behaviors (both nonverbal and verbal) as the information from which you draw your inferences and our attributions.

The emotions you experience and perceive in others are significant in affecting the development of relationships. For instance, when people describe their feelings to others, they do so in a way that is understandable to others. Usually people summarize their emotions as enduring states (e.g., "I love you") as opposed to momentary feelings (e.g., "I felt flush and a twinge when you looked at me the way you did") (Duck & Sants, 1983). Your emotions may also exert their greatest impact during periods of evolutionary change in relational development. That is, emotions most strongly affect relational development when the relationship is moving toward or away from a higher level of intimacy and intensity. Consequently, your emotions lead you to expect and think you are experiencing a greater change than is actually occurring.

CHARACTERISTICS OF INTERPERSONAL RELATIONSHIPS

When you are actually involved in interpersonal communication, you are not always aware of what is happening in the interaction. Only after you remove yourself from the interactional event can you reflect back on what happened and make some judgment about your relationship. In other words, despite the influence of prior expectations on your perceptions, you come to understand the meaning of your relationship retrospectively.

One of the most important skills of interpersonal communication involves being aware of what is happening in your relationship—in the patterns of interaction—as quickly as possible. Your immediate awareness of what your interaction means is probably lowest during the periods of evolutionary change in your relationship. But in order to enhance your awareness and interpretation of interaction, you need to know what to look for. Furthermore, you need to be on the lookout for the interactional phenomena that signal when a change in the relationship is occurring. The purpose of this section, then, is to discover what interactional elements to look for and then to see how those elements reflect changes of growth or decline in the relationship.

General Characteristics of Relational Interaction

The number of potential characteristics of the relationship dimension of communication is so large as to defy any listing. The following characteristics include only a few of the potential number of functions performed by communication in defining our interpersonal relationships and have been selected from a longer list (see Burgoon & Hale, 1984). These characteristic functions of communicative behaviors provide a starting point in developing your communicational skills. To understand what communication does is to understand what is going on when you interact with someone else.

Immediacy *Immediacy* is a catch-all term that refers to the connection between the interaction and the immediate situation. The more immediate the comment, the more directly that comment refers to the relationship, the other person, or the self of the communicator—in short, the elements of the immediate situation of interpersonal communication. Small talk, for instance, is low in verbal immediacy because it includes topics (such as the weather) far removed from self-interest or the relationship.

Comments expressing greater verbal immediacy often signal a change in the evolutionary development of the relationship. The transitional period of interaction toward either integration or disintegration typically includes an increase in the verbal immediacy of the interaction. Recall the opening comment of the bad script—"How do you like me so far?" It is high in verbal immediacy in that it refers directly to one person's feelings toward the other. It is also not appropriate to the getting-acquainted stage of relationship development precisely because it is too immediate (Baxter & Bullis, 1986). Later on, though, it may signal an attempt to move the relationship to another stage of development.

Recall the list of secondary characteristics of interaction discussed earlier: *intensity, intimacy, trust,* and *commitment.* You can probably think of a verbally immediate comment as referring quite directly to one or more of those characteristics. For example, each of the following comments is high in immediacy:

> "I had a great time tonight. Let's do it again real soon." (Intensity)
> "Talking with you is great fun. I think I'm beginning to like you." (Intimacy)

"Whatever you want to do tonight is fine with me. I'm sure I'll enjoy myself whatever you decide." (Trust)

"You mean more to me than anyone else. I want this to last forever." (Commitment)

Each of these comments signals a transitional period toward increasing integration in the relationship. Of course, comments could also signal a transition toward disintegration and still reflect high immediacy (such as "We may be getting too serious. Maybe we should stop seeing each other for a while").

"Immediate" interaction is so called because it refers directly to the relationship or to the self of one of the participants. A comment is immediate to the extent that it evaluates or assesses the relationship or the feeling of one of the partners toward the relationship or the other person. If you put into words what you are feeling toward the other person or the relationship, you are contributing to an increase in the immediacy of the interaction. Of course, immediacy is stronger when both partners contribute to the immediacy and reciprocate the other's feelings at approximately the same level of intensity, intimacy, trust, and commitment.

Immediacy characterizes nonverbal behaviors as well as verbal communication. For example, the behavioral postures in "quasi-courtship behavior" establish nonverbal immediacy in which the partners align themselves as "open" to each other (Scheflen, 1968). Other nonverbal indicators of immediacy might include prolonged eye gaze, smiling, nodding, and, of course touching (Mehrabian 1971, 1981). These behaviors, taken together, often result in perceptions of liking and closeness. And, because the meaning of any nonverbal behavior is subject to how it is perceived, it is impossible to say with accuracy which nonverbal behaviors are typically associated with interaction during periods of increasing intimacy.

The key to understanding immediacy as a sign of relational growth (and declining immediacy as a sign of relational decay) is to interpret nonverbal behaviors within some pattern of interaction. Specifically, that pattern is one in which the communicators seem to be at ease in behaving toward the other and in reciprocating the other person's behavior. Smiling is a good example of nonverbal immediacy that doesn't always reflect a greater degree of intimacy. New acquaintances smile at each other more frequently than do intimate couples. Intimate couples don't constantly feel the need to be on their best behavior, as do people who are trying to make a good first impression. Furthermore, all smiles are not the same. The smile of a beauty pageant contestant seems to be "pasted on," but a friend's smile seems warm and inviting.

Touching is another good example of nonverbal behavior that doesn't always reflect immediacy. Communication scholars Stanley Jones and Elaine Yarbrough (1985) write that the phenomenon of interpersonal touching is very ambiguous, even more so than has been believed. Precisely what touching means in interpersonal communication is extraordinarily difficult to answer. Touch can be interpreted as a sign of affection, support, dominance, appreciation, aggression, inclusion, confidentiality, attention getting, greeting, or a variety of other things. "Contextual factors are critical to the meanings of touch," according to Jones and Yarbrough (1985, p. 50). By "contextual factors" they mean the definition of the relationship, the timing of relational development, the verbal behaviors in which nonverbal behaviors are typically embedded, the pattern of both verbal and nonverbal interaction. For instance, Guerrero and Andersen (1991) found that stage of relationship and touch were related. Public touching increased between partners during an intermediate stage of development and then dropped off. The decrease was not associated with termination but with stability, suggesting that intimacy doesn't increase in a linear fashion but in fluctuating up-and-down patterns. In short, the meaning of touch (or any other nonverbal behavior, for that matter) will vary considerably from one communicative situation to another, from one interpersonal relationship to another, from one conversation to another.

Formality   In some communicative situations, you feel that you must constantly be on your guard. You feel inhibited and bound by the rules of the situation. These communicative situations—such as talking with someone you don't know particularly well, interviewing for a job with a person who has the power to hire you, interacting with an instructor about some classroom assignment—tend to generate interaction with a high degree of *formality.*

Formal situations make communicators conform to some set of rules restricting the freedom they have in contributing to the interaction. By contrast, informal situations allow communicators greater freedom of choice and provide them with some information as to what they might expect from the other person. Furthermore, you and your partner develop some informal interaction patterns that are unique to your particular relationship. In informal situations, you feel comfortable and at ease because you know what behaviors are appropriate. In formal situations, you don't feel comfortable because you don't know what to expect or what is expected of you.

Let us illustrate with a conversation Aub had with a student several years ago. Prior to this particular conversation, this student and Aub had established friendly relations and had talked at length about rather personal topics. On this particular day Aub became aware (for the first time) that the student was referring to him as "Dr. Fisher" and "Professor Fisher." Now you must understand that students and faculty colleagues alike called him "Aub" or "Dummy" or "Guy"—anything but some formal name. Aub asked him why he was suddenly being so formal, and he appeared surprised. He informed Aub that he had always used a formal title. Their past interaction had been so informal that Aub had somehow failed to notice this sign of formality in his address.

In a formal situation such as a job interview communicators conform to some set of rules restricting the freedom they have in contributing to the interaction.

The degree of formality in interaction is essentially a choice of what set of rules the relational partners use to govern their interaction. When communicators use rules from their situational context to determine appropriateness of their comments, their interaction is formal. When they develop their own rules to determine the appropriateness of their comments, their interaction is informal.

During periods of transition to a relational stage of greater integration, the interactants begin to develop their own rules to guide their interaction. As they recognize those self-created rules in their interaction, their interaction becomes increasingly less formal—that is, more informal. During transitional periods of disintegration, though, their interaction patterns reveal more formality and less informality. The relational partners begin to feel less comfortable in their interaction with each other, and their interaction becomes increasingly "polite." Interaction that reveals a move away from rules that made their relationship integrated is often a first sign that something is going wrong with their relationship.

Openness In relationships characterized by openness, the relational partners provide each other with information about their inner selves which influences their images of each other (Montgomery, 1984a). Openness is not necessarily the same as self-disclosing communication. Openness is a function of what is said, how it is said, and to whom it is said. For example, the amount of personal information gleaned from the remark, "I love you," depends on how it is said and the relational context. Self-disclosure is only characterized as verbal communication, and so it is only a part of openness.

Interaction is open to the extent that the partners tell each other about what is going on within them, often at that moment. In fact, one of the techniques that is often used in group work to increase openness is to flag the comment with a statement of openness, such as "I'd like to tell you what I'm thinking [feeling] at this very moment." A primary characteristic of openness is the expression of feelings.

Some people, most tend to believe, are more open than others. You think that some express their emotions more openly or let their emotions show. In this sense, openness is not so much a characteristic of the interaction as it is a characteristic of the interactant (more accurately, perhaps, of the "style" of the person's communication). Generally speaking, you think of an "open style" of communication more in terms of nonverbal behaviors than of verbalizing feelings. You generally believe that people who cry during sad movies, who laugh uproariously at funny jokes, who become visibly angry at news reports on television, are more open. They let their emotions show. They don't keep their feelings bottled up inside. They express what they feel.

The periods of transition as relationships become more integrated or disintegrated will reflect differing patterns of increasing or decreasing openness in the interaction. The typical assumption is that as a relationship moves toward being more integrated, the communicators will probably be more open in their interaction. Their information will probably also reflect an increase in the amount of intensity, involvement, or commitment to the relationship. And the reverse is probably true of a transitional period of interaction reflecting a change toward relational decline: The communicators will provide each other with less information about their feelings and their interaction will reflect less intensity, involvement, or commitment to the relationship. Closer examination of the research, however, does not provide overwhelming support for this global assumption (Baxter, 1988).

While communicators do acquire information about each other over the course of the relationship, direct open communication is not the norm. Communicators tend to enact indirect strategies in order to acquire information about themselves and the relationship. We discussed this tendency in Chapter 8 when we discussed initial interaction. Initially, vulnerability is the primary reason for indirect strategies (e.g., taboo topics, secret tests). Later, in more established relationships the primary reason for indirectness is the belief that directness is not necessary. Over time, the partners have come to assume that they already know each other, so why do they have to be direct? Nonverbal "mind reading" is not uncommon between those in

In informal situations communicators feel comfortable and at ease because they know what behaviors are appropriate.

established relationships (Baxter, 1988). During disintegration that is heading toward termination, indirectness emerges again as a preferred strategy. We will discuss these strategies in the next chapter.

The number of characteristics of relational interaction is enormous. To continue this discussion by adding more variables to the list would probably be more confusing than informative. The important point to be gleaned is that you should be able to detect a change in your relationship by watching out for changes in one or more of the characteristics of relational interaction. You can improve your skills in interpersonal communication to the extent that you become more aware of and sensitive toward these changes. You will probably first experience a feeling that something is "different" before you are able to pinpoint just what that difference is.

Growth in the Relationship

As your relationship becomes more integrated, you naturally will feel a greater involvement. That is, you begin to define your own self in terms of your relationship. As you and your partner involve more of your selves in the relationship, the quality of your interaction will also reflect increases in the secondary characteristics—higher levels of intensity, intimacy, trust, and commitment. As you involve more of your self in the relationship, you also constrain more of your freedom of behavioral choice. For instance, as you spend more time with a person, you choose to spend less time with other persons or by yourself. As you commit more of your self to the relationship, you also restrict your freedom to do other things in the future. In other words, you change your expectations concerning your future behaviors. Love, although a pleasant experience, does mean that individuals have to restructure their lives to accommodate another (Duck, 1986). Some find the disruption of "falling in love" problematic and have been known to develop skin problems and nervous disorders (Kemper & Bologh, 1981).

The most obvious change in interaction brought about by increased involvement is probably in the frequency of interaction, particularly face-to-face interaction. The number of opportunities to talk with each other increases markedly when partners are in a period of relational growth. You begin to seek each other out, to see each other more often, to find excuses to engage in interaction, to make plans for further interaction before the current interactional event comes to an end.

The variety of your interpersonal communication also increases during periods of relational growth. That is, your interactions occur in different situations and at different times. When two students start "getting serious" about each other, for example, they increase the variety of their interaction. They continue to go on dates, of course, but they soon find occasions to study together, to meet between classes for an exchange of greetings, to have lunch together, to visit each other's homes. The kinds of interaction and the variety of situations involving interaction increase during the transitional period of growth.

Emergent friendship is characterized by increased voluntary interaction and personalistic focus (Wright, 1978). Individuals make contact in friendly or informal interaction and move toward deliberate attempts to spend time together. Established friends continue to arrange time together even if it is inconvenient. Growth in friendship is also marked by the sense that each is interacting with a unique, irreplaceable individual. Hays (1984) discovered in his longitudinal study of friends that affection behavior or the expression of emotional bonds was the most stable behavior across developing friendships. The other behaviors he examined were companionship, support, and self-disclosure.

During a period of relational growth, the partners begin to resent the inherent discontinuity of their interaction. Before ending their interaction on any given occasion, they make specific plans for when they will see each other again. They don't let the conversation end with a ritualistic "See ya' around." They agree on some time and place for their next meeting before they leave each other's presence. One of them is more likely to part with a comment such as "Let's eat lunch together. How about the south door of the cafeteria, say about noon?" When not in each other's presence, the partners in a growing relationship don't necessarily experience uncontrollable anxiety. But when they do meet, they typically feel relief and some alleviation of anxiety at their reunion. In fact, they may even verbalize that feeling in their greeting remark—"I missed you" or "Miss me?"

Partners during periods of relational growth also begin to use the relationship to define their own self-interests, goals, or future behaviors. They may respond to a question such as "What are you going to do this weekend?" with a response similar to "I'm not sure yet. I'll have to check with Megan." When someone says, "I didn't know you liked to hike," an appropriate response might be "I didn't either until I tried it. Megan really likes to get out in the wilds, and I like it too." As involvement increases, the relational partners begin to set goals and make plans as a relational unit. They coordinate their free time so they can spend it together. They make plans for the future on the basis of their being together. As their relational involvement increases, they begin to extend their plans and goals farther into the future.

Another change in the interaction that occurs during periods of relational growth concerns what Mark Knapp (1984, pp. 231–232) calls "language patterns." We have called them strategies, or self-offers. Knapp indicates three such language patterns that "change as two people reach for greater intimacy": "absolutism," "repetition," and "tense." Statements containing *absolutism* reflect an extreme definition of the relationship or the situation, such as "I'll always love you" or "I'll never leave you." A boyfriend of one of Aub's daughters once told Aub in a moment of candor (which he has undoubtedly forgotten) "She is my one and only. I just can't live without her." He hasn't seen her for years!

Absolute statements do not typically reflect a relationship of high intimacy. Rather, they signal a relationship in a transitional period of integrative growth. Relational partners leave the growth stage and enter a period of high intimacy when their comments reflect "a more rational endorsement of the tentative nature of life and love in general" (Knapp, 1984, p. 231).

The second language pattern, *repetition*, also characterizes the relational interaction during periods of growth. During this "honeymoon" period, the partners are constantly expressing their affection and commitment to each other. They repeat their statements by using a variety of different ways of expressing their affection and commitment as well as repeating the same expressions again and again and again. People in a relationship that is evolving toward more intimacy apparently need to reinforce each other about their commitment. Thus, they repeat such statements more often. Partners in a mature relationship don't seem to need as much reinforcement.

The interaction in the relational growth period includes numerous references to the future, a characteristic of the language pattern of *tense*. Communicators apparently orient themselves to anticipating the future rather than dwell on what has occurred in the past. But they don't have much past, in the sense that they have just moved from a getting-acquainted stage to a period of increasing intimacy. They don't have much of a history of past interaction to look back on. On the other hand, the future is exciting, unknown, challenging—an uncharted area of great promise and potential. Consequently, their interaction reflects this future orientation: "When will I see you again?" "Isn't it about time we bought some new furniture?" "How about taking a camping trip next summer?"

By constantly orienting their relationship to the future, the partners are led to long-term commitments, even when they may not be aware of it. Aub's own personal experience comfirms this conclusion. He never did ask his wife to marry him. Furthermore, she claims that she didn't ask him to marry her. They did marry, though, and neither of them really knows how that came about. They began making plans of where to go, what job to take, and what to do after they graduated from college. They talked about what they'd do after they were married. They talked about where they would get married and who would marry them. But they apparently forgot to go through the step of asking and deciding to get married. Their interaction at that time was definitely oriented to the future—so much so, in fact, that it apparently affected the present.

Based on these language patterns, there are several ways you can effectively communicate your increasing commitment to another (Knapp & Vangelisti, 1992). One, you can continually restate your commitment in a different way each time. Second, you can use absolute statements. Third, you can refer to the future benefits of the relationship. In addition, Knapp and Vangelisti (1992) suggest that you express some commitment behavior in public, restate the commitment in more permanent forms such as in letters and cards, display some work or show that you have gone to some trouble, and don't always wait for the other to initiate expressions of commitment. As always, remember you should judge the appropriateness of these actions, considering the degree of directness you wish to use.

Decline in the Relationship

To some extent, a relationship in a transition period of disintegration is the reverse of a relationship in a transition period of integration. That is, a declining relationship will probably reflect lower levels of the characteristics of interaction quality. For example, the frequency of interactional events will decrease. More and longer gaps between interactions will occur. Partners will interact with lower levels of intensity, intimacy, trust, and commitment. But a relationship on the skids is also more than just the opposite of interaction patterns that signify growth.

Perhaps a metaphor can best illustrate that relational growth and decline are not the same process. When you start the engine of your automobile, you use the ignition switch. The engine begins turning over electrically, the fuel pump sends gas to the carburetor, the carburetor mixes fuel with air, the valves open to allow the fuel mixture to flow into the cylinder, the spark plug ignites the fuel, and the engine starts running.

But what happens when the engine breaks down? It is not simply the opposite of the starting process. For one thing, the engine is still running. However, the fuel lines may be clogged, and so the pump is unable to work properly. The carburetor may be dirty so that the fuel-air mixture is not OK. The spark plugs may be fouled or out of time so that the ignition sequence is wrong. In short, the engine continues to run, but it doesn't run properly. The driver will know that something is wrong; but—not being an expert mechanic—won't know what to do about it.

When a relationship begins to decline, in a very real sense it is "breaking down." The partners continue to interact, but their interaction is not smooth—it is "running rough." They are aware that something is wrong, but they aren't sure what to do about it. Two choices are immediately apparent: Keep it going until it stops completely, or try to fix it so that it runs more smoothly. Relationships and automobile engines are similar in this respect: You can let them go until they're beyond repair, or you can try to fix them.

Unfortunately, it is far easier to repair automobile engines than to remedy problems in interpersonal relationships. A mechanic can often find the faulty part and replace it with a brand new one, but a relational "mechanic" can't so easily repair a relationship. The process of interpersonal communication must retain the basic elements of the relationship (the selves of the individual communicators) even though they may show signs of wear or damage.

Little is known about the experience and interactional nature of *relational distance* (Helgeson, Shaver, & Dyer, 1987). Relational distance is not only the opposite of closeness; it requires some prior connection between partners which has become strained. That is, it occurs within an intimate context and is characterized by unpleasant feelings.

Helgeson, Shaver, and Dyer (1987) asked college-age females and males in same-sex and opposite-sex dyads to produce accounts of their distance experiences. Reported characterizations of distance were of disapproval or dissatisfaction with the relational partner. Both males and females thought of distance as resulting from annoying and hurtful behavior by the other (e.g., unavailability, inattentiveness, preoccupation, insensitiveness, or dating others). A decrease in joint activities and self-disclosure, although a part of relational distance, were not reported as primary reasons for distancing. Instead, neglect, insults, and going out with others were given as far more important reasons for distance behavior. The reported experience of distance in same-sex friendships wasn't as volatile an experience as it was for opposite-sex partners.

The experiences of distance are important to the relational dynamics because they can influence the behavior of the partners. Typical responses to distance were confrontation and attempts to get the partner to change. Arguments appear to be the reported strategic choice of males in both opposite- and same-sex relationships.

Some relationships also go into decline through no fault of the partners or their interaction. They decline because the situation has changed. For example, one of the partners moves to another city. A friend may get married or start a family and have less time to interact. Any number of contextual changes can account for a significant decrease in the amount of interaction or more frequent and longer gaps between the partners' interactional encounters. Environmental changes can affect a relationship just by not allowing it to grow or continue to flourish. As a result, the relationship declines through atrophy or lack of use.

Unlike periods of relational growth, periods of relational decay often send the partners to searching for something that has caused the relational problem. When a relationship is growing, the partners enjoy feelings of increasing integration. They rarely ask themselves why they have those feelings; they just enjoy them because the feelings themselves are so enjoyable. Relational breakdown is considerably different in this respect. The feelings the partners experience during such periods are not pleasant. In fact, such feelings as depression, self-doubt, anxiety, tension, disappointment, and betrayal are downright unpleasant. The normal response to unpleasant feelings is to get rid of them. And how do you do that? "Something must be making me feel bad," you say to yourself, "so I need to find out what is causing these feelings and do something about it."

Unfortunately, there is seldom a simple cause for the decline in any relationship (Knapp & Vangelisti, 1992). And even when you seem to find a cause of the problem, removing the cause is seldom enough to remedy the problem. It's like trying to put out a forest fire. Knowing what caused the fire (a smoldering campfire, for instance) does not help you to fight the fire that is now raging out of control several miles away. It may help you in your attempts to prevent forest fires in the future, but it won't help you put out the present fire.

To remedy a problem of relational decline is to discover the signs of it in the interaction patterns and do something about them. The solution to a relational problem lies in the patterns of communication, the exchange of self-offers. Whatever caused the problem in the first place is now irrelevant. The solution to the problem, then, is to do something to change the patterns of communication, to modify how the partners exchange their self-offers.

Relational breakdowns do not necessarily lead the partners to decide to terminate their relationship. In fact, most periods of relational decline are just disintegrative "lulls" in long-term relationships. During periods of relational decline, partners may try to reverse the trend and return to a period of relational growth. In that case, the period of decline is temporary and becomes a problem of how the partners can maintain the present definition of their relationship. In periods of relational decline, the partners may also attempt to remedy the problem by establishing a new definition of their relationship. That is, they retrospectively make sense of their relationship and redefine their past interaction to mean something different than they originally thought. After lovers quarrel or experience a lengthy period of decline in their romantic relationship, they may reassess their past interaction and decide that their relationship is not really love after all. They then proceed to redefine and enact their future relationship as "good friends."

Relational decline may occur in the middle of or immediately following a period of relational growth. For example, after the honeymoon, the newly married couple realize that they are entering a new period in their relationship. The future that they have talked about so often has become the present, and they need to define their relationship in light of that present. At one time the future had appeared to be brighter and rosier than the harsh reality of their present situation. For example, newly married couples discover they have financial problems they never encountered prior to marriage. The saying that "two can live as cheaply as one" is definitely not borne out in reality.

"After the honeymoon is over" is a phrase appropriate to any interpersonal relationship after a period of intense relational growth. It is not just for mixed-gender couples who have participated in a wedding ceremony. The posthoneymoon period typically implies some relational decline. To remedy these problems, partners often redefine their relationship. They look backward on their past interaction and make new sense of what it now means from the perspective of their present situation.

Adolescent couples often redefine their dating relationship after a period of relational growth and interpret it as something quite different from what they once thought it was. For instance, the newness of their relationship wears off, and they redefine their "true love" relationship to be only infatuation or a crush. The couple may continue to be good friends, or they may go their separate ways, still in search of the ideal partner. In either case, the experiences they shared in their past relationship haven't changed. But their definition of what those experiences meant does change. That is, they retrospectively paused to look back on their past interaction and made a different sense of those experiences. They solved a problem of relational decline by redefining their past relationship.

Redefining even a highly romantic relationship is not a very difficult thing to do. There are many different kinds of love, including brotherly love, erotic love, or unselfish altruistic love (sometimes designated by the Greek word "agape"), and kinship love. When a person says "I love you" to another, a typical first reaction is to consider that statement an expression of erotic love. But in retrospectively redefining a relationship, the partner can easily and rationally accept that the expression really referred to a platonic love instead. Consequently, the relationship once thought to be erotic love turns into close friendship. After redefining their relationship, the partners then change their interaction patterns to reflect their new relational definition.

Because a loving relationship may stem from different reasons, partners may cope with relational decline by attributing their past interactions to a different basis or reason. For instance, partners may retrospectively make sense of their past relationship by attributing it to a sense of gratitude rather than love. "She helped me out at a time when I needed help," he says. Thus, the partners redefine their relationship as one based on gratitude (trying to repay the other person) rather than love. Other bases of loving relationships that provide the partners with options to redefine what love meant in their past interaction include attributing their emotions to physical attraction ("He was absolutely gorgeous, but once I got to know him better, he turned out to be really dumb"), influence of the situation ("After he graduated, we sorta drifted apart—he didn't want to go to school dances and stuff"), overactive glands ("It wasn't really love—just lust"), or misperceptions of the other's feelings ("I thought he really loved me, but he was playing around with someone else on the sly").

Partners feel a need for redefinition only during periods of decline in their relationship. During periods of growth, they enjoy the interaction patterns and perceive no problems that need coping with. But when they feel their relationship begin to sour, partners feel the need to cope with the situation, if for no other reason than that they want to rid themselves of the unpleasant feelings that typically accompany relational breakdown. Most periods of relational decline do not lead to ending the relationship altogether. Rather, they typically lead to the participants reassessing the present state of their relationship and redefining what it was in the past. When redefinition occurs, the interactants once again engage in a process of retrospective sensemaking. They redefine their past interaction patterns by employing different attributions for their previous relationship. These techniques serve to protect each partner's self-concept and to keep the relationship going, typically with new patterns of interaction reflecting the revised definition of the relationship.

COMMON FACTORS IN RELATIONAL GROWTH AND DECLINE

The growth and declining stages of relational development are often characterized by a combination of factors working together in the interaction patterns of the relational partners. We now discuss the factors of self-disclosure, conflict, idealization, and turning points.

Self-Disclosure

We discussed self-disclosure earlier as a central component of Altman and Taylor's social penetration model. Self-disclosure was first conceptualized by psychologist Sydney Jourard in a book aptly titled *The Transparent Self* (1964). According to Jourard, self-disclosure is "the act of making yourself manifest, showing yourself so others can perceive you" (p. 19). Altman and Taylor's focus on self-disclosure was instrumental in promoting self-disclosure as a key component of relationship development. Some still consider the appropriate and controlled use of self-disclosure as the "main feature that stabilizes, establishes and develops relationships of all types" (Duck, 1991, p. 71). Self-disclosure remains a widely researched variable in interpersonal communication.

We will adopt a restricted definition of *self-disclosure* and use the term to refer only to information that one person tells another about her or his self "which the other person is unlikely to know or to discover from other sources" (Pearce & Sharp, 1973, p. 414). As mentioned previously, self-disclosure is not the same as openness; it is the verbal component of openness.

Self-disclosing communication embodies a real mystique in common mythology concerning communication in our society (see Bochner, 1984, pp. 600–601). Our romantic novels are filled with stories of first meetings between a woman and a man in which they reveal their innermost secrets and consequently fall madly, passionately, and immediately in love. A more objective understanding of self-disclosure reveals a far less formidable impact on interpersonal relationships. Despite an astounding interest and number of studies of self-disclosure in the fields of both psychology and communication (see Bochner, 1984; Chelune, 1979), the fact is that scholars really don't know nearly as much about it as they think they do. The following discussion attempts to provide a realistic look at self-disclosing communication and to give a sensible portrayal of its role in interpersonal communication from the individual as well as the relational viewpoint.

Self-Disclosure as a Personal Characteristic   It stands to reason that the person who knows more about yourself than anyone else is you. It also stands to reason that there are areas about yourself that may be known to others, but not yourself, as well as information that remains private only to you. In other words, all possible knowledge about yourself can be classified into two categories: public knowledge (what other people know) and private knowledge (what only you know). Self-disclosure, then, may be defined as your making public that knowledge which otherwise would be private only to you.

Joseph Luft (1969) has suggested four different classes of self-disclosure. Luft places his areas within a 2 × 2 matrix and calls it the Johari window—"window" because it represents a four-paned window and "Johari" because it was devised by *Joseph* Luft and *Harry* Ingram. Figure 9-3 depicts the Johari window, a representation of public and private knowledge of self.

Each person has some areas of self that she or he isn't aware of or prefers not to know about—the *unknown area.* Naturally, you can't disclose these portions of your self that you aren't aware of. Another area of your private self, the *blind area,* is a part of your self that you can't disclose to others, either, because this area contains information that others have about you but you don't have. This area is apparently that part of self-disclosure that leads other people to say that they "know you better than you know yourself."

The self-disclosure most significant to interpersonal communication is probably the information that is part of your perceived self-concept. When you share this information with another person through your communicative actions, intentionally or unintentionally, you move it from the *hidden area* to the *open area.* This shift is undoubtedly the self-disclosure intended by the widely accepted definition of the term—"making known to others information they wouldn't be able to know otherwise."

The public and private areas of self-knowledge that are significant to interpersonal communication are the perceived interpretations that each communicator possesses about her or his own self and the self of the other person. When you self-disclose you make manifest some aspect of your self. The other person, perceiving the behavior, infers something about you, and of course you do the same. But is the behavior a false or a genuine disclosure of the communicator's self? For instance, people tell you that you are gregarious and extroverted, but you say that you are shy. They say that

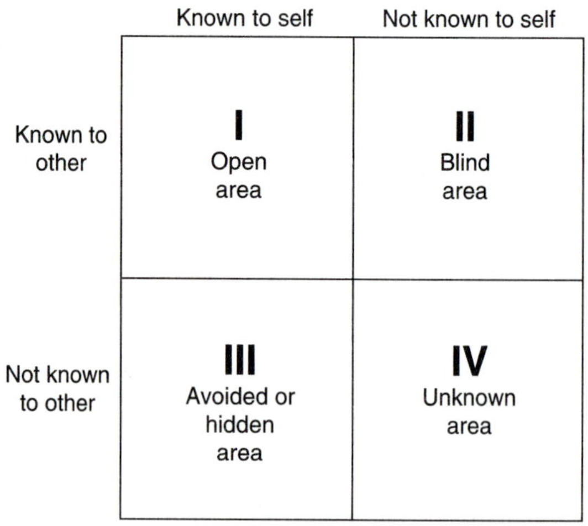

	Known to self	Not known to self
Known to other	**I** Open area	**II** Blind area
Not known to other	**III** Avoided or hidden area	**IV** Unknown area

FIGURE 9-3 Public and private knowledge of self (the Johari window).

your extroversion is a part of your blind area. You say it is a facade and isn't "really" you. Who is correct?

Whether they are right or wrong, whether the self-disclosure is false or genuine, is simply not important to the process of interpersonal communication. Your own self-perceptions may in fact disagree with others' perceptions and vice versa. It is the potential disagreement of perceptions, not which perceiver is "correct," that is important to interpersonal communication. What you perceive is "apparent knowledge" to you; what others perceive is "apparent knowledge" to them. Intrapersonally, the importance of your perceptions to interpersonal communication is whether your perceptions overlap. Self-disclosure, as a characteristic of the individual, is a part of the psychological process of perception. Although it is far more popular to characterize self-disclosure as a psychological phenomenon, it can be examined from an interactive or relational viewpoint (Cline, 1983).

Self-Disclosure as a Relational Characteristic   As we have pointed out, typical definitions of self-disclosure characterize it as the expression of some kind of personal information. It is far more unusual to portray self-disclosure as relational or interactive. Rebecca Cline and Sandra Petronio are two communication scholars with distinctive interactive approaches to self-disclosure and relational development.

Cline (1983) argues that self-disclosure is a form of relational communication. It functions sequentially to define both interactants within a relationship and those sequences of interaction do impact relational development. *Reciprocity* is the key to Cline's treatment of self-disclosure as a relational phenomenon.

The Norm of Reciprocity   Sociologist Alvin Gouldner (1960) has suggested that one of the most common norms in society is reciprocity. Reciprocity is the tendency to respond in kind to the other person. He likes you; you like him back. The term has been referred to as "response matching" (Argyle, 1969), the "dyadic effect" (Jourard, 1964) and compared to Leary's (1955) "interpersonal reflex." When applied to communicative behavior, reciprocity has been called the "best documented characteristic of self-disclosing communication" (Pearce & Sharp, 1973, p. 418). In other words, you self-disclose to another, and she or he will reciprocate by self-disclosing to you. The concept of reciprocity assumes *contingent* behavior and thus gives self-disclosure its relational character.

The force of the *norm of reciprocity* is hard to resist and tends to be positively valued in the relational literature. Wilmot (1980) identifies reciprocity as an essential ingredient of *successful* social relationships. Luft (1969) identifies reciprocal self-disclosure as *appropriate* self-disclosure. Argyle (1973) links it with *interpersonal trust*, explaining that individuals assume that if they help each other, such aid will be reciprocated. Berger and Bradac (1982) give it *strategic value.* Self-disclosure is viewed as "interactive knowledge gaining strategy" (p. 26) which works because people expect reciprocal exchange of information. Reciprocation is assumed to obligate individuals, thus promoting the exchange of information.

The norm of reciprocity is associated with relational development. For example, both Knapp (1984) and Wilmot (1980) speculate that as social relationships vary, so does reciprocity. Wilmot describes *encounter reciprocity* during initial interaction. Encounter reciprocity is the expectation that the other will respond to you and participate with you in the encounter. *Eventual reciprocity* occurs during later stages of relational development. Later in relationships, reciprocity may not be immediate. That is, partners may not always show immediate involvement with each other but later do so.

Cline (1983) investigated patterns of symmetrical and asymmetrical reciprocity in same-sex and cross-sex dyads during initial interaction. Symmetrical reciprocity occurs when both interactants reciprocate, whereas asymmetrical reciprocity occurs when only one interactant reciprocates. In the male-female dyads the negotiation of intimacy was achieved complementarily in patterns of asymmetrical reciprocity. The female responses in the study tended to accept the male's definition of the relationship, and their responses matched the intimacy level of previous male proposals. Male responses tended to reject female proposals to define the relationship. Female-female dyads showed a tendency toward symmetrical patterns of reciprocity in the negotiation of their intimacy. Their patterns displayed mutual attempts to define the relationship, with *both* partners offering intimacy proposals and intimacy responses. In male-male dyads there was little movement toward intimacy. Low levels of intimacy were proposed by interactants and often rejected with independent proposals of lesser intimacy. Neither partner appeared willing to let the other define the relationship. In other words, nonreciprocal behavior characterized the negotiation of intimacy in male-male dyads.

The norm of reciprocity appears to play a role in the development of relationships. Unfortunately there is not enough research to describe in detail how the norm functions in relational development, especially in long-term relationships. Sandra Petronio (1991) has developed a theory to explain how this idea of reciprocation is used by interactants to regulate privacy and intimacy in established relationships. She places the norm of reciprocity within the framework of boundary management.

Communication Boundary Management Theory   Petronio (1991) explains how couples strategically use self-disclosure of private information to negotiate intimacy in order to balance the tension between autonomy and connection. As we have discussed before, in close relationships people are faced with managing the opposing demands of moving close to one another (connecting) and of protecting self by moving away from other (autonomy). This dilemma gets manifested in the act of disclosing private information. Private information is information about your self that only you have a right to access. The disclosure of this kind of information is inherently risky because it can leave you vulnerable. Receiving this kind of information can also place the receiver in a vulnerable position because the act of disclosure is a move toward connection, and as such, it is a threat to another's autonomy.

In order to cope with the disclosure of private information and its opposing tensions, people construct boundaries. Controlling these boundaries help regulate the flow of private information between partners and thus protect the respective selves. The discloser of private information uses boundaries and so does the partner who receives the private information. As we mentioned earlier, self-disclosure assumes reciprocal responses of some sort. For instance, if you decide to disclose private information to a close friend you have, in essence, opened your communication boundary. Your disclosure implies that a response of some sort will follow. Whether the response from your friend meets your expectations depends on the level of boundary coordination between yourself and your friend. Patterns of boundary coordination may impact the quality of the relationship.

The communication boundary management theory rests on three assumptions. Relational partners exhibit tighter control of more private information. Second, they regulate their boundaries to minimize the risk of private information. Third, when their boundaries intersect, that is when disclosure occurs, the discloser uses criteria to decide the amount, the timing, and the recipient of the disclosure. The receiver also uses criteria to decide how to respond to the disclosure of private information. The receiver's decisions involve the balancing of individual autonomy with the intimacy of the disclosure.

When you are deciding whether to disclose, the regulation of your boundaries rests on five concerns: You will be concerned with (1) the strength of your desire to disclose, (2) your prediction as to what will happen as a result of disclosing, (3) the risk in disclosing to a particular individual, (4) the level of privacy of the information, and (5) your level of emotional control while disclosing. In addition, you decide whether to be indirect or direct in your disclosure. The receiver of your disclosure also regulates his or her boundaries by figuring out, (1) what it is you expect in return, (2) why you have disclosed (disclosure serves different functions), and (3) how to respond. Boundary coordination between yourself and another is a function of the fit between the expectations portrayed in your disclosive act and the response by the other. The degrees of fit range from satisfactory, to overcompensatory, deficient, and equivocal. Over time, patterns of fit may have consequences for the quality of the relationship.

Communication boundary management theory is important because it emphasizes the coordination of boundaries when private information is shared. In this theory both participants are players in the regulation of private information. This regulation is guided by a set of rules or criteria which shed some light on the myriad of factors that come into play in the regulation of effective disclosure. In addition, patterns of disclosure response are recognized as important factors in the development of relationships.

Some Concluding Thoughts   It should be clear that in order to understand the nature of interpersonal communication and provide a realistic basis for improving your own communicative practices, you need to adopt a realistic understanding of the role that self-disclosure plays in interpersonal communication. Toward that end, a few questions are in order.

1. *Is self-disclosure necessary for effective interpersonal communication?* According to Bochner (1982), "people believe it is appropriate to engage in high amounts of self-disclosure with others whom they like," and "people over-estimate the extent to which they self-disclose to others whom they like" (p. 118). In other words, friends may not exchange much self-disclosing information, but they *believe* they are doing so.

Self-disclosure isn't directly related to intimacy, but relationships developing toward intimacy typically include periods of high self-disclosure. Self-disclosure doesn't cause liking, but often if impressions are positive, then self-disclosure can enhance liking (Bochner, 1984). In fact, liking more often than not inhibits self-disclosure. We have discussed before the nature of indirectness between intimates as well as the amount of deception in close relationships.

Just because some self-disclosure is necessary in developing relationships, it doesn't follow that more self-disclosure is better. In a recent study of conversation in everyday life it was discovered that self-disclosure doesn't occur nearly as much as is presumed and much of the talk between intimates is nonintimate (Duck, Rutt, Hurst, & Strejc, 1991).

2. *Is self-disclosure desirable for effective interpersonal communication?* Clearly most people think so, without qualification. Sometimes, though, self-disclosure is quite undesirable. The timing of positive and negative disclosure and the pacing of deepening levels of self-disclosure is probably more important (Duck, 1991). Self-disclosure of negative information early in the relationship is not viewed as appropriate, for instance. You would be wise to exercise restraint in disclosing to others.

3. *Is self-disclosure important to effective interpersonal communication?* Again most people think so. And again, people need to qualify the answer. As they achieve a healthy and close relationship, partners will engage in self-disclosure along the way. But it is too readily assumed that self-disclosing communication causes (or at least leads to) healthy and close relation-

ships. As we saw in our discussion of boundary management, partners coordinate the regulation of private information in many ways, and some aren't beneficial to the relationship.

Bochner (1982) has previously written that "self-disclosure appears to be a highly overrated activity" (p. 121). The previous discussion about self-disclosure is intended to show that it is important to interpersonal communication. It is also intended to remove much of the magical quality so often attributed to self-disclosure when its significance and impact are overstated.

Conflict

For some reason mainstream American culture views conflict as rotten and nasty. Individuals, when asked, use only negative metaphors to describe conflicts in varying types of relationships (McCorkle & Mills, 1992). Typical metaphors include, "stubborn as a mule," "a tornado," "talking to a brick wall," "a festering splinter in your finger," "sinking ship with no lifeboat," "spinning top," "caught in a blender," "sliding down a razor blade," and "babysitting a seven year old" (McCorkle & Mills, 1992). Many of you with Euro-American backgrounds can probably recall parents saying things like "Nobody likes an arguer" and "Try to be 'nice' to people." Mainstream American society is somewhat two-faced regarding conflict. On the one hand, people are taught to develop a competitive fighting spirit and, as adolescents, encouraged to enter contests ranging from athletics, music, and speechmaking to drills and beauty pageants. At the same time, mainstream American culture tells people, "Try to be 'nice' to people. Conflict is bad."

It is an undeniable fact that conflict, particularly conflict in interpersonal communication, is so common as to be normal. Given our model of interpersonal communication, conflict is "a natural, inevitable occurrence in the continuous restructuring of social relationships" (Millar, Rogers, & Bavelas, 1984, p. 231). Every social relationship comprises individual human beings with different personalities, different self-concepts, different ideas, different emotions, different accounts of the relationship—a whole range of differences. As you get to know another person, you learn more about your partner's interests, attitudes, beliefs, values, and so on. The more you learn, the more likely you are to discover things that make you different, including things you dislike. You need to deal with the things that you dislike, or you risk being forever bothered by them.

During the period of integrative growth and change, the likelihood of significant conflict interaction is extremely high. The "glue" that bonds different individual selves together within a social relationship does not and cannot work when individuals deny that they are different. Remember that the dynamics of a social relationship revolve around the opposing tensions of separateness and interdependence. Intimate social bonds are, therefore, ultimately paradoxical:

> Moving closer to another person also, by necessity, means moving apart. That is, increasing awareness of, and confrontation with, the uniqueness of other. The more special two people become to each other the greater may be the pressure from both sides, to possess the other totally, or in popular phraseology, to "become one." And that indeed would mean the end of reciprocity. Intimacy, to be viable, thus requires the awareness and the acceptance of the stranger in the other. (Sprey, 1979, p. 724)

Individuals must create their unified relationship by managing their differences. Despite the appearance of similarities, individuals in even the closest and most intimate relationships will continue to be different. Their interaction characterized by patterns of separateness and connection is bound to include conflict.

Interpersonal Conflict: A Definition Keep in mind that within our model, conflict is *inter*personal. That is, *interpersonal conflict* requires a minimum of two people and must involve communication. No conflict can have any effect on the relationship unless the basis of the conflict involves both people, who disagree or are somehow differentiated from each other. Furthermore, the conflict can affect the relationship only if and when it appears in the form of argument, disagreement, or some form of incompatible acts occurring in the patterns of communication. Any other kind of conflict is simply not relevant or significant to interpersonal relationships or communication.

Millar, Rogers, and Bavelas (1984) conceptualize interpersonal conflict as a power struggle which becomes manifested in three uninterrupted one-up verbal behaviors. Conflict, described pragmatically, is an observable event occurring in sequences of behavior. They propose that the minimum pattern of conflict is composed of three consecutive one-up comments (see Chapter 6). The power struggle is manifested in the control dimensions of relationships. Recall that relationship-directed strategies which implicitly define the relationship in terms of which partner is "in charge" are known as control modes. One-up comments or domineering acts function to restrict the choices of the recipient, who then has the option to defer to the speaker's control (complementary interact) or match it with their own one-up act (symmetrical interact). The idea of a struggle implies at least three sequential one-up acts. That is, in a "conflict sequence, one interactant makes a definitional claim which is rejected by the other which, in turn, is opposed by the initial speaker" (Millar, Rogers, & Bavelas, 1984, p. 234). For example, you say to a friend, "I think that had we not met the way we did, we wouldn't be friends today." Your friend replies, "Well, maybe you wouldn't be but I would be." You then reply with the third one-up act, "No you wouldn't have been friends either."

Their description of conflict sequences allows for the identification of those sequences as well as the patterns prior to and after the conflict. Do not be misled, however, into thinking that relational conflict is as simple as it may *appear* to be in this description. Sillars and Weisberg (1987) point out that conflict in close, established relationships tends not to be straightforward and easily managed. Conflict in these relationships is more often chaotic and ambiguous, complicated by a variety of contextual factors. The disorganization of conflict is not simply captured in descriptions of conflict patterns. They explain three factors which contribute to the chaos and ambiguity of conflict in close relationships.

Interpersonal Conflict: Chaos and Ambiguity Conflict in close relationships often doesn't follow conventional rules of conflict presumed to exist for reasoned public argument. Relational partners in close relationships have developed their own understanding of how to "appropriately" do conflict. Nor are conventional rules of talk necessarily followed because in intense relational conflict, the partners can become less clear, orderly, and relevant and more emotional and impulsive (Sillars & Weisberg, 1987). Chaos and ambiguity in our interpersonal conflicts are more prevalent than may be expected and result from three factors: confusion over what the conflict is about, interactional complexity, and the nestedness of conflict in every day events.

What Is This Conflict About? Partners in close relationships usually don't engage in conflict over single issues, nor are they always clear about the source of their conflict (Sillars & Weisberg, 1987). Think of a recent conflict you have engaged in with a close friend. Did both of you perceive a conflict or only one of you? Did you both identify the same source of the conflict? How about the same reasons for the conflict? What were the perceptions of each other's behaviors and your individual attempts to deal with the conflict? Recognize as well that a myriad of issues are probably woven into the texture of your relationship. Any of these may be important to the conflict, for a variety of reasons that may not be shared by both of you. For example, husbands and wives will report different problem areas in their relationships (Scanzoni & Fox, 1980). Adding to the ambiguity surrounding interpersonal conflict is the realization that conflict often occurs on different levels. On the surface your conflict may appear to be caused by your forgetting to do something for your friend, but on a deeper level the issue is whether you now care as much for your friend as you used to. Millar et al. (1984, p. 235–236) provide an excellent example of how difficult it can be to identify the source of relational conflict.

MEGAN: What did you expect of me when we got married?
SYMON: Well, uh, I really didn't have any expectations of you.
MEGAN: I expected you to take care of me.

SYMON: Haven't I? (asked challengingly)
MEGAN: Yes. Have I complained?
SYMON: Yeah.
MEGAN: No! No.
SYMON: Silently!
MEGAN: No. No, no . . . no.
>   (Symon turns to the interviewer, after 15 seconds, and asks for the
>   next topic.)

What is the source of this conflict for Megan? What do her "no, no" remarks reveal about the "real" nature of this conflict? Is Megan disputing Symon's remark about her complaints? Is she disputing his implication that she does in fact complain, but silently? Is Megan trying to show disbelief in the manner in which the conversation is moving? Are her remarks an expression of embarrassment that these things are being said in the presence of a third party? Or is Megan disputing the account Symon is creating of the history of their relationship? Is it possible that the conflict could be about some combination of these issues? These are not easy questions to answer, and it is hard to ferret out the ambiguity inherent in many conflicts between intimates.

> ***How Do We Talk about These Issues?***   Chaos and ambiguity is further understood by the realization that there is no easy, orderly, clear manner of talking about these issues. The interactional organization of relational conflicts between intimates is complex (Sillars & Weisberg, 1987). How many times can you actually recall coming right out and dealing directly with a conflict with an intimate? Probably not very often. More than likely when faced with a difficult situation, you may have been rather irrelevant and incomplete in an attempt to steer clear of implicating yourself. At other times your conflicts may have involved numerous topic shifts as you and your partner struggled with the definition of the issues. At still other times your comments or the comments from your partner may have been ignored in the attempt to avoid direct rejection or acceptance of each other's comments. Patterns of relational conflict are variable and thus not easily described.

For one thing not all relational conflicts occur in clear, contingent patterns. Millar, Rogers, and Bavelas (1987), for example, describe such a pattern of contingency in their three one-up definition of conflict. Not all relational conflict, however, follows an immediately sequential pattern. For instance, Pike and Sillars (1985) discovered that some marital couples (those low in satisfaction) tended to use a "hit-and-run" pattern of expressing hostility. They expressed hostility at various times during the conversation except immediately after a partner's expression of hostility. Perhaps this is a way to approach and avoid a conflict—attack and then pull back.

Secondly, relational partners will engage in various patterns of topic management which don't make it easy for the partners to control the conflict. Let's take a look at some examples of ways partners can sequence the topics in conflict so that you can get an idea of how disorganized your intimate conflict can actually be. We will use the examples from Sillars and Weisberg (1987, pp. 154–156).

In *mutual contingency* both partners respond to each other and carry on with their own conflict agenda.

SYMON: We're not ever together.

MEGAN: Well, in the evenings, working the shift I work, we can't be together; I think we spend more time now than when we were first married.

SYMON: Yes, but during the week, if I want to go somewhere, we can't go together.

MEGAN: I have to work nights. I can't be there.

SYMON: You don't have to work nights. That was your own decision.

MEGAN: I did it for a reason. I get a better job, a raise, and more security. We're better off.

SYMON: Does that mean that you like not seeing me anymore?

MEGAN: No, I don't like it! But until some things change, that's the way it has to be.

In each case, the partner responded to the previous comment and then extended the issue, thereby broadening the focus of the conflict. For instance, Megan comments that she has to work nights. Symon responds by refuting her assertion and extends the issue by remarking that working nights is a matter of choice. Megan responds to the issue of choice and expands the focus by commenting on the quality of their life, and so forth.

In *asymmetrical contingency* one relational partner carries out his or her conflict agenda, while the other remains unaware of what is happening.

SYMON: Do you want to go back to gambling?

MEGAN: No. I like it, but I'm not going back to it.

SYMON: Why?

MEGAN: Well, I have obligations now.

SYMON: And you see those obligations as more important than gambling?

MEGAN: Right.

SYMON: You don't think there's anything that could cause you to go back to that again?

MEGAN: I don't think so.

SYMON: You're not sure are you?

MEGAN: I'm pretty sure. As a matter of fact I'll say I am sure.

SYMON: I don't want you going to horse races anymore.

In this example, Symon saves the main issue (he doesn't want Megan to go to the race track) until the end. He carries out his agenda under the guise of asking Megan about her gambling habit, and in the process he sets her up before he makes his request. Partners may do this to reduce possible objections to their arguments.

In *pseudo-contingency* patterns partners relate their comments to the immediately prior comment to show contingency but then drastically alter the focus.

SYMON: Your temper is not as bad as your pouting. Sometimes if something's wrong I have to drag it out of you. You just don't want to talk about it, or you just would rather sit and not discuss it.

MEGAN: I don't like to talk sometimes and maybe I should. Once in awhile I don't like some of your ideas because you take more time to think about things. I think I'm freer because when I get an idea that I'm going to do something, I just pursue it. I don't really think about it as much as you do.

Megan's response is a pretend, or pseudo-contingent, response to Symon because she acknowledges that his topic has relevancy, but then proceeds with her own conflict agenda.

Noncontingent reactions occur when partners don't bother to acknowledge each other's comments as they develop their own conflict agendas.

SYMON: You come from work and you're all upset. You take it all out on me. You just turn away from me and . . .

MEGAN: [interrupts] There's a lot of pressure these days. No wonder people are not living to be very old. They start worrying as soon as they get old enough to walk, and they worry until the day they die.

SYMON: They worry but they don't take it out on . . .

MEGAN: [interrupts] It's always been that way. You're always going to have worries about whether you have enough money to do this, to go there, or the house payment's due, the electric bill is due. There's always something. Money for this! Money for that! Always something.

While there is some topic continuity in this episode, Megan's comments disconfirm (Chapter 6) Symon because she ignores him as opposed to directly addressing the issue.

Intimate conflict is a complicated, often disorganized social event. When the conflicts follow the predictable "You did this–No I didn't–Yes you did" pattern, it is easier for the partners to anticipate responses. Note, however, that these patterns can become very rigid one-up patterns of a power struggle over the definition of the relationship and thus can damage the relationship (Millar, Rogers, & Bavelas, 1984). Further, interpersonal conflict can also occur in patterns which are hard to predict. These patterns can be very problematic for partners. Chaos can occur when partners continuously shift the focus of the conflict in various ways. Mild, less intense conflict is characterized by less topic shift and more control (Sillars & Weisberg, 1987). However, in intense conflicts, partners seeking to define the events in terms of their own agenda often shift focus in any number of ways.

Interpersonal Conflict Occurs in Context The third contributing factor to the disorganization and chaotic nature of intimate conflict is the fact that these conflicts occur in contexts which themselves aren't highly predictable. Recall that your personal relationships are unique and less formal than public relationships. Sillars and Weisberg (1987) explain that there are no set boundaries for intimate conflict. Often the conflict comes as a surprise to the partners, occurring any day or night and at all hours. Interestingly, Duck, Rutt, Hurst, and Strejc (1991) found that across relational types, Wednesday emerged as the day of the week when people reported more conversational conflict. Conflict is often a surprise to intimates because it is nested in daily life. Do you have a time set aside for sharing your problems with your friend or lover? Most people don't. Instead, conflicts occur *during* all sorts of daily activity which means its character and management is susceptible to the rhythms of those activities.

Interpersonal Conflict: Some Concluding Thoughts Don't be misled into believing that all is lost because conflict in your personal relationships is often improvised and ambiguous. Recognize, however, that there are no easy ways to manage most of these conflicts. One answer may be to avoid them altogether. This solution is not realistic because, as we pointed out earlier, conflict is normal and to be expected in interpersonal systems. In fact, partners in healthy social relationships find ways to promote and constrain conflict (Millar et al., 1984). Yes, conflict can harm the relationship if it is allowed to escalate into destructive patterns, as we mentioned earlier. Its benefits aren't always as obvious because many people remain constantly focused on a down slide to conflict. Conflict can help partners to see their similarities and differences, allowing them to build a relationship on the basis of a more complete understanding of each other. Conflict also allows relational partners to develop strategies for coping with adversity. The experience of having successfully met crises in the past serves to make the relational bond stronger in the future.

The avoidance of a stalemate in conflict interaction is probably the difference between conflict management and unsuccessful conflict management. Gottman (1982), for example, found that dissatisfied marital partners tended to respond to the partner's complaint with one of their own. Remember our discussion of the hostile comments followed by another hostile comment? Ting-Toomey (1983), in another study of marital couples, found that a maladjusted partner tended to confront the other with some complaint, and the typical response was for the partner to defend him- or herself or to confront the other back. In other words, unsuccessful conflict management means using a strategy that doesn't work and continuing to use it.

If conflict is managed successfully, a relationship can endure and may even be strengthened.

Unsuccessful conflict management reflects interaction that bogs down in repetition of the same pattern. The partners aren't managing their conflict. They stalemate the conflict, line up their defenses, and wait for the other to "give in." The best advice to give any dyad experiencing growth or decline is to keep the interaction going and try new actions to change the patterns. If your interaction stops without managing the conflict, then the partners have no opportunity to manage it.

Some conflicts, of course, may never be managed successfully. When they are unsuccessful, the conflict may cause the end of the relationship. Sometimes terminating their relationship is the only thing left for the partners to do. Sometimes it is the best alternative, too. However, when the partners believe the relationship is worth saving, they strive to manage their conflict interaction. When they do so successfully, their relationship is strengthened.

One last thought. Conflict in social relationships is not only an intricate, dynamic *inter*personal process, but it also is a cultural event (Sillars & Weisberg, 1987). You must be very careful to guard against using a single mainstream American standard to judge conflict and to choose your strategies of conflict management. The experience of conflict, its patterns, and the manner in which it is appropriately managed can vary tremendously from relationship to relationship and from culture to culture:

> Jews may seem argumentative; West Indians, Native Americans, and Scandanavians inexpressive; and the Irish or Japanese indirect and un-clear. Blue-collar families and many ethnic families may seem to lack true intimacy because of the intrusion of extended family and friends into the private affairs of a relationship. These relationships may also appear rigid because of a reliance on tradition and a passive problem-solving style. (Sillars & Weisberg, 1987, p. 162)

Conflict is truly a relational and cultural social event.

Idealization

Earlier discussions have implied that a period of relational growth may often include a series of misunderstandings. That is, the partners are so caught up in the joy of the moment that they tend to hear what they want to hear and see what they want to see. The period of relational growth induces very pleasant feelings, and those feelings may lead the partners to an *idealization* of the object of their affections (Hall & Taylor, 1976). When you idealize your partner, you are really perceiving a fictitious person—an "ideal partner" who doesn't really exist—instead of the "real" person who will always have good points and bad points.

Furthermore, the partner who is idealized tends to behave in a manner consistent with the idealization. That is, he or she constantly tries to live up to the partner's expectations. That doesn't necessarily mean that the partner is "faking" a different personality. The partner is simply portraying only a part of his or her self, the part that is most likely to give the other person the best impression. As a result, though, idealization leads one partner to have an incomplete and, to some extent, false impression of the other.

When "the honeymoon is over," the partners often realize that their relationship has been based on some misunderstandings. She discovers that he is not prince charming after all, and he discovers that his beautiful princess isn't as perfect as he thought. Both realize that their future together is not likely to follow the "happily ever after" scenario unless they can learn to see one another more realistically. The discovery that a partner is not perfect rarely signals the end of a relationship. In fact, idealizing the partner is rather common during periods of relational growth, and most relationships continue to develop after the partners discover their misunderstandings.

Generally speaking, a relationship that evolves through a series of misunderstandings will also evolve out of them, given enough time. As the partners continue to interact with each other, they discover and reveal increasingly more information about each other. The normal process of communication, allowed to continue, will reveal any misunderstandings that have developed from past interaction. The only problem occurs when the partners have committed themselves to their relationship beyond the point of being able to reassess and redefine the basis for their interpersonal relationship. But that makes the problem only more difficult, not impossible, to solve.

Unfortunately, all the secondary characteristics of interaction quality do not develop at the same rate. Intensity and intimacy, for example, typically evolve much more rapidly than trust and commitment. Idealizing a relationship generally implies high intensity and intimacy but not necessarily a corresponding high level of trust or commitment. Partners in an idealized relationship often withhold trust and commitment when they feel the relationship is "moving too fast." Consequently, when they discover their misunderstanding (which resulted from idealizing the other person) they "slack off" on their period of relational growth in order to get to know one another better. When that discovery occurs, the relationship proceeds from a period of rapid growth to a period of decline. But the period of decline typically means only that the level of intensity and intimacy reverts back to where it should have been in the first place—equivalent to the levels of trust and commitment.

In every case, the solution to relational problems created by idealization is continued interaction, continued development. And if the partners decide that their relationship doesn't warrant continued growth, they are still free to redefine their relationship and remain close acquaintances or "just friends."

Turning Points

The discussion of "turning points" began with Bolton in 1961. In his view of relationship development, turning points were a form of social interaction which impacted the course of relationship development. For Bolton, they marked shifts or transitions in the definitions of the relationship. Since then they have been referred to as "relational crises," "critical events," and "transition points." We defined *turning points* (Chapter 7) as any event connected with change in a relationship (Baxter & Bullis, 1986), and we consider turning points important in understanding relationship development. Their presence also is a reminder that social relationships contain elements of surprise, events that occur which interactants may or may not have any control over and which impact the dynamics of the relationship.

Planalp and Honeycutt (1985) investigated the nature and impact of turning points in established personal relationships (i.e., friendships and romantic relationships). They were interested in discovering events which increased uncertainty in personal relationships. Six turning points emerged from subject responses. "Competing relationships" was an event involving questions of partner loyalty. "Unexplained loss of contact or closeness" was an issue of uncertainty because one partner never understood why the other moved away or tired of the relationship. "Sexual behavior" included events in which one partner revealed their sexual orientation or made unexpected sexual advances. "Deception" involved lying about things such as drug or alcohol abuse. "Change in behavior or values" were events in which one partner discovered or observed behavior of the other contrary to existing impressions. For instance, one partner may observe the other engage in blatant racist behavior. And finally, "betraying a confidence" involved questions of trust.

All these turning points served to increase uncertainty in the relationship and did have an impact on both the intrapersonal and interpersonal levels. On the personal level, these critical events changed partner beliefs about the other and sometimes had a strong emotional impact. On the interpersonal level, communication was altered and there were relational consequences. Individuals reported communicative attempts to do something about the uncertainty. Some chose to talk about the event and its consequences, some avoided the event, some argued about it, and still others talked around it. Although some events (i.e., those which were highly charged emotionally and involved a major change in belief about the partner) did result in relational termination, not all these turning points resulted in negative consequences for the relationship. Critical events do occur in relationships increasing uncertainty and do impact the course of the relationship.

In another study by Baxter and Bullis (1986) turning points were studied in the context of one specific type of relationship and were used to test some assumptions about relational development. Romantic couples were asked to identify turning points in the course of their relationship and to specify the intensity of the event. Baxter and Bullis (1986) were also interested in using the turning point data to explore how the relationships moved through development and to see if the partners behaved in ways congruent with past research.

Romantic partners did identify several turning points (759 to be exact) in the course of their relationships such as "get-to-know time," "quality time," "external competition," "passion," "exclusivity," "serious commitment," and "sacrifice." The difference between "get-to-know time" and "quality time" further substantiated the fact that the amount of information is more important for romantic dyads, initially, followed by quality time later during development. The same shifting pattern holds true for friends (Hays, 1984). Physical affection during the "passion" turning point was important to the transition from platonic to romantic relationship. Someone Kathy knows once captured the idea behind this transition with the remark,

"The only difference between friends and lovers is where you place your hand." "Sacrifice" turning points, characterized by one partner giving of her- or himself, are important indications of caring for romantic dyads. And finally, loyalty and fidelity are marked by the turning points "external competition" and "exclusivity."

More important, the data revealed some interesting things about development. For instance, relationship development didn't follow the image of two people slowly peeling away layers of their onions as portrayed by the social penetration model. Development instead was characterized as a series of discrete events like the staircase image of Knapp's model. The same characterization of development emerged out of Conville's (1988) case study of one romantic dyad. Even more interesting is that it appears that within a turning point event, there is movement of positive and negative "explosions of commitment" (Baxter & Bullis, 1986). Conville (1988) suggests that turning points are themselves "interstages" between two broader stages with their own structure. This structure appears to be marked by the dynamics of dialectical tensions. These conclusions are speculative at this point because they are grounded in reports from subjects, and it is known that interactant accounts of development may differ from direct observation of relational behavior. Nonetheless, turning points offer a way for scholars to study the complex dynamics of relationship development.

Baxter and Bullis's (1986) study also confirmed two expectations about interactant behavior. One, 55 percent of the turning points reportedly involved direct talk, which may seem contrary to what is known about the preference for indirect talk about the relationship. Baxter and Bullis (1986) point out, however, that turning points are rare occurrences (one every two months or so), and some turning points such as "serious commitment" and "making up" would naturally involve direct talk. Second, the partners displayed that same amount of congruency between their perceptions of the turning points as would be expected from the research. And congruency of separate views is not necessary for satisfaction. Relational partners, contrary to popular belief, live in separate worlds *believing* they hold more congruent views than they actually do. As Sillars and Scott (1983) argue, congruency is not necessary for partner happiness, instead compatibility of separate views may be more important.

Not much work has been done in the area of turning points since Bolton identified these patterns as critical factors in relationship development. This is surprising given their obvious association with change in relationships. Also, most of the work has explored only romantic relationships. What are the turning points in friendships relationships? Do friendships shift in the same manner of other personal relationships? What is the interactive structure and function of these events in the total picture of relational change over time? These and other questions remain to be answered.

PATTERNS OF INTERACTION

Whether you communicate with friends or with partners who are fast becoming former friends, the strategies you use are amazingly similar. Your strategies reflect an emphasis on the self, typically the self of the partner. Generally speaking, the interaction of growing and decaying relationships allows the partners to compare their selves with each other. When the relationship is growing, the partners discover or emphasize the similarities of their selves. When the relationship is disintegrating, the differences between their selves become more important.

The important thing to remember is that similarities and differences in the individual selves of the communicators are present throughout the entire relationship. The interaction characterizing escalating relationships emphasizes the partners' similarities while ignoring or suppressing their differences. But those differences are significant in the interaction of partners whose relationship is in a period of decline, while their similarities are less significant. In both relational growth and relational decay, however, the partners use strategies that emphasize self even though the emphasis (on similarities or differences of self) differs.

Relational Issues and Strategies

Kathy Adams (1985) discovered in her investigation of relational interaction that friends tend to concentrate on self-as-other issues in their interaction with each other. They described their relationship with friends in the following manner:

> "We can do anything together, and she is fun and understanding."
>
> "We have a good warm relationship as friends. When we see each other, we can begin conversing as though we saw each other every day. Loren and I are alike. . . ."
>
> "Sara is easy to relate to. We hold things in common, and she is fun to be with and do things with."

"Friendship" is a term applied to a variety of different kinds of relationships with different levels of intimacy, intensity, trust, and commitment. Although they described their friendships similarly, these couples undoubtedly differed in characteristics of their interaction quality. Some of the couples may have been "best friends," and others may have been "just friends." In every case, though, they described their relationship in terms of their similarities. Friends tend to emphasize their similarities ("We are alike"), the things they have in common that make the other person easy to relate to.

Friends tend to be oriented to the other person. Hence, the interaction of friends includes many "you" statements, for example:

"Yeah, but there are things that you need."
"But you chose to do it alone."
"Like a con artist. Is that what you're saying?"
"Oh, I think your place is right here."

The interaction patterns of relationships in both relational growth and relational decline differ on the basis of whether they emphasize similarities or differences of the partners. Partners in friendships experiencing either decline or growth focus on self-as-other issues. Interaction during relational decline will also include many "you" statements, similar to the above comments. But even though the relational issues of their interaction are similar, partners in disintegrating relationships tend to use relational strategies to emphasize their differences. When you communicate with a friend, for example, you attempt to assimilate your self with your partner. When you communicate with a partner who is becoming less of a friend, you tend to differentiate your self from your partner. In both relationships, you interact by comparing your self with the self of your partner. The interaction patterns of relational growth and decline differ when the comparison leads to assimilating or differentiating the partners' selves.

The following interaction illustrates the assimilation of the partner's selves and is typical of the interaction of friends, that is, relationships escalating toward friendship:

SYMON: I don't know whether to take that one or to change to a weight training class. I just don't know.
MEGAN: Oh, if I were you, I'd stick with the exercise for fitness.

In this case, Megan is offering "advice" to Symon. Furthermore, Symon invited her to give him advice by stating clearly, "I just don't know." Megan's advising response thus functions to assimilate her self with Symon's self.

Another strategy that can serve to assimilate the selves is "supporting," as in the following interaction:

SYMON: I just took a chance and told him how I felt. I thought he might get mad or somethin' but he was really nice about it.
MEGAN: Good for you. You stuck up for your rights.
SYMON: Yeah, I guess so. It was kinda hard at first. You know, I wasn't sure what he'd do. He coulda really fried me.
MEGAN: I can imagine how hard it was for you. But you were right, and he was wrong. You gotta stand up for yourself when that happens. I'm proud of you.

In this interaction, Megan provides encouragement and support for Symon, who has told her about his own experience. By supporting her friend, Megan is assimilating her self with Symon's self. She expresses an emotion (pride) that she feels as a result of Symon's action. She tells Symon that she could experience the same feeling that he did ("I can imagine how hard it was for you").

This assimilating strategy is sometimes called "showing empathy." That is, you tell the other person that your self (emotions, feelings, and so forth) is similar to the other person's self. By offering sympathy, advice, and support, Megan expresses empathy or identifies (expresses similarity) her self with Symon's self.

The interaction patterns of declining friendships may appear to reflect "advising" or "supporting" strategies. However, the strategies in the context of the interaction pattern function to tell the other person how different their selves are. Note the differentiating strategies in the following excerpt from the interaction of partners whose relationship is on the skids:

SYMON: I don't know what I should do. I could sure use the extra money, but working on weekends? I just wouldn't have any free time. I just don't know.

MEGAN: Go ahead, do it. You'd have plenty of time during the week. You got all your evenings free, don't you?

SYMON: That's not the same, though. What can you do during the week? I like weekends to go fishing or camping or . . .

MEGAN: I know what you're thinking. You won't have any time to fool around with the boys. Big deal!

SYMON: No, that's not it. I just . . .

MEGAN: Come on. I know you too well. I can read you like a book. You just wanna pal around with your buddies.

SYMON: Well, that may be part of it. But I wouldn't have any weekends at all if I work all this overtime. I do a lotta things on weekends.

MEGAN: Now you're just feeling sorry for yourself. Money is too important to you. I know how you think. You'll do it.

This interaction includes comments from Megan that only *appear* to offer advice and support to Symon. But her comments don't show the similarities between the partners' selves. In fact, they actually differentiate her self from Symon's self. Megan attributes selfish motives to Symon, and Symon resists her telling him what he is feeling inside. Megan is not dissuaded, however, and continues to focus her comments on Symon's feelings. When she makes these comments, Megan implicitly distances her self from Symon's. After all, Megan doesn't want to "pal around" with Symon's buddies. By telling Symon what his feelings are, Megan demonstrates a difference in their selves and functions to emphasize something that makes their selves different rather than something they have in common.

Megan's comments also exhibit a strategy that appears to be "showing empathy" but actually functions quite differently. Note that several of her comments express what Symon's feelings or emotions are: "I know what you're thinking," "I can read you like a book," and "I know you too well." But these strategies don't "identify" Megan's self with Symon's self. Rather, they merely express Megan's claim that she "knows" Symon's self. This strategy is also known as "mind reading"—telling the other person what is going on within him or her. Megan tells Symon what he is thinking, what he is feeling, what his motives are. And Symon reacts to Megan's mind reading in a very typical manner. He says, in essence, "You don't know what I'm thinking. Don't tell me what I feel."

The normal response to people who tell you "they know you better than you know yourself" is to deny their mind-reading ability. You generally resent such comments, particularly when they tell you that your motives or feelings are less than perfect and particularly when they are correct. Nothing is more annoying than to hear someone tell you about feelings or motives that you do in fact have but don't want other people to know about. As long as people delude themselves that others aren't aware, people won't feel guilty about what they're feeling or thinking. As soon as you are forced to admit something uncomplimentary about yourself, you feel guilty or embarrassed. Your typical reaction is to resent the person who made you feel that way.

In each of the interaction samples above, the partners address self-as-other issues. Symon tells Megan about an experience or topic that is personal to him. Megan then orients to Symon and, through Symon, indirectly toward his personal experience. The partners also change roles so that they take turns presenting the personal experience. That is, Symon presents his experience to Megan and thus becomes the "other" for Megan's orientation. Later on in their interaction, Megan will introduce some personal topic and become the "other" toward which Symon orients his responsive strategies. Whether their relationship is growing or declining, the partners will focus their interaction on self-as-other issues. The principal difference between the growing and declining relationships is that in the latter the strategies in the interactional patterns emphasize the partners' differences whereas in the former their similarities are stressed.

Secret Tests

To a large extent, people in a changing relationship (either integrating or disintegrating) experience some uncertainty about the current state of their relationship. Each partner may wonder "How well are we doing? Is our relationship getting anywhere? Does my partner think, like I do, that we're having trouble?" To reduce their uncertainty about the relationship, partners devise strategies to gain some information about its status. Of course, you can't directly ask your partner about the relationship nearly as easily as you can ask her or him about information regarding self. Hence, you devise strategies that indirectly seek information about the relationship by concealing the true motive behind the strategy. Communication scholars Leslie Baxter and Bill Wilmot (1984) call such strategies *secret tests.*

The purpose of a secret test is to acquire information about the relationship, just as small-talk strategy seeks to acquire information about the other person's self. The most obvious test, of course, would be to ask the other person how she or he felt about you. Although many people in Baxter and Wilmot's survey of male-female relationships reported that they used direct-questioning strategies, any information acquired from direct questions is probably suspect. That is, if you were really uncertain about your partner's feelings toward you, would you unquestioningly accept the truth of the answer to your question "How do you really feel about me?" Strategies perceived to be most effective are probably those that secretly gain information about the relationship without your partner's knowledge.

A variety of "secret tests" are available to the person who wants to learn more about the current state of the relationship. The one that is most frequently used is called the *endurance test.* This strategy consists of drastically reducing the rewards for the other partner in the relationship or increasing the costs for remaining in the relationship. For example, a physical separation (not seeing each other for some period of time) tests the relationship's endurance. Does "absence make the heart grow fonder?" Or when you're "out of sight," are you also "out of mind?" Another endurance test is to ask your partner to be inconvenienced in some way, such as doing something for you that he or she would not normally or willingly do. A third type of endurance test would involve being rude toward your partner in order to determine whether he or she will sustain the relationship even after seeing your "worst side." Endurance tests all aim at discovering whether the relationship will endure after facing problems. If the partner is still around after you have used an endurance test, then you assume that your relationship is strong.

A second frequently used secret test is called a *triangle test.* This type of strategy, more likely to be used in male-female relationships, involves the use of a third party and places your partner in a situation in which his or her fidelity or jealousy is tested. Is your partner jealous when you see someone else, even if it's not a real date? Is your partner "true" to your relationship by choosing you over someone else? The earlier interaction excerpt involving Megan's mind-reading strategy may also reflect a secret test of the relationship. Megan accuses Symon of wanting weekends free to have fun with his buddies. Megan may be secretly testing the relationship by implicitly saying, "Who is more important to you—me or your buddies?" When Symon does not immediately respond by affirming his relationship with Megan, Megan may be thinking that he just failed her triangle test.

Another secret test uses *indirect* suggestion. For instance, you make some statement about the nature of the relationship but phrase it in such a way as to imply that you aren't really serious. For example, you might phrase your statement as though you were joking or just kidding around: "When we're married, you can get a great job and support me for the rest of my life. I think I'd like being a person of leisure." Or you can drop some hint about the state of the relationship and wait for your partner's response: "Boy, this party is really stuffy. I think I really prefer being alone with someone I really like than being in a crowd of strangers."

Joking or hinting is a strategy that indirectly asks the partner to respond with some statement that indicates the nature of the relationship. By taking the joke seriously or even extending the joke, the partner is telling you that the relationship is "on track" and still escalating. By taking the hint and leaving the party with you, the partner is saying that your relationship is in good shape. But if the partner ignores the hint, you may have cause for worry.

Baxter and Wilmot (1984) also discovered that women differ from men in their use of secret tests. For example, women reported testing their relationships more frequently than men. This result may indicate either of two different explanations. One, the social relationships of women may be different from those of men. Individuals' sex-role stereotypes lead them to believe that women are more socially oriented, and thus may be more "relationally attuned" than are men. On the other hand, the survey also revealed that women and men both reported that their partners (of the opposite sex) used about the same number of secret tests. Therefore, a second explanation is that women may not use any more strategies to assess their relationships than men do, but they *think* that they do.

The problem that continues to plague people's understanding of how women and men communicate is the potential and probable difference between what they *perceive* they do and what they actually *do* (Fisher, 1983; Ragan, 1989). Your perceptions, as earlier discussions have emphasized, are influenced by cultural stereotypes and socialized sex roles. The extent to which your actual behaviors, particularly communicative behaviors, are susceptible to those same cultural influences remains problematic.

Accounts

Strategies that provide an excuse or justification for one's own actions are, as you may recall, termed *accounts.* During the early stages of getting-acquainted communication, communicators frequently use accounts to interpret and justify their problematic actions. But the principal issue for interaction in the early stages is "self-as-object." When the relationship is in a stage of growth and decay, a prominent issue emerges—"self-as-other." During periods of growth and decay, partners orient their strategies toward the other person. Thus, when partners use *relational accounts* during these stages, they are attempting to interpret and sometimes justify each other's actions.

Accounts, in this broader sense, are essentially idealized perceptions or interpretations of the other person's behavior and the relationship. We have frequently mentioned in this chapter the retrospective sensemaking of relational partners. This sensemaking, or accounting, is like the "folklore" of your relationship. You and your partner essentially create your own history after you have lived it. Relational partners are said to "editorialize" their relationships as a function of circumstance and need (Duck & Pond, 1989). These relational accounts aren't reproduced so much as they are *reconstructed* (Miell, 1987). This means that they don't *re*present a description of relational reality, instead they *pre*sent a view of relational reality (Duck & Pond, 1989).

As you look back on your history of past interaction from the perspective of the present, you reconstruct certain events (perhaps that special date or that first argument) as having greater significance than they had at the time they happened. These accounts help you to make sense of your relationship. When you look back, whatever is happening in that moment of recollection, will influence what you find when you look back (Weick, 1979). For instance, relational partners predict the future of their relationship on the events of the last three days, not on their understanding of any long-standing character of their relationship (Miell, 1987).

The significance of past events results from your having attributed significance to them and presenting that view to another with the hope of possibly convincing her or him of that view. When people are getting to know each other, it is expected that the accounts of how they began will be discrepant. Later, however, their accounts of the beginning of their relationship show convergence (Duck & Miell, 1986). The work of relationships involves the constant negotiation and renegotiation of joint relational histories, or folklore. These retrospections function not only to make your relationships appear real and tangible, but they also influence how you and your relational partners see those relationships. People use these accounts to create a narrative of their lives and in so doing "market" their social relationships and tell stories about what is going on with them (Duck & Pond, 1989).

During a period of relational growth, you "account" for the relationship by idealizing your partner and, indirectly, the relationship. A time of relational growth, you recall, is like a honeymoon in which the partners are caught up in the joy of the moment. During periods of relational decay, you also tend to idealize your partner and the relationship, but you use a "negative ideal." You see your partner as a cad who never really liked you. You think your relationship was never really "true" friendship or romantic. You typically lay blame in your accounts on the other person—the perfect target for blame. The idealization and bias in these accounts are not memory losses but crucial rhetorical choices made by individuals trying to cope with the ending of a relationship (Duck, 1982).

These relational accounts appear during times of relational escalation. Expressions of affection (such as "I love you") and verbalized descriptions of the other person (such as "You are really a good friend") occur much more frequently during periods of relational growth. Their function is to provide a sense of continuity during a time of change (Duck & Pond, 1989).

Relational accounts as strategic moves in relational development do not have to be restricted to those strategies relational partners use to justify or excuse problematic behavior. In a much broader sense, relational accounts are used by relational partners to understand or make sense of their relationships (Harvey, Agostinelli, & Weber, 1989). Account making thus provides a rich context for understanding the patterns of interaction between relational partners.

SUMMARY

As people continue to interact with each other, they begin to create their interpersonal relationship. Continued interaction means continued development of their interaction toward a state of increased integration or a state of disintegration. Although relational growth and decay are different stages in the evolutionary process of relational development, they do have many characteristics in common. The difference between growth and decay is usually more in the pattern or sequence of interaction than in specific behaviors exhibited by the partners. Change is the one factor that remains constant in variable patterns of growth and decay. Change over the course of a relationship is predictable, unique, oblique to its happening, and involves an exchange of securities.

Charting the development of relationships is no easy task. Social penetration portrays change as a slow incremental process of individuals revealing more and more of themselves to each other. Self-disclosure plays a key role in this process. Knapp's staircase model of development portrays change as occurring in discrete steps characterized by qualitative changes in behavior. Understanding relational change is a difficult task compounded by the recognition that social relationships fluctuate through stages of growth and decay involving continual choice and commitment by partners. Interaction, for example, serves to constrain the choices of both partners in the relationship, but the partners in escalating relationships welcome these constraints, whereas those in deescalating relationships consider them confining.

The emotions of relational partners will change during periods of relational change. These internalized emotions are often mistaken for the definition of the relationship. In reality, the emotion is only an inference a partner makes about the relationship in order to make sense of it after the interaction has created it (and, of course, in order to make sense of it both during and after the interaction). An emotion may also be an attribution of the relationship in the sense that "If I feel this way, it must be love." In any case, however, the emotion is not the relationship but the reaction, either attribution or inference, of the individual relational partner to the communication and serves to make sense of the communication in terms of some feeling toward the other person.

Interaction comprises a number of different characteristics during periods of growth and decay. Among these components are immediacy, formality, and openness. A change in the relationship, toward integration or disintegration, involves a change in one or more of the components of the interaction. The partners in the relationship define their mutual relationship by looking backward (retrospective) on their interaction and making sense of it in terms of the relationship. When the interaction is in the process of changing, then, their definition of the relationship through retrospective sensemaking is also in the process of change.

The growth and declining stages of relational development are often characterized by a combination of factors working together in the interaction patterns of the relational partners. These factors include self-disclosure, interpersonal conflict, idealization, and turning points.

Interactional strategies include giving relational accounts, doing secret tests, and providing support and advice to the other. During a period of relational growth, a strategy that offers advice or support to the other person will express empathy to the partner. During a period of relational decay, though, that strategy may appear as "mind reading," which is typically resented by the other partner. Relational accounts are used by partners to make sense of their relationships and provide a context for understanding their interaction.

KEY TERMS

social penetration

breadth

depth

life-span developmental
    communication perspective

immediacy

formality

openness

relational distance

self-disclosure

open area

unknown area

blind area

hidden area

norm of reciprocity

encounter reciprocity   turning points
eventual reciprocity   secret tests
interpersonal conflict   endurance test
mutual contingency   triangle test
asymmetrical contingency   indirect test
psuedo-contingency   joking
noncontingent reactions   relational accounts
idealization

CHAPTER 10 Creating
Relationships—
Termination, or
"How Can I Leave
Thee? Let Me Count
the Ways."

Love's stricken "why"
Is all that love can speak—
Built of but just a syllable
The hugest hearts that break.

—Emily Dickinson

The end of a relationship is often a traumatic experience accompanied by emotional and physical consequences (Baxter, 1985). When marital partners divorce, for example, the entire family often feels the impact for years (Greenberg & Nay, 1982). Their entire lives change and must be reconstituted with different relationships. When good friends separate, they often experience great depression.

Because of the trauma associated with dissolving close relationships, people sometimes forget that they end far more of their relationships with not even a twinge of regret. In fact, the most common relational terminations occur immediately after a greeting ritual and a little small talk. You meet a new acquaintance, talk for a few moments, and terminate this brief relationship. Often you never see that person again, and you think nothing of it. Ending brief "new acquaintance" relationships also requires very little skill and is not of significant interest to you. After all, how much skill in interpersonal communication is needed to say "Goodbye" or "So long" or "Take care" or "See ya 'round" or "Have a nice day?"

Our concern in this chapter will be with relationships that terminate after having gone through a relatively extended period of evolutionary development. Ending a relationship that has achieved a relatively high level of integration (such as a friendship) does indeed require skill and relational strategies of interpersonal communication. We will leave the rituals involved in taking leave of new acquaintances to your own resources.

A few words about ending relationships is in order before we begin our

335

discussions in earnest. First, do not assume that you should always keep close relationships from terminating (Duck, 1991). When partners are involved in a destructive relationship, they should end it. All close relationships are not necessarily desirable or beneficial to the partners. Not all marriages, for example, should be saved. Some turn out to be terrible mistakes and aren't worth saving.

The noted playwright Henrik Ibsen detailed the story of a wife's leaving her husband in *A Doll House,* a theme that was scandalous in the late nineteenth century. Some historians of drama have suggested that the negative reactions to this play prompted Ibsen to write *Ghosts* shortly afterward. In this "sequel," Ibsen portrayed the story of a similar wife who remained in her suffocating marriage, and tragedy was the result. Ibsen was aware, long before his time, that some interpersonal relationships are harmful in a variety of ways. They may stifle the potential growth of one of the partners or be destructive in a variety of ways. When such relationships end, the aftermath can be a period of welcome freedom, renewed promise of a better future, and a better relational life (often for both partners) (Wilmot, 1980).

Second, relationships do not always terminate in a neat, orderly manner (Duck, 1987). The breakup of some relationships is often painful, totally unpredictable, and disorderly. The aftermath of relational termination is often a period of confusion for the partners. They feel a gap in their lives, an empty hole left by the departure of the partner. How the partners attempt to fill that void is often unpredictable, out of character, psychologically unfulfilling, and even harmful.

It is probably safe to say that, just as no two relationships evolve in precisely the same way, no two relationships will terminate in precisely the same way (Baxter, 1984). Every relationship is idiosyncratic and unique to some extent. One can probably say that no one set of strategies can or should be generalized to most relational terminations. Once a decision has been made by at least one relational partner to leave, there exist any number of possible paths the disengagement process can take (Baxter, 1984). The elements that make the relationship unique are important in determining the effectiveness and relevance of relational strategies used by the partners to terminate their relationships.

Third, a relationship often terminates despite the fact that one (and sometimes both) of the partners don't want it to end. This may happen because of circumstances beyond the control of the participants. For example, Kathy grew up in the military, and several times throughout her life she had to move away from friends. Not once did she want these friendships to end, but there was nothing she could do about the fact that her father had received new orders. At other times, a relationship may end because one or both of the partners consider termination to be better than keeping the relationship. Baxter (1984) discovered in her study of termination paths that unilateral termination was the most frequent path of termination, although, the occurrence of mutual termination may be underestimated (Wilmot, Carbaugh, & Baxter, 1985). New parents, for example, frequently discover that the arrival of their child forces them to terminate or drastically reduce the significance of other interpersonal relationships. In such cases, they choose the option of spending more time with family relationships and less time in casual, friendly relationships. Rose (1984), in her study of young-adult friendship endings, found that the most common turning point prior to the dissolution of male friendships is physical separation (e.g., one friend going to another school or moving away). For females it was the other friend dating or getting married.

Work relationships are among those which often terminate for reasons other than the desires of the partners. On several occasions in Aub's life, he had to terminate relationships with some really good friends, people with whom he was working. When he graduated from college, he left some good friends at the television station where he was working. When he returned to graduate school to pursue his Ph.D., he left people whom he liked very much. Kathy prolonged leaving Utah prior to receiving her Ph.D. because she not only dreaded leaving friends but also work associates whom she liked very much. She prolonged her stay by procrastinating on her dissertation much to the frustration of her committee, but she wasn't going to leave until it was necessary.

Our discussions in this chapter will attempt to make some sense of the "how" and "how come" of terminated relationships. Our discussions will include a few general metaphors that provide a framework for some typical patterns of relational termination. We will also be discussing the intrapersonal, contextual, and interpersonal factors associated with the end of close relationships and, often, the decision by the partners to terminate their relationship. The chapter will conclude with the now-familiar discussion of relational and communication strategies that have been associated with the final stage of developing relationships. Most of our discussion will focus on romantic heterosexual relationships (marital and nonmarital). There is still a tendency to study the termination processes of these relationships and not other types of relationships such as friendships, gay and lesbian relationships, work relationships, and so on.

METAPHORS OF RELATIONAL TERMINATION

Recall that the relationship itself has an identity separate from the identities of the individual human beings who participate in it. People think of the relationship as having a life of its own. Therefore, when a relationship is ending, people think of it as "dying." The metaphor of dying is often an appropriate way to visualize how relationships end (Owen, 1993). They may die suddenly, or they may waste away to nothing over an extended period of time (Baxter, 1984). Their death may cause great sorrow among the survivors (Douglas & Atwell, 1988). The "lifetime" of a relationship will continue to exist in the memories of the survivors. We can go on with this metaphor, but we think you've got the point.

Several scholars have attempted to picture the process involved in terminating relationships within the metaphor of death (e.g., Davis, 1973; Knapp, 1984). These images of relational termination are not actual descriptions of the process of relational termination, though. They are more like images or metaphors that people can use to understand some of the different ways that relationships might end. Not every terminated relationship will approximate one of these images, but most will probably reflect the characteristics of one of them.

Passing Away

Passing away is a term used by Knapp and Vangelisti (1992, pp. 294–297), which they adapted from Davis (1973) to describe one metaphor of relational termination. This type of relational termination is a long, slow, and gradual erosion of the relationship. Over a period of time (even years), the relationship loses its vitality. The partners continue in their relationship, but one day they look back on it and discover it isn't as good as it used to be. As in all retrospective sensemaking, the individuals may not realize during the period of its erosion that the relationship was in the process of passing away. But sooner or later, they look back and realize that the state of the relationship is not what it once was.

What causes people to grow apart from each other? What went wrong in the relationship? Why aren't things the way they used to be? Unfortunately, these questions have no simple answers. As a matter of fact, they may not even be the appropriate questions to ask. The problems involved in a relationship's passing away are unlikely to be found in some event or incident that "caused" the downward trend. The problems are generally to be found in the partners' lack of skills or efforts to maintain their relationship after it had evolved through a period of integration. They just didn't keep it going after it had its great start. In other words, the problems in a relationship that passes away are often not what the partners did, but what they failed to do.

Avoidance   When a relationship passes away, the partners have failed to deal with the ups and downs of their relational development. Every relationship, during its period of evolution, will go through periods of bliss and stress. Partners will find themselves happy at times and unhappy at others. In order to sustain the good times and get through the bad times, the partners develop rules or interactional patterns to manage the problems that threaten their relational bond. To the extent that they manage these problems (such as conflict) successfully, they develop a history of success and strengthen their relationship. However, the partners in some relationships become paranoid about stressful times (the "down" periods) in their relationship and don't want them to return. In fact, they will do anything to ensure that they don't return. And that may lead to entering the "passing away" process of relational termination.

One pair of friends, for instance, may have been distressed with some critical incident in their relationship. They may have had an argument that left them with feelings of depression. They may have gone through a period of stress, such as the loss of a job. By itself, the down period of their relationship is unimportant. But one or both of the partners may have disliked that period so much that they never want it (or something like it) to happen again. Hence, they develop rules to avoid the circumstances they associate with the bad times. If the distasteful experience in the past involved interpersonal conflict, for example, they tend to avoid those circumstances that might lead to arguments.

In essence, partners in relationships that are passing away cope with their problems by avoiding them—actually by failing to cope with them. Or they ignore problems when they arise and let them fester and continue to exist without being resolved. The result is that the very interactions that let their relationship evolve into a more highly integrated state are not allowed to continue. By avoiding problems, they think they won't have any more of them. But avoidance also means they won't have the experience of being strengthened by successfully solving problems. Soon their relationship becomes dull and boring. Close friendships have been found to end because of a decline in the quality of interaction. One aspect of this decline reported by close friends is boredom (Rose & Serafica, 1986). Nothing exciting ever happens, and their relationship begins to pass away. It doesn't die immediately; it just fades.

A relationship may also pass away when one or both of the partners avoid discussing something that is bothering them. Incrementalism is noted by Baxter (1984) as a reported signal of the beginning of relational termination. Relationships characterized by this sort of passing away reported "stockpiling of several relationship problems preceding the decision by at least one of the persons that the relationship should end" (p. 35). An example from Baxter's (1984) study illustrates this stockpiling:

> The first thing that upset me was that she didn't like my dog. I love my dog, and this bothered me. But we continued to see each other. Then I discovered that she had been married before. I started to wonder about how compatible we were, but we still continued as a couple. Then her former boyfriend started calling her up, which upset me because she didn't tell him about us. We argued a lot and things were tense between us. I finally decided that I'd had it and wanted out. (p. 35)

Each of these problems alone may seem trivial but together with a pattern of avoidance may be enough to move the relationship toward termination.

Consider another example. You may resent the fact that your roommate doesn't pick up dirty clothes, or doesn't help with washing dishes or cleaning the apartment. But you're afraid that your roommate will "take it the wrong way" if you voice your resentment. So you keep quiet. Furthermore, you tend to watch yourself (perhaps unconsciously) when you engage in conversation for fear that you will say something displeasing. The result is that you are likely to lower your trust and commitment to the relationship, and the relationship will lose some of its intensity and intimacy. Your roommate, not knowing what is wrong, also follows your lead and responds in the same reserved manner. Soon both of you realize that your friendship has lost its "zing" and decide to live somewhere else.

Looking back on what "caused" the passing-away stage, though, you would probably think that not helping to wash the dishes was pretty trivial stuff—certainly not important enough to cause you to break up. And you are correct. That incident is trivial by itself. But continually avoiding problems is not trivial. Avoidance soon becomes the strategy that is always used to deal with (or fail to deal with) the bad times in the relationship. The ultimate reason for your breakup is likely to be the pattern of avoidance, a pattern that is difficult to see even for one skilled in retrospective sensemaking. More importantly, you can't do anything about it after the relationship ends. The trick is not to develop the habit of avoidance in the first place.

Discontinuity and Decline in Quality of Interaction   The relationship that most commonly ends through passing away is the one in which friends are separated from each other for long periods of time. Discontinuity of interaction, you will recall, is a primary characteristic of relationships, but too much discontinuity can destroy the healthiest relationship. For instance, your best friend moves away, not necessarily far away, and your day-to-day interactions become less frequent. Soon your friendship deteriorates simply because you aren't able to continue frequent interaction.

Rose and Serafica (1986) studied the termination experiences of casual, close, and best friendships. Casual friendship often passed away due to a decrease in proximity. A decrease in proximity would also mean a decrease in accessibility between friends. The continuity of casual friendship was most susceptible to a decline in interaction due to a decrease in proximity. Close friendships tended to end because of a decline in both quantity and quality of interaction. Continuity was most impacted by such events as outside pressures, a change in the friend's social network (e.g., new friendships), or lack of effort by at least one of the friends to maintain the continuity. The quality of interaction between close friends suffered because of arguments, a loss of affection, boredom, betrayal, and discovery of significantly different values. The endings of best friends were similar to those of close friends except that they were less impacted by a decline in quantity of interaction. This should not be too surprising because we have mentioned before that quantity of interaction is more important initially in a relationship and then becomes less important. This is also the case across the life span. The elderly, if you will recall, don't base their definitions of their friendships on amount of interaction. Interestingly enough, Rose and Serafica (1986) found that people talk about best friends as self-maintaining and say that "true" best friendships never end. Those which did end were characterized as gradually ending or passing away.

In one of the only studies of gay and lesbian relational termination, Kurdek (1991) explored the possibility that these relationships may end differently than heterosexual romantic relationships. He surmised that due to some differences in the relationships their endings may be different. Gay and lesbian relationships tend to stay dyadic over the course of the relationship, unless children enter the family. These relationships also receive comparatively less support from families, and develop as a stigmatized relationship; they are characterized by a norm of partner equality, and few obstacles are seen as standing in the way of termination. He also speculated that due to gender stereotypes, lesbian relationships would sometimes end because of issues of distance and boundaries, whereas gay relationships would do so because of competition and sexuality issues.

In this preliminary study, interestingly, no differences were found between the gay and lesbian experience of relational termination and those reported by heterosexual couples. He also didn't find the gender stereotypes in the partner reports of termination. The most frequently reported reason for termination was partner nonresponsiveness. The most highly rated reason was emotional distancing or absence. In addition, the emotional impact of the ending can be assessed by examining the nature of the last five years of the relationship. There is some continuity between the partners' experience of the relationship and their subsequent experience of its ending.

A typical suggestion for avoiding such an end to a relationship is to advise the partners to remind each other frequently of their affection for each other. But keep in mind that passing away is a process that involves a gradual loss of intensity, intimacy, trust, and commitment over a long period of time. Relationships that pass away are often those which become dull and boring to the partners. Constant repetition of the same things (even "good" things) will also become dull and boring. To tell your partner constantly and repeatedly, "I love you" is to make the words dull and boring, without much meaning.

Partners in long-term, intimate relationships develop different ways of saying "I love you" without necessarily uttering those words. They help each other with menial tasks. They show concern (often just talking or listening with interest) about the things that interest the other. They surprise each other with spontaneous displays of affection. But even surprises get boring after a while if they are constantly repeated. The partners who don't let their relationship pass away are partners who create a variety of ways to show the intensity, intimacy, trust, and commitment in their relationship. The key word is *variety* in displaying their affection, not merely displays of affection by themselves.

Sudden Death

Sudden death (Davis, 1973; Knapp, 1984; Knapp & Vangelisti, 1992, pp. 298–301) is the second metaphor used to describe terminating relationships. Relationships terminate in sudden death when one partner becomes aware of some "new, surprising, and significant negatively charged information about a partner" (Duck, 1982, p. 7). The most obvious "negatively charged information" that immediately comes to mind is unfaithfulness—the discovery by one of the relational partners that the other is having an affair with someone else. This "critical incident" is captured in the following reflection: "From a mutual friend, she found out that I had been seeing other people while she was away at school. She confronted me and it was all over" (Baxter, 1984, p. 35). The unfaithful act of the partner is typically viewed as a serious betrayal of the intimacy, trust, and commitment in the relationship. The third person is also viewed as violating the relationship and is often considered to be just as "guilty" as the philandering partner. Unfaithfulness not only betrays the relationship but also violates the taboos of American society.

Of course, negative information does not necessarily involve the intervention of a third party in the relationship. One person may discover, for instance, that the partner is revealing confidential information to other people. Especially in highly intimate relationships, what goes on in the relationship is private to the partners. Partners consider that other people on the outside have no business knowing the innermost details of their relationship. Furthermore, relational partners know a great deal about each other because of the high degree of self-disclosing communication during the growth stages of their development. One person self-discloses to a partner with the expectation that such information is only for that partner's ears. To discover that the partner has told someone else is to believe that the partner has violated the trust inherent in the relationship. Intimates by virtue of the intricate nature of their bond carry a higher betrayal potential than nonintimates, and this can influence the character of their termination process (Baxter, 1985).

Intimates over the course of their relationship create all sorts of covenants governing how to behave. Some can be changed rather easily, but those considered more sacred by the partners if broken, can end the relationship rather suddenly (Knapp, 1984; Knapp & Vangelisti, 1992). However, covenants such as infidelity don't always lead to divorce, and betrayal of a confidence doesn't always result in the end of a relationship. In other words, the mere discovery of negative information about the partner does not necessarily result in sudden death of the relationship. In fact, many relationships continue to exist after such discovery. The question then becomes "How come?" How is it that some relationships die and others don't?

Negative information by itself cannot "cause" the sudden death of a relationship. The relational partners must "allow" the information to end the relationship. If they believe that their relationship is stronger or more important than the information, then they continue. But even when sudden death does not occur, the relationship is not the same as it was. The relationship evolves into a new definition. It may have less intensity, intimacy, trust, and commitment; but more likely it will have a different kind of intensity, intimacy, trust, and commitment. In some cases, the relationship may be even stronger.

Even the "sudden death" metaphor of relationship termination emphasizes the fact that relationships seldom completely die. They often continue, but in a redefined state. Wilmot (1980) explains that partners will often confuse the drastic changes in their relationships reflected in comments such as "she confronted me and it was over," "I got dumped last night," and "he called it off" with a termination. Instead, the relationship is redefined, which means that patterns of interaction become drastically altered and partners may even move away from each other. However, the relationship isn't "stopped dead in its tracks" (p. 169). Former marital partners often remain friends after a divorce. Some divorced couples say that they are even better friends with their former spouses after the divorce. Friends who were once close often continue to interact, but they have redefined their relationship as one of "just friends." True, if there is no more interaction, the relationship as defined is over, but the relationship that remains in the partners' memories lives on and will continue to influence their lives.

Sometimes relational partners continue to act out the relationship or "appear" to be together when in fact they aren't the loving partners they once were. Certain ties, like children, may keep partners together because termination is too difficult under those circumstances. Once those obligations are gone, the partners suddenly end the relationship—often to the dismay and shock of their friends and family. Kathy knew a couple in graduate school who represented to her the model of a perfect couple. No one, except the two selected friends, knew that their relationship was in trouble and that they were seeking a divorce. Wanting to keep gossip at a minimum, they had decided not to reveal their divorce to close friends until it was official. In the meantime they acted like husband and wife. Kathy, to this day, remembers her experience of total shock upon hearing about the end of their marriage. For Kathy, at the time of the news, the ending was unbearably "sudden."

One final comment about the "sudden death" metaphor of terminated relationships. Negative information about the partner is often used by one or more of the partners as an excuse to justify breakup after the fact. Persons accused of infidelity often claim that they were not unfaithful until long after the relationship had suffered from severe breakdown. They claim that their unfaithfulness was not really a violation of the relationship as much as it was a symptom of a relationship that had already ended for them. In their view, the relationship had already terminated before the act of unfaithfulness. In other words, the negative information about the partner is often seen as the cause of relational termination even though the relationship was already passing away.

Precisely what makes one relationship terminate and another continue is a matter of what the relational partners *do* when they are going through this stage. They may have little choice about whether the relationship terminates; they may continue to interact within a redefined relationship; or they may consciously decide to end it all. The termination of a relationship is an act of creating the end of the relationship through interpersonal communication. (Note the title of this chapter—"*Creating* Relationships—Termination.") In all cases relational termination is observable and interpretable as a process of interpersonal communication. Communication *is* the relationship, and termination is part of the process in the evolutionary development of many relationships (Baxter, 1985; Duck, 1987). Thus, termination of relationships is part of the process of interpersonal communication.

Preexisting Doom

Occasionally relationships terminate because the individuals are just not compatible. That is, for some reason the relationship appears to have developed beyond its optimum level. Although these instances of relational termination are not necessarily frequent, you probably know people who just "weren't meant for each other." Sooner or later, these couples discovered their mistake and dissolved their relationship—sometimes as friends and sometimes as enemies.

A relationship often has a way of "snowballing" beyond its normal rate of evolutionary development. The partners may have thought it was love at first sight, only to discover that they were nearsighted. In fact, that metaphor is not necessarily humorous. People may be attracted to each other for some superficial reason (such as physical attractiveness) and, in putting their best foot forward, behave differently in each other's presence than they would normally. As a result, the relationship is fine as long as they are in each other's presence. Over time, though, as they continue to interact and relax together, they discover things about each other that they don't particularly like. Partners in such relationships tend to attribute their emotions (such as love) to the relationship, only to discover, eventually, that their feelings are not the same as the relationship.

This image of relational termination goes by the label of *preexisting doom* (Duck, 1982, p. 5). That is, the relationship contains elements (typically within one or both of the partners and not easily observable) that threaten the relationship. As long as these elements continue to be hidden, the relationship will continue to develop. As soon as they are exposed, however, the relationship will probably terminate.

People perceive certain elements of another person's character, beliefs, attitudes, and the like. But they may fail to perceive (through selective perception) elements that are quite dissimilar with their selves or that they find distasteful. As long as those elements are never brought to the forefront of their perception, as long as they are not aware of those distasteful or dissimilar elements in the other person, these elements will not affect their interpersonal relationship. But when people do become aware of such elements, the relationship is in danger of ending.

You are typically attracted to (that is, you tend to like) those persons who are similar to you. It stands to reason, then, that a relationship between two people who are dissimilar in significant respects (for example, a devout Republican and devout Democrat, an active athlete and a passive lout) may develop quickly through a relatively strong integrative stage without the partners being aware of these dissimilarities. Later, when the leniency effect (Chapter 3) is overcome, they experience a severe decrease in their levels of intensity, intimacy, and commitment. Those dissimilar intrapersonal characteristics were present all along (preexisting), and discovery of these dissimilarities was always a risk. Serious incompatibility of the relational partners dooms the relationship.

Mere differences between relational partners, though, do not automatically lead to termination of the relationship. In fact, you probably know more than one happy couple who seem to be very different but continue to enjoy a happy relationship. How come? The tired saying that "opposites attract" just doesn't seem to be a satisfactory explanation. On the other hand, other explanations are apparent. For instance, incompatible partners may continue to enjoy a happy relationship without ever becoming aware of the differences that allegedly doom their relationship. Or they may discover their incompatibilities and find that their relationship is more important than the differences between them. Or one or both of the partners may actually change their self-concepts to reflect the relationship. There is a saying for this possibility, too: "This thing is bigger than both of us."

Generally speaking, no relationship that results in termination will fit neatly into one of these images—passing away, sudden death, or preexisting doom. But many relationships that "die" will have many of the characteristics of one of these metaphors. The important point to remember is that none of these metaphors lists causes of relational termination. Relationships that have many of the characteristics of each image do not always end and may be maintained for a long time. Moreover, a relationship that does reflect the characteristics of one of these metaphors will probably evolve into a redefined relationship that may be stronger or weaker. And many relationships that die do not stop completely but continue with greater interactional distance (more frequent and longer gaps between periods of face-to-face communication) and with a different definition (typically much less intensity, intimacy, trust, and commitment). Each of these models is best understood as a general pattern that captures how most terminated relationships evolve to the point of termination.

RELATIONAL BREAKDOWN—
"THE GATHERING STORM"

Imagine that you are a scholar interested in understanding how people dissolve their relationships, particularly relationships that have developed a relatively high degree of integration. In order to understand relational termination, you would have to observe and study interpersonal relationships that are in the process of terminating. But to do so is virtually impossible. Do you search for people who are about to break up, give them a tape recorder, and ask them to record their interpersonal communication while they are breaking up? Do you ask people whether they are about to break up and, if so, whether you can follow them around for a few months and observe them while their relationship disintegrates? Not very likely.

About the only available information concerning relational termination comes from surveys of people who have experienced a terminated relationship or who are asked to imagine one. Unfortunately, this information is subject to people's interpretations and perceptions of people. Their perceptions, particularly those expressed as answers on some survey form, are likely to reflect the attribution processes with which they protect their self-concepts, often placing blame on the other person or the situation. People are also likely to recollect what is a rather chaotic time as much more rational and logical than it was (Duck & Sants, 1983). In other words, your understanding of relational termination is likely to be of questionable validity, but it is all you have to go on.

Two communication scholars, Leslie Baxter and Steve Duck, have expressed concern over these issues. They both caution that too often relational termination is studied as a single event, not as a process that occurs over time. Hence, the focus is typically on what predicts termination and the outcomes of termination, not the dynamics of the actual termination (Baxter, 1985; Duck, 1987). Only since the mid-1980s have communication scholars turned their attention to the description and understanding of the interactional dynamics of termination. The information from much of the work concerns what people have experienced during the time immediately preceding and immediately following relationship termination. The following pages will discuss those experiences during the breakdown of the relationship—the period immediately preceding relational termination. We will then discuss the aftermath of relational termination, the period immediately following relational termination. Then, we will end by discussing the interactional dynamics of relational termination—the strategies which serve to accomplish the termination.

Intrapersonal Factors

A close interpersonal relationship exerts a powerful impact on the individuals who participate in it. In fact, the effect of a highly integrated relationship is psychologically similar to mutual "addiction." When the relationship terminates or breaks down, the partners often experience "withdrawal" symptoms. Our interest focuses more on the emotional, psychological, and behavioral symptoms of relational termination. These symptoms are evident during the period of time in which the integrated relationship is suffering breakdown. This period of relational deescalation is explained in five general phases by Steve Duck (1982, 1987, 1991) based on his review of the research in relational termination.

The Breakdown Phase   The *breakdown phase* describes the dissatisfaction of at least one participant with the relationship. In other words, one or both participants conclude that there is a problem with the relationship. At this point the issues are probably not discussed seriously with anyone. As you recall, relationships have their ups and downs, and people don't move to the next phase at every sign of trouble (Duck, 1991).

The Intrapsychic Phase   The *intrapsychic phase* focuses on the internalized feelings of each partner in terms of an emotional reaction to the other. Foremost in the individual's mind is an "I can't stand this any more" feeling. This is a time of emotional strife and internal struggle. The partner seriously questions the rewards or benefits of being in this relationship and is filled with anxiety, stress, self-doubt, and guilt. This early phase of relational breakdown may not be observable in the partner's actual behaviors, but if it is, that behavior is likely to reflect increased hostility, more value judgments, and the seeking of advice from friends and associates as to what to do. In fact, many of the letters to "Ann Landers" or "Dear Abby" read as though they were written by people in the middle of an intrapsychic phase of relational breakdown.

The important point of this phase is not to let the other partner in on what is going on. This is a phase of private brooding or sharing of problems with a confidant who will not tell the other (Duck, 1987). Communication with the other probably decreases and may increase in the partner's social network. The processes involved in the communicative accomplishment of comfort from others during this phase deserves closer attention by researchers (Duck, 1987). This is essentially a problem-solving stage for the relational partner and, if the problem is not solved, ends with the partner's decision to confront the other and express dissatisfaction.

The Dyadic Phase   The *dyadic phase* of relational breakdown begins with that confrontation. The participant tells the partner, in essence, "I'd be justified in withdrawing from this relationship. What should we do about it?" The interaction during this phase is likely to be rather negative, hostile, argumentative, and competitive (Duck, 1987). The issue at hand is no longer a matter for one individual to decide but is the joint decision of both relational partners: "Do we try to patch things up or go our separate ways?" The confronter can expect any number of things from the partner (Duck, 1991). The confronter may find someone who is oblivious to the problems or one who is also unhappy with the situation. The other may also have a different interpretation of relational events as well as attitudes and feelings about those events. The confronter may also find a partner who acknowledges the issues and is willing to work on it. Regardless of what the dissatisfied partner finds, this phase isn't easy.

   The dyadic phase of relational breakdown may be lengthy or relatively brief and will typically include a marked increase in the amount of personal talk and private discussion between the partners. They may seek the services of a third party (such as a counselor) to assist them, but their discussions remain highly personal. If the talks become too painful, the partners will avoid talking with each other altogether. When they do, they make the decision to dissolve their relationship by default. That is, in the absence of attempts to repair it, their relationship remains broken. This period may also include a trial separation in which the partners experiment with relational withdrawal. They may also attempt some experimental repair and see whether that works. During this phase there is some fluctuating between positive (repair) and negative (conflict) communication, although this oscillation between repair and termination is more likely in the previous phase (Baxter, 1984). The outcome of the dyadic phase is agreement on the response to the critical issue. That is, the partners either patch things up or split. If they patch things up, the phases of relational termination end (at least temporarily), and the relationship continues, although redefined. If they decide to split, the partners end the third phase.

The Social Phase   The *social phase* of relational breakdown involves some serious soul searching by the relational partners. They may have decided to terminate their relationship, but they aren't sure they've made the correct decision. During this period, they wonder what it will be like not to be together any more. They may go through periods of vacillating back and forth between reconciling and withdrawing, experimental repairs and experimental separations. They wonder about the future, and they are frightened about the unknown. They wonder what other people will think about their decision to break up and often avoid interacting with other friends and being exposed to their potentially negative reactions. At the same time, they feel the need to tell other people just why and how they have decided to break up. Perceived support from these social networks, or lack thereof, is an important influence on the rate of deescalation and the likelihood of termination (Felmlee, Sprecher, & Bussin, 1990).

The social phase is a period of great uncertainty and stress. Duck (1990) argues that it is this period that "makes or prevents the dissolution of the relationship" (p. 178). Early in this phase, confidants are sought out who may not know the other and who will not talk to the other about the relational problems. If these people cannot help, the person then seeks confidants who know the other and are capable of taking sides. In order to deal with the stress and uncertainty, partners will begin to assess blame for the breakup—typically faulting the other partner or the situation (rarely to the self). The content of communication becomes increasingly focused on the other and the relationship. The relational tone of the communication will probably be accusatory and complaining. Hindsight comments such as "I could've predicted this would happen" and "I knew from the beginning this might happen" will also increase in preparation for the next phase (Duck, 1991). The social phase of relational breakdown ends with the partners acknowledging to other people the impending death of their relationship. As this phase ends, the "whole world" has learned of the relational breakdown.

The Grave-Dressing Phase The *grave-dressing phase* of relational termination is a period of coping with the fact that the relationship is over. The individuals need to get their relationship behind them. They may have told other people one story, but they now find the need to create an acceptable story of the breakdown for themselves. This is a period of psychological reinterpretation and reperception of past events. It involves a great deal of retrospective analysis of the past relationship, but the purpose is not to make sense of the past. The primary purpose is to construct a rationale for the ending of the relationship, just as it was done for its existence, that satisfies the partner and others in the social network (Duck, 1991). This "ending story," or relational account (Chapter 9), must be both a worthwhile one, and it must be told carefully in order to present the teller as a worthy relational partner for the future.

Grave dressing involves a great deal of imagination and creativity.

Former partners must rationalize their past emotions and feelings so that they decrease the significance of their past relationship. This is not a period for attributing blame for the relational breakdown; it is a period of protecting the self-concept and associated feelings of guilt and doubts of self-worth that naturally arise from the death of a close relationship. This requires some rationalization that will help the partners explain their entire relationship from beginning to end. Typical ending stories include parts which portray the teller as knowing for some time the end was coming (Duck, 1987). In other words, these stories tell about some major problem in the relationship which couldn't be solved, despite the teller's efforts, and the final result was that the teller knew better than to stay in the relationship. Notice that the ending story has three elements: (1) the teller is not a fool, (2) the teller is capable of working on a relationship, and (3) the teller is a realist and knows when to quit (Duck, 1991). Partners who have trouble completing the grave-dressing phase will experience continued psychological stress and depression. If the outcome is not a successful protection and rebuilding of their self-concepts, they may find they need professional help from a psychotherapist.

The withdrawal symptoms experienced by individuals during the period of relational breakdown are often devastating to the partners. The impact is greater to the extent that the relationship was very well integrated and had achieved high levels of intensity, intimacy, trust, and commitment. Whether the relationship slowly passes away or dies suddenly does not particularly lessen the psychological stress felt by the relational partners during the period of relational breakdown. Keep in mind that these phases involve intrapersonal factors. They affect the interaction as the hostilities or self-doubts are expressed by the participants.

Interpersonal communication is insignificant in the intrapsychic phase, but it is extremely important during the dyadic phase. In this second phase, the strategies of relational termination come into play. This is the phase during which the participants determine whether they will indeed terminate their relationship, and it demands the highest degree of competence in interpersonal communication. Interpersonal communication skills are not necessarily used in attempts to repair the damage done to a relationship. Rather, they help the partners arrive at the most beneficial and appropriate decision in regard to termination. The decision that is best for the partners may well be to terminate their relationship.

Contextual Factors

The situation itself may exert a significant impact on whether and how rapidly a relationship terminates. Often the relational partners are victims of a changing context, and the relationship terminates even though the partners themselves make no decision to end it. We have already discussed contexts that enforce a greater interactional distance. That is, the context—such as moving to a new home or neighborhood, taking a different job in a different city, being away from home a lot—forces a physical separation on the partners. A number of factors can explain why the physical separation takes place. Keeping a relationship active requires communication, actual interaction in a face-to-face setting. When the opportunities for interaction decrease and a greater discontinuity of interaction occurs, the relationship has no opportunity to grow, change, and sustain itself. It eventually dies through disuse; it decays.

Surveys of factors leading to divorce have consistently placed environmental pressures on the marriage at or near the top of the list. Newly married partners, for example, face problems they never encountered during their integrative stage. Day-to-day financial pressures—paying for groceries, rent, automobile, clothing, health care, and so on—are probably chief among them. The birth of children creates significant pressures on the marriage too. Not only is the need for more money greater, but the couple experiences a significant decrease in the amount of free time they have. Without the time or the money to go on vacations or to have regular evenings out, they are confined to home for longer periods of time. That feeling of confinement is often transferred to the relationship itself, laying the groundwork for relational breakdown.

Norms and changes in society may also affect the relationship negatively. How many stories have you heard of marriages ending in divorce because of the changing roles of women? For the first years of her marriage, a woman is a typical housewife who stays home, cleans the house, makes the meals, and supports the rising career of her husband. Later, she feels a need to continue her education, goes to school, and lands an excellent job. She works to advance her career, but gradually her husband (who may have encouraged her to go back to school) may resent the fact that she has less free time to spend with him. The erosion of their relationship over several years may ultimately lead to termination and divorce.

As society encourages women entering the work force to pursue careers, more marital relationships will include spouses in separate but equal careers. Society's norms are gradually changing to accommodate these changes. But individuals who are members of those relationships may not have come to accept those changes. The traditional husband may resent and even be jealous of his wife's career, especially if it is more successful than his. The traditional wife may resent and even be jealous of her husband's career or, conversely, of her husband's insistence that she get a job. These resentments are seeds of the intrapsychic phase of relational breakdown. Furthermore, as the number of dual-career marriages increases, the time for free interaction between husbands and wives decreases. Thus, through no fault of their own, their relationship does not have as much opportunity to grow and develop and sustain itself. The pressures of society on such couples place additional strain on the relationship and may lead to relational breakdown.

Every interpersonal relationship exists within a network of other social relationships. Each partner has friends, relatives, acquaintances, and other relationships of his or her own. The partners together have friends and acquaintances they share in common. This network of interpersonal relationships is often called a "support system" for each or both of the relational partners. But these systems of social support are not support to both partners equally. Symons's friends are likely to be Megan's acquaintances, and Megan's friends are likely to be Symon's acquaintances. And they will both have friends and acquaintances as a relational pair. When these contextual social relationships are in conflict with one another, though, the relationship suffers.

The most common contextual support system comprises the kinship relations of each partner. Symon's family may or may not like Megan, but they will tend to be more supportive of Symon. Megan's family will similarly be more supportive of Megan. When these two support systems are in conflict, they strain the relationship. If it is a severe strain, the conflicting support systems will lead to relational breakdown. The fact that the support systems are in conflict does not, of course, necessarily "cause" relational breakdown, but it does exert pressure on the relationship. For instance, intimates (marital couples in this case) who don't perceive support or approval from family and friends and who don't like their partner's family and friends are more likely to end the relationship during breakdown than if they do perceive support and like their partner's family and friends (Felmlee, Sprecher, & Bussin, 1990).

Elements of the context may affect the relationship, but they can do so only when they are displayed in the form of actual communicative actions. Human beings have a remarkable resiliency when placed in an unfavorable context. Struggling young married couples look forward to a better future and proceed to strengthen their relationship while trying to survive an unpleasant present. People hear their friends tell them evil things about their relational partners and then compartmentalize those conversations so that they don't affect the interaction they have with their partners. In other words, humans have a remarkable ability to adapt to the situation in which they find themselves. When contextual pressures do lead to a relational breakdown, the explanation is not so much that the pressures were too great but that the partners' ability to adapt and cope was not great enough.

Interpersonal Factors

In some ways, ending a relationship is easier than beginning a relationship. For example, the beginning stages of relational development involve a great deal of uncertainty reduction—that is, acquiring information about the other person and controlling the kinds of information you give the other. Further, your job is complicated by a conjoint task: You not only must facilitate the perception that you are interested in a relationship with the other person, but also that you are a worthy investment (Baxter & Philpott, 1982). The stage of relational breakdown is comparatively easier because you have only to show that you aren't interested or that you are no longer a worthy investment; you don't have to do both (Baxter and Philpott, 1982). Also, you certainly don't need to "lose" information in order to end the relationship. To build a relationship requires effort at communicating. To end a relationship requires little effort; you can just stop communicating.

Unlike any other stage of relational development, one person can terminate a relationship. The integrative stage of relational development requires that both partners work to build and strengthen the relationship. One person cannot strengthen a relationship; it requires a minimum of two people working together in concert—*inter*action. However, one person has little control over the continuance of a relationship if the other person decides unilaterally that it is over. *Inter*action is necessary only to sustain the relationship and keep it moving along the stages of evolutionary development. Mere *action,* an intrapersonal decision by either one of the relational partners, is enough to terminate it.

The entrance of a competing third person may also lead to relational breakdown. In this case, one of the partners "chooses" between two alternatives—friend one or friend two. And that choice is necessary in closely bonded relationships, such as marriage or best friends. The third person may also function as a "medium of change," according to John LaGaipa (1982, p. 196). That is, one of the partners wants to end the relationship and initiates some interaction with a third person as a way of breaking it off. LaGaipa discovered, in a survey of adolescent dating relationships, that when a boy wished to break off with his girlfriend, he would start dating another girl. After the breakup, the girl would typically insist that the relationship was stable until the other girl came along. However, the boy would suggest a different interpretation—that he wanted to break up, and the easiest way to do it was to start dating someone else. Of course, the girl could start dating someone else in order to break up with her boyfriend, but adolescent dating rituals provide much more opportunity and freedom for boys to initiate dates with third persons. Adolescent boys generally have the option of initiating the date, and they typically avoid asking "someone else's girl" for a date.

The most significant interpersonal factor of relational breakdown is the rules or interaction patterns developed by relational partners during integration (Knapp, 1984, Knapp & Vangelisti, 1992). Every interpersonal relationship is unique to the extent that it develops, through continued interaction, its own rules and rituals defining that specific relationship. The partners may have pet names for each other. They may create their own special language to refer to particular things, and no one outside their relationship would have those same definitions. As their relationship begins to break down, their interaction includes fewer and fewer of these rituals and patterns. As the termination of their relationship nears, they tend to nullify these patterns, which have made their communication and their relationship unique. Failing to observe their own interaction patterns is virtually the same as failing to recognize the value of their relationship.

Some participants in relationships that are in the process of breaking down realize that something is wrong when they notice that their communication seems more "formal." They typically interpret that interaction in terms of their partner's becoming more "distant." Actually, they are recognizing the fact that the old familiar interaction patterns are missing. They no longer seem to be observing the rules established during their relational development. Their interaction isn't special any more; it isn't as close as it used to be. In other words, it's no longer different from that of other relationships, and those differences are what made their relationship special. The partners then wish they could go back to the way it used to be.

Whatever the circumstances leading to relational breakdown, relationships don't terminate on their own. They terminate when the communication between the partners changes. Communication may cease or be drastically reduced in amount. It may reflect new communication patterns that are destructive to the relationship. It may reflect interaction patterns that nullify the rules and rituals established earlier. In all cases, relationships don't terminate in people's heads or in the environment, although intrapersonal and contextual factors may precipitate the breakdown. Relationships terminate in the process of communication, the interaction patterns themselves. In fact, all phases in the evolutionary development of relationships are present in the patterns of interaction.

THE AFTERMATH—RESIDUES OF THE RELATIONSHIP

Communication creates, intensifies, and sustains a relationship; it also ends one. And as you know communication occurs in time, and that time always "marches on." As the relationship moves into the past, then, what are the residues that remain in the present? One axiom concerning interpersonal relationships is often neglected in the knowledge of common sense: *Close relationships do not "end"; they merely change.*

After the partners terminate their relationship, the relationship continues to exist in several forms. One, partners often continue to carry on some kind of relationship, to talk with one another, and to interact after they have terminated an intimate relationship. Although partners may remain friends after the termination, heterosexual and homosexual couples do report that the most frequent problem after termination is the relationship with former partners (Kurdek, 1991). Of course, their interaction is quite different from what it once was, and they now define their relationship very differently. Their past interaction patterns are events that continue to exist in the form of memories. No one can deny that those events in the past did, in fact, happen. Unlike a computer, human memory cannot easily be erased. A computer can "forget" a memory when the file is erased, and it will function as though the erased file had never existed. The memory of humans, though, works quite differently. You cannot "unknow" an intimate partner (Baxter, 1983). A close relationship will leave a deeply embedded stamp in the individual memories of the partners after relational termination. And, although humans cannot erase memories of significant events in the past, they can "change" their memory of events. Humans have the power to perceive, and perception allows them to create new memories or to redefine past events so that the remembered event is often very different from the event that actually happened. When computers change their memory, they have made an error. When humans do it, they are coping (Duck, 1982). Recall from Chapter 9 that relational accounts editorialize relationships as a function of circumstance and need. These accounts during and after termination are not only normative but also important coping strategies for dealing with a spoiled relationship (Cupach & Metts, 1986; Stephen, 1987).

When close relationships end, the partners must go through a "getting over it" stage. The emotions felt by both heterosexual and homosexual couples oscillate between the negative and positive (Kurdek, 1991). These include feelings of relief (from conflict) and feelings of personal growth as well as loneliness. Initial distress over the termination of heterosexual dating relationships is a function of satisfaction with the partner, perceived closeness to partner, and perceived ease of finding another partner (Frazier & Cook, 1993). Their adjustment to the loss of the relationship was a function of availability of social support, level of self-esteem, and perceived control of the events (Frazier & Cook, 1993). Being prepared for the termination plays an important role in how easily the posttermination stress is negotiated for both heterosexual and homosexual partners (Kurdek, 1991). It is important that the individual perceives some sense of control over the termination events.

This residue of the relationship is primarily a psychological reordering of memories and exists within the individual's psyche. But it has an interpersonal element, too. Besides rationalizing and redefining the past relationship so that it decreases in significance, the individual also moves the memory of the once-close relationship from the top of the stack to the bottom. In order to render the memory less easily accessible, the individual may seek out a variety of different partners to fill the void left by the partner's departure. As the person accumulates a variety of new relational partners, the memory of the formerly close relationship is submerged. It will never be erased completely, of course, but it will be brought to the top of the cognitive deck less often with each additional relational experience.

Seeking new and different relational experiences is a second coping mechanism, one that attempts to acquire so much relational information that the memory banks tend to overload. Soon all the relational partners begin to blur, so that the partner in the terminated relationship becomes just another blurry face in the crowd. In this way, the teenager breaks up with his or her "steady," for example, and proceeds to go on many dates with a variety of different people. But the coping teenager avoids going steady with any single one.

The emotional pain following the end of a close relationship is uncomfortable, and the idea is not to let it happen again—at least, not right away. Of course, the individual runs the risk of having a "rebound" relationship. In the eagerness to fill the void left by the departed partner, the individual may attempt to replace the "steady" with another as soon as possible. This coping mechanism short-circuits the time necessary for a close relationship to evolve through a lengthy integration phase. Consequently, rebound relationships are often quite unsatisfying and typically lead to another termination. After having failed twice, the partner's emotional pain is even greater and the damage to feelings of self-worth is even more severe.

A third way that individuals deal with the aftermath of relational termination is to seek out other relationships, but not as substitutes for the absent partner. Recall that each interpersonal relationship exists within a large network of overlapping social relationships. Recall that some of those overlapping relationships include the friends and acquaintances (social-support systems) of each partner. When a close interpersonal relationship dissolves, the other social relationships remain and become even more important for the individual partner. In times of psychological stress, human beings seek out interpersonal means to ease their intrapersonal discomfort.

In a study of relational loss, including death and the breakup of a romantic relationship, Feezel & Shepherd (1987) found that younger (college-age) and midlife individuals were more introspective about the loss and less likely to seek out others (family and friends) to talk about the loss than the elderly. For all three groups of individuals, friends were just as important as family for support. While friends were important across the life span, they were especially important for the college students in this study.

Often those relationships which serve as support systems become even closer as a result of their usefulness in these times of stress. In some ways, partners who function as support systems during the aftermath of relational termination do become substitutes for the other relational partner. Their continuity of interaction—as well as the trust and commitment of

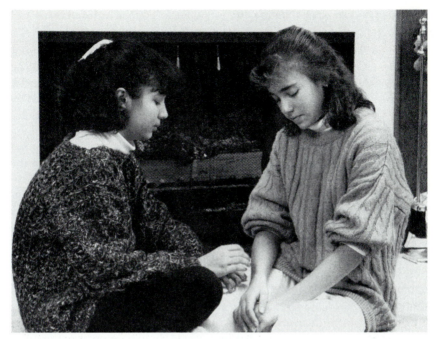

When a relationship ends, people often cultivate other relationships with friends or acquaintances.

their interaction—increases. Although the relationships are not precisely the same, the "good friend" who is there in time of need becomes an even better friend as a result.

For the most part, more is known about what happens during times of relational termination in terms of intrapersonal or psychological factors than of interpersonal ones (Banks, Altendorf, Greene, & Cody, 1987; Duck, 1987). We have noted the difficulty of securing information about what actually occurs in interpersonal communication during periods of relational breakdown. Interestingly, when Kathy was conducting her research on relational communication strategies, she discovered that one of the persons assisting her was going through a period of relational breakdown with his wife. Even though the opportunity was available, she never considered asking that person to record his discussions with his wife as they were arguing about their relational future. As a result, though, termination is primarily understood through the memories of people responding to surveys some time after they have experienced relational termination. Their responses are bound to reflect their psychological or intrapersonal feelings, which are often an inaccurate portrayal of their actual communication.

RELATIONAL STRATEGIES

Within the past decade, several communication scholars (including Banks, Altendorf, Greene, & Cody, 1987; Baxter, 1979, 1982, 1983, 1984, 1985, 1987a, 1987b; Baxter & Philpott, 1982; Cody, 1982; Ragan & Hopper, 1984; Wilmot, Carbaugh, & Baxter, 1985) have become interested in the strategies used by people to terminate their relationships during the dyadic phase of Duck's model of relational deescalation. They experienced the same problem, however, in attempting to observe how people interact when they are breaking off. They could not invade the privacy of people actually in the process of relational breakdown and observe their patterns of communication. Consequently, the information concerning disengagement strategies is largely in the form of responses to surveys asking people what they would do or say if they were in the situation of relational breakdown and wanted to end the relationship and also in material from diaries. This information concerning communicative strategies may be as suspect as the psychological information concerning relational breakdown. We have already discussed the fact that people tend to reinterpret their relationships after they have ended so that their memory of terminated relationships is generally quite different from the reality. Furthermore, people tend to respond to questions asking what they *would* do in a given situation with answers that reveal what they think they *should* do. As a result, the information from surveys may confirm commonsense beliefs rather than reveal actual communicative behavior. The following discussion summarizes information from a variety of scholarly studies and attempts to separate fact from fiction whenever the invalidity of the information seems evident.

For the most part, relational strategies used for the purpose of breaking off a relationship occur during the dyadic phase of relational breakdown, discussed earlier. Most of the interpersonal communication occurs during this phase of relational termination. The issue, of course, is whether to terminate the relationship or try to repair it. Communication during the dyadic phase is a process of negotiation as the partners decide the fate or future of their interpersonal relationship. During this phase the partners use some specific negotiation strategies directed toward resolving the issue of whether the relationship is "to be or not to be."

Direct Strategies

Several years ago singer Paul Simon suggested, "There must be fifty ways to leave your lover." Each "way" was a brief rhyming one-liner that gave advice to the person to end the relationship without fuss and without beating around the bush. "Drop off the key, Lee" was the favorite one-liner of Aub's oldest daughter whose name is, of course, Lee. Simon's lyrics advocated the use of relational strategies that told the partner directly that their relationship was over. In her studies of disengagement strategies, Leslie Baxter (1985) identified four kinds of direct strategies: fait accompli, state-of-the-relationship talk, attributional conflict, and negotiated farewell. These direct strategies differ in terms of whether they are one-sided or mutual.

Fait accompli and state-of-the-relationship talk are direct strategies used when only one of the relational partners desires to end the relationship. *Fait accompli* openly seeks to lay the issue of termination "on the table." For instance, "On the phone, I told him I was tired of seeing him and that I was bored with him. I said I never wanted to see him again" (Baxter, 1985, p. 249). You declare to your partner that you want to break off the relationship and there is no discussing it. You might explain your reasons for wanting to disengage. You tell your partner that it's all over. Fait accompli doesn't introduce the issue by suggesting that you want to patch things up. Rather, the strategy proposes a specific solution to the problems in the relationship—"let's end this relationship."

Like the fait accompli, the *state-of-the-relationship talk* openly seeks to lay the issue of termination "on the table," but isn't a final declaration. Instead, it is an open admission of dissatisfaction with the relationship and a desire to end the relationship with a mutual discussion of problems. Consider the following:

> He brought up the issue of breaking up by saying that the fights we'd been having lately were due to our different needs. . . . We talked about it a long time. . . . At the end of the talk, we both agreed that we should break up. (Baxter, 1985, p. 249)

State-of-the-relationship talk invites the other partner to disagree and suggest some repair. If the partner fails to disagree with the proposal or if the repair doesn't direct the relationship away from termination, the only thing to talk about is the alternative to break up.

When both partners wish to end the relationship, attributional conflict and negotiated farewell characterize their directness. Mutual desire to end a relationship doesn't guarantee that both partners agree on what caused the end of the relationship and who is responsible. *Attributional conflict* openly expresses the desire to end by describing a conflict which is seen as being the reason for the termination. This strategy is illustrated in this comment, "We had a most awful scene yelling and screaming at each other. . . . We both wanted out, but we were both angry with each other for causing the hurt" (Baxter, 1985, p. 249).

Not all direct termination strategies involve some interpersonal conflict. For instance, consider the following: "Our relationship had been having a lot of problems, and we both experienced them. We'd both had it, we went to dinner and had a good talk about what was going on" (Baxter,

1985, p. 249). This strategy, *negotiated farewell,* is characterized by an open discussion of the end of the relationship with no hostility or conflict.

Direct termination strategies include open assertions and reasons for terminating the relationship and may involve conflict. The meaning of openness during this stage of the relationship changes once again. Now, it is considered instrumental or necessary to signal the end, whereas during initiation it was considered risky, and during integration it was considered unnecessary because the partners already know each other (Baxter, 1988). The only way to consider possible repairs of the relationship at this point is to respond to a direct strategy by disagreeing with it. Hence, confrontive strategies, most often, lead directly to relational termination and sometimes interpersonal conflict. Interpersonal conflict, however, during relational dissolution is not met with as many repair attempts as it is during relational integration (Lloyd & Cate, 1985). During relational dissolution, conflict tends to focus on the other partner's faults and the unmanageable issues between the partners (Cupach & Metts, 1986). This kind of conflict doesn't promote the constructive management of interpersonal conflict nor does it decrease the likelihood of termination (Baxter, 1988).

Indirect Strategies

Baxter (1985) also categorized strategies of relational termination into indirect strategies. There are four prototypical strategies for indirectly ending a relationship: withdrawal, pseudo deescalation, cost escalation, and fading away. The purpose of most indirect strategies of relational termination is to behave in such a manner as to force the partner to realize that something is wrong. If an indirect strategy is successful, the partner soon gets the idea and brings up the issue of potential relational problems and the questions of breaking off. An indirect strategy gets the point across by changing the interactive behaviors that have typified the communication in the past. Their use differs as well on whether one or both parties desire to end the relationship.

Withdrawal, pseudo-deescalation, and cost escalation typify the one-sided indirect strategies. The object of *withdrawal* is to show your partner that some of your commitment to the relationship has been lost. You can do this by reducing the amount of interaction with the partner. You want to let your partner know that your relationship is in trouble, and so you don't interact as much. In fact, you go out of your way to avoid interaction. When opportunities to talk arise, you make excuses for not talking. As one respondent to Baxter (1985) said of the relationship, "I took a stand that related to too much homework for an excuse to avoid her. She then initiated notes to me which contained certain things that both of us didn't like about the relationship. I never answered the notes" (p. 248). The frequency of interaction between intimates (friends and romantics) can be quite high. When that frequency decreases drastically, both partners become aware that something is wrong.

A partner can withdraw from the relationship in other ways besides reducing the amount of interaction. The partner can also reduce the amount of intimacy of her or his communication. You can restrict your talk to topics of trivial importance. You don't ask your partner to do favors for you, and you find excuses not to do favors when your partner asks them of you. When you interact, you don't follow the rules that you and your partner have established during relational integration. You may stop using personal idioms such as terms of endearment or special names (e.g., "Babe," "Dear," and "Sweetie"). You don't follow the patterns that have become familiar in the past. In essence, you are indirectly giving your partner a message by being "polite." That is, you talk to your partner as though she or he were merely an acquaintance. Soon they will get the idea.

Pseudo deescalation is the second indirect strategy that is used when one partner wishes to end the relationship. Here one partner expresses the desire to redefine the relationship to include less closeness, while secretly intending never to see the other again. How many times have you told someone that you "just wanted to be friends," knowing that you were going to completely end the relationship?

Cost escalation is the third indirect strategy used in unilateral termination. Cost escalation includes those strategies in which one partner behaves in such a way as to decrease her or his value as a relational partner. In other words, you do things so that your partner will no longer want to be in a relationship with you. This strategy is captured in this comment, "I thought I would behave terribly for a while to make her like me less (Baxter, 1985, p. 248). The strategy is to get the other to initiate the termination without ever saying you want to break it off because of your "costly" behavior. This strategy may not be used as much as people think because it is more desirable to be seen as the disengager rather than as the disengaged (Hill, Rubin, & Peplau, 1976).

When the termination is mutual two strategies are typical: fading away and pseudo deescalation. *Fading away* occurs when both parties implicitly recognize the relationship is over:

> My lover was a married man who was visiting overnight on his way through Portland. On the way to the airport the next day, we hardly spoke at all. When we did speak it wasn't concerning our relationships. We both knew that it was over. . . . (Baxter, 1985, p. 248)

Pseudo-deescalation is the same as in the one-sided situation except that in this case both partners deceive each other about their desire to completely end the relationship while acting as if they are together. One respondent told Baxter (1985, p. 248), "We communicated the desire to try and continue the relationship ['just friends'], but I said this just to make the parting less painful, and he said it for the same reason."

Positive-Tone Strategies

In 1982 Baxter identified what she called "positive-tone" strategies. A *positive-tone strategy* intends to convey the message "Things aren't working out, but we can still be friends." The object is to disengage from the relationship while expressing some concern for the partner's feelings— their face. You might do this by telling the other person that you have enjoyed your relationship and will always have fond memories of it, but that you are really sorry that things just didn't work out. In other words, you attempt to tell your partner that the relationship was a good one, a positive one, and you regret that it must end.

Along with assuring your partner of the positive aspects of your relationship, a positive-tone strategy will also explicitly avoid laying any blame on the partner. In other words, you attribute the fault of relational breakdown to some other factor (typically an element of the situation) beyond the control of either of you. "I really hate to leave, but this new job is just too good to pass up." "We've really had fun together, and I'll really miss you." "We can still be good friends even if we are 1,500 miles apart." Both you and your partner know that the relationship is over. The physical separation and subsequent lack of interaction will ultimately lead to pro- gressively less interaction in the passing-away metaphor of termination. But the purpose of the strategy is satisfied because you both leave the relationship on a positive note and believe that "if only things had been different. . . ." Attributing the relational disengagement to the situation attempts to avoid letting the other person have any hard feelings about breaking up. The relationship continues to have a positive tone, but that tone will continue to exist only in your memories. And everyone knows that memories fade with the passage of time.

Later in her work on relational disengagement, Baxter (1985) posits that all relational strategies, direct and indirect, vary according to their positive- tone or "other orientation." Those strategies characterized by little to no other orientation are withdrawal, attributional conflict, fait accompli, and cost escalation. The most obvious example is cost escalation because one partner engages in negative behavior to move the other to terminate. Fait accompli doesn't allow the other any choice in the matter. Recall that distress during termination increases when the individual lacks control of the situation. In addition, these sorts of situations are a potential threat to face or to a person's self-esteem. The same can be said of withdrawal because a partner would have little control over the situation if it is difficult to get the disengager to interact. Attributional conflict involves open discussion of conflicts, which often involve blaming the other and thus don't show much other orientation.

The remaining strategies, state-of-the-relationship talk, pseudo escalation, fading away, and negotiated farewell, allow some face saving to occur (Baxter, 1985). Negotiated farewell is just that—"negotiated." Together, both parties create an account of the ending story which involves blaming external factors, self-blame, or shared blame and thus removes individual responsibility for the termination. Fading away provides a context for *both* parties to recognize that the relationship is over and that it should be allowed to die. Mutual pseudo deescalation allows both partners to recognize the social worth of the other ("Let's stay friends") and at the same time to save face by continuing to act as if they are still together. Unilateral pseudo deescalation at least steers clear of complete rejection of the other. Finally, state-of-the-relationship talk offers the other at least the pretense of discussing the termination and thus some perceived control of the disengagement process.

Misunderstanding Strategies

Normal communication occurs with few problems because the relational partners implicitly understand what is going on in the interaction, even though the precise meaning is not explicit. On the other hand, one of the partners always has the option of violating taken-for-granted understandings and of appearing to misunderstand. Whenever someone violates a norm or rule of interaction, the partner recognizes that violation as a departure from the ordinary.

The failure to understand what is typically understood very easily signifies that something is wrong with the interaction and, hence, with the relationship. For example:

SYMON: Hi. How ya doin'?
MEGAN: Whaddya mean, how'm I doin'? You know I don't feel good.
SYMON: Well, I didn't mean to . . .
MEGAN: You never "mean" to. You're so exasperating sometimes.
SYMON: How come you're so touchy?
MEGAN: I'm not touchy. I just don't feel good, that's all.
SYMON: Well, excyoooooooze me!

Poor Symon! He doesn't know what's going on. He was just making conversation, and Megan responds by violating all the rules of polite conversation. He can't understand why Megan is so touchy and finally gives up trying to understand. If something wasn't wrong with the relationship before, there is something wrong now.

Any violation of a norm, idiosyncratic or contextual (as in this instance), signifies a violation of the cooperation that is implicit whenever two people communicate with each other. A rule violation makes explicit a problem in communication. And when people have problems interacting with each other, they have problems in their relationship. After all, communicating is relating. To let the partner know that a problem exists in the relationship, a misunderstanding strategy makes that problem explicit by making it evident in the pattern of interaction.

Another misunderstanding strategy is to interact as though you just don't understand what your partner is telling you. The topic can be about anything: the relationship, the other's personal experience, the TV show you saw last night, or anything else. The strategy is to fail consistently to understand what your partner is trying to tell you. You are implicitly telling your partner that your relationship is in trouble. You are talking, but you just aren't "understanding" each other. Consider the following hypothetical interaction:

SYMON: Did you hear what happened to Jackie?
MEGAN: Jackie who?
SYMON: How many Jackies do we know? Jackie Smith, of course.
MEGAN: Jackie Smith? Oh yeah. What about her?
SYMON: She just won the big contest at Burger King.
MEGAN: What contest?
SYMON: The Burger King contest. The cards that you scrape off.
MEGAN: What do you mean "scrape off"?
SYMON: You take a coin and scrape the gray stuff off. You know.
MEGAN: At Burger King? What are they giving away?
SYMON: The big prize is a trip to Hawaii.
MEGAN: She's going to Hawaii? Really? That's great!
SYMON: No, that's the grand prize. She won $100.
MEGAN: I thought you said she won a trip to Hawaii.
SYMON: No. I said . . . Oh, just forget it.

Megan is making the conversation very difficult for poor Symon. She just fails to understand and continually asks questions, often of the "What do you mean" kind. After a while, Symon decides it isn't worth the effort any more and quits trying to tell the story.

If Symon and Megan have very many of these labored conversations, Symon will soon get the idea that they have a relational problem. They used to get along so well, he thinks, but now they seem to be incompatible. They just "don't seem to communicate" any more. If and when Symon comes to that conclusion, Megan will know that her "I just don't understand" strategy has worked. She has successfully disengaged herself from her relationship with Symon.

Preferred Strategies

According to the research (Baxter, 1982, 1985, 1987a; Cody, 1982; Wilmot, Carbaugh, & Baxter, 1985), people say to researchers that they prefer to use other-oriented strategies when they want to break up with friends or other close relationships. In general, they report that they would tend to avoid using the more negative strategies, particularly those involving open confrontation. The extent to which this preference holds true in "real life," though, is unknown. We can speculate that people responding to questionnaires would typically report that the best type of relational termination is one in which the partners leave without a "sour taste in the mouth." They want to part as friends and with no hard feelings. This is the kind of strategy that people think they *should* use, whether they actually use it or not. After all, feeling good about relational termination is probably preferable to feeling bad. And when people are given a choice about whether they want to feel good or bad, they are likely to say they would rather feel good.

But the end of a close relationship usually does include a period of "feeling bad." If the relationship has been close, it is only natural that partners will feel *withdrawal symptoms,* an empty feeling after the relationship breaks up. Some close relationships will involve partners who remain friends and have pleasant memories about the past. But we have little reason to believe that such "let's remain friends" endings are typical of most relationships that terminate. Banks, Altendorf, Greene, and Cody (1987) found that the positive tone of the termination strategy used by those who had experienced the breakup of a dating relationship wasn't associated with whether they remained friends. They surmise that the partners use a more positive tone or other orientation when the other partner is perceived as someone who won't deal well with the end of the relationship and is dependent on the disengager. Whether the partners remain friends may be a function of how believable the strategy appears to the target, what the target's response is to the strategy, and how both act in the early stages of dissolution. The literature remains unclear about the factors associated with remaining friends after termination.

The research findings also suggest that people prefer the use of indirect to direct strategies in initiating discussion of the issue of whether to terminate their relationship. The idea behind this strategy, remember, is that you let the other person think that something is wrong with the relationship. Furthermore, using an indirect strategy doesn't invite conflict or argument about breaking off the relationship. Continued use of indirect strategies, if successful, leads gradually to the belief that both partners would be better off if they did break up. It's just too much hassle to continue. The problem, of course, is that the persistent use of indirect strategies will extend the time required to end the relationship. The discussions may drag on and on and on, when direct strategies might have led to a "swift and merciful" decision to break up.

More direct strategies tend to be used when there is anticipated future contact, when the partner is not to blame for the end of the relationship, and when the relationship is especially close (Baxter, 1987a). Directness in these cases may be necessary because of the complexity of close relationships and the felt obligation to protect the face of the other. Although in less close relationships (e.g., nonromantic) being indirect is seen as polite, in closer relationships indirectness may be seen as impolite—the partner is owed a direct explanation for the exit (Baxter, 1985). Also, in close relationships there is greater chance of betrayal by the other, which can be a greater risk with indirect strategies. Finally, if the partners are to interact with each other in the future, they may need to be direct about the negotiation of that future interaction (Baxter, 1985). Regardless of the use of direct strategies in some situations, the indirect strategies remain the most prevalent choice reported by individuals (Baxter, 1987a).

When Baxter (1982) asked her respondents to express any regrets they had about their disengagement strategies, she found that reliance on indirect strategies was most frequently mentioned. These strategies are consistently the most preferred strategy, and yet they are often regretted. This is because indirect strategies tend to prolong the dissolution of what can be a painful process, and over time, negative responses by the other partner may increase (Baxter, 1985).

There's no getting around it. Breaking off a close relationship with your partner is likely to be a painful and difficult process, no matter what strategies are used to end it. Wilmot, Carbaugh, and Baxter (1985) argue that if partners want to experience less emotional turmoil and fewer regrets, it is best to work on the termination with the partner. However, those in contemporary American society often find themselves confronting a difficult dilemma. If mutual termination is not in the cards, the only alternative is a one-sided ending which will likely promote more negative emotions. American society on the other hand values directness, which is associated with close relationships. Interactants know that indirect strategies, even if they are regretted, are effective because they can allow a gradual, face-saving disengagement to unfold. Yet, interactants believe they "should" be more direct and open when terminating. Wilmot el al. (1985) remark that the dynamics of this contradiction between indirectness and directness in termination warrants further exploration.

To summarize, no two relationships are exactly alike. We know that relationships evolve differently and that one friendship is different to some extent from every other. We also know that no two relationships are likely to end in the same manner (see Baxter, 1984). Some relationships will terminate as a result of the actions of only one of the partners; others will terminate from the actions of both. Some relationships will terminate with the involvement of a third party, who may be a reason for the breakdown of the relationship or a strategy used by one of the partners to force a termination; others will involve no third person at all. Some relationships will terminate after a long period of relational breakdown and much discussion of the issue; others will terminate swiftly with little discussion. Some relationships will terminate on a positive note; others will terminate with bitter feelings. The differences among terminated relationships are large and varied. Some general similarities are also apparent.

One, relational termination takes time. It is a process, a part of the evolutionary process of relational development, not a single event. Part of the process involves interaction, and part involves psychological or intrapersonal conflict and reinterpretation of memories (Duck, 1987). Whether long or relatively brief, though, relational termination is a stage in a longer process and takes time.

Two, with all the talk of strategy you must not lose sight of the fact that not all termination is strategic (Duck, 1987). Participants many times do not have a clue as to what is happening (Duck & Miell, 1984), and when they do, there is no guarantee that mistakes won't be made. Relational termination between intimates can be extremely chaotic, and some research suggests that disengagement often occurs by accident (Baxter & Wilmot, 1985)—sometimes to the surprise of one partner.

Three, relationships don't merely "end"; they change. When relationships have evolved to a state of integration, they often continue to exist, though in a redefined form. That definition will typically include lowered levels of intensity, intimacy, trust, and commitment. Certainly the frequency and amount of interaction will decrease, and greater discontinuity of interaction will inevitably lead to gradually lower levels of interactional quality. Of course, some relationships terminate on a negative note and lead eventually to a total absence of communication between the partners. But even these relationships continue to exist in the memories of the partners, again after a process of intrapersonal redefinition and reinterpretation of the past events.

Four, ending an integrated relationship will inevitably leave some psychological scars on the individual self-concepts of the partners. No one can break off with a close friend and experience no aftermath, namely "withdrawal symptoms." The passage of time is necessary for the individuals to cope successfully with these withdrawal symptoms. Symptoms of relationship withdrawal may appear in the form of too much time available (the "empty" feeling), doubts about self-worth, lowered self-esteem, or other psychological scars. Humans have no way to eradicate memories of past events, but they can retrospectively change their perceptions of those events and wait for the memories to fade. The psychological aftermath of relational termination is also a process and requires time for its completion.

Five, in the absence of contextual changes (such as forced physical separation of the partners), relational termination rarely results from a reduction in the amount of interaction. When partners complain that they "just don't talk with each other any more," they are probably saying that they are becoming bored with their communication. Rarely does such a statement reflect a decrease in the actual amount of time spent in talking with each other. If it did, then partners in long-term continuing relationships would have the same complaint.

It is undoubtedly more accurate to say that communication stagnates rather than stops during relational breakdown and termination. Too much of the "same old thing" in the interaction (regardless of what it is) leads to boredom. Partners wonder what's wrong and feel that their relationship is not progressing. Relationships that fail to progress don't just stand still; they actually slide backward. Fresh water, if left to stand without being replenished with additional fresh water, will eventually turn into stagnant water. Relationships are just like that; they will stagnate if they are not revitalized by change.

Stagnation is also a process that takes time. It takes time for the partners to look back on their relationship and make sense of their interaction retrospectively. People are much better communicators when they are *developing* their relationships to high levels of intensity, intimacy, trust, and commitment. They are much less adept at *maintaining* their relationships at those levels. Maintaining interpersonal relationships at high levels involves the continuing process of *becoming* in the evolutionary development of interpersonal communication. And that is the subject of our discussions in the next chapter.

SUMMARY

Popular music of the past several decades offers conflicting advice on the stage of relational termination. According to Neil Sedaka, "Breaking up is hard to do," but Paul Simon disagreed when he sang "There must be fifty ways to leave a lover." Breaking up with a formerly well-integrated partner is a process that develops over time. It may include a gradual erosion of the relationship that "passes away," or it may entail a "sudden death" of the relationship when new and damaging information about one of the partners comes to light. Or the seeds of "preexisting doom" may be present throughout the entire relationship and finally result in breaking up.

The process of relational breakdown leading to termination typically goes through several phases. The *intrapsychic phase* involves intrapersonal struggle within one or both of the partners about whether to break off the relationship. During the *dyadic phase,* the partners discuss the issue of whether they want to break up. The partners let other people in their social network know about their relational breakdown in the *social phase* and then find the need to rearrange and reinterpret their terminated relationship intrapersonally again during the *grave-dressing phase.*

Relationships may break down for various reasons that exist within the minds of one or both partners, within the social context, and within the interpersonal interaction of the partners. The reasons for relational breakdown are difficult to pinpoint and typically include a variety of factors within all three sources. More important than the apparent reasons for relational breakdown is the process of interaction that leads to and results in relational termination, including the residues of the relationship left within the partners themselves and members of their social support systems.

Relational strategies used during the process of termination revolve around the issue of whether to end the relationship or to try to patch things up. Whether the relationship terminates or is repaired, the definition of the relationship will change rather than simply end. Relational strategies include direct strategies, indirect strategies, positive-tone strategies, and misunderstood strategies. Whereas most people report their preference for positive-tone strategies and indirect strategies, the indirect strategies are often regretted because they prolong the process. Although indirect strategies are the most preferred, direct strategies are preferred in closer relationships. Under any circumstances, however, the strategies people prefer may reflect what they think they should do rather than what they actually do when breaking up with someone. The use of positive-tone strategies, for example, is much more socially acceptable than the more negative-tone strategies.

Differences among terminated relationships are much more common than their similarities. Only a few general similarities are evident: One, relational termination takes time and is part of the process of relational development. Two, the process is not always rational and strategic. Three, relationships don't end so much as they change. Four, relational termination leaves psychological scars on the relational partners. Five, communication stagnates rather than stops, leading up to relational breakdown and termination.

KEY TERMS

passing away	state-of-the-relationship talk
sudden death	attributional conflict
preexisting doom	negotiated farewell
breakdown phase	withdrawal
intrapsychic phase	pseudo deescalation
dyadic phase	cost escalation
social phase	fading away
grave-dressing phase	positive-tone strategy
fait accompli	

CHAPTER 11

"Becoming" Relationships— Maintenance, or "For Better or Worse"

This poem goes on too long because our friendship has
been long, long for this life and these times, long
as art is long and uninterruptable,
and I would make it as long as I hope our friendship
lasts if I could make poems that long.

—Frank O'Hara

If someone were to ask you why that special someone was such a good friend, you would probably experience great difficulty in answering that question. In fact, the best answer to such a question may be "I don't know. She just is." For, what precisely makes someone a good friend is difficult to put into words. Many good friends confide in each other their innermost secrets, but others don't. Many good friends are together constantly and seem to do everything together, but others interact much less frequently. Many good friends seek each other out for practical help and advice, but others don't. Why are good friends such good friends? The answer is that they just are.

As difficult as it is to define the word "friend," though, it is even more difficult to explain what makes some friendships last while others don't. Some friendships last for years, and other friends grow apart from each other. How come? How do some friends maintain their relationships over such a long time? What is the secret of maintaining and keeping close relationships? Unfortunately, there are no simple answers to such questions. About the only thing that we can say without fear of being wrong is that there is no secret to keeping close relationships, but it does take a lot of work. Moreover, people who maintain close friendships often have no idea why. They just do.

Several years ago, Aub and a friend were commiserating with each other about the fact that so many of their mutual friends seemed to be getting divorced. His friend suggested that the basic reason their marriages remained intact was that they just never realized they had any option in the matter. They married "for better or worse" and assumed that whatever happened, they were in it "for the duration." His friend intended the

370

comment as an attempt at humor (a feeble attempt, to be sure), but his friend was *really* talking about the fundamental basis for maintaining a relationship.

Close relationships endure because the participants *choose* to make them last, even if choice is not based on a rational consideration of alternatives. That is, people don't necessarily stay in a relationship because of the "rewards" they receive or because they are aware of strong reasons for maintaining it. They maintain their relationships because they *choose* to maintain them. This is not really an answer to why people maintain their relationships as much as it is a statement about *how* they do so. In the words of Robert Bell (1981), "Sometimes friendships are maintained simply because they have existed for a long time" (p. 24). Similarly, Duck (in press) comments that personal relationships for much of their life "just are" and proceed, once they are engaged, "by reason of the simple advance of *time*" (emphasis his).

In this chapter we will attempt to shed some light on the "how" and the "how come" of enduring relationships. We hasten to add, though, that no one can claim to have a list of strategies that guarantee to keep every relationship together or to cure relationships that are deteriorating. If you expect to find some secret formula for maintaining relationships in this chapter, you will be sorely disappointed. No such formula exists. On the other hand, we do have some understanding of what characterizes relationships that "have existed for a long time," of what communication strategies are likely to characterize a long-term relationship, and of factors associated with long-term relationships.

In the following pages we will discuss the specific kinds of interpersonal relationships that have existed for a long time. We will discuss what it means to "maintain" a relationship in terms of its evolution over time and, specifically, the impact of the past on the present and future relationship. The evolving relationship is not a constant and steady progression but more like a roller-coaster ride of ups and downs.

Our discussions in this chapter will conclude with a description of some characteristics associated with very close relationships and the communicational strategies that typically occur in them. We won't know for sure that these strategies will guarantee how to keep a satisfying relationship, but we do know that using these strategies will enable us to improve our communication skills when we are involved in the process of maintaining a satisfying relationship. Even highly competent communicators will sometimes break up with their friends. Being competent in interpersonal communication will not guarantee success every time, but it will certainly shift the odds in your favor. One last note. As we mentioned in Chapter 10, ending a relationship doesn't mean that you or your partner were incompetent or that the relationship wasn't successful. Not all close personal relationships should or do "last forever," and success shouldn't always be equated with endurance.

THE NATURE OF RELATIONSHIP MAINTENANCE

Precisely what do we mean when we use the term "relationship mainte-nance?" What does it mean to *maintain* a relationship? Is a relationship maintained if it merely exists for a long time? And just how long is a long time, anyway? Certainly some relationships exist for a long time and require little work to keep them going. For example, you have probably had close acquaintances, such as school peers, work associates, or neighborhood acquaintances, for years. You see them one or two times a year but never talk with them at any other time. You may write letters to each other a few times during any given year, but you rarely write folksy letters—just business letters. And you have been acquaintances for a long time, maybe even years. It doesn't take much effort to keep these acquaintances going. Neither person goes out of the way to do so. Is this what we mean by "relationship maintenance"?

Naturally, some relationships (such as long-term acquaintances) can exist for a very long time, even an entire lifetime. But these relationships, though they have existed for a long time, have never evolved into a highly integrated relationship. The fact that they have been maintained is more a matter of coincidence than anything else. Kathy's long-distance profes-sional colleagues are acquaintances because they happen to attend the same professional conferences. Similarly, you develop acquaintanceships with people at work and keep them only because you happen to keep the same job for a long time. You see these people every day and can hardly avoid interacting with them, but you don't necessarily develop friendships with them. You live next door to people and develop acquaintanceships with them, but the relationship is based only on the coincidence that you happen to be neighbors. You may be on a first-name basis with the clerk at the checkout counter of the neighborhood grocery store, but that relationship exists only when and because you happen coincidentally to meet in the business of shopping for groceries.

Many relationships exist because the partners just happen to be in the same physical context at the same time. That context virtually requires interaction; hence, a relationship forms. But the relationship itself remains restricted to that physical context and does not typically extend into other contexts. Consequently, such relationships are simply a matter of coinci-dence: two people happen to be in the same place at the same time. If the context is one that the partners maintain for a long time, the relationship is "maintained," in a sense. But the relationship is bound to that context. The clerk gets a different job (that is, moves to another context), and the relationship ends. Relationships that are restricted to a coincidental context may be long-term relationships, but they are not very significant ones. As a result, we will not be considering them in this chapter's discussion of relationship maintenance.

You already know that the relationship known as friendship may include a wide variety of different kinds of relationships. A friendship may be an extremely close relationship with a high degree of intensity, intimacy, trust, and commitment (as in "best friends" or "close friends"). Or it may be a relationship with only a mediocre level of intensity, intimacy, trust, and commitment (as in "just friends"). Our discussions will emphasize those relationships that reflect a rather high level of these characteristics. In fact, our primary concern is with all interpersonal relationships with high interaction quality. These relationships include kinship and family relations, marital partners, and lovers under the general category of "very close relationships."

Remember that the very close interpersonal relationship is not the same as "liking" or "attraction." An interpersonal relationship is a bond that develops through and is defined by the communication or interaction patterns of the partners. You may like an acquaintance because that person has an attitude similar to your own, is physically attractive, lives near you, and is of nearly the same age and social status as you are. (You will recall that these are some of the factors associated with interpersonal attraction.)

But merely because you like a person does not mean that you have a close relationship with that person. Kathy likes many of her acquaintances and many people whom she has never met. But she does not have a close relationship with these people. You maintain close relationships with peo-

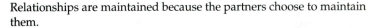

Relationships are maintained because the partners choose to maintain them.

ple by maintaining interpersonal communication, by talking with them. Talk takes center stage in the development (Duck & Pond, 1989) and maintenance of personal relationships (Duck, in press). In fact, Duck (in press) argues that talk is the very essence of relational maintenance. Through talk you and your relational partner share your world experiences, and in talk an ongoing story or image of the relationship is created and its reality is sustained. Talk makes "real" the relationship, and perhaps this is why partners in friend or family personal relationships report that its mere occurrence is far more important to relational continuance than its topics or content (Duck, Rutt, Hurst, & Strejc, 1991). They will also probably like them. But please don't confuse the intrapersonal emotion of liking with the interpersonal communication of relating. When relationships begin to fall apart, the emotion of liking also begins to decrease. The emotion of liking that the partners feel is a *result* of the relationship, but it is not the relationship itself.

Our primary concern is with those relationships that have evolved through the process of interpersonal communication to a relatively high level of integration. Rather than being based on mere coincidence, these relationships are maintained because the partners choose to maintain them. A general assumption of the relational maintenance research is that partners "seek to sustain desired relational definitions" (Canary & Stafford, 1993, p. 238). We will adapt this assumption and argue that partners choose to sustain desired relational definitions which emerge from interactional patterns between the partners. These relationships exist for a long time because the partners want them to exist. Our interest is in the long-term relationships that have undergone a process of change—from initial acquaintanceship and small talk to highly developed levels of interactional quality. Maintaining these relationships requires that the partners sometimes work to keep them in their communication. Friends, if they choose to remain friends, must choose to sometimes put forth the effort necessary to maintain their interaction (and, hence their interpersonal relationship) as friends.

We say "sometimes" work and "sometimes" put forth the effort because we don't believe that relational maintenance is *constant* work or effort. Relational maintenance is usually thought of as preventative work done by partners to sustain the status quo (e.g., Shea & Pearson, 1986), increase their liking for each other (e.g., Bell, Daly, & Gonzalez, 1987) or cope with the never-ending change of dialectical tension (Baxter, in press; Baxter & Dindia, 1990, Dindia and Baxter, 1987). The focus is predominantly on the interactional strategies partners use to maintain the current state of their relationship (e.g., Ayres, 1983; Canary & Stafford, 1992, 1993; Stafford & Canary, 1991). The overriding assumption of this strategic approach (except for the dialectical approach to maintenance) is that partners are always thinking, planning, and working to maintain their relationship or else it will fall apart (Duck, in press).

Relational partners, however, aren't always hard at work on strategically maintaining their relationships (Duck, in press). Just as your car doesn't need a mechanic under its hood all the time, you know that your close relationships don't always need a relational adviser nearby for them to thrive. Yes, relationships will unravel if partners don't work to keep them together, and they also sustain themselves naturally unless some event tears them apart. Relational maintenance, then, is composed of two elements: strategic work, or "servicing," and routine relational behavior (Duck, in press). We agree with Duck in his assertion that too often the routine life of relationships is forgotten. This is unfortunate because the time between servicings *is* the relationship to the partners. Although, much of our discussion will be on the strategic work of relational maintenance, we will be reminding you of the routine, nonmomentous interaction that also sustains your close personal relationships.

THE IMPACT OF "HISTORICITY"

Don't be too disturbed by the term "historicity." It is purely jargon, but the concept is an important one to keep in mind. We have consistently emphasized the fact that relationships evolve over a long period of time. During this evolutionary process, the relationship changes toward greater or less integration; but it is always changing. Occasionally we have referred to this evolutionary process as a constant state of *becoming*. Every set of relational partners, then, may be interacting at a particular point in time, but their interaction (and hence their relationship) at every point in time also reflects the entire history of their past interaction. The term used to describe how past history of interaction contributes to their present interaction is *historicity*. (If you are familiar with general system theory, you will recognize that we are using this term to embody the evolutionary characteristics of equifinality and multifinality.)

"Historicity" does not mean precisely the same as "history." As products of an American educational system, some of you were trained to think in linear terms, and some of you may think of history as a linear sequence of events. That is, you tend to see events as a chain reaction, each influencing each other, like dominoes falling in a long row. The bombing of Pearl Harbor, you think, "caused" World War II. The discovery of the burglary of the Democratic headquarters in the Watergate apartments, you think, "caused" Richard Nixon to resign as president of the United States. The poor condition of the economy, you think, "caused" George Bush to lose the 1992 presidential election to Bill Clinton. Asking a question "causes" the other person to provide an answer. This linear approach—where one event leads to and influences the next—is the way some people typically think of the "history" of chronological events.

The term "historicity" implies that a historical event does not necessarily influence another event to occur. In fact, the historical influence may actually move backward in time so that an anticipated future event actually influences a given event in the present. In this way, an event is influenced by another event that has not yet occurred. For example, "history" might explain that you experience hunger pains; therefore, you eat. "Historicity" might explain that you eat because you anticipate the enjoyable taste of the food—an event (experiencing the sensation of taste) that has not yet occurred!

So what does historicity mean? Essentially, it implies that the relationship at any point in time has evolved to its present state through past interaction patterns. However, there is absolutely no way of predicting, when those events occur, what that relationship is going to become. Many very close relationships began when two people hit it off immediately. They were attracted to each other right from the first and developed their friendship quickly and without difficulty. Other very close relationships, however, evolved from a rocky beginning. In fact, some good friends actually didn't like each other at first. But after they got to know each other, they became good friends. Other people were attracted to each other in a "love at first sight" beginning but grew to dislike each other after they got to know each other. You already know, therefore, that all or even most very close relationships do not begin in the same way. It logically follows, then, that you really can't predict what a relationship is likely to become on the basis of how it begins.

Research has demonstrated convincingly that it is virtually impossible to predict, on the basis of behaviors during the early stages of the relationship, how the relationship will turn out. For example, some people fervently believe that a more satisfying and lasting marriage is likely to develop when the couple live together for a time before they are married. Other people believe just as fervently that a more satisfying and lasting marriage is likelier to develop when a couple abstain from sexual activity until after they are married. Despite what anyone might believe, research results indicate that the early pattern of sexual activity (traditional, sexually moderate, or sexually liberal) provides absolutely no basis for predicting what the future relationship is likely to be. Researchers (Przybyla & Byrne, 1981) have concluded that "Individuals in each type of couple were equally likely to have broken up, continued dating, or married each other. There was no evidence that early sex inhibits the development of lasting commitments nor that a lasting relationship is necessarily facilitated by sexual abstinence or moderation" (p. 118).

So how does the history of past interaction contribute to the outcome of the relationship—that is, how the relationship turns out? First of all, the history of the interaction *is* the relationship. But the *meaning* of that relationship (and, hence, the meaning of the past interaction) is created through a process of retrospective sensemaking. People make sense of the interaction *after* they have interacted. You also know that you can even *re*define the meaning of the interaction (and, hence, the relationship) and thereby change what it means at any point in the process. Moreover, you are constantly making sense of the relationship/interaction throughout your history of interaction. You can't change the interaction patterns that have occurred in the past, but you can change the meaning or sense that you have of that interaction after it has occurred. Furthermore, that meaning is also likely to change as the patterns of interaction continue to occur.

This is what is meant by "historicity." Every relationship is a product of the past history of the interaction patterns that have been enacted by the participants. Those interaction patterns, though, are constantly changing, and their retrospective meaning is also constantly changing. Interpersonal communication or relationship contains more than mere history; it contains historicity.

Continuity—Not Consistency

There is an old saying that "The more things change, the more they stay the same." Although old sayings rarely have much value, this particular one is highly significant. The relationship is in a constant state of becoming, always changing and always different from one point to the next. The relationship is a process that is constantly occurring throughout time. You know that time does not and cannot stand still. It, too, is always moving, always changing and always different from one point to the next.

Let us illustrate this notion of the process of change through time. You buy a new car. It is beautiful. It is stylish. It runs beautifully. It has a shiny finish on the outside and gorgeous upholstery on the inside. It even smells like a new car. If time could stand still, that automobile would remain "new" forever. But time does not stand still. Eventually the shiny finish grows dull. The body becomes dented, and rust forms. The upholstery shows worn spots. The engine starts to use oil and develops a funny sound when it runs. The style of the car becomes outdated. And the smell of the car is often unpleasant. What happened? The car is the same car that it was when you bought it. It has the same engine, the same paint job, the same style, the same upholstery. But it has turned into an old clunker.

As the owner of the old clunker, you have several choices open to you. One, you can get rid of the old car and buy another new one. But you know that it will also grow old and wear out. Two, you can continue to drive the old clunker and be forever disappointed with it. But you know that you won't be enjoying yourself as long as you're driving it, and you still may have to get rid of it eventually. Three, you can maintain the present car. You select the third option and take the car to the body shop to have the dents and rust removed. You give the car a shiny new paint job. You have the engine repaired. You put seat covers on the upholstery. Soon you have the same old car, but it is now nearly the same as it was when it was brand new. Oh, the style may not be completely contemporary, but you like the style and are comfortable with it even though others (with brand-new cars) may think it is out of date. In short, the only way you can maintain the car like a new car is to keep changing it and repairing it. And the more you keep changing it, the more it stays the same as it was when it was new.

Relationships are just like that car. The only way to keep the relationship fresh and new is to keep changing it and repairing it. And the more you keep changing that relationship, the more it is likely to remain the same as it was. In order to "live happily ever after," you need to make sure that the relationship continues to change. Certainly the things that make you happy at ten years of age are not the same things that make you happy when you're twenty. And the things that make you happy at age twenty will change considerably if you remain happy at age thirty and forty and so on.

To keep a very close relationship from disintegrating and perhaps even terminating, you need to keep changing the interaction patterns that define the relationship. To illustrate, the interaction patterns of a very close relationship during the newlyweds' honeymoon are certainly not going to characterize a very close relationship during the couple's silver wedding anniversary. To maintain a satisfying marital relationship, the husband and wife must continually change their interaction patterns so that they maintain their level of satisfaction.

When the couple is first married, one or the other of them may work late or be absent from home in the evening hours or on weekends. They may not mind those periods of absence in the early years. After the birth of a child, however, the absent spouse is not present to help in the interaction patterns involved in raising a family. The partner may come to resent the absenteeism of the spouse and even redefine the past absenteeism (during the early years of the marriage) as a sign that the spouse never "really" cared about the marriage. To maintain the marriage as a very close relationship, the husband and wife must continually change their patterns of interaction.

The key to maintaining a relationship, then, is continuity rather than consistency. If you consistently do the same things over and over, regardless of how good they seemed at one time, they will soon become old and boring. Too much of a good thing will eventually turn into a bad thing. To be too consistent is to be boring. Recall from Chapter 10 that boredom is sometimes reported by friends and romantic partners as one reason for relational termination. Relationships need the shot in the arm provided by surprise and novelty. However, to be consistently novel or unpredictable can also be problematic (e.g., Planalp, Rutherford, & Honeycutt, 1988). Relational partners need to manage the tension between predictability and novelty, avoiding consistent patterns in either direction (Baxter, in press). To resist change and keep the same interaction patterns indefinitely is to allow the relationship to decay. But unlike the process of biological decay,

The key to relational endurance is continuity.

the process of decay in relationships can be reversed. A relationship that has started to deteriorate can, through appropriate changes in interaction patterns, get better and eventually be maintained as a good relationship once again.

People sometimes think that achieving the goal of a very close relationship is the most important part of the evolutionary process. That is simply not true. Achieving such a relationship is only a beginning; maintaining it is the next step. And maintenance is a never-ending component of the process of relational development. To put it simply, relationships are never finished (Duck, in press). Any of your relationships will always remain unfinished business. It requires some attention on the part of both participants. They need to be somewhat aware of their communication at all times and be on the lookout for signs of its growing stale. According to psychologist, I. L. Mangam (1981), "All shared understandings lack permanence and must be continually reaffirmed or renegotiated through personal means; rules, procedures, structure, and order itself are not automatic occurrences (however taken for granted they may appear) but rather must be worked at and sustained by the repeated acts of participants in the relationships that they create and maintain" (p. 200).

When a very close relationship starts to go wrong, the partners' first reaction is to return to the good old days when they were happy. They think that if they could just repeat the interaction that was instrumental in making their relationship satisfying, they would be happy again. This kind of remedy is probably doomed to failure. The couple does not have the same relationship that they once had. They can't go back; they must move forward. In other words, they must maintain the *continuity* of their relationship, their evolutionary process through time and into the future. If they can't repair the old relationship, then (just like the old car) they will probably decide to terminate it and go looking for a new one.

Keeping the relationship moving and changing (continuity)—not constant repetition (consistency) of the same old interaction patterns—is the key to successful maintenance of a relationship. Partners in stable friend and family relationships do report some degree of conversational continuity (Duck et al., 1991). Consistency leads to habits, and habits eventually become boring. Continuity leads to change. And the more things change, the more they stay the same.

Complexity—Not Simplicity

It is axiomatic that progress in evolutionary development leads to increasing complexity. Phrased simply, as something evolves or develops, it becomes more complex—that is, more differentiated. Evolution leads to greater variety. Let us illustrate the principle of complexity. When you developed your skill in using the English language, you became more complex. As your proficiency in the use of the language increased, you developed a larger vocabulary (more and different words and terms). You also learned more and different ways of saying the same thing, more and different ways of interpreting what other people said, more and different meanings of the same words or terms. In other words, your use of the

English language became more complex as your language proficiency evolved.

Throughout your career in the American system of education, you have been trained to believe that complexity is a problem that needs to be solved. You were given mathematical problems in your first year of algebra that involved simplifying equations or fractions in order to reduce the number of parts you were required to handle. The fewer parts you had to consider, the more easily you could find the answer. As a member of contemporary American culture, you have come to expect and even demand straight (that is, simple) answers to straight questions. You dislike "beating around the bush." A reverence for the importance of simplicity is a norm that pervades American society. Unfortunately, real life is not simple; it is highly complex. To demand simple solutions to real-life problems is to be disappointed when you discover that there aren't any.

Interpersonal relationships, during their beginning stages of development, are rather simple. The rules for doing small talk and carrying on polite conversations are relatively few. You can master them rather quickly. As a relationship evolves and becomes closer, though, you become less sure of the rules guiding your behavior. More importantly, you are confronted with a great deal of new information about the other person and, perhaps, about yourself. Whether you like it or not, you must learn to deal with an incredible variety of information and with the fact that you cannot easily predict where the relationship is going or guarantee how it will turn out. In short, you must learn to deal with a much higher level of complexity.

What do we mean when we say that the interaction in a very close relationship is more complex? Well, for one thing, people in close relationships use a greater variety of themes and topics when they interact (Owen, 1981). People in close relationships also use richer, more important, and positive symbols (e.g., certain behaviors, special places, events, objects, etc.) to identify their relationships. In addition, people in close relationships have already discovered vast quantities of psychological information about the other person during the course of their relationship. After their relationship has evolved into a close one, the partners' uncertainty about each other is no longer the issue it was in their initial interaction. At this point, they continue their interaction on other issues and topics. Hence, the issues and topics of interaction in very close relationships are more complex. For instance, in a study of the day-to-day dynamics of casual and close friends, Hays (1989) discovered that close friends interacted more, in a greater variety of settings and at a greater variety of times. Further, the complexity of relational endings also vary depending on the degree of relational closeness (e.g., Cupach & Metts, 1986).

People in close relationships are also aware that their relationship is fragile and subject to decay if they don't keep doing something about it.

People in close relationships have lived through that period of disappointment "after the honeymoon is over" and are aware of the failure of other close relationships. The partners know that merely expressing commitment to each other is not enough. The more serious problem is to cope with the difficulties of maintaining their commitment (see e.g., Knapp & Vangelisti, 1992, pp. 262–270).

The strategies of relationship maintenance are really coping strategies. People in a very close relationship are typically aware of the problems facing them in their attempts to keep their relationship together. As Owen (1984) found in his study of people in different relationships, "We can expect that everyone at one time or another discusses how relationships are, as some put it, 'washed-up,' 'hurting,' 'hopeless,' and 'scary' . . ." (p. 283). He found, "For dating individuals [relationships in early stages of development], fragile relations are a real and present threat" (p. 283). But married couples tended to think that their own satisfying relationship was different from other relationships that were in trouble. They felt theirs was a unique relationship. Friends vary in their level of awareness as well. We mentioned in Chapter 9 that friends experience a "mild existential terror" over the uncertainty of their friendships (Duck & Miell, 1986). In comparison, we mentioned in Chapter 10 that best friends tend to think about their friendships as "self-maintaining," needing minimal work to sustain them (Rose & Serafica, 1986).

Maintaining your own close relationship when you know that those of your friends are floundering is a little like being in a lifeboat in shark-infested waters. You know that you are safe in the boat, but the risk is always there. You can stay in the lifeboat and run the risk of not being saved. But that risk seems better than jumping overboard and swimming for safety. In your relationship, you cope with the situation by believing that you are unique (compared with other relationships that haven't made it), and that very uniqueness is what helps maintain your relationship.

In short, you cope with the difficulties that you know are present. If your attempts to maintain your relationship are not successful, you have failed to cope. The strategies associated with terminating relationships (Chapter 10) were also coping strategies to decide whether and how to end your relationship with another person. If you decide not to use the disengagement strategies and try to salvage the relationship, then the coping strategies attempt to repair damage that had been done.

But the coping strategies of relational maintenance do not attempt to repair past damage. Rather, maintenance strategies cope by not allowing damage to occur and not allowing the relationship to grow stale. To maintain a close relationship, strategic work in conjunction with routine behavior attempts to provide continuity—looking ahead to a brighter (or continued bright) future, rather than looking back to problems that have occurred in past interactions.

ROLLER-COASTER RELATIONSHIPS

People typically think of evolution or developmental change as constant and steady, like walking up a flight of stairs. You take one step at a time and eventually reach the top of the stairs. But a natural process of evolutionary change doesn't happen in a consistent manner. Rather, evolutionary change is a start-and-stop process of progress and regress, of spurts of change and lulls of no change. Biologically, for instance, your body developed from that of a small baby to its current adult size, but that development undoubtedly came in spurts of growth and in frustrating (to the child reaching puberty) periods of no growth at all.

When Aub was in the eighth grade, he was one of those adolescents who matured early and was shaving on a semiregular basis when his male classmates were still looking in the mirror for any trace of a whisker. He was singing songs two octaves below his classmates, who were still trying to keep their yodeling, breaking voices at the same pitch. He played forward on his eighth-grade basketball team; but when he graduated from high school, he was a guard (and a short one at that). He had his spurt of growth early and then watched as his other classmates passed him by. The center on his high school basketball team, for instance, sat on the bench in the eighth grade because he was too short.

Anyone who has ever tried to diet is fully aware of the uneven process of weight loss. You lose weight quickly at first, and then comes an agonizing period of no weight loss. In fact, while you are suffering on the diet, watching skinny people eat all they want, you step on the scales one morning and discover that you have actually gained weight overnight. Dieting is typically an evolutionary process of weight loss, weight gain, constant weight, weight loss, weight gain, and so forth. If dieters were to place the fluctuations of their weight on a line graph, that line would go up and down on a track similar to that of a roller coaster. To a dieter (just like the roller-coaster rider), the downward plunge is a time of great glee and the upward climb is boring and frustrating, made bearable only by the anticipation that there will be another exhilarating dive just ahead.

The evolutionary process in interpersonal relationships is like that roller coaster. The only difference is that the upward swing is the exhilarating part, while the downward plunge is frustrating and often unbearably depressing. There are, as you recall, forces that affect the relationship in opposite ways. Each participant, for example, has individual goals and motives that are not necessarily the same as those of the relationship. In fact, the responsibilities of being a member of the relationship may even conflict with the desires and goals of the individual participant.

Whenever individual people (with individual selves and self-interests) become members of an interpersonal relationship, they become subject to the tension between conflicting forces. Changes in the environment (such as the birth of a baby, loss of job, the apartment building going condo, moving to a new town, and so on) create tension and conflict with the present state of the relationship. The relationship then becomes a roller-coaster ride of rising and falling tension, increasing and decreasing conflict, good and bad times. The participants in the relationship cope with reality and quickly come to the realization that "happily ever after" really is a fairy tale.

Peaks and Valleys

Alan Alda has described his marriage as moving between periods of boredom and monotony in which he and his wife hardly paid any attention to each other and periods of "puppy love" in which they gloried in waves of emotional intimacy. The key to understanding this notion of waves, or peaks and valleys, is to be aware that the relationship undergoes the waves; individual members don't. The individual self is not undergoing any evolutionary change. The individual self is a member of the relationship that undergoes the change and is, therefore, caught up in the change. Certainly the individual will experience the change, and his or her self-concept will undoubtedly change along with it. But the peaks and valleys of the relationship are part of the *normal* process of evolutionary change and not the fault of one of the members. The soap opera romances and fairy tale fiction of the popular media have provided people with the notion that a very close relationship is a matter of interpersonal "chemistry." One individual is so suited to the other that their relationship will just "happen" as a matter of course. If it doesn't work out, then the "chemistry" must have been bad or they had a "personality conflict." At the same time, you hear occasionally about someone giving up a career or a huge inheritance for the sake of a romantic relationship, and you tend to distrust the intelligence of that person. When Edward VIII gave up the British throne because of his love for Wallis Simpson (an American divorcée), the world applauded the strength of his love but not so secretly wondered whether he was quite sane.

Oddly enough, people simultaneously hold the beliefs that (1) very close relationships are made in heaven but that (2) most of them don't work out that way in real life. You wait for the time when you can become involved in one of those relationships but know that it probably won't happen to you. Two psychologists, Arthur Colman and Libby Colman (1975), describe this frustration with the reality of "love" and our cultural ideal of it:

> Each of us becomes aware of love for another in brief, intense moments. Love peaks and then passes. Rarely can it be continuously experienced, for the traffic of our daily lives distracts us from the ecstasy of our relationship with another. We seem to acknowledge the peak moments of love as a great good, as something that gives meaning to life and brings us our most exquisite pleasures, but we are at the same time distrustful of its

reality. . . . We rarely think of love as something requiring work or discipline. (p. 3)

Maintaining a very close relationship with another person is not an easy task, but it *is* a task that requires some work and effort. The relationship is rarely a matter of personal chemistry or personalities that are suited to each other. Maintaining a very close relationship in real life is much more likely to be the result of the participants' hard work at keeping their relationship going and their participation in the routine daily life of their relationship. They cope with the tensions that result from the clash of intrapersonal and interpersonal motivations or environmental changes. They change their interactional patterns in order to cope with these tensions. They enjoy the peaks of those "brief, intense moments" of emotion and don't become unduly depressed or frightened during the valleys of relational routine. In every case, though, they are aware that the rising and falling periods during the relationship are part of the normal evolutionary process of relationship maintenance. And the emotional highs are always worth waiting for.

Tension and Conflict

Most people tend to distrust comments from people who say of their close friend or spouse, "We are so much alike, we never disagree with each other. In fact, we have never had an argument." Your first reaction is probably that the speaker is lying. If the speaker is telling the truth, you probably think that the relationship must be very dull indeed. It is hard to imagine a very close relationship that doesn't include some disagreement, conflict, and tension. If the relationship actually is entirely without tension, then it is also probably incapable of dealing with any conflict or tension that might arise. And the opportunities for conflict and tension to occur in a very close relationship are so numerous as to be virtually unavoidable.

Consider what a very close relationship is likely to be. These people spend a lot of time together. They have talked with each other so much and have self-disclosed so much that they know a great deal about each other, including those things that they don't particularly like. They have laid their selves on the line. They have risked a large portion of their self-concepts and invested their selves in this interpersonal relationship. In such a relationship, even a minor annoyance is likely to take on exaggerated importance. Even a little conflict can become a big argument.

In other words, the likelihood of tension and conflict in a very close relationship is much greater than in one that has not developed to such a high degree of intensity, intimacy, trust, and commitment (Cahn, 1992). For members of a close relationship not to experience any conflict, they must actively avoid or ignore sources of conflict when they do arise. If they do so, though, they will actually be making matters worse. Sooner or later a situation over which they have no control will arise (such as a change in the environment). When it does, they simply won't be prepared to deal interactionally with the resulting tension.

A relationship actually needs some tension and conflict in order to survive for a long time. Maintaining a relationship clearly implies that the participants have developed their own ways of dealing successfully and normally with conflict. Conflict doesn't have to be destructive. In fact conflict can actually help relationship maintenance and development if it is managed constructively (Duck, 1991). Relationship maintenance, then, involves the constructive *management,* not the *absence,* of conflict. Constructive management can refocus the relational partners on their interdependence and on what might have been lost if the relationship dissolved (Lloyd & Cate, 1985).

Let us warn you that we are about to introduce another piece of academic jargon—*cultural schismogenesis.* Now we could easily discuss the idea of schismogenesis without actually using the term itself. However, this term is often useful in answering that frequently asked question "What did you learn in college today?" If you are asked this, you can come back with a word that has five (count 'em) syllables and impress all your friends and neighbors. First, you need to know how to pronounce it correctly: skiz'-moh-jeh'-nuh-sis. Now for the definition.

Schismogenesis is a combination of two terms: schism and genesis. A *schism* is a "split" or "separation" between two things—in this case, between two people in a relationship. *Genesis* means "beginning." Hence, *schismogenesis* means the "beginning of a split between the two participants in an interpersonal relationship." Try using this term in a normal conversation sometime, preferably in an off-the-cuff manner, and you will be the hit of the party. You can even say that the noted anthropologist Gregory Bateson (1972) first used the term. (Rest assured that others will recognize your intellectualism when you attribute what you say to some experts and casually drop their names into the conversation.)

Bateson describes *cultural schismogenesis* (the beginning of a breakup in the culture or social relationship) as coming from either of two different sources: conflict or absence of conflict. In other words, conflict can certainly create tension between the relational partners and result in their splitting up. Common sense tells you that conflict between the partners can disrupt their relationship. But common sense might also tell you that the happiest and healthiest relationship is one that has no conflict at all. And this is where the principle of cultural schismogenesis becomes significant.

Schismogenesis is as much a threat to a relationship with no conflict as one with too much conflict. When two people in a relationship have absolutely no problems, tension, or conflict, they are just as likely to break up as those who have too much conflict. The total absence of tension characterizes a relationship that is monotonous, boring, and tedious. It is a relationship characterized by consistency (not continuity) and by simplicity (not complexity). It isn't going anywhere and will eventually decay.

Partners maintain their relationships and fight the threat of schismogenesis through the normal evolutionary process of peaks and valleys of development. Some research into communication patterns in developing relationships has illustrated how partners maintain their relationships through conflict-management peaks and valleys. Fisher and Drecksel (1983) observed the interaction patterns of male friends over an extended period of time and discovered that they alternated between periods of competition or conflict and periods of virtually no conflict. Apparently these male friends fluctuated between conflict and cooperation without realizing that they were doing so. In fact, if they had been asked whether they had any conflict, they might very well have responded that they got along beautifully and experienced none at all. When they interacted with each other in their competitive periods, they did so as a part of the normal process of their developing relationship. Because it was "normal," their conflict did not disrupt their relationship, and they probably moved in and out of competitive interaction patterns without thinking about it.

In other words, partners in a very close relationship interact with each other long enough to develop their own patterns and rules. They then come to recognize these patterns as the definition of their relationship. Probably without realizing it, they don't allow schismogenesis of either kind (too much or too little conflict) to develop. They have periods of conflict interaction, and they also have interaction without conflict. In fluctuating between these two periods, they develop their own methods of managing conflict. They don't let conflict get out of hand, and they don't avoid it when it occurs normally. By managing conflict in this way, they maintain their relationship and avoid falling victim to cultural schismogenesis.

The success of partners in developing their very close relationship is a direct result of the rules and norms that they have enacted and come to expect from their interaction with one another. Contrary to popular opinion, perhaps, research has consistently demonstrated that people's satisfaction with their close relationships is rarely associated with the "fit" of their individual personalities but is consistently associated with the way in which they interact, particularly in how they manage conflict situations (see Burgess, 1981, p. 189). For example, couples who use *integrative tactics* during conflict will not only experience communication satisfaction but also perceive their partner as communicatively competent (Canary & Cupach, 1988). In turn, these intrapersonal factors are associated with increased relational intimacy, trust, and satisfaction. Integrative tactics are characterized by a mutual rather than an individual orientation. They involve behavior which seeks a common ground and express trust and liking for the other. *Distributive tactics* during conflict, on the other hand, reduce relational trust, and have a significant impact on the relationship

(Canary & Cupach, 1988). These tactics are characterized by a competitive, personal orientation. They involve threats, shouting, and sarcasm. And Duck (1991) points out that even if the conflict is "won" by using distributive tactics, the relationship in the long run will probably be lost.

Precisely how relational partners manage their conflict will vary considerably from one couple to another. However, some of the interactional strategies and patterns (to be discussed later in this chapter) can be associated with many partners who are successful in their attempts to maintain close personal relationships.

Work and Play

Maintaining a close personal relationship is sometimes very serious business. It can require work and discipline, and relational partners are apparently aware of the work involved in relational development and maintenance. The root metaphor "relationship development as work" was the most frequently used metaphor by romantic couples to capture their experience of relational development (Baxter, 1992b). A little over 60 percent of the couples used this metaphor to capture their belief that effort and struggle are normal components of development. And in order to get the maximum amount of work accomplished, the relational partners have to play, too (Baxter, 1992a). Because they have been together for so long and interacted with each other so frequently, they are usually aware when their interaction is work and when it is play. Intimates develop intricate ways to signal to the other that their behavior is play (Glenn & Knapp, 1987). When it's play, they can relax and release any tension they might have. When their interaction involves work, they are managing their conflicts and further redefining their relationship.

Only partners in relatively close relationships know how to play in their interaction. People who haven't developed a rather high level of relational quality (intensity, intimacy, trust, and commitment) during their past interaction are less sure how the other will respond. They will be more likely to interact in patterns that demonstrate politeness and respect for the other person. They follow the norms of the larger social context or the culture— norms that tell people it is better to be "nice" than "not nice." But play in interpersonal communication is often "not nice," at least when compared with norms of the larger society.

For instance, good friends kid each other a lot; acquaintances don't. Good friends insult each other a lot; acquaintances don't. Good friends can call each other names and tell them they are wrong about something; acquaintances can't. Good friends frequently disagree and argue with each other; acquaintances don't.

What are the characteristics of play in communication? First and foremost, the same kidding themes occur and recur frequently during the history of the relationship. Second, both partners are aware of the "rules of the game." No one gets upset or bothered by the play but, instead, enjoys it. In fact, if one person gets tired of the theme, it will cease to exist and the partners will probably develop a new one. Third, the game involves a high degree of reciprocity. If Symon proceeds to kid Megan, the game will undoubtedly involve kidding from Megan in response. Fourth, the interactional episodes of play include only a small part of the entire interaction of the relational partners. Play is recreation and occurs as a break from the monotony of serious interaction in the relationship. Thus, the partners move back and forth between episodes of interactional play and periods of serious interaction. But periods of serious interaction undoubtedly make up most of the interaction in very close relationships.

People in close relationships often develop regular times in which they interact with each other as a form of relaxation. In some situations, this interaction time is called *banana time* (Roy, 1973). They don't need to say it, but both partners realize that this is a time for playing. Both partners realize that they need to interpret what they say to each other quite differently from the way they would at other times (Glenn & Knapp, 1987). Obviously they can't interpret each other's comments literally. After all, they're kidding each other.

Baxter (1992a) discovered several different forms of interactional play between close friends and romantic couples. Interactional play can take the form of insulting one another. Labeled as *verbal teasing,* comments during this play may sometimes appear, on the surface, to be devastatingly rude and even cruel. During verbal teasing play, partners kid each other about the relationship or about each other. Two female friends in Baxter's (1992a) study described their verbal teasing with this example (p. 346):

> My friend always teases me about this guy I like in our weight lifting class. She says things like 'He's looking right at you' so I'll turn red. I get even by teasing her about how often she falls in love. I'll say things like 'It's 2 o'clock now, time to change boyfriends.

Partners negotiate which topics are acceptable as kidding topics and which topics (central to their self concepts) aren't appropriate. Intimates develop their own specialized topics of play and their own idiosyncratic patterns of verbal teasing.

Another often-mentioned form of interactional play is *private verbal code play* (Baxter, 1992a). This form of play is characterized by verbal playfulness around any form of idiomatic expression. Recall from Chapter 7 that idioms are the specialized language of intimates, or their own personal jargon. These include playful nicknames, phrases for sexual activity, and private jokes. Kathy's best friends, two spouses, refer to each other as "Duck" and "Petri"—two dinosaurs from their favorite cartoon movie, *The Land before Time.* Interestingly these nicknames are only appropriate if the playful personality of each partner is being referenced, and only close friends can use the nicknames.

When intimates are *role playing,* another form of interactional play, one or both partners impersonate something or someone other than themselves. They can take on the identity of animals, movie stars, famous personalities, friends, and even each other. One dating couple in Baxter's (1992a) study talked about the great time they have following strangers around in their local shopping mall and imitating their walks.

Prosocial physical play occurs when intimates transform a conventional prosocial, or positive, action into play. This form of play is distinct because it is exclusively nonverbal (Baxter, 1992a). The kinds of prosocial behavior that come to mind are dances and greetings. A couple, in excitement, may mimic greeting gestures by playfully exaggerating the greeting ritual, such as wildly waving to each other.

When intimates transform conventional antisocial acts into playful ones they are engaging in *antisocial physical play.* These forms of play include hitting, mock fighting, stealing, and wrestling. Kathy and her best friend will sometimes carry on a mock boxing match which includes blows to the body that are carefully placed to avoid physical harm. When the blows do become harmful, play stops. Remember the all-too-typical comment from childhood, "Quit playing around before someone gets hurt?" Even America's President, Bill Clinton, is not beyond this form of intimate play. He once explained that he had received the four-inch scratch on his cheek from his daughter Chelsea by "playing with my daughter, I'm ashamed to say. Rolling around, acting like a child again. I reaffirm that I'm not a kid anymore."

Games and gossiping forms of play reflect typical differences between male and female friendship interaction. *Games* are intricately designed forms of play with rules and clear winners. For example, "pun-offs" between male friends in Baxter's (1992a) study occur when friends see who can come up with the best pun. Two female friends talked about *gossiping* as an enjoyable way of passing time with each other. They would nickname their friends after appropriate Walt Disney characters and inform each other about the recent escapades of these "characters." Verbal sparing and gossip aren't often appreciated by the opposite sex when in fact they should be recognized as important forms of intimate play between relational partners.

Public performances are occasional forms of play in which relational partners create and stage a performance for an audience. For example, a "lover's quarrel" may be staged for the purpose of watching the audience's anxiety (Baxter, 1992a). Public performances are important because they are something that both partners put together for their own entertainment.

Play between intimates is an important characteristic of the daily routine of close relationships which, as we mentioned before, is just as important to maintenance as the hard work put into relationships. This kind of routine behavior, however, hasn't received the same attention as children's play. Adult play, though not as thoroughly researched as children's play, is nothing to be ashamed of (note President Clinton's remarks). Play between intimates performs a valuable role in the daily routine maintenance of close relationships. Play, such as private verbal code play, is an important index of intimacy (Baxter, 1992a). Other forms of play such as gossiping and role playing allow the partners to distance their individual selves from their behavior, thus reducing their accountability. Gossiping, for example, is a way partners can indirectly inform each other about the qualities in people they value by commenting on the behavior of others. Constructive conflict management is also promoted by prosocial physical play and private verbal code play. Verbal teasing is an example of play probably more appropriate for very close relationships because it is high-risk play and could damage the relationship.

Play in close relationships serves multiple functions, and as you've seen, certain forms of play are more appropriate to certain kinds of functions. Baxter (1992a) argues that play and relational closeness are strongly associated with each other in both friendship and romantic relationships. These various forms of play allow partners to accomplish serious relational business while engaging in interaction that is relaxing and fun.

Play between intimates is an important characteristic of the daily routine of close relationships.

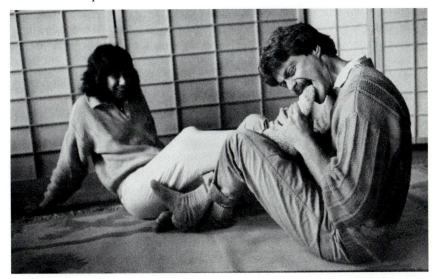

SPECIAL FRIENDSHIPS

You have probably noticed that our discussions in this chapter have frequently included the term "very close relationship." Some counselors use this term to refer to a specific kind of relationship with very high levels of intensity, intimacy, trust, and commitment. These relationships are not merely friendships; they are friendships that are extremely close—as in the case of "best friends." These relationships often (but not necessarily) include marital spouses and some family or kinship relations between, for example, brothers and sisters or parents and children.

Characteristics

What does a very close relationship look like? More accurately, perhaps, how do you go about creating one? After all, a special friendship does not magically come into being because people marry or are born into a close-knit family. Partners create and enact their very close relationship through the evolving historicity of their interaction. You just can't have such a relationship without working at it. Every marriage, for instance, is not a very close relationship. Mere conjugal love is not enough. Marital spouses or any other partners have this special kind of relationship only when they develop it through the process of interpersonal communication.

The first and most obvious characteristic of a very close relationship is that it endures. It is a special friendship that has lasted for a long time. But not all enduring relationships are special. Psychologist John Reisman (1981) has described three types of enduring friendships: "associative," "receptive," and "reciprocal" ones. The first two have endured but not necessarily because they are very close. An *associative friendship* endures because of circumstances that bring the partners together. Associative friendships include relationships with colleagues at work, at church, at school and members of the same club, athletic team, fraternity, or sorority. The sense of commitment that each partner feels toward the other is due to the situation (belonging to the same club). A *receptive friendship* is based on a difference in status or control. One member is the giver and the other is the taker. Leaders and followers create receptive friendships, as do instructors and students, mentors and trainees, masters and apprentices, or any set of people whose relationship is based on a relational difference of complementary roles in which one person is the giver and the other is the receiver.

A very close relationship is most likely to be a *reciprocal friendship* rather than an associative or receptive one. Partners in a reciprocal friendship feel a commitment specifically to their interpersonal relationship. Moreover, reciprocal friends tend to consider themselves as equals (symmetrical) in the relationship. They will switch back and forth between giving and receiving roles and will typically not maintain one role throughout the relationship.

To illustrate, a marital relationship is more likely to be a reciprocal relationship if the partners share their roles fairly equally. Husband and wife will both, at various times, take on the role of babysitter, housecleaner, meal preparer, lawn mower, furniture arranger, grocery shopper, and breadwinner. This is not to say that the "traditional" marriage (in which the husband goes off to work and the wife takes care of the house and children) cannot be a very close relationship. But it is a receptive friendship based on role differences. It is much easier for partners in a reciprocal friendship to create the interaction patterns of equality that are more typically the basis of a very close relationship.

A second characteristic of a very close relationship is the deep emotional attachment each partner feels toward the other and to the relationship itself. That emotion is typically called "love," even though partners in same-sex relationships generally don't use that specific term. But what does love look like in the interaction patterns of partners in a very close relationship? That question is difficult to answer. We might normally suppose that very close friends would self-disclose to each other or would seek out the very close friend for help in times of trouble. But we already know that very close friends self-disclose to each other much less than they did when they were in the earlier stage of integration. And some close friends turn to each other for help, but probably just as many others do not. (See O'Connor & Brown, 1984, especially p. 172). So how do partners exhibit "love" in very close relationships?

Obviously one very close relationship may be quite different from another. Best friends, for example, tend to be grounded more in affection than other friendships and are more self-maintaining and less likely to end because of a lack of contact (Rose & Serafica, 1986). They tend to be long-standing and more exclusive in nature than other friendships (Rawlins & Holl, 1987). A *best friendship*, more than any other friendship, is "the one perceived to share the closest emotional intimacy and the most unique relationship" (Kalbfleisch, 1993, p. 192). In her study of the public testimonials of female best friends (only a few males volunteered for the study), Kalbfleisch (1993) found that best friends were described, in order, as honest or trustworthy, fun-loving and humorous, loyal or compassionate, like a family member, and physically attractive.

Consistently best friends not only list honesty and trustworthiness as central to the friendship but also its playfulness (e.g., David & Todd, 1982). Hays (1986) found that fun and relaxation is used by close friends to evaluate the progression of the friendship. Their enjoyment of each other is fundamental to their friendship. Kalbfleisch (1993) found that best friends didn't describe their friendship as work, like romantic pairs have been found to do. Remember, best friends consider their friendships self-maintaining. Their "love" endures because, (1) the friends are together for so long, (2) the friends support each other in times of crisis, (3) the friends are similar and complementary to each other, or (4) the friends share a significant ritual that forever seals the friendship (Kalbfleisch, 1993). Although the maintenance of close friendships may appear not to be as difficult or as much work as that of romantic couples, remember that activities such as play do accomplish the very serious business of relational maintenance; they just do so in a different manner. The lesson to be learned is that the activity of relational maintenance varies across social contexts or relationships.

Moreover, love means something different to the partners at different stages in the evolution of a very close relationship and across the life span. In the early stages, the feeling is one of excitement and anticipation of the good things that the future will bring. In the middle stages, the feeling is one of exhilaration and happiness because the partners have confronted, struggled with, and solved their problems. Anticipation of the future is still bright. As people grow older in a very long-term friendship, however, their feeling of love looks very different.

When he observed long-term married couples, Olson (1981) discovered that these partners seemed to regard love as a feeling of being very comfortable in the relationship. They felt no need to talk with each other as much as they once did. Their feeling toward the relationship may have reflected less excitement and anticipation, but it was probably no less intense. In the later stages of an enduring very close relationship, partners are comfortable in the presence of each other. They are comfortable in the relationship and would continue to experience a great feeling of emptiness if the partner were absent. The relationship itself continues to reflect high communalism, or oneness, but the emotional symptom of love internalized within each of the partners is different. But change is a normal occurrence in the evolutionary development of a relationship. And change in the emotional attachment of friends is another symptom of the continuity of the relationship. Recall that continuity (and change) is part of maintaining a relationship.

Gender and Very Close Relationships

In our earlier discussion of this topic we reached the conclusion that we typically perceive and believe that men and women communicate differently. When the gender issue is examined at the interpersonal level, however, the conclusion is quite the contrary. Generally, whether one is male or female does not have much influence on the process of interpersonal communication or the development of interpersonal relationships. Although the impact is slight, gender probably influences communication most when the partners are members of a very close relationship. Close male friends do interact differently than either close female friends or close male-female friends. In most cases, those differences tend to be somewhat superficial. When Duck and Wright (1992) explored the everyday conversations between male and female same-sex friends, they discovered remarkable similarities between the sexes—contrary to what many have been led to believe. The differences appear to be quantitative not qualitative. Both males and female friends see everyday friendship talk as performing the same purposes. Duck and Wright (1992) caution researchers to be careful in their interpretations of how males and females use conversation in friendship.

As with every discussion that attempts to make some generalizations about friendships, keep in mind that each very close relationship has its own unique historicity. There is a considerable amount of variation among interpersonal relationships and patterns of communication. Nevertheless, some observations about what is typical of certain kinds of relationships are possible. The following discussion of the influence of gender on interpersonal relationships refers only to those typical characteristics. And in light of our previous comments, we caution you not to assume that these typical differences between male and female friendships are due exclusively to the gender of the participants. Further, any friendship involving specific individuals is likely to differ in some respects from the typical male friendship, female friendship, or male-female friendship.

Male Friendships   One thirty-five-year-old male described his friendships with other males in the following manner: "There is a special quality to being friends with men and it wouldn't be the same with women. With my male friends there is something special—I don't know what, but it isn't there with women" (Bell, 1981, p. 78).

Some years ago, Betty Friedan wrote a book with the provocative title, *The Feminine Mystique.* Its counterpart for males (the "masculine mystique") is more commonly known by the Spanish word, "machismo." It is the social stereotype of males in western society and goes something like this: The "real man" is strong and brave. He is athletic, aggressive, and never reveals his emotions; he is "cool," doesn't cry, and never eats quiche. Of course, machismo is a myth believed by some members of American culture rather than a realistic description of how men behave. For one thing, many masculine men like quiche and have been seen to cry on numerous occasions. Most men probably behave in a manner quite unlike the machismo myth. Nevertheless, some elements of machismo influence the interaction of males in very close relationships.

Males learn the mystique of machismo just by being members of our society. Small boys are given guns, footballs, and toy trucks as their first toys. They are expected and encouraged to participate in athletic teams even before they go to school and are rewarded for this. Most schools now have both boys' and girls' basketball, soccer, and track teams; but "everybody knows" that the boys' teams are really "where it's at." Girls are rarely allowed to be members of "macho" athletic teams that involve physical contact, such as football, wrestling, or hockey. You occasionally read stories in the newspapers of girls who have to go to court to earn their right to participate in such sports. Boys are expected and encouraged to be athletes; girls are still actively discouraged.

The result is that boys have the frequent experience of being members of a team. They learn quickly the value of teamwork and becoming a good team player. Consequently, boys come to associate friendships with team membership, activity, role relations, and "doing." Boys learn to suppress their emotions (to "play with pain") and individual goals for the sake of the team. Athletics and the team dominate the socialization of males in contemporary American society.

Not surprisingly, adult males develop friendships with other males around organized activities (Pogrebin, 1987). Male friends participate in games, go bowling, go fishing or hunting, and play poker. Each has a role to play in the "game" of friendships. Hence, the interaction in male friendships often revolves around kidding themes, insults, verbal aggressiveness. That aggressiveness even takes the form of physical aggression. Male friends often develop aggressive greeting rituals that involve hitting each other with clenched fists, slapping each other on the back, clapping each other on the shoulders. Talk between male friends is often loud and boisterous. Their interaction is very similar to that of a "game"—reciprocated aggressive activities.

One theme characterizing the interaction of male friends is "locker-room talk." Allegedly, this kind of interaction frequently occurs in the informal communication of men when they are in locker rooms, but the term is more likely to refer to any all-male talk. Locker-room talk typically includes profanity, telling of dirty stories, verbal aggression, and a lot of needling or kidding exchanges. One favorite topic of conversation is (of course) women. The stereotypical rating system (from 1 to 10) that men apparently use to rate women is typical of the way locker-room talk treats the topic of women. This kind of interaction is crude and consistent with the mystique of machismo. Most males have undoubtedly participated in locker-room talk, even if they have never seen the inside of a locker room.

Because of the cultural influence of team membership, males often have friendships in groups of three or more. Moreover, males often prefer to interact with their friends in groups. Aub often (but not as often as he liked) went fishing or skiing with three or more people. In planning such activities, they typically attempted to get three or more people to participate, but only two people was okay, too. Male friends are not necessarily uncomfortable in pairs, but the presence of three or more males in friendly activities or interactions is quite typical.

It has been said that male friendships are not as close as those of male-female or female-female pairs. To a large extent, this is probably true. At least, it is more difficult for males to develop very close relationships with other males for several reasons. One, the games that males play in their interaction are frequently competitive, and competition is rarely the principal basis on which very close relationships are built. Two, the team aspect of male friendships encourages partners to relate with each other in terms of roles, and roles lead to receptive rather than reciprocal friendships. Three, because male friendships often occur in groups of three or more, males don't have as many one-on-one interactional opportunities. Consequently, the closeness of their friendship is diluted by sheer numbers. Male friendships can certainly develop into very close relationships, but it may be more difficult.

Female Friendships   One forty-year-old woman described her friendships with other women in the following manner:

> Womanness does matter because of the same socialization. All of us have experienced being crapped on. But I don't think it is any sort of basic femaleness. But I certainly have become aware of women as sisters. Sisters in the sense of so many common experiences. I have also come to really feel good about my women friends. (Bell, 1981, p. 63)

If male friendships are commonly thought to be less "personal," less "revealing," and less emotionally "attached," the common view of female friendships is just the reverse. People think of women friends as being more expressive and more intimate. Women, people believe, tend to reveal more of their selves to other women, to confide more in other women, and to express their emotions more freely with other women. Women, according to some "feminine mystique," are much more likely to have very close relationships with each other.

In one sense, though, American culture tends to think friendships among women are somehow inferior to friendships among men. Our society sees conversation among women as involving topics of decidedly trivial importance. Meredith Wilson immortalized women talk in the musical comedy *The Music Man*, by comparing such talk with that of chickens in his song, "Pick a Little, Talk a Little." "Hen talk" allegedly deals with such topics as exchanging recipes, the latest soap operas, giving birth to babies, what store is having a sale, the latest fashion in clothes, and gossip. On the other hand, "rooster talk" treating such topics as automobiles, sports scores, and hunting season can hardly be considered very profound.

The past few decades have strongly influenced the relationships of women in our society. The women's movement has engendered a sense of sisterhood among many women, a sense that is explicit in the woman's earlier description of her friendships. The latest census figures predict that by the year 2000, over 50 percent of the workforce will be composed of women and minorities. Already over 50 percent of college students are women. Dual-career marriages, with both husband and wife working in equivalent jobs, are commonplace. Latest census figures also show that many more women than ever before are not remarrying after divorce. No longer can society expect that a married woman's most significant relationship will be with her husband. Most women today, like most men, have very close relationships outside marriage. If men have a unique bond of maleness that comes from being team members, women also have a unique bond that comes from their being women in a male-oriented society. Men have their mystique of machismo, and women have their mystique of sisterhood (see, e.g., O'Connor, 1992).

Are friendships between women more expressive and self-disclosing than male friendships? Certainly female friends do not typically engage in the verbal and nonverbal aggressiveness demonstrated in the interaction of male friends. Hugging and kissing constitute a typical greeting ritual of female friends, just as hitting and backslapping are typical greeting rituals of male friends. During a conversation, women are also more apt to touch their partners. This is typically a casual touch in which one friend might lay her hand on the other's arm. Further, women will often sit closer together when they are interacting with women friends. Consequently, we tend to think that the interaction characterizing typical female friendships is more expressive and more intimate than that typical of male friendships.

Intimacy and expressiveness are also more easily demonstrated with just two people in a one-to-one situation. Women typically do not have "team" friendships. Rather, females typically have one-on-one friendships. When only two people are involved, the interaction tends to be more personalized, more oriented to the self of the individual communicator. Hence, women tend to perceive their friendships as being more intensely personal. In the two-person interaction, women are more likely to express their emotional attachment to the other person.

Whether women's friendships are "closer" as a result of their expressiveness will probably never be totally clear. But expressions of emotion are probably more explicit in the interaction patterns of female friendships than in those of males. And the interaction patterns of women (for example, touching and sitting close together) will "look like" they are closer and more expressive.

Male-Female Friendships   The following comment comes from a forty-year-old male: "I have always felt I could be much closer to a woman as a friend than to any man. It is a real gut feeling I have. I feel that in general women care more about their friends than men do" (Bell, 1981, p. 111). And this comment from a twenty-six-year-old female: "Some of my male friendships have had to end because of attempts to move it into the bedroom. I have never had one male friend who accepted the friendship without wanting to move into sexual involvement" (Bell, 1981, p. 106).

An unfortunate but probably true comment on American culture is that very close relationships (outside marriage) are overwhelmingly between members of the same sex—both males or both females (Pogrebin, 1987). As the above comment illustrates, a male-female friendship is expected to focus on sexual relations. When a boy and girl are friends in high school, for instance, all their other friends (both male and female) assume they are "going together." When fire and police departments went "coed" across the country, some of the most vocal critics of the change were the wives of police officers and firefighters who feared there would be "hanky panky" between their husbands and female work partners. For some reason, our society assumes that males can be good friends and females can be good friends, but a male and female together will inevitably be lovers.

The culture in which Americans live has certainly encouraged the belief that friendships between males and females are expected to lead to some bonded relationship, principally marriage. Popular romantic novels, TV soap operas, and movies confirm the cultural expectation that boys and girls grow up to be husbands and wives. In fact, the recent avalanche of movies focusing on adolescents (probably beginning with *Porky's* and all the subsequent rip-offs) lead the audience to believe that sex is the only thing on the minds of adolescent boys (and probably girls). Even in the highly popular movie, *When Harry Met Sally,* the friendship between Harry and Sally ended in a marriage, once again implying that male and female close friends are "doomed" to eventual romance and marriage.

Probably the most significant single factor accounting for the comparative rarity of male-female friendships is the sex-role stereotyping prevalent in our society. When a man and woman (of virtually any age from junior high on up) meet for the first time, their typical first response to each other is on the basis of sexual attractiveness. Adolescent girls are as likely as boys to rate specimens of the other sex on a scale from 1 to 10. Hence, unlike same-sex friendships, a male-female relationship begins its evolutionary development from initial interaction that is heavily influenced by the sexual dimension. These cultural expectations lead the partners to be aware at all times that the potential for sexual involvement is always there. And that potential gets in the way of the developing relationship.

The expectations and stereotypes of relational partners in a male-female friendship are also in the process of change as society slowly changes its views of sex roles. Indeed, a decade-old study at a midwestern college indicates that males tend to have greater confidence in their nonromantic friendships with females than in their male friendships, a finding that would have been unthinkable not too long ago. Nevertheless, the number of nonromantic friendships between males and females, compared with same-sex friendships, is extremely small. But, in the words of Bob Dylan, "the times they are achanging." Pogrebin (1987) notes that those with satisfying cross-sex friendships are probably unique in themselves in some way or the situation is unique. She concludes that (1) those in cross-sex friendships probably haven't had sex with each other, (2) they have had enough contact with the opposite sex to find him or her a "regular human being," (3) their context facilitates their equality, or (4) at least one of the friends doesn't conform to sex-role stereotyping.

So far, we have said little about very close relationships when the members are married. Certainly, marital spouses can also be friends, but the mere exchange of marriage vows does not automatically create a very close relationship. Yet spouses do spend a great deal of time interacting with each other and thus have a greater opportunity to develop an extremely close relationship. It also stands to reason that sheer amount of interaction does not create a very close relationship, but it does provide an opportunity for development significantly greater than most other relationships. More important to the relationship than the amount of time spent interacting are, of course, the strategies used to maintain the relationship and the pattern of interaction when the relational partners are actually communicating with each other. And that is the topic for discussion in the next and final section of this chapter.

To repeat, the actual communication of males and females (with each other and with individuals of the opposite sex) is not all that different, though people often think it is. Males and females may be quite different biologically, but they probably aren't very different when it comes to how they communicate in interpersonal situations. Despite what you might believe from the conventional wisdom of American society, communication scholars (for example, Baxter, 1979; Ayres, 1980, 1983; Fisher, 1983; Ragan, 1989) have consistently discovered little difference in how males and females communicate. Duck and Wright (1992) said it best when they said that

> not all relationships are the same, not all measures of behavior in relationships indicate the same effects, not all the same things are true of a given sex in one type of relationship that are true in other relationships, but in many respects the sexes are the same in what they do in same-sex friendships. (p. 12)

There are differences, to be sure, but those differences often turn out to be trivial and insignificant. When it comes to strategies and patterns of interaction, the gender of the communicators doesn't appear to be a significant factor.

RELATIONAL THEMES AND STRATEGIES

The following descriptions of very close relationships come from people in Adams's (1985) study of relational strategies:

> My favorite person, lover, friend, and pal. Carl is also my biggest pain and frustration. I absolutely adore him. Our relationship is warm, loving and understanding. Carl and I have come a long way together. We've had our share of hardships and easy times. Now our relationship is eternally oriented because we are both determined to make it so.

What sort of strategies are used by people in very close relationships when they are engaged in normal communication with one another? What are the interaction patterns that characterize the process of communication of people trying to maintain their very close relationship? As you might imagine, questions such as these are very difficult to answer, since it is not easy to record people's everyday conversations. Furthermore, the interaction patterns of people in such relationships are constantly changing in order to maintain continuity. Recall the earlier discussion of roller-coaster relationships.

The relational themes and interactional strategies discussed in the following pages are primarily very close relationships of marital couples in her study. The descriptions of two of these relationships that introduced this discussion are from wives describing their relationships with husbands.

Some of these couples are in the early years of their marriages; some have been married for decades. The thing they all have in common is the fact that their relationship is very close, in addition to being bonded through an exchange of marriage vows. The following discussion, then, treats typical interactional patterns relevant to themes and strategies. What it lacks is the evolutionary development of continuity—the changes in the interaction patterns the partners enacted in order to maintain their relationship. That continuity of change undoubtedly is different for each couple. Even though we will not be able to grasp that notion of "the more it changes, the more it stays the same," you can still gain some understanding of how people in very close relationships maintain their relationship in typical patterns of interaction.

Self-as-Relational Issues

An individual in a very close relationship will typically define much of his or her own self-concept in terms of the relationship. Consequently, each partner creates and enacts a self that is bound up in the relationship and, to a great extent, defined by it. Following are some comments from several typical interactions that reflect the self-as-relational theme:

I think I'm ready to go to bed, you mind?

It would be nice if you could go with me, and we could spend a day or two.

That's another couple we should have over real soon.

Have we decided which ones we want?

We need at least a four-seater, though.

We don't want to go without a charge card.

Each of these comments begins implicitly from the speaker's assumption that "I define my own individual activity in terms of what you do." In fact, what is really an individual activity becomes defined as a joint activity involving the partner. For example, the first comment tells the other person about an individual activity (going to bed) but still asks the other person for "permission" ("you mind?"). Now the partner is not *really* asking for permission to go to bed, but he does seem to be defining his own individual activity in terms of a joint activity. In asking "you mind?" he is implicitly defining his individual activity in terms of what they do together and acknowledges the fact that he is doing it alone.

Many of the comments define personal wants, desires, or motives in terms of wants and desires and motives which they both have as a single relationship. "We need" and "we don't want" are statements about what are essentially individual and intrapersonal notions—needs and wants. But the partner defines his or her own intrapersonal needs and wants as though they "belonged to" them both together. Each partner thus serves to define his or her individual self-concept and individual activities in terms of what they mean in the context of the relationship.

In this way, the partners create and enact a relationship that is as "real" as their own intrapersonal selves. Each of them has an entire system of intrapersonal wants, needs, motives, and desires, but they also attribute those same wants, needs, motives, and desires to the relationship (the "we"). Precisely to whom those wants and needs belong (to the two selves coincidentally or the relationship as a whole) is difficult to say. The result is that the theme of the interaction pattern tends to blur any real distinction between the things that belong to the individual self and those that belong to the relationship—in other words, self-as-relational issues.

Strategies

People in very close relationships probably use more strategies than communicators in any other kind of relationship. And in maintaining their relationship, they probably use a greater variety of strategies (complexity) in their interaction than at any other time of their relationship. If maintenance requires change and continuity of their interaction, then it stands to reason that people will use everything at their disposal to keep a very close relationship going. And the more strategies you have in your repertoire of communicative behaviors, the more choices you have at your disposal to interact appropriately. Recall, too, that maintaining a relationship involves continuity, not consistent use of the same strategies and interaction patterns for an extended period of time.

Interdependent Selves Individuals maintain a very close relationship by using strategies that encourage interdependence, the sense of unity or togetherness of the partners. Of course, they can achieve interdependence by doing things together—that is, planning and participating in a joint activity. The following hypothetical conversation demonstrates the interdependence that comes from doing things together:

A: Let's do something this weekend. Whaddya say?

B: Yeah. I'd like that. Maybe we could take in a movie or something.

A: I was thinking of making a real night of it. I could pick you up after work and we could get something to eat. You know, a nice restaurant and . . .

B: That sounds good. I've always wanted to go to that new French restaurant on Third. I've heard it's good.

A: Well, okay, but I was sorta looking forward to a good steak.

B: Then let's go to Angelo's. We haven't been there for a long time. And the food is good.

B: That's not far away from the Orpheum, either. I wonder what's playing.

A: How about a play, instead? The Acting Company's got a new play on right now.

B: Where do they put their plays on? I know they used to be in the Capitol building, but . . .

A: I think they're in that old school on the north side now. They probably use the stage in the old gym or something.

B: What time you off work? I can get there by 5:30 at least, even if the traffic is bad.

This conversation logically progresses from the first suggestion of "doing something together" to making complete plans for an entire evening. The conversation focuses on a single activity in which both people will engage. Their strategy is based on doing one activity, a common activity involving both partners.

Partners can also achieve interdependence of their individual selves through coordinating their otherwise individual and independent actions. The following is the conversation of two people who have different things to do but synchronize their individual activities in order to maintain their interdependent relationship:

A: The boss told me today that he wants me to work late tomorrow night. I'm afraid I won't be home until late.

B: Really? When will you be through?

A: I'm not sure. I really don't know what he wants me to do. I suppose by seven at least.

B: I can pick you up when you're through. I can spend a little extra time at the office, myself.

A: If you're at the office, I could call you when we're through. That's better than trying to set a definite time.

B: No problem. I'll just be sitting at my desk working.

A: On second thought, why don't I take the bus? Or someone can give me a ride. There's a lot of people who live out in that direction.

B: It's no problem, really. I can use the extra time at work.

A: Well, this way you don't have to worry about leaving something in the middle. And you don't have to go out of your way to pick me up.

B: Okay, but I bet we leave work about the same time.

Interdependence so strongly characterizes the interaction of people in a very close relationship that one partner typically doesn't consider planning any activities without considering the plans of the other. Whether the activity is one in which both will participate or one that is essentially independent of the partner, the interaction will consider both partners in planning.

In a way, interdependence implies that each partner recognizes a sense of "being accountable" to the other. What one person does will affect what the other does, and each partner recognizes that fact of their relationship. Even when the partners do not attempt to coordinate their individual activities, they will probably inform each other what they are doing or plan to do. They don't necessarily ask for each other's permission or approval, but they do recognize the interdependence and mutual accountability of their actions to each other. In a very real sense, the actions of each partner take on meaning only with respect to the other person.

Responsive Strategies   People in virtually every relationship, from acquaintance to "very close relationship," will respond to the comments of the other. But the nature of that responsiveness will be different, depending on the level of interaction quality (intensity, intimacy, trust, and commitment). Partners in acquaintanceships (or any relationship relatively low in interaction quality) respond to each other in a parallel or coincidental manner—similar to "That same thing happened to me, too." In a "very close relationship," partners are responsive within the feeling of interdependence—similar to "If it happens to you, it's just like it happened to me." Occasionally this interdependent responsiveness seems like "empathy," but it is really much more than that. This responsiveness goes beyond "feeling" empathy and involves "acting" interdependently.

One way in which partners in very close relationships demonstrate responsiveness is in "advising" or offering advice to the other. On some occasions, one of the partners will request the advice:

SYMON: I just can't seem to get rid of this headache. You think I should see a doctor?

MEGAN: You've been taking aspirins for days, and they haven't worked. You ought to get it taken care of.

On other occasions, the partner offers advice even when the other person has not requested any:

SYMON: Sometimes I just hate to go to work in the morning. It just isn't fun anymore.

MEGAN: Why not quit? With your skills you can get another job easy. I sure wouldn't keep a job that made me so unhappy. It's not worth it.

A second way for people in a very close relationship to demonstrate their responsive interdependence is by "supporting" and "showing approval." Perhaps the strongest form of providing support is that of being an advocate for the other. Megan's comment above, for instance, is really a statement that supports Symon by being his advocate. Megan expresses her advocacy with the line, "With your skills you can get another job easy." Partners can also serve as each other's advocates by defending and rationalizing the other's actions or feelings:

SYMON: I don't know why, but I just couldn't make myself concentrate. I just know I flunked that test, and I knew the answers, too.

MEGAN: I bet you didn't flunk it. You just didn't do as well on it as you wanted. You're too smart to flunk it.

SYMON: Oh, I flunked it all right. I know what answers I missed and what ones I left blank.

MEGAN: You just blanked, that's all. Remember you didn't get much sleep the night before. You were tired.

SYMON: Yeah, but I still flunked it.

MEGAN: Your other scores are good, aren't they? And you've still got the final coming up. I bet you ace the final.

SYMON: Well, I suppose. That test is only 10 percent of the grade. But still . . .

MEGAN: Don't worry about it. Ace the final and you're home free.

A partner can also be supportive of the other person by providing assistance by "reproaching" or "repairing" the other's comments or actions. When you feel that the other person in a very close relationship has made a mistake or an error in judgment, you feel that you have made the mistake yourself. Hence, you respond by correcting the error. The correction may be as simple as making a minor repair in the information:

SYMON: The color was kinda pink like that sweater of yours.
MEGAN: You mean my angora? I'd call it a light orange.
SYMON: Yeah, kinda light orange. It was really pretty.

Sometimes the partner asks for the repair so that the story being told is really a joint activity:

SYMON: It happened last week sometime, wasn't it, Megan?
MEGAN: Tuesday night I think. Right after the news was over.
SYMON: That's right. Tuesday, and it was pretty late at night.

Individuals in a very close relationship experience no problem in correcting the other or offering reproaches when they feel they are needed. Neither partner wants the other to make a mistake. Hence, the partner will offer a reproach in response to what is considered an error. Consider the following interaction:

SYMON: Can you believe that guy? He voted for that idiot when he knew the guy was crooked.
MEGAN: What makes you think he was crooked? You certainly liked his stand on the environmental protection bill last session.
SYMON: But that was different. He's just trying to protect all those defense contractors. He'll vote for anything with big bucks for more bombs.
MEGAN: Maybe he's just voting in the best interests of the people who elected him. After all, those contractors provide a lot of jobs for people in the state. And what would happen to the state taxes if they didn't get that contract?
SYMON: Yeah, well maybe. I'm still not convinced, though.

The point of the responsive strategy is not that each partner always approves or supports the other. Rather, the responsive strategy is a contribution to the interaction that consistently recognizes the worth of the other individual's opinion, desire, or self (a form of confirmation). Sometimes that strategy translates into a response that explicitly supports the partner, and sometimes it means that the appropriate response is a reproach or repair. The individuals in a very close relationship do not take the attitude of "my partner—right or wrong." Instead, they adopt the responsive attitude of "my partner—always be appropriately responsive."

Remember schismogenesis—creating a relational problem through a too consistent and monotonous interaction pattern? Always expressing support and approval of the partner's actions indiscriminately and too consistently is likely to lead to schismogenesis. In fact, too much supportiveness will eventually lead to a comment such as "Just once I'd like to hear you disagree with me!" Of course, finding fault with the other all the time is equally as destructive—"All you ever do is nag, nag, nag!" Before the interaction gets to the point of disrupting the relationship, though, one of the partners in a very close relationship is more likely to point out the potential harm of that action to the relationship, as in the following interaction:

SYMON: You should stand up for your rights more often. Tell him what you really think.

MEGAN: I wish you wouldn't always tell me what I oughta do. I'm not a kid any more, you know.

SYMON: Oh, I didn't mean to tell you what to do. I just get so mad sometimes when people don't respect who you are.

MEGAN: I know. And I really want your advice sometimes. It's just that some things I have to work out for myself.

SYMON: Okay. I don't want you to think that I'm dictating to you. You gotta make your own decisions.

MEGAN: It's okay. It's just that sometimes . . .

SYMON: I understand. I won't give you advice unless you ask for it. But remember you can ask for my help anytime. I really do want to help.

MEGAN: And I appreciate that. I really will ask you, too, when I can't do it by myself.

The most appealing element of the interpersonal communication pattern that maintains long-term relationships is the fact that the partners feel no inhibitions in interacting with each other. They feel almost absolute freedom to say what they want whenever they want without fear of doing something wrong. In fact, they also realize that the partner will maintain the very close relationship even when they are wrong. They don't have to worry about arguing or being in conflict with each other, because they know that mere disagreement will not damage their relationship. They've worked out their differences in the past, and they are confident they will work them out in the future. The lack of inhibitions in their interaction may be the most significant part of relationship maintenance: the partners are totally comfortable in their interaction with each other.

The last line of the novel *Love Story*, popular well over a decade ago, has become almost a cliché: "Love is never having to say you're sorry." We have never fully understood that line and have never really believed it. The line could probably be rewritten, though, to describe more accurately the interaction patterns which serve to maintain a very close relationship. "Love is never *having* to say you're sorry or anything else. Love is *being comfortable* in saying you're sorry or anything else."

SUMMARY

Maintaining interpersonal relationships is often little more than staying together for an extended period of time. Although many acquaintanceships last for years, those relationships require little maintenance and continue largely as a matter of coincidence: Both partners are in the same place at the same time. Maintenance of close personal relationships on the other hand is a complex process that varies across relationships and throughout the course of a relationship. The process involves both hard work and routine behavior.

Every relationship is a product of its "historicity." The outcome, or later developmental stage, of a relationship can rarely be predicted on the basis of the way it started. Nevertheless, every relationship evolves to what it has become through the stages of its earlier patterns. Relationships that continue to maintain themselves continue to change in order to remain the same. Long-term friendships are also characterized by complexity, rather than simplicity, in their interaction patterns.

The maintenance process of long-term relationships is like a roller coaster in that it tends to fluctuate back and forth between different patterns of characteristic interaction as partners choose to seek desired relational definitions. Relationships remain finished business as partners experience emotional highs in brief, intense moments after long periods of routine behavior. They fluctuate back and forth between periods of conflict and cooperation. They intersperse periods of serious interaction with periods of different forms of interactional play. Throughout these peaks and valleys, the ups and downs of interaction, the partners in close personal relationships ward off the potential breakdown of their relationship that comes from too much of the same thing—the monotony of "cultural schismogenesis."

Special friendships are very close relationships between people who experience high levels of intensity, intimacy, trust, and commitment. They may be best friendships which can include spouses and family. Participants experience a feeling of closeness to each other and are comfortable with each other during their interaction. The interaction of very close relationships differs somewhat on the basis of whether the partners are both males, both females, or male and female. The sex-role stereotypes of contemporary American culture affect friendships especially when the close friends are cross-sex friends. Generally speaking, though, the influence of gender on the interaction patterns of members in very close relationships is believed to be much stronger than it actually is.

The interactional theme that characterizes the maintenance stage of close friendships focuses on the interdependence of the relational partners. Typically, individual communicators in the process of maintaining a very close relationship discuss self-as-relational themes and emphasize the interdependence of their individual selves—in planning and performing joint activities or synchronizing their independent and individual activities with each other. Relational strategies used to maintain close friendships involve the support and approval of the other person as well as offering reproaches and repairs. All types of these strategies could be generalized as "responsive strategies," in which each individual responds to the other individual with respect and self-interest. Strategies used to maintain close friendships are also very numerous. The greatest variety of strategies is used to maintain close relationships, and the partners feel comfortable in using as many of them as they want or need.

KEY TERMS

historicity

cultural schismogenesis

integrative tactics

distributive tactics

banana time

verbal teasing

private verbal code play

role playing

prosocial physical play

antisocial physical play

games

gossiping

public performances

associative friendship

receptive friendship

reciprocal friendship

best friendship

Glossary

accident One of three situations in which social contact occurs. An accident involves the happenstance contact between people.

accounts Accounts are strategies which tell the other person explicitly the reason or reasons for the behavior.

acquaintanceship The day-to-day relational context that is not developed into an in-depth interpersonal encounter.

analogical code This code, associated with nonverbal behavior, is made up of (1) infinite and (2) a continuous range of (3) naturally derived values.

antisocial physical play When intimates transform conventional antisocial acts into playful ones.

appropriateness A dimension of communicative competence that refers to the nonviolation of expected rules or norms of others or of the interaction with others.

associative friendships Friendships that endure because of circumstances that bring the partners together, such as relationships with colleagues at work, at church, at school, and members of the same club, etc.

asymmetrical contingency A form of topic management when one relational partner carries out his or her conflict agenda while the other remains unaware of what is happening.

asynchrony When actions do not fit together into a pattern.

attribution A perceptual process of assigning reasons or causes to another's behavior.

attributional conflict Openly expresses the desire to end the relationship by describing a conflict which is seen as being the reason for the termination.

back region One of two regions of self-presentation. "Back" refers to a person's behind-the-scenes' behavior, the private self.

banana time People in close relationships often develop regular time in which they interact with each other as a form of relaxation.

411

best friendship   The friendship perceived to share the closest emotional intimacy and the most unique relationship.

blind area   The area of self that is known to others but not to the individual.

breadth   Refers to the number of different topics covered during interpersonal communication.

breakdown phase   This phase of relational termination describes the dissatisfaction of at least one participant with the relationship.

business   A situation which requires social contact and which focuses the conversation on topics that are part of the situation.

ceremony   A situation involving a ritual in which one person supports the other.

change signals   A category of tie-signs that are sequences of acts that members of the relationship create and in which they participate together.

code perspective   This perspective rests on the assumption that individuals do not directly experience "reality" but construct meaning. They construct this meaning with codes.

codes   Codes are flexible and highly adaptable cognitive models that are highly individual and reflect our experiences and shared knowledge which are activated in interaction and provide communicators with various choices.

commitment   The quality of the interaction that reveals the extent to which relational partners are dedicated to the relationship.

communicative competence   Refers to appropriate and effective interaction whether enabled by personal abilities and performance or attributed by observer(s).

competence   The understanding of the grammatical rules and proper use of standard language.

complementary   A control mode pattern based on difference—one person in charge and the other person agreeing with the definition.

compliance-gaining strategies   These other-directed strategies attempt to persuade or manipulate another person.

conceptual filters   These filters are the internal states of individuals, which can be described as beliefs, attitudes, images, self-concepts, motives, needs, cognitions, personalities, and so on.

confirmation   Other-directed strategy which attempts to tell the other person that her or his self-image is worthwhile or acceptable.

connotative meaning   An individual's affective meaning or emotional experience associated with a word.

constitutive rule   A type of rule which stipulates the actions that must occur in order for a particular activity to exist. These rules enact an activity.

content   The "what" aspect of a message which refers to the ideas or information conveyed in the message.

context   A component of the pragmatic model of interpersonal communication that refers to anything and everything which needs to be taken into account when attempting to understand patterns of behavior.

control modes   Relationship-directed strategies that implicitly define the relationship in terms of which participant is "in charge."

convergence   Occurs when interactants use language to adapt to any number of features of another's speech style.

conversational preserve   The right of an individual to exert some control over who can summon him or her into talk and when this can be accomplished.

cost escalation   An indirect termination strategy in which one partner behaves in such a way as to decrease her or his value as a relational partner.

cultural schismogenesis   The beginning of a breakup in a culture or social relationship coming from either of two different sources: conflict or absence of conflict.

decoration features   These features comprise those elements of the physical contexts that can typically be manipulated or changed.

denotative meaning   The conventional or formal meaning of a word typically found in the dictionary.

depth   Refers to a deeper or more personal level of conversation within any given topical area.

design features   These features comprise those elements of the physical contexts that are built into the setting.

determinism   A view of environmental influence which posits that aspects of the context influence the behaviors and perceptions of humans, perhaps without their conscious awareness.

dialectical contradictions   Dialectical contradictions are dual opposing tendencies which mutually negate each other, and yet they are interdependent. Examples of these tendencies include individuation and socialization, openness and closedness, and stability and change.

dialogic listening   An example of relational listening which displays a genuine awareness of the relationship between two people—it is the use of "our," with a focus on what happens between partners and the relational present.

digital code   This code, associated with verbal behavior, is linguistic and made up of a (1) finite set of (2) discrete and (3) arbitrarily defined units.

disclaimers   Disclaimers are a type of flagging that function to manage impressions and protect the identities of individuals by attempting to avoid potential problems such as misunderstanding, misinterpretations, conflict, embarrassment, and so on.

disconfirmation   These other-directed strategies attempt to deny the other person as a source of the message and even her or his existence or significance.

discontinuity   Events that occur with certain lapses in time between them.

dislike criteria   A set of criteria or standards used to judge whether an individual will be disapproved of as a potential friend.

disqualifying response   A disconfirming response which is a put-down of another's intelligence, trustworthiness, significance, and so on.

disregard criteria   A set of criteria or standards used to judge whether an individual will be ignored as a potential friend.

distributive tactics   Conflict tactics characterized by a competitive personal orientation. These tactics can reduce relational trust and have a significant impact on the relationship.

divergence   Occurs when interactants use language to stress the speech differences between them.

dyad   A small social grouping comprising two people.

dyadic phase   This phase of the relational breakdown begins with a confrontation that may be lengthy or relatively brief and typically includes a marked increase in the amount of personal talk and private discussion between the partners.

ecology of attraction   The process of recognizing which situations and circumstances are best for fostering first impressions.

effectiveness   A dimension of communicative competence that refers to the accomplishment of desirable or preferred outcomes.

egocentric bias   A judgmental bias used in retroactive sensemaking of past events.

enact   People enact communication when they act toward the other person and experience the other person's acting toward them.

encounter reciprocity   A form of reciprocity referring to the expectation that the other will respond to you and participate with you in the encounter.

endurance test   This secret test strategy consists of drastically reducing the rewards for the other partner in the relationship or increasing the costs for remaining in the relationship.

entropy   An irreversible force or tendency within a system to decrease its order over time.

environmental interactionalism   A view of the environment which posits that the meaning of the context is socially created or defined by humans in their actions toward and within the context.

equifinality   A central component of a system describing the fact that the outputs of an open system are different from the initial inputs.

error of assumedness   This error occurs when people generalize from one relationship to another. This error occurs when a person assumes that an observed difference between two relationships is why those relationships are in fact different.

eventual reciprocity   A form of reciprocity occurring during the later stages of the relational development.

external self   The part of self observable to others; an individual's behaviors or actions.

face   The public self-image a person claims for her- or himself.

fading away   An indirect termination strategy occurring when both parties implicitly recognize that the relationship is over.

fait accompli   A direct termination strategy which openly seeks to lay the issue of termination on the table.

false consensus bias   The belief that other people will do and say the same as themselves in a given situation.

flagging Strategies which tell the other person what function a comment plays in the interaction.

flexibility A dimension of communicative competence that refers to the ability of people to adapt their repertoire of behavior to the guidelines of those situations, relationships, and partners that they interact with.

formality A general characteristic of relational interaction referring to situations in which the communicators conform to some set of rules restricting the freedom they have in contributing to the interaction.

friendship This relational context is voluntary, personal or privately negotiated, and collaborative; it emphasizes equality.

front region One of two regions of self-presentation. "Front" refers to that part of self that is observable or publicly visible to others.

games Games are intricately designed forms of play with rules and clear winners.

global uncertainty An overall uncertainty or doubtfulness about acquaintanceship in general.

goal-directed strategy A strategy which attempts to adapt to a communicative situation that does not appear to be fulfilling a person's goals.

gossiping A form of intimate play characterized by talking about other people in the partner's social network.

grave-dressing phase The phase of a relational termination that is a period of coping with the fact that the relationship is over.

halo effect A response set in which people overgeneralize another's behavior in one situation to other situations about which they know nothing.

hidden area The area of self that is known to the person but not known to others.

hierarchy A property of a system highlighting the fact that no system occurs in isolation, but within an imbedded order of systems.

historicity The term used to describe how the past history of an interaction contributes to the interaction.

holon Sub wholes of a system characterized by the dual tendency of self-assertiveness and synthesis.

I The "I" aspect of self which is the active agent or the subject of action; the active self.

ideal self A person's imaginative construction of who he or she wants to be or ought to be.

idealization When you idealize your partner, you are really perceiving a fictitious person—an "ideal partner" who doesn't really exist—instead of the "real" person who will always have good points and bad points.

impervious response A disconfirming response which denies the validity of what the other is saying.

implicit personality theory The use of a person's five senses and the other person's behavioral cues to make a psychological assessment of the other person.

impression management When people behave socially with another person and manage their impressions of that person.

indexical expressions   The linguistic techniques that perform the indexing function.

indexicality   Indexicality refers to the contextual nature of objects and events.

indifferent response   A disconfirming response which denies another's existence or the existence of the relationship.

indirect test   This secret test occurs when a person makes a statement about the nature of the relationship but phrases it in such a way as to imply that he or she isn't really serious.

information preserve   The set of facts about an individual to which the individual expects to control access while in the presence of others.

informational issues   The information about the other person that needs to be attained in the beginning of a relationship.

innovative context   This socializing context encourages creativity and innovation on the part of the person becoming socialized.

instructional context   This socializing context involves learning about the nature of objects and other people.

integrative tactics   Conflict tactics characterized by mutual behavior which seeks a common ground and expresses trust and liking for the other.

intensity   The strength or potency of a relationship.

internal self   The part of self hidden from observation; the psychological and cognitive processes of an individual.

interpersonal conflict   Conflict requiring a minimum of two people and involving communication. It is an observable event within a sequence of behavior composed of three consecutive one-up comments.

interpersonal communication   Interpersonal communication is the process of creating social relationships between at least two people by acting in concert with one another.

interpersonal (intrapersonal) context   In this socializing context the individuals learn to become aware of their own emotions, inner selves, innermost feelings, and how to deal with them.

interpersonal perception   Interpersonal perception involves person perception and the social coordination of partners toward each other and a common issue: congruency.

interpersonal system   The relational level of interpersonal communication found in the patterns of behavior between interacting individuals.

intimacy   The depth of an individual's attachment or close association.

intrapersonal system   The individual level of interpersonal communication found within individual cognitive and psychological processes. Also, the smallest system composed of the individual human being.

intrapersonal view   A view of interpersonal communication occurring from the individual's standpoint or perspective. This insider view of interpersonal communication is also known as a psychological understanding of human communication.

intrapsychic phase   This phase of relational termination focuses on the internalized feelings of each partner in terms of an emotional reaction to the other.

issue   A question that, until answered, is a topic to be negotiated or resolved.

issue-directed strategy   A strategy that attempts to exert some control over the content of the information or the flow of information being discussed.

joking   A secret test strategy that indirectly asks the partner to respond with some statement that indicates the nature of the relationship.

kinship   The relational context based on the connections of biological relations.

langue   An abstract system shared by all members of a language-speaking community which enables them to speak.

leniency effect   A response set which occurs when people allow their relationship with another to affect their perceptions of the other partner.

life-span developmental communication perspective   A fundamental premise of this perspective is that the understanding of any communicative phenomenon is predicated first on understanding the development of that phenomenon.

markers   A category of tie-signs which are acts or events that lay claim to parts of a relationship.

me   The "me" is the aspect of self which is an object or a person's reflective self.

metacommunication   A behavioral message that conveys ideas or information and simultaneously comments on how the ideas are to be taken.

mindfulness   Remaining open to the variety of possible interpretations in any given context and being willing to create new interpretations.

mindlessness   Acting as if information were true regardless of its context.

model   An analogy or a metaphor that stands for something real.

mutual contingency   A form of topic management when both partners respond to each other and carry on with their own conflict agenda.

mutually shared field   When individuals perceive each other, they are simultaneously engaged in the same process of person perception.

negative face   A person's claim to carry out actions without interference from others.

negotiated farewell   A direct termination strategy characterized by an open discussion of the end of the relationship with no hostility or conflict.

noncontingent reactions   A form of topic management occurring when partners don't bother to acknowledge each other's comments as they develop their own conflict agendas.

nonsummativity   A central property of a system describing the ability of the system to take on an identity separate from its individual components.

norm of reciprocity   The tendency to respond in kind to the other person.

one-across comment   A type of control mode referring to equivalence-defining comments.

one-down comment   A type of control mode that defers to the speaker's one-up comment.

one-up comment A type of control mode that contains an imperative or gives instructions.

open area The area of self that is known to the person and to others.

open system An open system is characterized by a high degree of continuous exchange with its environment. This characteristic is also known as openness.

opening moves Occur during the first few exchanges of interaction and serve to start the relationship.

openness A general characteristic of relational interaction describing when partners provide each other with information about their inner selves which influences their image of each other.

other-directed strategy These strategies focus the interaction on the other person.

parole Language use in communication, or the way members of the community actually speak.

passing away This type of relational termination is a long, slow, and gradual erosion of the relationship.

perception The psychological process associated with interpretation and assigning meanings to persons and objects.

perceptual sets A cognitive process individuals use to form an overall impression of another person from incomplete information.

performance The social use of language, including all the revisions and violations of standard rules typical in any given social context.

personal space Territorial personal distance, varying in size and indicating degrees of interpersonal relationship.

physical context The context composed of design, decoration, and the presence or absence of other people. Also defined as a context that consists of directly observable objects, and so its identification is rarely a problem in interpersonal communication.

politeness Politeness occurs when individuals acknowledge and accept each other's self-image.

positive face A person's claim to a self-image or desire to be approved and appreciated by other interactants.

positive-tone strategy A termination strategy meant to convey the message that the relationship is ending while expressing concern for the other.

pragmatic code A kind of cognitive model or code linked to individual oral tradition that resembles spoken language.

pragmatic model of interpersonal communication A model of interpersonal communication composed of three interdependent components: individuals, relationship, and context. The primary thrust of the model is a focus on the sequences of interaction occurring at the dyadic level.

pragmatic view An approach to the study of interpersonal communication, adapted from general system theory, with an exclusive focus on observable behavior between people.

preexisting doom   A sense that the relationship contains elements which threaten the existence of the relationship.

private verbal code play   The form of play that is characterized by verbal playfulness around any form of specialized language of intimates or their own personal jargon.

proactive responses   A person's actions toward the environment.

process   A characteristic of interpersonal communication referring to the dynamic, ongoing, ever-changing, and continuous nature of its interdependent components.

prosocial physical play   When intimates transform a conventional prosocial or positive action into play.

proxemics   Is the term used to describe space and distance in human interaction.

pseudo contingency   A form of topic management in which partners relate their comments to the immediately prior comment to show contingency, but then drastically alter the focus.

pseudo deescalation   An indirect termination strategy used when one partner expresses the desire to redefine the relationship to include less closeness all the while secretly intending never to see the other again.

psychological models of communication   These models locate interpersonal communication and thus the relationship within the individual. The relationship is the "background" for the individual as "figure."

public performance   Forms of intimate play in which relational partners create and stage a performance for an audience.

punctuation   A term used to refer to the order imposed on a sequence of behavior.

reactive responses   A person's reaction to stimuli from the environment.

receptive friendship   Friendship based on a difference in status or control.

reciprocal friendship   When partners feel a commitment specifically to their interpersonal relationship.

reciprocity   The quality of interaction in which each interactant in turn exchanges the other's definition of their relationship.

recurrence   An event that may occur again and again at different times.

reflexivity   Language that serves to identify members of a particular social context and in turn the members of that particular social context identified with it.

regulative context   This socializing context involves the learning of authoritative relationships and the rules of conduct that regulate the larger society as well as a small group of friends.

regulative rule   A type of rule created during an activity. These rules guide preexisting activity.

relational accounts   People use accounts to create a narrative of their lives and, in so doing, "market" their social relationships and tell stories about what is going on with them.

relational contexts   These contexts describe the different types of connections between participants in interpersonal communication.

relational distance   Occurs when the prior connection between partners becomes strained and is characterized by unpleasant feelings.

relational issues   These issues address "Who am I in relation to you?" and "Who are you in relation to me?"

relational listening   A quality of listening which extends beyond attention and good skill. During relational listening one or both partners are responsive to the needs and feelings expressed in the interaction.

relationship   The "how" of a message which comments on how the ideas or content of the message is to be taken. The aspect of the message signals how an individual defines the relationship which in turn guides how to interpret the content.

relationship-directed strategy   This strategy functions directly to define the relationship with another person.

residues   The outcome of a relationship which is internalized in the form of an emotional response, a memory, or a perceptual definition of the relationship.

response sets   A part of the perceptual set relevant to the person perception which involves making inferential leaps from the other person's behavior to our own behavioral response.

retrospective sensemaking   Occurs when people give meaning to behaviors after they occur. This form of sensemaking is what is typically done to define behaviors and the relationship.

rituals   A category of tie-signs which are a set of behaviors or events that have been repeated so often that both partners know the meaning of how it confirms the existence of the relationship. Also, opening moves which are perfunctory, conventionalized acts through which an individual portrays his or her respect and regard for some object of ultimate value or to its stand-in.

role playing   A form of intimate play when one or both partners impersonate something or someone other than themselves.

roles   Roles provide guidelines for behavior or what the social context designates as appropriate behavior in specific relationships.

rule   A followable prescription that indicates what behavior is obligated, preferred, or prohibited in certain contexts.

schema   The framework into which a person places all known information about his or her "self" in any given situation.

secret tests   When a person devises strategies that indirectly seek information about the relationship by concealing the true motive behind the strategy.

self-as-object issue   Interaction that is essentially conversation in which each communicator defines his or her self in relation to a common topic.

self-as-other issue   Interaction that occurs when one person tells the other about his or her experiences and the other person talks about those same experiences.

self-as-relational issue The negotiation within a relationship that addresses the relationship that binds the partners together.

self-concept That part of the self which a person conceptualizes as a set of relatively stable self-characterizations.

self-directed strategy This strategy is used by interactants to tell the other person how to interpret their self-offers.

self-disclosure The act of making yourself manifest, showing yourself so others can perceive you.

self-esteem The term used to denote a person's evaluative perception of self; it is an inherent part of a person's self-concept.

self-fulfilling prophecy A behavioral confirmation process in which the person's actions, which are based on preconceived assumptions and beliefs, can set up the behaviors of others to validate those very preconceived notions.

self-handicapping strategy A form of self-protection in which an individual attributes a potential threat to the self-concept to some external cause that doesn't affect the self-concept.

self-schemata Cognitive generalizations about the self, derived from past experience, that organize and guide the processing of self-related information contained in an individual's social experience.

self A person's organization of accumulated experiences which provides the basis for personal action.

sensemaking Sensemaking is the ability to make sense out of everything, even nonsense. It is the ability to organize events into patterns that give the events meaning.

situation-directed strategy Coping strategies that allow the communicator to define the situation so that he or she no longer feels a victim of circumstances.

small talk Routine behavior which transpires in conversation, often but not necessarily between new acquaintances and in the very first phase of a developing relationship.

social context Consists of people and the influences of those people who make up a particular social system. The people may not be physically present when interpersonal communication takes place. Also, the learned norms, values, beliefs, and traditions of society.

social contracts Relational context which contain an overt obligation on the part of members not present in any other relational context. For example, marital couples are "legally married" and therefore subject to certain obligations.

social penetration Provides insight into how self-disclosure is linked with developing intimacy or liking.

social phase This phase of relational termination describes the need to tell other people just why and how the partners decided to break up.

social system A type of system which occurs any time an individual's actions become interconnected. A social system can be as small as a dyad or as large as an entire society.

socialization   The institutions that teach or pass on the social contexts.

speech accommodation theory   Explains the reasons for and the consequences of such speech accommodating phenomena as style switching.

state-of-the-relationship talk   A direct termination strategy used when the dyad openly seeks to lay the issue of termination on the table but not to make a final declaration.

stereotypes   A widespread belief based on common sense.

strategy   The fundamental unit of interpersonal communication which can potentially affect the negotiated outcome of the relationship.

style   A person's language-in-use in a particular social context, or the way a person participates in communication.

style switching   A person's ability to change his or her use of language from the conventions of one social context to another.

sudden death   When one partner becomes aware of some new, surprising, and significant negatively charged information about a partner and the relationship ends.

symmetrical   A control mode pattern in which neither party gains or relinquishes the position of control or changes who is in charge of the relationship; a relationship based on equality.

synchrony   Events that fit together in a logical progression.

syntactic code   A kind of cognitive model or code associated with formal, planned, and literate language use.

system   A system functions as a whole by virtue of the interdependence of its parts.

systems theory   A loosely organized and highly abstract set of principles that serve to direct our thinking about communicative processes.

territoriality   The assumption of property rights toward some geographical area.

tie-signs   Relationship-directed strategies which refer to objects, acts, events, and expressions that provide evidence of a relational bond that exists between two or more people.

triangle test   This secret test strategy involves the use of a third party and places your partner in a situation in which his or her fidelity or jealously is tested.

trust   The extent to which partners freely engage in high-risk behaviors when interacting with each other.

turning points   Any event or occurrence that is associated with a change in a relationship.

uncertainty reduction   An attempt to discover appropriate communicative behaviors.

unknown area   The area of self that is not known to the person or to others.

verbal immediacy   A general characteristic of relational interaction referring to the connection between the interaction and the immediate situation.

verbal teasing   A form of intimate play characterized by playful, insulting behavior.

wholeness   A central property of a system describing the fact that the components of a system affect all other components.

withdrawal   An indirect termination strategy used to show your partner that some of your commitment to the relationship has been lost.

work   This relational context develops when people work together. The context is considered a matter of coincidence.

References

Adams, K. L. (1985). "Communication as negotiation: A study of strategic interaction in social relationships." Doctoral dissertation, University of Utah, 1986. *Dissertation Abstracts International, 46,* 10A.

Adler, R. B., & Towne, N. (1993). *Looking out/Looking in,* 7th ed. Forth Worth, TX: Harcourt Brace Jovanovich.

Allport, G. W. (1962). Psychological models for guidance. *Harvard Educational Review, 32,* 373–381.

Allport, G. W. (1968). The historical background of modern social psychology. In G. Lindzey & E. Aranson (Eds.), *Handbook of social psychology,* 2d ed., Vol. 1, pp. 1–80. Reading, MA: Addison-Wesley.

Altman, I. (1975). *The environment and social behavior.* Monterey, CA: Brooks/Cole.

Altman, I., Nelson, P., & Lett, E. (1972). The ecology of home environments. *Catalog of selected documents in psychology.* Washington: American Psychological Association.

Altman, I., & Taylor, D. A. (1973). *Social penetration.* New York: Holt.

Andersen, P. A. (1986). Consciousness, cognition, and communication. *Western Journal of Speech Communication, 50,* 87–101.

Andersen, P. A. (1991). When one cannot not communicate: A challenge to Motley's traditional communication postulates. *Communication Studies, 42,* 309–325.

Andreyeva, G. M., & Gozman, L. J. (1981). Interpersonal relationships and social context. In S. Duck & R. Gilmour (Eds.), *Personal relationships 1: Studying personal relationships,* pp. 47–66. New York: Academic Press.

Antaki, C. (1987). Performed and unperformable: A guide to accounts of relationships. In R. Burnett, P. McPhee, & D. Clarke (Eds.), *Accounting for relationships,* pp. 97–113. London: Methuen.

Ardrey, R. (1970). *The territorial imperative.* New York: Atheneum.

Argyle, M. (1969). *Social interaction.* Chicago: Aldine.

Argyle, M. (1973). The meeting of personalities. In C. D. Mortensen (Ed.), *Basic readings in communication theory,* pp. 243–263. New York: Harper & Row.

Athay, M., & Darley, J. M. (1981). Toward an interaction-centered theory of personality. In N. Cantor & J. F. Kihlstrom (Eds.), *Personality, cognition, and social interaction,* pp. 281–308. Hillsdale, NJ: Erlbaum.

425

Ayres, J. (1980). Relationship stages and sex as a factor of dwell time. *Western Journal of Speech Communication, 44,* 233–240.

Ayres, J. (1983). Strategies to maintain relationships: Their identification and perceived usage. *Communication Quarterly, 31,* 62–67.

Banks, S. P., Altendorf, D. M., Greene, J. O., & Cody, M. J. (1987). An examination of relationship disengagement: Perception, breakup strategies and outcomes. *Western Journal of Speech Communication, 51,* 19–41.

Baratz, J. C. (1970). Teaching reading in an urban negro school system. In F. Williams (Ed.), *Language and poverty.* Chicago: Markham.

Bar-Hillel, J. (1954). Indexical expressions. *Mind, 63,* 359–379.

Barnlund, D. C. (1981). Toward an ecology of communication. In C. Wilder-Mott & J. Weaklund (Eds.), *Rigor and imagination,* pp. 87–126. New York: Praeger.

Bateson, G. (1972). *Culture contact and schismogenesis: Steps to an ecology of mind.* New York: Chandler.

Bateson, G. (1978, Summer). The pattern which connects. *The CoEvolution Quarterly,* pp. 4–15.

Bateson, G. (1979). *Mind and nature: A necessary unity.* New York: Dutton.

Bavelas, J. B. (1984, May). "Researching pragmatics, seventeen years later." Paper presented at the annual meeting of International Communication Association, San Francisco.

Bavelas, J. B. (1988, February). "Notes for special session." Paper presented at the annual meeting of the Western Speech Communication Association, San Diego.

Bavelas, J. B. (1990). Behaving and communicating: A reply to Motley. *Western Journal of Speech Communication, 54,* 593–602.

Bavelas, J. B., Black, A., Chovil, N., Lemery, C. R., & Mullett, J. (1988). Form and function in motor mimicry: Topographic evidence that the primary function is communicative. *Human Communication Research, 14,* 275–299.

Bavelas, J. B., Black, A., Lemery, C. R., MacInnis, S., & Mullet, J. (1986). Experimental methods for studying "elementary motor mimicry." *Journal of Nonverbal Behavior, 10,* 102–119.

Bavelas, J. B., Black, A., Lemery, C. R., & Mullett, J. (1986). "I show how you feel." Motor mimicry as a communicator act. *Journal of Personality and Social Psychology, 50,* 322–329.

Baxter, L. A. (1979). Self disclosure as a relationship disengagement strategy: An exploratory investigation. *Human Communication Research, 5,* 215–222.

Baxter, L. A. (1982). Strategies for ending relationships: Two studies. *Western Journal of Speech Communication, 46,* 223–241.

Baxter, L. A. (1983). Relationship disengagement: An examination of the reversal hypothesis. *Western Journal of Speech Communication, 47,* 85–98.

Baxter, L. A. (1984). Trajectories of relationship disengagement. *Journal of Social and Personal Relationships, 1,* 29–48.

Baxter, L. A. (1985). Accomplishing relationship disengagement. In S. Duck & D. Perlmann (Eds.), *Understanding personal relationships,* pp. 243–265. Newbury Park, CA: Sage.

Baxter, L. A. (1987a). Cognition and communication in the relationship process. In R. Burnett, P. McGhee, & D. Clarke (Eds.), *Accounting for relationships,* pp. 192–212. London: Methuen.

Baxter, L. A. (1987b). Self disclosure and relationship disengagement. In V. J. Derlega & J. Berg (Eds.), *Self-disclosure: Theory, research and therapy*, pp. 155–174.

Baxter, L. A. (1988). A dialectical perspective on communication strategies in relationship development. In S. W. Duck, D. F. Hay, S. E. Hobfell, W. Iches, & B. Montgomery (Eds.), *Handbook of personal relationships*, pp. 257–273. New York: Wiley.

Baxter, L. A. (1990). Dialectical contradictions in relationship development. *Journal of Social and Personal relationships, 7,* 69–88.

Baxter, L. A. (1992a). Forms and functions of intimate play in personal relationships. *Human Communication Research, 18,* 336–363.

Baxter, L. A. (1992b). Root metaphors in accounts of developing romantic relationships. *Journal of Social and Personal Relationships, 9,* 253–279.

Baxter, L. A. (in press). A dialogic approach to relationship maintenance. In D. J. Canary & L. Safford (Eds.), *Communication and relationship maintenance.* New York: Academic Press.

Baxter, L. A., & Bullis, C. (1986). Turning points in developing romantic relationships. *Human Communication Research, 12,* 469–494.

Baxter, L. A., & Dindia, K. (1990). Marital partners' perceptions of marital maintenance strategies. *Journal of Social and Personal Relationships, 7,* 187–208.

Baxter, L. A., & Philpott, J. (1982). Attribution-based strategies of reinitiating and terminating relationships. *Communication Quarterly, 30,* 217–224.

Baxter, L. A., & Wilmot, W. W. (1984). "Secret tests": Social strategies for acquiring information about the state of the relationship. *Human Communication Research, 11,* 171–202.

Baxter, L. A., & Wilmot, W. (1985). Taboo topics in close relationships. *Journal of Social and Personal Relationships, 2,* 253–269.

Beach, W. A. (1983). Background understandings and the situated accomplishment of conversational telling-expansion. In K. T. Craig & K. Tracy (Eds.), *Conversational coherence: Form, structure, and strategy*, pp. 196–221. Beverly Hills: Sage.

Beach, W. A., & Dunning, D. G. (1982). Pre-indexing and conversational organization. *Quarterly Journal of Speech, 68,* 170–185.

Beattie, G. (1983). *Talk: An analysis of speech and non-verbal behavior in conversation.* Milton Keynes, England: Open University Press.

Beebe, L. (1981). Social and situational factors affecting communicative strategy of dialect code-switching. *International Journal of the Sociology of Language, 32,* 139–149.

Bell, R. A., Buerkel-Ruthfuss, N. L., & Gore, K. E. (1987). Did you bring the yarmulke for the cabbage patch kid? The idiomatic communication of young lovers. *Human Communication Research, 14,* 47–67.

Bell, R. A., & Daly, J. (1984). The affinity-seeking function of communication. *Communication Monographs, 51,* 91–115.

Bell, R. A., Daly, J. A., & Gonzalez, C. (1987). Affinity maintenance in marriage and its relationship to women's marital satisfaction. *Journal of Marriage and the Family, 49,* 445–454.

Bell, R. R. (1981). *Worlds of friendship.* Beverly Hills: Sage.

Bennis, W. (1979). Toward better interpersonal relationships. In W. Bennis, J. Van Maanen, E. H. Schein, & F. I. Steele (Eds.), *Essays in interpersonal dynamics*, pp. 182–205. Homewood, IL: Dorsey.

Berger, C. R. (1979). Beyond initial interaction: Uncertainty, understanding, and the development of interpersonal relationships. In H. Giles & R. St. Clair (Eds.), *Language and social psychology*, pp. 122–144. Oxford: Blackwell.

Berger, C. R. (1987a). Planning and scheming: Strategies for initiating relationships. In R. Burnett, P. McGhee, & D. Clarke (Eds.), *Accounting for relationships*, pp. 158–174. London: Methuen.

Berger, C. R. (1987b). Self-conception and social information processing. In J. C. McCroskey & J. A. Daley (Eds.), *Personality and interpersonal communication*, pp. 275–304. Newbury Park, CA: Sage.

Berger, C. R. (1987c). Communicating under uncertainty. In M. F. Roloff & G. R. Miller (Eds.), *Interpersonal processes: New directions in communicative research*, pp. 39–62. Newbury Park, CA: Sage.

Berger, C., & Bradac, J. (1982). *Language and social knowledge: Uncertainty in social relations*. London: Arnold.

Berger, C., & Calabrese, R. (1975). Some explorations in initial interaction and beyond: Toward a developmental theory of interpersonal communication. *Human Communication Research, 1,* 99–112.

Berger, C. R., & Kellermann, K. (1989). Personal opacity and social information gathering: Explorations in strategic communication. *Communication Research, 16,* 314–351.

Berglas, S., & Jones, E. E. (1978). Drug choice as an externalization strategy in response to noncontingent success. *Journal of Personality and Social Psychology, 36,* 405–417.

Berko, R. M., Wolvin, A. D., & Wolvin, D. R. (1981). *Communication: A social and career focus,* 2d ed. Boston: Houghton Mifflin.

Berlo, D. K. (1960). *The process of communication.* New York. Holt, Rinehart, & Winston.

Bernstein, B. (1972). Social class, language and socialization. In P. P. Giglioli (Ed.), *Language and social context: Selected readings,* pp. 157–178. New York: Penguin.

Berscheid, E., & Walster, E. H. (1974). Physical attractiveness. In L. Berkowitz (Ed.), *Advances in experimental social psychology,* Vol. 7, pp. 158–215. New York: Academic Press.

Bettini, L. M., & Nussbaum, J. F. (1991, November). "Life-span developmental communication: Toward a theoretical perspective." Paper presented at the annual Speech Communication Association convention, Atlanta.

Bettini, L., Patterson, B. R., Nussbaum, J., & Norton, M. L. (1991, November). "The meaning and measurement of friendship across the life-span." Paper presented at the annual Speech Communication Association convention, Atlanta.

Birdwhistell, R. (1959). Contributions of linguistic-kinesic studies to understanding of schizophrenia. In A. Auerback (Ed.), *Schizophrenia: An integrated approach,* pp. 99–123. New York: Ronald Press.

Birdwhistell, R. L. (1970). *Kinesics and context: Essays on body motion communication.* Philadelphia: University of Pennsylvania Press.

Blumer, H. (1969). *Symbolic interactionism: Perspective and method.* Englewood Cliffs, NJ: Prentice-Hall.

Bochner, A. P. (1982). On the efficacy of openness in close relationships. In M. Burgoon (Ed.), *Communication yearbook 5,* pp. 109–124. New Brunswick, NJ: Transaction.

Bochner, A. P. (1984). The functions of human communication in interpersonal bonding. In L. L. Arnold & J. W. Bowers (Eds.), *Handbook of rhetorical and communication theory*, pp. 544–621. Boston: Allyn & Bacon.

Bochner, A. P. (1991). On the paradigm that would not die. In J. A. Andersen (Ed.), *Communication yearbook 14*, pp. 484–491. Newbury Park, CA: Sage.

Bolton, C. D. (1961). Mate selection as the development of a relationship. *Marriage and Family Living, 23*, 234–240.

Bowers, J. W., Metts, S. M., & Duncanson, W. T. (1985). Emotion and interpersonal communication. In M. L. Knapp & G. R. Miller (Eds.), *Handbook of interpersonal communication*, pp. 500–550. Beverly Hills: Sage.

Bradac, J. J. (1983). The language of lovers, flovers, and friends: Communicating in personal and social relationships. *Journal of Language and Social Psychology, 2*, 141–162.

Brown, P., & Levinson, S. (1978). Universals in language usage. Politeness phenomena. In E. Goody (Ed.), *Questions and politeness.* Cambridge: Cambridge University Press.

Brown, P., & Levinson, S. (1987). *Politeness: Some universals in language usage.* London: Cambridge University Press.

Buhrke, R. A., & Fuqua, D. R. (1987). Sex differences in same and cross-sex supportive relationships. *Sex Roles, 17*, 339–352.

Burgess, R. L. (1981). Relationships in marriage and the family. In S. Duck & R. Gilmour (Eds.), *Personal relationships 1: Studying personal relationships*, pp. 179–196. New York: Academic Press.

Burgoon, J. K. (1985). Nonverbal signals. In M. L. Knapp & G. R. Miller (Eds.), *Handbook of interpersonal communication*, pp. 344–390. Beverly Hills: Sage.

Burgoon, J. K., & Hale, J. L. (1984). The fundamental topoi of relational communication. *Communication Monographs, 51*, 193–214.

Burgoon, J. K., & Koper, R. J. (1984). Nonverbal and relational communication with reticence. *Human Communication Research, 10*, 601–626.

Burgoon, J. K., & Saine, J. (1978). *The unspoken dialogue: An introduction to nonverbal communication.* Boston: Houghton-Mifflin.

Byers, P. (1977). A personal view of nonverbal communication. *Theory into Practice, 16*, 134–140.

Cahn, D. D. (1992). *Conflict in intimate relationships.* New York: Guilford Press.

Camden, C., Motley, M. T., & Wilson, A. (1984). White lies in interpersonal communication: A taxonomy and preliminary investigation of social motivations. *Western Journal of Speech Communication, 48*, 309–325.

Canary, D. J., & Cupach, W. R. (1988). Relational and episodic characteristics associated with conflict tactics. *Journal of Social and Personal Relationships, 5*, 305–325.

Canary, D. J., & Spitzberg, B. H. (1989). A model of competence perceptions of conflict strategies. *Human Communication Research, 15*, 630–649.

Canary, D. J., & Stafford, L. (1992). Relational maintenance strategies and equity in marriage. *Communication Monographs, 59*, 243–267.

Canary, D. J., & Stafford, L. (1993). Preservation of relational characteristics: Maintenance strategies, equity, and laws of control. In P. J. Kalbfleisch (Ed.), *Interpersonal communication: Evolving interpersonal relationships*, pp. 237–260. New York: Erlbaum.

Cappella, J. N., & Palmer, M. T. (1990). Attitude similarity, relational history, and attraction: The mediating effects of kinesic and vocal behaviors. *Communication Monographs, 57,* 161–183.

Cappella, J. N., & Palmer, M. T. (1992). The effect of partner's conversation on the association between similarity and attraction. *Communication Monographs, 59,* 180–189.

Capra, F. (1982). *The turning point.* New York: Simon and Schuster.

Chelune, G. J. (Ed.). (1979). *Self-disclosure.* San Francisco: Jossey-Bass.

Chomsky, N. (1965). *Aspects of the theory of syntax.* Cambridge, MA: MIT Press.

Chovil, N. (1991). "Social determinants of facial displays." *Journal of Nonverbal Behavior, 15,* 141–154.

Cissna, K. N. L., & Sieburg, L. (1981). Patterns of interactional confirmation and disconfirmation. In C. Wilder-Mott & J. H. Weakland (Eds.), *Rigor & imagination: Essays from the legacy of Gregory Bateson,* pp. 253–282. New York: Praeger.

Clevenger, T. (1991). Can one not communicate? A conflict of models. *Communication Studies, 42,* 340–353.

Cline, R. J. (1983). The acquaintance process as relational communication. In R. Bostrom (Ed.), *Communication Yearbook 7,* pp. 396–413. Beverly Hills: Sage.

Cochran, S. D., & Mayes, U. M. (1990). Sex, lies and HIV. *New England Journal of Medicine, 322,* 774–775.

Cody, M. J. (1982). A typology of disengagement strategies and an examination of the role intimacy, reactions to inequity and relational problems play in strategy selection. *Communication Monographs, 49,* 148–170.

Cohen, J. (1969). *Sensation and perception. I. Vision.* Chicago: Rand McNally.

Collins, O., & Collins, J. M. (1973). *Interaction and social structure.* The Hague: Mouton.

Colman, A. D., & Colman, L. L. (1975). *Love and ecstasy.* New York: Seabury.

Condon, W. S. (1980). The relation of interactional synchrony to cognitive and emotional processes. In M. R. Key (Ed.), *The relationship of verbal and nonverbal communication,* pp. 49–65. The Hague: Mouton.

Condon, W. S., & Ogston, W. D. (1966). Sound film analysis of normal and pathological behavior patterns. *Journal of Nervous and Mental Disease, 143,* 338–347.

Conville, R. L. (1983). Second-order development in interpersonal communication. *Human Communication Research, 9,* 195–207.

Conville, R. L. (1988). Relational transitions: An inquiry into their structure and function. *Journal of Social and Personal Relationships, 5,* 423–437.

Cooley, C. H. (1922). *Human nature and the social order,* rev. ed. New York: Scribners.

Coupland, N. (1985). "Hark, hark the lark": Social motivations for phonological style shifting. *Language and Communication, 5,* 153–171.

Crable, R. E. (1981). *One to another: A guidebook for interpersonal communication.* New York: Harper & Row.

Cronbach, L. J. (1955). Processes affecting scores on "understanding of other," and assumed similarity. *Psychological Bulletin, 52,* 177–193.

Cunningham, J. D., & Antill, J. K. (1981). Love in developing romantic relationships. In S. Duck & R. Gilmour (Eds.), *Personal relationships 2: Developing personal relationships,* pp. 27–51. New York: Academic Press.

Cupach, W. R., & Metts, S. (1986). Accounts of relational dissolution: A comparison of marital and non-marital relationships. *Communication Monographs, 53,* 311–334.

Dance, F. E. X. (1970). A helical model of communication. In K. K. Sereno & C. D. Mortensen (Eds.), *Foundations of communication theory,* pp. 103–107. New York: Harper & Row.

Davis, M. S. (1973). *Intimate relations.* New York: Free Press.

Davis, M. (Ed.). (1982). *Interaction rhythms.* New York: Human Science Press.

Davis, K. E., & Todd, M. (1982). Friendship and love relations. *Advances in Descriptive Psychology, 2,* 79–122.

Denzin, N. K. (1970). Rules of conduct and the study of deviant behavior. In G. J. McCall, M. M. McCall, N. K. Denzin, G. D. Suttles, & S. B. Kurth (Eds.), *Social relationships,* pp. 62–94. Chicago: Aldine.

Diez, M. E. (1986). Negotiation competence: A conceptualization of the rules of negotiation interaction. In D. G. Ellis & W. A. Donohue (Eds.), *Contemporary issues in language and discourse processes,* pp. 223–237. Hillsdale, NJ: Erlbaum.

Dindia, K., & Baxter, L. A. (1987). Strategies for maintaining and repairing marital relationships. *Journal of Social and Personal Relationships, 4,* 143–158.

Donohue, W. A. (1981). Development of a model of rule use in negotiation interaction. *Communication Monographs, 48,* 106–120.

Donohue, W. A., Diez, M. E., & Hamilton, M. (1984). An expanded model of communication rule use in negotiation. *Human Communication Research, 10,* 403–425.

Douglas, J. D., & Atwell, F. C. (1988). *Love, intimacy, and sex.* Newbury Park, CA: Sage.

Douglas, W. (1984). Initial interaction scripts: When knowing is behaving. *Human Communication Research, 11,* 203–220.

Douglas, W. (1987). Affinity-testing in initial interactions. *Journal of Social and Personal Relationships, 4,* 3–15.

Douglas, W. (1991). Expectations about initial interaction: An examination of the effects of global uncertainty. *Human Communication Research, 17,* 355–384.

Drake, G. (1980). The social role of slang. In H. Giles, W. P. Relansar, & P. M. Smith (Eds.), *Language: Social psychological perspectives,* pp. 63–70. Oxford: Pergamon.

Duck, S. W. (1973). *Personal relationships and personal constructs: A study of friendship formation.* New York: Wiley.

Duck, S. W. (1977). *The study of acquaintance.* Westmead, England: Saxon House.

Duck, S. W. (1982). A topography of relationship disengagement and dissolution. In S. Duck (Ed.), *Personal relationships 4: Dissolving personal relationships,* pp. 1–30. New York: Academic Press.

Duck, S. (1986). *Human relationships: An introduction to social psychology.* London: Sage.

Duck, S. (1987). How to lose friends without influencing people. In M. E. Roloff & G. R. Miller (Eds.), *Interpersonal processes: New directions in communication research,* pp. 278–298. Newbury Park, CA: Sage.

Duck, S. W. (1991). *Understanding relationships.* New York: Guilford Press.

Duck, S. W. (in press). Steady as (s)he goes: Relational maintenance as a shared meaning system. In D. J. Canary & L. Stafford (Eds.), *Communication and relationship maintenance.* New York: Academic Press.

Duck, S., & Barnes, M. K. (1992). Disagreeing about agreement: Reconciling differences about similarity. *Communication Monographs, 59,* 199–208.

Duck, S. W., & Miell, D. E. (1984). Towards an understanding of relationship development and breakdown. In H. Tajfel, C. Fraser, & J. Jasper (Eds.), *The social dimension: European perspectives on social psychology,* pp. 228–249. Cambridge: Cambridge University Press.

Duck, S. W., & Miell, D. E. (1986). Charting the development of personal relationships. In R. Gilmour & S. W. Duck (Eds.), *The emerging field of personal relationships,* pp. 133–144. Hillsdale, NJ: Erlbaum.

Duck, S., & Pond, K. (1989). Friends, romans, countrymen, lend me your retrospections. In C. Hendrick (Ed.), *Close relationships,* pp. 17–38. Newbury Park, CA: Sage.

Duck, S., Rutt, D. J., Hurst, M. H., & Strejc, H. (1991). Some evident truths about conversations in everyday relationships: All communications are not created equal. *Human Communication Research, 18,* 228–267.

Duck, S. W. & Sants, H. K. A. (1983). On the origin of the specious: Are personal relationships really interpersonal states? *Journal of Social and Clinical Psychology, 1,* 27–41.

Duck, S., & Wright, P. (1992, February). "Men's and women's communication in friendship: Are there really sex differences?" Paper presented at the annual convention of the Western Speech Communication Association, Boise, ID.

Duncan, H. D. (1967). The search for a social theory of communication in American sociology. In F. E. X. Dance (Ed.), *Human communication theory,* pp. 236–263. New York: Holt, Rinehart and Winston.

Duval, S., & Wicklund, R. A. (1972). *A theory of objective self-awareness.* New York: Academic Press.

Edwards, J. R. (1985). *Language, society and identity.* Oxford: Blackwell.

Edwards, J. R., & Giles, H. (1984). Applications of the social psychology of language: Socio-linguistics and education. In P. Trudgill (Ed.), *Applied sociolinguistics,* pp. 119–158. London: Academic Press.

Eiser, J. R. (1983). From attributions to behavior. In M. Hewstane (Ed.), *Attribution theory: Social and functional extensions,* pp. 160–169. Oxford: Blackwell.

Ellis, D. G. (1992a). *From language to communication.* Hillsdale, NJ: Erlbaum.

Ellis, D. G. (1992b). Syntactic and pragmatic codes in communication. *Communication Theory, 2,* 1–23.

Ellis, D. G., & Hamilton, M. (1985). Syntactic and pragmatic code usage in interpersonal communication. *Communication Monographs, 52,* 264–279.

Emmert, P., & Donaghy, W. C. (1981). *Human communication: Elements and contexts.* Reading, MA: Addison-Wesley.

Faules, D. K., & Alexander, D. C. (1978). *Communication and social behavior: A symbolic interaction perspective.* Reading, MA: Addison-Wesley.

Feezel, J. D., & Shepherd, P. E. (1987). Cross-generational coping with interpersonal relationship loss. *Western Journal of Speech Communication, 51,* 317–327.

Felmlee, D., Sprecher, S., & Bussin, E. (1990). The dissolution of intimate relationships: A hazard model. *Social Psychology Quarterly, 53,* 13–30.

Festinger, L., Schachter, S., & Back, K. (1950). *Social pressures in informal groups: A study of human factors in housing.* New York: Harper & Row.

Fincham, F. D. (1983). Clinical applications of attribution theory: Problems and prospects. In M. Hewston (Ed.), *Attribution theory: Social and functional extensions,* pp. 187–203. Oxford: Blackwell.

Fisher, B. A. (1978). *Perspectives on human communication.* New York: Macmillan.

Fisher, B. A. (1981). Implications of the "interactional view" for communication theory. In C. Wilder-Mott & J. H. Weakland (Eds.), *Rigor and imagination,* pp. 195–209. New York: Praeger.

Fisher, B. A. (1983). Differential effects of sexual composition and interactional context on interaction patterns in dyads. *Human Communication Research, 9,* 225–238.

Fisher, B. A. (1985, August). Pragmatics of meaning. In J. R. Cox, M. O. Sillars, & G. B. Walker (Eds.). *Argument and social practice: Proceedings of the Fourth SCA/ACA Conference on Argumentation,* pp. 511–522. Annandale, VA: Speech Communication Association.

Fisher, B. A., & Drecksel, G. L. (1983). A cyclical model of developing relationships: A study of relational control interaction. *Communication Monographs, 50,* 66–78.

Fiske, S. T. (1980). Attention and weight in person perception: The impact of negative and extreme behavior. *Journal of Personality and Social Psychology, 38,* 889–908.

Fitzpatrick, M. A. (1988). *Between husbands and wives.* Beverly Hills: Sage.

Fitzpatrick, M. A., & Winke, J. (1979). You always hurt the one you love: Strategies and tactics in interpersonal conflict. *Communication Quarterly, 38,* 618–628.

Frazier, P. A., & Cook, S. W. (1993). Correlates of distress following heterosexual relationship dissolution. *Journal of Social and Personal Relationships, 10,* 55–67.

Gamble, T., & Gamble, M. (1984). *Communication works.* New York: Random House.

Garfinkel, H. (1967). *Studies in ethnomethodology.* Englewood Cliffs, NJ: Prentice-Hall.

Geertz, C. (1975). On the nature of anthropological understanding. *American Scientist, 63,* 47–53.

Gelman, R., & Spelke, E. (1981). The development of thoughts about animate and inanimate objects: Implications for research on social cognition. In J. Flavell & L. Ross (Eds.), *Social cognitive development.* Cambridge: Cambridge University Press.

Gergen, K. J. (1968). Personal consistency and the presentation of self. In C. Gordon & K. J. Gergen (Eds.), *The self in social interaction, Vol. 1: Classic and contemporary perspectives,* pp. 299–308. New York: Wiley.

Giles, H. (1973). Accent mobility: A model and some data. *Anthological Linguistics, 15,* 87–105.

Giles, H., Bourhis, R. Y., & Taylor, D. M. (1977). Towards a theory of language in ethnic group relations. In H. Giles (Ed.), *Language, ethnicity and intergroup relations,* pp. 307–348. London: Academic Press.

Giles, H., & Johnson, P. (1986). Perceived threat, ethnic commitment, and inter-ethnic language behavior. In Y. Y. Kim (Ed.), *Current studies in interethnic communication,* pp. 91–116. Newbury Park, CA: Sage.

Giles, H., Mulac, A., Bradac, J. J., & Johnson, P. (1987). Speech accommodation theory: The first decade and beyond. In M. L. McLaughlin (Ed.), *Communication yearbook 10,* pp. 13–48. Newbury Park, CA: Sage.

Giles, H., Scherer, K. R., & Taylor, D. M. (1979). Speech markers in social interaction. In K. R. Scherer & H. Giles (Eds.), *Social markers in speech*, pp. 343–381. Cambridge: Cambridge University Press.

Giles, H., & Wiemann, J. M. (1987). Language, social comparison, and power. In C. Berger & S. H. Chaffee (Eds.), *Handbook of communication science*, pp. 350–384. Newbury Park: Sage.

Glaser, L. E. (1992, May 17). Photo can tell "the ugly truth" beyond words. *Fresno Bee*, Fresno, CA, p. B5.

Glenn, P. J., & Knapp, M. L. (1987). The interactive framing of play in adult conversations. *Communication Quarterly, 35*, 48–66.

Goffman, E. (1959). *The presentation of self in everyday life*. Garden City, NY: Doubleday.

Goffman, E. (1963). *Behavior in public places: Notes on the social organization of gatherings*. New York: Free Press.

Goffman, E. (1971). *Relations in public: Microstudies of the public order*. New York: Basic Books.

Goss, B., & O'Hair, D. (1988). *Communicating in interpersonal relationships*. New York: Macmillan.

Gottman, J. M. (1982). Emotional responsiveness in marital conversations. *Journal of Communication, 32*, 108–120.

Gouldner, A. W. (1960). The norm of reciprocity: A preliminary statement. *American Sociological Review, 25*, 161–171.

Graziano, W. G., & Musser, L. M. (1982). The joining and the parting of the ways. In S. Duck (Ed.), *Personal relationships 4: Dissolving personal relationships*, pp. 75–106. New York: Academic Press.

Greenberg, E. F., & Nay, W. R. (1982). The intergenerational transmission of marital instability reconsidered. *Journal of Marriage and the Family, 44*, 335–347.

Gudykunst, W. B. (1987). Cross-cultural comparisons. In C. R. Berger & S. H. Chaffee (Eds.), *Handbook of communication science*, pp. 847–889. Newbury Park, CA: Sage.

Gudykunst, W. B., & Kim, Y. (1984). *Communicating with strangers*. New York: Random House.

Gudykunst, W., & Nishida, T. (1984). Individual and cultural influence on uncertainty reduction. *Communication Monographs, 51*, 23–36.

Gudykunst, W. B., Ting-Toomey, S., & Chua, E. (1988). *Culture and interpersonal communication*. Newbury Park, CA: Sage.

Guerrero, L. K., & Andersen, P. A. (1991). The waxing and waning of relational intimacy: Touch as a function of relational stage, gender and touch avoidance. *Journal of Social and Personal Relationships, 8*, 147–165.

Gumperz, J., & Hymes, D. (Eds.) (1972). *Directions in sociolinguistics*. New York: Holt, Rinehart, & Winston.

Hall, A. D., & Fagen, R. E. (1968). Definition of a system. In W. Buckley (Ed.), *Modern systems research for the behavioral scientist*, pp. 81–92. Chicago: Aldine.

Hall, E. T. (1966). *The hidden dimension*. New York: Doubleday.

Hall, J. A., & Taylor, S. E. (1976). When love is blind: Maintaining idealized images of one's spouse. *Human Relations, 29*, 751–762.

Hanson, N. R. (1967). Observation and interpretation. In S. Morganbesser (Ed.), *Philosophy of today's science*, pp. 89–99. New York: Basic Books.

Harvey, J. H., Agostinelli, A.L., & Weber, A. L. (1989). Account-making and the formation of expectations about close relationships. In C. Hendrick (Ed.), *Close relationships*, pp. 39–62. Newbury Park, CA: Sage.

Harvey, J. H., Weber, W. L., Yarkin, K. L., & Stewart, B. E. (1982). In S. W. Duck (Ed.), *Personal relationships 4: Dissolving personal relationships*, pp. 107–126. New York: Academic Press.

Hatfield, E. (1984). The dangers of intimacy. In V. J. Derlega (Ed.), *Communication, intimacy and close relationships*, pp. 207–220. Orlando, FL: Academic Press.

Hays, R. B. (1984). The development and maintenance of friendship. *Journal of Social and Personal Relationships, 1,* 75–98.

Hays, R. B. (1989). The day-to-day functioning of close versus casual friendships. *Journal of Social and Personal Relationships, 6,* 21–37.

Hayward, G. D. (1977). "An overview of psychological concepts of 'home'." Paper presented to the annual conference of the Environmental Design Research Association, Urbana, IL.

Helgeson, V. S., Shaver, P., & Dyer, M. (1987). Prototypes of intimacy and distance in same-sex and opposite sex relationships. *Journal of Social and Personal Relationships, 4,* 195–233.

Heritage, J. (1984). *Garfinkel and ethnomethodology.* Cambridge: Polity Press.

Heshka, S., & Nelson, Y. (1974). Interpersonal speaking distance as a function of age, sex, and relationship. *Sociometry, 35,* 92–104.

Hewitt, J., & Stokes, R. (1975). Disclaimers. *American Sociological Review, 40,* 1–11.

Hewstone, M. (1983). Attribution theory and common-sense explanations: An introductory overview. In M. Houston (Ed.), *Attribution theory: Social and functional extensions*, pp. 1–26. Oxford: Blackwell.

Hickson, J. (1985). Psychological research on empathy: In search of an elusive phenomenon. *Psychological Reports, 57,* 91–94.

Hill, C. T., Rubin, Z., & Peplau, L. A. (1976). Breakups before marriage: The end of 103 affairs. *Journal of Social Issues, 32,* 147–168.

Hinde, R. A. (1979). *Towards understanding relationships.* London: Academic Press.

Hoelter, J. W. (1985). A structural theory of personal consistency. *Social Psychology Quarterly, 48,* 118–129.

Hofstede, G., & Bond, M. (1984). Hofstede's culture dimensions: An independent validation using Rokeach's value survey. *Journal of Cross-Cultural Psychology, 15,* 417–433.

Homans, G. (1961). *Social behavior: Its elementary forms.* New York: Harcourt Brace Jovanovich.

Honey, P. (1976). *Face to face: A practical guide to interactive skills.* London: Institute of Personnel Management.

Hopper, R. (1981). The taken-for-granted. *Human Communication Research, 12,* 195–211.

Hopper, R., Knapp, M., & Scott, L. (1981). Couples' personal idioms: Exploring intimate talk. *Journal of Communication, 31*(1), 23–33.

Hsu, F. (1985). The self in cross-cultural perspective. In A. Marsella, G. Devos, & F. Hsu (Eds.), *Culture and self: Asian and western perspectives.* New York: Tavistock.

Ichheiser, F. (1970). *Appearances and realities: Misunderstanding in human relations.* San Francisco: Jossey-Bass.

Infante, D. A., Rancer, A. S., & Womak, D. F. (1990). *Building communication theory.* Prospect Heights, IL: Waveland Press.

Jantsch, E. (1980). *The self-organizing universe.* New York: Pergamon.

Johnson, F. (1985). The western concept of self. In A. Marsella, G. Devos, & F. Hsu (Eds.), *Culture and self: Asian and western perspectives,* pp. 91–138. New York: Tavistock.

Johnson, G. D., Palileo, G. J., & Gray, N. B. (1992). "Date rape" on a southern campus: Reports from 1991. *Sociology and Social Research, 76,* 37–43.

Jones, E. E., & Nisbett, R. E. (1971). *The actor and the observer: Divergent perceptions of the causes of behavior.* Morristown, NJ: General Learning Press.

Jones, S. E., & Yarbrough, A. E. (1985). A naturalistic study of the meanings of touch. *Communication Monographs, 52,* 19–56.

Joos, M. (1967). *The five clocks,* 3d ed. New York: Harcourt, Brace & World.

Jourard, S. (1964). *The transparent self.* New York: Van Nostrand.

Kalbfleisch, P. J. (1993). Public portrayals of enduring friendships. In P. J. Kalbfleisch (Ed.), *Interpersonal communication: Evolving interpersonal relationships,* pp. 198–212. Hillsdale, NJ: Erlbaum.

Kellermann, K. (1989). The negativity effect in interaction: It's all in your point of view. *Human Communication Research, 15,* 147–183.

Kellermann, K. (1992). Communication: Inherently strategic and primarily automatic. *Communication Monographs, 59,* 288–300.

Kellermann, K., & Reynolds, R. (1990). When ignorance is bliss: The role of motivation to reduce uncertainty in uncertainty reduction theory. *Human Communication Research, 17,* 5–73.

Kelley, H. H. (1979). *Personal relationships: Their structures and processes.* Hillsdale, NJ: Erlbaum.

Kelley, H. H., & Thibaut, J. W. (1978). *Interpersonal relations: A theory of interdependence.* New York: Wiley.

Kemper, T. D., & Bologh, R. W. (1981). What do you get when you fall in love? Some health status effects. *Sociology of Health and Illness, 3,* 72–88.

King, J. (1983). Attribution theory and the health belief model. In M. Hewstone (Ed.), *Attribution theory: Social and functional extensions,* pp. 170–184. Oxford: Blackwell.

King, R. G. (1979). *Fundamentals of human communication.* New York: Macmillan.

Kitchens, J. T., Herron, T. P., & Behnke, R. R. (1976). "Effects of visual environmental aesthetics on interpersonal attraction." Paper presented to the annual meeting of the Southern Speech Communication Association, San Antonio, TX.

Knapp, M. L. (1978). *Nonverbal communication in human interaction,* 2d ed. New York: Holt, Rinehart, & Winston.

Knapp, M. L. (1980). *Essentials of nonverbal communication.* New York: Holt, Rinehart & Winston.

Knapp, M. L. (1984). *Interpersonal communication and human relationships.* Boston: Allyn & Bacon.

Knapp, M. L., & Vangelisti, A. L. (1992). *Interpersonal communication and human relationships,* 2d ed. Boston: Allyn & Bacon.

Koestler, A. (1978). *Janus: A summing up.* New York: Random House.

Kolligian, J., Jr. (1990). Perceived fraudulence as a dimension of perceived incompetence. In R. J. Sternberg & J. Kolligian (Eds.), *Competence considered*, pp. 261–285. New Haven, CT: Yale University Press.

Koury, R. (1993, February 20). The "feminist" knows about role reversal. The *Fresno Bee*, Fresno, CA, p. B1.

Kreckel, M. (1981). *Communicative acts and shared knowledge in natural discourse*. New York: Academic Press.

Krivonos, P. D., & Knapp, M. L. (1975). Initiating communication: What do you say when you say hello? *Central States Speech Journal, 26,* 115–125.

Kuhn, M., & McPartland, T. S. (1954). An empirical investigation of self-attitudes. *American Sociological Review, 19,* 58–76.

Kuiper, N. A., & Derry, P. A. (1981). The self as a cognitive prototype: An application to person perception and depression. In N. C. Cantor & J. F. Kihlstrom (Eds.), *Personality, cognition, and social interaction,* pp. 215–232. Hillsdale, NJ: Erlbaum.

Kurdek, L. A. (1991). The dissolution of gay and lesbian couples. *Journal of Social and Personal Relationships, 8,* 265–278.

Kurth, S. B. (1970). Friendships and friendly relations. In G. J. McCall, M. M. McCall, N. K. Denzin, G. D. Suttles, & S. B. Kurth (Eds.), *Social relationships,* pp. 136–170. Chicago: Aldine.

Labov, W. (1966). *The social stratification of English in New York City.* Washington: Center for Applied Linguistics.

Labov, W. (1972). The logic of nonstandard English. In P. P. Giglioli (Ed.), *Language and social context: Selected readings,* pp. 179–215. New York: Penguin.

LaGaipa, J. J. (1977). Interpersonal attraction and social exchange. In S. Duck (Ed.), *Theory and practice in interpersonal attraction,* pp. 129–164. London: Academic Press.

LaGaipa, J. J. (1981). A systems approach to personal relationships. In S. W. Duck & R. Gilmour (Eds.), *Personal relationships 4: Dissolving personal relationships,* pp. 67–89. New York: Academic Press.

LaGaipa, J. J. (1982). Rules and rituals in disengaging from relationships. In S. W. Duck (Ed.), *Personal relationships 4: Dissolving personal relationships,* pp. 189–121. New York: Academic Press.

Laing, R. D. (1971). *Self and others.* New York: Pantheon Books.

Landman, J., & Manis, M. (1983). Social cognition: Some historical and theoretical perspectives. In L. Berkowitz (Ed.), *Advances in experimental social psychology,* Vol. 16, pp. 49–123. New York: Academic Press.

Langer, E. J. (1989). *Mindfulness.* Reading, MA: Addison-Wesley.

Lauer, R. H., & Handel, W. H. (1977). *Social psychology: The theory and application of symbolic interactionsism.* Boston: Houghton Mifflin.

Laver, J. (1981). Linguistic routines and politeness in greeting and parting. In F. Coulmas (Ed.), *Conversational routine,* pp. 289–318. The Hague: Mouton.

Leary, T. (1955). The theory and measurement methodology of interpersonal communication. *Psychiatry, 18,* 147–161.

Leeds-Hurwitz, W. (1992). *Communication in everyday life: A social interpretation,* 3d ed. Norwood, NJ: Ablex.

Leiter, K. (1980). *A primer on ethnomethodology.* New York: Oxford.

Levine, T. R., & McCornack, S. A. (1991). The dark side of trust: Conceptualizing and measuring types of communicative suspicion. *Communication Quarterly, 39,* 367–372.

Lindbergh, A. M. (1975). *Gift from the sea*, 2d ed. New York: Vintage Books.

Littlejohn, S. W. (1992). *Theories of human communication*, 4th ed. Belmont, CA: Wadsworth.

Lloyd, S. A., & Cate, R. M. (1985). The developmental course of conflict in dissolution of premarital relationships. *Journal of Social and Personal Relationships, 2,* 179–194.

Luft, J. (1969). *Of human interaction: The Johari window*. Palo Alto, CA: Mayfield.

Luft, J. (1970). *Group process: An introduction to group dynamics*. Palo Alto, CA: National Press.

Mangam, I. L. (1981). Relationships at work: A matter of tension and tolerance. In S. Duck & R. Gilmour (Eds.), *Personal relationships 1: Studying personal relationships,* pp. 197–214. New York: Academic Press.

Markus, H. (1977). Self-schemata and processing information about the self. *Journal of Personality and Social Psychology, 35,* 63–78.

Markus, H., & Smith, J. (1981). The influence of self-schemata on the perception of others. In N. C. Cantor & J. F. Kihlstrom (Eds.), *Personality, cognition, and social interaction,* pp. 233–262. Hillsdale, NJ: Erlbaum.

Marston, P. J., Hecht, M. L., & Robers, T. (1987). "True love ways": The subjective experience and communication of romantic love. *Journal of Social and Personal Relationships, 4,* 387–407.

Marwell, G., & Schmitt, D. R. (1967). Dimensions of compliance-gaining behavior: An empirical analysis. *Sociometry, 30,* 350–364.

Maslow, A. H., & Mintz, N. L. (1956). Effects of esthetic surroundings: I. Initial effects of three esthetic conditions upon perceiving "energy" and "well-being" in faces. *Journal of Psychology, 41,* 247–254.

McCall, G. J. (1987). The self-concept and interpersonal communication. In M. E. Roloff & G. R. Miller (Eds.), *Interpersonal processes: New directions in communication research,* pp. 63–76. Newbury Park, CA: Sage.

McCall, G. J. (1988). The organizational life cycle of relationships. In S. W. Duck, D. F. Hay, S. E. Hobfell, W. Iches, & B. Montgomery (Eds.), *A handbook of personal relationships,* pp. 467–484. New York: Wiley.

McCall, G. J., & Simmons, J. L. (1978). *Identities and interactions: An examination of human associations in everyday life,* rev. ed. New York: Free Press.

McCorkle, S., & Mills, J. L. (1992). Rowboat in a hurricane: Metaphors of interpersonal conflict management. *Communication Reports, 5,* 57–66.

McCroskey, J. C., Richmond, V. P., & Daly, J. A. (1975). The development of a measure of perceived homophily in interpersonal communication. *Human Communication Research, 1,* 323–332.

Mclaughlin, M. L., Cody, M. J., & Rosenstein, N. E. (1983). Account sequences in conversations between strangers. *Communication Monographs, 50,* 102–125.

Mead, G. H. (1913). The social self. *Journal of Philosophy, Psychology and Scientific Methods, 10,* 374–380.

Mead, G. H. (1934). *Mind, self and society from the standpoint of a social behaviorist*. Chicago: University of Chicago Press.

Mehrabian, A. (1971). *Silent messages: Implicit communication of emotion and attitudes*. Belmont, CA: Wadsworth.

Mehrabian, A. (1981). *Silent messages: Implicit communication of emotion and attitudes,* 2d ed. Belmont, CA: Wadsworth.

Mercer, N., Mercer, E., & Mears, R. (1979). Linguistic and cultural affiliation. In H. Giles & B. Saint-Jacques (Eds.), *Language and ethnic relations,* pp. 15–26. Oxford: Pergamon.

Merton, R. K. (1948). The self-fulfilling prophecy. *Anitoch Review, 8,* 193–210.

Miceli, M. (1992). How to make someone feel guilty: Strategies of guilt advancement and their goals. *Journal of the Theory of Social Behavior, 22,* 81–104.

Miell, D. (1987). Remembering relationship development: Constructing a context for interaction. In R. Burnett, P. McGhee, & P. Clarke (Eds.), *Accounting for relationships: Explanation, representation and knowledge,* pp. 60–73. London: Methuen.

Miell, D., & Duck, S. (1986). Strategies in developing friendships. In V. J. Derlega, & B. A. Winstead (Eds.), *Friendships and social interaction,* pp. 129–143. New York: Springer-Verlag.

Millar, F. E., & Rogers, L. E. (1976). A relational approach to interpersonal communication. In G. R. Miller (Ed.), *Explorations in interpersonal communication,* pp. 87–103. Beverly Hills: Sage.

Millar, F. E., & Rogers, L. E. (1987). Relational dimensions of interpersonal dynamics. In M. E. Roloff and G. R. Miller (Eds.), *Interpersonal processes: New directions in communication research,* pp. 117–139. Newbury Park, CA: Sage.

Millar, F. E., Rogers, L. E., & Bavelas, J. B. (1984). Identifying patterns of verbal conflict in interpersonal dynamics. *Western Journal of Speech Communication, 48,* 231–246.

Miller, G. A. (1956). The magical number seven, plus or minus two: Some limits on our capacity for processing information. *Psychological Review, 63,* 81–97.

Miller, G., Boster, F., Roloff, M., & Siebold, D. (1977). Compliance-gaining message strategies: A typology and some findings concerning effects of situational differences. *Communication Monographs, 44,* 37–51.

Miller, G., Boster, F., Roloff, M., & Siebold, D. (1987). MBRS rekindled: Some thoughts on compliance gaining in interpersonal settings. In M. E. Roloff & G. R. Miller (Eds.), *Interpersonal processes: New directions in communication research,* pp. 89–116. Newbury Park, CA: Sage.

Milroy, L. (1980). *Language and social networks.* Oxford: Blackwell.

Mintz, N. L. (1956). Effects of esthetic surroundings: I. Prolonged and repeated experience in a "beautiful" and "ugly" room. *Journal of Psychology, 41,* 459–466.

Mischel, W. (1973). Toward a cognitive social learning reconceptualization of personality. *Psychological Review, 80,* 252–283.

Mishler, E. G. (1979). Meaning in context: Is there any other kind? *Harvard Educational Review, 49,* 1–19.

Montgomery, B. M. (1984a). Behavioral characteristics predicting self and peer perceptions of open communication. *Communication Quarterly, 32,* 233–242.

Montgomery, B. M. (1984b). Individual differences and relational interdependencies in social interaction. *Human Communication Research, 11,* 33–60.

Montgomery, B. M. (1988). Quality communication in personal relationships. In S. Duck, D. Hay, S. Hobfoll, W. Ickes, & B. Montgomery (Eds.), *A handbook of personal relationships,* pp. 343–362. New York: Wiley.

Morris, C. (1946). *Signs, language and behavior.* Englewood Cliffs, NJ: Prentice-Hall.

Motley, M. T. (1990). On whether one can (not) not communicate: An examination via traditional communication postulates. *Western Journal of Speech Communication, 54,* 1–20.

Newman, H. (1981). Communication within ongoing intimate relationships: An attributional perspective. *Personality and Social Psychological Bulletin, 7,* 59–70.

Nofsinger, R. (1976). On answering questions indirectly: Some rules in the grammar of doing conversation. *Human Communication Research, 2,* 172–181.

Nofsinger, R. E. (1989). Collaborating on context. Invoking alluded-to shared knowledge. *Western Journal of Speech Communication, 53,* 227–241.

Nussbaum, J. F. (1989). Life-span communication: An introduction. In J. F. Nussbaum (Ed.), *Life-span communication: Normative processes,* pp. 1–4. Hillsdale, NJ: Erlbaum.

Ochs, E. (1979). Introduction: What child language can contribute to pragmatics. In E. Ochs & B. Schieffelin (Eds.), *Developmental pragmatics.* New York: Academic Press.

O'Connor, P. (1992). *Friendships between women: A critical review.* New York: Guilford Press.

O'Connor, P., & Brown, G. W. (1984). Supportive relationships: Fact or fancy? *Journal of Social and Personal Relationships, 1,* 159–176.

Olson, C. D. (1981). "Artifacts in the home and relational communication: A preliminary report." M.S. thesis, University of Utah.

Olstand, K. (1975). Brave new man: A basis for discussion. In J. Petras (Ed.), *Sex: male/Gender: masculine.* Port Washington, NY: Alfred.

O'Keefe, B. J., & Delia, J. G. (1985). Psychological and interactional dimensions of communicative development. In H. Giles & R. St. Clair (Eds.), *Recent advances in language, communication and social psychology,* pp. 41–85. London: Erlbaum.

Osgood, C., Suci, G., & Tannenbaum, P. (1957). *The measurement of meaning.* Urbana, IL: University of Illinois Press.

Owen, W. F. (1981). Interpretive themes in relational communication. *Quarterly Journal of Speech, 67,* 274–286.

Owen, W. F. (1993). Metaphors in accounts of romantic relationship terminations. In P. J. Kalbfleisch (Ed.), *Interpersonal communication: Evolving interpersonal relationships,* pp. 261–278. Hillsdale, NJ: Erlbaum.

Parks, M. (1982). Ideology in interpersonal communication: Off the couch and into the world. In M. Burgoon (Ed.), *Communication yearbook 5,* pp. 79–108. New Brunswick, NJ: Transaction.

Parks, M. R. (1985). Interpersonal communication and the quest for personal competence. In M. L. Knapp & G. R. Miller (Eds.), *Handbook of interpersonal communication,* pp. 171–201. Beverly Hills: Sage.

Parsons, T. (1951). *The social system.* New York: Free Press.

Pearce, W. B., Cronen, V. E., & Conklin, F. (1979). On what to look at when analyzing communication: A hierarchical model of actors' meanings. *Communication, 4,* 195–220.

Pearce, W. B., & Sharp, S. M. (1973). Self-disclosing communications. *Journal of Communication, 23,* 409–425.

Pendell, S. D. (1976). "The influence of room design on small group communication." Doctoral dissertation, University of Utah, 1976. *Dissertation Abstracts International, 37,* 10A.

Petronio, S. (1991). Communication boundary management: A theoretical model of managing disclosure of private information between marital couples. *Communication Theory, 1,* 311–335.

Phillips, G. M. (1984). A competent view of "competence." *Communication Education, 33,* 24–36.

Phillips, G., & Wood, J. (1983). *Communication and human relationships: The study of interpersonal relationships.* New York: Macmillan.

Pike, G. R., & Sillars, A. L. (1985). Reciprocity of marital communication. *Journal of Social and Personal Relationships, 2,* 303–324.

Piland, J. (1986, February). "Relational commitment: The expression of commitment in marriage." Paper presented at the Western Speech Communication Association Convention, Tucson, AZ.

Planalp, S., & Hewes, D. F. (1982). A cognitive approach to communication theory: *Cog ito ergo dico?* In M. Burgoon (Ed.), *Communication yearbook 5,* pp. 49–77. New Brunswick, NJ: Transaction.

Planalp, S., & Honeycutt, J. M. (1985). Events that increase uncertainty in personal relationships. *Human Communication Research, 11,* 593–603.

Planalp, S., Rutherford, D. K., & Honeycutt, J. (1988). Events that increase uncertainty in relationships: Replication and extension. *Human Communication Research, 14,* 516–547.

Platt, J. (1977). Review of H. Giles & P. F. Powesland, Speech style and social evaluation. *Lingua, 28,* 98–100.

Platt, J., & Weber, H. (1984). Speech convergence miscarried: An investigation into inappropriate accommodation strategies. *International Journal of the Sociology of Language, 46,* 131–146.

Pogrebin, L. (1987). *Among friends: Who we like, why we like them, and what we do with them.* New York: McGraw-Hill.

Prather, H. (1970). *Notes to myself.* Lafayette, CA: Real People Press.

Przybyla, D. P. J., & Byrne, D. (1981). Sexual relationships. In S. Duck & R. Gilmour (Eds.), *Personal relationships 1: Studying personal relationships,* pp. 67–89. New York: Academic Press.

Ragan, S. L. (1989). Communication between the sexes: A consideration of sex differences in adult communication. In J. F. Nussbaum (Ed.), *Life-span communication: Normative processes,* pp. 179–193. Hillsdale, NJ: Erlbaum.

Ragan, S. L., & Hopper, R. (1984). Ways to leave your lover: A conversational analysis of literature. *Communication Quarterly, 32,* 310–317.

Raph, J. B. (1967). Language and speech deficits in culturally disadvantaged children, and their implication for the speech clinician. *Journal of Speech and Hearing Disorders, 32,* 203–214.

Rapoport, A. (1968). Foward. In W. Buckley (Ed.), *Modern systems research for the behavioral scientist,* pp. VII–XXII. Chicago: Aldine.

Rathjen, D. P., & Foreyt, J. P. (Eds.). (1980). *Social competence: Interventions for children and adults.* New York: Pergamon.

Rawlins, W. K. (1983a). Openness as problematic in ongoing friendships: Two conversational dilemmas. *Communication Monographs, 50,* 1–13.

Rawlins, W. K. (1983b). Negotiating close friendships: The dialectic of conjunctive freedoms. *Human Communication Research, 9,* 255–266.

Rawlins, W. K. (1989). A dialectical analysis of the tensions, functions, and strategic challenges of communication in young friendships. In J. A. Andersen (Ed.), *Communication yearbook 12*, pp. 157–189. Newbury Park, CA: Sage.

Rawlins, W. K. (1992). *Friendship matters: Communication, dialectics, and the life course.* New York: Aldine De Gruyter.

Rawlins, W. K., & Holl, M. R. (1987). The communicative achievement of friendship during adolescence: Predicaments of trust and evaluation. *Western Journal of Speech Communication, 51,* 345–363.

Rawlins, W. K., & Holl, M. (1988). Adolescent's interactions with parents and friends; Dialectics of temporal perspective and evaluation. *Journal of Social and Personal Relationships, 5,* 27–46.

Read, K. (1955). Morality and the concept of the person among Gahuku-kama. *Oceania, 25,* 233–282.

Reis, H. T., Nezlek, J., & Wheeler, L. (1980). Physical attractiveness and social interaction. *Journal of Personality and Social Psychology, 38,* 604–614.

Reisman, J. M. (1981). Adult friendships. In S. Duck & R. Gilmour (Eds.), *Personal relationships 2: Developing personal relationships,* pp. 205–230. New York: Academic Press.

Rieke, R. D., & Sillars, M. O. (1993). *Argumentation and critical decision making,* 3d ed. Glenview, IL: HarperCollins.

Roach, C. A., & Wyatt, N. J. (1988). *Successful listening.* Glenview, IL: HarperCollins.

Robert, M. (1982). *Managing conflict: From the inside out.* San Diego: Learning Concepts.

Rodin, M. J. (1982). Non-engagement, failure to engage, and disengagement. In S. Duck (Ed.), *Personal relationships 4: Dissolving personal relationships,* pp. 31–49. New York: Academic Press.

Rogers, T. B. (1981). A model of the self as an aspect of the human information processing system. In N. C. Cantor & J. F. Kihlstrom (Eds.), *Personality, cognition, and social interaction,* pp. 193–214. Hillsdale, NJ: Erlbaum.

Rogers, L. E. (1989, April). "The relational dance: The study of process and pattern." *Proceedings of the 16th annual student conference in communication,* California State University, Fresno.

Rogers, L. E., & Farace, R. V. (1975). Analysis of relational communication in dyads: New measurement procedures. *Human Communication Research, 1,* 222–239.

Roloff, M. E. (1981). *Interpersonal communication: The social exchange approach.* Beverly Hills: Sage.

Roloff, M. E., & Cloven, D. H. (1990). The chilling effect in interpersonal relationship: The reluctance to speak one's mind. In D. D. Cahn (Ed.), *Intimates in conflict: A communication perspective,* pp. 49–76. Hillsdale, NJ: Erlbaum.

Roscoe, B., Cavanaugh, L. E., & Kennedy, D. R. (1988). Dating infidelity: Behavior reasons and consequence. *Adolescence, 23,* 35–43.

Rose, S. M. (1984). How friendships end: Patterns among young adults. *Journal of Social and Personal Relationships, 1,* 267–277.

Rose, S., & Serafica, F. C. (1986). Keeping and ending casual, close and best friendships. *Journal of Social and Personal Relationships, 3,* 275–288.

Rosegrant, T. J., & McCroskey, J. C. (1975). The effect of race and sex on proxemics behavior in an interview setting. *Southern Speech Communication Journal, 40,* 408–420.

Rosenbaum, M. E. (1986). The repulsion hypothesis: On the nondevelopment of relationships. *Journal of Personality and Social Psychology, 51,* 1156–1166.

Rosenfeld, L., & Civikly, J. (1976). *With words unspoken: The nonverbal experience.* New York: Holt, Rinehart, & Winston.

Roy, D. F. (1973). "Banana time"—Job satisfaction and informal interaction. In W. G. Bennis, D. E. Berlow, E. H. Schein, & F. I. Steele (Eds.), *Interpersonal dynamics: Essays and readings on human interaction,* 3d ed., pp. 403–417. Homewood, IL: Dorsey.

Ruben, B. (1984). *Communication and human behavior.* New York: Macmillan.

Rubin, R. B. (1985). The validity of the communication competency assessment instrument. *Communication Monographs, 52,* 173–185.

Sanders, R. E. (1992). Conversation, computation, and the human factor. *Human Communication Research, 18,* 623–636.

Sapir, E. (1949). The unconscious patterning of behavior in society. In D. Mandelbaum (Ed.), *Selected writing of Edward Sapir in language, culture and personality,* pp. 544–559. Berkeley: University of California Press.

Saussure, F. de. (1916). *Course in general linguistics* (W. Baskin, trans.). New York: McGraw-Hill.

Sawyer, J., & Guetzkow, H. (1965). Bargaining and negotiation in international relations. In H. C. Kelman (Ed.), *International behavior: A social psychological analysis,* pp. 464–520. New York: Holt, Rinehart, and Winston.

Scanzoni, J., & Fox, G. L. (1980). Sex roles, family and society: The seventies and beyond. *Journal of Marriage and the Family, 42,* 743–756.

Scheflen, A. E. (1968). Quasi-courtship behavior in psychotherapy. In W. G. Bennis, E. H. Schein, F. I. Steele, & D. E. Berlow (Eds.), *Interpersonal dynamics: Essays and readings on human interaction,* rev. ed., pp. 182–196. Homewood, IL: Dorsey.

Scheflen, A. E. (1972). *Body language and social order: Communication as behavioral control.* Englewood Cliffs, NJ: Prentice-Hall.

Scheflen, A. E. (1974). *How behavior means.* Garden City, NY: Doubleday.

Schegloff, E., & Sacks, H. (1973). Opening up closings. *Semiotica, 8,* 289–327.

Schiffrin, D. (1977). Opening encounters. *American Sociological Review, 42,* 676–691.

Searle, J. (1969). *Speech acts: An essay in the philosophy of language.* Cambridge: Cambridge University Press.

Shannon, C., & Weaver, W. (1949). *The mathematical theory of communication.* Urbana: University of Illinois Press.

Shea, B. C., & Pearson, J. C. (1986). The effects of relationship type, partner intent, and gender on the selection of relationship maintenance strategies. *Communication Monographs, 53,* 354–364.

Sheehy, G. (1974). *Passages: Predictable crises of adult life.* New York: Dutton.

Shimanoff, S. B. (1980). *Communication rules: Theory and research.* Beverly Hills: Sage.

Sillars, A. L. (1985). Interpersonal perception in relationships. In W. Ickes (Ed.), *Compatible and incompatible relationships,* pp. 277–305. New York: Springer-Verlag.

Sillars, A. L., Pike, G. R., Jones, T. S., & Murphy, M. A. (1984). Communication and understanding in marriage. *Human Communication Research, 10,* 317–350.

Sillars, A., & Scott, M. (1983). Interpersonal perception between intimates: An integrative review. *Human Communication Research, 10,* 153–176.

Sillars, A. L., & Weisberg, J. (1987). Conflict as a social skill. In M. Roloff and G. R. Miller (eds.), *Interpersonal processes: New directions in communication research*, pp. 140–171. Newbury Park, CA: Sage.

Simmel, G. (1902). The number of members as determining the sociological form of a group (A. Small, trans.). *American Journal of Sociology, 8*, 158–196.

Simmel, G. (1950). *The sociology of Georg Simmel* (K. H. Wolff, trans.). New York: Free Press.

Smilowitz, M. (1986). "Confirming communication in supervisor/subordinate dyads." Doctoral dissertation, University of Utah, 1985. *Dissertation Abstracts International, 45*, 12A.

Snyder, M. (1974). Self-monitoring of expressive behavior. *Journal of Personality and Social Psychology, 30*, 526–537.

Snyder, M. (1981). On the influence of individuals on situations. In N. C. Cantor & J. F. Kihlstrom (Eds.), *Personality, cognition, and social interaction*, pp. 309–329. Hillsdale, NJ: Erlbaum.

Sommer, R. (1969). *Personal space: The behavioral basis of design*. Englewood Cliffs, NJ: Prentice-Hall.

Spitzberg, B. H. (1993a, February). "The dark side of (in)competence." Paper presented at the Western Speech Communication Association Conference, Albuquerque, NM.

Spitzberg, B. H. (1993b). The dialectics of (in)competence. *Journal of Social and Personal Relationships, 9*, 137–158.

Spitzberg, B. H., & Cupach, W. R. (1984). *Interpersonal communication competence*. Beverly Hills: Sage.

Spitzberg, B. H., & Cupach, W. R. (1989). *Handbook of interpersonal competence research*. New York: Springer-Verlag.

Spitzberg, G. H., & Hecht, M. L. (1984). A component model of relational competence. *Human Communication Research, 10*, 575–600.

Sprey, J. (1971). On the management of conflict in families. *Journal of Marriage and the Family, 33*, 722–731.

Stafford, L., & Canary, D. J. (1991). Maintenance strategies and romantic relationships type, gender, and relational characteristics. *Journal of Social and Personal Relationships, 8*, 217–242.

Stephen, J. D. (1985). Fixed-sequence and circular-caused models of relationship development: Divergent views on the role of communication in intimacy. *Journal of Marriage and the Family, 47*, 955–963.

Stephen, T. (1987). Attribution and adjustment to relationship termination. *Journal of Social and Personal Relationships, 4*, 47–61.

Stewart, J., & D'Angelo, G. (1988). *Together: Communicating interpersonally*, 3d ed. New York: Random House.

Stewart, J., & Thomas, M. (1990). Dialogic listening: Sculpting mutual meanings. In J. Stewart (Ed.), *Bridges not walls: A book about interpersonal communication*, 5th ed., pp. 192–210. New York: McGraw-Hill.

Street, R. L. (1982). Evaluation of noncontent speech accommodation. *Language and Communication, 2*, 13–31.

Sunnafrank, M. (1992). On debunking the attitude similarity myth. *Communication Monographs, 59*, 164–179.

Sunnafrank, M. J., & Miller, G. R. (1981). The role of initial conversations in determining attraction to similar and dissimilar strangers. *Human Communication Research, 8,* 16–25.

Tannen, D. (1990). *You just don't understand: Women and men in conversation.* New York: Morrow.

Taylor, D. M., Meynard, R., & Rheault, E. (1977). Threat to identity and second language learning. In H. Giles (Ed.), *Language, ethnicity and intergroup relations* (pp. 99–118). London: Academic Press.

Taylor, S. E. (1989). *Positive illusions: Creative self-deception and the healthy mind.* New York: Basic Books.

Thibaut, J., & Kelley, H. (1959). *The social psychology of groups.* New York: Wiley.

Ting-Toomey, S. (1983). An analysis of verbal communication patterns in high and low marital adjustment groups. *Human Communication Research, 9,* 306–319.

Trenholm, S. (1991). *Human communication theory,* 2d ed. Englewood Cliffs, NJ: Prentice-Hall.

Trenholm, S., & Jensen, A. (1992). *Interpersonal communication,* 2d ed. Belmont, CA: Wadsworth.

Trudgill, P. (1975). *Accent, dialect and the school.* London: Arnold.

Turner, R. E., Edgley, C., & Olmstead, G. (1975). Information control in conversations: Honesty is not always the best policy. *Kansas Journal of Sociology, 11,* 69–89.

Tversky, A., & Kohneman, D. (1973). Availability: A heuristic for judging frequency and probability. *Cognitive Psychology, 5,* 207–232.

Tyler, S. (1978). *The said and the unsaid: Mind, meaning and culture.* New York: Academic Press.

Vanlear, C. A. Jr., & Trujillo, N. (1986). On becoming acquainted: A longitudinal study of social judgement processes. *Journal of Social and Personal Relationships, 3,* 375–392.

Van Maanen, J. (1979). On the understanding of interpersonal relations. In W. Bennis, J. Van Maanen, E. H. Schein, & F. I. Steele (Eds.), *Essays in interpersonal dynamics,* pp. 13–42. Homewood, IL: Dorsey.

von Bertalanffy, L. (1967). *Robots, men and minds.* New York: Braziller.

von Bertalanffy, L. (1968). *General system theory: Foundations, development, applications.* New York: Braziller.

von Bertalanffy, L. (1975). *Perspectives on general system theory.* New York: Braziller.

Walster, E. (1970). The effect of self-esteem on liking for dates of various social desirabilities. *Journal of Experimental Social Psychology, 6,* 248–253.

Ward, S. A., Bluman D. C., & Dauria, A. F. (1982). Rhetorical sensitivity recast: Theoretical assumptions of an informal interpersonal rhetoric. *Communication Quarterly, 30,* 189–195.

Watchel, P. (1973). Psychodynamics, behavior therapy and the implacable experimenter: An inquiry into the consistency of personality. *Journal of Abnormal Psychology, 82,* 324–334.

Watson, O. M. (1970). *Proxemic behavior: A cross-cultural study.* The Hague: Mouton.

Watzlawick, P. (1976). *How real is real: Confusion, disinformation, communication.* New York: Vintage Books.

Watzlawick, P., Beavin, J. H., & Jackson, D. D. (1967). *Pragmatics of human communication: A study of interactional patterns, pathologies and paradoxes.* New York: Norton.

Watzlawick, P., & Weakland, J. H. (1977). *The interactional view: Studies at the Mental Research Institute, Palo Alto, 1965–1974.* New York: Norton.

Weick, K. E. (1977). Enactment processes in organizations. In B. W. Starn & G. R. Salancik (Eds.), *New direction in organizational behavior,* pp. 267–300. Chicago: St. Clair Press.

Weick, K. (1979). *The social psychology of organizing,* 2d ed. Reading, MA: Addison-Wesley.

Weiss, P. A. (1969). The living system: Determinism stratified. In A. Koestler & J. R. Smythies (Eds.), *Beyond reductionism: New perspectives in the life sciences,* pp. 3–55. New York: Macmillan.

Werner, C. M., Altman, I., & Brown, B. (1992). A transactional approach to interpersonal relations: Physical environments, social context and temporal qualities. *Journal of Social and Personal Relationships, 9,* 297–323.

Wheeless, L. R., Wheeless, V. E., & Baus, R. (1984). Sexual communication, communication satisfaction, and solidarity in the development stages of intimate relationships. *Western Journal of Speech Communication, 48,* 217–230.

Wiemann, J. M. (1977). Explication and test of model of communicative competence. *Human Communication Research, 3,* 195–213.

Wiemann, J. M., & Kelly, C. W. (1981). Pragmatics of interpersonal competence. In C. Wilder-Mott & J. H. Weakland (Eds.), *Rigor & imagination: Essays from the legacy of Gregory Bateson,* pp. 283–298. New York: Praeger.

Wiener, M., Devoe, S., Rubinow, S., & Geller, J. (1972). Nonverbal behavior and nonverbal communication. *Psychological Review, 79,* 185–214.

Wilkinson, S. (1987). Explorations of self and other in a developing relationship. In R. Burnett, P. McGhee, & D. Clarke (Eds.), *Accounting for relationships,* pp. 40–59. London: Methuen.

Wilmot, W. W. (1980). *Dyadic communication,* 2d ed. Reading, MA: Addison-Wesley.

Wilmot, W. W., Carbaugh, D. A., & Baxter, L. A. (1985). Communicative strategies used to terminate romantic relationships. *Western Journal of Speech Communication, 49,* 204–216.

Wilmot, W. W., & Sillars, A. L. (1989). Developmental issues in personal relationships. In J. F. Nussbaum (Ed.), *Life-span communication: Normative processes,* pp. 119–135. Hillsdale, NJ: Erlbaum.

Wolvin, A. D., & Coakley, L. G. (1985). *Listening,* 2d ed. Dubuque, IA: Brown.

Wright, P. H. (1978). Toward a theory of friendship based on a conception of self. *Human Communication Research, 4,* 196–207.

Zunin, L. (1972). *Contact: The first four minutes.* Los Angeles: Nash.

Indexes

Author Index

Adams, K. L. 175, 184, 186, 187, 189, 191,
    266, 325, 357, 401
Adler, R. B., 62
Agostinelli, A. L., 332
Alexander, D. C., 53, 54
Allport, G. W., 53, 159
Altendorf, D. M., 357, 358, 365
Altman, I., 95, 105, 280, 281
Andersen, P. A., 142, 219, 296
Andreyeva, G. M., 122
Antaki, C.,194
Antill, J. K., 51
Ardrey, R., 102
Argyle, M., 63, 65, 309
Athay, M., 223
Atwell, F. C., 338
Ayres, J., 374, 400

Back, K., 104
Banks, S. P., 357, 358, 365
Bar-Hillel, J., 143
Baratz, J. C., 147
Barnes, M. K., 246, 247
Barnlund, D. C., 35
Bateson, G., 12, 35, 39, 386
Baus, R., 230
Bavelas, J. B., 4, 10, 11, 142, 149, 158, 159, 160,
    161, 227, 313, 314, 315, 316, 318, 319
Baxter, L. A., 33, 137, 170, 214, 235, 257,
    258, 259, 263, 265, 274, 278, 284, 285,
    286, 294, 299, 322–338, 339, 342, 344,
    346, 348, 353, 355, 358–363, 365–367,
    374, 378, 388, 389, 390, 400
Beach, W. A., 96, 113, 144, 145, 149,
    195

Beattie, G., 134
Beavin, J. H., 9, 10, 13, 18, 20, 32, 153,
    154, 199
Beebe, L., 151
Behnke, R. R., 100
Bell, R. A., 136, 259, 374
Bell, R. R., 371, 395, 397, 399
Berger, C. R., 66, 67, 68, 69, 70, 93, 184,
    215, 257, 258, 310
Berglas, S., 70
Berko, R. M., 132
Berlo, D. K., 20
Bernstein, B., 113
Berseheid, E., 118, 243
Bettini, L. M., 286, 287
Bettini, L., 287
Birdwhistell, R. L., 19, 156, 172
Black, A., 159, 160
Bluman D. C., 151
Blumer, H., 54,
Bochner, A. P., 239, 245, 257, 284, 285, 287,
    307, 312, 313
Bologh, R. W., 300
Bolton, C. D., 274, 275
Bond, M., 65
Boster, F., 196–198
Bourhis, R. Y., 150
Bowers, J. W., 289, 310
Bradac, J. J., 138, 150, 151
Brown, B., 95
Brown, G. W., 393
Brown, P., 252
Buerkel-Ruthfuss, N. L., 136
Buhrke, R. A., 120
Bullis, C., 259, 265, 278, 294, 322,
    323, 324

449

Subject Index